# Sinclair on
# Warranties and Indemnities on
# Share and Asset Sales

AUSTRALIA
Law Book Co.
Sydney


CANADA and USA
Carswell
Toronto


NEW ZEALAND
Brookers
Wellington


SINGAPORE and MALAYSIA
Sweet & Maxwell Asia
Singapore and Kuala Lumpur

# Sinclair on
# Warranties and Indemnities on
# Share and Asset Sales

*Sixth Edition*

**General Editor**
Robert Thompson

London
Sweet & Maxwell
2005

Fifth Edition 2001
Sixth Edition 2005

Published by Sweet & Maxwell Limited of
100 Avenue Road, Swiss Cottage, London, NW3 3PF
(http://www.sweetandmaxwell.co.uk)

Typeset by Interactive Sciences Ltd, Gloucester
Printed and bound in Great Britain by Athenaeum Press Ltd., Gateshead, Tyne & Wear

No natural forests were destroyed to make this product:
only farmed timber was used and replanted.

A CIP catalogue record for this book is available from the British Library

ISBN 0 421 862602

# Preface to the Sixth Edition

The last edition of this work was published in 2001. In this sixth edition, new chapters on completion accounts and valuation have been included. The purpose of their inclusion is to give the vendors' and the purchaser's solicitors an insight into these key areas which are often overlooked when negotiating the terms of the warranties and indemnities or in otherwise seeking to shift the risk of an issue from one party to the other.

The text has been revised to take account of legislative changes since September 2001 and to reflect changes in convention and drafting since then. This is particularly so in the form of tax deed and the legal due diligence questionnaire. Significant changes to the warranties discussed in Ch.7 have been made to reflect either changes in law since the last edition or a shift in focus or convention. Chapter 8 and Appendix 5 have been substantially updated to reflect not only changes to common form warranties on the purchase of a business but also increasing reliance on indemnities in this area as a means of addressing risk.

The purpose of the book remains the same, to assist all parties who have to deal with a sale and purchase agreement ("sale agreement") for either a company or business to do so with confidence and an understanding of the relevant issues.

For the purchaser's solicitors, who would normally prepare the first draft of any sale agreement, the book is designed to provide precedents of suitable warranties and indemnities from which a tailored and appropriate draft can be prepared. Far more respect is gained from sending out a bespoke draft as opposed to sending the vendors' advisors a full-scale precedent which makes no effort to address the particular circumstances of the transaction and has simply been printed off from the firm's precedent bank. Current convention is to prepare a more balanced first draft which seeks to address the specifics of the transaction rather than the old approach of sending out an aggressive purchaser's first draft. The suggested qualifications in favour of the vendors should assist with that process.

For the vendors' solicitors the guidance that accompanies many of the warranties will enable them to consider their impact, determine their relevance to the target company or business and, where appropriate, suggest amendments that may need to be made to moderate the sometimes harsh effect of some of them.

Even for those that have significant experience of this area, the book performs a useful function in broadening the understanding as to the origin of certain warranties and indemnities, which are now largely taken for granted, and as a reference for checking the wording of a particular warranty or clause that has been sought.

The views expressed as to the fairness of the various clauses or the appropriateness of any suggested amendments are subjective, albeit in most cases they reflect current convention.

In editing this work I have enjoyed significant contributions from many of my colleagues and partners throughout my firm and I am grateful to them. Two that should be fairly highlighted for special mention are my partner Paul Christian who has been responsible for tax input and my assistant Jo Stephenson who has been an invaluable help throughout.

The law is stated as at January 24, 2005.

Robert Thompson
January 2005

# Introduction

The book is largely organised around precedents of clauses and documents, accompanied by commentary. In the precedents, words which begin with a capital letter are assumed to be defined terms; the definitions in para.4–01 have been adopted. The words and phrases which are included in square brackets in the precedents are suggested amendments for the benefit of the party to whom the first draft, which would not include the bracketed additions, is presented. Where relevant and for ease of interpretation, the clauses have been highlighted in bold to differentiate the wording of these from the accompanying commentaries and explanations.

The precedents deal primarily with the sale of shares of a company but, without overloading the text with obvious variations, the amendments which are applicable to the sale of a business have generally been indicated. In the text, the company which is being sold is referred to as "the target company". The vendors of the shares are described as such throughout the book and it is assumed that they are the persons giving the warranties. When they are not it would be appropriate to differentiate between them in the sale and purchase agreement by reference to vendors and warrantors. The word covenantors is used in the tax deed.

To assist readers who wish to make use of, or be reminded about the precedents, these are collected together in the Appendices. In particular, Appendix 9 contains the various clauses discussed in Chs 1 to 4, whilst Appendix 10 repeats the warranties and undertakings by the purchaser which are examined in Ch.11.

The following initials are used in relation to particular statutes:

| | |
|---|---|
| CA | Companies Act |
| CAA | Capital Allowances Act |
| FA | Finance Act |
| ICTA | Income and Corporation Taxes Act |
| IHTA | Inheritance Tax Act |
| IT(EP)A | Income Tax (Earnings and Pensions) Act 2003 |
| LPA | Law of Property Act |
| TMA | Taxes Management Act |
| TCGA | Taxation of Chargeable Gains Act |
| VATA | Value Added Tax Act |

The initials VAT refer to value added tax, the initials SDLT refer to stamp duty land tax and the initials ESC refer to an Inland Revenue extra statutory concession.

The chapters are arranged into a logical chronology beginning with the history and function of warranties and indemnities. The book then considers the various parties to the sale and purchase agreement and some of the nuances between them. There then follows a chapter which explains the rights and liabilities that arise from a breach of warranty and the particular issues that need to be considered in relation to this. The warranties are then introduced by some general points before moving on to a detailed consideration of tax, property and general warranties applying in a share sale. Warranties applicable to an assets deal are then separately considered before moving on to a detailed review of disclosure letters, their purpose and affect. The next chapter then focuses on the form of tax deed by providing a detailed review of a modern format of this. This is followed by a chapter dedicated to the warranties, undertakings and indemnities which might in certain circumstances be requested by the purchaser. Finally, two new chapters have been added to deal with completion accounts and valuation so as to give the reader an insight into how the negotiation of warranties and indemnities may be affected by completion accounts where a transaction includes these, and to put the warranties and indemnities in context by reference to how the target company or business was valued.

# Contents

Page

## APPENDICES

# Table of Cases

# Table of Statutes

# Table of Statutory Instruments

# Table of European Legislation

# CHAPTER 1

# History and Function of Warranties and Indemnities

## PURPOSE OF WARRANTIES

Apart from the limited rights given under the sale of goods legislation and the **1–01** Financial Services and Markets Act 2000, the purchaser of the share capital or business of a company receives no protection under the law if the bargain turns out to be not what it expected unless there has been misrepresentation by the vendors. The concept is embodied in the somewhat dated Latin tag *caveat emptor*, which effectively means that it is for the purchaser to decide what protection it requires and that it is not for the law to provide it. In both types of purchases, the effect is to leave the purchaser generally at risk that the assets which it thinks it is acquiring, either directly in the case of the purchase of a business or indirectly in the case of the purchase of share capital, are less than it believed or subject to unexpected defects. In the case of the purchase of shares, the purchaser has the further risk that the company is subject to unknown or unduly onerous liabilities.

This difference arises because, in general, the liabilities of a company are unaffected by changes in the identity of its owners and the purchaser effectively acquires all assets, rights and liabilities of the company by acquiring its share capital. Where the transaction relates to the purchase of assets, however, it is most unusual for the purchaser to become subject to liabilities of the business unless they are expressly taken over by it. A notable exception to this general rule is that the purchaser will take on employment liabilities if the Transfer of Undertakings (Protection of Employment) Regulations 1981 apply.

It is therefore customary for the purchaser of a private company or a business **1–02** to receive some form of assurances from the vendors as to the assets of the company or the business and, where the acquisition is of the shares of a company, as to the liabilities which attach to the target company. Over the years there has been a steady expansion in the scope of the assurances that purchasers require, agreements relating to these purchases tend to be very extensive, with a large part being in the nature of warranties.

It is sometimes suggested that a major purpose of the extensive warranties in the normal sale agreement is to bring to the attention of the vendors the points which are likely to be of concern to the purchaser. The process of checking the warranties for the purposes of disclosing against them is designed to bring out all potential problems; the parties will be able to negotiate, before the sale, as to what impact these should make on the transaction. In this way, the chances of acrimonious disputes arising after completion are reduced. Where the transaction involves completion accounts, disclosure of a liability against the warranties may not be the end of the matter. Please see Ch.12 for further discussion of this.

**1–03** It should never be overlooked that the main purpose and effect of the warranties is to impose legal liability upon the vendors and to provide the purchaser with a remedy if statements made about the company prove to be incorrect and the value of it reduced. In effect, the warranties allocate risk, as between the vendors and the purchaser, in relation to the target company whose assets or shares are being purchased. To the extent that warranties are given, the vendors accept the liability; in so far as warranties are not given or are restricted in their scope, the purchaser takes the risk. The negotiation of the warranties is often referred to as the "battle of the risks" for this reason. The "risk" can also be addressed through indemnities or adjustments being made to the price through a completion accounts mechanism.

There are nevertheless normally some warranties which in practice will not entitle the purchaser to any damages in the event of a breach. The only purpose of including these warranties is the checklist function. Examples of such warranties are those which are invariably rendered ineffective by the disclosure letter (see cl.1.10.1 in para.7–23, relating to the memorandum and articles of association of the target company, and general disclosure (4) in para.9–07) or those where a breach would not normally mean that the purchaser suffers any loss (see cl.3.3.1 in para.7–61, relating to bank accounts).

**1–04** Although the principle of *caveat emptor* applies equally to acquisitions of listed shares and shares of private companies, it has nevertheless been generally accepted by bidders for listed companies that they do not get warranties. Occasionally, if there is a large controlling shareholding, the bidder may receive some kind of limited protection but in general the bid is made blind. There is no clear reason why a purchaser of a listed company should be prepared to take on board the risk of deficiencies in the assets or the existence of undisclosed liabilities whilst not being prepared to do so if it is purchasing a private company or a business.

It might be thought that one reason for the difference of approach arises from the fact that many private companies are operated in a somewhat more casual manner than public companies, but this view would not explain why it is that, for example, the purchaser of a wholly-owned subsidiary of a listed company would expect the full warranties that apply on any purchase of a private company, or why the purchaser of a business from a listed group requires warranty protection. It is also difficult to explain the difference on the grounds that more information is available in relation to listed companies as, unless circulars have had to be sent out by the listed company in accordance with Stock Exchange requirements which give more detail than would appear in the accounts, there is usually no greater access to information concerning the affairs of a listed group than of a private group.

**1–05** Nevertheless, the distinction is well-accepted and it is very rare that the vendors of an unlisted company or a business will manage to avoid having to give large-scale warranties; but it is reasonable for the vendors to require the purchaser to justify each warranty that is sought rather than their having to demonstrate that the deletion or qualification of the warranty is fair. In striking contrast to the widespread acceptance of the obligation to give vendor warranties is the fact that it is unusual for the vendors to seek warranties from the purchaser when the purchase consideration is satisfied wholly or partly by the allotment of shares in the purchaser. If the consideration shares constitute a significant proportion of the purchaser's total capital, the vendors should consider with the utmost care whether they should oppose the standard practice and seek the protection of warranties. An indication of warranties that might be suitable for this purpose is provided in Appendix 3.

## THE ORIGIN OF INDEMNITIES

The concept of warranties is that the purchaser should receive compensation for any loss of bargain it may suffer as a result of a breach of the warranties. In effect, the warranties give rise to an adjustment in the purchase price and therefore concern only the vendors and the purchaser. In the case where there is a sale of shares, the target company itself is not directly involved.   **1–06**

While historically this was generally considered satisfactory, it was recognised some years ago that there were two particular types of liabilities where, on a share sale, the target company, rather than the purchaser, should receive the benefit of an indemnity from the vendors. These related to statutory liabilities for taxation which were imposed upon a company in respect of benefits derived or liabilities avoided by a shareholder. The company was required to discharge a taxation liability which was really nothing to do with it without being given a corresponding statutory right of recovery or reimbursement.

The first of these provisions was FA 1940, s.46, which in certain circumstances imposed a liability to estate duty on the death of a person who had, during his lifetime, transferred property to the company. The company could be liable to estate duty in respect of benefits derived by the deceased, but it had no right to recover the estate duty from his estate. The second case arose under the Income Tax Act 1952, s.245 in respect of liability arising from surtax assessments. In that case, if a closely held company did not pay adequate dividends, an assessment in respect of surtax (being the equivalent of higher rate tax) could be made on the company based upon the surtax that would have been paid by the shareholders if full dividends had been distributed. Again, no statutory right of recovery existed for the company.

In both cases, therefore, as the company could incur a liability which should really have fallen upon another party, it is perfectly reasonable for the purchaser to require the vendors to provide an indemnity in respect of those liabilities. It is consistent with this analysis that the question of indemnities in favour of the purchaser of a company's business has never arisen, as the purchaser does not take over the tax liabilities of the vendor in these transactions.   **1–07**

Over the years, this simple principle has become obscured and what started off as an indemnity against specific secondary taxation liabilities, where there was no right of recovery, gradually became extended so that it is now more or less invariably applied to all taxation liabilities of the target company.

In addition, because damages for breach of warranty might not put the purchaser in a position to rectify the problem without cost to itself, for example if the defect in one of the acquired assets does not affect the overall value of the company, an indemnity, which gives rise to an automatic right to payment in prescribed circumstances, may be sought by a purchaser.

**1–08**    In the event of a claim under an indemnity, the court will assess whether the specified event has occurred and how much should be paid to fix the problem by reference to the terms of the indemnity itself, which are usually more favourable to the claimant than the position would otherwise be at common law. There is usually no need to prove a link between the liability and the value of the company and the indemnity clause will commonly provide for recovery of costs and expenses, including legal fees, which might otherwise be irrecoverable. Indemnities are, therefore, often used where a specific problem has been identified and it is agreed that the risk will be borne by the vendors.

An additional point which is sometimes made to justify the use of indemnities as an alternative or in addition to the warranties concerns the effect of the purchaser's knowledge on its right to damages for breach of a warranty. In recent years the generally accepted position has been that if the purchaser is aware when it enters into the sale agreement that a warranty is incorrect, its entitlement to damages is likely to be reduced accordingly (see *Eurocopy plc v Teesdale and others* [1992] BCLC 1067 and para.4–24). Where a purchaser chooses to act through an agent for the purpose of an acquisition, the actual knowledge of the agent, to the extent that it is knowledge within the scope of the purpose for which the agent is acting, will be treated as the knowledge of the purchaser (see *Infiniteland Ltd and another v Artisan Contracting Limited and another* [2004] EWHC 955, Ch D). However, it should be noted that the *Eurocopy* decision was a ruling on a preliminary matter only and not a final decision on the effectiveness of a clause that seeks to prevent knowledge of a purchaser from prejudicing a claim made by it under the warranties where it has actual knowledge of facts not disclosed to the appropriate standard in the disclosure letter. In *Infiniteland* the High Court rejected the argument that as a general rule if the purchaser knew something and still completed the deal it could not claim for breach of warranty no matter what the terms of the agreement, although in that case, as the purchaser had the requisite actual knowledge, the reference in the agreement to actual knowledge of the purchaser limiting the extent of the warranties defeated the warranty claim. Notwithstanding the *Infiniteland* decision, in view of *Eurocopy*, where a purchaser has knowledge of facts that would constitute a breach of warranty, it should not be assumed that it will automatically have a claim for breach of warranty if the relevant facts are not stated in the disclosure letter. The safest course of action will be to cover the issue of what will and what will not defeat a warranty claim in the sale agreement.

These issues do not arise in relation to indemnities, as knowledge of the purchaser is irrelevant and in the absence of agreement to the contrary—which would be unusual—the extent of the loss suffered by the purchaser is irrelevant.

If a liability has been disclosed against a particular warranty it is not possible to undo that knowledge by seeking to delete the disclosure. The way to address the risk in favour of the purchaser is for the vendor to provide an appropriate indemnity in respect of the matter. A purchaser may seek to provide that all warranties are given on an indemnity basis, but this should always be resisted by vendors, particularly in the light of the *Eurocopy* decision and the fact that such a basis potentially allows an unscrupulous purchaser to profit from its bargain, given that many of the matters that are covered by warranties will not have been remotely relevant to its initial valuation of the company but on an indemnity basis may give rise to a claw back of consideration.

## OVERLAP OF WARRANTIES AND INDEMNITIES ON SHARE SALES

Although the concepts of warranties and indemnities have developed along rather different routes, they will inevitably overlap to some extent. The warranties given to the purchaser will deal with numerous matters covering all aspects of the target company including, in particular, taxation liabilities of it. The tax liabilities will also generally be covered by the indemnity or tax deed (as it is more usually termed). **1–09**

In addition there may then be further indemnities to cover the risk of either disclosed matters where the purchaser is not prepared to accept the risk, or matters of concern to the purchaser that have arisen during due diligence. It used to be convention to seek that any indemnities were given in favour of the target company. Any payments made pursuant to those indemnities would then often give rise to further taxation problems, as the target company had to pay tax on receipt of the indemnity payments and the purchaser would usually insist that any such payments were therefore grossed up to cover the additional tax. To alleviate these issues it is now almost universal practice to provide indemnities in favour of the purchaser alone.

It is generally preferable from the vendors' point of view that liability should arise under the warranties rather than the indemnities (see further para.3–26). In cases where the vendors are also the covenantors under the tax deed, the vendors might wish to have inserted a suitable clause in both the sale agreement and the tax deed such as follows:

### [1A] Claims under Warranties to precede claims under the Tax Deed

**If a claim may be made by the Purchaser in respect of an act, event or default, both under the Warranties and under the Tax Deed, the claim shall first be made under the Warranties. Any amount payable under the Tax Deed to the Purchaser in respect of the claim shall be reduced to the extent of the amount payable under the Warranties. The provisions of clause [ ] of** **1–10**

**the Tax Deed shall apply as if the claim were wholly made under the Tax Deed.**

The position for the vendors will be more complicated if the vendors and the covenantors differ or if, as sometimes occurs under tax deeds, different minimum or maximum levels of liability apply. This is considered further in para.3–16.

Nowadays the tax warranties are almost exclusively used for the purposes of requiring disclosure of specific tax issues or liabilities. Once such disclosures have been made, then subject to them meeting the required level of disclosure the relevant warranty will be rendered ineffectual. However, the tax deed will provide that the relevant disclosed tax liability is required to be paid to the purchaser on an indemnity basis. Clause 1A would be ineffective in this case as no warranty claim could be made (on the assumption there had been fair disclosure) and so a claim for the full amount under the tax deed would remain intact.

The usual purpose of cl.1A is to require a purchaser to prove its loss (as opposed to the matter being indemnified in the tax deed) and to make any claim subject to the full "suite" of warranty protection provisions which would usually apply against the warranties, including financial deductibles. These will often not apply to the tax deed.

**1–11**    The purpose of the third sentence in the clause is to ensure that the conduct of claims in relation to taxation warranties is given to the vendors in the same manner as with the tax deed (see para.11–14 for a further discussion of this). It may be omitted where a corresponding right is given to the vendors under the sale agreement in relation to claims for breach of warranty. There are, in addition, other provisions of the tax deed which might usefully be added to cl.1A, such as cl.6 of the deed discussed at para.10–06. It will also be appropriate to ensure that the parties are clear about whether or not liability will arise if expected reliefs are not available (see the discussion on cl.1.5 of the deed at para.10–14).

## PREPARATION OF THE SALE AGREEMENT

**1–12**    Historically, it has been normal practice for the sale agreement to be drafted in the first instance by the solicitors acting for the purchaser. However, if the share capital or business of the target company is being sold by way of an auction process, which is becoming increasingly common where there is likely to be significant interest in the target company or business, the vendors' solicitors will provide the first draft agreement. Moreover, the widespread use of word-processing and electronic transmission of documentation means that both solicitors acting for the vendors and those acting for the purchaser may systematically amend a document in transit between them, with the result that any notion of "ownership" of it is eroded. Often, at the outset of a transaction, the solicitors have limited information available to them concerning the target company or the business and there is sometimes a tendency to prepare the agreement using a standard form which may be inappropriate to the actual circumstances. However, this should not be the case in an auction process where any draft should be carefully tailored to reflect the business or target company being sold and provide a balance of risk apportionment in terms of the warranties and indemnities offered. Ideally, any draft should be prepared on the basis of detailed information regarding the target company or the business and this may be obtained either from an accountant's long form report, if one is available, or, more usually, from a legal due diligence questionnaire, substantially in the form set out in Appendix 1, which should be sent to the vendors or their solicitors before drafting starts.

# CHAPTER 2
# Parties

## THE VENDORS

**2–01** In the case of the sale of shares of a company, the vendors will be the owners of the shares. The main continuing liability for the vendors will arise in relation to the warranties and indemnities although there are likely to be other provisions, such as restrictions on the activities which they may carry on in the period immediately following the sale, that continue to affect them. Where the vendor is a small subsidiary in a large group, the purchaser may wish to obtain the covenant of the parent company to support these obligations. This is discussed further in para.3–13.

In the case of a sale of shares the purchaser at least has the comfort that the vendor will receive the proceeds of sale subject only to any related taxation liability. In the case of the sale of a business, however, the position is quite different. The vendor, which will be the company whose business is being sold, will dispose of the assets of the business but remain subject to its liabilities. Indeed, the vendor may have no net assets when the liabilities are taken into account and, even where there are net assets, it may be expected that these will rapidly be extracted by the owners of the company if the effect of the sale is to leave it as a non-trading shell.

## CORPORATE VENDORS

**2–02** When accepting warranties and indemnities from a corporate vendor, the purchaser should consider not only the vendor's initial covenant status but also the extent to which it can deplete its assets and reduce the worth of its covenant by the payment of dividends. When determining the funds available for distribution by way of dividend, it is not necessary for the company to make provision for contingent liabilities, such as those which might arise under the warranties, unless there is reason to believe that the liability is likely to accrue (see CA 1985, s.270). The purchaser could thus find itself with a warranty claim against a vendor which has substantially reduced its net worth by the payment of dividends. As such, if a corporate vendor's assets are largely in the form of distributable reserves, the purchaser should consider the desirability of imposing a restriction upon the vendor in relation to the making of distributions during the warranty period. The form of such a restriction would follow that suggested in relation to trustee shareholders in para.2–06, but it will be of limited value unless the company's net assets are of the same order as the amount that could be involved in a warranty claim. An alternative or additional approach would be to seek a parent company or other shareholder guarantee.

The directors of a corporate vendor will need to be satisfied that it has the **2–03** necessary powers under its memorandum of association to enter into the transaction and to give the warranties. Generally this will not be a matter of doubt as, if the vendor has the power to hold the shares of the target company or, as the case may be, to carry on the business with the assets which are the subject matter of the sale, then it will also have the power to sell the shares or assets and to enter into such commitments as are a normal attribute of such a sale. The purchaser need not concern itself at all with this question as it will be protected by CA 1985, ss.35–35B.

With a view to obtaining further protection, purchasers sometimes seek warranties to the effect that the vendor has the power to enter into the sale agreement. This is a pointless approach since if the vendor does not have power to enter into the agreement it will, of necessity, not have power to give the warranty. There is a further discussion of this in para.7–04 in relation to cl.1.1.

## EXECUTIVE SHAREHOLDERS

In determining who should give the warranties on a share sale and how the **2–04** liability should be divided among the vendors, the most straightforward case arises where the vendors are also executives of the target company. In that event, the persons who are accepting responsibility for the warranties are those who are also receiving the benefit of the sale. It is generally appropriate in such a case that normal joint and several or, at any rate, pro rata liability should apply. However, as indicated in para.3–15, it may be desirable to modify this broad principle in special cases, for example where liability under the warranties is attributable to benefits received by one of the shareholders and not by the others.

The position becomes more complicated if there is a difference between the persons who are the vendors and those who have knowledge about the affairs of the target company. The extreme example of this would arise where a subsidiary, which operates entirely independently, is sold by a corporate vendor and the management remains with the subsidiary. It is in this kind of circumstance that the real function of warranties, which is to impose liability upon the vendors and not merely to extract information about the target company, is shown at its clearest. When considering the warranties, the vendors will doubtless request information from the executives of the target company but it would be unreasonable in practice to impose financial risk upon them in relation to their replies as they obtain no corresponding financial benefit.

In between these two extreme cases arises the common situation where some **2–05** of the vendors are passive investors, such as trustees, while others are active executives. If some of the vendors are venture capitalists, it is usually the case that they will resist giving any warranties at all, other than warranties relating to their own share ownership, which should always be given, leaving the executive vendors with the greater burden of risk. While this might be thought fair in principle, as they have the means of verifying generally whether the warranties are likely to be breached, it is suggested that this view is flawed, as if an unexpected liability arose, then all the shareholders of the target company would have suffered a diminution in the value of their investment if they had not sold the target company. By analogy, therefore, they should each bear pro rata the loss arising if the liability results in a breach of warranty. In practice a purchaser will usually accept a lower claims maximum against the executive vendors so that they cannot be made liable for more than they in aggregate receive.

While this seems to be clearly in accordance with principle where the warranties are in an absolute form, it is often the case that some of the warranties are qualified so that they apply only if there is an undisclosed liability of which one or more of the vendors was aware. In such a case, it would seem to be appropriate that the party who was aware of the liability but deliberately failed to disclose it should alone be penalised although he might argue that, by failing to disclose the liability, he has avoided a possible renegotiation of the purchase terms by the purchaser. This question is considered further in para.4–19. Deliberate non-disclosure is likely to be a high-risk strategy as it often removes the benefit of any warranty protection provisions that have been negotiated in favour of the vendors and can give rise to the commission of a criminal offence under the Financial Services and Markets Act 2000.

## TRUSTEE VENDORS

2–06   Similar principles to those which apply to corporate vendors of shares arise in the case of sales by trustees or personal representatives, although in a more extreme form. A purchaser from a corporate vendor at least has the comfort that, in the absence of special circumstances, the paid-up share capital cannot be distributed but no similar restrictions exist in relation to trusts. The purchaser might wish to restrain the trustees or personal representatives from making distributions during the warranty period but this is unlikely to be acceptable to them. An alternative approach is to require that, in the event of a distribution being made, it must be on terms that the recipient of the distribution accepts pro rata responsibility under the warranties and indemnities. A suitable clause for this purpose follows, it being assumed that "Trust" and "Trustees" are defined terms:

### [2A] Restrictions on distributions by trustee Vendors

2–07   **The liability of the Trustees under the Warranties is limited to the net value from time to time of the capital of the Trust, after deduction of sums due to the Inland Revenue and costs and fees properly chargeable against the capital of the Trust. The Trustees may not distribute capital of the Trust, other than for the payment of those sums, costs and fees, whilst a claim under the Warranties is outstanding or prior to the expiration of the time limit for making a claim, unless an undertaking in favour of the Purchaser is obtained from a beneficiary, in a form satisfactory to the Purchaser, by which the beneficiary accepts joint and several liability with the Trustees to the extent of the value of the distribution.**

Trustees will often prefer to amend this restriction so that they will be released from warranty liability to the extent that the recipient of a capital distribution agrees to be bound by the warranties. They will normally also seek to remove or restrict the liability of a trustee retiring or dying and will seek to restrict the liability to a defined period, normally not exceeding six years.

The remaining vendors may wish to protect themselves from suffering, as a result of this limitation, a larger proportion of any claim than is fairly attributable to their shareholding. For further discussion of this point see para.2–20.

An additional matter for trustee vendors to consider is whether they can give warranties and indemnities without incurring personal liability to the beneficiaries. No difficulty will arise in the case of an express power to give the warranties and indemnities being granted by the trust instrument. This would normally be included in trusts based upon modern precedents, but older trust deeds or those less comprehensively drafted may not contain such administrative provisions.

It may be argued, however, that no implied power exists but it is suggested that this approach fails to have regard to the true purpose of warranties. In effect they operate to adjust the purchase price and there can be no real doubt that trustees who have power to sell can negotiate a price which is adjusted according to the true value of the asset sold. The point is perhaps less clear in relation to the indemnities, and trustees might be well advised to decline to give indemnities or to obtain a Court order under the Trustee Act 1925, s.57.

A separate potential problem for purchasers from trustees arises under the Insolvency Act 1986. For further details reference should be made to the discussion of cl.1.2.4 in para.7–08.

## MANAGEMENT BUY-OUTS

This is another situation where there is normally a separation between ownership on the one hand and knowledge on the other. It might be thought that the management who are buying the target company and therefore know most about its affairs should not have the benefit of warranties from a vendor who ultimately would rely upon the management to provide the very information which is warranted. It is suggested, however, that the correct way to proceed under these circumstances is to divide the normal warranties into two broad categories.

**2–08**

First, there are the warranties which relate to matters independent of the activities of the management. These would include, in particular, the title of the target company to its assets, the title of the vendor to the shares, taxation liabilities and possibly the accuracy of the accounts.

The second group of warranties would be those which concern the management of the company such as the details of the employment contracts and, probably, day-to-day trading matters. Although there may be difficulty in determining whether a particular warranty falls into one category rather than the other, it is suggested that in principle the vendor should accept responsibility for the first group of warranties but not the second. The management should be made aware that any party providing funding for the acquisition will itself require warranties from the management which will inevitably go far beyond those given by the vendor.

## RECEIVERS AND ADMINISTRATORS

**2–09**　When an administrative receiver or administrator is appointed in respect of a company the administrator or receiver may, on occasion, hive-down the assets and continuing activities into a new subsidiary for the purpose of trading. This is most common in businesses such as hotels and retail businesses where it is damaging to customer confidence for the customers to be aware that the business is in administration or receivership. When a hive-down has occurred the receiver or administrator may on occasion sell the new subsidiary as opposed to the assets themselves. In these circumstances the administrator or receiver will not be prepared to provide any significant warranties in relation to the shares or the trading of the subsidiary. The only warranties which would normally be available would relate to the title of the shares being sold, the authorised and issued share capital of the target company (including any options outstanding), and compliance with statutory obligations in relation to the formation of the target company. A purchaser should also request a general warranty that the target company is not carrying on any activities other than those pursuant to the hive-down agreement. On occasion the administrators or receivers will, as a matter of policy, refuse to provide even these warranties and will offer instead vague assurances, sometimes only of a verbal nature, the benefits of which are negated by various exclusions in the sale agreement. Buying from receivers or administrators is high risk as the only comfort that can be obtained is through due diligence rather than any warranty or indemnity cover.

## SUBSCRIPTION FOR SHARES

**2–10**　Different principles arise where there is a subscription for, rather than a sale of, shares. In that event, the shareholders who existed before the injection of new capital receive no direct benefit from the payment for the new shares. Indeed, if the subscription price is a fair market value for the new shares, then the existing shareholders will not even receive an indirect benefit. The subscriber for the new shares is entitled to be satisfied that the price attributed to the new shares is correct and it will therefore wish to receive the normal warranties. The most logical party to give the warranties in this case will be the target company which is issuing the shares, as it will have received the consideration paid by the subscribers. If there are undisclosed liabilities then the subscription price will have been overstated and a refund should be made to the subscriber.

While on the face of it this may seem to provide a straightforward solution, the subscriber may find itself in a dilemma. Normally an issue of new shares takes place in circumstances where the money is required by the target company for its business activities, and there could be serious implications if the expected funds proved not to be available. The subscriber could therefore find that it suffers both from the unexpected liability which makes the value of the shares for which it subscribed less than at first appeared, and from the disadvantage of prejudicing the target company, in which it now has a stake, by causing it to pay back what could well be much needed resources. A further point which has to be borne in mind by the subscriber is that the target company will be able to refund only such part of the subscription money as constitutes a premium on the nominal value of the shares, as a greater refund would mean that the target company was allotting its shares at a discount.

It would seem that, in practice, where funds are provided by an institutional **2–11** investor, logic is ignored and the existing shareholders are required, as a term of the finance being made available, to give warranties in favour of the investor. The taxation position arising from a claim in these circumstances appears to be unsatisfactory for the shareholders, as they will receive no relief for the payment made; in particular it is suggested that the payment will not be taken into account in computing their capital gains tax liability on an eventual disposal of their own shareholdings, as none of the headings for computing allowable expenditure under TCGA 1992, s.38 will apply. Similarly, the payment may be treated disadvantageously for the subscriber in that, being paid otherwise than by a vendor to a purchaser, it may be treated as a capital receipt arising on a disposal of the right to receive it (see para.3–26).

## SUBSEQUENT DISPOSALS BY THE PURCHASER

The warranties are given to the purchaser and it may happen that the purchaser **2–12** itself disposes of all or part of the target company or the business which it has purchased before learning that it has a claim for a breach of warranty. The question will then arise whether the purchaser has suffered any loss as a result of the breach. It is considered that, where there has been a sale of the target company by the purchaser and the circumstances of that sale are such that there is no corresponding liability upon the purchaser in respect of the breach of warranty, then the purchaser cannot claim from the original vendors as it will have suffered no loss from the breach.

If, however, as would be normal, the purchaser has itself given warranties to its sub-purchaser then it is suggested that, in the absence of special provision, the liability of the original vendors would be equal to the lesser of the loss which the purchaser would have suffered if it had retained the target company and the loss which it has to make good to the sub-purchaser by reason of the warranties given on the sub-sale. If the sale agreement expressly provides that the warranties shall enure for the benefit of the purchaser's successors in title to the shares of the target company itself, or for the benefit of a sub-purchaser of the business, it is considered that the liability of the vendors will remain unaltered even if the purchaser ceases to own the target company or the acquired business.

This principle may well not be acceptable to the vendors, who may take the **2–13** view that the warranties which they give are not to be treated as assets capable of being sold by the purchaser. In general, a prohibition against assignment will be effective, although in cases where the parties can be taken to have contemplated that a subsequent sale of the shares or assets might occur, the purchaser may be taken to have acquired the warranties for the benefit of its successors in title (*Linden Gardens Ltd v (1) Lenesta Sludge Disposals Ltd (2) McLauglin & Harvey (3) Ashwell Construction Co. Ltd; (1) St Martins Property Corporation Ltd (2) St Martins Property Investments Ltd v Sir Robert McAlpine & Sons Ltd* [1994] 1 AC 85).

The position is complicated further by the Contracts (Rights of Third Parties) Act 1999, by virtue of which, if the sale agreement expressly provides that a term may be enforceable by a third party, then the relevant term will be enforceable by that party or, if a term purports to confer a benefit on a third party, there will be a rebuttable presumption that the relevant term will be enforceable by that third party. A purchaser contemplating an onward sale of the target company or acquired business might consider use of the Act. However, since generally rights under the Act are less satisfactory than rights conferred directly, it is in the interests of both the purchaser and, if third parties are not to be entitled to warranty protection, the vendors, to make the position totally clear. In reality application of the Contracts (Rights of Third Party) Act 1999 is in the vast majority of instances excluded from transactions. Clause 2D provides suitable wording for achieving this. Without such an exclusion, not only will a third party be able to enforce relevant terms of the sale agreement (subject to the provisions of the Act) but there would seem to be nothing in principle to stop them assigning those rights. If the Contracts (Rights of Third Party) Act 1999 is not to be excluded and there are relevant provisions in the sale agreement, this right of assignment should be excluded.

If assignment by the purchaser is to be prohibited the following clause should be included:

## [2B] No assignment of Warranties

2–14    **The Purchaser shall not be entitled to assign the Warranties and shall not be taken to hold the benefit of the Warranties for its successors in title to [the Shares] [the Assets].**

If assignment of the benefit of the agreement is permitted, the vendors should seek to ensure expressly that their liability under the warranties cannot be increased. A suitable qualification to the assignment clause is:

## [2C] Liability of Vendors to assignee

2–15    **If the benefit of the Warranties is assigned, the liability of the Vendors shall be no greater than it would have been had the Purchaser remained the owner of [the Shares] [the Business] and retained the benefit of the Warranties.**

If this approach is accepted, the vendors may want to make it clear that they will be entitled to avail themselves of any defences and rights of set-off that would otherwise be available to them in the event that a claim for breach of warranty is made. In these circumstances they should consider the insertion of the words **"and the Vendors shall be entitled to rely upon the defences and to exercise the rights that would have been available to the Vendors"** prior to the words **"had the Purchaser remained"** in cl.2C. From the purchaser's point of view, the principle involved would appear to be reasonable but practical difficulties can arise.

Where the damages resulting from a breach of warranty are not clearly quantifiable, a claim under the warranties may necessitate both the plaintiff and the original purchaser having to prove what damage they have suffered or, in the case of the original purchaser, would have suffered if the shares or business had been retained. Apart from this, the sub-purchaser will not normally have the means to compel the purchaser to quantify its notional loss unless the sub-sale agreement expressly includes an obligation to do so. The sub-purchaser would generally prefer, therefore, not to take an assignment of the warranties but instead to seek to impose full liability on its vendor (see also para.4–11).

The position in relation to indemnities on share sales is different in those cases **2–16** (which used to be the normal position but are increasingly less common) where the benefit of the indemnities belongs to the target company itself. If there is a sub-sale of the target company, the obligations under the tax deed will remain unaffected. In view of this, the covenantors may wish to consider whether they should restrict their liabilities so that the indemnity lapses in the event of a change of control of the target company. From the covenantors' point of view, this is not an unreasonable request. The outcome of disputes between the target company and the Inland Revenue may well depend upon the view that the Revenue take of the owners of the target company and, if the target company comes into the hands of an unsavoury purchaser, the covenantors could be prejudiced.

On the other hand, the purchaser will argue that the indemnity provided by the covenantors is an asset of the target company, and if the indemnity were to lapse on a sale then the target company would be devalued. While on the face of it this argument seems convincing, in practice it is most unlikely that the value of a company is ever determined on the basis of whether or not there exists an indemnity against past tax liabilities. In most cases the issue will not arise as indemnities are now routinely offered and accepted by the purchaser only.

Unless the parties have specifically agreed that the Contracts (Rights of Third **2–17** Parties) Act 1999 is to apply to the transaction, a provision excluding its application should be included in the sale agreement and the tax deed, as follows:

## [2D] Exclusion of the Contracts (Rights of Third Parties) Act 1999

**A person which is not a party to this [Agreement] [Tax Deed] has no right 2–18 under the Contracts (Rights of Third Parties) Act 1999 to enforce any of its terms but this does not affect the rights or remedies of a third party which exist or are available apart from that Act.**

## CHANGES IN CONTROL OF THE PURCHASER

**2–19**  Although the circumstances are different, the vendors and covenantors should also have regard to their position if there should be a change in control of the purchaser. They may consider that, whereas they were happy to give the warranties and indemnities in circumstances involving a specific known purchaser, they would not be content to rely upon the way that these would be enforced by an unknown party who took over control of the purchaser.

A second point arises from the fact that the warranties and indemnities, while primarily imposing liabilities upon the vendors and covenantors, will also impose certain obligations upon the purchaser. These relate to such matters as giving the conduct of litigation to the vendors and covenantors and reimbursing the covenantors with any repayments of tax following a successful appeal. The vendors and covenantors may therefore be concerned that the financial status of the purchaser and its ability to perform its obligations might be reduced following a change of control.

Accordingly, it is understandable if the vendors and covenantors should wish to provide that their liability should cease if there were a change of control of the purchaser. In general, the purchaser would not be prepared to accept this restriction as it is irrelevant to the purchaser itself who controls it. However, the question is really one that has to be debated with the owners of the purchaser and, if the purchaser is owned by a small group of individuals and their families, they should in practice have limited grounds for objecting to the concept. There will often be difficulty in deciding upon a suitable definition of "control" for this purpose and, even if the owners of the purchaser are sympathetic to the proposal, this may prevent agreement being reached.

## CONFLICTS OF INTEREST BETWEEN VENDORS AND COVENANTORS

**2–20**  In the case of a sale of a business, there is in the vast majority of cases one clear vendor and no problem of conflict should arise. The position will often be different where there is a share sale and, although it is usual to look upon the vendors and the covenantors as a single composite body who can readily be advised by one solicitor, this may not be the case for a variety of reasons. Some of those are dealt with above and relate primarily to cases where there are differences between the financial benefits which are derived from the transaction and the information which is available for dealing with the warranties.

Vendors may also be concerned where there are trustee vendors whose liability is restricted to the trust assets and, between themselves, the vendors and the covenantors may wish to provide for special treatment of liabilities arising from warranties and indemnities which are in some way related to benefits which have been enjoyed by members of the company. Typical examples relate to indemnities in respect of employee benefits or loans to participators (ICTA 1988, s.419). In these circumstances, the vendors may wish, amongst themselves, to consider including in the agreement in relation to the warranties the following provision:

## [2E] Sharing of liability between Vendors

**Without affecting their joint and several liability under this Agreement, the**    2–21
**Vendors agree that, as between themselves, any one person shall bear only**
**his appropriate part of a liability which arises in relation to the Warranties.**
**For this purpose "appropriate part" means:**

**[2E.1] in the case of a liability which is fairly attributable to, or which arises**
**by reason of, income or benefits received by, or the act or default of, that**
**person or persons connected with him (not themselves being any of the**
**Vendors): the whole liability; and**

**[2E.2] in any other case that proportion of the liability that the number of**
**the Shares sold by him bears to the total number of the Shares.**

This clause assumes that the agreement includes a suitable definition of "connected", such as that contained in ICTA 1988, s.839.

A similar provision could also be included in the tax deed. In extreme cases of a conflict of interest between the parties, they should consider the desirability of separate professional representation. See also the discussion of joint and several liability in para.3–15.

A purchaser may, however, prefer for such matters to be dealt with in a separate contribution deed prepared by the respective vendors' advisors so as to avoid any confusion on the otherwise clear basis of liability between itself and the relevant vendors.

# Chapter 3

# Rights and Liabilities

## Breach of Warranty or Misrepresentation

**3–01**   The entitlement of the purchaser, who finds that the company or business is not as it anticipated, to claim damages for breach of contract will depend on the scope of the warranties expressly or impliedly given to it. The contractual remedy for a breach will generally be damages or, rather exceptionally, rescission. Both of these are discussed below.

As an alternative remedy, the purchaser might be able to claim rescission or damages on the grounds of misrepresentation by the vendors. The purchaser is fully protected against fraudulent misrepresentation but the position is more complicated if the misrepresentation is either wholly innocent or, whilst not fraudulent, is the result of negligence by the person making the representation. The rights of the purchaser are governed by the Misrepresentation Act 1967 and a detailed analysis can be found in any of the standard books on contract law. There are, however, certain points which need to be considered in the context of a transaction where there is a detailed legal agreement between the parties which includes specifically prepared and negotiated warranties.

**3–02**   If the misrepresentation was negligent, the purchaser, as an alternative or in addition to rescission, has a right to damages, computed on the same basis as if the misrepresentation had been fraudulent (s.2(1)). In the case of an innocent misrepresentation, damages may be awarded in place of rescission (s.2(2)).

As the purchaser who has the benefit of warranties in an acquisition agreement is in principle protected by the agreement, it might be thought that, in the absence of fraud, the purchaser would not have the right to seek relief for a breach of warranty by claiming, instead, for misrepresentation. This, however, is not the case as the rights under the contract and under the Misrepresentation Act are cumulative and the latter may be excluded only to the extent that the exclusion satisfies the test of reasonableness (s.3).

There are two particular implications for the vendors which arise from the concurrent rights under the contract and under the Act:

(1)   The measure of damages is different in the two cases.

(2)   The provisions of the contract limiting the time within which claims for breach of warranty may be brought (see para.3–18) and imposing floors and ceilings on the claims (see paras 3–20 and 3–23) will not apply to claims for misrepresentation unless expressly stated otherwise. If the restrictions

were extended to claims for misrepresentation they might even be rendered invalid by s.3.

In the past, attempts have been made to exclude liability for misrepresentation **3–03** by incorporating into the contract a clause to the effect that the contract represents the whole agreement between the parties in relation to the subject matter of the transaction and that the purchaser acknowledges that it has not relied on any representations which are not included as warranties. Such a clause is often termed an "entire agreement clause". The effect of such a clause was considered in *Thomas Witter Ltd v TBP Industries Ltd* [1996] 2 All E.R. 573. It was held that an entire agreement clause was ineffectual in excluding the right of the purchaser to make a claim based upon misrepresentation even though the representations in question were included as express warranties. In particular the clause was unreasonable within the meaning of s.3 because it purported to exclude claims based on misrepresentation even where there was fraud. However, in *E A Grimstead & Son Ltd v McGarrigan* [1998–99] Info. T.L.R. 384 the Court of Appeal found *obiter* that an entire agreement clause that did not carve out fraudulent misrepresentation from the exclusion was reasonable in the context in which it was used, this being in circumstances of a commercial contract between experienced parties of equal bargaining power, where the parties had entered into the arrangement with (most importantly) the benefit of professional advice. (Chadwick L.J.'s reasoning in that case was that it was reasonable to assume that the parties desired commercial certainty, that the bargaining between them would be found in the documents that they had signed and that the price to be paid reflected the commercial risk which each party was prepared to accept. It was legitimate and commercially desirable that both parties should be able to measure the risk and agree the price on the basis of the warranties that had been given and accepted.) This is an approach that was supported by the High Court in *Government of Zanzibar v British Aerospace* [2000] W.L.R. 2333 and the Court of Appeal in *Watford Electronics Ltd v Sanderson CFL Ltd* [2001] EWCA Civ 317. However, notwithstanding that judicial thinking in these cases would tend to suggest that where parties have entered into arrangements with the benefit of professional advice the approach in *Thomas Witter* would no longer be followed, in the interests of certainty it is nonetheless common practice for the entire agreement clauses to include a carve out for fraudulent misrepresentation. A properly drafted and reasonable entire agreement clause which deals with this point should effectively operate to exclude innocent or negligent misrepresentation claims.

# RESCISSION

The circumstances in which a right to rescind the sale agreement will arise are **3–04** complex and it is not the purpose of this discussion to provide a detailed analysis of them. In practice, however, rescission is primarily a remedy against misrepresentation and is generally of limited value. The essential requirement is that the parties should be capable of being restored substantially to their original position. This will often not be possible once completion of the sale has taken place. Also the purchaser will lose its right of rescission if, once it discovers the misrepresentation, it nevertheless takes action which effectively affirms the contract. Normally the purchaser will continue the running of the target company or the acquired business whilst it is considering its rights and thus is likely to be deemed to have adopted the sale. In practice therefore rescission is not a realistic option once completion has taken place.

Rescission is, however, a significant remedy where there is an interval between contract and completion. In that event, it is customary by the use of *interregnum* provisions to restrict the method of conducting the businesses of the target company, or the business that is being acquired, so that the interests of the vendors and the purchaser are adequately recognised during the intervening period. An example of clauses which might be adopted in this situation are set out in Appendix 2 and, although they are drafted in the context of a share purchase, they may be readily adapted to a purchase of assets. If, prior to completion, it is found that the warranted circumstances do not exist, either because they never did or because of a change which occurs in relation to the target company or the business, it is normal for the purchaser to be given an express right to rescind in terms such as the following:

### [3A] Right to rescind prior to Completion

**3–05**   **The Purchaser may rescind this Agreement by notice in writing to the Vendors or the Vendors' solicitors if prior to Completion:**

**[3A.1]**   **it appears that the Warranties were not or have ceased to be accurate [in all material respects]; or**

**[3A.2]**   **an act or event occurs which, had it occurred on or before today's date, would have had the effect that there would have been a [material] breach of the Warranties; or**

**[3A.3]**   **there is a [material] breach or non-fulfilment of the Warranties which (being capable of remedy) is not remedied prior to Completion.**

Although in practice it should be possible to achieve an effective rescission prior to completion without too much difficulty, in some cases the vendors may prefer to complete the sale and suffer a reduction in the sale price as a result of a warranty claim. This could be the case, for example, if the simple act of announcing the exchange of contracts had such an unsettling effect on staff, suppliers or customers that the business could not readily be resumed under the original ownership if the sale did not proceed. If a right of rescission is accepted, cl.3A should be amended by the vendors by the addition of the words in square brackets, although materiality would usually be defined by reference to financial criteria.

To avoid the argument that the failure by the purchaser to exercise a right of rescission amounts to a waiver of its right to claim for damages, it is helpful to include an express denial of waiver as in cl.4T. For a further discussion as to the circumstances in which the remedy is available and the effect of a rescission, reference should be made to any of the leading works on contract law.

# DAMAGES

The remedy which is normally sought by a purchaser where there is a breach of **3–06** warranty is compensation by the payment of damages. The measure of damages will be determined on the normal principles of contract law or, if the claim is based on misrepresentation, on the rules relating to claims in tort. The standard textbooks should be consulted for a detailed analysis of the principles involved in determining the quantum of damages in any particular case. The basic rule in contract is that the purchaser should be compensated for its loss of bargain; in the case of a claim in tort, the damages will be such as will put the purchaser back in the same position that it would have been in if the representation had not been made. Normally the measure of damages will be the same whether the purchase has been effected for cash or for shares of the purchaser.

A considerable complication arises in the case of a business sale if the sale agreement adopts the normal practice of allocating the purchase consideration amongst the various categories of assets being sold. It is often advantageous for the purchaser's tax position to attribute the minimum acceptable amount to the goodwill (see the comments in para.3–28). If the breach of warranty is of such a nature that the value of the goodwill is diminished, it is difficult as a general principle to see how the purchaser can claim a loss greater than the amount allocated to the goodwill. The purchaser would have to argue that the values attributed to the other assets, such as stocks, are valid only if the company is in a sound commercial position. If the breach of warranty has an adverse effect on the business as a whole, it might be the case that a different valuation should have been applied to the other assets. To assist the purchaser in arguing that proposition, it could seek to include the following clause (for the purposes of which the definitions of "Goodwill" and "Assets" in Pt 1 of Appendix 5 are used):

## [3B] Purchaser's loss on breach of Warranty

**If a Warranty does not relate to the value, or to anything affecting the value, 3–07 of the Assets other than the Goodwill, the loss suffered by the Purchaser as a result of a breach of the Warranty shall be determined as if the value of each of the Assets (other than the Goodwill) was not that stated in clause [ ] but the lesser value that they would have had if the sale of the Business had been a forced sale and the reduction in the value of those Assets was additional consideration given for the Goodwill. If the parties are unable to agree to the adjustments to be made under this clause, the matter shall be referred to an independent firm of accountants nominated by the President of the Institute of Chartered Accountants in England and Wales for their**

**determination as independent experts [and not as arbitrators and the Arbitration Act 1996 shall not apply] and, in the absence of manifest error, their determination shall be final.**

Apart from this special consideration in relation to business sales, the parties may find it convenient to provide expressly as to how damages are to be quantified in a particular case. A clause dealing with this is the following:

## [3C] Measure of damages for breaches of Warranty

3–08 **Without limiting the rights of the Purchaser or its ability to claim damages on any basis if there is a breach of Warranty or any of the Warranties is untrue or misleading, if [the Company incurs or becomes subject to a liability or an increase in any liability which it would not have incurred or been subject to had the breach not occurred or] the value of any asset of the Company is less or becomes less than the value would have been had the breach not occurred then the Vendors undertake to the Purchaser to pay to the Purchaser (as the Purchaser elects) in cash on demand a sum equal to the liability or increased liability, or the reduction in the value of the asset (as appropriate), or the reduction in the value of the Shares caused by the breach.**

This clause effectively gives the purchaser the right to choose between the normal measure of damages for breach of contract and the indemnity basis of damages. If normal damages would exceed the amount paid by way of indemnity, the purchaser's right to the additional compensation is preserved. The vendors will usually wish for a damages basis to apply while a purchaser will usually favour an indemnity basis. Current convention follows a damages basis in most circumstances. Usually the sale agreement is silent on the measure of damages to apply which preserves the common law basis of damages.

3–09 The clause may be used in the case of the purchase of a business although, in that case, the words in square brackets will not be relevant.

Where the consideration for the acquisition is the allotment of shares of the purchaser, the effect of a payment of damages is somewhat obscure. The consideration for the allotment will be the transfer of the shares of the target company or the business of the vendor company. If, in the event, the value of the target company or the business proves to be less than the par value of the consideration shares, then it might be thought that the purchaser will be in the rather unfortunate position of having allotted its shares for a consideration of less than par which, of course, is not permitted. It is suggested that in practice this should not give rise to a difficulty as, if the directors of the purchaser company, acting bona fide and on the basis of a valuation of the target company or the business, have allotted shares which they thought were for a consideration at least equal to par, then there can be no criticism if it proves to be the case that the consideration was less than par. A further protection in practice arises under CA 1985, s.103 which requires non-cash consideration for the issue of shares of a public limited company to be valued before the allotment takes place.

So far as the vendors are concerned, the consideration which they receive will **3–10** be in the form of securities of the purchaser which have a variable value. If compensation has to be paid under the warranties and, at the time that the claim is made, the consideration shares have fallen in value, the vendors might wish to take advantage of the provisions of CA 1985, Pt V, which permit a company to purchase its own shares. The vendors might suggest that, in the event of a warranty claim arising, the claim should be satisfied by the purchaser re-purchasing an appropriate number of the consideration shares for a nil purchase price. In this way, the vendors will be put in the same position as if the target company had been correctly valued in the first instance and the number of the consideration shares reduced accordingly.

The vendors will wish the purchaser to limit its claim for damages on a breach of warranty to the net loss it suffers, taking into account any unexpected benefits which the target company or business enjoys. It might well seem reasonable that the purchaser should not complain about the bad without giving credit for the good, and a possible clause in the case of a share sale is the following:

## [3D] Credit for improvements

**The liability of the Vendors under the Warranties shall be reduced by:** **3–11**

[3D.1] **an amount equal to the value or additional value of any fixed assets (apart from the Properties and goodwill) owned at Completion which were not included in the Accounts or were included at less than market value after deducting (in the case of assets acquired after the Balance Sheet Date) their cost of acquisition [and Taxation which would arise on their disposal at those values];**

[3D.2] **the amount of or by which Taxation for which the Company is accountable is extinguished or reduced as a result of the claim giving rise to the liability;**

[3D.3] **the amount by which a provision for Taxation [not being a provision for deferred Taxation], bad or doubtful debts or contingent or other liabilities contained in the Accounts proves after Completion to have been excessive, except by reason of a reduction in tax rates [or as a result of an event occurring, or action taken by the Purchaser or the Company,] after Completion;**

[3D.4] **the amount of debts paid which had been previously written off [less attributable Taxation];**

[3D.5] **the amount of credits, recoveries or other benefits which have been or will be received or obtained by the Company by reason of the matters giving rise to the liability.**

Only the first of the above sub-paragraphs might be relevant in relation to a **3–12** business sale depending upon the actual terms agreed. (In such circumstances

"Goodwill" should be a defined term. The definition of "Goodwill" in Pt 1 of
Appendix 5 would be suitable for these purposes).

The concept of this clause is not particularly fair if the purchase price for the
shares has been calculated otherwise than on the basis of the asset value of the
target company. Even in that event it is difficult to see how the reduction can be
quantified in any but the simplest case. This, of itself, is not an adequate reason
to reject it as an arbitration procedure (for example permitting the target company's auditors to certify the adjustment) can be included. If the purchaser
accepts the clause, it should add the words in square brackets to make a rather
crude adjustment for the tax implications and to avoid the vendors benefiting
from reductions in taxation liability which were not attributable to circumstances
existing before completion. In relation to this last point, the vendors would not
normally be entitled to savings which result from a retrospective reduction in the
corporation tax rate or the carry-back by the target company of subsequent losses.
Similarly, the adequacy of a provision for deferred taxation will depend on later
events and should not affect the liability of the vendors whether it proves to be
excessive or inadequate.

## Security in Relation to the Warranties

3–13    The vendors will have a potential liability to the purchaser for perhaps the whole
amount of the consideration which they receive and this liability might contingently exist for a number of years. This is particularly so in the case of the
obligations under the tax deed which customarily continue for at least six years.
The purchaser should review the ability of the vendors in the case of a share sale
or the vendor in the case of a business sale to meet claims which might be
quantified only after a considerable period of time. This is of particular concern
where some or all of the vendors may be looking to retire abroad. Where the
transaction involves the sale of a business, the ability of the vendor company to
meet warranty claims needs particular attention, as the liabilities retained by the
vendor will invariably, and often drastically, reduce the net assets which it has
available.

The purchaser might wish to consider whether it should require security for
these liabilities. In relation to the tax deed, it is in practice impossible for the
purchaser to require the covenantors to provide any significant amount of security for the whole of the six-year period. There is a possibility that the vendors
will agree to provide security for the life of the warranties if this is sufficiently
short. It is not unusual in the case of a share sale, but less likely on a business
sale, for part of the purchase price to be retained in an escrow account for some
period to enable the purchaser to determine whether warranty claims are in fact
likely to arise. This is usually appropriate where there is a risk that the sale
proceeds are likely to be difficult to trace.

3–14    If the consideration is in the form of shares of the purchaser, the most suitable
security is a charge on those shares. This, however, cannot be given in favour of
the purchaser if it is a public limited company (CA 1985, s.150). A charge on the
consideration shares in favour of the target company to support claims under the

tax deed will be effective, as s.150 does not restrict charges in favour of the public company's subsidiaries. In the case of private companies it is common for the articles to amend regulation 11 in Table A of the Companies (Table A to F) Regs 1985 (SI 1985 No. 805) so that the company has a lien on the shares held by a member in respect of all sums which he owes to the company. To take advantage of the same principle for securing warranty claims it would be possible for the purchaser to sub-sell the shares and assign the warranties to a subsidiary, which would take a charge or lien to secure potential claims. This solution is not free from difficulties and reference should be made to para.2–12.

While it is obvious that the purchaser has a risk in respect of these unsecured liabilities, it is often overlooked that the vendors and covenantors are also at risk in respect of the obligations of the purchaser under the warranties and under the tax deed. This point arises particularly under the tax deed where it is not unusual for a tax liability to arise because of a decision of a lower court only to find that this is reversed on appeal to a higher court. In those circumstances, the payments under the tax deed may pass backwards and forwards between the covenantors and the purchaser.

## JOINT AND SEVERAL LIABILITY

In the absence of express provisions to the contrary, where two or more parties      **3–15**
undertake the same obligation they are considered to have assumed liability jointly with each other (*White v Tyndall* (1888) 13 A.C. 263). This presumption can be rebutted by an express statement in the sale agreement, and in the case of the sale of shares it is almost invariable for the purchaser to request that the warranties and the covenants under the tax deed are given on a joint and several basis by the vendors and the covenantors.

The broad effect of this is well known. The purchaser or target company, having the benefit of the warranty or indemnity, can recover against any one of the vendors or covenantors leaving him to exercise his right to obtain a contribution from the other vendors or covenantors. This right of contribution is given under the Civil Liability (Contribution) Act 1978 and entitles the court to determine a just and equitable basis for allocating the liability amongst the vendors and the covenantors. More commonly the liability is shared between the vendors or covenantors by a specific deed of contribution drawn up by their advisors and reflecting what has been agreed as just and equitable between them. Purchasers, or their advisers, commonly set great store by the apparent advantage of joint and several liability, since it offers the purchaser the flexibility to sue all or some of the vendors or covenantors for the full amount. In the normal case, however, the ultimate effect is to shift from the purchaser to the vendors the risk that, if a claim is made, a vendor may not be traceable or may not be able to meet his share of the liability.

If, as is commonly the position, the vendors and covenantors are one and the      **3–16**
same and the consideration is paid to them pro rata to their shareholdings, the statutory concept of liability sharing will give rise to no difficulty. The following are some examples of cases where complications arise:

(1) If some of the vendors are not required to give the warranties and indemnities or different maximum claim levels apply, as frequently happens in the case of trustee shareholders (see para.2–06). While in that event it may normally be the case that the liability will be apportioned among those vendors who do give the warranties, or who are not able to take advantage of a reduced maximum, in proportion to the consideration which they receive, this may be unfair. If, for example, the target company is owned by two families and one of the families holds a large number of their shares through a trust, then the family for whose benefit the trust exists should accept responsibility for liability which would have fallen upon the trustees if they had given the warranties.

(2) If the share capital of the target company consists of preference shares and ordinary shares. It would normally be appropriate for liability under the warranties to be borne only by the ordinary shareholders. Preference shares usually have a fixed value and beyond their fixed value do not ordinarily participate in the overall equity value.

(3) If the claim under the warranty results from benefits received by one of the vendors, such as a distribution from the target company. In that event, it would be appropriate for the liability under the warranty to be borne by the shareholder who has received the corresponding advantage.

Accordingly, where the sale is not a straightforward case of all the vendors giving the warranties and indemnities, the vendors and covenantors should come to an agreement amongst themselves determining how liability should be apportioned. This contribution agreement may be included in the sale agreement and tax deed so as to bind the purchaser, although usually a purchaser will not wish to be a party to this. A clause which partly deals with this is suggested in para.2–21 and this may suffice where the position is not particularly complicated. If, however, there are significant differences in the interests of the parties or, for example, one shareholder is willing to accept liability under the warranties in respect both of his or her own holding and those of other members of his family or his trustees, then the clause will have to be altered.

**3–17**    It will also be necessary in a complicated case to determine how any provisions relating to a floor for claims should apply (see para.3–20). In the absence of a special arrangement, it would seem that the floor for claims would operate for the benefit of the parties who are liable in relation to the first claim which happens to be made. A fairer arrangement would be for the vendors and covenantors to agree amongst themselves that the benefit of any floor should apply pro rata to the liabilities which they incur. Even this may not be wholly satisfactory in cases where, for example, a warranty liability arises specifically because of a benefit which has been received by one shareholder and where the other shareholders have had nothing to do with it.

If the vendors are successful in making inroads into the basic concept of joint and several liability, there are two approaches which they might adopt. The more extreme is to provide that each vendor is liable only for an appropriate proportion of any claim—normally being the proportion which he receives of the total purchase price. A more modest alternative would be to provide that the total liability of each vendor has a ceiling, which would usually be the amount of the sale proceeds which he actually receives. It is a matter for negotiation to determine whether one of these approaches—and if so which—should apply.

## PERIODS OF LIMITATION

The normal period of limitation within which an action must be brought is six    **3–18** years, if the right arises under a document which is not a deed, and 12 years if there is a deed. It is usual for the period to be reduced to two or three years in respect of the non-taxation warranties on a share sale and to six or seven years for the tax warranties and for the tax deed. The underlying principle is that one or two audits of the target company should identify most defects which existed at the time of the sale but, as the statutory limitation period for taxation matters is six years from the end of the relevant accounting period (TMA 1970, s.34) (in the absence of special factors such as fraud), a six-year period from the end of the accounting period should apply to the tax deed and the tax warranties.

Sometimes a purchaser may seek to differentiate between limitation periods for different types of warranties, for instance environmental, where a longer period than the two or three years normally requested may be sought. It will be a matter for negotiation in each particular case whether these matters should be dealt with differently than claims based on other warranties but, as a matter of drafting, it is possible to specify different limitation periods for any of the warranties. More often, if a purchaser has a particular concern it will request an indemnity rather than a warranty and the limitations, if any, that apply to that will be a matter for negotiation.

In the case of a business sale, there are sound reasons for arguing that the statutory periods should not be altered. Although the purchaser is not concerned about the emergence of undisclosed liabilities (except indirectly where these could have an adverse impact on goodwill), deficiencies in the assets acquired may come to light less quickly than in the case of a share sale. This is because the purchaser of a company acquires all its files and other papers which will assist in the verification of the ownership of assets. In the case of a business purchase, the purchaser has no information about the ownership of assets other than that which it is able to obtain from the vendor and problems may not arise or be capable of identification for an indefinite period.

It is consistent with this principle that the tax warranties should have the same limitation period as the tax deed. As the vendors will normally prefer claims which can be brought under either heading to be based on the warranties (see para.1–09) this approach should be satisfactory to both parties. A suitable clause dealing with this aspect in relation to the warranties on a share sale is as follows:

### [3E] Time limit for Warranty claims

**A claim shall not be brought by the Purchaser in respect of a breach of the**    **3–19**
**Warranties unless notice of the claim (specifying in reasonable detail the**

circumstances which give rise to the claim, the breach that results and the amount claimed) has been given to the Vendors before the expiration of the appropriate period. The claim shall be deemed to have been withdrawn (if it has not been previously satisfied, settled or withdrawn) one year [six months] after the expiration of the appropriate period, unless proceedings in respect of it have commenced by being issued and served on any of the Vendors. For the purpose of this clause, the "appropriate period":

[3E.1]      in respect of claims which could have been brought by the Purchaser under the Tax Deed is seven years from the Balance Sheet Date;

[3E.2]      in respect of claims which arise under clauses [ ] or [ ] of Schedule [ ] is [ ] years from Completion;

[3E.3]      in respect of other claims is [two years from Completion] [the period ending nine months after the end of the first accounting period of the Company to begin after Completion].

The vendors might reasonably require that the period specified in cl.3E.1 should be six years from the end of the last complete accounting period but, if the indemnities relate also to liabilities of the current period, it is logical that the six years should run from the end of the current period. The choice of the alternative periods specified in cl.3E.3 will depend upon how much of the current accounting period of the target company has expired at completion. Clause 3E.2 would be used where specific warranties have been identified as having a longer limitation period.

In the case of the sale of a business, the first sub-clause will not be relevant. Apart from imposing a time limit for claims, a major purpose of this clause is to ensure that the purchaser cannot maintain an open position by giving a general notice of claims at the end of the period. The vendors are justified in requiring a claim to be made in sufficiently specific terms to ensure that it is bona fide. The purchaser cannot reasonably object to the restriction—although the exact period of limitation is a matter for negotiation—but it must be careful to ensure that, when a claim is made, the precise procedure specified in the clause is followed.

## Minimum Level of Liability

**3–20**     To avoid the trouble of trivial claims, it is usual for the vendors to require, and for the purchaser to accept, that small claims are completely excluded and that claims should not be brought unless they exceed a specified floor. Trivial claims are usually referred to as *de minimis* and the floor as a "threshold" or "basket". There is, however, no absolute convention as to whether, once the minimum level is exceeded, the claim can relate to the full amount or only to the excess. More often than not it will be the full amount. If the rationale for having a floor really is simply the avoidance of small claims, then once claims exceed the minimum the liability should be for the full amount. An alternative view is that the floor operates as a kind of margin of error allowed to the vendors, on which basis only the excess liability should be discharged.

A clause which takes the second approach is as follows:

## [3F] Exclusion of small claims

**The Vendors shall not be liable in respect of a claim brought by the**   **3–21**
**Purchaser for a breach of the Warranties unless their liability for all claims**
**would exceed in aggregate £[ ] and in that event they shall be liable only for**
**the excess.**

If the first approach is adopted, it would suffice to omit the last part of this clause commencing with the words **"and in that event . . . "**. It is preferable, however, for the purchaser to make the position absolutely clear by substituting for those words the following:

**" . . . and in that event they shall be liable for the whole of the claims and not**
**merely the excess."**

If the vendors wish all small claims to be disregarded, even if claims in aggregate exceed the agreed floor, the clause should read as follows:

**The Vendors shall not be liable in respect of a claim brought by the**
**Purchaser for a breach of the Warranties where the liability would not**
**exceed £[ ]. The Vendors shall not be liable in respect of other claims unless**
**their liability for all the other claims would exceed in aggregate £[ ] and, in**
**that event, they shall be liable only for the excess. [For the purpose of this**
**clause, all claims arising from a particular set of circumstances shall be**
**treated as one claim.]**

The purchaser would wish to add the last sentence so as to avoid the possibility   **3–22**
that a series of claims, which while individually small are large in aggregate, could be excluded even though arising from the same cause. An example would be if there were a large number of small claims made against the target company as a result of defects in goods manufactured by it.

It should be noted that neither version of cl.3F will necessarily be effective in protecting the vendors from being involved in claims which the purchaser genuinely believes will exceed the floor even if, in the event, the liability is held to be for a lesser amount and the vendors are accordingly absolved. An unscrupulous purchaser could with comparative ease claim an amount in excess of the minimum level in the belief that the vendors, to avoid the nuisance of litigation, would be prepared to make a payment in settlement even though the liability is likely in fact to be below the minimum level.

A similar clause can be used in the tax deed, although the concept underlying the tax indemnities is such that it would normally be appropriate for the covenantors to be liable for the full amount of the claim on a pound for pound basis without any financial deductibles. Sometimes the purchaser may be persuaded to agree a "floor" to apply to the tax deed but rarely any *de minimis*. There is little logic to this position although the usual justification is that a tax liability is an actual liability which the company will need to pay rather than a loss of some element of "bargain" as might be the case in a warranty claim. However, often the distinction is not clear cut, for example where a tax relief which was not treated as an "asset" by the purchaser has been lost and gives rise to an indemnity payment under the tax deed. The purchaser would in any event wish any financial limit to be in the aggregate, and not to apply separately to claims under the warranties and the tax deed. This would be achieved by adding **"or by the Purchaser under the Tax Deed"** after the words **"by the Purchaser for a breach of the Warranties"** in cl.3F. This wording will not be appropriate if the vendors and covenantors are not identical and in that event separate floors would have to be agreed. The clause would, in any case, need a cross-reference in the tax deed.

If the purchaser agrees to a floor for claims, this could affect its view on amendments which the vendors might wish to make to the warranties. It is frequently suggested by the vendors that certain warranties should be amended so that they apply only to "material" matters (see, for example, cl.1.14 in para. 7–31). From the purchaser's point of view, however, such a qualification would provide a double margin of error for the vendors if there is also a minimum claims clause in the sale agreement; but, for the vendors, it is undesirable for the protection offered by the clause to be whittled away by the cumulative effect of small items in relation to which the purchaser has no real concern.

## Maximum Level of Liability

3–23    The vendors commonly seek a ceiling (or "cap") on their liability under the warranties and indemnities. This is usually fixed at the amount of the consideration paid for the target company or business, on the somewhat questionable basis that the purchaser should not actually have to be paid to take it over.

This argument, although generally accepted, is not necessarily appropriate from the purchaser's point of view for a number of reasons:

(1) In many cases the real consideration given by the purchaser is not only the price actually paid but also any further sums specifically provided at the time of the purchase, for example sums required to repay loans made to the target company by the vendors or to obtain the release of guarantees given by the vendors.

(2) The purchaser will normally provide funds for the subsequent development of the target company or business, thereby increasing the total amount invested by it.

(3) If the vendors had retained the target company and liabilities materialised which effectively gave the group a negative value, the vendors could not necessarily have avoided the obligation to make up the difference by

allowing the group to be wound up. If the vendors are individuals, there will frequently be personal guarantees outstanding and, if there is a corporate vendor, the insolvent liquidation of a subsidiary could result in an event of default under financial and other agreements.

It is sometimes suggested, by way of justification for the ceiling, that at worst the purchaser could recover from the vendors the cost of its purchase and avoid any further liability by allowing the target company or business to be liquidated. This, however, is rarely a real choice open to a purchaser for reasons similar to those mentioned in para.(3). In particular, in the case of the purchase of a business, the purchaser will be able to contemplate a liquidation only if it was established purely for the purpose of carrying on the acquired business and had no other activities. As with many of the questions relating to the scope of warranties, it is ultimately a question for the parties as to where the residual risk of unexpected problems should lie.     **3–24**

The simplest form of a clause imposing a ceiling on claims, which would have to be included in both the sale agreement and the tax deed, is:

## [3G] Ceiling on claims

**The total liability of [the Vendors and the Covenantors], arising by reason of claims under the Warranties or the Tax Deed, shall not exceed £[ ].**     **3–25**

The purchaser would wish to be able to recover the aggregate of the purchase price and all other sums laid out by it at the time of the acquisition. Merely to state a ceiling which exceeds the purchase price payable for the shares or business—because, for example, it includes the amount of loans repaid to the vendors at completion or obligations of the business for which the purchaser accepts responsibility—will not give the purchaser the automatic right to take those additional amounts into account in determining its entitlement to damages (see also para.3–06).

If the agreed limit is to be the purchaser's total investment, cl.3G could be expanded by replacing the reference to "**£[ ]**" by:

**"an amount equal to the aggregate of £[ ] and the amounts which the Purchaser provides for the Company to enable it to discharge its liabilities to the Vendor and any other expenditure reasonably incurred by the Purchaser in consummation of the transactions contemplated in this Agreement."**

The advantage of stating a specific sum is clarity but if the purchase price is not quantifiable at the date of the sale agreement (for example, because there is additional consideration payable according to future profits) it might be appropriate to replace the reference to a specific sum by:

**"an amount equal to the total consideration paid for [the Shares][the Business]."**

The above formulations are adequate, in principle, where there is a cash purchase. If, however, the consideration consists wholly or partly of shares or loan stock of the purchaser, it might be fairer, though complex, to fix the ceiling at the value of the consideration securities at the date of claim.

## TAXATION TREATMENT OF PAYMENTS UNDER WARRANTIES AND INDEMNITIES IN CONNECTION WITH SHARE PURCHASES

**3–26**   In general, the vendors will hold the shares of the target company as a capital asset and the proceeds of sale will be brought into account in a capital gains tax computation. A partial recognition of the taxation implications is contained in TCGA 1992, s.49. This provides that, in the first instance, no account is taken of any contingent liability in respect of a warranty or representation made on a sale of property other than land. If and when a liability materialises, a retrospective adjustment is made.

Accordingly, a payment under a warranty operates retrospectively to effect a reduction in the purchase consideration. The vendor's chargeable receipt is decreased and a corresponding reduction is made to the purchaser's base cost with, on an eventual sale of the shares, a related increase in its chargeable gain at that time. This is clear enough if the consideration is cash, but the position is more obscure if the disposal is wholly or partly by way of exchange for shares or other securities of the purchaser. In such circumstances, it is suggested, and it is understood to be the view of the Inland Revenue, that:

(1) where the vendor receives wholly securities of the purchaser, the warranty payment is treated as additional consideration given for those securities under TCGA 1992, s.128(1), being the section giving a roll-over on a capital reorganisation;

(2) where the vendor receives a mixture of securities and cash, the payment will be apportioned pro rata and dealt with partly under s.128(1) and partly under s.49.

It is considered that in the rather unusual case of the shares of the target company being held by the vendor as trading stock, a warranty payment will be treated as a revenue expense.

Different principles apply to payments under the tax deed where, unusually, it is structured such that the indemnity is in favour of the target company rather than the purchaser. The legal position, which derives from the decision in *Zim Properties Limited v Procter* [1985] S.T.C. 90, has been recognised by the Inland Revenue as giving rise to some unintended results. In that case it was held that a right to compensation arising from the negligence of a solicitor constituted an asset. The receipt of the compensation resulted in a disposal of the asset for the amount received. By analogy, it would seem that the contingent right to receive an indemnity payment is an asset of the target company of which disposal is made when the payment is received.

As the right would have been acquired for no consideration and without a **3–27** corresponding disposal, no allowable expenditure can be brought into account to reduce the chargeable gain (TCGA 1992, s.17). The whole payment is thus taxable. On December 19, 1988 the Inland Revenue published a concession (ESC D33) to the effect that payments made by the vendor, whether under a warranty or an indemnity, to the purchaser (or, at its direction, to the target company) will be dealt with under TCGA 1992, s.49. However, ESC D33 does not deal specifically with payments to the target company in its own right and therefore such payments may be treated as giving rise to a gain, on the disposal of the right, which is not exempt from capital gains tax.

Although this concession removes a potential liability arising from payments to the purchaser made under indemnities, payments to the target company are not of themselves within the concession and will generally be subject to corporation tax on the full amount of the payment without any deduction for the cost of acquiring the right to the payments. Furthermore, the covenantors will receive no tax relief for the indemnity payments made to the target company.

It is therefore generally in the interests of all the parties, so far as tax is concerned, that a claim should be made by the purchaser under the warranties or indemnities and not by the target company, under the indemnities. In most cases this will not be an issue as indemnities are rarely now given in favour of the target company for these reasons. See para.1–10 for a suggested clause to cover the point.

## Taxation Treatment of Payments under Warranties in Connection with Business Sales

A major difference between share and business purchases is that while the former **3–28** involves the acquisition of a single category of assets, the latter relates to a mixture of assets with widely differing commercial and tax characteristics. Certainly for tax purposes, and probably also for balance sheet reasons, both the vendor and the purchaser will have to allocate the price amongst the assets which are sold. Although it is not essential that they should adopt the same allocation, the agreement of the Inland Revenue will be more readily forthcoming if the purchase price is attributed to the different assets by the sale agreement. The Inland Revenue will not normally dispute the allocation in the agreement unless it is manifestly unreasonable and is excessively motivated by tax considerations.

For the purchaser it will usually be advantageous to minimise the part of the price paid for goodwill and to maximise the part of the consideration that is apportioned to stocks as this will reduce the taxable profits on the eventual sale of the stocks. The vendor has a more difficult tax analysis as much will depend upon the base cost for the purpose of chargeable gains of the goodwill sold by it. If the base cost is high, the vendor may prefer the purchase price to be attributed to the goodwill as this could result in a lower tax bill than if the price is dealt with as a profit on the sale of trading stock.

**3–29**    Where a payment has to be made under a warranty claim, it will not always be obvious which of the purchased assets is affected. A number of warranties, such as those relating to trading relationships and employees, clearly affect the value of the goodwill and it is likely that this is true of most of the warranties which do not specifically concern particular assets. The impact of this on the amount of damages that can be claimed on a breach of warranty is discussed in para.3–06.

If the warranty payment relates to a capital asset, the taxation implications will arise under the legislation in respect of corporation tax on chargeable gains and will be similar to those applicable to share sales as discussed in the preceding section. There is a difficulty, however, if the warranty payment exceeds the amount of the purchase price allocated to the asset involved. This will often arise if the claim affects the value of the goodwill of the business and the common practice of allocating a nominal value to the goodwill has been adopted. In that case, no relief will be obtained by the vendor for the excess of the amount of the claim over the allocated price.

**3–30**    Where the claim concerns trading assets such as stock, the tax liability will be determined in accordance with the normal rules for corporation tax purposes. The taxable profits will initially be determined on the basis of the allocation of the purchase consideration set out in the sale agreement, unless it is clearly unrealistic, and no deduction will be made at that stage for contingent liabilities under the warranties unless the likelihood of a claim being made is so great that normal accountancy practice would require the making of a provision. If by the time the claim is made and settled the vendor has ceased to trade, the warranty payment will be made otherwise than for the purposes of a trade and accordingly will not carry tax relief.

The above tax analysis is an additional reason for the vendor to seek a very short warranty period where there is the sale of a business (see also the discussion in para.3–18). If the claim can be quantified before the accounts for the period in which the sale takes place are adopted, it may be possible to adjust the accounts to provide for the claim.

## Insurance

**3–31**    Insurance cover used to be widely available against liability in respect of warranties for both vendors and purchasers. However, the insurance market has now hardened and, while insurance cover is still available in most cases, generally it is not economic or worthwhile given the exceptions to cover, the level of premiums and the insurers' general requirements. Cover when available is usually expensive and carves out most of the warranties that might ordinarily give rise to unexpected warranty claims. The premium itself will depend on what view the insurers and their lawyers take of "the risk" by reference to the agreed form of sale agreement (and in particular the negotiated warranties and warranty protection provisions), the disclosure letter and the tax deed.

In most cases, if the vendors' advisors have negotiated a balanced set of warranties, undertaken a rigorous disclosure exercise and produced a full disclosure letter, then the risk of successful post-completion warranty claims is fairly minimal.

# CHAPTER 4

# General Points Relating to Warranties

## DEFINED TERMS

**4-01**  To facilitate the drafting of the warranties it is normal to make use of a number of defined terms. In this book, the term **"Company"** (meaning the target company) is used generally in the draft clauses.

Typical examples of further definitions are set out below and these definitions are used in the warranties and indemnities and draft clauses discussed throughout the book.

### [4A] Definitions

**In this Agreement, the following expressions have the meanings stated namely:**

**"Accounts" means the audited balance sheet, as at the Balance Sheet Date, and audited profit and loss account for the year ended on the Balance Sheet Date of the Company together with the directors and auditors reports and notes in relation to them.**

In the case of a business sale, this definition should be amended so that it refers to the accounts of the vendor.

It should be borne in mind by the vendors that, by virtue of this definition, the accounts warranty will also cover the report of the directors.

**"Accounting Standards" means SSAPs, FRSs, UITF Abstracts, SORPs and all other generally accepted accounting principles applicable to a United Kingdom company.**

**"this Agreement" means this agreement for the sale and purchase of the Shares.**

If the general interpretation clauses do not make it clear that schedules are included as part of the agreement then such wording could be added to this definition.

**"Associate" means:**

**(1) (in relation to an individual);**

**(1.1)  the individual's spouse, brother, sister or parent;**

**(1.2)  a company which is directly or indirectly controlled (within the meaning of ICTA 1988, s.840) by the individual or a person who is the individual's spouse, brother, sister or parent, or by any two or more of them;**

**(2)  (in relation to a company) a Subsidiary or holding company of the Company, and any other Subsidiary of a holding company of the Company; "holding company" bearing the meaning in CA 1985, s.736.**

This definition can take any one of many similar forms.

**"Balance Sheet Date" means [ ] 200[ ] (being the date as at and to which the Accounts were prepared).**

**"Business Day" means any day other than Saturdays and Sundays and bank holidays during which clearing banks are open for business in the City of London.**

This definition is usually only relevant if there is a gap between contracts and completion where conditions are to be satisfied and completion is expressed to take place on the next "Business Day" following satisfaction of the conditions. The definition may also be used where deferred payments are to be made to ensure that such payments are made on business days when banks are open for business.

**"CA 1985" means the Companies Act 1985.**

**"CAA 2001" means the Capital Allowances Act 2001.**

**"Companies Acts" means CA 1985, the former Companies Acts (within the meaning of CA 1985, s.735(1)) and the Companies Act 1989.**

This is a consolidating definition.

**"Completion" means completion of the purchase of [the Shares] [the Business].**

**"Computer Systems" means all hardware, firmware, peripherals, communication links, storage media, networking equipment and other equipment used in conjunction with it together with all computer software and all related object and source codes and databases.**

As most businesses are increasingly reliant on their information technology and computer systems it is usual to include specific warranties relating to them. Such warranties are included in para.7–245. Vendors are unlikely to want to give any warranties in relation to their information technology infrastructure to the extent that information technology is shared with others, for example if it is provided by third party service providers. However, the purchaser will still expect information to be provided in relation to the shared information technology infrastructure during the due diligence process even if no warranties are given in relation to it.

**"Confidential Business Information" means all or any information relating to:**

**(1)  the business methods, corporate plans, management systems, finances, new business opportunities or development projects of the Company;**

**(2)  the marketing or sales of any present or future product of the Company;**

**(3)  any trade secrets or other information relating to the provision of any product or services of the Company to which the Company attaches confidentiality or in respect of which it holds an obligation of confidentiality to any third party.**

This is an extremely wide definition which will usually relate not only to the warranties but also to the restrictions. In the case of a business sale this is usually defined as the "Knowhow".

**"Connected Person" has the same meaning as in ICTA 1988, s.839.**

Various statutory definitions of "control" may be adopted—s.840 is reasonable in that it covers the ability, whether through voting power or otherwise, to control the conduct of affairs.

**"Disclosure Letter" means the disclosure letter of today's date from the Vendors to the Purchaser in the agreed form.**

As to the form and content of the disclosure letter, see Ch.9.

**"Encumbrance" means any encumbrance or security interest of any kind whatsoever including without limitation a mortgage, charge, pledge, lien, hypothecation, restriction, right to acquire, right of pre-emption, option, conversion right, third party right or interest, right of set-off or counter-claim, equity, trust arrangement or any other type of preferential agreement (such as a retention of title arrangement) having similar effect or any other rights exercisable by or claims by third parties.**

**"Environment" means the environment as defined in the Environmental Protection Act 1990, s.1(2) and includes any or all of the following media: air, water and land and the medium of air includes the air within buildings and the air within other natural or man-made structures above or below ground and the medium of water includes ground water and acquifers.**

"Environmental Claim" means any claim, notice of violation, prosecution, demand, action, official warning, abatement or other order or notice (conditional or otherwise) relating to any Environmental Matters or Environmental Liabilities and any other notification or order requiring compliance with the terms of any Environmental Licence or Environmental Laws.

"Environmental Damage" means any pollution, contamination, degradation, damage or injury caused by, related to or arising from or in connection with the presence, generation, use, handling, processing, treatment, storage, transportation, disposal or release of any Hazardous Substance.

"Environmental Laws" means any Official Requirements relating to the protection of the Environment or the control or prevention or remedying of Environmental Damage or the control of Hazardous Substances.

"Environmental Liabilities" means any liabilities, responsibilities, claims, losses, costs (including remedial, removal, response, abatement, clean-up, investigative and/or monitoring costs), damages, expenses, charges, assessments, liens, penalties and fines which are incurred by, asserted against or imposed upon a person as a result of or in connection with any violation of or non-compliance with Environmental Laws (including the failure to procure or violation of any Environmental Licence required by Environmental Laws); or any Environmental Damage.

"Environmental Licence" means any permit, licence, authorisation, consent or other approval obtained or which ought to have been obtained pursuant to any Environmental Laws at any time by the Company and/or in relation to the business carried on by the Company.

"Environmental Matters" means any of the following (1) any generation, deposit, keeping, treatment, transportation, transmission, handling or manufacture of any Hazardous Substances; (2) damage to property, nuisances, noise, defective premises or health and safety at work or elsewhere; (3) the carrying out of a development (as defined in the Town and Country Planning Act 1990, s.55(1)); and (4) the pollution, conservation or protection of the Environment whether relating to man or any living organisms supported by the Environment or any other matter whatsoever affecting the Environment or any part of it.

The environmental definitions are extremely wide and great care should be taken by the vendors when reviewing them for the purposes of the warranties. Where the purchaser requires an indemnity in respect of a specific or all environmental matters then these definitions will double for that.

"FA" means the Finance Act.

**"FRS" means a financial reporting standard adopted or issued by The Accounting Standards Board Limited or such other body or bodies as are prescribed for the purposes of CA 1985, s.256.**

The Accounting Standards Board Limited is the prescribed body for the issue of statements of standard accounting practice for the purposes of CA 1985, s.256.

**"Hazardous Substances" means any solid, liquid, gas, noise and any other substance or thing which causes or may cause harm (alone or in combination with any other substance) to the Environment or any structure, thing or living organism within the Environment including any substance regulated under any Environmental Law.**

**"ICTA 1988" means the Income and Corporation Taxes Act 1988.**

**"Intellectual Property Rights" means all copyright, moral rights, design rights, registered designs, database rights, [semiconductor topography rights], patents, utility models, business names, trade marks, service marks, trade names, rights arising in domain names, knowhow, trade secrets and rights in confidential information and any other intellectual property rights or rights of a similar nature (in each case whether or not registered) and all applications for any of them which may subsist anywhere in the world.**

As this definition will form the basis of a warranty, the vendors should consider whether its scope is unduly wide and whether certain of the rights referred to are inappropriate, for example semiconductor topography rights. In particular, the general words **"and any other intellectual property rights or rights of a similar nature . . . which may subsist anywhere in the world"** may be unacceptable if the target company carries on business in a number of foreign jurisdictions. Conversely, the purchaser will want to ensure that it acquires all relevant intellectual property rights existing anywhere in the world.

**"ITA 1984" means the Inheritance Tax Act 1984.**

**"IT(EP)A 2003" means the Income Tax (Earnings and Pensions) Act 2003.**

**"LPMPA 1994" means the Law of Property (Miscellaneous Provisions) Act 1994.**

**"Management Accounts" means the unaudited balance sheet of the Company as at [ ] and the unaudited profit and loss account for the period ended on [ ] copies of which are attached to the Disclosure Letter.**

The period of the management accounts should run from the date of the last audited accounts to the date of the most recent management accounts. In the case of a sale of part of the business of a company, it may not be possible to extract relevant information from the last accounts, in which case the purchaser will be reliant upon management accounts produced in respect of the business to be acquired. In these circumstances, the purchaser may require that the management accounts cover a longer period, for example, two or three years.

**"Non-Taxation Warranties" means those warranties set out in Schedule 4 other than the Taxation Warranties.**

The purpose of differentiating between non-taxation and taxation warranties is to apply different limitation periods and perhaps warranty limitation provisions between the two.

**"Official Requirement" means any law, statute, ordinance, pact, decree, treaty, code, rule, regulation, directive, order, notice or official published plan or policy with legal or actual force in any geographical area and/or for any class of persons.**

**"Planning Acts" means the Town and Country Planning Act 1990, the Planning (Listed Buildings and Conservation Areas) Act 1990, the Planning (Hazardous Substances) Act 1990 (as amended) and the Planning and Compensation Act 1991.**

**"Properties" means the properties briefly described in Schedule [ ].**

**"Sensitive Payments" means (whether or not illegal) (1) commercial bribes, bribes or kickbacks paid to any person including central or local government officials, trade union officials or employees; (2) amounts received with an understanding that rebates or refunds will be made in contravention of the laws of any jurisdiction either directly or through a third party; (3) political contributions; (4) payments or commitments (whether made in the form of commissions, payments or fees for goods received or otherwise) made with the understanding or under circumstances that would indicate that all or part thereof is to be paid by the recipient to central or local government officials or as a commercial bribe, influence, payment or kickback; and (5) any payment deemed illegal under the Prevention of Corruption Acts 1889 to 1916.**

This definition will be of particular relevance when dealing with a target company that operates in the public sector. The definition will form the basis of a warranty to the effect that no such payments have been made.

**"Shares" means the whole of the issued and allotted share capital of the Company as at Completion.**

This definition will be relevant only on a share sale and the reference to "allotted" shares is unnecessary unless shares have been allotted—perhaps on provisional allotment letters—but without the allottees having been entered in the register of members (*National Westminster Bank plc and another v IRC* [1994] 3 W.L.R. 159).

**"Subsidiary" means a subsidiary as defined in CA 1985, s.736.**

The CA 1989 introduced the concept of "subsidiary undertaking" in relation to consolidated accounts. This is a wider term than "subsidiary" since it includes certain partnerships and, additionally, applies a test involving participating interests, dominant influence and unified management. If the target company does have subsidiary undertakings which are not also subsidiaries, the definition could read:

**"Subsidiary Undertaking" means a subsidiary undertaking as defined in CA 1985, s.258.**

The definition is unlikely to be required on a business sale.

**"SORP" means a statement of recommended practice issued by The Accounting Standards Board Limited or such other body or bodies as are prescribed for the purposes of CA 1985, s.256.**

**"SSAP" means a statement of standard accounting practice published by the accounting standards committee of CCAB Limited and adopted by The Accounting Standards Board Limited.**

Although new accounting standards are now identified as FRSs, the use of the acronym SSAP is still required as many of the standards identified by a SSAP number are extant.

**"Taxation" means all forms of taxation, duties, imposts, governmental charges (whether international, national or local) and levies whatsoever and whenever created, enacted or imposed and whether of the United Kingdom or elsewhere and without prejudice to the generality of that expression includes:**

(1) **income tax, corporation tax, capital gains tax, capital transfer tax, inheritance tax, stamp duty, stamp duty reserve tax, rates, value added tax, customs and other import duties, insurance premium tax, national insurance contributions and any payment whatsoever which the Company may be or become bound to make to any Taxation Authority or any other person as a result of any enactment relating to taxation and any other taxes, duties or levies supplementing or replacing any of the above; and**

(2) **all costs, charges, interests, fines, penalties and expenses incidental or relating to any taxation, duties, imposts, charges and levies whatsoever (including without limitation any such described above).**

The wide scope of the definition of **"Taxation"** can have unexpected results, particularly in relation to the more general warranties such as cl.1.1 in para.5–03. There is no compelling reason why the definition should extend beyond income tax, corporation tax, capital gains tax, inheritance tax and value added tax and, perhaps, their overseas equivalents.

**"Taxation Authority" means the Inland Revenue, HM Customs and Excise or any statutory or governmental authority or body (whether in the United Kingdom or elsewhere) involved in the collection or administration of Taxation.**

**"Tax Deed" means a tax deed in the form set out in Schedule [ ].**

As explained in Ch.10, the problematic tax treatment of payments made under the indemnity to the target company in relation to unexpected tax liabilities has now resulted in their usually being made to the purchaser rather than the target company. Payments made in this way, although computed on an indemnity basis, are not really in the nature of an indemnity so far as the purchaser is concerned.

**"Tax Warranties" means the warranties in paragraphs [ ] to [ ] of Schedule [ ].**

A definition referring specifically to those of the warranties dealing with taxation will be required if, as suggested in para.3–18, there is a longer period of limitation applicable to them than to the warranties generally.

**"TCGA 1992" means the Taxation of Chargeable Gains Act 1992.**

**"TMA 1970" means the Taxes Management Act 1970.**

**"UITF Abstract" means an abstract issued by the Urgent Issues Task Force of The Accounting Standard Board Limited or such other body or bodies as are prescribed for the purposes of CA 1985, s.256.**

**"VATA 1994" means the Value Added Tax Act 1994.**

**"Warranties" means the [obligations,] warranties[, representations and undertakings] of the Vendors contained in [this Agreement][[clause [ ] and] Schedule [ ]].**

It is assumed that the warranties discussed in the following chapters are contained in a schedule. This is the usual and most convenient way of dealing with the warranties.

This definition needs careful attention. The agreement will invariably contain a clause similar to cl.4C which imposes an obligation on the vendors in relation to "the Warranties" which is of considerable importance. A general definition such as the above, if the words in brackets on the first line are included, as is often the case, obscures the commitments which are undertaken. When it is being reviewed, the following points should be taken into account:

(1) The warranty obligations accepted by the vendors will apply not only to warranties as normally understood but also to other obligations imposed upon them by the agreement by virtue of the drafting of this definition.

(2) The final draft of the sale agreement, after it has been amended by the vendors' solicitors, will usually include restrictions on the period within which claims for breach of the "warranties" must be brought and on the amounts which can be claimed (see paras 3–18 to 3–25). The definition of "Warranties" set out above would extend, for example, to the obligations on the vendors under covenants restricting the activities they can carry on after completion of the sale. This is not usually intended or likely to be acceptable to the purchaser.

(3) Any given problem may entitle the purchaser to alternative remedies either for breach of contract or for misrepresentation (see para.3–01). The restrictions on the time within which claims may be brought (see para.3–18) and any floor and ceiling to claims (see paras 3–20 and 3–23) will automatically apply to all claims however they are based. Subject to the problem posed by the Misrepresentation Act 1967, s.3 (as discussed in para.3–01), which prohibits reductions in the liabilities of the representor unless they are reasonable, the vendors will accordingly wish to extend the definition of "Warranties", at least for the purposes of the clauses of the agreements which incorporate these exclusions, so that it includes non-fraudulent representations on which the purchaser has relied and is not limited to representations **"contained in this Agreement"**.

Conversely most vendors will wish to exclude liability for non fraudulent misrepresentation and with a carefully drafted entire agreement clause (which does not purport to exclude fraudulent misrepresentation (see para.3–03 for further discussion of this)) that should be perfectly possible. In most cases both the purchaser and the vendor will want to achieve certainty in relation to the warranties and the limitations that are to apply to them. The use of the definition without the words in brackets achieves this by ensuring that the limitation provisions only apply to the warranties themselves rather than other parts of the agreement. Care also needs to be taken to ensure that the fundamental title warranties are not eroded by the warranty protection provisions. This can easily be achieved by making it clear that the relevant provisions do not apply to these fundamental warranties.

**"Warranty Claim" means any claim made by the Purchaser for breach of any of the Warranties.**

In addition to the definitions suggested above, the following are often  **4–02**
included:

**"month" means a calendar month.**

**the singular includes the plural and vice versa.**

**the masculine includes the feminine and vice versa.**

Express definitions are in fact not required as they are contained in LPA 1925,
s.61 and apply, unless excluded, for the purpose of documents executed after the
commencement of the Act. S.61 also provides that "person" includes a corporation but does not expressly include partnerships (see Interpretation Act 1978,
Schedule 1). Where this could be a matter of concern, it would be appropriate to
add:

**"Person" includes a firm or other body of persons.**

## STATUTORY REFERENCES

It is usual to find a definition concerning the statutory provisions referred to in the  **4–03**
warranties and indemnities substantially in the following form:

### [4B] Statutory references

**References to any statute, or to any statutory provision, statutory instru-
ment, order or regulation made thereunder, includes that statute, provision,
instrument, order or regulation as amended, modified, consolidated, re-
enacted or replaced from time to time, whether before or after the date of
this Agreement and also includes any previous statute, statutory provision,
instrument, order or regulation, amended, modified, consolidated, re-
enacted or replaced by such statute, provision, instrument, order or regulation.**

As drafted, this clause would cause the vendors and covenantors to bear the  **4–04**
risk of retrospective legislation causing, or increasing, a liability under the
warranties or indemnities. This is generally inconsistent with the principle that,
as from the exchange of contracts (or, at any rate, completion), the business of the
target company (or the business which is being acquired) is conducted at the risk
of the purchaser. Another circumstance in which an unexpected result can arise
is where liability under a warranty, which depends on a statutory reference, may
arise only some considerable time after the date of the agreement. An example
is in the case of a warranty as to contamination which may state that there is no
liability on the target company arising from environmental laws. If this reference
to laws is deemed to incorporate changes enacted after the date of the agreement,
the vendors may find that the scope of their liability is greatly increased as a
result of legislative developments. The vendors or covenantors should therefore

amend this definition by reversing the phrases in brackets—re-enactments applying only if they do not modify the original legislation—and modifications being effective only if the relevant provisions are enacted before the date of the agreement.

An alternative way of limiting the effect of retrospective legislation is for the vendors to add the following words to the above clause:

**" ... except to the extent that an amendment, modification, consolidation, re-enactment or replacement enacted after today's date would extend or increase the liability of the Vendors under the Warranties [or of the Covenantors under the Tax Deed]."**

The reference to the tax deed will be necessary if the deed adopts by reference the definitions contained in the sale agreement.

The purchaser should take into account that it is not unusual for legislation to take effect from an earlier date, being the date upon which a public announcement was made of the intention to bring in the legislation in question. This is particularly common with taxation matters and, indeed, the Finance Act each year will for the most part operate retrospectively to the date of the relevant budget speech and, in the case of tax anti-avoidance measures, will often apply from the date on which the proposal to introduce legislation was announced. The purchaser should at least consider amending the suggested alternative wording so that it refers to legislation taking effect, rather than being enacted, after the date of the agreement.

## The Warranty Obligation

**4–05**    It is convenient, and normal practice, for the warranties to be set out in a separate schedule, as will be seen from the definition of "Warranties" in para.4–01. The schedule would be adopted by a clause in the body of the agreement as follows:

### [4C] The Warranties

**The Vendors [jointly and severally] warrant and [represent] to the Purchaser that, save as [fully, fairly and accurately] [fairly] [disclosed] [set out] in the Disclosure Letter, the Warranties are true in all respects.**

It is now universal practice to agree the warranties without seeking to amend the terms of them by reference to factual matters which are known to conflict with them. Qualifications to the warranties which are not intended simply to alter the drafting are collected together in the disclosure letter. Clause 4C accordingly provides for the warranties to be read subject to the disclosures. The use of the words "fully, fairly and accurately", "fairly" and "disclosed" is discussed in detail in Ch.9.

**4–06**    In addition, cl.4C by inclusion of the word "represent" provides for the warranties to constitute representations as well as warranties. This provides the purchaser with additional remedies for breach of warranty at common law and under the Misrepresentation Act 1967 if the relevant representations have been relied upon. (See Ch.3 for the remedies available in cases of misrepresentation). In practice, however, recission is unlikely to be available by the time the representation has been found to be wrong, in which case the purchaser's remedy will be to seek damages—the same as if the warranties were not also representations. The vendors will nonetheless wish to delete references to representations and to include an entire agreement clause excluding liability for representations made (see Ch.3).

In a case where there is doubt about the abilities of the target company or the purchaser to continue in business, the vendors might wish to qualify the warranty by adding the words:

" ... and all the Warranties are given on the basis that [the Company will carry on its business as a going concern] [the Business will be carried as a going concern]."

The purpose of this addition is to avoid any possibility that the vendors should bear extra liabilities which arise only by reason of a cessation of business—such as redundancy payments to employees or balancing charges in respect of plant and equipment—and should be acceptable to the purchaser.

## IMPLIED WARRANTIES AS TO TITLE

The Law of Property (Miscellaneous Provisions) Act 1994 provides for certain **4–07** covenants to be implied in an instrument effecting a disposition of assets where the disposition is expressed to be made **"with full title guarantee"** or **"with limited title guarantee"**. In both cases the implied covenants may be limited or extended by the instrument itself.

The covenants implied by using the formula **"with full title guarantee"** are that:

(1) the person making the disposition has the right to dispose of the asset as he purports to (s.2(1));

(2) he will at his own cost do all that he reasonably can to give the person to whom he disposes of the asset the title he purports to give (s.2(2)); and

(3) the disposer is disposing of the asset free from all charges and encumbrances and from all other rights exercisable by third parties other than rights which the disposer does not and could not reasonably be expected to know about (s.3(1)).

The first two of these covenants are also implied by the words **"with limited **4–08** title guarantee"**. The third covenant is instead that the disposer has not since the last disposition for value:

(1) charged or incumbered the asset by means of a charge or incumbrance which subsists when he makes the disposition; or

(2) granted third party rights in relation to the asset which subsist; or

(3) suffered the asset to be charged or incumbered or subjected to third party rights;

and that he is not aware that anyone else has done so since the last disposition for value (s.3(3)).

In both cases the covenants do not apply to anything of which the person to whom the disposition is made is actually aware when the disposition is made, or which is a necessary consequence of the facts which are then actually known by him (s.6(2)).

**4–09**　　The covenants implied by the limited title guarantee are unlikely to be sufficient for most purchasers but the full title guarantee may be acceptable. If the words are used the following points arise:

(1) The covenants are impliedly given by the vendor. While this is appropriate in the case of a business sale, it may not be correct in relation to a share sale if the vendors and the parties giving the warranties are not the same.

(2) Warranties by a vendor as to title, such as cll.1.2.1 and 1.2.2 in paras 7–05 and 7–06 will not be required.

(3) The purchaser will wish to amend the implied covenants by excluding the reference to the knowledge of the disposer which appears in s.3(1) and the exception in respect of matters of which the purchaser is aware which is provided by s.6(2). A suitable clause for this purpose is the following:

## [4D] Restriction on implied covenants

**4–10**　　**The express assurance in clause [ ] as to freedom from encumbrances and the covenants implied in that clause by sections 2 and 3 of the LPMPA 1994 shall apply to anything falling within the scope of such assurances and covenants notwithstanding that the Vendors do not know or could not reasonably be expected to know about it, or, at the time of transfer, it is within the actual knowledge, or is a necessary consequence of facts then within the actual knowledge of the Purchaser, and the operation of the covenants implied by sections 2 and 3 of the LPMPA 1994 shall be deemed to be extended so as not to exclude the liability of the Vendors thereunder in any of such circumstances.**

From the point of view of both parties it will often be preferable to omit the implied covenants entirely and to rely instead on express warranties which take account of the circumstances relevant to the particular transaction. In practice most sale agreements contain both.

## RESTRICTION OF WARRANTIES TO PERIOD OF OWNERSHIP

The form of many warranties is such that there could be a breach however long **4–11**
ago the occurrence of the relevant event. An example is a warranty that all
statutory returns have been properly made and filed (see para.7–27, cl.1.11.1). If
the period of ownership or involvement of the vendors has been short, they may
wish to seek to avoid liability for defects attributable to an earlier period and the
following provision might be appropriate in these circumstances.

### [4E] Application of Warranties to past events

**The Vendors shall not be liable, in relation to a breach of the Warranties, if  4–12
and to the extent that the breach is primarily attributable to anything which
occurred prior to [ ].**

Although the vendors may seek to justify the principle underlying this clause on
the basis that they cannot warrant the correctness of statements where they have
no means of knowing whether or not they are accurate, this argument, which is
based on the checklist function of the warranties, is flawed. Either the vendors or
the purchaser must accept the risk of inaccuracy and, if neither of them has
knowledge of the applicable facts, they must decide by negotiation where the risk
is to lie. If the purchaser accepts the principle, the wording of cl.4E is more likely
to be approved if **"primarily"** is omitted or replaced by "wholly". In addition,
the purchaser should require the vendors to assign to it, or to enforce for its
benefit, any warranties in relation to the target company or business which were
obtained when the vendors made their acquisition (see para.2–12). In practice
most purchasers would expect the vendors to bear the risk in these circumstances.

The vendors may also wish to restrict the warranties so that liability will not
arise if a breach of warranty results from the combined effect of events both
before and after completion. A suitable clause is as follows:

### [4F] Effect of post-Completion events

**The Vendors shall not be liable for a claim under the Warranties which  4–13
would not have arisen but for anything occurring after Completion.**

See also the discussion on cll.1.10 and 3.1.12 of the tax deed in Ch.10, which
deal with the same point.

## DATE OF APPLICATION OF WARRANTIES

Although completion may follow immediately upon the exchange of the con-  **4–14**
tracts for the purchase of the target company or business, it is sometimes the case
that there is an interval between contracts and completion. This may arise, for
example, because certain consents are required, or where the consideration is to
be satisfied by a placing of shares. Where an interval exists, the target company

or business will usually continue to be run by the vendors although normally this will be for the benefit, and at the risk, of the purchaser.

The purchaser may therefore wish to include provisions in the sale agreement which restrict the way in which the business of the target company or the acquired business may be conducted in the intervening period (*interregnum* provisions) (see Appendix 2 which contains an example of generic provisions that would be suitable in such circumstances). In addition the purchaser will wish the warranties contained in the sale agreement to apply both at the date of the exchange of contracts and at completion and perhaps even at every moment in between. The first of these dates is relevant as the purchaser will, in part, be relying upon the warranties in deciding to enter into the sale agreement. It is also appropriate, from the purchaser's point of view, for the warranties to be extended to completion as the purchaser will be committed to proceed with the transaction whatever external changes occur and it will therefore wish to protect itself so far as possible by passing the risk of changes to the vendors.

As the vendors will generally control the target company or business until completion, it is difficult for them to resist some extension of the warranties to completion. It is likely that the vendors will be presented with clauses to cover these aspects similar to those which follow in this section. Great care needs to be taken by the vendors in extending the warranties to completion as that will substantially erode the usual basis that the company or business is carried on after exchange of contracts at the purchaser's risk.

## [4G] Events occurring prior to Completion

4–15   **[Each of the Vendors] [The Vendor] will promptly disclose in writing to the Purchaser any [material] circumstance which arises, or becomes known to [him] [her] [it], prior to Completion and is inconsistent [in a material respect] with any of the Warranties or the disclosures in the Disclosure Letter, or which might be material to be known by a purchaser for value of [the Shares] [the Business].**

The purchaser will be justified in seeking to include this clause where it has a right to rescind the contract if a breach of warranty occurs or is identified prior to completion. The purchaser might also wish to retain the clause in any case on the basis that, if difficulties arise before completion, notification should be given to it so that it can plan appropriate corrective action. Whilst this argument has some validity, the vendors might reasonably object to putting themselves in a position where a failure to comply with the clause could give rise to a claim for damages. Furthermore, they should not underestimate the considerable practical difficulty of keeping constantly in mind the wording of lengthy and technical warranties.

The purchaser will probably insist that any disclosure under this provision is in writing so that there can be no dispute afterwards as to whether the disclosure has taken place. The vendors should ensure therefore that a written record is made of any relevant discussions which take place with the purchaser between contracts and completion.

The clause as drafted refers to all the warranties and the vendors should consider each warranty specifically to determine whether or not the obligations imposed by the clause should extend to that warranty. The vendors should also consider inserting the qualifying words in square brackets.

The suggested wording would require a disclosure of information which is in **4–16** the public domain and which does not relate specifically to the target company or business. Thus, for example, there might during the interval between contracts and completion be an announcement of new legislation to be introduced with effect from the date of the announcement. This could render a warranty incorrect but the vendors should not be required to make a disclosure of the announcement. It is therefore suggested that the vendors should consider qualifying the clause by adding the words:

**"being a circumstance relating specifically to [the Company] [the Business]."**

The vendors would also wish to consider carefully whether the words **"or which might be material to be known by a purchaser for value of [the Shares] [the Business]"** are acceptable as they have no way of knowing what might affect a purchaser in general rather than the actual purchaser. Even to amend the clause so that it applies only to matters which might be material to be known by the actual purchaser may not be acceptable, as the vendors may have little information about the purchaser's reasons for acquiring the target company or business. The second clause which the purchaser would wish to include in cases of deferred completion, in addition to any express restrictions such as are contained in Appendix 2, would be to the following effect:

## [4H] Conduct of the Company pending Completion

**The Vendors shall procure that, save as may be necessary to give effect to  4–17 this Agreement, the Company shall not, before Completion, without the prior written consent of the Purchaser [knowingly] do, procure or allow anything which might constitute or result in a [material] breach of the Warranties, or make any of them inaccurate or misleading, if they were given at Completion.**

The equivalent wording in the case of a business sale would be:

**"Save as may be necessary to give effect to this Agreement, the Vendor shall not, before Completion, without the written consent of the Purchaser [knowingly] do, procure or allow anything which might constitute or result in a [material] breach of the Warranties, or make any of them inaccurate or misleading, if they were given at Completion".**

The purpose of this provision is to apply the warranties on a continuing basis throughout the interval between exchange of contracts and completion. It is accordingly an onerous clause, to be viewed with caution by the vendors. If they accept it in principle they should at least make sure that extraordinary transactions are avoided during the period between contracts and completion. It would also be realistic for the vendors to qualify the clause by adding the following wording:

**"[The Vendors] [The Vendor] shall not, however, be liable under this clause for a breach which arises from the usual course of [business of the Company] [the Business]."**

An example of an event which would come within this sentence is a routine change in the identity of named employees (for example, cl.6.1.1 in para.7–160). The vendors should also consider making the qualifications shown in square brackets and whether the word **"might"** should be replaced by **"would"** or **"would be likely to"**. The third clause which the purchaser will require, whether the interval between contracts and completion is short or long, is along the following lines:

### [4I] Warranties to apply at Completion

4–18 **Each of the Warranties shall be deemed to be repeated, with any necessary modification, immediately before the time of Completion, with reference to the facts then existing.**

This clause differs from cl.4H in that it takes no account of whether any change has been caused by the vendors or was within their control. It is inconsistent with the concept, which is standard in conveyancing practice, that the risk of adverse events occurring which are outside the control of the vendors passes to the purchaser on exchange of contracts, a concept which is usually heavily eroded on share transactions by the combined effect of the interregnum provisions and the repetition of the warranties up to the point of completion. Clause 4H is as far as the vendors would normally wish to go.

Even if the clause is accepted, it is desirable to consider each warranty individually to determine whether or not it is appropriate for it to be extended in this way.

## VENDORS' KNOWLEDGE

4–19 It is usual for certain of the warranties requested by the purchaser to be qualified so that they apply only to the best of the knowledge and belief of the vendors, or only so far as the vendors are aware of the relevant facts or circumstances, and it is even more usual for the vendors' solicitors to try to amend the warranties, either generally or to a significant extent, in this way. This is probably unnecessary, as it would appear from *William Sindall plc v Cambridgeshire County Council* [1994] 1 W.L.R. 1016 that, if there is a duty on the vendor to make disclosures, a statement that the vendor is not aware of something implies that it has made such investigation as might reasonably be expected to be made by or under the guidance of a prudent vendor. Nevertheless, to ensure that full enquiry is made by the vendors before expressing their knowledge and belief it is useful to add a specific provision to the following effect:

## [4J] Full enquiry by the Vendors

**Where a Warranty refers to the knowledge, information, awareness or belief   4–20
of the Vendors, each of the Vendors undertakes that they have made full
enquiry into the subject matter of the Warranty and it shall not be a defence
that the Vendors did not appreciate the relevance of any particular matter.**

The last part of this clause is intended to make it clear that the lack of knowledge is determined objectively. The vendors should replace **"full enquiry into the subject matter of the Warranty"** with either **"due and careful enquiry"** or **"such enquiry into the subject matter of the Warranty as is reasonable in the context of the sale of the [Shares] [Business]"**. Unless the wording is qualified in the latter way, the clause could mean, for example, that before warranting that there is no investigation planned by the taxation authorities, the vendors should request the authorities to confirm that this is so.

Often the vendors' advisors will wish to achieve certainty in relation to the level of enquiry the vendors have to make in order to satisfy the relevant standard. This is often done by stating the persons or entities of whom enquiry has to be made (for example solicitors, accountants, insurance brokers, sur-veyors, bankers and the like together with a defined list of executives and/or employees). If this course is acceptable to a purchaser it will need to be satisfied that the relevant entities or persons are sufficient to glean all relevant information from. Usually an objective standard without reference to a defined list will be the purchaser's preference.

A problem arises where the relevant knowledge is that possessed by a com-   **4–21**
pany. This occurs most generally in the case of a business sale where the vendor, and the only party giving the warranties, will invariably be a company. The point can also exist in relation to share sales, particularly if the target company is a wholly owned subsidiary. Although it is not possible to provide a simple rule for identifying the individual whose knowledge is treated in a particular case as being that of the company, certain broad principles can be identified. What has to be determined, by applying the usual canons of interpretation is whose knowledge for the particular purpose was intended to count as that of the company (*Meridian Global Funds Management Asia Ltd v Securities Commis-sion* [1995] 2 BCLC 116). In the Meridian case, the knowledge of some senior investment managers was treated as being that of the company. The Court of Appeal in *El Ajou v Dollar Landholdings plc (No.1)* [1994] 1 BCLC 464 held that it is necessary to identify the person having actual management and control in relation to the particular act. The clearest technique for resolving the matter is to specify the individuals whose knowledge is attributed to the company and it may also be appropriate to state the warranties in relation to which named individuals are treated as having relevant knowledge. It might be reasonable, for

example, to state that the knowledge of any director is taken into account for all the warranties but that senior executives who are not directors are treated as relevant only in relation to those areas for which they have executive responsibility. A clause to that effect is the following:

## [4K] Knowledge of the Vendor

4–22    **In determining whether the Vendor has the knowledge referred to in a Warranty it shall be treated as knowing:**

**[4K.1] anything which is known to any of its directors; and**

**[4K.2] anything which is known to the persons listed in Schedule [ ] but, in respect of each of the individuals named, only in relation to those of the Warranties which are specified against his name in that Schedule.**

This clause deals only with the knowledge of the vendor. While the concept of belief sits rather awkwardly with a corporate vendor, if it is to be included cl.4K should be extended to cover the attribution to the company of the beliefs of the specified individuals.

Other difficult questions can arise in the case of a sale of shares where one of the vendors is in default in this respect, because of deliberate concealment, oversight or negligent failure to make due enquiry, but the remaining vendors are not. The normal form of this qualification to the warranties would result in all the vendors in such a case being in breach.

If the purchaser accepts a warranty qualified in this manner, then essentially it is seeking to protect itself against deliberate concealment or negligence by the vendors in reviewing the affairs of the target company in relation to the warranty. If, therefore, only one vendor has access to the relevant information, the purchaser's objective is to prevent him being fraudulent or negligent. This is largely unnecessary because of the remedies available where there has been misrepresentation (see the discussion in para.3–01). For clarity, the purchaser might prefer to add the following clause:

## [4L] Awareness of one of the Vendors

4–23    **If one of the Vendors is or could reasonably have been aware that there was a breach of a Warranty which refers to the knowledge, information, awareness or belief of the Vendors, he shall be liable for a fraction of the Purchaser's loss arising from that breach equal to the fraction of the Shares which are sold by him.**

The effect of cl.4L on the minimum level for making claims (see para.3–20) should be considered carefully. The purchaser would wish to add the following to cl.4L:

**In determining whether claims exceed the amount specified in clause 3F, the whole of the loss, and not just the fraction, shall be taken into account.**

## EFFECT OF INVESTIGATION

In most transactions, financial and legal due diligence will be undertaken on the **4–24** target company. It is usual for the factual replies to enquiries submitted as part of the due diligence process to be warranted as true and accurate. Most vendors will be reluctant to warrant the accuracy of the due diligence reports themselves, even if they have been disclosed, as they will often contain the subjective views of those who undertook the due diligence which the vendors would not wish to underwrite.

The purchaser will normally wish to include the following clause:

### [4M] Effect of investigation or waiver of liability

**The remedies of the Purchaser in respect of a breach of the Warranties shall** **4–25** **not be affected by any investigation made, or to be made, by or on behalf of the Purchaser into [the affairs of the Company] [the Business], or by the Purchaser rescinding, or failing to rescind, this Agreement or anything else other than a specific and duly authorised written waiver or release.**

It is questionable whether the exclusion will be effective to protect a purchaser who had knowledge of the relevant circumstances when entering into the purchase contract (*Eurocopy plc v Teesdale and others* [1992] BCLC 1067) either itself or through its agent (*Infiniteland Ltd and another v Artisan Contracting Ltd and another* [2004] EWHC 955—although see commentary at para.1–08 in relation to this) and the knowledge would make it difficult for the purchaser to show that it suffered damage as a result of the breach. The vendors, nevertheless, cannot fairly object to this clause as it is normally in the interests of both parties that qualifications to the warranties should be in writing in the disclosure letter. The vendors might reasonably require that the words "duly authorised" are omitted as it may in practice be difficult to ascertain whether due authority has been obtained.

## PARTLY-OWNED SUBSIDIARIES

If the target company has subsidiaries, one of which is partly owned, the **4–26** purchaser's entitlement to damages where a breach of warranty occurs in relation to that subsidiary will be adjusted automatically. It would not normally be necessary, therefore, to make any special provision in relation to the warranties to cover partial ownership unless—exceptionally—the partly-owned subsidiary is under the control of a third party and not of the purchaser, perhaps because of special voting rights.

A different position arises in respect of the tax indemnities. If no special arrangement is made, the covenantors will have to compensate the purchaser in full, even though the purchaser effectively derives only a proportionate part of the benefit. The dilemma can be resolved by making the indemnity relate to an appropriate proportion of any claim that is made.

## EJUSDEM GENERIS RULE

4–27    The following clause is quite frequently to be found in share sale (and, indeed, other) agreements:

**[4N] *Ejusdem generis* rule**

4–28    **In construing this Agreement the so-called "ejusdem generis rule" does not apply and accordingly the interpretation of general words is not restricted by:**

**[4N.1] being preceded by words indicating a particular class of acts, matters or things; or**

**[4N.2] being followed by particular examples.**

This rule originates from the decision of Tenterden C.J. in *Sandiman v Breach* (1827) 7 B & C 96 who said "Where general words follow particular ones, the rule is to construe them as applicable to persons *ejusdem generis*". The rule has not been consistently applied, particularly in modern times, but care is needed where a list of examples precedes a general word, or a general word is followed by specific examples. These qualifications will be unnecessary except in the rare cases where there is a real doubt as to whether it is intended that the general operation of the wording is to be restricted. While, as a matter of drafting technique, it is better to ensure that the doubt does not arise, the use of a clause such as the above, or qualifying **"including"** by a phrase such as **"but without limitation"**, provides an alternative approach.

## FOREIGN COMPANIES OR BUSINESS

4–29    Where the target company or business has limited overseas activities, the warranties considered in Chs 7 and 8 will generally be suitable. If, however, there is a material overseas involvement, it is desirable for local advice to be obtained as to the equivalent matters to be covered by the warranties so far as they relate to the overseas jurisdictions. For this purpose it should be borne in mind that the law in Scotland is not necessarily the same as in England and Wales.

     A somewhat shorthand approach which may reasonably be adopted if the overseas involvement is slight is to include the following clause:

**[4O] Overseas companies or businesses**

4–30    **The Warranties apply, with any necessary modification, to [that part of the Company's business as is carried on] [any part of the Business carried on] outside England and Wales, and for the purpose of construction:**

**[4O.1] a reference to a statutory provision enacted, or accounting principle applying, in England and Wales includes a reference to the corresponding**

provision in the local legislation and (where relevant) to a generally accepted accounting principle; and

[4O.2] **a reference to a governmental, or administrative, authority or agency includes a reference to the equivalent local governmental, or administrative, authority or agency.**

This is very much a broad brush approach and will be unlikely to provide the purchaser with suitable protection if the overseas activities are more than minimal.

## EXCLUSIONS

It will normally be agreed that the warranties do not apply, for example, to **4–31** matters disclosed in the target company's or, in the case of a business sale, the vendor's accounts or on file at the Companies Registry. These qualifications to the warranties can be set out in the agreement but it is more usual to list them in the disclosure letter (see cl.4C and Ch.9).

Another circumstance which could operate to exclude liability for a breach of warranty is where the purchaser has failed to act in accordance with the instructions of the vendors in relation to the conduct of disputes relating to the subject matter of the warranty. A suitable clause for this purpose is the following:

### [4P] Failure to follow Vendors' instructions

**The Purchaser shall not be entitled to make a claim in respect of a Warranty** **4–32** **if it fails after due warning to act in accordance with the reasonable instructions of the Vendors in conducting a dispute in relation to the subject matter of the claim in accordance with clause [ ].**

The clause referred to in the above clause is one giving conduct of claims to the vendors (see para.11–14). The purchaser should not readily agree to this clause. If it fails to perform its obligations the vendors will in any case be entitled to appropriate compensation for the breach. The sanction imposed by cl.4P is too onerous and inflexible. Often a purchaser will not be prepared to give the vendor conduct of claims or if it does it will be subject to so many safeguards that the worth of having conduct is severely eroded.

## GENERAL CLAUSES

Where, on a sale of shares, the vendors are not closely involved in the manage- **4–33** ment of the target company, they will normally base their reaction to the draft warranties, and the preparation of the disclosure letter, on information provided to them by the company's management. If this information is negligently prepared and as a result the purchaser is able to mount a successful claim under the warranties or for misrepresentation, the vendors might have a counter-claim against either the target company or the directors of the target company for negligence in providing the relevant information. Such a claim would operate to the detriment of the purchaser and it is therefore usual for the purchaser to exclude that right. A clause dealing with this point is as follows:

## [4Q] Information supplied to Vendors

4–34    **Information supplied by the Company or its professional advisers to the Vendors, or their agents, representatives or advisers, in connection with the Warranties and the Disclosure Letter, or otherwise in relation to the business and affairs of the Company, is not deemed to be a representation by the Company to the Vendors as to its accuracy, and the Vendors may not make a claim against the Company, its officers or employees or its professional advisors in respect of that information.**

Although the waiver may not be effective as far as the company is concerned, it not being a party to the sale agreement, in the event of a claim being made the purchaser would be able to sue for breach and claim damages if loss could be established.

Another clause of general relevance is:

## [4R] Warranties independent

4–35    **Each of the Warranties is independent of other Warranties [and undertakings] and, unless the contrary is expressly stated, no clause in this Agreement limits the extent or application of another clause.**

Inevitably there will be a degree of overlap in the warranties and the purpose of the first part of this clause is to eliminate any suggestion that might otherwise exist to the effect that a qualification to one warranty operates to reduce the scope of an overlapping warranty. The vendors should treat each warranty on its own merits and make amendments to them on that basis. In view of the overlap that occurs between warranties, the vendors will wish to ensure that the disclosures contained in the disclosure letter are not interpreted as being limited to specific warranties but qualify the warranties generally (see Ch.9).

The second half of the clause, even with the words between the commas, is unnecessary and potentially harmful to the vendors. They should therefore delete it.

## [4S] Warranties to survive Completion

4–36    **Each of the Warranties, other than a Warranty fully performed at Completion, shall remain in full force and effect notwithstanding Completion.**

The purpose of this provision is to avoid the concept of merger of a contract into the completion document. If an executory contract is to be implemented by a subsequent deed, the general principle is that the real completed contract is to be found in the deed and the contract ceases to be relevant except for the purpose of construing the deed (*Leggott v Barrett* (1880) L.R. 15 Ch D 306). This rule is subject to the qualification that those terms of the contract which are not intended to be performed by the deed are not merged with it (*Knight Sugar Company Ltd v The Alberta Railway Irrigation Co* [1938] 1 All E.R. 266).

As there is no deed with which the contract for sale of the company can merge, the principle would seem to be inapplicable to share sales although it is possible that by analogy the courts may apply it to completion of a share sale. There is a greater possibility of its applying to a business sale. Furthermore, the whole tenor of the warranties is that they should survive, and be enforceable after completion. While it could therefore be argued that cl.4S is strictly superfluous, given the fact that it is possible that the courts may apply the principle to a share sale a prudent purchaser would be well advised to incorporate the clause. While it is primarily the terms relating to enforcement of the warranties that the purchaser will be concerned with, given that there are likely to be other unperformed terms of the sale agreement at completion the purchaser ought to consider amending the clause to cover the whole of the sale agreement and not just the warranties. The following wording would be suitable for this:

**The provisions of this Agreement, insofar as the same have not been fully performed at Completion, shall remain in full force and effect not withstanding Completion.**

## [4T] Delay in enforcing Warranties

**A failure by the Purchaser to exercise, or a delay by it in exercising, a right**   4–37
**in respect of a Warranty shall not operate as a waiver of the right or Warranty, and a single or partial exercise of a right shall not preclude another or further exercise of the right or the exercise of another right.**

This provision might be unduly favourable to the purchaser in a case where the warranties have no significant time limit as the purchaser might then be entitled to raise a claim many years after it became aware of it. If, as is normal, a reasonable time limit is imposed within which claims must be brought, then the clause has little practical significance.

## [4U] Purchaser's Warranty

**The Purchaser has not already formulated, and does not presently have any**   4–38
**actual knowledge (save as fairly disclosed in the Disclosure Letter) of any circumstances which it knows would presently entitle it to make, a Warranty Claim.**

The use of this warranty by vendors' advisers has been more popular since *Eurocopy plc v Teesdale and others* [1992] B.C.L.C. 1067. The warranty is designed to put the common law position under *Eurocopy* into contractual effect.

There are many alternative forms of this warranty but the wording used here is likely to be acceptable to both the vendors and the purchaser. The provision or otherwise of this warranty is a question of bargaining position between the parties. Most purchasers will be wary of conceding the warranty while most vendors will want the comfort of it.

# Chapter 5

# Taxation Warranties

## Introduction

A large number of the warranties normally required by a purchaser of a company  **5–01** relate to tax. Whilst it would be possible to deal with all taxation matters in a few general paragraphs (as in the short form warranties set out in Appendix 7), it is particularly in relation to taxation that the value of the checklist concept of warranties demonstrates itself. By listing all taxation sections which it considers to be relevant, the purchaser assists the vendors in checking systematically whether any circumstances have arisen which ought to be brought to its attention.

Disclosure of any relevant matters will usually negate any warranty claim. However, the tax deed will still catch any tax liability that the target company has in relation to the warranted matters. Disclosures rarely operate to take effect against the tax deed and the purchaser's knowledge will be irrelevant to any claim made under the tax deed.

Even where warranty claims can be made for tax matters they will rarely be made if the matter is covered by the tax deed as under the tax deed there is neither a need to prove loss (as will often be the case for a breach of warranty) nor a need to overcome the "suite" of warranty protection provisions that there will usually be, including in particular the financial deductibles. In most cases these will not apply to the tax deed.

In this chapter we set out and discuss the tax warranties which might be required if an active trading company is being purchased. The following is a list of the headings which are covered:

| Clause | Title |
|--------|-------|
| 1 | **Returns and clearances** |
| 2 | **PAYE and other deductions at source** |
| 3 | **Penalties** |
| 4 | **Claims, elections, liabilities and reliefs** |
| 5 | **Unremittable income and capital gains** |
| 6 | **Tax avoidance** |
| 7 | **Depreciatory transactions and value shifting** |
| 8 | **Disallowance of deductions** |
| 9 | **Transactions not at arm's length** |
| 10 | **Disallowance of losses** |
| 11 | **Loan relationships** |
| 12 | **Distributions** |

| 13 | Close companies |
| 14 | Sale and leaseback of land |
| 15 | Payments from pension funds |
| 16 | Group relief and group surrenders |
| 17 | Acquisitions from group members |
| 18 | Demergers and purchase of own shares |
| 19 | Stock dividends |
| 20 | Capital allowances |
| 21 | Base values and acquisition costs |
| 22 | Replacement of business assets |
| 23 | Chargeable gains: special cases |
| 24 | Capital losses and limited partnerships |
| 25 | Gifts involving group companies |
| 26 | Foreign businesses |
| 27 | Foreign loan interest |
| 28 | Value added tax |
| 29 | Inheritance tax |
| 30 | Stamp duty and stamp duty land tax |
| 31 | Disclosure requirements |

5–02 As a result of inertia, standard form documents often continue to include warranties relating to specific tax liabilities long after the relevant legislation has been abolished. An indication of the more common examples and of a number of special taxes which are not reviewed in detail in this chapter appear in para.5–118.

In considering the tax warranties, the vendors' solicitors and the target company's auditors will need to work closely together. A review of tax computations and returns for the past six years is normally desirable.

The warranties considered below adopt the definitions in para.4–01.

## Detailed Consideration

### 1 Returns and clearances

5–03 **1.1 All returns, notifications, computations and payments which should have been made or given by the Company for a Taxation purpose were made or given within the requisite periods and were [in all material aspects] up-to-date, correct and on a proper basis; and none of them is, or is likely to be, the subject of a [material] dispute with the Inland Revenue or other Taxation Authorities.**

Apart from the returns which have been required under FA 1988, Sch.18, Pt II (Company tax return) since July 1, 1999 when self-assessment became operative (and before that returns of profits under TMA 1970, s.11 (Return of profits)), the principal returns relate to income tax deducted from payments which must be returned under ICTA 1988, Sch.16 (Collection of income tax on company payments which are not distributions), non-qualifying distributions, within 14 days of the accounting period under ICTA 1988, s.234 (Information relating to distributions), and employees' earnings (such as forms P11D) under TMA 1970, s.15 (Return of employees' earnings, etc.) and the Income Tax (Pay As You Earn) Regulations 2003. For accounting periods ending on or prior to April 5, 2003, FA 1988, s.85 (Information) required a company in which an employee acquired shares under an unapproved employee share scheme and, if different, the employing company, to give notice to the Inland Revenue of the acquisition within 30 days of the end of the year of assessment. If in such accounting periods a chargeable event occured under FA 1988, s.78 (Charge where restrictions removed etc.) in relation to the shares, or the employee received a special benefit within s.80 (Charge on special benefits), notice had to be given within 60 days of the relevant event. Section 421(J) IT(EP)A 2003 now provides for various reportable events in relation to employment securities (including the acquisition of securities and chargeable events relating to restricted and convertible securities) to be notified to the Revenue where the relevant event occurred after April 6, 2003.

If a company carries out a transaction which is covered by ICTA 1988, s.765 **5–04** (Migration etc. of companies) but is excluded by s.765A (Movements of capital between residents of Member States), details have to be provided to the Inland Revenue within six months (see Statement of Practice SP2/92 dated February 28, 1992).

Accounts and returns generally have to be filed 12 months after the end of the accounting period to which they relate (FA 1998, Sch.18, para.14 (Filing Date)).

Other taxation returns include, in particular, those relating to VAT. For example, a change in the particulars registered for VAT purposes must be notified within 30 days (Value Added Tax Regulations 1995 (SI 1995 No. 2518) regulation 5(2), as amended).

The vendors should be cautious about giving this warranty as it is unlikely in practice that all returns will have been made precisely within the statutory time limits. This is, nevertheless, a matter of some relevance to the purchaser in view of the onerous interest charges and penalties which are imposed as a result of late payment of tax. Furthermore, the target company may have made special arrangements regarding certain returns such as P11Ds. These arrangements should either be disclosed or excluded from the warranty. The vendors must bear in mind the width of the defined term **"Taxation"**. If, for example, the uniform business rate falls within the definition, it will be necessary to make a disclosure of any dispute with the rating authorities.

The reference to returns not being **"likely"** to be the subject of a dispute needs care. In view of the approach taken by the courts in relation to tax avoidance arrangements, it might be anticipated that any arrangements which have been entered into on an artificial basis or which have been largely motivated by tax avoidance reasons will be possible targets for Inland Revenue attack however firm the theoretical basis upon which they rest.

The vendors may wish, in any event, to qualify the warranty by the addition of the words in square brackets.

**5–05**    **1.2 All particulars furnished to the Taxation Authorities, in connection with an application for consent or clearance on behalf of the Company, or affecting the Company, fully and accurately disclosed everything material to their decision; the consent or clearance is valid and effective; and the transactions for which the consent or clearance was obtained have been carried into effect (if at all) only in accordance with the terms of the application and the consent or clearance.**

The primary consent referred to was that required under ICTA 1988, s.765 (Migration, etc., of companies). This section related to the migration of companies, transfers of businesses abroad and the issue of shares or debentures by a foreign subsidiary, but was repealed (without the title of the section being amended to reflect the change) in relation to the first two categories by FA 1988. Implementation of a transaction without the necessary consent being obtained can give rise to a criminal offence.

**5–06**    Clearances are given on various matters under ICTA 1988, s.215 (Advance clearance by Board of distributions and payments) in relation to demergers; ICTA 1988, s.225 (Advance clearance of payments by Board) in respect of purchases of own shares; ICTA 1988, s.707 (Procedure for clearance in advance) in respect of transactions in securities; ICTA 1988, s.776 (Transactions in land: taxation of capital gains); TCGA 1992, s.138 (Company reconstructions and amalgamations: Procedure for clearance in advance) and s.139 (Reconstruction involving transfer of business) in relation to capital gains tax on company reconstructions.

Apart from the statutory clearances, it is sometimes possible to obtain informal rulings from the Inland Revenue, Customs and Excise and the Stamp Office either on general points or on the specific facts of a particular case. It should be emphasised that these rulings cannot be relied upon and that the relevant departments do not consider themselves bound by them. The vendors should not therefore be expected to accept responsibility for the effectiveness of any informal clearance obtained in this way.

As this warranty relates only to applications made by the target company, it is largely a question of fact whether a breach could arise. The warranty will accordingly present little difficulty for the vendors in normal circumstances, although it would be a sensible precaution to limit the warranty to the preceding six years or some shorter period. This warranty has increased importance from the purchaser's perspective following *R. v Inland Revenue Commissioners, ex parte Matrix Securities Ltd* (1994) S.T.C. 272 (HL) which showed that incomplete information will invalidate an Inland Revenue clearance or consent.

**5–07**    **1.3 The Company has not taken any action which has had, or might have, the result of altering or prejudicing for a period commencing after the Balance Sheet Date an arrangement or agreement which it has with a Taxation Authority.**

In practice, the taxation authorities frequently agree to arrangements which are designed to operate on a broadly equitable basis and do not require that a strict detailed application of the legislation is adopted. Examples arise in relation to the treatment of expenses, benefits to directors and employees, valuation of stocks and depreciation of assets. Arrangements of this kind may be terminated at any time but it is important for the purchaser to be aware of any changes which have occurred after the end of the last accounting period.

The vendors should consider carefully whether the clause should be limited so that it is restricted to actions which, to their knowledge, have altered such arrangements, and the word **"might"** should be replaced by **"will"**. They should also seek to restrict the warranty to arrangements agreed with the Inland Revenue and Customs and Excise.

**1.4 There has been no determination under TMA 1970, s.41A (Determina-** **5–08** **tion procedure) or FA 1998, Schedule 18, Part V (Revenue determinations and assessments) of the amount of tax payable by the Company.**

Schedule 18 of FA 1998 allows the Inspector to make a determination as to the amount of corporation tax payable or as to the amount of any element which goes into the calculation of tax liability, including, for example, profits, sets-offs and reliefs. The time limit for such a determination is six years from the end of the relevant accounting period.

As the warranty covers a factual question in relation to which the purchaser will have a legitimate interest, the vendors might reasonably be expected to accept the warranty.

**1.5 The Company is not obliged to pay corporation tax in quarterly** **5–09** **instalments under the provisions of the Corporation Tax (Instalment Payments) Regulations 1998 (SI 1998 No. 3175) and TMA 1970, s.59E.**

Under the corporation tax self assessment regime companies (and groups) whose tax liabilities exceed a certain level are required to make payments of their corporation tax liabilities in instalments. Payments are made on an estimate of the actual liability and any excess or shortfall in relation to the amount which should have been paid (determined when the tax return for the accounting period is submitted) attracts interest until such time as it is correct.

**1.6 The Company has not entered into any group payment arrangements** **5–10** **under FA 1998, s.36.**

If the target company is part of a group payment arrangement it is important to ensure that the arrangement is amended when the target company comes out of the vendors' group and that payment arrangements are made in relation to the purchaser's group.

## 2 PAYE and other deductions at source

**5–11   2.1 The Company has properly operated the PAYE system, by duly deducting tax from all payments made, or treated as made, to its employees or former employees, and accounting to the Inland Revenue for all tax deducted by it and for all tax chargeable on benefits provided for its employees or former employees.**

This warranty applies not only in relation to the normal PAYE system which now operates under IT(EP)A 2003, s.684 (PAYE Regulations) in relation to employment income of employees, but also in relation to certain benefits in kind, such as cash vouchers and readily convertible assets, and the special charges on employment related securities. This is all dealt with in IT(EP)A 2003, Pt 11. The PAYE system also applies to certain workers engaged through agencies (IT(EP)A 2003, s.688 (Agency Workers)). A number of special provisions apply dealing with a variety of unusual cases, including those where payments are made by intermediaries or to employees of non-United Kingdom employers (IT(EP)A 2003, ss.687 and 689 respectively).

**5–12**   Sections 703–707 IT(EP)A 2003 replace the procedure in ICTA 1988, s.206A (PAYE settlement agreements), a statutory procedure to enable employers to adopt a simplified method for settling the liability of employees in respect of tax on certain benefits.

Although the purchaser is entitled to be satisfied that PAYE requirements have been properly carried out and are up to date, it will in practice often be the case that minor infringements of the regulations have occurred. Furthermore, the last part of the clause, which refers to tax chargeable on employees' benefits, is unlikely to be satisfied in practice. The vendors may wish to qualify the warranty by providing that no significant failures to operate the system have occurred but, if a floor to claims has been agreed as described in para.3–20, the purchaser might reasonably take the position that this adequately protects the vendors against trivial claims being made under the warranty without a qualification also being necessary.

**5–13   2.2 The Company has complied fully with all its obligations relating to Class 1 and Class 1A National Insurance Contributions, both primary and secondary.**

Since Class 1A National Insurance Contributions have been made applicable to most benefits not otherwise subject to National Insurance and National Insurance avoidance schemes have become increasingly common, it has become important to obtain this kind of warranty.

**5–14   2.3 The Company has complied with the following sections and regulations made under them:**

**FA 1995, ss.126 (U.K. Representatives of non-residents), 127 (Persons not treated as U.K. Representatives) and Schedule 23 (Obligations etc. imposed on U.K. Representatives);**

**ICTA 1988, s.349 (Payments not out of profits or gains brought into charge to income tax, and annual interest) and s.350 (Charge to tax where payments made under s.349);**
**ICTA 1988, s.524 (Taxation of receipts from sale of patent rights);**
**ICTA 1988, s.536 (Taxation of royalties where owner abroad);**
**ICTA 1988, ss.555–558 (Entertainers and sportsmen);**
**ICTA 1988, ss.559–567 (Sub-contractors in the construction industry);**
**ICTA 1988, s.582 (Funding bonds issued in respect of interest on certain debts);**
**ICTA 1988, s.733 (Persons entitled to exemptions);**
**ICTA 1988, s.736A and Schedule 23A (Manufactured dividends and interest);**
**ICTA 1988, s.777 (Provisions supplementary to ss.775 and 776).**

Without going into the full details of the scope of these sections, their broad significance is as follows:

- FA 1995, Sch.23 and ss.126 and 127: under these provisions a United Kingdom branch or agency which is the representative of a non-resident can be liable for taxation in respect of profits or gains arising through or from that branch or agency.

- ICTA 1988, ss.349 and 350: these sections provide a withholding tax system in relation to interest and annual payments. FA 2001 introduced a new s.349A which gives a broad exemption from such withholdings for payments between companies if the payer reasonably believes the payee is United Kingdom resident for tax purposes.

- ICTA 1988, s.524: this relates to payment of the proceeds of sale of a United Kingdom patent to a person resident outside the United Kingdom. The exemption at s.349A also applies to deductions under this section.

- ICTA 1988, s.536: this relates to payment of copyright royalties to a person resident outside the United Kingdom.

- ICTA 1988, ss.555–558: basic rate income tax must be deducted from payments made to non-resident entertainers or sportsmen for United Kingdom appearances.

- ICTA 1988, ss.559–567: these sections relate to the obligation to deduct tax from payments to certain sub-contractors in the construction industry.

- ICTA 1988, s.582: this relates to funding bonds issued in lieu of interest.

- ICTA 1988, s.733: this provision qualifies s.732 (Dealers in securities), which provides that certain dealers in securities who buy securities cum-interest have to deduct an appropriate amount of interest received in computing profits or losses. If, however, the purchaser is exempt from tax (for example, a charity or pension fund) this amount is treated under s.733 as being chargeable to tax and a withholding obligation arises.

- ICTA 1988, s.736A and Sch.23A: where, under a contract or arrangement for the transfer of securities, one party is required to pay amounts which represent dividends on shares or interest on United Kingdom securities of non-United Kingdom companies, the payments are treated as annual payments from which tax must be withheld and accounted for.

- ICTA 1988, s.777: where ICTA 1988, s.775 (Sale by individual of income derived from his personal activities) or s.776 (Transactions in land: taxation of capital gains) applies, the Inland Revenue may direct under s.777(9) that tax should be withheld.

5–15    It will be seen that many of these provisions apply only in exceptional circumstances and it would be appropriate for both parties to omit references which cannot apply to the target company.

5–16    **2.4 No liability to National Insurance Contributions or obligation to account for income tax under the PAYE system could fall on the Company as a result of a chargeable event (within the meaning of IT(EP)A 2003, Part 7) before, at or after Completion in respect of securities and interests in securities made available or securities options granted to an employee or director prior to Completion.**

Part 7 of IT(EP)A 2003 introduces a regime in relation to employment related restricted securities and convertible securities (and interests in such securities) under which an income tax charge may arise in respect of various chargeable events. Where the relevant securities constitute readily convertible assets, the target company may be liable to account for the income tax under PAYE and pay National Insurance Contributions. Under the regime it is possible to make various elections which mitigate the future income tax relating to such securities and take future gains or losses into the capital gains regime.

5–17    **2.5 No officer or employee of the Company participates in any scheme approved under IT(EP)A 2003, Schedules 2 (Approved share incentive plans), 3 (Approved SAYE option schemes), or 4 (Approved CSOP schemes) or has any unapproved options (whether under IT(EP)A 2003, Schedule 5 (Enterprise Managing Incentives) or otherwise) or is a beneficiary or potential beneficiary of a qualifying employee share ownership trust as defined in FA 1989, Schedule 5 (employee share ownership trust).**

Employee participation schemes have become a common part of the remuneration packages offered by companies of all sizes. This warranty can be used for fact-finding but further examination of any scheme will be required.

5–18    **2.6 [The Disclosure Letter contains full particulars of all elections in force in relation to the Company under ICTA 1988, s.247 (Dividends etc., paid by** one member of a group to another) and no assessment may be made under that section on the Company in respect of advance corporation tax which ought to have been paid or income tax which ought to have been deducted.]

In relation to distributions made on or before April 5, 1999, where one company owned more than 50 per cent of the ordinary share capital of another, they could jointly elect under s.247 for dividends to be paid without accounting for ACT. United Kingdom resident companies could still elect that payments between them, which are deductible in relation to the payer company for corporation tax purposes, should be made without deduction of income tax subject to certain provisions. This warranty should only be included if there is a risk that dividends were paid intra-group prior to April 6, 1999.

## 3 Penalties

**3.1 The Company has not paid or, since the Balance Sheet Date, become**   **5–19**
**liable to pay a penalty or interest under any statute relating to Taxation.**

The prime examples of penalties or interest in relation to the corporation tax self-assessment regime arise under FA 1998, s.117 and Sch.18, paras 17 and 18, and in relation to accounting periods ending before July 1, 1999, under TMA 1970, Part X (Penalties, etc.). The most common penalties arise in relation to failing to make proper returns, making incorrect returns or paying tax after the due date. Stringent penalty provisions apply in relation to VAT under VATA 1994, s.63 (Penalty for misdeclaration or neglect resulting in VAT loss for one accounting period equalling or exceeding certain amounts), s.64 (Repeated misdeclarations) and s.67 (Failure to notify and unauthorised issue of invoices). Stamp duty penalties can arise for late stamping, under Stamp Act 1891, s.15 (Penalty upon stamping instruments after execution). FA 2003, Sch.10 (Stamp duty land tax: returns, enquiries, assessment and appeals) provides for penalties in relation to stamp duty land tax.

    It is important that the width of the definition of "Taxation" (when referring to payments due under any statute relating to Taxation) should be taken into account by the vendors and they might wish to restrict the warranty to corporation tax penalties. Penalties relating to VAT are covered in cl.29.

    **3.2 The Company has not been the subject of an investigation, discovery**   **5–20**
**or access order by or involving a Taxation Authority and there are no**
**circumstances which make it likely that an investigation, discovery or order**
**will be made.**

The Inspector of Taxes can make a "discovery" under TMA 1970, s.29 (Assessment where loss of tax discovered) within six years unless the point has been agreed under s.54 (Settling of appeals by agreement). If there has been fraud or wilful default, a "back-duty" investigation can be made for up to 20 years under s.36 (Fraudulent or negligent conduct). An access order permitting the removal of documents may be made under VATA 1994, Sch.11, para.11 (Order for access to recorded information etc.).

The vendors might reasonably object to this warranty on the basis that it is irrelevant in so far as it relates to past investigations. Although there is some justification for the purchaser requesting a warranty about future enquiries, the wording is so wide that the vendors should be most cautious in accepting it. It is common to qualify the wording of this warranty in relation to routine PAYE and VAT inspections.

*4 Claims, elections, liabilities and reliefs*

**5–21**    **4.1 The Disclosure Letter contains full details of all matters relating to Taxation in respect of which the Company (either alone or jointly with another person) is, or at Completion will be, entitled:**

     **4.1.1**    **to make a claim (including a supplementary claim) for, disclaimer of or election for relief under any statute relating to Taxation;**

     **4.1.2**    **to appeal against an assessment to or a determination affecting Taxation;**

     **4.1.3**    **to apply for the postponement of Taxation.**

It is important that the purchaser should be aware of any outstanding rights that exist in relation to the target company to make claims, elections, appeals or applications as described so that the necessary action can be taken before any time limits expire. Clause 4.1.1 refers specifically to supplementary claims, which may be made under FA 1998, Sch.18, para.56 (Supplementary claim or election) if a claim has already been made and a mistake is discovered. Disclaimers arise, for example in relation to capital allowances as mentioned below. Appeals can cover not only assessments but also numerous other matters relevant to taxation liability, such as the existence of a group structure for corporation tax or VAT purposes, or whether a company is trading or carrying on an investment business.

**5–22**    Generally, in relation to corporation tax, claims, etc. may be made at any time within six years after the relevant event or accounting period. The main provisions which impose shorter time limits are the following:

Claims

- Appeals: generally a 30-day limit applies.

- Capital allowances: claims for capital allowances which are available primarily against a specified class of income to be set-off against other income must be made within two years from the end of the relevant accounting period (CAA 2001. ss.259–260 (Special Leasing)). Under corporation tax self-assessment. which applies to accounting periods on or after July 1, 1999, claims for capital allowances must be included in a company tax return. Claims may normally be made, amended or withdrawn up to the first anniversary of the filing date for the relevant company tax return (FA 1998, Sch.18, Part IX).

- Capital gains: if the value of an asset becomes negligible, a claim may be made for the asset to be treated as if it had been sold and reacquired at market value. The claim may be made retrospectively to an accounting period which ended not more than 24 months before the date of the claim (TCGA 1992, s.24(2) (Disposals where assets lost or destroyed, or become of negligible value)).

- Group relief: claims must be included in the relevant company tax return (FA 1998, Sch.18, Part IX).

- Loan relationships: non-trading deficits on a company's loan relationships may be treated in a variety of different ways as provided by FA 1996, s.83 (Non-trading deficit on loan relationships) and Sch.8 (Loan relationships: claims relating to deficits). Claims must be made within two years of the end of the relevant period or within such further period as the Board of the Inland Revenue may allow.

- Losses on unquoted shares in trading companies: a claim may be made by an investment company to apply against its income a loss on shares subscribed by it within two years after the end of the accounting period in which the loss occurs (ICTA 1988, s.573 (Relief for companies)).

- Trading losses: a claim to set-off losses incurred in a trade against other profits of the same accounting period, or to carry the losses back to the preceding three accounting periods, must be made within two years of the end of the accounting period in which the loss is made (ICTA 1988, s.393 (Losses other than terminal losses) and s.393A (Losses set off against profits of the same, or an earlier, accounting period)).

- VAT bad debt relief: if VAT is accounted for on a debt which is written off by the creditor, it may, on a claim being made, be recovered provided a period of six months has elapsed since the supply (VATA 1994, s.36 (Bad debts)). The effect of the warranty is to cover cases where a debt has actually been written off; cl.28.2 deals with those debts which, being at least six months old, could be written off, thereby giving rise to a right to claim relief.

## Elections

- Advance corporation tax and shadow advance corporation tax: since the abolition of ACT with effect from April 6, 1999 companies pay dividends without accounting for ACT, and so an election to do so is no longer necessary. While a company with unrelieved surplus ACT as at April 6, 1999 will fall within the shadow ACT regime (the Corporation Tax

(Treatment of Unrelieved Surplus ACT) Regulations 1999), companies may opt out of the shadow ACT system (regulations 4 and 5).

- Corporation tax: see the commentary on cl.5 in relation to unremittable income. Two companies in a group may, by giving notice to the Inspector before the refund has been made, elect that a tax refund to which one of them is entitled is surrendered to the other (FA 1989, s.102 (Surrender of company tax refund etc., within group)).

- Capital allowances: CAA 2001, s.569 (Election to treat sale as being for alternative amount) gives the transferor and transferee in relation to sales of equipment the right in certain cases to elect that the assets are treated for capital allowances purposes as transferred at their written down values and not market values. The election must be made within two years of the transfer. A similar election on a transfer of trade may be made under s.266 (Elections where predecessor and successor are connected persons). An election may be made for certain equipment to be treated as short-life assets, thereby enabling capital allowances to be computed as if those assets were used for a separate notional trade. The election must be made not later than two years after the end of the period in which the expenditure was incurred (CAA 2001, s.85 (Election for short-life assets treatment: procedure)).

5–23    If an equipment lessor incurs expenditure on fixtures and the lessee has an interest in the relevant property so that he would have been entitled to claim capital allowances under CAA 2001, s.176 (Persons who are treated as owners of fixtures: person with interest in relevant land having fixtures for purposes of qualifying activities) had he himself incurred the expenditure, the lessor and lessee may elect that the fixtures should be treated as belonging to the lessor. The effect of this will be to entitle the lessor to the capital allowances. The election must be made within two years of the end of the period in which the lessor incurs the expenditure (CAA 2001, s.177 (Equipment lessors)). Where machinery or plant has become a fixture and the lessor grants a lease under which the lessee incurs expenditure on fixtures in relation to which, had the lessor incurred the expenditure, it would have been entitled to allowances, the lessor and lessee may elect for the fixture to be treated as if it belonged to the lessee. The election must be made within two years from the grant of the lease (CAA 2001, s.183 (Incoming lessee: where lessor entitled to allowances)).

- Capital gains: if an asset was acquired before April 6, 1965, an election may be made within two years of its disposal (or within such further period as the Board of the Inland Revenue may by notice allow) to have the gain or loss based on its market value at that date and not determined by applying straight-line growth (TCGA 1992, Sch.2, para.17 (Election for valuation at April 6, 1965)). An election may be made under TCGA 1992, s.35 (Assets held on March 31, 1982 (including assets held on April 6, 1965)) to have the capital gains and losses on assets held on March 31, 1982 determined by reference to their value at that date without regard to the original acquisition cost. The election may be made within two years of the end of the period in which the first relevant disposal occurs (see also cl.21.2). An election may be made under TCGA 1992, Sch.4 (Deferred charges on gains before March 31, 1982) for certain rolled-over or postponed capital gains to be halved. The election must be made within two years of the end of the accounting period in which there is a disposal, or deemed disposal, of the relevant asset.

- Capital losses: TCGA 1992, s.171A allows two group members to elect to be treated as if an asset had been transferred between them immediately prior to its disposal to a third party. This election can only be made if the company making the disposal could have made a no gain/no loss transfer to the other group company at that time (see cl.17.1). The election must be made less than two years after the end of the relevant accounting period.

- VAT: an election may be made to waive exemption from value added tax in relation to certain property transactions (see cl.28.4).

## Postponement

- If a company believes it is being overcharged by an amendment of a self assessment, it may within 30 days of the issue of the amendment apply for payment to be postponed pending hearing of the appeal. The 30-day period can be extended where there is a change of circumstances which is believed to have caused the overcharge (TMA 1970, s.55 (Recovery of tax not postponed)). The short time scale applicable in most cases makes it unlikely that a right to apply for postponement will, in practice, ever need to be disclosed.

A claim to postpone the taxation on chargeable gains arising on a transfer of the trade of a United Kingdom company, which is carried on abroad, to a non-resident in exchange for securities may be made under TCGA 1992, s.140 (Postponement of charge on transfer of assets to non-resident company) or s.140C (Transfer of a non-UK trade) if both parties to the transfer are resident in member states (see cl.26.1). If a company which is resident in one member state transfers a United Kingdom trade to another company which is resident in another member state in exchange for securities of the transferee, they may jointly claim that the transferee takes over the base cost of the transferor (TCGA 1992, s.140A (Transfer of a UK trade)).

This warranty is so widely drawn, both in its express terms and by reason of the definition of "Taxation", that it will often be difficult for the vendors to ensure compliance. They should seek to limit the warranty so that it applies to specified statutory provisions only.

**4.2 The Company has not made a claim under TCGA 1992, s.24(2)** 5–24
**(Disposals where assets lost or destroyed, or become of negligible value) or**

**exercised an option to pay tax by instalments under s.280 (Consideration payable by instalments).**

If a capital asset becomes negligible in value the owner may claim under s.24(2) to be treated as if the asset had been sold and immediately reacquired at that value. Section 280 applies where the purchase consideration on a disposal is payable over a period exceeding 18 months. At the option of the person making the disposal the tax may be paid by instalments over a period of up to eight years. Clause 4.1 covers entitlements to make claims whereas this warranty deals with claims which have already been made.

The purchaser will have an interest in knowing about these claims but the vendors may wish to limit the application of the clause to claims within the previous six years or to cases where the asset in relation to which a s.24 claim was made is still owned or where instalments remain outstanding under s.280.

**5–25**      **4.3 The Company is not, nor will it become, liable to pay, or to reimburse or indemnify another person in respect of, Taxation in consequence of the failure by any other person (not being the Company) to discharge the Taxation, where the Taxation relates to a profit, income or gain arising or deemed to have arisen or anything occurring or deemed to have occurred (whether wholly or partly) prior to Completion.**

There are several statutory provisions whereby a company can be liable for the payment of corporation tax or VAT which is the primary responsibility of another company. The main ones are the following:

- ICTA 1988, s.419 (Loans to participators etc.): this is considered in relation to cl.13.3.

- ICTA 1988, s.767A (Change in company ownership: corporation tax): if the ownership of a company changes after November 30, 1993 and corporation tax for a period which began before the change remains unpaid six months after the date of the corporation tax assessment, the tax may be collected from a person who during the three years preceding the change of ownership had control of it or from a company controlled by that person. For the section to apply there must have been either a major change in the activities of the company which owes the tax associated with a transfer of assets to a connected party or a cessation of the company's trade. The person required to pay the tax has a right of recovery from the company which owed it (s.767B (Change of company ownership: supplementary)).

- TCGA 1992, s.137(4) (Restriction on application of ss.135 and 136): s.135 (Exchange of securities for those in another company) and 136 (Scheme of Reconstruction involving issue of securities) provide a roll-over for capital gains tax purposes on certain company reconstructions and amalgamations. Section 137 restricts the relief so that it is not available if the transaction was carried out mainly for the purpose of avoiding tax. If s.137 applies and the transferor fails to pay the resulting tax within six months of the due date, it may be assessed at any time within two years on a holder of the securities which acquired them by intra-group transfer.

- TCGA 1992, s.139 (Reconstruction involving transfer of business): a bona fide reconstruction involving a transfer of one company's business to another can be disregarded. If, however, the transfer was not effected for bona fide commercial reasons, the tax arising from the transfer can be recovered from the transferee.

- TCGA 1992, s.189 (Capital distribution of chargeable gains: recovery of tax from shareholder): this is discussed in relation to cl.12.3.

- TCGA 1992, s.190 (Tax recoverable from another group company or controlling director): this relates to circumstances where a chargeable gain has accrued to a company when it is a member of a group. If the company does not pay the corporation tax within six months of the due date it can be recovered from the principal company of the group or any other company which, at any one time within two years ending with the disposal, was another member of the group and owned the relevant asset. This liability will accordingly be relevant only if the company primarily responsible for the payment of the taxation is not a member of the target company's group of companies. A controlling director of the company may also be liable in certain circumstances.

- FA 2000 substituted a new version of TCGA 1992, s.190, for gains accruing on or after April 1, 2000. Section 190 now provides that if the United Kingdom corporation tax liability of a non-resident company remains unpaid more than six months after the due date, corporation tax may be recovered from:
  (1) the principal company of the group;
  (2) any other company which, at any time during the 12 months before the gain accrued, was a member of the group and owned all or part of the asset (or an underlying asset); and/or
  (3) any person who is a controlling director of the taxpayer company or a company controlling the taxpayer company, or was such a controlling director during the 12 months before the gain accrued.

In respect of accounting periods ending on or after April 1, 2000, FA 2000, Sch.28 provides that if the United Kingdom corporation tax liability of a non-resident company remains unpaid more than six months after the due date, that corporation tax liability may be recovered from other companies with which it is (or was) associated. The Inland Revenue can recover the outstanding tax liability from a company within the same group, a member of a consortium which owned the non-resident company at any time in the relevant period or a member of the same group as a company which was a member of a consortium which owned the non-resident company at any time in the relevant period. In the latter two instances only a proportion, determined by reference to the relevant consortium member's share in the consortium, can be recovered.

The relevant period begins the later of 12 months before the start of the non-resident company's accounting period and April 1, 2000 and ends when the unpaid tax first became payable. The Inland Revenue has three years after the date when the non-resident company's liability is finally determined within which to serve notice seeking recovery.

Where there is a clawback of stamp duty where relief under FA 1930, s.42 or FA 1986, s.76 is withdrawn pursuant to FA 2002, ss.111 and 113, the stamp duty which then becomes payable can be recovered under FA 2002 Schs 34 and 35 from the transferor company, any company which at the relevant time was a member of the same group as the transferee company and was above it in the group structure and any controlling director of the transferee company. Similar provisions apply in relation to SDLT under FA 2003, Sch.7.

- VATA 1994, s.43 (Groups of companies): companies in a group for which there is a group registration are jointly and severally liable for the group's VAT, which is primarily payable by the representative member of the group.

Further minor sections to which this warranty would apply are dealt with in Appendix 8.

The purchaser has a real interest in this warranty only if there is no statutory right of reimbursement (as to which see Appendix 8) or if the covenant of the person against whom the right exists is of doubtful strength. The vendors should include an obligation on the purchaser to procure that the target company pursues any right of recovery which it has against third parties. The vendors should also consider whether the extension of the warranty to future events, arising from the phrase **"will become"**, is acceptable. Finally, the warranty should fairly be restricted to taxation in the usual narrow sense.

5–26     **4.4 No relief from Taxation has been claimed by or given to the Company, or taken into account in determining the provision for Taxation in the Accounts, which could be withdrawn, postponed or restricted as a result of anything occurring after Completion [which is not a deliberate act or omission, or a circumstance deliberately created, by the relevant Company after Completion for the purpose of effecting the withdrawal, postponement or restriction].**

The purpose of this warranty is to cover the very unusual case where relief available before completion may be at risk because of action occurring after completion. This could occur if within the three years preceding the sale of the target company to the purchaser there had been another change of ownership.

If the purchaser allows a major change to occur in the nature or conduct of the trade of the target company before the three years expire, losses carried forward from a period prior to the first alteration in ownership could be prejudiced by the operation of ICTA 1988, s.768 (Change in ownership of company: disallowance of trading losses) and s.768A (Change in ownership: disallowance of carry back of trading losses). Inland Revenue Statement of Practice SP10/91 explains the basis on which the Inland Revenue interprets the term "a major change in the nature or conduct of a trade".

While the purchaser would wish to be covered against the withdrawal of past   **5–27** reliefs as an inadvertent result of transactions occurring after completion, the vendors might fairly consider that it is up to the purchaser to ensure that no such circumstances arise. To cover this, the words in square brackets could be added. Furthermore, the warranty is reasonable only if the loss of the relief results in an immediate liability to taxation. The withdrawal of relief should otherwise not be the subject of a warranty unless a representation has been made that reliefs would remain available.

It may be necessary to consider the interplay of this warranty, if given, with any general provision dealing with liabilities which are the result of events both before and after completion (see, for example, para.4–12).

## 5 Unremittable income and capital gains

**5.1 The Company has not received or become entitled to income which is**   **5–28** **"unremittable income" within the meaning of ICTA 1988, s.584 (Relief for unremittable overseas income) or a gain to which TCGA 1992, s.279 (Foreign assets: delayed remittances) could apply [and which has not been remitted to the United Kingdom].**

Income is unremittable for the purposes of s.584 if it cannot be brought to the United Kingdom because of the laws of the territory in which the income has arisen, executive action of the government of that territory or the impossibility of obtaining foreign currency in the territory. In those circumstances, the taxpayer may apply by notice, given before the relevant assessment has become final and conclusive, for the United Kingdom tax liability on the income to be held over until it becomes remittable. TCGA 1992, s.279 applies similar rules in relation to chargeable gains accruing from the disposal of assets in foreign territories where the gains cannot be remitted.

The purchaser will wish to ensure not only that it is notified of any claims which have been made and which therefore give rise to a contingent liability when remittance occurs or could occur, but also that claims have been made where the legislation permits them. The vendors may wish to qualify the warranty by the words in square brackets to cover cases where claims were made in the past but the gains were subsequently remitted and the tax paid. It will also be noted that the warranty effectively relates not only to cases where claims have been made but also to circumstances where they could have been made. The vendors may wish to restrict the clause so that they merely warrant that no claims have been made.

If the vendors accept that the warranty applies to cases where there is an unexercised right to make a claim, they should, in the case of a target company which has overseas business activities, ensure that any extension of the warranties to completion does not cover this part of the clause.

### 6 Tax avoidance

**5–29**  **6.1 The Company has not, since the Balance Sheet Date, engaged in, or been a party to, a scheme or arrangement of which the main purpose, or one of the main purposes, was the avoidance of, or a reduction in liability to, Taxation.**

While it might be possible for the vendors to satisfy themselves whether or not the target company has engaged in transactions intended to avoid taxation, they would not normally be able to give a warranty in relation to a reduction of tax liability. Many ordinary commercial transactions are structured in a way that will minimise the taxation impact and it would be reasonable for the vendors to require the purchaser to specify the circumstances in which it is interested. The warranty is particularly dangerous as a result of the very wide definition of "Taxation" adopted by para.4–01. The sections listed in cl.6.2 would seem to deal comprehensively with all relevant anti-avoidance legislation and to provide the purchaser with adequate protection.

**5–30**  **6.2 The Company has not been a party to, or otherwise involved in, a transaction to which any of the following could apply:**

> **ICTA 1988, s.56 (Transactions in deposits with and without certificates or in debts);**
> **ICTA 1988, s.399 (Dealings in commodity futures etc.: withdrawal of loss relief);**
> **ICTA 1988, ss.116 (Arrangements for transferring relief), 395 (Leasing contracts and company reconstructions) and 410 (Arrangements for transfer of company to another group or consortium);**
> **ICTA 1988, s.730 (Transfers of income arising from securities);**
> **ICTA 1988, ss.731–735 (Purchase and sale of securities);**
> **ICTA 1988, s.736 (Company dealing in securities: distribution materially reducing value of holding);**
> **ICTA 1988, s.767A (Change in company ownership: corporation tax);**
> **ICTA 1988, s.774 (Transactions between dealing company and associated company);**
> **ICTA 1988, s.779 (Sale and lease-back: limitation on tax reliefs);**
> **ICTA 1988, s.781 (Assets leased to traders and others);**
> **ICTA 1988, s.786 (Transactions associated with loans or credit);**
> **CAA 2001, Part 2, Chapter 17, ss.218, 221–224, 232(1), 241–243 or 246(1) (Anti Avoidance);**
> **CAA 2001, s.5 (When capital expenditure is incurred);**
> **TCGA 1992, s.29 (Value shifting: General provisions); and**
> **TCGA 1992, s.106 (Disposal of shares and securities by company within prescribed period of acquisition).**

The following gives a brief indication of the scope of the provisions listed in **5–31** this warranty:

- ICTA 1988, s.56: this section taxes under Sch.D, Case VI the profit on the disposal of deposits unless the property is taxable as a trading receipt.

- ICTA 1988, s.399: this section counteracts certain artificial arrangements for obtaining tax relief by dealing in commodities, financial futures or traded options.

- ICTA 1988, ss.116, 395 and 410: this series of anti-avoidance provisions prevents the surrender of group relief where there is a partnership of companies and one partner receives a benefit in relation to its share of the losses of the partnership, where leasing contracts may be transferred or where arrangements exist which could cause a group structure to be broken.

- ICTA 1988, s.730: this relates to a sale of the income from a security without the security itself being sold.

- ICTA 1988, ss.731–735: these provisions relate to reverse bond washing where a purchaser buys securities cum-interest and later resells them, in the meantime receiving interest. The anti-avoidance provisions will apply unless the transaction involved the exercise of a traded or financial option on normal commercial terms or the time between the purchase and sale exceeds six months or, if the purchase and sale were effected at the current market price and were not in pursuance of an arrangement, one month.

- ICTA 1988, s.736: where, as a result of a dividend being declared on shares held by a dealing company as trading stock, a fall in the value of the shares occurs, the loss is not allowed as a deduction. The shareholding in question must amount to more than ten per cent of all holdings of the same class of shares in the company.

- ICTA 1988, s.767A: this section is briefly summarised in the commentary on cl.4.3. The purpose of the provision is to prevent the abuse arising from the purchase of companies with tax losses which could be used to shelter the profits of the purchaser, followed by the extraction of funds from the loss making company. Although the reduction of the assets of the company will have taken place quite properly, the effect would be to leave the company without any funds to discharge the tax liability arising from the transaction if the Revenue were to be successful in challenging its effectiveness.

- ICTA 1988, s.774: where there are transactions between a dealing company and an associated company which is not a dealing company, certain deductions, which are allowed for the dealing company but would otherwise not be taxed in the hands of the associated company, will be treated as taxable income of the associated company.

- ICTA 1988, s.779: this limits the tax deduction allowed in relation to a sale and leaseback transaction to a commercial rent for the premises.

- ICTA 1988, s.781: this section applies where a tax deduction is available in respect of payments under a lease of an asset and the payer receives a capital sum under the lease or the lessor's interest belongs to an associate of the payer who has received the capital sum.

- ICTA 1988, s.786: this section prevents tax relief being obtained on certain types of quasi-interest payments.

- CAA 2001, Pt II, c.17: qualifying expenditure for the purposes of claiming writing down allowances can be restricted by anti-avoidance provisions where, in particular, sale and leaseback transactions occur.

- CAA 2001, s.5: capital expenditure is treated as incurred when the obligation to pay becomes unconditional. If, however, the obligation arises on a date earlier than that which accords with normal commercial usage and the sole or main benefit of the arrangement was to ensure that the capital allowances were available in an earlier period, the relevant date is the date for payment and not the date of obligation.

- TCGA 1992, s.29: a disposal occurs for capital gains tax purposes where a person exercises control to pass value out of shares in a company into other shares in the company.

- TCGA 1992, s.106: bed and breakfast deals by companies where securities comprising not less than two per cent of the issued share capital in question are sold and reacquired within a one-month period in the case of Stock Exchange transactions or a six-month period in other cases, are disregarded for capital gains tax purposes.

5–32    Certain statutory provisions are sometimes included in warranties such as the above which are wholly inappropriate. These include:

- ICTA 1988, ss.739–746: (Transfer of assets abroad) which in certain circumstances can impose liability on a United Kingdom resident individual in respect of income arising to a non-resident;

- ICTA 1988, s.775: (Sale by individual of income derived from his personal activities) which treats as income what would otherwise be a capital sum resulting from a sale by an individual of their future income arising from his or her earning capacity in certain activities.

The vendors should be cautious about accepting any liability in relation to the matters covered by this warranty. Many of the sections will clearly not apply to normal trading companies and should be deleted. Those sections which could, in the particular circumstances of the target company, have some relevance should be retained only if the terms of the sale are such that it is fair for the vendors to accept the risk of liabilities arising.

**6.3 The Company has not, since the Balance Sheet Date, been a party to** 5–33
**a transaction to which any of the following provisions have been, or could**
**be, applied other than transactions in respect of which all necessary consents**
**or clearances were obtained:**

**ICTA 1988, ss.703–709 (Cancellation of tax advantages from certain**
**transactions in securities);**
**ICTA 1988, s.765 (Migration, etc., of companies);**
**ICTA 1988, s.776 (Transactions in land: taxation of capital gains);**
**TCGA 1992, ss.135–138 (Company reconstructions); or**
**TCGA 1992, s.139 (Reconstruction involving transfer of business).**

The above sections all relate to anti-avoidance measures and provide clearance
procedures. They are of necessity extremely complex and the following is only
a very broad summary of their scope:

- ICTA 1988, ss.703–709: this is a very onerous group of provisions which
  enables tax advantages arising from transactions in securities to be counteracted. Clearances may be obtained under s.707.

- ICTA 1988, s.765: it is a criminal offence for a United Kingdom resident
  company to permit the issue of shares or debentures by, or to transfer
  shares or debentures of, a non-resident subsidiary of a United Kingdom
  resident company, unless Treasury consent is obtained.

- ICTA 1988, s.776: this relates to transactions involving a disposal of
  assets representing the value of land where a capital gain would otherwise
  arise. There is a limited right to obtain a clearance under s.776(11).

- TCGA 1992, ss.135–138: these sections provide roll-over relief for capital gains tax purposes where there is a reconstruction. Clearance can be
  obtained under s.138.

- TCGA 1992, s.139: the purpose of s.139 is to disregard for taxation
  purposes a reconstruction which involves the transfer of the whole or part
  of a company's business to another company for a consideration involving only the transfer of liabilities. The section will not apply, however, if
  the reconstruction was effected otherwise than for bona fide commercial
  reasons or with a view to avoiding tax. Subsection (5) provides that a
  clearance may be obtained under s.138 (Procedure for clearance in
  advance).

Although these anti-avoidance provisions are widely drawn, particularly those
contained in ss.703–707 and s.776, the vendors should generally be in a position
to determine whether the warranty can be given. If, however, there is any doubt
as to whether any of the sections apply, it would be appropriate for the vendors
to make a full disclosure and for the purchaser to be required to assess the
likelihood of an infringement having occurred.

### 7 Depreciatory transactions and value shifting

**5–34**  **7.1 No allowable loss, which may accrue on the disposal of an asset by the Company, is likely to be reduced by reason of TCGA 1992, s.176 (Depreciatory transactions within a group) or s.177 (Dividend stripping).**

Section 176 of TCGA 1992 relates to depreciatory transactions within a group where a disposal of assets takes place at less than market value. If the effect of the transaction is to reduce the value of the shares of the company, any allowable loss for capital gains tax purposes occurring on a disposal of the shares within the following six years will be reduced by an amount reflecting the depreciatory transaction. Section 177 extends this concept to dividend stripping where a dividend is paid and, as a result, a loss would arise on a disposal of the shares in the company paying the dividend.

The only effect of those sections in the present context is to restrict the allowable loss that would otherwise occur. While in principle it would seem fair that the purchaser should not suffer if the sections apply, nevertheless the vendors might reasonably argue that, unless the arrangements relating to the sale of the target company specifically envisaged that allowable losses would occur on disposals of assets, the purchaser will not suffer if an allowable loss is restricted.

**5–35**     **7.2 No chargeable gain or allowable loss arising on a disposal by the Company is likely to be adjusted under TCGA 1992, s.30 (Tax-free benefits).**

Section 30 provides for an adjustment to the consideration received on a disposal of an asset where an arrangement exists whereby the value of the asset has been materially reduced and the person disposing of it receives a tax-free benefit. Under s.30(2), where a parent company disposes of shares in a subsidiary a reduction in the value of certain assets other than those shares may be taken into account in determining the chargeable gain or allowable loss arising on the disposal. The relevant assets are those owned by a member of the parent's group and the circumstances must be such that their reduction in value causes a material decrease in the value of the shares.

This provision is of a narrow scope and, provided the vendors carefully review any transactions which might fall within this section, they should have no difficulty in agreeing the warranty. Nevertheless, the vendors might reasonably consider that the warranty should apply only in so far as s.30 gives rise to an increased chargeable gain and not to a reduction in an allowable loss.

**5–36**     **7.3 No reduction in the value of the shares of the Company has occurred as a result of:**

**7.3.1**    **the payment of a dividend after March 13, 1989 out of chargeable profits within the meaning of TCGA 1992, s.31 (Distributions within a group followed by a disposal of shares) as extended by TCGA 1992, s.31A (Asset-holding company leaving the group); or**

**7.3.2    a transfer of an asset in circumstances within TCGA 1992, s.32(2) (Disposals within a group followed by a disposal of shares).**

Section 31 provides that the provisions referred to in cl.7.2 apply where there is a group dividend and the dividend is paid out of "chargeable profits", being primarily accounting profits which are non-taxable because they result from either an intra-group transfer or a re-valuation of assets.

Section 31 does not apply unless the asset with enhanced value is no longer owned, immediately after the disposal, by the company that has made the disposal or by an associated company of it. TCGA 1992, s.31A provides for a charge to tax if, at any time within the six years following the first disposal of the asset, the company owning the asset in question leaves the group of which it was a member at the time of the disposal or ceases to be a 75 per cent subsidiary, or an effective 75 per cent subsidiary, of a member of that group.

Section 32 applies the value shifting rules to a sale of shares where the value of the shares has been reduced by an intra-group transfer of an asset for a consideration which is less than both market value and original cost. The section does not apply if the transfer was for bona fide commercial reasons and not as part of a scheme to avoid tax.

This warranty will only be material in circumstances where the target company has subsidiaries and will be relevant on a disposal of the target company's shares in a subsidiary. In such circumstances the vendors will be entitled to resist the warranty if either the purchase price for the target company has not been determined with regard to the potential tax liability if a subsidiary is sold off or no disposal of any subsidiaries is contemplated.

## 8 Disallowance of deductions

**8.1 No rents, interest, annual payments or other sums of an income nature paid, or payable, since the Balance Sheet Date by the Company or which the Company is under an obligation to pay are, or may be, wholly or partially disallowable as deductions in computing profits or as charges on income, for the purposes of corporation tax, by reason of ICTA 1988, ss.74 (General rules as to deductions not allowable), 125 (Annual payments for non-taxable consideration), 338–338B (Charges on income deducted from total profits), 770A (Transaction not at arm's length), 779 (Sale and lease-back: limitation on tax reliefs), 781 (Assets leased to traders and others), 787 (Restriction of relief for payments of interest) or otherwise.**    5–37

The purpose of this provision is to protect the purchaser against unexpected    5–38 circumstances in which the profits of the target company earned since the balance sheet date and shown, for example, in interim or management accounts are less than the taxable profits because of the disallowance of deductions. It also covers the possibility that there are payments to be made under a contractual liability which it might reasonably expect to be, but which in the event are not, deductible for taxation purposes. It should be noted that the statutory provisions specified are by way of example only and that the warranty extends by virtue of the words

**"or otherwise"** to any cause which gives rise to non-deductibility whether or not falling within those sections. The warranty is restricted to payments made after the balance sheet date as earlier payments are adequately covered by other warranties, such as cl.2.1.2.7 in para.7–40.

The sections specified are those which are most likely to apply and are as follows:

- s.74: this sets out the basic rule that expenses are not deductible unless wholly and exclusively laid out for the purposes of the trade and also excludes a large number of other items.

- s.125: an anti-avoidance provision intended to attack the so-called reverse annuity schemes. An annual payment is deductible only if the consideration for which it is made is taxable as income.

- s.338: certain payments which would normally be charges on income are excluded from being allowed as deductions including, for example, interest paid to a non-resident which is not paid under deduction of tax (except in certain circumstances).

- s.770A: this provides (together with Sch.28AA) for the substitution of market prices for actual prices where transactions take place on non-arm's length terms between parties, one of whom participates in the management, control or capital of both. Such participation may be direct or indirect. It will normally result in an increase in the amount treated as received but might occasionally give rise to a reduction.

- s.779: if land is subject to a sale and lease-back, the rent is not deductible to the extent that it exceeds a commercial amount.

- s.781: if a trader makes deductible payments for the use of an asset leased to him, any capital sum received by him under the lease will be taxed under Sch.D, Case VI to the extent of the deduction.

- s.787: another anti-avoidance provision, introduced to prevent the deduction of interest in the case of artificial arrangements designed to obtain a benefit from interest deductions.

While this warranty is unlikely to affect most companies, care is needed, particularly in relation to s.74 and to the **"or otherwise"** sweeping-up words.

*9 Transactions not at arm's length*

5–39  **9.1 The Company has not [since the Balance Sheet Date] carried out, or been engaged in, a transaction or arrangement to which ICTA 1988, s.770A (Transaction not at arm's length) and Schedule 28AA (Provision not at arm's length) has been or may be applied.**

ICTA 1988, s.770A and Sch.28AA apply to transactions on non-arm's length terms between persons, one of whom participates in the management, control or capital of the other, or where the same person or persons participate in the management, control or capital of both. Such participation may be direct or indirect. The term **"transactions"** is very broadly defined. It includes arrangements, understandings and mutual practices, whether or not intended to be legally enforceable. There can be a series of transactions between two persons even if, for example, there is no transaction to which both those persons are parties. Under corporation tax self-assessment there is a risk of substantial penalties in this area.

Until April 1, 2004 these rules did not affect transactions between parties wholly in the United Kingdom; however FA 2004, ss.30–37 and Sch.5 extended the rules to cover such situations. A broad exemption for small and medium sized enterprises was also introduced which is expected to protect the affairs of most United Kingdom businesses. Taxpayers can make Advance Pricing Agreements with the Inland Revenue to secure confidence as to the tax treatment of their pricing policies (FA 1999, ss.85–87). The transfer pricing rules also affect excessive debt financing of companies which was previously dealt with by thin capitalisation rules. All adjustments made under the transfer pricing rules are made in the self assessment tax returns of the taxpayers involved (both sides of the transaction) and the usual penalties apply for fraud or negligence in completing those returns.

This is a wide warranty but in principle there is no reason, under corporation **5–40** tax self-assessment, why this warranty should not be given.

It would be reasonable for the vendors to limit this clause to events after the balance sheet date, as earlier transactions will be effectively covered by a warranty such as cl.2.1.2.7 in para.7–40.

**9.2 The Company has not disposed of or acquired an asset in such** **5–41** **circumstances that TCGA 1992, s.17 (Disposals and acquisitions treated as made at market value) could apply.**

The basic effect of s.17 is to substitute market value for the actual consideration where an asset is acquired or disposed of otherwise than by a bargain made at arm's length unless there was no corresponding disposal (as where shares of a company are subscribed).

As regards assets acquired, the vendors may argue that the purchaser's only interest is to ensure there is no unexpected tax charge on the disposal of the assets on the basis that the acquisition cost for capital gains tax purposes is less than the cost appearing in the last accounts. This is already covered by the warranty set out at cl.21.1 and similar considerations to the ones detailed there will apply.

## 10 Disallowance of losses

**10.1 There has not been in the past three years a major change in the nature** **5–42** **or conduct of the trade or business of the Company such as might prevent the carry forward or back of trading losses or excess management expenses by reason of the application of ICTA 1988, s.768A (Change in ownership: disallowance of carry back of trading losses) or s.768B (Change in ownership of investment company: deductions generally).**

**5–43** The sections referred to in this warranty are among several provisions of the tax legislation where the concept of a major change in the nature or conduct of a trade or business is relevant. The effect of the sections referred to is as follows:

- ICTA 1988, s.768: this applies a restriction in relation to the carry forward of a trading loss under ICTA 1988, s.393 (Losses other than terminal losses) if, in any period of three years, there is both a change in the ownership of the company and a major change in the nature or conduct of its trade.

- ICTA 1988, s.768A: extends the restriction in s.768 to the carry back of losses to an earlier accounting period under ICTA 1988, s.393A (Losses: set off against the same, or an earlier, accounting period).

- ICTA 1988, s.768B: this prevents excess management expenses from a period before the change of ownership being deducted in determining the taxable profits for a later period if, in a period of six years beginning three years before the change in ownership, there is both a change in the ownership of the company and a major change in the nature or conduct of its trade.

The concept is also relevant in relation to ICTA 1988, s.767A (Change in company ownership: corporation tax), which is covered in cl.6.2. As mentioned above the Inland Revenue has explained the basis on which it interprets the phrase "major change in the nature or conduct of a trade or business" in Statement of Practice 10/91, as amended in April 1996.

**5–44** The vendors should resist giving this warranty unless the negotiations relating to the sale of the target company have taken into account the availability of losses. If the vendors do agree to the clause, they should bear in mind that the loss of the relief may be the result of a gradual series of events taking place over the period spanning the sale of the shares. The vendors would therefore wish to confine the warranty to a loss of relief which is solely attributable to events occurring prior to completion and to replace **"might"** by **"will"**. Furthermore, it may be desirable to include a specific provision as to how the purchaser's loss in the event of a disallowance is to be computed (see para.3–06).

*11 Loan relationships*

**5–45** **11.1 If the Company is a party to a loan relationship (within the meaning of FA 1996, s.81 (Meaning of "loan relationship" etc.)) it uses as respects the loan relationship in its statutory accounts a basis of accounting which is or equates to an authorised accounting method under FA 1996, s.85 (Authorised accounting methods).**

Under FA 1996, Ch.II, all profits and losses arising from loan relationships of companies are dealt with under a new regime. A company has a loan relationship if it stands in the position of a creditor or debtor as regards a money debt and the debt is one arising from a transaction for the lending of money. Generally, the taxation treatment will follow the accounting treatment provided this complies with one of two authorised accounting methods. The first of these, which is of general application, is the accruals method, and the other is mark to market. If the accounting method used by a company for statutory accounts does not comply with the definitions of authorised accounting methods contained in s.85, the taxation position will be determined in accordance with an accounting basis which equates to an authorised accruals basis in accordance with FA 1996, s.86 (Application of accounting methods).

It is a matter of legitimate concern to the purchaser to be satisfied that the accounting treatment used by the Company in respect of its loan relationships is authorised so that its taxation liabilities will be based upon the accounting profits and losses. The vendors should have no difficulty in knowing whether the accounting method used by the target company satisfies the requirements of s.85 but, if there is any possibility that a different accounting method will have to be used for determining tax liability under s.86, the vendors will need to be satisfied as to the implications that might arise by giving this warranty. From the vendors' point of view, it will be better for them to make a disclosure of any differences between the statutory accounting method and the authorised accounting method and leave it to the purchaser to determine what taxation implications result.

**11.2 The Company has not, in respect of a loan relationship within the** **5–46**
**meaning of FA 1996, s.81 (Meaning of "loan relationship" etc.), applied:**

**11.2.1** **an authorised accounting method inconsistently or otherwise in a materially different way in successive accounting periods; or**
**11.2.2** **used a different authorised accounting method for the same or successive accounting periods as provided by FA 1996, s.89 (Inconsistent application of accounting methods).**

The effect of s.89 was to ensure that if there is a change in an authorised accounting method, an adjustment is made by way of a balancing debit or balancing credit in the second accounting period. Essentially, the debit or credit is the difference between the aggregate of the debits and credits given in respect of the loan relationship in previous accounting periods determined on the basis of the existing method as compared with those which would have arisen under the new method. FA1996, s.89 was repealed with effect for accounting periods beginning after September 30, 2002.

The vendors will generally prefer to disclose any changes in the accounting method which might be relevant for the purposes of s.89 and to leave it to the purchaser to determine the tax consequences.

**11.3 The Company is not required to use an authorised accruals basis of** **5–47**
**accounting as respects a creditor relationship by virtue of FA 1996, s.87**
**(Accounting method where parties have a connection).**

If the parties to a loan relationship have a connection within the meaning of s.87—broadly arising through common control—they are required to use an authorised accruals basis of accounting. In such a case FA 1996, Sch.9, para.6 (Bad debts etc., where parties have a connection) requires the accounting treatment to proceed on the basis that the debt is good. The normal provision in para.5 (Bad debts etc.), which modifies the assumption that the debt will be paid in full if the debt is bad or released, does not generally apply. Furthermore, if interest on such a loan is not paid within 12 months of the end of the accounting period in which it would be normally treated as accruing, the accruals method of accounting is modified so that no deduction is allowed until the interest is paid (FA 1996, Sch.9, para.2 (Late interest)).

Because of the wide definition of "connection" the purchaser may be adversely affected by paras 2 and 6, particularly in group situations where the target company is merely one member of the vendor's group and the loan relationship exists between the target company and companies which are not the subject of the sale. As the vendors should have no difficulty in determining whether or not a loan relationship exists between the parties having the relevant connection, they should be able to give the warranty although they might reasonably be concerned as to the exposure that they accept by doing so.

5–48     **11.4 The Company is not subject to a restriction as to the amount of the loss that it may bring into account in respect of a loan relationship by virtue of FA 1996, Schedule 9, paragraph 10 (Imported losses etc.).**

The purpose of this paragraph is to restrict relief that is available under an authorised accruals basis where the losses in question relate to periods when the loan relationship was not subject to United Kingdom taxation. For this purpose, the loss is referable to such a period if the company which is seeking to benefit from the loss would not have been subject to tax on a profit or gain arising from the loan relationship.

The circumstances giving rise to a restriction under this paragraph are sufficiently unusual that the vendors should be fully aware if the paragraph could apply. Nevertheless, it would be reasonable for them, as an alternative to giving a warranty, to make a full disclosure of the circumstances and to leave it to the purchaser to evaluate the potential exposure. In any case, unless the purchase has been negotiated on the basis that the purchaser is expecting to benefit from the availability of the losses arising from the relationship, it is unlikely that the purchaser would suffer any loss as a result of the restriction being applied.

5–49     **11.5 The Company has not acquired or disposed of rights or liabilities in respect of a loan relationship where the company from which it made the acquisition or to which it made the disposal was a member of the same group of companies within the meaning of FA 1996, Schedule 9, paragraph 12 (Continuity of treatment: groups etc.).**

If the rights or liabilities under a loan relationship are transferred within a group, the transaction is ignored for the purposes of the loan relationship legislation. The transferee company takes over the entitlement to debits and credits arising from the relationship.

Accordingly, if the target company has been a party to the transfer of a loan relationship, the taxation treatment might work unfairly so far as it is concerned. A disposing company may have incurred tax liabilities without receiving these subsequent taxation benefits and the converse may occur where there is the acquisition of the debt. The purchaser is entitled to be informed of circumstances where a transaction has occurred which could give rise to disadvantages to the target company under this paragraph but the vendors may reasonably feel that, if such transaction has occurred, the correct way to deal with any potential problems is for a disclosure to be made to the purchaser which can then evaluate the potential tax risk.

**11.6 The Company has not been a party to a loan relationship which had**   **5–50**
**an unallowable purpose within the meaning of FA 1996, Schedule 9, paragraph 13 (Loan relationships for unallowable purposes).**

This is an anti-avoidance provision which deals with cases where the purposes for which a loan relationship was entered into included a purpose which was not among the business or commercial purposes of the company. If the paragraph applies, the effect is to exclude relief for debits which result from the transaction.

This paragraph gave rise to considerable debate at the time it was enacted. Even though the final form of the provision is much narrower than was originally proposed, it is still uncertain in its scope and exposes borrowers to risk of non-deduction. Whether this risk should be borne by the vendors or the purchaser is a matter for negotiation between them.

## 12 Distributions

**12.1 The Company has not repaid, or agreed to repay, or redeemed, or**   **5–51**
**agreed to redeem, any of its shares, or capitalised, or agreed to capitalise, in the form of redeemable shares or debentures, any profits or reserves.**

Repayments of share capital are treated as distributions under ICTA 1988, s.209(2)(b) (Meaning of "distribution") to the extent of any premium over the amount paid up on the shares. A bonus issue of redeemable share capital or securities is treated as a distribution under ICTA 1988, s.209(2)(c). If a company has repaid share capital since April 6, 1965, and subsequently issues new shares by way of bonus, the amount treated as paid up on the new shares is, to the extent of the capital repayment, treated as a distribution (ICTA 1988, s.210 (Bonus issue following repayment of share capital)). The provisions relating to bonus issues do not apply after a period of ten years except in the case of closely held companies or where redeemable share capital is involved (ICTA 1988, ss.210 and 211 (Matters to be treated or not to be treated as repayments of share capital)).

**12.2 No outstanding security, within the meaning of ICTA 1988, s.254**   **5–52**
**(Interpretation of Part VI (Company distributions, tax credits, etc.)) of the Company was issued in such circumstances that the interest payable on it, or**

**any other payment in respect of it, falls to be treated as a distribution under ICTA 1988, s.209 (Meaning of "distribution").**

A security comes within the definition contained in ICTA 1988, s.254 even if no security is created or evidenced by it. Various circumstances are specified in s.209 as a result of which interest and other payments on securities are treated as a distribution. In particular, the consideration given for the use of the principal money secured is a distribution to the extent that it exceeds a reasonable commercial return. Another rather special case arises under s.209(2)(e)(vii) (introduced by F(No. 2)A 1992, s.31 (Equity notes)) in relation to equity notes. These are securities having a term of more than 50 years or no repayment date. If the notes are held by a company which is associated with or is a funder of the issuing company, the interest is treated as a distribution unless paid to a company within the charge to corporation tax. Although aimed at loan stock which is really in the nature of equity and which seeks to achieve an interest deduction for payments which are in the nature of dividends, the legislation is drawn in extremely wide terms and needs to be approached with caution. Interest which is deemed to be a distribution is not deductible in computing taxable profits or as a charge on income.

5–53  **12.3 The Company has not received a capital distribution to which TCGA 1992, s.189 (Capital distribution of chargeable gains: recovery of tax from shareholder) could apply.**

Section 189 has a limited impact as it relates to capital distributions by a company which are not treated as income of the recipient. There are few such distributions which are not caught by ICTA, 1988, s.209 (Meaning of "distribution"). The effect of s.189 is that, if the target company has received a capital distribution from a connected company which represents the proceeds of a disposal giving rise to a chargeable gain, then corporation tax on the chargeable gain of the distributing company may be recovered from the target company to the extent that the gain is represented by the distribution. As the target company has a statutory right of reimbursement, it is questionable whether the vendors should ever be expected to accept this liability unless the distributing company is one which is controlled by them. In any event, the vendors should provide that the target company should pursue its right of recovery and, in an appropriate case, assign the benefit of it to the vendors (see para.11–09).

*13 Close companies*

5–54 **13.1 The Company is not, nor was it at any time during the six years ended on the Balance Sheet Date, a close company as defined in ICTA 1988, s.414 (Close companies).**

The purchaser will wish to be satisfied that the target company does not have any outstanding liabilities attributable to a period of close company status. If the warranty can be given in this simple form, it will avoid the necessity for more detailed warranties covering the specific provisions relating to close companies.

If this warranty is not appropriate, the alternative warranties set out in the following clauses will have to be considered.

**13.2 No distribution within ICTA 1988, s.418 ("Distribution" to include**   5–55
**certain expenses of close companies) has been made by the Company [since**
**the Balance Sheet Date].**

Section 418 treats as a distribution by a close company expenses incurred in providing benefits in kind for participators and their associates which are not otherwise taxed. The value of the benefits will be non-deductible for taxation purposes. If the clause is accepted by the vendors, they should consider restricting its application to an appropriate period, such as the broken period following the balance sheet date.

This clause will rarely apply, as the benefit will normally be taxable as income of the recipient under IT(EP)A 2003 Pt 3 (Employment Income: Earning and benefits etc. treated as earnings). As any liability which does not arise will be attributable to benefits which have been enjoyed by participators in the target company, it is difficult for the vendors to resist the warranty. It may, however, be appropriate for the vendors to agree among themselves that, if the liability is attributable to the benefits received by one of them, he alone should be responsible for liability under the warranty (see para.3–15).

**13.3 No loan or advance within ICTA 1988, Part XI, Chapter II (Charges**   5–56
**to tax in connection with loans) has been made [and remains outstanding],**
**or agreed to, by the Company, [and the Company has not, since the Balance**
**Sheet Date, released or written off the whole or part of the debt in respect**
**of such a loan or advance.]**

Chapter II comprises ss.419–422. A loan by a close company to an individual who is a participator or his associate, otherwise than in the ordinary course of a lending business, gives rise to a tax charge equal to 25 per cent of the loan under s.419 (Loans to participators etc.). The tax is recoverable when the loan is repaid or if the debt in respect of the loan is written off.

Although the section primarily relates to loans to individuals, it is extended to apply also to loans made to companies in a fiduciary capacity and, until March 31, 1996, to non-resident companies (s.419(6) and FA 1996, s.173 (Loans to participators etc.)). Indirect loans are covered by s.419(5). Section 422 (Extension of s.419 to loans by companies controlled by close companies) is an anti-avoidance provision which prevents s.419 being circumvented by indirect loans through controlled companies. If the debt attributable to a loan or advance which falls within s.419 is to any extent released or written off, the amount released or written off is treated as income of the debtor under s.421 (Taxation of borrower when loan under s.419 released etc.). If that is relevant, the additional words in brackets should be added to the warranties to flush out any relevant transactions.

The vendors cannot reasonably resist giving this warranty, but they should consider the desirability of an agreement between themselves that, where the offending loan has been enjoyed by only one of the vendors, or his associates, he should bear the ultimate responsibility for the warranty (see para.3–15). Furthermore, a provision should be inserted in the sale agreement requiring the purchaser to make a refund if and when the tax is recovered on the repayment of the loan.

The part of the warranty relating to the release or writing-off of the debt is, however, irrelevant to the purchaser as the resulting tax liability falls only upon the debtor.

It should be noted that the purchaser will not in fact be prejudiced if the loan was made at a date prior to the balance sheet date as any tax payment will have been made or shown as a liability. The right of recovery of the tax paid will thus constitute a windfall benefit for the purchaser, unless it has been specifically taken into account. Far from warranting that no such loan has been made, the vendors may wish to provide that they alone should benefit as and when the tax recovery is received. Different principles will apply if the loan was made after the balance sheet date, since the payment of tax under the section will not then have been apparent to the purchaser.

### 14 Sale and leaseback of land

**5–57**    **14.1 The Company has not, since the Balance Sheet Date, entered into a transaction to which the provisions of ICTA 1988, s.780 (Sale and leaseback: taxation of consideration received) have been, or could be, applied.**

The effect of s.780 is to tax as income part of the sale consideration received where a short lease, having less than 50 years to run, is sold on a leaseback for a term not exceeding 15 years. The warranty is restricted to transactions occurring after the balance sheet date as any earlier transaction will be shown in the tax provision. In these circumstances, the vendors should have no difficulty in agreeing to the warranty.

### 15 Payments from pension funds

**5–58**    **15.1 The Company has not received a payment out of funds held for the purposes of an exempt approved scheme in respect of which an amount is recoverable by the Inland Revenue under ICTA 1988, s.601 (Charge to tax: payments to employers).**

If a payment out of a pension fund is made to an employer—typically because of over-funding—a tax charge of currently 35 per cent of the payment is made under s.601. The charge is treated as if it were income tax under Sch.D, Case VI (ICTA 1988, s.602 (Regulations relating to surpluses)).

In practice it will generally be quite clear, in practice, whether a s.601 payment has been received and, if it has, whether an outstanding amount remains recoverable. However, in cases of doubt the underlying fairness of the warranty will need to be analysed. The purchaser should have no ground for complaint if a s.601 payment has been received unless it has—incorrectly—been led to believe that the corresponding assessment has been discharged. To make the warranty fit with this approach, the following wording could be added:

**"but this clause shall not apply unless the amount received was included as an asset of the Company in the Accounts without the amount recoverable being included as a liability."**

Where there is to be a gap between contracts and completion it would be inappropriate to extend this warranty to the completion date because, if a payment is received after the contract date, the target company will have benefited from the net receipt.

This section, s.7 is due to be repealed with effect from April 6, 2006 following FA 2004, subject to transitional provisions and savings in FA 2004, Sch.36.

## 16 Group relief and group surrenders

This section, s.7 and part of s.17 are only relevant when the target company has been or is part of a group of companies. Although this is not expressed to be the case for the target company referred to throughout the book, it was considered useful to include these to cover a group situation. A suitable definition for "Group Companies" might be the Company and Subsidiaries of the Company, "Subsidiary" already having been defined. In certain circumstances it would also be appropriate to include a holding company of the Company in the definition as well.

**5–59**

**16.1 The Group Companies comprise a group for the purposes of ICTA 1988, s.402 (Surrender of relief between members of groups and consortia) and there is nothing in ICTA 1988, s.410 (Arrangements for transfer of company to another group or consortium) which precludes a Group Company from being regarded as a member of the group.**

**5–60**

For group relief purposes, companies comprise a group where there is a common shareholding of not less than 75 per cent of the ordinary share capital. As of April 1, 2000 a group may now include non-resident companies (ICTA 1988, ss.402 (3A), (3B), 413(2), (3)). Although cross border loss relief is not yet recognised, The European Court of Justice case law in this area is constantly evolving as cases come before it.

ICTA 1988, s.413 (Interpretation of Chapter IV), as amplified by Sch.18 (Group relief: equity holders and profits or assets available for distribution), lays down detailed requirements for ensuring that a true 75 per cent relationship exists in relation to dividend rights and rights on a winding-up. In determining rights to dividends and on a winding-up, the interests of "equity holders" are taken into account and these include not only shareholders but also certain classes of loan creditors.

By virtue of FA 2000, Sch.18 was amended such that the economic ownership tests were extended and certain ratchet loans which were regarded as non-commercial are now considered to be "normal commercial loans". This latter change applies to both loans after and those in existence at March 21, 2000, and

**5–61**

has the effect that a company borrowing money where the rate of interest payable might increase as its results deteriorate no longer risks being de-grouped by reason of such a loan (para.1(5E)).

5–62    The economic ownership tests have also been amended to reflect the potential inclusion of non-resident companies. The amendments adjust the tests in relation to limited rights (ICTA, Sch.18, para.4) and option arrangements (ICTA, Sch.18, para.5) to take into account rights which have effect by reference to whether or not the profits being distributed relate to the non-resident company's United Kingdom trade. See also ICTA 1988, Sch.18, para.5F.

Even where a group appears to exist, the anti-avoidance provisions contained in s.410 could result in one or more of the companies being treated as not being members of the group. The provision is extremely complex but broadly operates as follows. If there is an arrangement which could result in one of the companies leaving the group and becoming related to another company, or where a third company takes over the trade of one of the companies, the companies will not be treated as a group from the time of the arrangement. The term "arrangement" is not defined other than to state that it includes "arrangements of any kind whether in writing or not" (ICTA 1988, s.410(5)). It is clear that arrangements do not need to be legally enforceable (see Inland Revenue Statement of Practice 3/93) but that in the context of negotiations for the disposal of shares, although they do not need to be binding, they must be capable of taking effect, such as a non-binding agreement made subject to contract (see *Scottish and Universal Newspapers Ltd v Fisher (Inspector of Taxes)* [1996] S.T.C.(S.C.D.) 311). Furthermore, if the disposal requires shareholder approval, "arrangements" will not arise until the approval is given or the directors become aware that it will be forthcoming. However, the courts have held that the group relief relationship is broken only for the period while the "arrangements" for the target company to leave the group exist (see *Shepherd (Inspector of Taxes) v Law Land plc* [1990] S.T.C. 795).

Notwithstanding the difficulties of interpretation which exist in relation to these provisions, the vendors should generally be able to see clearly whether any member of the target company's group of companies may be treated as not being a member of the group for group relief purposes. Care will have to be taken if unusual loans have been made to a member of the target group by a non-member or if there have been any arrangements to sell off one of the members of the group separately from the other members.

Nevertheless, the vendors might reasonably question the appropriateness of giving this warranty to the purchaser unless surrenders of group relief amongst the members of the target group are contemplated.

5–63    **16.2 The Company has not, since the Balance Sheet Date, made or agreed to make, otherwise than to or from another Group Company a surrender of, or claim for, group relief under ICTA 1988, Part X, Chapter IV (Group relief).**

5–64    A member of a 75 per cent group may surrender its losses to other members of the group and the losses thus surrendered are deducted from the taxable profits of the claimant companies. Claims for group relief must be made within two years from the end of the surrendering company's accounting period to which the claim relates. It is therefore possible for surrenders or claims to have been made since the balance sheet date in respect of the last two complete accounting periods of the target company.

The purchaser will wish to know about any surrenders or claims since the balance sheet date as these will not necessarily appear in the latest accounts. It should be noted that because of the anti-avoidance provisions of ICTA 1988, s.410, referred to above, if the negotiations relating to the sale of the target company commenced prior to the balance sheet date, the actual accounting period will be treated as consisting of two notional periods respectively ending and commencing when the arrangements came into existence. This could prevent a full surrender of group relief for the last accounting period.

**16.3 No Group Company is liable to make or entitled to receive a payment for group relief otherwise than to or from another Group Company.** 5–65

If a company having excess losses is a member of a group and surrenders its losses to another company—the claimant company—it is usual for the claimant company to pay for the surrender. A payment for group relief is disregarded for tax purposes, so long as it does not exceed the amount of the losses surrendered (ICTA 1988, s.402(6) (Surrender of relief between members of groups and consortia)). A liability or entitlement will be relevant only if it involves a company outside the target group, such as a corporate vendor. If it is the target group which is entitled to receive the payment, the vendors will wish to consider the question of security.

**16.4 The Company has not made or received a payment for group relief (otherwise than to or from another Group Company), which may be liable to be refunded in whole or in part.** 5–66

If a surrender of group relief proves ultimately to be ineffective, perhaps because losses which were thought to exist are not in fact available or because of a defect in the group structure, the surrendering company will normally be required to repay, in whole or in part, the payment made for the surrender. Accordingly, until the surrender has been agreed with the Inland Revenue, the surrendering company is contingently liable to make a refund and, if this liability is to a company which is not a member of the target group, the purchaser will wish to know about it. The vendors should have no difficulty with the warranty in relation to payments made or received but may wish to redraft it as follows:

**All claims for group relief by any Group Company either have been agreed with the Inland Revenue or are detailed in the Disclosure Letter.**

An alternative warranty covering the same point in relation to group relief is:

**All claims for group relief made by each Group Company [(otherwise than as a result of a surrender of group relief by another Group Company)] were**

**valid and have been, or will be, allowed by way of relief from corporation tax.**

This wording is likely to be acceptable in so far as it relates to past claims, but the vendors should seek the deletion of **"or will be"**.

5–67        **16.5 If any member of the Group Company only became a member after the Balance Sheet Date, the apportionment of profits and losses will be made under ICTA 1988, s.403B (Apportionments under s.403A) on a time basis according to the respective lengths of the component accounting periods.**

If a member of the target group joined the group after the balance sheet date, there is a restriction under ss.403A and 403B on the losses that may be surrendered and the profits that may be sheltered in respect of the joining company and any other member of the group. Only a proportion of the losses of the surrendering company may be surrendered and only a proportion of the profits of the claimant company may be sheltered. In each case, the basic rule is that the proportion should be determined on a time apportioned basis according to the fraction of each company's accounting period which overlaps the other. However, s.403B provides that, instead of apportionment on a time basis, such other method shall be used as appears just and reasonable, if it appears that time apportionment would work unreasonably or unjustly.

This warranty will, accordingly, be relevant only if there is a member of the target group which became a member after the balance sheet date. Even in that event, the purchaser would not be entitled to the warranty unless it was part of the agreement between the parties that group relief would be surrendered or claimed by the company which joined the target group in respect of the overlapping accounting period.

5–68        **16.6 The Company is not restricted in relation to the surrendering of group relief by ICTA 1988, s.404 (Limitation of group relief in relation to certain dual resident companies).**

Section 404 was introduced in 1987 to prevent the exploitation of tax losses in more than one jurisdiction ("double-dipping"). A company could be simultaneously resident in two countries because of different criteria adopted by those countries in determining residence. A loss arising in one country could give tax relief in both. As s.404 applies to specific—usually contrived—circumstances of an unusual nature, the vendors will generally know whether the warranty can be given, although they might fairly question why the purchaser should be entitled to it.

5–69        **16.7 The Company has not agreed to surrender, otherwise than to another Group Company, any right to receive a tax refund under FA 1989, s.102 (Surrender of company tax refund, etc., within group).**

Under the pay-and-file system, there is a liability to pay interest on tax underpaid and a corresponding right to receive interest on tax overpaid. As, however, the rate of interest to be paid will be higher than the rate to be received, it may be in the interests of a group to take advantage of s.102, whereby one member of a group will be able to surrender its right to receive a repayment to another member which has underpaid its tax. For a surrender to be made, both companies have to be members of a 75 per cent group, for the purposes of group relief, throughout the relevant accounting period. Notice must be given jointly by both companies specifying the amount of the refund which is to be surrendered. When a valid notice has been given, the recipient company will be treated as having paid an amount of corporation tax for the relevant accounting period equal to the part of the prospective refund which has been surrendered.

This warranty is unlikely to give any difficulty to the parties but will operate as a useful reminder to ensure that the benefit of any refund is properly taken into account when analysing the asset value of the target company.

## 17 Acquisitions from group members

**17.1 The Company does not own an asset which was acquired from another company [not being a Group Company], which was, at the time, a member of the same group of companies (as defined in TCGA 1992, s.170 (Groups of companies: interpretation of ss.170–181)) as the relevant Group Company, and which owned that asset otherwise than as trading stock within TCGA 1992, s.173 (Transfers within a group: trading stock).** 5–70

Section 170 defines a group as comprising a principal company and its 75 per cent subsidiaries. The specified percentage relates to ordinary share capital as defined in ICTA 1988, s.838 (Subsidiaries), and the group may with effect from April 1, 2000 include non-resident companies.

Where an asset held as a capital asset is transferred between members of a group, the transfer will be deemed to have taken place at the base cost for capital gains tax purposes of the transferor company (TCGA 1992, s.171 (Transfers within a group: general provisions)). If the transferor held the asset as a capital asset and the transferee acquires it as trading stock, then the transferee is entitled to choose either to treat as an immediate chargeable gain an amount equal to the change in value between the date of acquisition by the transferor and the date of transfer or, by election, to avoid the corporation tax liability on the chargeable gain but to have its eventual trading profits or losses computed as if its acquisition cost was equal to the purchase price originally paid by the transferor company (thus creating a no gain/no loss transfer). If the transferee has made the election in circumstances where the asset has increased in value, thereby having avoided an immediate liability to tax at the cost of a deferred but potentially greater liability, the company will have a hidden additional liability to taxation against which the purchaser is entitled to the benefit of a warranty. If, on the other hand, the asset has decreased in value when the transfer takes place, the election may convert what would otherwise be a capital loss into a more flexible trading loss. From April 1, 2000, a transfer of an asset between two members of a group will be a no gain/no loss transfer only if the relevant asset is, and as a result of the transfer remains, within the scope of United Kingdom corporation tax.

Significantly, the incorporation of a United Kingdom branch of a non-resident company which is achieved by the transfer of the assets of the branch to a United Kingdom resident subsidiary company in exchange for an issue of new shares by the United Kingdom subsidiary to the non-resident company, will be treated as a no gain/no loss transfer. Consequently, TCGA 1992, s.172, under which it was possible to elect for such treatment, has been repealed. The new regime, however, allows no right of election, and as a result the incorporation of a branch in the manner described will always potentially give rise to a degrouping charge if the United Kingdom subsidiary subsequently leaves the group.

5–71    The vendors cannot reasonably resist giving this warranty but it may be difficult to ensure that no assets are held by a member of the target group which were not originally acquired from another company which was previously in the same group. The vendors may accordingly prefer to insert the bracketed words which exclude from the warranty transfers between members of the target group, although the purchaser will wish to know about group transfers so that it can avoid inadvertently triggering a liability under TCGA 1992, s.179 (Company ceasing to be member of group: post-appointed day cases), as described in relation to cl.17.2. The vendors may reasonably consider that, in the absence of special circumstances, the purchaser is nevertheless not entitled to the protection of a warranty.

5–72    **17.2 The execution or completion of this Agreement will not result in profit or gain being deemed to accrue to the Company for Taxation purposes, whether under TCGA 1992, s.179 (Company ceasing to be member of group: post-appointed day cases) or otherwise.**

The effect of s.179 is to impose a liability to corporation tax on chargeable gains where a company, which has acquired a capital asset from another group company, ceases to be a member of the same group while still owning the asset. The company leaving the group is treated as having, immediately it left, disposed of and reacquired the asset at its then market value. The section applies only if the ending of the group structure occurs within six years of the transfer of the asset. Following FA 2000, the basic conditions for the operation of the degrouping charge have changed to take account of the amended grouping provisions. The degrouping charge will generally operate so as to claw back relief given in respect of intra-group no gain/no loss transfers within the previous six years. However, the relevant asset need not be transferred to the company leaving the group by way of intra-group transfer, and it will be sufficient that the transferee company leaves the same group of which the transferor company was a member at the time of transfer. These changes apply to assets acquired on or after April 1, 2000, but the old rules and the previous form of s.179 remain relevant to assets acquired before that date (FA 2000, Sch.29, para.4(6) (De-grouping charge)).

This warranty will not normally be relevant, unless there is a corporate vendor, as the sections do not apply if the transferor and transferee of the asset are both members of the target group.

The words **"or otherwise"** which appear at the end of this warranty may need special consideration. The purchaser will wish to include these words to cover any possible liability which might arise by a termination of the group structure, such as contractual arrangements between one or more members of the vendor group which come to an end on the sale of the target company and which, by so doing, give rise to tax liability. These circumstances would be quite exceptional and it would not be possible for the purchaser to know of the circumstances unless they were specifically disclosed to it. The vendors, however, should reasonably be expected to be aware of any taxation implications which can arise by virtue of any unusual arrangements which exist between the target company and other companies.

The vendors should take account of the possibility that, owing to the wide definition of "Taxation" in para.4–01, a liability could arise in an overseas jurisdiction.

## 18 Demergers and purchase of own shares

**18.1 The Company has not been engaged in, or been a party to, any of the transactions set out in ICTA 1988, ss.213–218 (Demergers), nor has it made or received a chargeable payment as defined in s.214 (Chargeable payments connected with exempt distributions).**   5–73

Sections 213–218 provide for certain types of demergers to be exempt from treatment as distributions. Essentially, exempt distributions are those arising from a transfer by a company to its members of the shares of one or more of its 75 per cent subsidiaries or the transfer by a company of its trade, or of one or more of its 75 per cent subsidiaries, to another company in exchange for shares issued to its members. Exemption will be lost if within five years there is a chargeable payment, namely a non-taxable payment, made in connection with its shares otherwise than for bona fide commercial reasons. Provision is made for obtaining advance clearance (see also cl.1.2).

If a demerger has occurred to which the sections apply, the vendors should be able to argue that they should nevertheless not be liable for any tax resulting from the demerger or a subsequent chargeable payment as the purchaser, being aware of the transaction by reason of disclosure, would be able to ensure that no liability subsequently occurred.

**18.2 The Company has not redeemed, repaid or purchased or agreed to redeem, repay or purchase, any of its own shares.**   5–74

ICTA 1988, ss.219–229 (Purchase of own shares) provide that a purchase of its own shares by an unquoted company which is a trading company or the holding company of a trading group does not give rise to a distribution if the purpose is to benefit the company's trade. Section 225 (Advance clearance of payments by Board) provides a clearance procedure.

The purchaser will wish to ensure that a purchase of its own shares by the target company was not a distribution giving rise to a liability to advance corporation tax if occurring prior to April 6, 1999. The vendors will normally have the benefit of a clearance in which case the warranty will amount to a representation that the clearance was properly obtained (see cl.1.2). If no clearance was obtained in relation to any of the transactions falling within the warranty, the vendors will need to consider very carefully whether the exemption conditions in ss.219–229 were satisfied.

### 19 Stock dividends

5–75 **19.1 The Company has not issued share capital to which the provisions of ICTA 1988, s.249 (Stock dividends treated as income) or TCGA, s.142 (Capital gains on stock dividends) could apply and the Company does not own any such share capital.**

The purpose of s.249 is to avoid the tax advantages which would otherwise derive from arrangements whereby shareholders, who did not wish to receive unearned income on their shares, were offered the opportunity to take bonus shares in substitution for, and of equal value to, the dividends they would otherwise have received on the shares. Section 249 effectively treats bonus issues received in this way as taxable income, but only higher rate tax is payable. TCGA 1992, s.142 allows the amount taxed in this way to be treated as expenditure on the bonus shares acquired. As the tax liability affects only individuals, the warranty is substantially irrelevant except in so far as there is an administrative obligation upon the company to make appropriate returns. In view of the curious drafting of s.249, which could apply to normal bonus issues, the vendors may find it difficult to give the warranty with absolute confidence if the target company has issued bonus shares in the past. As the purchaser will be aware, from its searches and the other warranties, of the capital history of the target company, it should be prepared to accept the risk of s.249 applying as the only disadvantage relates to the administration involved in making the appropriate returns.

### 20 Capital allowances

5–76 **20.1 All expenditure which the Company has incurred or may incur under a subsisting commitment on the provision of machinery or plant has qualified or will qualify (if not deductible as a trading expense of a trade carried on by the Company) for writing-down allowances under CAA 2001, Part 2, Chapter 5 (Allowances and Charges).**

Expenditure on machinery and plant incurred by a person carrying on a trade for the purpose of the trade qualifies for writing-down allowances. These are usually at the rate of 25 per cent of the excess of qualifying expenditure over disposal value for the relevant accounting period. However, first year allowances in excess of this are available on certain types of expenditure, particularly expenditure by small and medium-sized enterprises.

Special rules which may restrict or exclude the availability of capital allowances apply to lessors, particularly where the lessee is non-resident (CAA 2001, Pt 2 Ch.11 (Overseas Leasing)).

In general, the vendors will be able to accept this warranty unless the target company claims allowances by virtue of being equipment lessors. Nevertheless, unless the availability of allowances has been a factor in settling the purchase price, they might reasonably take the view that they should not be required to guarantee future tax reliefs.

**20.2 No event has occurred since the Balance Sheet Date which may be treated as a notional sale by the Company of machinery or plant pursuant to CAA 2001, ss.61 (Disposal events and disposal values) or 72 (Disposal values).** 5–77

If a company discontinues its trade or sells its equipment at less than market price (unless between connected persons) or the equipment ceases to be used for the purposes of trade, it is deemed to have sold the equipment at market value. Any balancing charge or allowance is determined on that basis. The purchaser is entitled to ensure that tax will not be calculated on the basis of notional rather than actual proceeds and the vendors should readily be able to ascertain if these sections could apply. The warranty can be limited to events since the balance sheet date as the accounts for completed periods should cover any adjustment by an appropriate tax provision.

**20.3 No capital allowances made or to be made to the Company in respect of capital expenditure already incurred or to be incurred under a subsisting commitment arise from special leasing (as defined in CAA 2001, s.19) or qualifying non-trade expenditure (as defined in CAA 2001, s.469) on patents.** 5–78

Generally, capital allowances are given effect by allowing them as an expense of the trade. In the two situations referred to in the clause allowances can only be set against income from that specific asset. Special leasing is leasing otherwise than in the course of a qualifying activity and qualifying non-trade expenditure is expenditure on patents otherwise than for the purposes of a trade.

**20.4 Since the Balance Sheet Date the Company has not done, or omitted to do, or agreed to do, or permitted to be done, an act as a result of which a balancing allowance or a balancing charge may be brought into account for capital allowances purposes, or there may be a recovery of excess relief under CAA 2001, s.111 (Excess allowances: standard recovery mechanism).** 5–79

In general, capital allowances are available on a pool basis. If a company's qualifying expenditure in an accounting period (being expenditure on which writing-down allowances arise) is less than the disposal value which is to be brought into account for that period, a balancing charge arises on the amount of the difference. A disposal value arises if the equipment ceases to belong to the company or the company permanently ceases the trade for which the equipment is used. A different basis applies in relation to short-life assets (essentially those with a useful life of less than four years) where an election is made under CAA 2001, s.83 (Meaning of "short-life asset"). In that event each asset is treated as comprising a separate pool and a balancing charge or allowance arises on the disposal of the individual asset.

CAA 2001, s.109 (Assets leased outside the United Kingdom) provides that assets are eligible for writing-down allowances at the reduced rate of 10 per cent on machinery and plant if during the requisite period (in this case, 10 years from when the asset is brought into use) they are let on a long-term basis to foreign lessors who do not carry on a United Kingdom trade. Excess relief can arise on assets initially leased in the United Kingdom if, during the requisite period, the equipment is leased to a non-resident. Section 111 treats the excess as if it were a balancing charge.

The vendors should normally have no difficulty in knowing if this warranty would be infringed.

5–80      **20.5 The Company is not in dispute with any person as to any entitlement to capital allowances under CAA 2001, Part 2, Chapter 14 (Fixtures) and at the date of this Agreement as far as the Vendors are aware there are no circumstances which might give rise to such a dispute.**

CAA 2001, Pt 2, Ch.14 (Fixtures), sets out rules for determining entitlement to capital allowances on expenditure on fixtures among parties having different interests in land. As disputes can arise, the Special Commissioners can determine whether or not equipment has become a fixture. The parties affected by the decision are entitled to take part in the hearing.

Although the vendors will generally be in a position to know whether a dispute can arise in relation to claims for allowances on expenditure on fixtures, they may nevertheless consider that, unless the anticipated relief has been a factor in the sale negotiations, the purchaser is not entitled to the protection of this warranty.

*21 Base values and acquisition costs*

5–81      **21.1 If each of the capital assets of the Company was disposed of at Completion for a consideration equal to its book value in, or adopted for the purpose of, the Accounts, no liability to corporation tax on chargeable gains and, on the assumption that the expenditure on each asset was incurred for the purpose of a separate trade, no balancing charge under CAA 2001 would arise; and, for the purpose of determining the liability to corporation tax on chargeable gains, there shall be disregarded reliefs and allowances available to the Company other than amounts falling to be deducted under TCGA 1992, s.38 (Acquisition and disposal costs etc.).**

5–82      TCGA 1992, s.38 defines the categories of allowable expenditure which are deductible in determining the amount of a chargeable gain. The purpose of the last part of this clause is to require deductions which are not allowable expenditure, such as carry-forward losses, to be disregarded in determining whether the disposal would give rise to a chargeable gain.

The value of the capital assets of the target company as shown in its last accounts may exceed the value for capital gains tax or capital allowances purposes, for example because the value has been written up in the books, or because of transfers from connected persons (TCGA 1992, s.18 (Transactions between connected persons)); deemed disposals under s.24 (Disposals where assets lost or destroyed, or become of negligible value); roll-over under ss.126–136 (Reorganisation of share capital, conversion of securities etc.), reconstruction (s.139 (Reconstruction involving transfer of business)); transfers of a trade within s.140 (Postponement of charge on transfer of assets to non-resident company); or group transfers (s.171 (Transfers within a group: general provisions)).

Other relevant provisions are TCGA 1992, s.39 (Exclusion of expenditure by reference to tax on income), which excludes from the allowable expenditure for capital gains tax purposes sums which are deductible as a trading expense; s.42 (Part disposals), which apportions the original expenditure between the part disposed of and the part retained on the occasion of a part disposal; and s.43 (Assets derived from other assets) which provides that an "appropriate proportion" of the allowable expenditure incurred on the original asset shall be treated as having been incurred on a new asset whose value is derived from the original asset. The vendors might fairly require that the indexation allowance, which adjusts the allowable expenditure by changes in the retail prices index under TCGA 1992, s.53 (The indexation allowance and interpretative provisions), should not be disregarded.

Balancing charges arise under CAA 2001, ss.318–320 (Calculation of balancing adjustments), in respect of industrial buildings, and under s. 56 (Amount of allowances and charges), where machinery or plant in respect of which capital allowances have been obtained are disposed of or cease to be used for trading purposes. The consideration brought into account will be the market value of the equipment or, if there is an arm's length disposal, the proceeds of sale. The warranty will apply if the book value exceeds the balance of qualifying expenditure available for writing-down allowances. Particular care may be required if a target company owns machinery or plant which was acquired from a connected company. In that event, an election may have been made to apply CAA 2001, s.266 (Election where predecessor and successor are connected persons) so that, for capital allowances purposes, the transfer was effectively disregarded.  **5–83**

The vendors should generally have no difficulty, in principle, in checking on the matters covered by this clause, although a substantial amount of work may be involved. They might nevertheless reasonably consider that, unless the sale of the target company was negotiated with regard to the taxation results of a sale of fixed assets, the purchaser is not entitled to the protection of this warranty.

If the purchaser insists on retaining the clause, it might be appropriate to provide that a breach of warranty arises only if an increased liability is incurred on a disposal, within a limited period of perhaps one year, of an asset to which the warranty applied.

**5–84**     **21.2 The Company has not made an election under TCGA 1992, s.35 (Assets held on 31 March, 1982 (including assets held on 6 April, 1965)) for capital gains and losses on all the assets held by it on 31 March, 1982 to be computed by reference only to their market value on that date.**

A general rebasing for capital gains tax purposes to March 1982 was introduced in 1988. All the target company's assets will be treated for computing capital gains as if they were sold and reacquired for their market value on that date. Unless the company elects otherwise, rebasing does not take place if it would result in a gain in place of a smaller gain or a loss, or if it would result in a loss and there would otherwise have been a smaller loss or a gain. The election had to be made by April 1990 or within two years of the end of the accounting period in which the first relevant disposal occurs and must relate to all assets which were held in March 1982. An election is irrevocable. In relation to companies within a 75 per cent group, the election may be made only by the principal company (TCGA 1992, Sch.3, para.8 (Elections under s.35(5): group of companies)).

This warranty has a valuable information function for the purchaser but the vendors might reasonably object to accepting the commitment which the warranty imposes, even though it will usually be a clear matter of record as to whether an election has been made. This warranty is often included by the purchaser even when wholly irrelevant, for example because the target company was incorporated after 1982. In such circumstances it should be deleted.

**5–85**     **21.3 The Company has not since the Balance Sheet Date engaged in a transaction in respect of which there may be substituted, for Taxation purposes, a different consideration for the actual consideration given or received by it.**

This warranty is intended to cover cases where the actual profit or gain made by the target company on a transaction differs from the taxable profit. In general, this will not be material for transactions which have been completed prior to the balance sheet date as the taxation position will be reflected in the accounts. For transactions occurring after that date, the purchaser will wish to know that there will not be a liability to tax on a profit or gain of a greater amount than that which has actually accrued.

The vendors should insist on the deletion of this provision and require the purchaser to rely on the warranties which specifically deal with those statutory provisions that enable actual considerations paid or received to be replaced by notional amounts (see particularly cll.9 and 21.4). If the warranty stands, it should be limited to "taxation" in a narrower sense than the definition in para.4–01.

**5–86**     **21.4 In determining the liability to corporation tax on chargeable gains in respect of any asset which has been acquired by the Company, or which the**

Company has agreed to acquire (whether conditionally, contingently or otherwise):

**21.4.1** the sums allowable as a deduction will be determined solely in accordance with TCGA 1992, ss.38 (Acquisition and disposal costs etc.) and 53 (The indexation allowance and interpretative provisions);

**21.4.2** the amount or value of the consideration, determined in accordance with s.38(1)(a), will not be less than the amount or value of the consideration actually given by the Company for the asset; and

**21.4.3** the amount of any expenditure on enhancing the value of that asset, determined in accordance with s.38(1)(b) will not be less than the amount or value of all expenditure actually incurred by the Company on the asset.

In determining liability to capital gains tax, a deduction is made for allowable expenditure, determined in accordance with s.38. This expenditure comprises the consideration given wholly and exclusively for the acquisition of the asset or, where the asset was not acquired, consideration wholly and exclusively incurred in providing the asset, expenditure wholly and exclusively incurred in enhancing the value of the asset or preserving title to it, and costs incidental to the disposal. Section 53 provides for the unindexed gain or loss to be adjusted by taking into account an indexation allowance. This is broadly equal to the actual expenditure multiplied by the rise in the retail prices index over the period of ownership.

Numerous provisions in the capital gains tax legislation provide for the substitution of a deemed acquisition cost for the true cost or for the disallowance of certain expenditures.

While on the face of it it might seem reasonable for the purchaser to require a warranty that the gain on a disposal of a capital asset will not, for capital gains tax purposes, exceed the true gain, it is doubtful in fact whether the requirement is fair. The purchaser will be affected only if and when a disposal of the asset occurs and, unless its disposal has been specifically contemplated in the course of the negotiations leading to the purchase of the target company, the vendors might reasonably consider that the possibility of a disposal should be disregarded. In any case, a disposal may not take place for a considerable time and the purchaser should not be entitled to a claim under the warranties if no loss would result to it in the foreseeable future. Indeed, under general principles relating to the quantification of damages for breach of warranty, it is doubtful whether the purchaser could make a significant claim unless the contemplation of the parties was that a disposal would take place within a foreseeable time.

**21.5 No asset owned, or agreed to be acquired, by the Company (other**     5–87
**than plant and machinery in respect of which it is entitled to capital allowances) is a wasting asset within TCGA 1992, s.44 (Meaning of "wasting asset").**

The significance of this warranty is that the allowable expenditure on a wasting asset, being plant or machinery or substantially any other asset with a predictable life not exceeding 50 years, is reduced over the expected life of the asset. Accordingly the chargeable gain arising on the disposal will exceed the actual gain (TCGA 1992, s.46 (Straightline restriction of allowable expenditure)). This provision does not apply to assets qualifying for capital allowances (TCGA 1992, s.47 (Wasting assets qualifying for capital allowances)).

As with the previous warranty, it is unreasonable in general for the purchaser to require this warranty in cases where the parties have not expressly contemplated that a disposal of the assets in question would take place. If such a disposal is in mind, it would be appropriate for a more precise agreement to be reached between the parties as to how any increased taxation liability resulting from an asset being a wasting asset should be borne.

**5–88**    **21.6 The Company has not joined in the making of a claim under TCGA 1992, s.140A (Transfer of a U.K. trade) in relation to the transfer to it of the whole or part of a trade carried on within the United Kingdom.**

A United Kingdom company which transfers the whole or part of the trade carried on by it in the United Kingdom to a company resident in another member state, in exchange for securities of the transferee, may elect jointly with the transferee for roll-over relief. The effect of the relief is that the transfer is deemed to take place at the base cost of the transferor. The transferee accordingly has a greater prospective liability to corporation tax on chargeable gains arising on a subsequent disposal than it would incur if the consideration paid by it were treated as its base cost.

The purchaser is entitled to know of circumstances where there is a hidden potential liability to tax. The vendors should have no difficulty in giving the warranty in cases where no acquisition of the kind covered by the section has taken place, particularly as the purchaser is unlikely to suffer loss even if the warranty is breached unless the parties had in mind a disposal of the acquired business.

*22 Replacement of business assets*

**5–89**    **22.1 The Company has not made a claim under TCGA 1992, ss.23 (Receipt of compensation and insurance money not treated as a disposal), 152 (Replacement of business assets: Roll-over relief), 153 (Assets only partly replaced), 154 (New assets which are depreciating assets), 175 (Replacement of business assets by members of a group) or 247 (Roll-over relief on compulsory acquisition) which would affect the amount of the chargeable gain or allowable loss which would, but for the claim, have arisen on a disposal of any of its assets.**

Roll-over relief for capital gains tax purposes in relation to disposals of assets, which are replaced by qualifying business assets within a period of one year before the disposal and three years afterwards, is given under TCGA 1992, ss.152–154. The consideration received on the disposal of the old asset is treated as being reduced so as to give rise to neither a gain nor a loss and the consideration given on the acquisition of the new assets as being reduced to an equal extent. There are, however, special rules where depreciating assets are involved (s.154).

Section 247 extends the relief in relation to land disposed of as a result of a compulsory acquisition. Under s.175 all the trades carried on by a group of companies are treated as a single trade.

Section 23 provides a form of roll-over, where compensation or insurance proceeds arising on the loss of or damage to an asset are applied in restoring or replacing the asset.

The vendors should have no difficulty in giving this warranty as the information will be a matter of record. They might, nevertheless, wish to consider whether the purchaser would ever expect to incur any increased liability by reason of a roll-over as, in the case of an expanding business, there might be no reason to suppose that a recapture would ever occur.

## 23 Chargeable gains: special cases

**23.1 The Company is not owed a debt (not being a debt on a security), upon**   **5–90**
**the disposal or satisfaction of which a liability to corporation tax on chargea-**
**ble gains will arise under TCGA 1992, s.251 (Debts: General provisions).**

A debt does not normally constitute a chargeable asset although, as discussed in relation to cl.23.2, certain qualifying loans can give rise to an allowable loss. Accordingly, in the exceptional event of a disposal or satisfaction of the debt giving rise to a gain, there will not be a tax liability unless the gain constitutes income. The general rule does not, however, apply to a debt on a security or a debt where the creditor was not the person to whom the liability was first incurred. The meaning of a debt on a security is obscure as the somewhat circular definition, which is in TCGA 1992, s.132 (Equation of converted securities and new holding), provides that security includes loan stock of a company, whether or not secured.

If, therefore, a target company owns a debt which has the characteristics of a security or a debt which was acquired by it from the original creditor, a liability to capital gains tax could arise which would not be anticipated by the purchaser. The clause should present no difficulty for the vendors. Although it may be doubtful as to what debts are debts on a security for the purpose of this clause, it will rarely be possible for a debt in respect of which a target company is the original creditor to give rise to a gain. In so far as the warranty relates to debts owing to a target company in circumstances where it was not the original creditor, it will generally be clear if a potential liability exists.

**23.2 The Company has not claimed nor is it entitled to claim under TCGA**   **5–91**
**1992, ss.253 (Relief for loans to traders) or 254 (Relief for debts on qualify-**
**ing corporate bonds) that an allowable loss has accrued in respect of a loan**
**made by it.**

As is indicated above, debts normally fall outside the scope of the capital gains tax legislation. Exceptions are made in respect of "qualifying loans", that is loans to United Kingdom traders who use the loans for the purposes of trade, and qualifying corporate bonds, which are sterling securities carrying not more than a commercial rate of interest (see TCGA 1992, s.117 (Meaning of "qualifying corporate bond") for the detailed definition). If the loan or bond becomes to any extent irrecoverable and it is still owned by the original creditor an allowable loss may be claimed. If, after a s.253 claim, a recovery is made, a chargeable gain accrues equal to so much of the allowable loss as corresponds to the amount recovered.

Section 254 has been repealed in relation to loans made on or after March 17, 1998 and accordingly will often no longer be relevant.

It may be difficult for the vendors to know if a claim can be made in relation to an outstanding loan. In any case, as the effect is to give rise to an allowable loss the vendors could reasonably maintain that they should not be responsible for ensuring that the purchaser can obtain the benefit of it unless the sale terms have contemplated otherwise. Conversely, the purchaser is entitled to know if recovery of a bad debt would result in a tax charge although the vendors could argue that, if an unanticipated recovery is made, there should be no objection to it being taxed.

On this basis the vendors should at least delete **"is entitled to claim"** and possibly seek to exclude the whole warranty.

5–92     **23.3 The Company does not own rights, or an interest in rights, under a policy of assurance or contract for a deferred annuity on the life of any person of which it is not the original beneficial owner.**

A disposal of a life assurance policy or deferred annuity does not give rise to a chargeable gain unless the disposal is by a person who is not the original owner and acquired the rights for actual consideration (TCGA 1992, s.210 (Life assurance and deferred annuities)). The warranty is intended to protect the purchaser from an unexpected tax liability but, unless specific representations were made that such an asset existed and would generate a tax-free gain, the vendors should reject the clause.

5–93     **23.4 No part of the consideration given by the Company for a new holding of shares (within the meaning of TCGA 1992, s.126 (Reorganisation or reduction of share capital: Application of ss.127–131) will be disregarded by virtue of s.128(2) (Consideration given or received by holder).**

The broad effect of s.128 is to treat consideration given by a person on acquiring a new holding of securities as a result of a reorganisation as being part of the cost of acquiring the original holding of shares. If, however, the transaction is not at arm's length, the new consideration is taken into account only in so far as it does not exceed the increase in the value of the new holding as compared with the value of the original holding immediately prior to the reorganisation. The implications of this qualification can be widespread and would have an unexpected effect where, for example, a minority shareholder takes up a rights issue, since the resultant increase in the value of his shareholding is unlikely to match precisely the consideration put up for the new shares.

While the purchaser is entitled to be satisfied that no expenditure will be disallowed for capital gains tax purposes, the vendors should treat this provision with the utmost care and an analysis of the possible impact of s.128(2) on any rights issues that have involved the target company should be made. The vendors might also reasonably consider that the purchaser should not be entitled to compensation for a breach of this warranty unless the parties specifically contemplated a disposal of the shares concerned.

**23.5 No asset owned by the Company has been the subject of a deemed**   5–94
**disposal under TCGA 1992, Schedule 2 (Assets held on 6 April, 1965), so as**
**to restrict the extent to which the gain or loss, over the period of ownership,**
**may be apportioned by reference to straightline growth.**

If a capital asset, not being a quoted security or land reflecting development value, was owned on April 6, 1965, when capital gains tax was introduced, the taxpayer can normally elect to have the ultimate gain or loss arising on a disposal determined in one of two ways. The straightline growth method treats the gain or loss as having accrued steadily over the whole period of ownership and only that part attributed to the post-April 1965 period is brought into the computation. Alternatively, the asset is deemed to have been sold and repurchased at market value on April 6, 1965.

The straightline apportionment method, which will be advantageous if the rate of growth has increased, is lost when a part disposal occurs (TCGA 1992, Sch.2, para.16(8) (Apportionment by reference to straightline growth of gain or loss over period of ownership)), or if there is a reorganisation of share capital which gives rise to a holding of shares of a different class (para.19 (Reorganisation of share capital, conversion of securities, etc.)) or, if assets are transferred to a close company by a person having control over it, in so far as the value of the shares of the close company on a subsequent transfer reflects a profit on the assets transferred (para.21 (Assets transferred to close companies)).

The significance of the right to time apportionment has been greatly reduced by the rebasing of capital gains tax to 1982. Even where the loss of the right to time apportionment is disadvantageous, it is generally unreasonable to require this warranty to be given unless a disposal of assets, which were acquired by a target company before April 6, 1965, is in the contemplation of the parties and the purchaser has reasonably relied upon the availability of the apportionment method.

Again this warranty is often irrelevant as the target company will often not have capital assets acquired before April 6, 1965.

*24 Capital losses and limited partnerships*

**24.1 The Company has not incurred a capital loss to which TCGA 1992,**   5–95
**s.18(3) (Transactions between connected persons) is applicable.**

This section applies to a capital loss arising on a disposal of an asset to a connected person. The loss can be set-off only against chargeable gains arising on a disposal of chargeable assets to the same connected person.

The vendors should resist this warranty unless the purchase price for the target company reflects the value of expected losses.

**5–96     24.2 The Company is not treated as a limited partner under ICTA 1988, s.118 (Restriction on relief: companies).**

A company which is a limited partner in a partnership is not entitled to relief for losses, capital allowances or charges on income to an extent greater than its contribution to the partnership. A company is, for this purpose, a limited partner not only if it is registered as such under the Limited Partnership Act 1907, but also if it is a general partner which is not entitled to take part in the management but is entitled to have its liabilities over a specified limit reimbursed by a third party. A company will also be treated as a limited partner if it carries on a trade jointly overseas and the local law prohibits participation in management and restricts liability. The breadth of the definition can cause a joint venture to constitute a limited partnership for this purpose.

The vendors should resist giving this warranty, particularly if there is any risk that the section could apply.

*25 Gifts involving group companies*

**5–97   25.1 The Company has not received assets by way of gift as mentioned in TCGA 1992, s.282 (Recovery of tax from donee).**

Section 282 entitles the Inland Revenue to recover from a donee the capital gains tax which should be paid by the donor on the making of a gift. The donee has a statutory right of recovery from the donor. Although the purchaser is entitled to protect itself against an unexpected liability under this section, the vendors should ensure that they are given the benefit of the right of recovery . See also cl.29.1 regarding the inheritance tax implications.

*26 Foreign businesses*

**5–98   26.1 The Company has not made a claim under TCGA 1992, s.140 (Postponement of charge on transfer of assets to non-resident company) or s.140C (Transfer of a non-U.K. trade) in relation to the transfer of the whole or part of a trade which it carried on outside the United Kingdom through a branch or agency.**

Section 140 applies where a United Kingdom resident company carrying on a trade outside the United Kingdom transfers all or part of it to a non-resident company in exchange for shares or loan stock of the non-resident company. Provided the United Kingdom resident company controls at least one quarter of the ordinary share capital of the transferee, the transferor may make a claim for the gains and losses to be aggregated. The net gain is then deemed to arise on a single transaction and the chargeable gain is rolled over until the transferor disposes of the relevant assets or the transferee disposes of the shares it acquires. There is thus a contingent additional liability to tax which will arise if and when there is a disposal of the securities, provided that the disposal occurs within a period of six years.

Section 140C provides similar alternative relief where a United Kingdom resident company transfers to a company resident in another member state the whole or part of a trade carried on by the transferor outside the United Kingdom but within the EU.

This kind of transaction is perhaps becoming more common given the tendency of EU law to reduce discrimination between residents of different member states. The warranty will not, however, be relevant in a transaction where there is no cross-border aspect. **5–99**

**26.2 No notice under ICTA 1988, s.747 (Imputation of chargeable profits 5–100 and creditable tax of controlled foreign companies) has been received by the Company and no circumstances exist which would entitle the Inland Revenue to apportion profits of a controlled foreign company to the Company under ICTA 1988, s.752 (Apportionment of chargeable profits and creditable tax) as extended by ICTA 1988, ss.752A (Relevant interests), 752B (Section 752(3): the percentage of shares which a relevant interest represents) and 752C (Interpretation of apportionment provisions).**

A controlled foreign company is one that is resident outside the United Kingdom, but controlled by persons resident in the United Kingdom, and which is subject to a level of taxation in the country of its residence which is less than a specified fraction of the corresponding level of taxation in the United Kingdom. An apportionment of the profits of the company may be made amongst United Kingdom residents according to their interests in the company unless either the company distributes by way of dividend at least half of its trading profits, is engaged in specified exempt activities or is quoted on a recognised stock exchange. When this legislation was introduced, the rate of corporation tax in the United Kingdom was 45 per cent and the fraction was one-half. Following the reduction in the corporation tax rate that has occurred since then, the fraction was increased to three-quarters by FA 1993, s.119 (Controlled foreign companies).

Although the vendors will have no difficulty with the first half of this clause, which relates to the factual question of whether a notice has been received, the second half may cause problems. The power of the Inland Revenue to make a direction as to whether the provisions apply was removed by FA 1998, such that the provisions will automatically apply if the relevant criteria are met.

## 27 Foreign loan interest

**27.1 The Company has not received foreign loan interest on which double 5–101 taxation relief will, or may, be restricted under ICTA 1988, ss.798 (Restriction of relief on certain interest and dividends), 798A (Adjustments of interest and dividends for spared tax etc.) and 798B (Meaning of "financial expenditure").**

The purpose of the earlier version of s.798 was to restrict taxation advantages received, in particular by banks, where loans were made to persons resident outside the United Kingdom and the expenses of making the loan were deductible in determining the United Kingdom taxable profit of the lender. In general, the lender was entitled to a foreign tax credit up to the full United Kingdom corporation tax rate if it suffered overseas tax on the interest even if, owing to "tax sparing" agreements with the United Kingdom, overseas tax was not in fact paid but was treated for double tax relief as though it had been.

A new version of s.798 applies to foreign interest or foreign dividends paid on or after March 17, 1998, subject to transitional exceptions. If the new version of s.798 is applicable, ss.798A and 798B are also applicable. "Financial expenditure" incurred by the lender or an associated company or person must be deducted from the interest or dividends receivable, and the limit on tax credit must be calculated on the net amount. Moreover, the amount of foreign withholding tax which may be credited is limited to 15 per cent of the gross amount of the interest or dividends concerned.

In view of the rather special circumstances in which these sections apply, the warranty will rarely be appropriate.

*28 Value added tax*

**5–102**  **28.1 In relation to value added tax the Company:**

**28.1.1 has duly registered and is a taxable person;**

A taxable person is one who makes or intends to make taxable supplies of goods or services in the United Kingdom, other than exempt supplies (VATA 1994, s.4 (Scope of VAT on taxable supplies)). The level of taxable supplies at which registration becomes necessary is specified in VATA 1994, Sch.1 (Registration in respect of taxable supplies) and is updated frequently. There should in general be no difficulty in determining whether registration is required and has been effected.

**5–103**  **28.1.2 has complied, in all material respects, with all statutory requirements, orders, provisions, directions and conditions;**

There are extensive regulations controlling the operation of VAT, and the vendors may find difficulty in satisfying themselves that all of them have been followed. Nevertheless, the purchaser is entitled to be sure that no unexpected liability to VAT will arise and ultimately it is a question of where the risk should lie, as between the parties, of any VAT return being incorrect or not having been properly made.

**5–104**  **28.1.3 maintains complete, correct and up-to-date records as required by the applicable legislation;**

The obligations to keep records are set out with reasonable clarity in VATA 1994, Sch.11, para.6 (Duty to keep records) and Notice No. 700. The vendors should not have difficulty in accepting this warranty.

**28.1.4 has not been required by the Commissioners of Customs and Excise**    5–105
**to give security;**

The Commissioners are entitled, under the provisions of VATA 1994, Sch.11, para.4(2) (Power to require security and production of evidence), to require that security is given of such amount and in such manner as they may determine. Clearly the purchaser will be extremely concerned if security has been required, as it will reflect badly either on the way that the target company has conducted its value added tax payments in the past, or, alternatively, on its credit standing.

**28.1.5 has not applied for treatment as a member of a group which**    5–106
**includes another company; and**

A group of companies may elect for treatment as if they were a single entity under VATA 1994, s.43 (Groups of companies). It is important to bear in mind that a consequence of group registration is that each member of the group is jointly and severally liable for all VAT payable in respect of the activities of the group. The purchaser will therefore wish to know whether the target company has at any stage been a member of a group for VAT purposes. Companies can form VAT groups only if each company is established or has a fixed establishment in the United Kingdom and one company controls the other (within the terms of CA 1985, s.736) or one person (which may be one individual or a number of individuals in partnership) controls all of them (VATA 1994, s.43A(1) (Groups: eligibility)).

**28.1.6 the Company is not, nor has it agreed to become, an agent (for the**    5–107
**purposes of VATA 1994, s.47 (Agents etc.)) for the supply of goods for a**
**person who is not a taxable person.**

The effect of s.47 is to make an agent liable for VAT if his principal is a non-taxable person in two circumstances. These are that:

(1) goods are acquired from another member state by the non-taxable person and the agent acts in relation to the acquisition and supplies the goods in his own name for his principal; or

(2) goods are imported from a place outside the member states and supplied by the agent in his own name.

As the agent incurs liability for his or her principal, it is reasonable for the purchaser to require that the vendors give this warranty. Since the subject matter is a question of fact, the vendors will normally have no difficulty in determining whether the warranty could be infringed.

**28.2 The Disclosure Letter sets out accurate and complete particulars of**    5–108
**claims for bad debt relief which have been made and remain outstanding, or**

**which may be made, by the Company under VATA 1994, s.36 (Bad debts) and of any debts which, if written off, would give a right to claim relief.**

Value added tax has to be paid over to Customs and Excise following the rendering of an invoice regardless of whether payment is then received. If payment is never received, the VAT may be recovered under s.36. A number of requirements have to be satisfied, principally that the debt has been written off as bad and that at least six months have elapsed from the time of the supply. The purchaser has a limited interest in claims for relief which have been made but is concerned to make due application where a debt could be written off but no action has been taken. The vendors should be cautious about warranting that all claims which can be made are disclosed as they may have no ready means of knowing whether the required circumstances exist.

5–109    **28.3 The Company has not, during the past 12 or 24 months respectively, received a surcharge liability notice under VATA 1994, s.59 (The default surcharge) or a penalty liability notice under s.64 (Repeated misdeclarations) nor may it be liable to a penalty under s.63 (Penalty for misdeclaration or neglect resulting in VAT loss for one accounting period equalling or exceeding certain amounts).**

A default surcharge notice may be served on a taxable person if he fails to furnish a return for a prescribed accounting period or to pay the VAT shown on the return. The surcharge is a specified percentage—varying between two per cent and 15 per cent according to the number of periods for which there is a default—of the outstanding VAT.

A penalty liability notice may be served if there is a "material inaccuracy" for a period, that is a return which understates liability to VAT or overstates the entitlement to credits to an extent greater than £500,000 or 10 per cent of the VAT for the period. If, following the notice, two further material defaults occur within the next eight periods, there is a penalty of 15 per cent of the VAT involved.

If a return is made which understates liability to VAT or overstates entitlement to repayment of credits and the amount of tax involved exceeds certain limits, a penalty may be charged under s.63.

It is clearly reasonable that the purchaser should be informed if either category of notice has been received by a target company or if there have been defaults which could result in liability to penalties.

5–110    **28.4 No election to waive exemption from value added tax in relation to any of the Properties has been made by the Company or a predecessor in title under VATA 1994, Schedule 10, paragraph 2 (Election to waive exemption).**

A number of transactions in relation to land are exempt from VAT under VATA 1994, Sch.9, Group 1 (Exemptions—Land). The election to waive exemption, which is generally known as the "option to tax", enables input tax to be recovered in circumstances where it would otherwise be lost as a result of the partial exemption provisions. In general the exercise of the option is irrevocable and the purchaser will be entitled to the information.

As it is a question of fact whether the option has been exercised, the vendors should have no difficulty with the warranty but, as an alternative, they may seek to obtain confirmation from Customs and Excise as to whether there has been an exercise of the option in relation to each of the target company's properties.

### 29 Inheritance tax

**29.1 The Company has not made a transfer of value (as defined in IHTA 1984, s.3 (Transfers of value)) [otherwise than for the purposes, or in the course, of its business].**
5–111

A transfer of value by a target company will be relevant only if it is a close company in which case the provisions of IHTA 1984, s.94 (Charge on participators), could apply. Under that section, the amount transferred by the close company, less the amounts received by the participators in the company, is apportioned amongst the participators according to their respective rights and interests and the company has the primary liability for any resulting inheritance tax.

Broadly speaking, liability arises under this section only if the gift has been made otherwise than to the participators. There are many *ex gratia* payments which may be made by a company for bona fide commercial reasons and the vendors might reasonably consider that they should not be penalised if they have had no benefit themselves and if the liability arises as a result of actions carried out for the benefit of the target company. To cover this point, the vendors might wish to add the bracketed words although this will not protect them from their statutory secondary liability which arises if the target company, which is primarily liable, fails to pay.

The purchaser is unlikely to accept the additional words on the ground that any such liability should entitle it to a reduction in the purchase consideration paid for the target company.

**29.2 No Inland Revenue charge for unpaid inheritance tax (as provided by IHTA 1984, ss.237 and 238 (Inland Revenue charge for unpaid tax)) exists over an asset of the Company or in relation to any shares in the capital of the Company.**
5–112

The Inland Revenue entitlement to a charge for unpaid inheritance tax is not only relevant to close companies. The Inland Revenue is entitled to a charge on any property involved in a transfer (s.237) and this could attach to assets owned by a target company. A purchaser of property subject to a charge takes free of the charge if he is not aware of it (s.238) and, while this would normally result in the purchaser taking free of any charge on the shares which are being sold, it would not assist in relation to assets of the target company which were charged. If the warranty cannot readily be given, it may be appropriate for the purchaser to require that, before exchange of contracts, the vendors obtain a certificate of discharge under IHTA 1984, s.239 (Certificates of discharge).

### 30 Stamp duty and stamp duty land tax

**5–113**    **30.1 The Company has not within the past three years made a claim for relief or exemption under FA 1930, s.42 (Relief from transfer stamp duty in case of transfer of property as between associated companies), FA 1995, s.151 (Leases etc. between associated bodies corporate) or FA 1986, ss.75–77 (Acquisitions: reliefs).**

FA 1930, s.42, as amended by FA 1995, s.149 (Transfer: associated bodies), provides relief from stamp duty on a conveyance or transfer where assets are transferred within a group where at least 75 per cent of the share capital of the companies concerned is in common ownership. Although there is no obligation to maintain the group relationship for any specific period, the relief will be withdrawn if it appears that it was not the intention of the transferor and the transferee to remain associated (FA 1967, s.27 (Conveyances and transfers on sale: reduction of duty, and amendment of provisions for exemption)). FA 2000, s.123 (Transfer of property between associated companies: Great Britain) introduced changes such that relief for intra-group transfers will be available only if the parent company has a substantial economic interest in its subsidiary, the existence of which will be assessed by reference to ICTA 1988, Sch.18 (Group relief: equity holders and profits or assets available for distribution).

FA 1995, s.151 essentially provides a similar relief for leases between companies in common ownership. FA 1986 ss.75–77 provide for relief from stamp duty on certain reorganisations of companies and their businesses. As these reliefs were being used to avoid stamp duty, legislation was introduced in FA 2002, ss.111–113. These sections provide that where there was a transfer to which one of the reliefs applied and the transferee company left the transferor's group within 3 years of the transfer, the relief would be effectively clawed back and stamp duty become payable.

For the purchaser it will be important to know that any disposal after completion will not trigger a clawback of stamp duty relief. It should be relatively easy for the vendors to obtain the necessary information to disclose, however, the vendors may object in principle to this warranty if post acquisition disposals are not expressly contemplated.

**5–114**    **30.2 All documents in the possession of the Company, or which the Company is entitled to require the production of, and which confer any right upon the Company or are necessary to establish the title of the Company to any asset, have been stamped and any applicable stamp duties or charges in respect of such documents have been accounted for and paid, and no such documents which are outside of the United Kingdom would attract stamp duty if they were brought into the United Kingdom.**

It is now quite common to require an all-encompassing warranty from the vendors in relation to the stamping of documents. By virtue of FA 1999, FA 2003 and FA 2004, stamp duty has been abolished in the transfer of all assets other than shares, marketable securities and partnership interests.

In respect of real property FA 2003 (as amended by FA 2004 and various regulations) introduced SDLT from December 1, 2003. The major difference between SDLT and stamp duty is that payment of SDLT is obligatory and the tax is effectively within the self assessment scheme. There are automatic penalties and interest for late filing and the Revenue have power to open enquiries on a return to see whether it has been completed appropriately.

The rate of SDLT is in general terms the same as stamp duty on the transfer of freeholds but there is a radically new system for leases.

**30.3 Stamp duty land tax has been paid in full in respect of all estates or interests in land acquired on or after December 1, 2003 by the Company and there are no contingent liabilities or requirements to submit a further land transaction return in relation to:**   5–115

**30.3.1 properties acquired as a going concern for the purposes of VATA, s.49 (Taxation of going concerns);**

**30.3.2 unascertainable future consideration;**

**30.3.3 transactions capable of being treated as linked for the purposes of FA 2003, s.108 (Linked transactions);**

**30.3.4 turnover leases;**

**30.3.5 leases subject to a rent review within five years of grant;**

**30.3.6 leases the assignment of which would be deemed to be the grant of a new lease; or**

**30.3.7 any other arrangement capable of giving rise to a further charge to stamp duty land tax.**

It is quite common for the purchaser to seek a warranty to the effect that SDLT has been properly administered. This is particularly important given that the payment of it is obligatory.

A further feature of SDLT which was not part of the stamp duty regime is that there is in certain circumstances an obligation to file further returns after the initial return has been filed. These situations are listed above at cll.30.3.1–30.3.7. It is important for the purchaser to know what future returns may be necessary, not only so that it can assess any contingent liability but also so that it can ensure that the target company will not breach any of the administration requirements.

**30.4 The Company has not claimed relief from stamp duty land tax under FA 2003, Schedule 7, Part 1 (group relief) or Part 2 (reconstruction and acquisition relief), (Stamp Duty Land Tax: Group Relief and Reconstruction and Acquisition Reliefs) in relation to any estate or interest in land that has been transferred to it.**   5–116

The comments at cl.30.1 apply equally to the position in relation to group relief and reconstruction and acquisition relief under the SDLT regime.

*31 Disclosure Requirements*

**5–117**  **31.1 The Company has not notified the Inland Revenue of any notifiable arrangement or notifiable proposal (as defined by FA 2004, s.306 (Meaning of "notifiable arrangements" and "notifiable proposal")) for the purposes of the Tax Avoidance Schemes (Information) Regulations 2004 and there are no circumstances in which any such disclosure should have been made by the Company.**

**31.2 The Company has not implemented any proposal or entered into any arrangements which are notifiable pursuant to FA 2004, ss.309 (Duty of person dealing with promoter outside United Kingdom) or 310 (Duty of parties to notifiable arrangements not involving promoter) and has not included any scheme reference on any of its tax returns pursuant to FA 2004, s.313 (Duty to parties to notifiable arrangements to notify Board of number, etc.) and there are no circumstances in which such notification or inclusion of a reference should have been made by the Company.**

Following the introduction of disclosure requirements in FA 2004, it is important to now obtain this kind of warranty in order to find out what, if any, schemes have been disclosed and also to cover the situation where a scheme should have been disclosed but has not been. It is unlikely in most cases that the clauses will be relevant except where the target company is a major corporation which devises its own tax planning. The vendors should not have any problem giving the warranty.

# OBSOLETE PROVISIONS AND LIMITED APPLICATION TAXES

**5–118**  The convenience of standard forms is such that warranties continue to make their appearance in relation to obsolete taxation matters long after any liability or dispute can arise. The following are taxes and taxation provisions which have ceased to be relevant:

- Estate duty: the predecessor of inheritance tax in respect of deaths prior to March 1975.
- Capital transfer tax: now redesignated as inheritance tax.
- Special charge: a one off surcharge on 1967/68 investment income.
- Selective employment tax: imposed upon employers until 1973.
- Purchase tax: replaced in 1973 by value added tax.
- Development gains tax: applied to certain developments which took place before August 1976.
- Development land tax: abolished in relation to disposals occurring after March 1985.

- Capital duty: abolished from March 1988.

Reliefs which have been withdrawn include:        **5–119**

- Stock relief: withdrawn for accounting periods beginning after March 1984.

- Relief from transfer stamp duty on the amalgamation of companies under FA 1927, ss.55 (replaced by narrower reliefs under FA 1986, s.75 (Acquisitions: reliefs) and 77 (Acquisition of target company's share capital)).

From 1973 to 1999, companies paying dividends were required to pay part of        **5–120** their corporation tax liability at the same time (ACT). The ACT paid during the year was then available to be set against their corporation tax liability at the normal time for payment of that liability. This regime was withdrawn with the introduction of corporation tax self assessment instalment payments. It was possible to build up surplus (unrelieved) ACT by paying ACT on dividends in excess of the tax liability for the period; there were various restrictions on the use of surplus ACT. In order to allow relief of the surplus ACT which companies were carrying forward, a 'shadow ACT' system was introduced which allows set off of surplus ACT broadly in the same way as before the ACT regime was abolished. However, companies are no longer required to pay tax at the time of paying dividends. Large companies may have surplus ACT carried forward for some time to come.

Until 1988, close companies were liable to "apportionments" if insufficient dividends were paid in accordance with the ICTA 1988, Pt XI, Ch.III and Sch.19. These provisions were repealed in relation to accounting periods which began after March 31, 1989 and, in the absence of fraud, will now no longer be relevant. They entitled the Inland Revenue to recover amounts equivalent to higher rate income tax and advance corporation tax if, without good cause, a close company failed to make a distribution of its investment or estate income. If distributions of the required level were not made, the best protection that could be given against an assessment was a clearance. This was binding upon the Inland Revenue only if the information accompanying the request for the clearance and any further particulars furnished to the Inspector of Taxes made full and accurate disclosure of all facts and considerations which were material to be known.

Finally, mention should be made of ICTA 1970, s.279, which dealt with cases        **5–121** where a subsidiary company left a group following a reorganisation or reconstruction which took place within the preceding six years. The section does not apply to a reconstruction occurring after April 1977.

A number of taxes have very limited application and are not considered separately in this book. It should nevertheless be borne in mind that the wide definition of "Taxation" adopted in para.4–01 and in relation to the tax deed in Ch.10 will have the effect that all these taxes are automatically covered by many of the tax warranties and by the tax indemnity. The taxes which are not discussed include:

(1) air passenger duty;

(2) excise duties, other than VAT;

(3) insurance premium tax;

(4) landfill tax; and

(5) petroleum revenue tax.

# CHAPTER 6

# Property Warranties

## PURPOSE IN THE CASE OF BUSINESS AND SHARE PURCHASES

In the case of the purchase of a business, the procedures adopted in relation to properties included in the assets which are being purchased will be no different from those of a property purchase which is not connected with a business sale. The usual surveys and searches should take place and the contract and completion documents will conform to normal conveyancing practice. It is possible that warranties will be sought which would not normally be relevant to a simple property purchase if there are aspects of the properties which impact on the value of the goodwill of the business. The warranties that might be considered are included in Appendix 5, which provides precedents of the warranties appropriate for the purchase of a business. In general, however, it would be unusual in the case of the purchase of a business for the purchaser to seek or the vendors to give substantial property warranties. **6–01**

The practice in relation to a share purchase in a case where the assets of the target company include properties is rather different, as are the remedies. The general concept of property warranties is to support the assumption made by the prudent purchaser that the target company's title to its property is good and marketable. How this will apply in any given case depends on a variety of factors, but will usually revolve around the issues of saleability (can the target company sell, let or otherwise dispose of it?); value (will the target company be able to dispose at a price equal to a proper valuation placed upon it, or obtain loan finance at expected levels upon the security of the property?); and use and enjoyment (in the normal course of events will the target company be able to carry on its business there?). **6–02**

These issues overlap substantially. If there are factors preventing or hampering a sale, the value otherwise ascribed to the property will be reduced. If the property is required as a place of business, it may well lose its ascribed value if its use as such cannot be continued, and so on. Nevertheless the emphasis of the warranty protection which is sought may, in appropriate circumstances, be concentrated on one or more, rather than all, of these issues and, while the purchaser may request, and accept if it is offered, wide-ranging property warranty protection, the vendors will wish to limit their liability. In any event the vendors should be concerned to offer no more than the purchaser reasonably requires, having regard to the purposes for which the property is intended to serve the target company under the ownership of the purchaser and the extent to which the value or use of the property has been a factor in determining the price **6–03** paid by the purchaser. A fuller understanding of some of the principles of valuation may be obtained by reference to Ch.13.

## TYPES OF PROTECTION ON TITLE TO PROPERTY

**6–04**   There are three conventional ways in which the purchaser of shares may wish to be satisfied that the target company has a good and marketable title to its properties. It may, through its own solicitor, carry out an investigation of title; it may rely upon warranty protection; or it may accept a certificate of title from the target company's solicitor.

A full set of property warranties obtained from the vendors serves as a substitute for an investigation of title to the properties made by the solicitor acting for the purchaser. If the purchaser has the opportunity to make an investigation of title itself, why should it seek the protection of property warranties? If the target company's solicitor is in a position to give a certificate of title, what need then for property warranties or an investigation of title?

There is, of course, no general answer to these questions for circumstances will vary in every case, but it is pertinent to examine the functions of property warranty protection, investigation of title and certificates of title, and the issues involved in deciding which measures or mix of measures to adopt. Each is dealt with in turn below.

## WARRANTY PROTECTION

**6–05**   In the case of full property warranties, the principal function will be to provide to the purchaser, by way of damages, protection against the presence of factors in relation to the properties which were not known to the purchaser at the time of the acquisition of the target company and which detrimentally affect it. Provided the vendors have the financial substance to support the warranty liability, the purchaser has recourse through the warranties for any loss arising from breach.

There is another, practical, function; if warranties are given, the purchaser may be relieved of the need to investigate title, but there are other practical considerations which are examined below.

## INVESTIGATION OF TITLE

**6–06**   The purchaser, through its solicitor, will carry out the same investigative conveyancing procedures as it would if it were to acquire the properties as such rather than the target company and will satisfy itself on all relevant matters. It will not enjoy the same protection in damages against the vendors since, in the absence of property warranties, it would not even enjoy the benefit of normal covenants for title implied by a vendor selling the property with full title guarantee (see para.4–07). There is no purchase of the property, only the purchase of shares. There may be some responsibility placed on the vendors by a general warranty with respect to disclosure so that liability is incurred by the vendors for failure to bring to the attention of the purchaser material matters (if such a warranty were given), or a warranty that such information as has been disclosed is accurate and complete. Liability for breach of those warranties would then be similar to liability for damages for misrepresentation by a vendor of property in answer to preliminary enquiries. Indeed, even without such general warranties, there may be liability for damages for misrepresentation under the Misrepresentation Act 1967 (see para.3–01) although in most cases this will now be limited to fraudulent misrepresentation by effective use of entire agreement clauses (see para.3–03).

The function of an investigation of the target company's title to its properties, in isolation, is to allow the purchaser the opportunity of doing the job thoroughly for itself, through its own professional adviser, whom it knows and trusts. The purchaser may prefer to deal with the matter in this way, but it may have no choice if the vendors refuse to give any property warranties or give only limited property warranties.

## CERTIFICATE OF TITLE

**6–07** A certificate of title is given by the target company's solicitor and, if properly drawn, covers the same ground as a full set of property warranties or the subject matter of a report of the purchaser's solicitor if he had investigated title. The purchaser relies not on its own solicitor but on the certificate of the target company's solicitor. The purchaser's protection is based on a right of action for negligence against the solicitor. In theory, the target company and the vendors would not be liable for the negligence of the target company's solicitor in the absence of some general warranty given in support. In practice, the target company or the vendors might well be joined as co-defendants in an action for negligence since the relevant part of the certificate may have been based upon inaccurate information provided by the vendors amounting to misrepresentation.

The function of a certificate of title is to cover the subject matter of an investigation of title and to relieve the purchaser of the need to make one.

## WARRANTIES, INVESTIGATION OR CERTIFICATE?

**6–08** In terms of content, there should be little difference between a full set of property warranties, an unqualified certificate of title and the report of the purchaser's solicitor following an investigation of title. What factors then determine the choice between them, and would it be appropriate to combine or mix them? How comprehensive should their content be? The decision should be influenced by a number of considerations which are set out below.

## Remedies and Protection Provided

**6–09**  In a single choice between warranties, investigation of title and a certificate of title, the purchaser probably achieves the greatest legal protection from a full set of property warranties. If the vendors have the financial substance to discharge any liability arising from breach, the purchaser obtains something akin to insurance. However, it would not generally be prudent for the purchaser to ignore the perils of litigation in pursuing warranty claims, nor to indulge the belief that the vendors will always be able to pay, nor more generally to disregard the adage "prevention is better than cure". Far better therefore for the purchaser to combine full warranty protection with its own solicitor's investigation of title. Conversely, the vendors will wish to avoid, so far as they may do in the circumstances, assuming any liability. If there is a balance of negotiating power between the parties and all other factors are equal, the vendors' best position is to require the purchaser to investigate title, and only to warrant that the information given in answer to enquiries made by the purchaser's solicitor in the course of investigation is to the best of the knowledge and belief of the vendors true and accurate. In that way, there is a fair division of responsibilities between the parties, a balance between the need for prudent enquiry and an obligation to answer fully and accurately. Timing will usually play an important part and interfere with the ideal position from the vendors' point of view. Often the purchaser's solicitors will be unable to undertake a full investigation of title in the available time and therefore the vendors will have to "fill in the gaps" by appropriate warranty protection.

**6–10**  The offer or availability of a certificate of title from the solicitor to the target company is usually determined by considerations of timing and convenience but, dealt with in this setting, the purchaser is simply substituting the report of the target company's solicitor for that of its own solicitor following an investigation. Its remedy for a defective report from its own solicitor, or inaccuracies in the certificate of title from the target company's solicitor, is an action for negligence. In practice, the target company's solicitor will usually endeavour to qualify the certificate by incorporating certain exemptions and even disclaimers. As a general proposition, the purchaser should require a warranty from the vendors confirming the accuracy and completeness of the certificate of title and, where the certificate is qualified, specific warranty protection to cover the gaps which it leaves. In that way the purchaser has the double protection of the warranty from the vendors and the solicitor's insurance cover against negligence.

Similar considerations apply to investigations of title. The purchaser's solicitor will obviously not seek to exempt himself from liability as such but will point out any areas which are not satisfactory. Warranty protection should be sought from the vendors on these specific matters. It is considered that an investigation of title is a more satisfactory protection to a purchaser than a certificate of title. The purchaser's own solicitor can be as thorough and searching as the purchaser requires and will represent the purchaser as such. The purchaser and its solicitor, between them, set the depth of investigation. The target company's solicitor, in producing a certificate of title, is not answerable to the purchaser in the same way and does not act for it. Furthermore, not every inaccuracy or mistake in a certificate of title is necessarily the result of a failure by the target company's solicitor to take reasonable care, giving rise to liability for negligence.

## IMPORTANCE OF THE PROPERTY

The transaction, in form, is a purchase of shares—the acquisition of the target **6–11** company. The properties may, at one end of the scale, be the only assets of substance (as they would be on the acquisition of a property investment company) or at the other merely one group of assets of scant importance (for example surplus premises held on an unprotected lease due to expire within a short period). A useful guide as to the properties' importance in the transaction is whether the price for the target company is calculated by reference to the net asset value of the target company or is determined according to its profitability. If the former, the significance of the properties would probably be greater. However, it should not be forgotten that a property of little capital value (say one held upon a lease at a full market rental) may nevertheless be vital to the running of the business of the target company.

In any case where the properties are of substantial importance and where all other factors are equal, it is recommended that the purchaser should carry out an investigation of title and should seek such warranty protection from the vendors as it can get, settling for no less than warranties dealing with the areas of defect or uncertainty unearthed by the investigation, plus a general warranty that all information given to the purchaser's solicitor upon such investigation is accurate and complete.

## TIMING AND CONVENIENCE

Often all other considerations have to give way to the timing of a transaction; **6–12** with the urgency such that it dictates what can be done in the time allotted. If the target company's solicitor can give a certificate of title in time and it is convenient for him to do so, then that course will be far quicker than the making of an investigation of title, which is seldom speedy. On many occasions, it will not be convenient for a certificate of title to be given or practicable for an investigation to be carried out. In such circumstances, a full set of property warranties comes into its own; the parties are forced to fall back on that route by the practicalities of the deal.

The choice between the certificate of title and the investigation of title is often grounded on issues of convenience alone, although it is rare that questions of timing are not also involved. The complexity of title, coupled with the familiarity with the properties and the knowledge of the target company's solicitor, may make the offer of a certificate of title appropriate, particularly if the properties are not of crucial importance.

# COST

**6–13**  An investigation of title can be a costly process. Again, if the significance of the properties is only incidental, it may be satisfactory to save cost and rely on warranty protection only.

# BARGAINING POWER

**6–14**  In many cases the determining factor will be simply the relative bargaining strengths of the parties. Reluctant vendors, much courted by an anxious purchaser, can afford to give less away in warranties than in a case where there are both willing vendors and a willing purchaser. At the other extreme, hard pressed vendors anxious to unload the target company on to a diffident purchaser may assume all sorts of liability under stringent warranties for the short-term benefits of disposing of the target company, taking on the risk of long-term liability if all is not what it appears to be in relation to the properties.

# SCOPE OF WARRANTY PROTECTION

**6–15**  It has been stated that the purpose of property warranties is to support the assumption made by the prudent purchaser that the target company's title to its property is good and marketable. The meaning of "good and marketable title" has now to be examined.

A vendor of land is under an obligation to show good title. He must prove that he is entitled to and is selling the legal estate in land for the appropriate tenure (*i.e.* freehold or leasehold), free from encumbrances or defects save as is otherwise provided or disclosed. In the case of registered land, the vendor must show that he is registered as the proprietor of the property with absolute title. If title to the property is unregistered, he must be able to deduce a chain of title to the legal estate commencing not less than 15 years earlier with a good root—that is a document of title which deals with the legal and beneficial ownership of the property, identifies the property and contains nothing to cast doubt on the title of the disposing party. Anything less, or any qualification, must be provided for or disclosed.

**6–16**      The inclusion of the words "and marketable" involves a separate requirement by implying that there is an absence of other factors relating to the property, either rendering it commercially unsaleable or impairing its saleability. The limited nature of the requirement to show good title is thus opened out to general aspects of marketability. By analogy with the sale of land, the purchaser is concerned with much more than mere title upon an investigation. It will have the property surveyed in order to be advised upon its state and condition. It will, through its solicitor, make searches in the Register of Local Land Charges and enquiries to the local authority to ascertain, for example, whether the property will be or is likely to be compulsorily acquired and to find out information on planning matters, highway rights and obligations, drainage, compliance or non-compliance with statutory requirements in relation to the property, and the like.

It will submit through its solicitor preliminary enquiries to the vendor on a large and wide range of issues and its solicitor will, if the circumstances are appropriate, make additional searches in the Index Map and Parcels Index at HM Land Registry and in the registers of common land and town or village greens. It may also enquire with the Coal Authority to find out about the presence of mining activity in the area and subsidence. For the most part these procedures deal with issues and matters which have little to do with title as such; they are designed to ascertain information about the property generally, so that the purchaser will be able to assess the value of the property for the purposes of the purchase or for obtaining mortgage finance, the likelihood of imminently having to carry out repairs and maintenance, the suitability of the land for the purchaser's requirements and the problems that might arise on resale. An investigation of title is in practice, therefore, not limited to matters of ownership and is much more extensive. It is submitted that all these matters are encompassed by the expression "good and marketable title".

It follows that, if as a substitute for an investigation of title the purchaser is offered a full set of property warranties, those warranties should cover the matters which would have been dealt with on an investigation of title by the purchaser of the target company; that is an exercise in parallel with the investigation that is carried out by a purchaser of land. Indeed, if title is warranted as good and marketable, the circle is completed.

## PURCHASE OF SHARES AND PURCHASE OF LAND

The scope of a full set of property warranties is purposely set as widely as **6–17** possible, not only to confer requisite protection but also to compel disclosure of information by the vendors beforehand in order to avoid liability which they might otherwise incur. In such circumstances, the purchaser is given the opportunity of reviewing relevant information about the property of the target company before the point of legal commitment to acquire the target company and, if appropriate, may withdraw or renegotiate. Once contracts are exchanged, the purchaser's only remedy is in damages or rescission. The purchaser of land with registered title has the additional benefit of procedural protections afforded by a title pre-completion search at HM Land Registry which will give the purchaser of land priority for a specified period within which to register its transfer. With this priority, the purchaser of land is then protected against any other transaction not similarly protected by an earlier search. It will also allow the purchaser of land the opportunity to raise with the vendor and address before completion the existence of any adverse entries submitted to HM Land Registry for registration and not previously disclosed by the vendors.

## ANALYSIS OF WARRANTIES

**6–18**    The warranties in this chapter are prepared in connection with a share purchase and, although some of them may be of interest to a purchaser of a business, it is unusual in such transactions for extensive property warranties to be requested or given.

If, in the case of a share sale, the properties are not of significant importance, short form warranties may be appropriate as set out in Appendix 7. The rest of this chapter deals with long form warranties. The full set of property warranties is so designed as to cover the complete range of circumstances in which any property asset of the target company may be utilised, from pure investment to occupation for the purposes of the target company's business. Each warranty is drafted to deal with a single issue, or group of issues, so that, if it is inapplicable to a particular transaction, it may usually be deleted without repercussion in relation to any other warranty. The issue raised by each warranty may be substantive and provide specific protection to the purchaser, or its primary purpose may be to draw forth necessary information and to give general protection to the purchaser against the absence of, or inaccurate, disclosure.

The form of the property warranties presupposes that, by way of appropriate schedules, each property is described, the principal terms of leases under which the target company holds the property or of tenancies to which the target company holds the reversion are itemised and details of encumbrances and latent defects in title given. Accordingly, a number of warranties are in negative form so that their presence will elicit the disclosure of important information which might otherwise not be forthcoming. That aspect will be of even more importance when the commercial purpose of the purchaser in acquiring the target company is not primarily directed to its property assets and little or no investigation of title or enquiry about them has been made.

**6–19**    Some suggestions are made as to how the vendors may modify the full severity of certain warranties. As the protection sought runs in parallel with an investigation of title which would be made on a purchase of land, the view is taken in general that, if information would reasonably be expected to be obtained from the vendors in that context, then the equivalent warranty protection should be provided by the vendors.

The warranties discussed in the following paragraphs are as follows:

| *Clause* | *Title* |
|---|---|
| 1 | Title |
| 2 | Encumbrances |
| 3 | Planning matters |
| 4 | Statutory obligations |
| 5 | Adverse orders |
| 6 | Condition of the Properties |
| 7 | Insurance |
| 8 | Leasehold properties |

9      Tenancies

The clauses set out below adopt the definitions appearing in para.4–01.

*1 Title*

The warranties grouped under this heading deal principally with matters of    **6–20**
ownership and tenure. They are intended to cause the vendors to provide full
information about the properties in the target company's portfolio under the
sanction of liability for damages for failure to disclose and inaccurate disclosure.

**1.1 The Properties comprise all the properties owned, occupied or other-
wise used by the Company in connection with its business.**

This warranty is provided as a checklist to ensure that every property owned,
occupied or used by the target company is identified. It is unlikely that the
purchaser will have an entitlement to damages if the warranty is incorrect unless
the undisclosed properties carry liabilities, for example under repairing covenants or under any mortgage secured thereon.

Ownership means that the freehold interest in, or a lease of the property, is
held. The right to occupy or use a property may be an incident of holding either
the freehold or leasehold interest or may be enjoyed under a licence granted
by the owner. A licence creates no interest as such in a property but merely
permits the licensee to occupy or to use and enjoy it according to the terms laid
down in the licence.

The information required to be given should be readily available and the
purchaser is entitled to it.

**1.2 Those of the Properties which are occupied or otherwise used by the
Company in connection with its business are occupied or used by right of
ownership or under lease or licence, the terms of which permit the occupation or use.**

In contrast with the warranty in cl.1.1, which is concerned with identifying all    **6–21**
the properties, the issue here is lawful use and occupation. Use or occupation
which is not permitted may amount to trespass and be actionable in damages.
Title may be in the course of being acquired by adverse possession. The
purchaser requires, and should insist upon, protection against circumstances in
which such occupation or use may be unexpectedly terminated by persons having
a better title to the property.

**1.3 The Company is the legal and beneficial owner of the Properties.**

Ownership of the freehold or a leasehold interest may be vested in a nominee for
the absolute benefit of another or held upon certain other express or implied trusts
for another party. In either case the beneficial ownership would be vested in that

other party. The purchaser must therefore be assured that the property of the target company is held beneficially. In addition, on a sale of land the beneficial ownership passes to the purchaser as from the date of contract. Protection against the undisclosed presence of beneficial interests which are not held by the target company, and the possibility of onerous trust obligations attached to the legal interest in property, is an extension of the general principle that a vendor of land is required to make good title free from undisclosed encumbrances.

6–22      **1.4 The information contained in Schedule [ ] as to the tenure of each of the Properties, the principal terms of the leases or licences held by the Company and the principal terms of the tenancies and licences subject to and with the benefit of which the Properties are held, is complete and accurate.**

"Tenure" means a freehold or leasehold estate in land but does not include a licence.

Possession of a property usually connotes either the right of use and occupation or the receipt of rents and profits (see LPA 1925, s.205) and this clause follows that concept.

The information to be provided under this clause is fundamental but will rarely be difficult to obtain.

6–23      **1.5 The Company has a good and marketable title to each of the Properties.**

The meaning of good and marketable title has already been considered (see para.6–15). The purpose of a full set of property warranties is to ensure that the purchaser is protected against a bad or unmarketable title of the target company to its properties. This warranty, which is all embracing, not only duplicates the protection provided by other more specific warranties but also "sweeps up" other areas of liability which may not be covered by the aggregate effect of the particular liability imposed by other individual warranties.

The vendors may properly seek to limit the wide and unlimited ambit of the use of "marketable". They may point to the presence of large numbers of other warranties dealing with specific aspects of marketability which, they might argue, give adequate protection. If "marketable" is not to be omitted, then a more limited form of warranty might be acceptable, such as:

**The Company has good title to the Properties and, so far as the Vendors are aware, there is nothing which renders the Properties unmarketable.**

In this way, the protection against unmarketable property is narrowed to those circumstances which are known, or constructively known, to the vendors.

6–24      **1.6 [The Company is the proprietor of the Properties registered at HM Land Registry with absolute title.] [None of the Properties is registered at HM Land Registry.]**

These alternative forms of warranty are primarily for the purposes of information and will require adaptation to accord with the circumstances. Both forms may be applicable. They are intended to serve in place of an official certificate of search in the Index Map and Parcels Index at HM Land Registry; such a certificate states whether the land is registered and, if registered, whether as freehold or leasehold land, or otherwise as the case may be, and in the case of leasehold land also states the date of and parties to the lease.

A transfer for value of freehold land, or of a lease having more than seven years unexpired, or the grant of a lease for more than seven years, which are not already registered at HM Land Registry, must be registered within two months, failing which the title of the owner to the legal estate in the land becomes void. The Chief Land Registrar has a discretion, however, to extend the period of registration (Land Registration Act 2002, s.6(5)).

A person may be registered as proprietor with absolute title or possessory title and, in the case of leaseholds only, there is an additional category of good leasehold title. It is beyond the scope of this commentary to explore the differences between these forms of title. However, there is no better registered title than absolute. With absolute title, the property is vested in the proprietor subject only to entries on the register and to overriding interests (one of the most important overriding interests is a lease for a term of seven years or less).

The use of the second alternative form will cause the vendors to disclose title which is possessory or qualified (and, in the case of a lease, a good leasehold title) and which may have adverse implications for value or disposability.

**1.7 Each lease of the Properties granted for more than 7 years is either**  6–25
**registered at HM Land Registry with absolute title or not registered because**
**it was not registrable at the time of grant and no event has occurred in**
**consequence of which first registration of title should have been effected.**

This warranty provides, in relation to leasehold properties, similar protection to that afforded under cl.1.6. A lease granted for more than seven years must be registered at HM Land Registry. Failure to do so within two months renders the legal estate created by the lease void, although the Chief Land Registrar has a discretion to extend the period of registration (Land Registration Act 2002, s.6(5)).

## 2 Encumbrances

**2.1 The Properties are free from mortgages, debentures, charges, rent**  6–26
**charges, liens or other encumbrances.**

This clause is principally directed to encumbrances which secure upon land some financial liability, either of the target company itself or of some other party.

A mortgage connotes a document or deed which transfers a legal or equitable interest, with a provision for redemption so that, upon repayment of a loan or performance of some other obligation, the transfer becomes void or the interest is re-transferred. It is distinguished from a common law lien, which is the right to retain possession of the property or the deeds of the property and which confers no right upon the holder to sell or otherwise deal with it. An equitable lien may in certain circumstances result in a court ordering a sale of land upon the application of the holder and is therefore less effective in comparison to the powers of enforcement vested in a mortgage. A charge is a species of mortgage, but transfers nothing; the chargee nevertheless holds an interest in the property conferring upon him the power of sale or other forms of enforcement according to the circumstances. A debenture is a comprehensive term for a document issued by a company evidencing an indebtedness, which is normally, but not necessarily, secured by a charge over property. A rent charge does not secure repayment of money, but is an annual or periodic payment secured on the charged land. It allows the chargee to enforce the burden of positive covenants against the owner for the time being of the charged land, which otherwise would not run with the land, or to secure payment for the cost of services provided by the chargee without the creation of a lease.

The various terms used in this clause substantially overlap therefore, and are intended principally to cover all circumstances where the land may be taken in execution in order to enforce the security.

The circumstances in which any encumbrance may be created or arise are legion. They range, for example, from an ordinary mortgage, given to secure a loan, to a charge imposed by statute to secure property taxes. This warranty applies equally to a rent charge or annuity issuing out of land, as it does to a charge by the target company to secure a guarantee given for the benefit of a third party. Nevertheless the vendors should be aware of all relevant information and a purchaser is entitled to the protection afforded in order to obtain the equivalent of good title.

**6–27    2.2 The Properties are not subject to outgoings, other than business rates, water rates and insurance premiums and additionally, in the case of lease-hold properties, rent and service charges.**

The term **"outgoings"** covers all forms of recurring and non-recurring liability incidental to land ownership or occupation. They will usually arise under statute. It includes, for example, an obligation of a frontager to contribute to the cost of making up a road for dedication as a public highway and unoccupied property rate. The outgoings specifically referred to in the warranty may be regarded as being usual; all others, being unusual, should be disclosed. This information is normally requested in, and given in reply to, preliminary enquiries preparatory to a purchase of land.

In relation to leasehold properties, rent and service charges are usual and, therefore, do not need to be disclosed in this limited context. However, they are of vital importance in relation to value and are dealt with in cll.8 and 9.

**6–28    2.3 The Properties are free of restrictive covenants, stipulations, ease-ments, *profits à prendre*, wayleaves, licences, grants, restrictions, overriding interests or other similar rights vested in third parties.**

This clause is primarily addressed to non-financial encumbrances over land which are commonly encountered. They are of a kind which enable parties in whom they are vested either to use the land owned by another or to prevent its use in some manner by the owner.

A restrictive covenant prevents the owner of land from using or enjoying his land in some specified way. The burden of the covenant runs with the land in equity and affects the current owner at any time. It is enforceable by injunction by the owner of the land which enjoys the benefit. A covenant not to use land for a particular trade or business could be of vital importance to the purchaser of the target company wishing to change or expand its business conducted on the land in breach of the restriction. A covenant not to build would present a major obstacle to a purchaser needing to develop the land of the target company.

Easements are rights which one landowner holding the "dominant" land may exercise over the "servient" land of another which is adjoining or nearby. The most common examples of easements are rights of way and rights of light. The acquisition of the target company with a view to the development of its properties may give rise to important questions on these issues. The presence of a right of way or of light over land may prevent or restrict the land's development. Conversely a right of access may be essential to use of land without which its value would be heavily reduced. A wayleave is a right enjoyed by permission of the owner which is usually granted to a public utility to authorise, for example, the passage of cables, pipes or conduits through or over land, for which a nominal rent is often paid. A licence, in this context, is a permission to use or occupy land.
**6–29**

All other terms used in this warranty involve some minor extension of, or difference from, these concepts which encumber land. The reference to "other similar rights" would normally include options over land although these are specifically dealt with in cl.2.5.

Certain encumbrances will be specifically noted on the title to a property, and the vendors will have no difficulty in disclosing their presence. That is not true, however, of all such matters and it is customary on the sale of land for a vendor to endeavour to limit liability for non-disclosure of or inability to define all such burdens. Typical examples are the passage of services in, on or under land, and drainage rights. By analogy, it is legitimate for the vendors to endeavour to limit their liabilities in the same way. They may argue that they should only be fairly responsible for restrictions which inhibit existing use.

**2.4 Where any of the matters referred to in clauses [2.1, 2.2 and 2.3] are disclosed in the Disclosure Letter, the obligations and liabilities imposed and arising under them have been performed and discharged and no payments in respect of them are outstanding.**
**6–30**

The presence of such third party rights may, of course, be perfectly acceptable to the purchaser and have been taken into account. Nevertheless the purchaser will be concerned to be protected against the failure of the target company to discharge its obligations and liabilities in relation to those rights.

While this protection may properly be sought by the purchaser the vendors should endeavour to restrict liability to material matters. In its unrestricted form, the clause allows the purchaser to claim redress on minor matters except in so far as trivial claims are excluded by a clause imposing a floor on claims (see para.3–20).

**6–31**      **2.5 The Properties are free of options or rights of pre-emption.**

An option to purchase a property, or to take up a lease, creates an equitable interest in land which requires registration as a land charge in the case of unregistered land, or noting on the charges register relating to the title to registered land, in order to secure full protection to the option-holder. The protection provided by this warranty overlaps with that provided under cl.2.6. A right of pre-emption, or right of first refusal, however, does not create a registrable interest in land (at least not before it is exercised and, indeed, will not become exercisable unless and until the vendor ever decides to sell). They are conveniently dealt with together, even though their technical character and consequences in conveyancing terms are different.

This information should be known to the vendors and the purchaser is entitled to it.

**6–32**      **2.6 There are no local land charges, land charges, cautions, inhibitions or notices registered against the Properties and there is nothing which is capable of registration against them.**

These are matters which would be covered by searches in the Register of Local Land Charges maintained by local authorities, the Land Charges Registry in the case of unregistered title to land, and HM Land Registry where the title to land is registered. The principal purpose of this warranty is to provide protection in a case where the purchaser has not had time to make the usual searches.

The matters referred to either create charges over land or are procedural devices to protect certain rights of third parties against it. For example, an option or restrictive covenant is registrable as a land charge in the case of unregistered land or is protected by notice or caution if title is registered. Without such registration, the option or restrictive covenant would be void against a purchaser of the legal estate in the land. The emphasis of the warranty is therefore concentrated upon the procedures to protect encumbrances.

The scope of this warranty is so wide that the vendors will be reluctant to give it in all but exceptional cases and only then if the property is not of great importance. The vendors should do so only against the background of recent searches made by them or on their behalf so that they will be able to avoid liability by making full disclosure of what searches by the purchaser would themselves reveal. In any event, it will be legitimate for the vendors to limit liability to their actual or constructive knowledge and to information of which they ought reasonably to be aware.

The vendors should be careful to omit **"local land charges"** from any renewal of the warranty at completion if there is an interval between contracts and completion; the purchaser would otherwise be placed in a better position than a purchaser of land.

### 3 Planning matters

Planning matters are creatures of statute and could logically be included in the group of warranties which appear under the heading "statutory obligations"; they have separate treatment in this arrangement of headings as being of fundamental importance. The value of property depends on how it may lawfully be used. This grouping accords to planning matters their proper significance and compels the vendors to consider them individually.

**6–33**

#### 3.1 The use of each of the Properties is the permitted use for the purposes of the Planning Acts.

A permitted use is one which is authorised by the grant of planning permission or for which planning permission is deemed to have been granted. The object of this clause is to protect the purchaser not only from the inconvenience arising from enforcement proceedings taken by a planning authority to terminate an unauthorised use but also against the loss of value to a property if its existing use has to be discontinued.

**"Permitted use"** should be distinguished from "lawful use", a term introduced by the Planning and Compensation Act 1991, which replaced "established use". Lawful use is one which has not been authorised by planning permission but has been rendered immune from enforcement proceedings by the passage of time (in the case of commercial uses continuous use for 10 years since the breach of planning control began) and through a successful application for a certificate of Lawful Use or Development. Where the suggested warranty is not applicable, it is suggested that a certificate of lawful use should be obtained.

The penalty for giving this warranty recklessly may be very severe. However, the vendors should have the relevant information available to them and they would be expected to give it in answer to preliminary enquiries were they vendors of land. If the vendors are in any doubt, they should either make full disclosure of the circumstances or seek to limit their liability in an appropriate manner.

#### 3.2 Planning permission has been obtained, or is deemed to have been granted, for the purpose of the Planning Acts with respect to the development of the Properties; no planning permission has been suspended or called in and no application for planning permission is awaiting a decision.

**6–34**

This clause overlaps with the warranty in cl.3.1, since it would by itself cover issues of permitted user, but its emphasis is upon development of the target company's properties.

**"Development"** is defined by the Town and Country Planning Act 1990, s.55 which, broadly speaking, is divided into two categories. The first is the carrying out of building, engineering, mining or other operations in, on, over or under

**6–35**

land. The second category is the making of a material change in the use of buildings or land. Planning permission is required for all such development unless it is deemed to have been granted by the Town and Country Planning General Permitted Development Order 1995 (SIs 1995 Nos 418 and 419 (as amended)) or the Town and Country Planning (Use Classes) Order 1987 (SI 1987 No. 764 (as amended)). The General Permitted Development Order lays down a number of different classes of development for which planning permission is automatically granted provided these rights have not been removed and various criteria met. Certain developments within the curtilage of a dwellinghouse, the erection of certain gates and fences, the erection of temporary buildings and uses in connection with the carrying out of other development are examples of classes of permitted development under the Order. Under the Use Classes Order, there are now some 11 categories of use. Planning permission is deemed to be granted for any change of use to another within the same class and also for changes to other classes in certain instances, again subject to the rights not having been removed.

Under planning law it is possible for a planning application for which there is a resolution to approve to be called in or to be suspended. The wording of the clause has been extended to cover these potentially damaging circumstances although their occurrence is comparatively rare. The clause, which for the most part concentrates upon substantive protection for the purchaser, changes course by adding that no application for planning permission is awaiting a decision; this is essentially for information only.

This information would normally be revealed in searches in the Register of Local Land Charges but such is its importance that preliminary enquiries on the subject are also normally addressed to a vendor of land.

The vendors cannot easily resist the inclusion of a warranty in this form, since the target company should have accurate records of the development which it has carried out or of detailed enquiries made upon the acquisition of a property if it was developed before it came into the target company's ownership. Disclosure of circumstances casting doubt is particularly important.

**6–36**    **3.3 Building regulation consents have been obtained with respect to all development of and alterations and improvements to the Properties.**

This is not strictly speaking a planning matter, but it relates to development and is conveniently grouped with the other warranties under this heading.

Building regulation consents must be obtained for most building operations under numerous statutes and by-laws, many of them applying only in the locality of the property. This not only extends to major development of a property but also to comparatively minor alterations and improvements. Alterations and improvements to properties not requiring planning permission may nevertheless involve building regulation consents. The expressions used connote differences of scale and **"development"** should be construed as applying to forms of development other than mere alterations and improvements to properties. Altera-tions are distinguished from improvements as being building activities which do not add anything to property. For example, the demolition of an outhouse and the bricking up of a wall would be alterations; the addition of a new storey to an existing building would be an improvement.

The purchaser is entitled to this protection. By analogy, a purchaser of land would require the information.

### 3.4 The Company has complied and is complying with planning permissions and statutory orders and regulations with respect to the Properties.      6–37

This clause overlaps substantially with the ground covered by previous warranties under this heading but the emphasis of this clause is upon compliance, not only with consents which have been obtained but also with requirements of the law. As such, it provides substantial protection for the purchaser.

The vendors should think carefully before giving this warranty since it is in absolute and general terms. They would be well advised, even if they are confident that no major breach or non-observance on the part of the target company has taken place, to introduce qualifying words to limit its scope. A purchaser would normally accept compliance **"in all material respects"** as being sufficient for its purposes.

### 3.5 The Company has complied and is complying with all agreements and all planning obligations made in respect of the Properties under the Town and Country Planning Act 1971, s.52 and under the Town and Country Planning Act 1990, s.106.      6–38

Irrespective of the powers to control development by granting or withholding planning permission or imposing conditions upon the grant of planning permission, a planning authority may also enter into agreements with landowners, restricting or regulating the development of land either permanently or for temporary periods. These agreements are enforceable against successors in title to the land.

The agreements have now become commonplace on large or important developments, and planning permissions often contain a condition that such an agreement must be entered into particularly in order to secure planning gain (*i.e.* some additional but related gain to the community, subject to a qualification that it must relate to the proposed development and be necessary to the grant of planning permission). A common example is the provision of car parking accommodation for members of the public.

The warranty may properly be requested from the vendors who should have full information about the target company's activities in this respect.

### 3.6 The Company has complied and is complying with all agreements made under the Highways Act 1980, s.38 with respect to the Properties.      6–39

Again, this matter is conveniently included under this group of warranties although it has little to do with town and country planning in its strict sense.

Frequently, and in particular with reference to housing estate development, the Local Authority requires that a new road be made up and, once it has been completed and maintained for a period to the satisfaction of the Highway Authority, it will be declared a highway repairable by the public. Under s.38 agreements, a specification for the road, the manner of construction and its maintenance to the satisfaction of the Highway Authority are generally laid down. Security from the developer is usually required in the form either of a deposit of cash or of a performance bond provided by a financial institution. Full disclosure of such obligations on the part of the target company is obviously of administrative and financial importance to the purchaser.

The vendors would not normally be justified in resisting the giving of this warranty where applicable, since it relates to information which they should have readily available and would be required to provide were they vendors of land.

**6–40**    **3.7 None of the Properties is listed as being of special historic or architectural importance or located in a conservation area.**

This information would be revealed by a search in the Register of Local Land Charges. The Secretary of State for Culture, Media and Sport compiles lists of buildings of special architectural or historic interest. It is an offence to demolish, alter or extend a listed building without a listed building consent or to damage such a building. While a building may not be so listed, it may be within a conservation area—that is an area of special architectural or historic interest with a character or appearance which ought to be preserved and which is designated as such an area by the Local Planning Authority. No building in such an area may be demolished without consent and trees in the area are protected as if they were subject to a tree preservation order.

These issues can be of critical importance if the target company is being acquired for the purpose of the redevelopment of its properties. In such an event, however, the vendors should require the purchaser to make an investigation of title, since the property assets of the target company will be of fundamental importance. Therefore the warranty will usually be deleted or omitted. Furthermore, if the disclosure letter treats as being disclosed all matters which would be revealed in a search (see, for example, paragraph (2) of the disclosure letter discussed in para.9–07) then this warranty will be valueless.

### 4 Statutory obligations

**6–41**    **4.1 The Company has complied and is complying with all applicable statutory and by-law requirements with respect to the Properties of the Public Health Acts, the Shops Acts 1950 to 1965, the Factories Act 1961, the Offices, Shops and Railway Premises Act 1963, the Fire Precautions Act 1971, the Health and Safety at Work etc. Act 1974, Environmental Protection Act 1990, Part IIA, the Sunday Trading Act 1994, the Disability Discrimination Act 1995 and any other legislation current or previous currently affecting the Properties and any other [applicable or] relevant orders, regulations or directions of a competent authority affecting the Properties.**

These are essentially checklist items but impose potentially substantial liability upon the vendors for failure to disclose or inaccurate disclosure.

In contrast with the reference to compliance with the building regulation consents and by-laws raised under the "planning matters" group of warranties, compliance with statutory and by-law requirements in this clause is intended to relate to use and enjoyment of the properties and not to their development, although the wording is wide enough to cover development obligations. The statutes specifically mentioned in this warranty lay down regulations as to how certain properties may be used and enjoyed. They are largely concerned with safety precautions and good working conditions.

As with all warranties which state generally that "compliance has been made", the liability is virtually limitless. If the warranty is to be given, the vendors should seek to limit it to those matters of which they are aware. This is another example of a warranty which should be given only where the properties are not of great importance or issues of timing or the strength of the purchaser's bargaining power allow the vendors little freedom to manoeuvre. In all other circumstances, it should be for the purchaser to satisfy itself.

**4.2 There is no outstanding or unperformed obligation with respect to the**   **6–42**
**Properties, compliance with which is necessary to satisfy the requirements**
**(whether formal or informal) of a competent authority exercising statutory**
**or delegated powers.**

This warranty overlaps with the protection given under cl.4.1. However, that clause is essentially directed to the application of the general law to property, whereas this warranty relates to specific requirements which competent authorities in exercise of their powers have laid down in respect of the properties of the target company. It is one thing to infringe the requirements of the general law and another to fail to comply with the requirements of competent authorities exercising their powers specifically in relation to a property. These requirements ought to be known to the vendors and the protection sought by the purchaser is sufficiently specific not to be resisted. The vendors might properly seek to limit the scope of the warranty by reference to materiality.

**4.3 No licences are required in relation to any of the Properties.**   **6–43**

This warranty is intended to cause disclosure to be made of licences required with respect to any particular use of property or to the business carried on upon property. It essentially duplicates cl.4.15.l in para.7–123 and, unless the activities carried out on the premises are such as to require special licensing, it need not be repeated here.

*5 Adverse orders*

The two warranties appearing under this heading could logically be allocated to "encumbrances" and "planning matters". It is considered, however, that this grouping is more convenient and draws better attention to their subject matter.

6–44    **5.1 There are no compulsory purchase notices, orders or resolutions affecting the Properties and [to the best of the knowledge and belief of the Vendors] there are no circumstances likely to lead to any being made.**

This clause relates to matters which would be revealed in the Register of Local Land Charges in answer to the standard CON 29 enquiries invariably submitted as part of the Local Authority search. Accordingly, the warranty would be rendered inoperative by most disclosure letters (for example paragraph (2) in para.9–07). The warranty is in two parts. Because the second part relates to circumstances which may lead to such notices, orders or resolutions being made, it should be limited by the addition of the words in square brackets.

If the purchaser has time to make searches, the vendors should be reluctant to give this warranty.

6–45    **5.2 There are no closing, demolition or clearance orders, enforcement notices or stop notices affecting the Properties and [to the best of the knowledge and belief of the Vendors] there are no circumstances likely to lead to any being made.**

Closing, demolition and clearance orders are mainly to do with safety regulations and slum clearance under the Public Health Acts. Enforcement notices and stop notices are procedures under the Planning Acts to prevent infringements of planning control. An enforcement notice can require the demolition or alteration of buildings or works, the discontinuance of any use of land or the carrying out on land of any building operations or other operations. An enforcement notice may be accompanied by a stop notice, the effect of which is to prohibit any person on whom it is served from carrying out or continuing any specified operations on land.

The existence of such orders or the service of such notices should be information known or available to the vendors, but they are matters upon which the purchaser should make searches and, if there is time for that to be done, the vendors should resist giving this warranty. If the vendors are to give the warranty they should seek the insertion of the wording in brackets.

*6 Condition of the Properties*

6–46    On a purchase of land, the purchaser normally has no remedy against the vendor for any grievance arising out of the state and condition of the property acquired. The prudent purchaser will therefore carry out a survey of the property prior to entering into a contract to acquire it. It may make preliminary enquiries about the state and condition of the property, which are customarily parried by the vendor's solicitor who usually answers that the purchaser must rely upon its own inspection. The group of warranties under this heading gives the purchaser of the target company protection which it would not normally be able to obtain if it were to buy land. Their inclusion ought therefore to be resisted by the vendors, save in exceptional and appropriate circumstances.

**6.1 The buildings and other structures on the Properties are in good and substantial repair and fit for the purposes for which they are used.**

The standard of repair required by this warranty adopts the formula often seen in leases and is often described as a full repairing obligation. Certainly there would be a breach of the warranty if any but the most minor repairs are required to be done.

The warranty is likely to be acceptable only if the purchase price of the target company reflects a value of the properties depending upon their being in good condition.

**6.2 No structure on the Properties has been affected by structural damage 6–47 or electrical defects or by timber infestation or disease.**

These circumstances would normally be investigated on the survey of land. The vendors should therefore resist the inclusion of this warranty but, if it is retained, it should be limited to a reasonable period in the past.

**6.3 No structure on the Properties contains in its fabric high alumina 6–48 cement, blue asbestos, calcium chloride accelerator, wood wool slabs used as permanent shuttering or other deleterious material.**

In the post-war period, a number of building substances were used by the construction industry which have since proved to be unsound and which have rendered certain larger constructions susceptible to collapse. They are usually the subject of a preliminary enquiry to a vendor of land.

If the target company has built the properties, then the vendors should have the relevant information. If the target company acquired them, it may have replies to preliminary enquiries made on its behalf at the time of acquisition. In those circumstances the vendors may feel themselves able to give the warranty, but in all other circumstances they should resist doing so.

**6.4 There are no disputes with a neighbouring owner with respect to 6–49 boundary walls and fences, or with a third party with respect to easements or rights over or benefitting the Properties.**

In the purchase of land, a standard preliminary enquiry is made on these matters. Support may be required for a boundary wall, and disputes over rights of way, rights of light and access to the property are often key issues when development proposals are about to be implemented.

The vendors cannot easily resist giving this warranty since it is information which should be available to them.

**6.5 The principal means of access to the Properties are over roads which 6–50 have been taken over by the local or other highway authority and which are maintainable at the public expense, and no means of access to the Properties is shared with another party or subject to rights of determination by another party.**

The purchaser will want to know whether there is any liability to repair and maintain any road on to which a property abuts and if there is any potential liability to the cost of making up the road in order that it should be adopted by the highway authority. The second part of the warranty is concerned with whether a right of access may be lost.

The wording used is an amalgamation of enquiries which are normally directed to the Local Land Charges Department and raised by way of preliminary enquiries on the purchase of land.

**6–51**     **6.6 Each of the Properties enjoys the mains services of water, drainage, electricity and gas.**

This is normally the subject of a preliminary enquiry on the purchase of land. The vendors should give this information.

**6–52**     **6.7 [To the best of the knowledge and belief of the Vendors] none of the Properties is located in an area or subject to circumstances particularly susceptible to flooding.**

These circumstances would normally be investigated on the survey of land and by enquiry of the Environment Agency. The vendors should endeavour to qualify the warranty by adding the wording in brackets.

**6–53**     **6.8 The Properties are not subject to rights of common.**

This warranty is usually only applicable to land in country areas. An example is the right to pasture cattle on the land. This would be dealt with on a purchase of land by a search in the registers of common land and town or village greens.

**6–54**     **6.9 [To the best of the knowledge and belief of the Vendors] the Properties are not affected by mining activity.**

A prudent purchaser of land in areas which are or might be affected by sub-sidence due to mining activity can make a search with the Coal Authority which will certify, or otherwise give information as to, mining activity, past present and, as at the date of the search, any known future proposals in the area, and whether or not the property could be affected by subsidence. The vendors should endeav-our to exclude this warranty, or to qualify it by introducing the wording in brackets.

*7 Insurance*

**6–55**     Although the question of proper insurance is of particular significance in relation to properties, the following clauses overlap the warranties in cl.8.4 in para.7–218. The vendors should seek to eliminate the duplication.

**7.1 The Properties are covered by insurance of a type usually available in the United Kingdom insurance market against a comprehensive range of risks**

**(including subsidence and terrorism) in their full reinstatement values and against third party and public liabilities and professional fees to an adequate extent and, where any of the Properties are let, for not less than three years' loss of rent or such greater period as may be specified in the tenancies affecting the Properties.**

Reinstatement value is based upon the cost of rebuilding the buildings or structures insured. It is customary to insure for loss of rent from premises for a period long enough to allow for the reconstruction of buildings which have been totally destroyed. These amounts are measurable according to current building costs and rental values. Third party and public liability insurances cover injury or damage to personal property and as such the cover to be provided should be adequate.

If the purchaser has had time and opportunity to consider these questions, the vendors may properly resist giving the warranty.

**7.2 All premiums due in respect of insurance policies relating to the Properties have been duly paid and, where the Properties are let, the premiums are recoverable in full from the tenants pursuant to the tenancies affecting the Properties and nothing has arisen which would vitiate the policies or permit the insurers to avoid them.**          6–56

The warranty in cl.7.1 deals with the cover afforded by the policies; this clause is concerned in part with the payment of premiums and additionally with the validity of the policies. This last matter is not always easily determined and that element of the clause may reasonably be resisted by the vendors.

**7.3 The information in the Disclosure Letter with respect to insurance policies is complete and accurate.**

This clause presupposes that insurance details will have been supplied by the vendors. The vendors should have no difficulty with the clause provided that the relevant information is purely factual.

## 8 Leasehold properties

The warranties under this heading relate to leases held by the target company. A lease creates a tenancy, but the expression "tenancies" has been used for the heading for the warranties in cl.9 which relate to leases subject to and with the benefit of which the properties are held so that income is derived from them. It is emphasised that this distinction is neither technical nor even proper; it is merely a convenient way, in this context, of labelling them.          6–57

On an assurance of leasehold land by a vendor conveying with full title guarantee, further covenants are implied in addition to the covenants as to right to convey, further assurance and freedom from undisclosed encumbrances. These are that the lease is subsisting, that there are no breaches of the tenant's covenants and that there is nothing rendering the lease liable to forfeiture. The warranties under this heading are based on and expand upon those covenants.

Details of the leases held by the company will have been given, and are referred to in cl.1.4.

**6–58** **8.1 The Company has paid the rent and performed [in all material respects] the covenants on the part of the tenant and the conditions contained in any leases (which expression in this clause [8] includes underleases) under which the Properties are held, the last demands for rent (or receipts, if issued) were unqualified and all the leases are in full force.**

The expression **"leases"** is extended to underleases so that it includes all derivative underleases.

The clause borrows the assumption made in the LPA 1925, s.45(2) that on the sale of a lease the production of the receipt for the last payment of rent due under the lease before the date of actual completion of the purchase causes the purchaser to assume, unless the contrary appears, that all the covenants and provisions of the lease have been duly performed and observed up to the date of actual completion of the purchase. This provides a mechanism for completion of the purchase of land to take place, notwithstanding that there may in fact be a breach of such covenants. Following on from that procedure, it used to be customary, and is still good estate management practice, for any known breach of covenant to be recorded on a receipt for rent given by the landlord or his agent. The production of an unqualified receipt for rent is therefore some, but limited, comfort that there is no material breach of covenant outstanding.

The vendors cannot easily resist giving this warranty but may properly endeavour to qualify it by introducing the words in square brackets.

**6–59** **8.2 All licences, consents and approvals required from the landlords and any superior landlords under leases of the Properties have been obtained, and the tenant's covenants therein have been performed [in all material respects].**

Leases invariably contain tenant's covenants which involve the obtaining of the prior consent or approval of the landlord. The most common instances are assignments and sublettings of the premises demised by the lease, the making of alterations to the premises and a change in the user of the premises. Licences granting permission in respect of such matters usually contain additional tenant's covenants. The purchaser of the target company will be equally concerned that additional covenants imposed by such licences and approvals have been performed. As minor breaches can easily occur, the vendors should seek to qualify this warranty by the addition of the words in square brackets.

**6–60** **8.3 There are no rent reviews in progress under leases of the Properties held by the Company.**

In general, time is not of the essence for a rent review unless it is expressly or impliedly made so. It is therefore possible for rent reviews to take place long after their appointed date.

**8.4 No obligation necessary to comply with a notice or other requirement**     6–61
**[properly] given by the landlord under a lease of any of the Properties is**
**outstanding and unperformed.**

The scope of this clause overlaps with the protection provided under cll.8.1 and
8.2, but its emphasis is concentrated upon notices which have been given by the
landlord. It has in contemplation, primarily, notices given under the LPA 1925,
s.146, which are a procedural prerequisite to forfeiture of a lease for breach of
covenant, other than in the case of non-payment of rent. The landlord must serve
a notice on the tenant specifying the particular breach complained of and if the
breach is capable of remedy requiring the tenant to remedy the breach, and in any
case requiring the tenant to make compensation in money for the breach. If the
tenant fails within a reasonable time to remedy a breach which is capable of
remedy to the landlord's satisfaction and to make reasonable monetary compensation, the landlord is entitled to exercise its right of re-entry or forfeiture,
subject to the powers of the court to award relief. The vendors might reasonably
require the insertion of the word **"properly"** as indicated.

**8.5 There is no obligation to reinstate any of the Properties by removing**     6–62
**an alteration made to it by the Company or a predecessor in title to the**
**Company.**

It is good estate management practice for a landlord to require in the grant of a
licence permitting alterations that the premises should, if the landlord so requires,
be reinstated at the expiration or earlier determination of the lease. The origins
of this requirement are in the Landlord and Tenant Act 1927, Pt I, which allows
a tenant to claim compensation for improvements to premises in appropriate
cases by complying with the very cumbersome procedure laid down by the Act.
The imposition of covenants requiring the reinstatement of the premises enabled
the landlord to avoid paying compensation for improvements in appropriate
cases. While this part of the Act is now seldom used, the practice of requiring
reinstatement has been continued as a practical, useful tool in the hands of a
landlord who may not wish to retain the "improvement" even if issues of
compensation are not also involved.

**8.6 The Company has not entered into an authorised guarantee agreement**     6–63
**under the Landlord and Tenant (Covenants) Act 1995, s.16 in respect of any**
**property.**

Section 16 was introduced in connection with the abolition by that Act of the
doctrine of privity of contract in relation to leases granted on or after January 1,
1996. Under s.16, the landlord may require the tenant, in accordance with the
terms of the lease, to enter into an authorised guarantee agreement when assigning the lease. While the Act provides for the release of a tenant on an assignment
it allows, in specified circumstances, the entering into of an authorised guarantee
agreement by the tenant guaranteeing the performance of the tenant's covenants
by the assignee. The guarantee may relate only to the performance of the

immediate assignee and may subsist only for the period during which the lease remains vested in the immediate assignee.

The purchaser will be able to ascertain whether any of the leases of properties held at the date of the share sale contain a provision relating to an authorised guarantee agreement but it has no ready means of determining the position in relation to leases which have already been assigned. As it will be a question of fact whether the target company has entered into an agreement, the vendors should have no difficulty in giving the warranty although, in appropriate cases, they would wish to restrict the application of the warranty to assignments which have taken place while the company has been in their ownership.

**6–64**    **8.7 The Company has not had the right to call for an overriding lease of any property under the Landlord and Tenant (Covenants) Act 1995, s.19.**

Section 19 provides that a former tenant or its guarantor which has incurred liability under the tenant's covenants in a lease as a result of a default by the assignee may, on discharging the liability, call for an overriding lease to be granted to it, subject to and with the benefit of the existing lease. It could be an important matter for the purchaser to be aware of but, as the vendors may not know that circumstances exist entitling the target company to call for the lease, the warranty should be qualified so that it applies only to the best of their knowledge.

**6–65**    **8.8 The Company has not entered into an agreement with the lessor of any of the Properties specifying circumstances in which it would be reasonable for the lessor to withhold its consent to an assignment in accordance with the Landlord and Tenant Act 1927, s.19(1A).**

Section 19(1A) was inserted into the Landlord and Tenant Act 1927 by the Landlord and Tenant (Covenants) Act 1995, s.22 to lessen the impact on landlords of the abolition of privity of contract in leases granted on or after January 1, 1996. The section permits a landlord to agree with the tenant, either in the lease or in a separate document, permitted circumstances in which the landlord may reasonably withhold consent to an assignment. The circumstances which may be specified are restricted so that, for example, it may not include matters which are to be determined by the landlord unless there is a reasonableness test.

The purchaser will be particularly concerned about the existence of such an agreement which is separate from the lease itself and the vendors should generally be able to give the warranty without difficulty.

### 9 Tenancies

**6–66**    **9.1 The Properties are held subject to and with the benefit of the tenancies (which expression in this clause [9] includes subtenancies) as set out in Schedule [ ] and no others.**

The principal terms of the tenancies will have been specified; cl.1.4 compels such disclosure.

**9.2 With respect to the tenancies, the Disclosure Letter contains partic-    6–67
ulars of:**

**9.2.1    the rent and any rent reviews and, with respect to rent reviews, the date for giving notice of exercise of the reviews and the operative review date;**

**9.2.2    the term and rights to break or renew the term;**

**9.2.3    the obligations of the landlord and tenant in respect of outgoings, repairs, insurance, services and service charges;**

**9.2.4    options or pre-emption rights;**

**9.2.5    the user required or permitted;**

The information disclosed in cll.9.2.1 to 9.2.5 is essential for administrative and management purposes. As an alternative, the vendors could produce to the purchaser copies of the relevant leases and warrant them to be accurate.

Where the properties are held for investment purposes, this information will be crucial. The maintenance and potential growth of value in a property centres upon the right to review rent and the full recovery from tenants of the cost of repair, maintenance, insurance and the provision of services.

**9.2.6    the entitlement of a tenant of the Properties to compensation either    6–68
on quitting the premises, for improvements or otherwise;**

A tenant of business premises will be entitled under the Landlord and Tenant Act 1954, s.37 (as amended) to compensation on quitting the premises in certain circumstances. For example, if the landlord terminates the business tenancy at the appropriate time and opposes the grant of a new tenancy on the grounds that it requires the premises for its own business, or that upon the termination of the current tenancy it intends to demolish or reconstruct the premises, then the right to such compensation accrues. The procedure for obtaining compensation for improvements under the Landlord and Tenant Act 1927, Pt I has already been mentioned. The purchaser will be entitled to know of any potential liability of the target company for such compensation.

**9.2.7    any unusual provisions; and**                                        6–69

Usual covenants in a lease are those which "occur in ordinary use" and depend on the facts of each particular case. In an open contract for the grant of a lease containing usual covenants, the court will allow evidence of what is current practice in leases of premises of that type and in that locality. The purpose of this information is to place the onus upon the vendors to bring to the attention of the purchaser any provisions which are not in accordance with current practice. The vendors might object to its indeterminate nature and refuse to give it if the purchaser has time to investigate. The alternative is for the vendors to produce the leases to the purchaser, which can then evaluate the provisions for itself.

**6–70** **9.2.8    short particulars of subtenancies derived out of the tenancies [of which the Vendors are aware].**

This information is particularly important in determining the existence of business tenancies under the Landlord and Tenant Act 1954, Pt II. A subtenant in occupation of the premises for the purposes of his business enjoys rights of renewal as conferred by the Act but a tenant, having sublet and not occupying any part of the premises, has no such security of tenure. A landlord usually has this information, but it would be proper for the warranty to be qualified by the addition of the words in square brackets.

**6–71**    **9.3 The Vendors are not aware of a material or persistent breach of covenant by a tenant of the Properties.**

This information is of importance to a purchaser and enables it to assess the covenant strength of the tenant and its effect on the value of the property. In addition, persistent delay in paying rent or other substantial breaches of covenant by the tenant constitute grounds of opposition by the target company to the grant by the court of a new tenancy under the Landlord and Tenant Act 1954, Pt II.

**9.4 The Company has not at any time:**

**9.4.1    surrendered any lease, licence or tenancy to the landlord without first satisfying itself that the landlord had good title to accept such surrender and without receiving from the landlord an absolute release from all liability arising under such lease, licence or tenancy;**

**9.4.2    assigned, or otherwise disposed of, any lease, licence or tenancy without receiving a full and effective indemnity from the assignee or transferee in respect of its liability under such lease, licence or tenancy;**

**9.4.3    been a guarantor of a tenant's liability under any lease, licence or tenancy; or**

**9.4.4    assigned or otherwise disposed of any leasehold property in such a way that it retains any other residual liability in respect thereof.**

This clause is designed to flush out any residual liability that the target company may have in respect of any premises formerly occupied by it. In practice it is unlikely to cause the vendors any difficulty and will simply require disclosure of any relevant matters.

# CHAPTER 7

# Typical Long Form Commercial Warranties on Share Sales

## INTRODUCTION

The form that warranties may take where the shares of an active trading company **7–01** are purchased is infinitely variable, and no standard set of warranties can be entirely suitable for every case. In selecting which warranties are appropriate for a particular transaction, it is helpful to have a comprehensive standard form available which can be suitably edited to deal with that transaction. For a systematic approach, it is essential, as well as being good practice, for the warranties to be grouped into sections dealing with related subject matters. The following is an example of the headings which might usefully be considered other than in relation to taxation and properties (which are dealt with separately in Chs 5 and 6), each paragraph being analysed in some detail further on in this chapter. The warranties themselves are repeated in Appendix 4, with the omission of the amendments which are included within square brackets and which are put forward to assist and protect the vendors.

## SHORT FORM WARRANTIES

**7–02** If the target company's affairs are comparatively simple or if the consideration for the company is modest, the use of extensive warranties may not only be inappropriate but actually counter-productive. A shorter set of warranties would be suitable in such cases and a precedent is contained in Appendix 7. The precedent essentially takes the long-form warranties and condenses them down into a set of warranties which, while much shorter, cover for the most part the same areas. The effect of this is to put the burden on the vendors and their advisers to consider fully the potential scope of each of the warranties, as the warranties themselves will not direct their minds specifically to all relevant areas. The purchaser will enjoy a similar level of cover as if long-form warranties had been used, but save the costs of negotiating long-form warranties and, to unsuspecting vendors, the purchaser may appear to be more reasonable.

While the warranties in Appendix 7 would be particularly useful in a low value transaction where little is known of the target company, in circumstances where details are known and the target company's affairs are relatively simple, consideration should be given as to whether it would be preferable to tailor the long-form warranties to cover relevant areas to try to ensure that all relevant disclosures are made so as to enable the purchaser to consider the disclosed matters carefully.

## ANALYSIS OF INDIVIDUAL WARRANTIES

**7–03** In the following detailed analysis of typical warranties it is assumed that the vendors and warrantors are one and the same, that the purchase relates to the shares of a trading company and that the purchaser is a company. The definitions in para.4–01 are adopted, and defined terms are printed with a capital first letter. Where words are included in square brackets it is assumed in most cases that the warranty is prepared by the purchaser's solicitors without those words and that the vendors might wish to add them.

# 1 Preliminary

## 1.1 Capacity and authority of the Vendors

**1.1.1 Each Vendor has full power and authority to enter into and perform    7–04
this Agreement, the Tax Deed and all other documents to be executed by
them pursuant to this Agreement which constitute, or when executed will
constitute, obligations binding on each Vendor in accordance with their
terms.**

Lack of power, or incapacity, can arise in the case of infants, bankrupts, trustees,
persons of unsound mind and companies which do not have appropriate provisions in their memoranda of association. Where a vendor is a foreign entity, it
would be advisable to obtain an opinion letter from a lawyer qualified in the
relevant jurisdiction as to the existence of the required capacity.

If the vendors are not all parties to the tax deed, the drafting of this warranty
will need amendment.

Where there is a sole vendor who is also the warrantor, the warranty has no
function except to operate by way of a reminder to the purchaser's advisers to
check the capacity of the vendor. If the vendor lacks capacity to enter into the
agreement, he/it will also lack capacity to give the warranty. The provision has
legal value in practice only where there are a number of vendors and each vendor
accepts responsibility for any incapacity of another vendor, or where the vendors
and warrantors differ. If there is any risk attached to this matter, it seems
appropriate that it should fall upon the vendors who are, in principle, obtaining
the benefit of the sale of the target company rather than the purchaser.

## 1.2 Ownership of Shares

**1.2.1 The Shares are fully paid or credited as fully paid and will, at Comple-    7–05
tion, constitute the whole of the issued and allotted share capital of the
Company.**

Issued shares are shares in respect of which an entry has been made in the register
of members. Allotted shares are shares which have been allotted by a company
and are held on letters of allotment, but have not been registered. Shares are fully
paid if they are subscribed for cash and are credited as fully paid if allotted for
a non-cash consideration, including in particular a capitalisation of reserves. If
shares are not fully paid, there is a contingent liability under the Insolvency Act
1986, s.74 upon holders and certain past holders to pay up the shares on an
insolvency. The warranty may also have particular relevance in relation to a
target company which is a public limited company, as CA 1985, s.101 requires
the shares of a plc to be paid up to the extent of at least one quarter of their
nominal value.

**1.2.2 The Vendors have the right to transfer to the Purchaser (without the    7–06
consent of any third party) and will on Completion transfer the legal and
beneficial title to the Shares.**

It is only the legal ownership, that is the ownership conferred by entry in the register of members, of the shares of the target company that is strictly relevant. This is because the persons entered in the register are defined to be the members of the company (CA 1985, s.22). The reference to beneficial ownership will often be inappropriate, for example if the vendors include trustees or the target is a wholly owned subsidiary and one of the vendors is the nominee for the holding company. If for good reason the vendors wish to omit the reference to beneficial ownership, the purchaser should not be concerned. This warranty will be superfluous if the vendors are expressed to sell with full title guarantee (see para.4–07) unless the vendors and the warrantors are not the same persons.

7–07    **1.2.3 There is not now existing nor is there any agreement to create any Encumbrance on or affecting shares of the Company.**

**"Encumbrance"** is defined to include not only those matters that would normally be considered to be encumbrances in the ordinary English meaning of the word but also more esoteric matters which might arguably not ordinarily amount to an encumbrance. There are minor, and largely irrelevant, differences between the various types of encumbrances in the way that they might apply to shares. If share certificates are handed over for the purpose of securing a debt, the transaction strictly gives rise to a pledge. A lien exists where the certificates are held by a person to whom a debt is owed, such as a banker who happens to be holding the certificates on behalf of a customer indebted to the bank, without a formal charge being created. In relation to a bank, it would appear to be correct to confine the concept of a lien to a right which attaches to documents coming into the bank's possession otherwise than directly in relation to the indebtedness. A lien on the shares held by a vendor may also exist if he is indebted to the target company and its articles of association provide for a lien even where the shares are fully paid.

A charge or other encumbrance on shares is not registrable under CA 1985, s.395, unless given for the purpose of securing an issue of debentures, and the normal rules applicable to bona fide purchasers without notice will therefore apply. If the purchaser is to take free of such a charge of which it did not have actual notice, it must be able to show that the lack of notice was bona fide and this warranty will assist it in doing so. Furthermore, from a practical point of view, the purchaser will wish to ensure that the vendors are reminded to check whether the shares are charged so that arrangements can be made to deliver the shares, free of encumbrances, at completion. The vendors cannot reasonably resist the warranty and would in practice gain nothing by doing so.

If the shares were the subject of a "chargeable transfer" under IHTA 1984 and tax arising on the transfer remains unpaid, the shares will be subject to a charge to secure the tax (see the comments on cl.29.2 in para.5–112). This warranty will be effectively redundant if there are covenants as to title implied by the vendors selling with full title guarantee (see para.4–07). The purchaser may nevertheless wish to have both protections if the warrantors and the vendors are not the same persons.

**1.2.4 None of the Shares was, or represents assets which were, the subject**   7–08
**of a transfer at an undervalue (within the meaning of the Insolvency Act**
**1986, ss.238 or 339) within the past five years.**

If an asset is transferred at an undervalue "at a relevant time" and the transferor
becomes bankrupt, goes into liquidation or administration, the court may order
the asset to be revested in the transferor (s.238 in relation to companies and s.339
in relation to individuals). The "relevant time" is five years prior to the presenta-
tion of the bankruptcy petition (s.341) or two years prior to the liquidation
(s.240), provided that the transferor was then insolvent or was an individual who
became bankrupt within two years of the transfer. Even if the transferor, being an
individual, was solvent at the time of the transfer, the transfer may be set aside
if bankruptcy occurs within two years. An order cannot be made against an
owner of the asset who acquired the asset in good faith and for value. Until ss.238
and 339 were amended by the Insolvency (No 2) Act 1994, the purchaser also
had to buy without knowledge of the "relevant circumstances". These are
defined in ss.241(3) and 342(4). In particular, in respect of a transfer by an
individual within two years of his bankruptcy, the only knowledge that was
required for a purchaser to be at risk was of the fact that the transfer was at an
undervalue. This would have been apparent, for example, in cases where shares
were held by trustees if the share transfers by which they acquired their holdings
indicated a nil consideration. This caused a serious difficulty in the case of a wide
range of transactions but, as a result of the change made by the 1994 Act, the
problem can be disregarded except in two special cases. The first of these is
where the buyers are associates of, or connected with, the person who has made
the transfer at an undervalue. The second case arises if the purchaser of property
which has been the subject of a transfer at an undervalue knew of the transaction
and that the transferor is, or is about to be, subject to insolvency proceedings.

There remains a small risk to a purchaser, for a period of two years after a
transfer has been made to trustees, that the transferor may become bankrupt and
steps taken to set the transfer aside. As the purchaser is safe if it did not know
of the transfer and of the insolvency proceedings, the warranty helps to demonstrate that it did not have the requisite knowledge if the acquisition should be
contested. From the point of view of the vendors, there may be some concern
about each of them having to accept responsibility in relation to the history of the
previous transfers of the shares unless they are all well known to each other.
Purchasers should however be alert to the fact that as a result of due diligence
they may become aware or may be held to be on notice of these issues notwithstanding the warranty.

**1.2.5 None of the Shares was allotted at a discount.**   7–09

Allotment at a discount, that is for a consideration of less than par, is unlikely to
have occurred if the shares were allotted for cash. However, if the consideration
was the transfer of assets or provision of services, the possibility of a breach is
more real. The purchaser will avoid liability to make good any shortfall under

CA 1985, s.112 if it is a bona fide purchaser without notice (s.112(3)) and the warranty will help to establish this defence should it be required.

### 1.3  Share capital

**7–10**  **1.3.1 No share or loan capital has been issued or allotted or agreed to be issued or allotted by the Company since the Balance Sheet Date.**

This warranty is designed to elicit disclosure of any share or loan transactions which have occurred since the last accounts were prepared.

**7–11**  **1.3.2 The Company has not at any time repaid, redeemed or purchased any or its own shares, reduced its share capital or capitalised any reserves or profits (or agreed to do the same).**

The purchaser will wish to check that prior transactions have been properly undertaken to ensure that there is no risk arising from any of them and that the vendors have good title to the shares they are purporting to sell. For instance, a prior buy back of shares which was not properly undertaken in accordance with the requirements of CA 1985 is likely to be void. The consequence of this is that the prior owners of the relevant shares will still be the owners of the shares and the company will have paid out money for no benefit. This can cause significant complications, particularly if the prior owners cannot be located or are not co-operative, as their involvement will inevitably be needed in correcting the position and no prudent purchaser will want to enter into a transaction with the vendors unless it is satisfied that they do in fact have good title to sell all of the relevant shares.

**7–12**  **1.3.3 The Company has not at any time provided financial assistance pursuant to CA 1985, ss.151 and 158.**

Private limited companies (as opposed to public companies which are not) are permitted to give financial assistance subject to compliance with the relevant provisions of CA 1985 (usually referred to as a "whitewash").

A prudent purchaser will wish to ensure that the procedures were properly followed as the consequences of breach or failure to follow them will mean that the provision of the financial assistance was unlawful, any agreement or charge given as part of the financial assistance will potentially be void, and the directors of the company may be guilty of a criminal offence.

### 1.4  Details of the Company

**7–13**  **1.4.1 The information relating to the Company in Schedule [ ] is accurate and complete [in respect of the matters dealt with].**

Information which it is appropriate to include in the schedule would be details of the company number, date of incorporation, authorised, issued and allotted share capitals, registered office, directors, secretary, auditors and accounting reference date. A cautious vendor might reasonably object to the statement that the information is "complete" on the ground that it is for the purchaser to specify precisely what particulars are required. The vendors may take some comfort from the additional words in brackets.

### 1.4.2 The Company has not at any time had only one member.     7–14

Section 24 of CA 1985, imposes personal liability, in certain circumstances, on any person who is the sole member of a company which carries on business for more than six months. In accordance with the 12th Company Law Directive, the Companies (Single Member Private Limited Companies) Regulations 1992 (51 No 1699) were brought into effect on July 15, 1992 for the purpose of allowing private companies limited by shares or guarantee to be formed by one person or to have one member.

Certain requirements have to be satisfied in the case of such a company. In particular, entries have to be made in the register of members when the company either becomes or ceases to be a single member company (CA 1985, s.352A). Contracts with a sole member who is also a director have to be recorded (s.322B), as do decisions which would otherwise require a resolution of shareholders in a meeting or a written resolution (s.382B).

In general the warranty will give no difficulty. If, however, the company has had a single member, particularly after the regulations came into effect, then the warranty should be amended so as to provide that the requirements referred to above have been duly satisfied. If there has been a failure to comply with the requirements in question, the omissions should be rectified before the sale takes place.

## 1.5 Directors and shadow directors

### 1.5.1 The only directors of the Company are the persons listed as such in     7–15 Schedule [ ].

This is essentially a simple question of fact but the vendors should bear in mind that the definition of "director" in CA 1985, s.741 includes a person occupying the position of a director by whatever name called. This warranty primarily performs a checklist function as it is unlikely that a breach would give rise to a claim for damages.

### 1.5.2 No person is or has been a shadow director (within the meaning of     7–16 CA 1985, s.741) of the Company but not treated as one of its directors for all the purposes of CA 1985.

A shadow director of a company is a person who is not a director but in accordance with whose instructions the directors of the company are accustomed to act. As the statutory definition of "director" includes a person occupying the position of a director by whatever name called (CA 1985, s.741), the concept of a shadow director must be even wider. Section 741(3) expressly excludes a parent company from falling within the definition for most purposes. In practice, therefore, a shadow directorship is most likely to occur in family companies and the purchaser will wish to be aware of arrangements giving rise to a shadow directorship so that they may be terminated. It may be noted that this definition is also relevant for the purposes of CA 1985, s.317, relating to the disclosure by a director of his or her interests in a contract with the company, and CA 1985, s.318, which requires directors' service contracts to be open for inspection.

### 1.6 Subsidiaries and branches

**7–17   1.6.1 The Company:**

**1.6.1.1  is not the holder or beneficial owner of, nor has it agreed to acquire, share or loan capital of a body corporate[ ]; and**

An agreement to acquire an asset will be relevant if it results in an outstanding liability. In any other case it might be thought that a purchaser will not be concerned if, in the event, the target company has more subsidiaries than were disclosed. However, the purchaser will often be subject to group borrowing restrictions and a heavily geared new subsidiary could have an important impact on the purchaser's gearing ratios. There may also be other cases where such additional companies would be objectionable. Thus, for example, the undisclosed companies might be engaged in activities which are not consistent with other activities of the purchaser, or be in serious financial difficulty so that the purchaser might then face the embarrassment of inadvertently becoming the owner of insolvent companies. Two further examples are where the undisclosed shares are only partly paid or are shares in an unlimited company.

**7–18   1.6.1.2  has not outside the United Kingdom a branch, agency or place of business, or a permanent establishment (as that expression is currently defined in the relevant double taxation relief order).**

The term **"permanent establishment"** is used in most double tax treaties but the definitions vary. In general, a permanent establishment exists if there is a fixed place of business and will usually include a branch or office or an agency where the agent has, and habitually exercises, power to conclude contracts on behalf of his principal.

This provision is relevant for a number of reasons. Clearly if the warranty is incorrect there is a potential taxation liability in the overseas jurisdictions concerned and, if significant activities are involved, it would be prudent to obtain local advice as to the precise implications. However, in addition to taxation matters, any overseas branch will involve a consideration of the regulations applying in the overseas jurisdiction to business activities carried on by foreigners, including such matters as registration requirements and work permits. A foreign branch may also be subject to local exchange control restrictions which would prevent or inhibit repatriation of profits (see also cl.4.4.2).

### 1.7 Options over the Company's capital

**7–19   1.7.1 Apart from this Agreement, there are no agreements or arrangements which provide for the issue, allotment or transfer of, or grant a right**

**(whether conditional or otherwise) to call for the issue, allotment or transfer of share or loan capital of the Company. No claim has been made by any person to be entitled to any of the foregoing.**

It might be thought sufficient to refer to outstanding "agreements" to acquire shares or loan capital but the purchaser would nevertheless wish to extend the warranty to cover arrangements. This is because unilateral obligations, such as the grant of an option, may be said not to constitute agreements. Equally preemption rights (where shareholders agree to sell shares to each other on a first refusal basis) are often set out in the articles of association of a company and it is not usual to regard the articles as an agreement. This point could be met by replacing **"agreements or arrangements"** with **"obligations"**. The warranty expressly excludes the sale agreement as otherwise the agreement to sell the target company itself would strictly conflict with the warranty, although it is difficult to see how a breach of the warranty in that respect could give rise to a claim for damages.

## 1.8 Commissions

**1.8.1 No one is entitled to receive from the Company a finder's fee, broker-**    7–20
**age or other commission in connection with the sale and purchase of the Shares under this Agreement.**

Section 151 of CA 1985, makes it illegal for a company to give financial assistance in connection with the purchase of its own shares or the shares of its holding company. Payment of a commission, particularly if payable by a subsidiary of the target company, could therefore result in an infringement of the section. In certain cases, for example involving local authorities, it is also possible that payment of the commission could involve corruption and the warranty would minimise any possibility of the purchaser being involved in this corruption. (Warranty 4.25.1 below deals with the issue of 'sensitive payments'.) This warranty also serves the practical function of reducing the chances of a subsequent dispute as to who is liable for any broker's fees and is quite often extended to cover legal fees to ensure that no personal fees of the shareholders are being met by the target company.

## 1.9 Elective and written resolutions

**1.9.1 The Company has not passed an elective resolution under CA 1985,**    7–21
**s.379A which remains in force.**

A private company may elect, by unanimous resolution:

(1) to reduce the restrictions imposed by CA 1985, s.80 on the number of shares which may be allotted by directors and the period of their authority;

(2) to dispense with the obligations under CA 1985, s.252 to lay accounts before shareholders in a general meeting;

(3) to dispense with the holding of annual general meetings;

(4) to reduce from 95 per cent to 90 per cent the holdings of shares which must belong to shareholders consenting to a meeting being held at short notice; and/or

(5) to dispense with the annual appointment of auditors.

The elective regime, even if adopted, is optional and no harm results if it is ignored. The warranty accordingly has value merely for information purposes but the vendors will normally have no reasonable grounds for rejecting it.

7–22     **1.9.2 The Company has complied with CA 1985, s.381B by giving notice to its auditors of all written resolutions passed or to be passed by it from April 1, 1990 to June 18, 1996 and the auditors gave no notice of objection.**

It has long been the practice for articles of association to provide for resolutions to be effective if signed by all shareholders. A similar statutory regime was introduced by CA 1989, as CA 1985, ss.381A–C, with the addition of a safeguard in relation to auditors. The legislation originally provided that a signed resolution under this procedure would not be effective unless and until the auditors had been notified of it and either confirmed that it did not concern them or failed to react within seven days. This administrative requirement was unfortunate as a third party had no way of knowing whether the procedure had been followed, whether the auditors did object or what was the timing of when the resolution became effective. The position was altered by the Deregulation (Resolutions of Private Companies) Order 1996 so that the validity of the resolution is no longer affected by failure to notify the auditors. A further difficulty with the original legislation was the possibility that the statutory procedure overrode any equivalent provisions in a company's articles of association (see CA 1985, s.381C(1)). This doubt has also been removed by the Order.

   The warranty is accordingly of no relevance in relation to resolutions passed after June 19, 1996, being the date when the Order came into force. Written resolutions apparently passed after the sections came into force on April 1, 1990 and before June 19, 1996 must still be treated with caution. The warranty will help the checking process, as the vendors will need to review their records before accepting it. If doubt exists regarding any particular resolution, the parties should consider whether possible deficiencies could be rectified by an appropriate ratification by the shareholders.

*1.10 Memoranda and articles of association, statutory books and resolutions*

7–23   **1.10.1 The copy of the memorandum and articles of association of the Company attached to the Disclosure Letter is accurate and complete and has**

**embodied in it, or attached to it, a copy of every resolution which is referred to in CA 1985, s.380(2).**

Section 380 applies to:

(1) special resolutions;

(2) extraordinary resolutions;

(3) elective resolutions and resolutions revoking an elective resolution;

(4) resolutions or agreements which have been agreed to by all the members but which, if not so agreed to, would not have been effective unless passed as special or extraordinary resolutions;

(5) resolutions or agreements which have been agreed to by all the members of a class of shareholders but which, if not so agreed to, would not have been effective unless passed by some particular majority or otherwise in some particular manner, and all resolutions that effectively bind all of the members of any class of shareholders though not agreed to by all those members;

(6) a directors' resolution to change the company's name following a direction of the Secretary of State;

(7) resolutions creating, varying, revoking or renewing the authority of directors to allot shares;

(8) a directors' resolution altering the company's memorandum on the company ceasing to be a public company following acquisition of its own shares;

(9) resolutions creating, varying, revoking or renewing a s.166 authority (market purchase of own shares);

(10) resolutions requiring the company to be wound up voluntarily;

(11) resolutions to re-register old public companies; and

(12) directors' resolutions allowing title to a public company's shares to be evidenced and transferred without written instrument.

The purchaser will normally have made a search at the Companies Registry against the company but it remains a possibility that the memoranda and articles of association which are shown on the files are not correct. This could be as a result of a failure to file resolutions or arise from the fact that the resolutions do not have to be filed before a lapse of 15 days from the date of passing. There is therefore always the possibility that a company's file will not be up to date.

It will be noted that the warranty requires the copies of the memoranda and articles of association to be annexed to the disclosure letter so that there is no question as to the copies which are warranted. If the disclosure letter contains the normal exclusion from the scope of the warranties of matters which appear on the file at the Companies Registry (see, for example, paragraph (3) in para.9–09), the first half of this warranty will for all practical purposes be rendered inoperative.

**7–24    1.10.2 The register of members and other statutory books of the Company have been properly kept and contain an accurate and complete record of the matters with which they should deal.**

The statutory books of a company are the register of members (CA 1985, s.352), overseas branch register (if one is kept) (s.362), index of members where the number of members exceed 50 (s.354), register of debenture holders (s.190), register of charges (s.407), register of directors and secretary (s.288), register of directors' interests (s.325) and register of interests in shares (s.213). As it is quite possible that minor, irrelevant inaccuracies exist in the statutory books, for example in listing other directorships of a past director, the vendors might wish to qualify the warranty so that immaterial errors are excluded. However, in practice it is most unlikely that such errors could entitle the purchaser to make a claim and the vendors should therefore be able to leave the warranty unchanged without undue concern.

**7–25    1.10.3 No notice or allegation has been received that the statutory books of the Company are incorrect or should be rectified.**

Powers of rectification of the registers of members and charges exist under CA 1985, ss.359 and 404. Although the purchaser is substantially protected by the warranties as to charges and in respect of title to the shares and ownership of the subsidiaries, it is also of importance to the purchaser that the registered particulars are not in dispute.

**7–26    1.10.4 Since the Balance Sheet Date, no alteration has been made to the memorandum or articles of association of the Company and no resolution has been passed by its shareholders (other than resolutions relating to routine business at annual general meetings).**

Until a new form of Table A was introduced by the Companies (Tables A to F) Regulations 1985 (SI 1985 No 805) a distinction was made between special and other business at annual general meetings. Any business was special other than declaring a dividend, considering the accounts, electing directors in place of those retiring and appointing auditors. This distinction no longer appears in Table A, although the articles of association of a company may, either expressly or by adoption of a previous form of Table A, retain the concept. The use of the word **"routine"** would appear satisfactory to cover the resolutions mentioned for any normal company.

The copies of the memoranda and articles of association of the target company whose accuracy is warranted under cl.1.10.1 should reveal most relevant resolutions passed by them and the dates on which they were passed. Nevertheless the purchaser is entitled to be specifically satisfied that no change has taken place in the memoranda and articles of association since the last accounts were prepared as in certain cases a change could affect the treatment of the accounts. Thus, for example, an amendment to the memorandum of association of an investment company to make it into a trading company could alter the tax treatment of its fixed assets. It is also possible for an ordinary resolution to have been passed, for example giving approval to substantial property transactions involving directors under CA 1985, s.320, where there is no obligation to file the resolution.

## 1.11 Documents filed

**1.11.1 All returns, particulars, resolutions and documents required by CA   7–27
1985 [or other legislation] to be filed with the Registrar of Companies [or other authority] in respect of the Company have been duly filed and were accurate and complete.**

The filing obligations imposed by CA 1985 are extensive and it is not realistic to attempt to list all of them. While the purchaser is entitled to be satisfied that these obligations have been fully performed, to ensure both freedom from default penalties and that the searches against the target company will be complete, the actual wording of the warranty is quite onerous. It is not unusual for filing of annual returns and accounts to be late but the vendors should be able to disclose all cases of late filing, at any rate within a reasonably recent period.

The extension of the warranty to filing obligations under legislation other than CA 1985 and the reference to **"other legislation"** are so wide in their scope that they are unlikely to be acceptable to the vendors. Indeed, the warranty could be interpreted as applying even to the filing of tax returns. The vendors may find the warranty more acceptable by the inclusion of the words in brackets.

**1.11.2 All charges in favour of the Company have (if appropriate) been   7–28
registered in accordance with the provisions of CA 1985, Part XII.**

Most, but not all, charges created by a company (or to which property acquired by a company is already subject) must be registered within 21 days to be effective. Chapter I of Part XII (ss.395–409) relates to registration of charges by companies registered in England and Wales; Ch.II (ss.410–424) containing similar provisions for companies registered in Scotland. Sections 395 and 410 provide that a registerable charge which is not duly registered is void against a liquidator or administrator and any creditor of the company, and any money secured by the charge becomes immediately payable. Furthermore, if a registerable change is not registered within the prescribed time limits, the company and each officer of the company is liable to a default fine. The effect of ss.409 and 424 is to extend the filing obligation to charges on property in the United

Kingdom which are created, and to charges on property in the United Kingdom which is acquired by an overseas company with an established place of business in the United Kingdom. In *Slavenburg's Bank NV v Intercontinental Natural Resources Ltd* [1980] 1 All E.R. 955, it was decided that the obligation to register a charge created over an asset in England, of a kind described in s.395, applied to all overseas companies having a place of business in England, and that lack of registration under the predecessor of CA 1985, Pt XXIII (which relates to registration of overseas companies) was not conclusive as to the existence of a place of business. Following this decision the cautious view has been to register charges over United Kingdom property created by unregistered overseas companies, the Registrars maintaining the information in the "Slavenburg register".

Sections 395–424 are to be substituted by Companies Act 1989, Sch.15, Pt IV which inserts new CA 1985, ss.703A–N. (As at the time of writing these provisions had not been enacted.) The new provisions resolve the ambiguity that has existed, making it clear that only those overseas companies that have registered as having an established place of business in the United Kingdom under CA 1985 are required to register charges over property in the United Kingdom. (The new sections will also govern the position in relation to overseas companies opening branches in the United Kingdom.)

## 1.12  Possession of documents

**7–29**   **1.12.1 All the title deeds relating to the assets of the Company, an executed copy of all [subsisting written] agreements to which the Company is a party and the original copies of all other documents [which are in force or otherwise relevant to the Company and] which are owned by, or which ought to be in the possession of, the Company are in its possession [or under its control].**

In practice this warranty would normally require modification or the making of disclosures as documents are frequently held by solicitors and bankers as well as by the company itself; alternatively, the final words in brackets could be added to the clause. From an administrative point of view it is obviously important for the purchaser to know where relevant documents are held but there could also be a legal significance in the warranty in that documents held by a third party could give rise to a lien, for example for unpaid fees. The vendors would probably wish to restrict this warranty in relation to documents which are not title deeds, either by deleting the reference to **"other documents"** or by limiting the warranty so that it applies only to documents of material importance to the assets or business of the target company. The words in square brackets are additional amendments which are worth consideration by the vendors.

## 1.13  Investigations

**7–30**   **1.13.1 No investigation or enquiry by, or on behalf of, a governmental or other body in respect of the affairs of the Company is taking place or**

**pending and the Vendors are not aware of any fact or matter that could lead to any such investigation or enquiry.**

The most important form of investigation would be under the powers of the Competition Commission or the EU's European Commission. Extensive powers of investigation also exist under CA 1985, ss.431 and 432. The vendors may not know whether an enquiry is pending and as such that part of the warranty should either be deleted or be qualified by reference to the vendors' knowledge.

### 1.14 Information disclosed to Purchaser correct

**1.14.1 All [material] [written] information given [by any of the Vendors, the 7–31 Vendors' solicitors or the Company's auditors to the Purchaser, the Purchaser's solicitors or the Purchaser's accountants relating to the business, affairs, assets and liabilities of the Company was and is accurate and complete [in all material respects] and opinions, expectations and beliefs included in the information are honestly held and have been arrived at on a reasonable basis after full enquiry] [by the Vendors' solicitors in the form of replies to pre-contract enquiries was when given and is now accurate and complete [in all material respects]].**

The purchaser will wish to achieve the greatest possible cover from this clause by including all information, whether or not committed to writing. The vendors will be interested in maximising certainty by restricting the warranty to written information or even by specifically listing the information which is warranted. They should, in addition, be very cautious about accepting responsibility for information provided by the professional advisers. Although the vendors will also wish to confine the warranty to material matters, for example by making the amendments in square brackets, the purchaser might reasonably maintain, if there is a floor to warranty claims as described in para.3–20, that this provides adequate protection for the vendors against trivial claims. Additionally the vendors should consider whether the word **"affairs"** is reasonable, in that its very breadth can give rise to difficulties in interpretation, and whether it is for them or the purchaser to be responsible for determining whether the information was complete.

The second part of the warranty relating to opinions, expectations and beliefs places a heavy burden upon vendors not involved in the day-to-day running of the company. However, it is not unreasonable for the purchaser to seek protection in respect of matters which are not purely factual. The vendors might seek to restrict the nature and extent of the enquiry undertaken (see cl.4K).

As the warranty relates to information provided by any of the vendors, they should also consider obtaining a mutual confirmation, perhaps in an agreement of the kind described in para.3–16, that each of them is satisfied that the warranty is correct in relation to information given by him. In view of the wide ranging nature of this warranty it will often be restricted to the formal replies to the legal due diligence questionnaire. This can be achieved by amending the warranty so that it relates only to the words contained in the last set of brackets. A well-advised vendor would usually require anything that the purchaser required to be warranted to be dealt with in a specific warranty on the issue.

7–32    **1.14.2 [So far as the Vendors are aware] there are no material facts or circumstances in relation to the assets, business or financial condition of the Company which have not been fully and fairly disclosed in writing to the Purchaser or the Purchaser's solicitors and which, if disclosed, might reasonably have been expected to affect the decision of the Purchaser to enter into this Agreement.**

This is the infamous sweeping-up warranty which is intended to cover any matters not specifically dealt with by the detailed warranties. The fairness or otherwise of this warranty depends entirely on the commercial position of the parties as the objective is to impose upon the vendors the risk of any residual problems not dealt with by the specific warranties. As previously indicated, although the warranties serve a valuable purpose as a checklist, their primary function from a legal point of view is to ensure that the risk that there might exist adverse factors relating to the target company, which were unknown or had not been disclosed, lies on either the vendors or the purchaser on an agreed basis. It will be a matter for negotiation to determine how this residual risk should be borne or shared. At very least, the vendors will wish to avoid giving an absolute warranty by adding the words in square brackets. They should also carefully review the phrase **"fully and fairly"** as it could mean that a disclosure made in good faith was nevertheless ineffective. This warranty is to be contrasted with the immediately preceding one, since in the present case the vendors will prefer to omit the reference to writing. The parties should carefully consider whether it is more appropriate to refer to the decision of **"the Purchaser"** or **"a purchaser"** to provide for either a subjective or objective view.

In most cases where there are full warranties dealing specifically with all areas of importance to a purchaser, this warranty, even in amended form, will not be given by the vendors and it is difficult in such circumstances for the purchaser to justify its inclusion.

## 2  Accounts

### 2.1  The Accounts

7–33    **2.1.1 The Accounts were prepared in accordance with the historical cost convention and with the requirements of all relevant statutes and generally accepted accounting practices; and on the same bases and policies of accounting as adopted for the purpose of preparing the audited accounts of the Company in respect of the preceding three accounting periods.**

Although the accounts will include a statement as to the accounting policies adopted in their preparation, it is appropriate for a warranty to be given that this is a correct statement. The warranty requires that the Accounts (which will usually be the most recent audited accounts or the most recent annual accounts where the target company's accounts are not required to be audited and the ones upon which some or all of the financial valuation will have been based) are warranted as having been prepared in accordance with the historical cost convention and more particularly UK GAAP (by reference to generally accepted accounting practices and that the three prior sets of accounts have been produced consistently.

### 2.1.2 The Accounts:

#### 2.1.2.1  give a true and fair view of the assets and liabilities and state of          7–34 affairs of the Company at the Balance Sheet Date and its profits and cash flow for the period ended on that date;

It is sometimes suggested that the wording of this warranty should be to the effect that the accounts are "true and accurate". This should not be an acceptable form of the warranty, as the statutory obligation under CA 1985, ss.226 and 227 is that the accounts should give a true and fair view of the state of affairs of the company as at the end of the financial year and of the profit or loss for that year. No accounts can claim to provide an "accurate" view and a warranty that the accounts are accurate would be unrealistic. The vendors should endeavour to follow the precise wording that appears in the auditors' reports and might prefer to replace **"give"** by **"gave"**.

#### 2.1.2.2  comply with the requirements of CA 1985;          7–35

The accounts of a company must be presented in one of the forms prescribed in CA 1985, Sch.4, although banking, shipping and insurance companies may choose to use the format in Sch.9.

#### 2.1.2.3  comply with current Accounting Standards;          7–36

The reference to **"Accounting Standards"** includes all FRSs SSAPs, SORPs and UITF Abstracts.

SSAPs were the forerunners of FRSs, the latter being developed by the Accounting Standards Board ("the ASB"). Some SSAPs have been replaced by FRSs, others remain in force. A list can be found on the ASB web site at *www.asb.org.uk*. Normally the accounts would specify where they do not comply with the FRSs but a warranty of compliance is desirable. The vendors should have no difficulty in obtaining from the auditors of the target company details of all necessary disclosures if there has not been full compliance with the FRSs. Alternatively, the warranty could be amended to read:

**"complied with all the FRSs which were at the relevant time applicable to a United Kingdom company."**

The Urgent Issues Task Force (UITF) Abstracts set out the consensus reached by the UITF (a sub-committee of the ASB) on significant accounting issues where unsatisfactory or conflicting interpretations of an existing standard or legislative requirement have developed or appear likely to develop. The UITF Abstracts do not amend or override the accounting standards or other statements adopted or issued by the ASB and are read in conjunction with them. Although the UITF Abstracts are not envisaged by the Companies Acts, it is the expectation of the Consultative Committee of Accountancy Bodies, the ASB and the accountancy profession that they will be observed and it is, therefore, reasonable for a purchaser to require a warranty as to compliance.

Statements of Recommended Practices ("SORPs") are generally issued on subjects on which it is not decided appropriate to issue an accounting standard at that time. They usually relate to auditing specific areas of industry. They do not have mandatory status but are considered "best practice" when they apply. If the target company is in one of the specialist sectors where SORPs are relevant then the warranty will obtain confirmation of compliance or disclosure of non-compliance.

If the vendors wished to achieve greater certainty on cl.2.1.3 they could substitute the defined term **"Accounting Standards"** for **"and with the requirements of all relevant statutes and generally accepted accounting practices"** and then delete cll.2.1.2.2 and 2.1.2.3.

7–37 **2.1.2.4 are not affected by extraordinary, exceptional or non-recurring items;**

Although there is no statutory definition of **"extraordinary items"**, they were defined in SSAP 6 as being derived from events or transactions outside the ordinary activities of the business which were both material and expected not to occur frequently or regularly. They did not include an item which, although exceptional in size or incidence and therefore requiring separate disclosure under CA 1985, Sch.4, para.57(3), derived from the ordinary activities of the business. **"Exceptional items"** were defined in SSAP 6 as deriving from events and transactions which fell within the ordinary activities of the company but which, because of their size or incidence, needed to be disclosed in order to present a true and fair view. This distinction was changed by FRS 3, which has replaced SSAP 6. Extraordinary items now require "a high degree of abnormality" and, as a result, will in future be extremely rare.

As the warranties will invariably include provisions along the lines of cll.2.1.2.1 and 2.1.2.3, this clause adds nothing of value to the purchaser. Indeed, the subjective nature of the concepts referred to in the clause make it difficult for the vendors to accept the clause in its absolute form without amendment.

7–38 **2.1.2.5 fully disclose all the assets of the Company on the Balance Sheet Date;**

Accounts will not necessarily show all assets, for example goodwill which has accrued but has not been shown in the accounts. It would be appropriate for the vendors to qualify this warranty by stating that assets are disclosed to the extent required by CA 1985 and the appropriate FRS and to delete the word **"fully"**. In any event, the purchaser is unlikely to have valid ground for complaint if the warranty proves to be incorrect.

This warranty overlaps, to some extent, the provisions of cl.8.1.1.

**2.1.2.6 [to the extent required by CA 1985 and the relevant FRSs] 7–39 provide or reserve in full for all liabilities and capital commitments of the Company outstanding at the Balance Sheet Date, including contingent, unquantified or disputed liabilities; and**

Provisions for liabilities and charges must be shown as a separate main heading in the balance sheet. These provisions are defined in CA 1985, Sch.4, para.89 as any amounts retained as reasonably necessary for the purpose of providing for a liability or loss which is either likely to be incurred, or certain to be incurred but uncertain as to amount or as to the date on which it will arise. Capital commitments must be noted under CA 1985, Sch.4, para.50(3), if they are contracted for.

FRS 12, which has replaced SSAP 18, has completed the process of moving United Kingdom accounting practice from a decision-based to a commitment-based approach to making provisions. The standard aims to ensure that appropriate recognition criteria and measurement bases are applied to provisions and to contingent assets and liabilities and that disclosure in respect of their nature, timing and amount is sufficient. A contingency is defined as a condition which exists at the balance sheet date where the outcome will be confirmed only on the occurrence of one or more uncertain future events. A material contingent loss should be accrued in the accounts where it is probable that a future event will confirm a loss which can be estimated with reasonable accuracy. Any other material contingent loss should be noted unless the possibility of loss is remote.

As the accounts will of necessity show commitments and liabilities only to the extent required by CA 1985 and the relevant FRS, it would be appropriate for the vendors to amend the warranty by the addition of the bracketed words and the deletion of **"in full"**.

**2.1.2.7 provide or reserve, in accordance with the principles set out in 7–40 the notes included in the Accounts, for all Taxation liable to be assessed on the Company, or for which it may be accountable, in respect of the period ended on the Balance Sheet Date.**

FRS 16 has superseded SSAP 8, which became outdated with the abolition of advanced corporation tax (ACT) early in 1999. It requires that current tax is recognised in the profit and loss account except to the extent that it relates to gains or losses that have been recognised directly in the statement of total recognised gains and losses. The standard is mandatory for accounting periods ending on or after March 23, 2000 and there are transitional arrangements for unrelieved ACT. FRS 19 superseded SSAP 15 for accounting periods ending on or after January 23, 2002. FRS 19 requires that deferred taxation be provided for on a "full provision" basis as opposed to the "partial provision" basis previously required under SSAP 15. The new requirements are designed to bring United Kingdom accounting practice more in line with international requirements although conceptual differences remain.

While the purchaser will wish to ensure that the taxation provisions in the accounts have been accurately prepared, the vendors may prefer to delete this warranty on the basis that the purchaser should rely on the lengthy, detailed tax warranties. If the warranty is given, the vendors should bear in the mind the wide definition of "Taxation" and should amend the wording so that it states that the provision for taxation complies with the applicable FRS.

**7–41     2.1.3 The amount included in the Accounts in respect of each asset, whether fixed or current, did not exceed its purchase price or production cost (within the meaning of CA 1985, Schedule 4) or (in the case of current assets) its [estimated] net realisable value at the Balance Sheet Date.**

Schedule 4 requires that, under the historical cost convention, fixed assets are shown at their purchase price or production cost, less any provision for depreciation or diminution in value. Current assets are shown at purchase price or production cost, or at net realisable value if lower. The determination of purchase price or production costs is to be made in accordance with paras 26 to 28 of the schedule.

The reference to the net realisable value of the assets should be qualified by the vendors by the addition of the word **"estimated"**, as indicated.

*2.2 Valuation of stock in trade and work in progress*

**7–42   2.2.1 In the Accounts and in the accounts of the Company for the three preceding financial years, the stock in trade and work in progress of the Company was treated in accordance with SSAP 9.**

SSAP 9 provides a comprehensive statement as to the determination of the value for accounts purposes of stocks and work in progress. The basic requirement is that these should be stated at the lower of cost and net realisable value of the separate items concerned or of groups of similar items. Long-term contract work in progress is valued at net cost less foreseeable losses and progress payments on account. As there is a subjective element involved in these requirements, the purchaser would generally have difficulty in proving a breach unless the accounts were clearly prepared negligently or on the basis of values which no reasonable person could have thought to be correct.

**7–43     2.2.2 In the Accounts slow-moving stock in trade was written down as appropriate and redundant, obsolete, obsolescent and defective stock was wholly written off and the value attributable to any other stock did not exceed the lower of cost and net realisable value at the Balance Sheet Date.**

Appendix 1 to SSAP 9, dealing with practical considerations in relation to the valuation of stocks and work in progress, provides that the main circumstances in which the net realisable value is likely to be less than cost are where there is an increase in costs or fall in selling price, physical deterioration, obsolescence, a decision to manufacture or sell at a loss, or errors in production or purchasing. If stocks are unlikely to be sold within the normal turnover period, the resulting increased likelihood of deterioration or obsolescence should be taken into account. Although the last accounts should therefore have taken into consideration the factors mentioned in this clause, the vendors should resist the warranty on the grounds that it involves highly subjective judgments and that the purchaser is adequately protected by cl.2.2.1.

**2.2.3 In valuing work in progress in the Accounts no value was attributed    7–44
in respect of eventual profit and adequate provision was made for such losses
as were at the time of signature of the Accounts by the directors of the
Company foreseeable as arising or likely to arise on completion and/or
realisation thereof.**

This warranty focuses on the work in progress dealt with in cl.2.2.1. It is designed to flush out early attributions of profit and adequate provision for losses on work in progress.

## 2.3 Depreciation of fixed assets

**2.3.1 In the Accounts and in the accounts of the Company for the three    7–45
preceding financial years, the fixed assets of the Company were depreciated
in accordance with FRS 15.**

FRS 15, which has superseded SSAP 12, deals with the accounting treatment required to provide for depreciation of tangible fixed assets, other than investment properties. The standard seeks consistency in the initial measurement, valuation and depreciation of fixed assets and introduces some new requirements aimed at precluding perceived abuses. Broadly speaking, tangible fixed assets are initially recorded at cost and then depreciated on a systematic basis over their useful economic lives. A significant change is that FRS 15 introduces a formal framework for revaluation, which must be carried out on a periodic basis.

## 2.4 Deferred Taxation

**2.4.1 Where provision for deferred Taxation is not made in the Accounts, full    7–46
details of the amounts of deferred Taxation have been disclosed in the
Disclosure Letter.**

For a short summary of FRS19, which deals with deferred taxation, see the commentary on cl.2.1.2.8. Although the purchaser might reasonably seem to be entitled to full details of deferred taxation which is not shown in the accounts, the vendors should consider carefully whether the purchaser would suffer a loss, and therefore be entitled to the protection of a warranty, if these details proved for any reason to be incorrect.

### 2.5  Accounting reference date

**7–47    2.5.1 The accounting reference date of the Company for the purposes of CA 1985, s.224 is, and has always been, [ ].**

The accounting reference date of a company is defined by s.224, being the date in the calendar year on which the accounting reference period of the company is to be treated as coming to an end. There are complicated provisions in CA 1985, s.225 defining the circumstances in which an accounting reference date may be changed and these may be of significance in taxation matters. In principle, an accounting period for taxation purposes ends when the accounting period ends in accordance with CA 1985. If, however, the period of the accounts is for more than 12 months, the first 12 months are treated as one accounting period for taxation purposes and the balance of the period as another (ICTA 1988, s.12). As it may be essential for taxation purposes to extend or shorten an accounting period to ensure that profits or losses arise in the appropriate period, the restrictions contained in s.225 could be important. The vendors should ask the purchaser for a clear statement of the reason why it requires this warranty so that a determination can be made of the resulting exposure which they would incur.

### 2.6  Management Accounts

**7–48    2.6.1 The Management Accounts have been prepared in accordance with accounting policies consistent with those used in the preparation of the Accounts, with all due care and on a basis consistent with the management accounts of the Company prepared in the preceding [year]. The cumulative profits, assets and liabilities of the Company stated in the Management Accounts have not been [materially] misstated.**

The wording of this warranty is likely to be the subject of much negotiation between the vendors and the purchaser. As with the last accounts, the vendors will be most reluctant to warrant the management accounts as "accurate" for the reasons given with respect to cl.2.1.2.1 and further because the procedures used in their preparation are likely to be less rigorous than those at audit. The aim of the wording at the start of the warranty which refers to consistency with the last accounts is to flush out, by disclosure, differences between the accounting policies adopted in the management accounts and those in the last accounts which will in most instances have been audited. The parties would do well to remind themselves of the requirement of CA 1985, s.221 which requires a company to keep accounts which disclose with reasonable accuracy, at any time, the financial position of the company at that time.

**7–49**    The vendors might seek to avoid giving any warranties with regard to the management accounts, beyond confirmation of compliance with CA 1985, s.221 (see cl.2.7.1.4), particularly when completion accounts are to be prepared in respect of the period from the Balance Sheet Date to completion.

The purchaser might argue with some justification that the "materiality" qualification is unnecessary if the agreement includes *de minimis* provisions.

Given that the management accounts will usually be annexed to the disclosure letter, the vendors will need to be careful that they do not indirectly warrant their accuracy by virtue of general wording in the disclosure letter of the type discussed in Ch.9.

## 2.7  Books and records

### 2.7.1 The accounting and other records of the Company:          7–50

#### 2.7.1.1  are in its exclusive ownership and direct control;

Section 222 of CA 1985 requires that the accounting records of a company are kept at its registered office or at such other place as the directors think fit. If the records are kept abroad, the company must send certain accounts and returns to be kept in Great Britain.

The purpose of this warranty is primarily as a reminder, to ensure that the purchaser will obtain possession of all the books and records of the target company. An example of circumstances where this might otherwise be overlooked is where the target company is a subsidiary of a corporate vendor and the books of the target company are maintained, perhaps on a computer, by the parent company which is not being sold.

The reference to "other records" should be considered carefully by the vendors in view of its potentially wide reaching scope. It may also be appropriate to restrict the warranty to accounts and other records of not more than a certain age, particularly as CA 1985, s.222 requires private companies to preserve their accounting records for only three years, as compared with six years for public companies.

#### 2.7.1.2  have been fully, properly and accurately kept and completed;          7–51

On the face of it this is an onerous warranty in that it is most unlikely in practice that any records will be entirely free from deficiencies. On the other hand, if these are of a minimal nature they will in practice not result in any liability under the warranty as the purchaser will suffer no loss.

#### 2.7.1.3  are accurate in all material respects;          7–52

Even with the qualification **"in all material respects"**, this is an onerous warranty. The purchaser will generally have relied only on the accuracy of the accounts and will invariably have various warranties in this respect. The vendors might reasonably argue that the purchaser is not entitled to further protection.

#### 2.7.1.4  show a true and fair view of its trading transactions and its          7–53
#### financial, contractual and trading position.

Section 2211 of CA 1985 requires that the accounting records which every company is obliged to keep should disclose with reasonable accuracy, at any time, the financial position of the company at that time. As the books will provide on a daily basis a less comprehensive picture than the true and fair view of the annual accounts, it is apparent that the statutory obligation is less onerous than the requirements of this warranty. The vendors may seek to limit this warranty to the requirements of s.221.

**7–54**     **2.7.2 Full disclosure has been made to the Company's auditors and all previous auditors of the Company of all matters relevant to the preparation of the Accounts and any previous audited financial statements of the Company.**

The preparation of audited accounts requires disclosure to the auditors by the directors of all relevant matters. If the directors have been remiss either deliberately or negligently then it is likely that the accounts will be inaccurate. This warranty is designed to cover that scenario. In practice the vendors will have little difficulty in giving this warranty when they are also the directors. Where they are not they might seek to qualify it by awareness.

## 3  Finance

### 3.1  Capital commitments

**7–55**     **3.1.1 No commitments on capital account were outstanding at the Balance Sheet Date and, since then, the Company has not [to any material extent] made, or agreed to make capital expenditure, incurred or agreed to incur capital commitments, or disposed of or agreed to dispose of capital assets (or any interest in them).**

Unless qualified by the reference to materiality as indicated in square brackets, this clause will normally be unduly onerous. Although the purchaser might argue that the purpose of the warranties floor (see para.3–20), if there is one, is to avoid the necessity of qualifying the warranty in this way, the vendors might reasonably maintain that the warranty, if unqualified, would result in unfair and inappropriate inroads being made into the cushion provided by the floor. If the warranty is amended, it would be as well, in cases of doubt, to clarify what is intended by **"material"**. This will not usually give rise to difficulty but, where there is a programme of capital purchases, it may be as well to insert a specific sum per item and an aggregate limit below which disclosure is not required.

### 3.2  Bank and other borrowings

**7–56**     **3.2.1 Particulars of all money borrowed by the Company are set out in the Disclosure Letter. The Company does not have any bank borrowings which exceed applicable overdraft limits (and has not had any that have done so during the last 12 months).**

The purchaser will want to know details of all money borrowed by the target company, not least to ensure that the company does not have any borrowings that it is not already aware of.

It is important for the purchaser to know whether a temporary accommodation has been given to the company by its bankers allowing it to exceed its normal facilities. It will, however, be appreciated that overdrafts are invariably repayable on demand and a facility can normally be withdrawn at any time. It is accordingly unlikely that the purchaser could prove any loss if the warranty was breached as, in general, the only sanction for the bank would be to exercise the right it has in any case to call for immediate repayment. The last part of the clause is designed to elicit details of prior excesses and should allow the purchaser to determine whether current facilties are sufficient.

**3.2.2 The total amount borrowed by the Company (as determined in**   7–57
**accordance with the provisions of the relevant documents) does not exceed**
**any limitation on borrowing powers contained in its articles of association or**
**in a debenture or other document.**

In practice, a breach of borrowing limits imposed by a loan stock or debenture trust deed has more serious implications than a breach of borrowing limits contained in the articles of association. Most trust deeds contain a provision entitling the lenders or trustees to call in the loan immediately in the event of an infringement of the borrowing restrictions. If there is particular concern about this, the purchaser should examine any such restrictions to satisfy itself, so far as possible, that no breach has occurred. If there has been a breach and the right to call in a loan or debenture is exercised as a result, the compensation for breach of warranty is unlikely to provide much satisfaction.

**3.2.3 The Company does not have outstanding nor has it agreed to create**   7–58
**or issue any loan capital nor has it factored or discounted its debts or**
**engaged in financing of a type which would not require to be shown or fully**
**reflected in the Accounts or borrowed money which it has not repaid, save**
**for borrowings not exceeding the amounts shown in the Accounts.**

Debt factoring or invoice discounting involves the sale of debts and, where factoring has taken place, it would be appropriate to ensure that the target company has not given a warranty that the debts will be recoverable in full or to any specified extent. Factoring is a method of financing which may be off-balance sheet and the purchaser will be entitled to ensure that all financing arrangements by the target company have been fully disclosed.

**3.2.4 The Company has not since the Balance Sheet Date repaid or**   7–59
**become liable to repay any loan or other indebtedness in advance of its**
**stated maturity.**

This warranty should present little difficulty to the vendors and, as the continuing availability of facilities may be of some importance to the purchaser, there will normally be no reasonable basis for objecting to it.

7–60     **3.2.5 The Company has not received notice (whether formal or informal) [which remains outstanding] from any lenders of money, requiring repayment or intimating the enforcement of security which it holds over assets of the Company; and [so far as the Vendors are aware] there are no circumstances likely to give rise to such a notice.**

The purchaser is entitled to ensure that financial facilities apparently available to the target company have not been withdrawn but, without the qualifications of the words in square brackets, the vendors might reasonably consider the clause to be too onerous.

### 3.3 Bank accounts

7–61 **3.3.1 Statements of all the bank accounts of the Company, showing their balances as at a date not more than seven days before today's date, have been supplied to the Purchaser.**

The delivery to the purchaser of up-to-date bank statements will be of interest only if the purchaser is able to carry out a reconciliation with the financial statements which have been provided to it. Even then the warranty serves little purpose as it is unlikely that a breach would entitle the purchaser to any damages.

7–62     **3.3.2 Since the date of each statement, there have been no payments out of the account to which the statement relates, except for payments in the normal course of business; and the balances on current accounts are not substantially different from the balances shown in the statements.**

Insofar as this provision relates to transactions which have occurred up to the date of the sale agreement, it is not difficult for the vendors to check the accuracy of the warranty although they will need to consider carefully what payments are within the normal course of business. Nevertheless, the vendors might reasonably consider that this is not a matter upon which the purchaser is entitled to a warranty if there are clauses in the agreement corresponding to cl.4.1 which covers in some detail the activities which have occurred between the balance sheet date and the date of the agreement. Furthermore, if the warranty is extended so that it applies also at completion (when there is a gap between contracts and completion) and there is a delay of any significance between the date of the signing of the contract and the date of completion, this will amount in effect to a cash flow warranty. In the case of a normal trading company where a material interval is involved, it would be unreasonable to expect the vendors to give a warranty as to the precise cash position at completion since this will depend upon a variety of arbitrary events. Where the transaction involves completion accounts, cash in hand will simply form part of the overall net assets. The cash position may be far more important where the transaction has been structured on a "debt and cash free" basis. In these circumstances the gross price that has been agreed will be adjusted by reference to the level of debt (as a deduction off the price) and by the addition of "excess cash" which would normally be determined by reference to any excess over normal working capital requirements. An example of this is contained in Ch.13.

## 3.4 Continuation of facilities

**3.4.1 The Disclosure Letter sets out full details of (and there are attached to it accurate copies of all documents relating to) all debentures, acceptance credits, loans or other financial facilities outstanding or available to the Company (referred to in this clause as the "Facilities") and of any limits or restrictions to which they are subject.**                                    7–63

Although the purchaser should require production of copies of all documents relating to material financing facilities, the vendors should not expect simply by producing the documents to avoid an obligation, under a warranty corresponding to cl.4.16.1, to disclose to the purchaser specifically provisions in the facility documents of a particularly onerous nature. It is not clear that the purchaser would normally have any remedy if the disclosure omitted a facility.

**3.4.2 There has been no contravention of, or non-compliance with, the terms of the Facilities.**                                                         7–64

In practice it is not always possible to avoid minor infringements of the extensive restrictions which are to be found in some facility documents and the vendors and the purchaser will need to negotiate as to which of them carries the ultimate risk that a minor infringement gives a creditor the right to terminate a facility or call in a loan.

**3.4.3 No steps for the early repayment of sums outstanding under the Facilities have been taken or threatened and [so far as the Vendors are aware] no circumstances have occurred which give rise to an obligation to make, or would permit the calling for, early repayment.**                        7–65

This provision will need qualification if a threat has been made in the past but withdrawn; in that event it would be appropriate to add the words **"and not withdrawn"** after **"threatened"** and **"which remain outstanding"** after **"occurred"**. The vendors may wish to limit the warranty by adding the words in brackets given its wide ranging nature.

**3.4.4 There have not been and are no circumstances known to the Vendors whereby the continuation of any of the Facilities might be prejudiced or their terms altered.**                                                          7–66

This warranty is drafted so that the knowledge of the vendors is stated to relate to the circumstances and not to the impact that the circumstances will have on the continued availability of the facilities. The vendors may wish to consider altering the wording so that it reads:

**There have been and are no circumstances which, so far as the Vendors are aware, are likely to prejudice the continuation of any of the Facilities or to give rise to an alteration in their terms.**

7–67     **3.4.5 None of the Facilities is dependent on the guarantee or indemnity of, or security provided by, a third party.**

This provides an important reminder to both parties. The vendors will wish to ensure that any guarantee or security given by a third party is released when the sale takes place while the purchaser will require details of any such circumstances so that it can consider what alternative arrangements should be made.

## 3.5 Debts

7–68   **3.5.1 No part of the amounts included in debtors in the Accounts, or subsequently recorded in the books of the Company as owing by a debtor, is overdue by more than 90 days, has been released on terms that the debtor pays less than the full book value of his debt, has been written off, has had a credit issued against it or has proved to be, or is regarded as, wholly or partly irrecoverable.**

This is substantially a straightforward factual matter insofar as it relates to the position of debtors at the date of the exchange of the agreement but careful consideration will be necessary if there is a general clause in the agreement which extends the warranties to the completion date. In such a case, the vendors should, if possible, provide that the extension does not apply to this warranty. Alternatively, they should ensure that the length of the period which is specified in the warranty, as being the maximum period for which debtors are overdue, takes into account the anticipated duration of the interval between contracts and completion when there is to be a gap between the two.

7–69     **3.5.2 The amounts due from [trade] debtors as at Completion [(less the amount of any relevant provision or reserve, determined on the same basis as that applied in the Accounts and disclosed in the Disclosure Letter)] will be recoverable in full, in the normal course of business, and in any event not later than 60 days after Completion; and none of the debts is subject to a right of counterclaim or set-off, or withholding or other deduction except to the extent of the provision or reserve.**

This warranty is unusual in that it extends to events that will be determined only after completion, when the vendors will no longer have control over the target company. The collection of debts after completion is largely in the hands of the purchaser and, if the target company continues to trade with a slow payer, there may be disputes as to whether a payment by the debtor relates to any particular debt. The vendors might wish to provide that, unless a debtor appropriates a payment to a specific debt, then payments by the debtor are treated as discharging older rather than more recent debts (see para.11–07).

This provision amounts to a guarantee of outstanding debts and will not be appropriate unless in some manner the purchase price for the target company was determined on the basis that the debts would be good. If the vendors agree to give the warranty, they should consider restricting it to trade debtors if there are other debts, such as loans, outstanding. They should also require that any debt which falls within the warranty should be assigned to them for a consideration which would in particular take account of any threshold for warranty claims which may have been agreed. If, following the assignment, the debt proves to be bad, it is likely that the vendors will be entitled to an allowable loss for capital gains tax purposes since they would not be the original creditors in relation to the debt. This area involves quite difficult questions which are analysed in more detail in para.11–09.

The vendors should be entitled to qualify the warranty by the addition of the words in the second pair of brackets.

**3.5.3 Complete and accurate details, including repayment terms, of loans made by the Company which remain outstanding are set out in the Disclosure Letter and all the loans will be repaid in full by their maturity dates.** 7–70

The first part of this warranty has little more than informational value but the second part effectively amounts to a guarantee by the vendors and is unlikely to be acceptable to them. If the concept is agreed, the wording should at least be qualified by wording such as **"provided that no time or indulgence is granted to the debtors"**.

**3.5.4 The Company has not made a loan or quasi-loan contrary to CA 1985.** 7–71

Loans to directors, and similar arrangements, are prohibited by CA 1985, ss.330–340. A quasi-loan, which is defined in s.331, arises if the target company agrees to pay a sum to a third party for the benefit of a director who is then himself liable to reimburse the target company. Quasi-loans are prohibited for a "relevant" company, that is a company which either is not itself a private company or is in a group, some member of which is not a private company. This definition is capable of having unexpected results in that a company, which on the face of it is part of a private group, may find that it is a relevant company because a fellow subsidiary happens to be a plc. If the target company's group of companies does not contain any company which is a relevant company, the reference to a quasi-loan could be replaced by a warranty that no company in the target company's group of companies is a relevant company within the meaning of s.331.

**3.5.5 The Company has not made a loan, which remains outstanding, on terms entitling it to receive either a rate of interest varying with, or a share of, the profits of a business.** 7–72

A loan to a person engaged in a business on the terms described in this clause is *prima facie* evidence of a partnership (Partnership Act 1890, s.2). Unless the loan agreement is in writing signed by all the parties, the lender's right of recovery is postponed to all other creditors of the borrower. The implications of a loan of this nature for the purchaser are obvious and it is reasonable for the purchaser to seek protection. If the terms of a loan are such that it is unclear whether it could fall within s.2, the details could be disclosed to the purchaser and the parties could negotiate as to who should take the risk of difficulty.

### 3.6 Liabilities

7–73    **3.6.1 The Company has no outstanding liabilities (including disputed or contingent liabilities) other than the liabilities disclosed in the Accounts or incurred, in the normal course of business, since the Balance Sheet Date.**

A liability is outstanding so long as it remains in existence and the vendors will wish to consider carefully what liabilities could be covered by this warranty. It will be noted that the exclusion for transactions in the course of business relates only to those which were incurred since the last accounts date. The vendors should amend the warranty so that all liabilities incurred in the normal course of business are excluded, whenever they arose (but see the discussion in relation to cl.4.1.1.1). Furthermore, as the accounts will disclose liabilities only so far as required by the appropriate accounting conventions, the vendors should exclude liabilities which on normal accounting principles would not have appeared in the last accounts.

7–74    **3.6.2 The Company has not been the tenant of, or a guarantor in respect of, a leasehold property which is not one of the Properties.**

If a target company was the original lessee of premises under a lease granted before January 1, 1996, it will remain contingently liable to the lessor by virtue of the privity of contract between them, notwithstanding a subsequent assignment. Even if it were not the original lessee it will normally, upon taking the assignment of the lease, have given covenants for indemnity to its predecessor in title. There is therefore a contingent liability in the event of the current tenant defaulting under the lease. In the case of leases granted on or after January 1, 1996, the assignee of a lease ceases to be liable except to the extent of any liability arising under an authorised guarantee agreement (Landlord and Tenant (Covenants) Act 1995; see also cl.8.6 in para.6–63).

If a disclosure has to be made under this warranty in relation to a substantial lease, the purchaser may wish to consider the quality of the covenant of the present tenant so that an analysis can be made of the likelihood of a default which would involve the target company.

7–75    **3.6.3 There has been no exercise, purported exercise or claim for any Encumbrance over any of the assets of the Company and there is no dispute directly or indirectly relating to any assets.**

"**Encumbrance**" is widely defined. The purchaser will be concerned to ensure that there is no claim over or dispute in respect of any of the assets of the target company.

## 3.7 Working capital

**3.7.1 Having regard to the Facilities (as defined in clause [3.4.1]), the     7–76
Company has sufficient working capital to carry on its business, in its
present form and at its present level of turnover, for 12 months after
Completion and to carry out, in accordance with their terms, all outstanding
commitments.**

The first part of this warranty closely follows the statement that has to be given by directors of a company when making a public issue and the vendors must carry out a careful cash flow analysis if they are to give it. The vendors might require that a definition of working capital is included, such as "debtors, prepayments and stock, less creditors and accruals". The second part of the warranty will depend on events after completion, including the way the purchaser procures that the target company fulfils its subsisting obligations, and is not something to which the vendors should readily agree. Although the warranty is onerous, it must be recognised that a purchaser will have difficulty in ever showing a breach of warranty unless it can demonstrate that the assumptions made in preparing the cash flow statement were, or should have been, known by the vendors to have been incorrect. In assessing whether such a warranty has been breached, in circumstances where the actual outcome differs from the projected figures, the court will ask whether the forecast in question was a reasonable interpretation of the relevant information. If it concludes that it was, then there will have been no breach of warranty (see *Lion Nathan Ltd and others v CC Bottlers Ltd and others* [1996] 2 B.C.L.C. 371). It would also be appropriate for the vendors to include a statement of the assumptions upon which the cash flow statement is believed to be correct, such as no major insolvencies among customers, no significant changes in tax rates and no events occurring of a general nature which would cause a properly prepared cash flow forecast to be rendered inaccurate.

## 3.8 Dividends and distributions

**3.8.1 Since the Balance Sheet Date, no dividend or other distribution (as     7–77
defined in ICTA 1988, Part VI and s.418) has been, or is treated as having
been, declared, paid or made by the Company.**

ICTA 1988, Pt VI (and particularly s.209) contains extensive definitions of "distributions" which include not only dividends but also any distributions out of assets and such special cases as issues of bonus redeemable shares. Section 418 brings within the definition expenditure incurred in providing benefits for shareholders in close companies.

The purpose of this warranty is to protect the purchaser against deliberate reductions in shareholders' funds occurring in the period between the end of the last accounting period and contracts. Often a purchaser will require a certain level of net assets at completion. This warranty would require disclosure of any "distributions" in favour of the shareholders since the end of the last accounting period, allowing the purchaser to check that the likely level of net assets will be as expected.

Although the warranty is intended to deal with dividends as understood for CA purposes, it is nevertheless convenient, for the purchaser, to extend the concept of dividends to include the wide tax definition of distributions. The vendors might prefer to amend the warranty so that it relates only to dividends and distributions within the meaning of CA 1985. The purchaser cannot reasonably object to such an amendment as the taxation implications of other distributions will be covered by the detailed tax warranties.

7–78    **3.8.2 All dividends and distributions declared, made or paid by the Company were declared, made or paid in accordance with its articles of association and the applicable provisions of CA 1985 and in accordance with any agreements or arrangements between the Company, its shareholders or any third party regulating the payment or declaration of dividends.**

If a dividend has been improperly paid, it will normally be recoverable by the paying company. In general a purchaser will not be concerned about this aspect, since any defect in a dividend payment by a target company can operate only to the benefit of that company. The warranty will, however, be of significance to a purchaser if, for example, there are different classes of shares, as a shareholder who has not received the appropriate payment could have a claim against the target company. Similarly, if dividends have been paid improperly by reference to a shareholders agreement, that could result in a claim against the company, it often being a party to such arrangements.

The clause, as expressed, applies to the whole term of existence of the target company and, unless the target company is comparatively newly formed, the vendors should consider restricting the warranty to a reasonable past period.

*3.9 Government grants*

7–79    **3.9.1 The Company has not in the last 6 years applied for, or received, a grant, subsidy or financial assistance from any government department or agency, or a local or other authority.**

Many grants are repayable if certain conditions are not fulfilled and the vendors should have no difficulty in determining whether this warranty applies. The purchaser will wish to know what conditions remain outstanding so that it can review its plans for the target company with them in mind. There are also certain taxation implications which can arise in relation to grants. Thus, for example, if the grant is made in connection with the acquisition of plant or machinery generally capital allowances will be obtained only on the net amount (CAA 2001 s.532). A write-off of a government investment in a company reduces the company's tax losses as at the end of the accounting period ending last before the write-off date (ICTA 1988, s.400).

## 4 Trading and contracts

### 4.1 Changes in business activities and financial position since the Balance Sheet Date

#### 4.1.1 Since the Balance Sheet Date: 7–80

**4.1.1.1 the business of the Company has been continued in its normal course [as regards the nature, extent and manner of carrying it on] with a view to maintaining the business as a going concern and without entering into any transaction assuming any liability or making any payment which is not provided for in the Accounts or which is not in the normal course of its business;**

The purchaser is entitled to be sure that the target company has carried on its business in the normal manner since the balance sheet date and will also wish to ensure that it continues to do so up to completion. To refer to continuing in "the ordinary course of business" would provide the purchaser with little protection as it is clear from such cases as in *Borax Company, Re* [1901] 1 Ch 326 that almost any transaction within the powers of a company, short of a disposal of its whole business, can be in the ordinary course. It is therefore desirable from the purchaser's point of view to refer to "normal" or "ordinary and proper". For the vendors these concepts are not clear unless the target company has acted in a purely routine manner and they would need to satisfy themselves that there is no problem in identifying what constitutes the "normal" course of the business. They may also wish to add the words in square brackets which limit the scope of the warranty, although each of the words **"nature"**, **"extent"** and **"manner"** would need to be considered carefully if the words are to be added.

**4.1.1.2 there has been no deterioration in the turnover, or financial or 7–81 trading position [or prospects, of the Company [except as a result of factors generally affecting similar businesses] [to a similar extent];**

While there should be little difficulty in practice in determining whether turnover has been maintained, this will not necessarily be a fair warranty if trade is of a seasonal nature. Greater difficulty may be experienced in warranting the financial and trading position of the target company in view of the vagueness of these concepts and the fact that the accuracy of the warranty would be very dependent on events occurring after completion. **"Prospects"** would rarely be warranted by the vendors. It would usually be appropriate for them to add the words in the second pair of square brackets, in which case the purchaser should add a qualification such as that in the second pair.

**4.1.1.3 the Company has not by doing, or omitting to do, anything 7–82 [materially] prejudiced its goodwill;**

This warranty, which may at first sight seem to be comparatively innocuous, is in fact potentially very onerous. If goodwill is a measure of the ability to generate profits, then a warranty as to the maintenance of goodwill amounts to a warranty as to the ability to maintain profitability. In addition, in an active business many routine transactions may, in the event, have unexpected repercussions. The clause is accordingly unlikely to be acceptable to the vendors, even with the addition of **"materially"**. If the vendors are compelled to give a warranty along these lines, they should try to limit the clause so that it relates only to things done and not to things omitted.

**7–83**    **4.1.1.4 the Company has not entered into any capital transaction as seller, purchaser, lessor or lessee or otherwise undertaken any material commitment on its capital account;**

This warranty requires disclosure of capital transactions arising after the balance sheet date which are likely to be of interest to the purchaser. The vendors would not normally have an issue with this warranty.

**7–84**    **4.1.1.5 of the plant, machinery, fixtures, fittings, equipment, vehicles, furniture, property, materials and other assets (not being included in the current assets) included in the Accounts or acquired by the Company since the Balance Sheet Date:**

**4.1.1.5.1 none has been sold or disposed of at a figure lower than book value or an open market arm's length value whichever is the higher;**

**4.1.1.5.2 none has been or has been agreed to be let on hire or hire purchase or sold on deferred terms; and**

These warranties are targeted at eliciting details of any transactions involving the assets included in the accounts or those that have been acquired since then which it would not be routine for the company to dispose of. Normally the warranty would not give rise to concern for the vendors and would simply require disclosure of relevant transactions.

**7–85**    **4.1.1.6 the Company has paid its creditors in accordance with their respective credit terms; and there are no amounts owing by it which have been due for more than 60 [90] days.**

The first half of this warranty would imply an analysis of the credit terms of every supplier with whom the target company has dealings. The vendors may prefer to amend the wording so as to provide that creditors have been paid in accordance with the normal practice of the target company. If this approach is adopted, the purchaser might accept it if the warranty is extended such that the vendors confirm that no claims have been made or are pending under the Late Payment of Commercial Debts (Interest) Act 1998, which incorporates into business supply contracts an implied term that overdue debts carry fixed statutory interest. The second half of the warranty relating to outstanding amounts is purely factual and, while there may be difficulty in checking every small item, this problem will be minimal if a sufficiently long period is specified.

### 4.1.2 The value of the net realisable assets of the Company is not less than at the Balance Sheet Date.

7–86

Although **"net realisable assets"** is not defined and no method for determining **"value"** is provided, in effect the warranty amounts to a statement that the target company has not made losses or suffered a reduction in the value of its fixed assets since the balance sheet date. In practice the purchaser would have great difficulty in verifying whether this warranty had been breached but, nevertheless, unless the purchase of the target company has been negotiated on the basis that a representation is made as to the net asset position of the target company at the date of contracts or completion, the vendors should not accept the clause. Furthermore, the parties may agree to the omission of such a warranty if completion accounts are to be prepared. However, if it is accepted, the vendors should ensure that the terms mentioned above are clearly defined.

## 4.2 Vendors' other interests and liabilities

### 4.2.1 The Vendors and their Associates are not, directly or indirectly, interested in any business, other than that now carried on by the Company, which is or is likely to be competitive with the business of the Company, apart from interests in securities [normally] listed on the London Stock Exchange, or dealt in on its alternative investment market, and in respect of which the Vendors, with their Associates, are interested in less than three per cent of any class of the securities in that company.

7–87

The warranty refers to the vendors but, in cases where the warrantors are not the same persons as the vendors, consideration will have to be given to the question of precisely what interest the purchaser is trying to protect. The body of the sale agreement will normally contain a restrictive covenant which will prohibit the vendors from carrying on competing activities within a specified area and for a specified period. The vendors might reasonably consider that, if a restrictive covenant is given, the purchaser derives as much protection as it is entitled to receive against possible competitive activities under that provision. This warranty, while covering similar ground to the normal restrictive covenant, is also wider in its scope and the vendors should particularly give careful consideration to the acceptability of the reference to **"Associates"** and the use of the words **"are likely to be"**. In addition, the insertion of the word **"normally"** as indicated in square brackets would be a desirable precaution for the vendors to cover the case where an investment in a listed company falls outside the strict wording of the warranty by reason of a temporary suspension of the listing. From the purchaser's point of view it will have a legitimate interest in finding out about any potentially competing activities prior to completion so that it can address them in the restrictions it seeks or otherwise as part of the negotiations.

**7–88    4.2.2 None of the Vendors, or their Associates, is indebted to the Company.**

The purpose of this warranty is primarily to provide a reminder that the purchaser would normally expect all indebtedness of the vendors and their associates to the target company to be cleared. The vendors may wish to amend this clause so that it provides instead that any such indebtedness will be discharged by completion. It may be noted that a breach of the warranty would not usually give rise to a loss provided that the debtor is able to meet the liability.

## 4.3 Effect of sale of Shares

**7–89    4.3.1 The Vendors are not aware, and have no grounds for believing, that after Completion (whether by reason of an existing agreement or arrangement or as a result of the acquisition of the Company by the Purchaser):**

**4.3.1.1 a supplier of the Company will cease, or be entitled to cease, supplying it or may substantially reduce its level of supplies;**

**4.3.1.2 a customer of the Company will cease, or be entitled to cease, to deal with it or may substantially reduce its level of business;**

**4.3.1.3 a supplier or customer of the Company will seek to impose or negotiate materially different terms of trading from those currently enjoyed by the Company;**

**4.3.1.4 the Company will lose a right or benefit which it enjoys; or**

**4.3.1.5 any officer or senior employee of the Company will leave its employment.**

While the purchaser will generally wish to know if the purchase of the target company is likely to have an adverse effect on relationships with suppliers and customers, the vendors may wish to qualify the warranty by limiting it to suppliers and customers which are material to the company either by virtue of the type of goods involved or because of the percentage of total supplies or sales which the group obtains from that supplier or makes to that customer. The vendors would usually wish to limit the effect of the warranty further by making it clear that no actual enquiry has been made of the customers, suppliers or employees. This would not be unusual given the need to preserve confidentiality with most transactions until they are completed.

**7–90    4.3.2 Compliance with this Agreement will not:**

**4.3.2.1 breach or constitute a default under an agreement or arrangement to which the Company is a party, or any provision of the memorandum or articles of association of the Company, or any security**

**interest, lease, contract or order, judgment, award, injunction, regulation or other restriction or obligation of any kind affecting the Company;**

Save in respect of banking and finance documentation (which will often contain a change of control provision) it would be unusual for the change in control of the target company to give rise, of itself, to a breach of an agreement binding the target company. A corporate vendor may find that it will breach a trust deed if it sells the target company without the appropriate approvals but such a breach should not affect the target company. The only provisions of a normal share sale agreement which may require attention in the context of this warranty would usually be an obligation for directors to retire (which may involve a wrongful dismissal by the target company) or terms which adversely affect employees' pension rights. The vendors should be cautious about the reference to **"any other restriction"** although, in practice, it is unlikely that they will not be aware of anything which might operate to prevent the sale.

**4.3.2.2 relieve any person from any [material] obligation to the Com-   7–91
pany (whether contractual or otherwise), or enable any person
to determine any such obligation [or any right or benefit
enjoyed by the Company, or to exercise a right in respect of the
Company];**

The purchaser is entitled to a warranty that no significant agreements will, by reason of the change of control of the target company, be terminable. The vendors should, however, delete the words in brackets and restrict the warranty to material contractual obligations.

**4.3.2.3 result in any present or future indebtedness of the Company   7–92
becoming, or becoming capable of being declared, due and
payable prior to its stated maturity or loan facilities being
withdrawn; or**

The vendors should have no difficulty in checking all facility letters and loan agreements to find whether a change in control would cause an early repayment obligation to arise. The most common circumstance would be where there is a corporate vendor which has guaranteed the indebtedness but as to this see cl.3.4.5. It is unlikely that, apart from the sale itself of the target company, any other provision of the share sale agreement would be relevant. See also cl.3.2.5.

**4.3.2.4 result in the creation, imposition, crystallisation or enforcement   7–93
of any Encumbrance on any of the assets of the Company.**

To some extent this overlaps with cl.4.3.2.1 although there is a technical difference. In practice it is not likely to be an issue in the context of change of control when any relevant matters will be required to be disclosed and, if material, appropriate consents obtained.

## 4.4 Business conducted properly

**7–94  4.4.1 The Company has carried on business and conducted its affairs in compliance with CA 1985 and all other statutory obligations and in accordance with its memorandum and articles of association and all other documents to which it is, or has been, a party.**

While the vendors might reasonably accept responsibility for conduct of affairs in accordance with the memoranda and articles of association of the target company, they should be extremely cautious about agreeing to represent that all statutory obligations and obligations arising under all **"other documents"** have been properly performed. If the purchaser has particular concerns regarding a specific document or transaction, then the vendors could reasonably require that the document or transaction in question is identified in the warranty and that others are excluded. Alternatively, the warranty could be restricted to certain specific categories of documents, such as loan agreements or leases. The vendors should also consider whether it would be appropriate to restrict the application of the warranty to the reasonably recent past.

**7–95   4.4.2 The Company has the power and is duly qualified to carry on business in all jurisdictions in which it carries on business.**

While this warranty is reasonable in principle, the vendors should be careful in considering the phrase **"carries on business"**. If, for example, the target company has overseas distributors, they might under local law be deemed to be carrying on business in the countries where the distributors operate. In cases of doubt the vendors could seek to exclude business activities which are limited to dealing with distributors and agents. Alternatively, the warranty could be brought more closely into line with cl.1.6.1.2.

If the overseas activities of the target company are significant, the purchaser should consider extending this warranty by also specifying the particular overseas requirements with which it is primarily concerned. Local advice will usually be required to identify these.

## 4.5 Joint ventures and partnerships

**7–96  4.5.1 The Company is not, nor has it agreed to become, a party in or member of a joint venture, consortium, partnership or other unincorporated association or other profit or income sharing arrangement [(other than recognised trade associations)].**

Membership of a partnership will be relevant because of the exposure that arises from the joint and several liability for the obligations of the other partners. Although joint and several liability should be unusual in the case of a joint venture or consortium, care should be taken with contractual or unincorporated joint ventures because agreement by the joint venturers to share either profits or losses will be *prima facie* evidence of a partnership. It is also possible that there could be a joint venture or consortium operating outside the United Kingdom in jurisdictions where joint and several liability exists even though there is no partnership. Additionally, the terms of a joint venture could include a surrender of rights by the target company, for example by granting control to another participant in the venture. The reference to trade associations may be a convenient way of avoiding the necessity of making a specific disclosure if such memberships exist.

### 4.6 Agency agreements and agreements restricting business

**4.6.1 The Company is not a party to an agency, distributorship, marketing,     7–97
purchasing, manufacturing or licensing agreement or arrangement, or a
restrictive agreement or arrangement, under which part of its business is
carried on or which restricts its freedom to carry on its business as it thinks
fit.**

In so far as the warranty refers to agreements, it is largely an administrative task to review existing agreements to see whether any relevant restrictions exist. It is reasonable for the purchaser to require this review to be undertaken by the vendors who will, or should, have the information necessary to enable them to ensure that the review is comprehensive. Difficulty will arise if agreements have not been properly documented and exist either in the form of correspondence or as a result of a course of conduct. In such cases, however, the existence of a relevant restriction would be most unusual.

The vendors should carefully consider whether the references to **"arrangement"** are acceptable, as they might take the view that an unenforceable arrangement would not adversely affect the purchaser. However, from the purchaser's point of view commercial prudence may make it important to adhere to informal arrangements and a suitable compromise might be to include only those arrangements which are material to the businesses of the target company.

The vendors may prefer to omit agreements or arrangements for the licence of third party intellectual property rights to members of the target company's group of companies as many, if not all of the licences, will include restrictions as to the use of the licensed intellectual property rights. If this is the case, the words **"(other than any agreement or arrangement relating to the use of any Intellectual Property Rights)"** should be added after the word **"arrangement"** on the second line. However, such an amendment is likely to be resisted by the purchaser who will want to understand the nature of any restrictions upon the conduct of the business.

**4.6.2 The Company is not subject to any undertaking or assurance which     7–98
it has given to a court or government agency which is still in force.**

The importance of court undertakings is self-evident. Undertakings given to government agencies are rare in practice in the United Kingdom although they may be given for the purpose of obtaining a grant or other assistance (see cl.3.9). Different considerations will arise if material business activities are conducted outside the United Kingdom in which case undertakings to government agencies may be commonplace but nonetheless important.

### 4.7  Unfair trade and restrictive practices

7–99    **4.7.1 The Company is not nor has it been a party to or concerned in any agreement, practice or arrangement (whether legally binding or not) which is or was:**

#### 4.7.1.1 in contravention of the Trade Descriptions Act 1968;

The Trade Descriptions Act 1968 makes it an offence to apply to goods, in the course of a trade or business, a false or misleading trade description. The warranty will be inappropriate for a company which does not manufacture or market goods.

7–100    #### 4.7.1.2 in contravention of the Fair Trading Act 1973 Part XI as amended by the Trading Schemes Act 1996;

The Fair Trading Act 1973, Pt XI deals with "pyramid selling". Essentially this involves methods of selling otherwise than on business premises where inducements are given to the sellers for introducing other participants or meeting certain targets. There should be little difficulty in determining whether the activities of the target company are such as might fall within the scope of this legislation but, if they do, detailed consideration will have to be given to the precise wording of the legislation, which is complex and obscure in many aspects.

7–101    #### 4.7.1.3 in contravention of the Consumer Credit Act 1974;

The Consumer Credit Act 1974 essentially deals with credit agreements which involve a personal credit not exceeding £25,000 and hire agreements which do not require the hirer to make payments exceeding £25,000. Part III of the Act establishes a system of licensing consumer credit businesses and consumer hire businesses. Part IV regulates advertisements and Part V deals with the formalities which are to be complied with when regulated credit and hire agreements are entered into. If a target company does deal in consumer credit or consumer hire transactions, it will be necessary for the vendors to review its activities to ensure that the statutory formalities have been met.

7–102    #### 4.7.1.4 in contravention of or invalidated (in whole or in part) by the Competition Act 1998;

The Competition Act 1998 repealed the Restrictive Trade Practices Acts 1976 and 1977, the Restrictive Trade Practices Court Act 1976, the Resale Prices Act 1976 and the anti-competitive provisions of the Competition Act 1980 (which allowed investigation by the old Monopolies and Mergers Commission of certain anti-competitive practices). The Act replaced this legislation with two prohibitions based closely on EU law; namely, a prohibition on anti-competitive agreements and arrangements that have or are capable of having an effect on trade within the United Kingdom (based on Article 81 (formerly Article 85) of the Treaty of Rome); and, a prohibition against the abuse of a dominant position that has or is capable of having an effect on trade within the United Kingdom (based on Article 82 (formerly Article 86) of the Treaty of Rome). Under the Act the Office of Fair Trading, under the Director General of Fair Trading was given substantial new enforcement powers, including the ability to conduct "dawn raids" and to impose significant fines upon infringing undertakings. The Office of Director General of Fair Trading was abolished by the Enterprise Act 2002 (for further details of which please see commentary below). The Act compels all United Kingdom authorities involved in its application to ensure, so far as is possible, that questions arising under the Act are dealt with in a manner consistent with the way in which Articles 81 and 82 have been and are interpreted by the European Court of Justice and the European Commission.

The Act excludes from its remit mergers as defined in the Fair Trading Act and also concentrations, which fall within the exclusive jurisdiction of the EU Commission under the EC Merger Regulations.

### 4.7.1.5 in contravention of the Enterprise Act 2002;      7–103

The Enterprise Act 2002 repealed the monopoly and merger provisions of the Fair Trading Act 1973, introduced new systems of merger control and market investigations (giving the Competition Authority the power to make final decisions on merger and market investigations) and changed the institutional framework of United Kingdom competition authorities (replacing the Director General of Fair Trading with the Office of Fair Trading (having a variety of functions under the Competition Act 1998 and the Enterprise Act 2002) and establishing the Competition Appeal Tribunal to which appeals/reviews of the decisions of the Competition Commission, Office of Fair Trading, Secretary of State (whose powers in relation to competition law matters are significantly reduced by the Enterprise Act), and sectoral regulators can be made).

### 4.7.1.6 in contravention of the Treaty of Rome;      7–104

Articles 81 and 82 (formerly Articles 85 and 86) of the Treaty of Rome render void various agreements which may affect trade between member states and which have the object or effect of preventing, restricting or distorting competition in the EU. Any abuse by one or more undertakings having a dominant position within the EU is prohibited in so far as it may affect trade between member states. The detailed provisions are extremely complex and subject to ongoing development (for example, the application of Articles 81 and 82 was fundamentally changed on May 1, 2004 when Council Regulation 1/2003 (the EC Modernisation Regulation) came into force) and as such specialist works dealing with the Treaty of Rome should be consulted. The vendors should in any event amend this warranty so that it refers only to Articles 81 and 82 as there are other minor provisions, such as Articles 28 (dealing with free movement of goods) and 87 (anti-dumping), which could be covered.

### 4.7.1.7 or in contravention of any regulations, orders, notices or directions made thereunder, or otherwise registerable, unenforceable      7–105

**or void or renders the Company or any of its officers liable to administrative, civil or criminal proceedings under any anti-trust, anti-monopoly or anti-cartel, trade regulation or similar legislation or regulation in any jurisdiction where the Company carries on business.**

This broad provision is intended primarily to deal with non-United Kingdom legislation as the specific provisions discussed above deal comprehensively with United Kingdom legislation. Unless the target company engages in a considerable degree of activity within a jurisdiction where it is known that there is significant anti-trust legislation, the vendors might reasonably decline to give this warranty.

The legislation on competition law is complex and as such reference should be made to specialist works dealing with competition law, or appropriate specialist advice taken, if there is a possibility that the target company may be involved in anti-competitive practices.

### 4.8 Litigation

7–106    **4.8.1 Neither the Company nor any person for whose acts or defaults the Company is or may be vicariously liable are engaged in litigation, arbitration, administrative or criminal proceedings [except for collection of debts not exceeding an aggregate of £[ ]]; there are no proceedings pending or threatened, either by or against the Company or such persons; and [so far as the Vendors are aware] there is nothing which is likely to give rise to such proceedings.**

The vendors should have no difficulty in confirming that the target company is not engaged in litigation. The purpose of the exclusion of small debt collecting is to avoid lengthy disclosures for minor debt collecting matters. The vendors should, however, consider carefully the implications of the part of the warranty which refers to circumstances likely to give rise to proceedings. At the very least the vendors might wish to qualify this part of the warranty by the inclusion of awareness as suggested by the words in brackets but, furthermore, the vendors may feel, in a complex business, that it is not realistic for them to express a view as to whether litigation is likely. Many vendors are concerned by the extension of the warranty to threats of litigation. In many businesses, such threats are common but rarely give rise to litigation.

7–107    **4.8.2 The Company is not subject to any order or judgment given by any court or governmental agency (local or national).**

The vendors will usually have no difficulty in confirming these matters as they are largely factual and should be known to the target company.

7–108    **4.8.3 There are no claims pending or threatened or capable of arising against the Company by an employee or workman or third party in respect of any accident or injury which are not fully covered by valid insurance.**

This warranty needs to be viewed carefully by the vendors in conjunction with their insurance brokers or advisers. The vendors would be wise to separate the warranty into several elements. The first should deal with actual notice of any such claims which should be straightforward. The second would be that the vendors have no actual knowledge of any circumstances which might give rise to a claim and which would not be covered by insurance. The vendors may object to the extension of this warranty into the realms of adequacy of insurance given the separate insurance warranties and the ability of the purchaser to satisfy itself in due diligence as to the adequacy or otherwise of the target company's insurance.

**4.8.4 There is no dispute with any government (local or national) or     7–109 agency or body acting on behalf of such government or other authority in the United Kingdom or elsewhere in relation to the affairs of the Company and [so far as the Vendors are aware] there are no facts or circumstances which may give rise to such a dispute.**

The first part of the warranty is factual and should not be an issue for the vendors. Please see comments above at cl.4.8.1 in relation to the vendors position on warranties which refer to circumstances likely to give rise to proceedings which will apply equally here in relation to the last part of this clause. As suggested above, the second part of the clause could be moderated by the vendors by the inclusion of an awareness qualification.

**4.8.5 Neither the Company nor any current or former employee, officer or     7–110 agent of the Company has been convicted of an offence in relation to the Company and no employee or officer has been convicted of an offence that reflects upon the reputation of the Company or their suitability for holding the position that they hold in the Company.**

With the suite of legislation that can give rise to criminal offences that can be committed by a target company or its officers or directors (common examples are breach of data protection, working time regulations, environmental legislation and financial assistance), the purchaser will have a legitimate interest in seeking any relevant disclosure. In relation to previous conduct the purchaser will be interested to see the level of fines that the company has paid and whether the conduct is likely to be a continuing issue. On change of control the purchaser's directors and officers will usually assume the position of the target company's directors and officers and will be concerned to ensure that there is no continuing criminal exposure for them. The vendors might wish to qualify the part of the warranty that relates to officers and employees, particularly former ones, by reference to knowledge.

## 4.9 Winding-up

**4.9.1 The Company is not insolvent or unable to pay its debts within the     7–111 meaning of the Insolvency Act 1986, s.123 (the references in that section to proving to the satisfaction of the court being disregarded).**

There is no single definition of "insolvency", but a company will generally be taken to be insolvent if either it is unable to pay its debts as they fall due (Insolvency Act 1986, s.123(1)(e)) or there is an excess of liabilities over assets (s.123(2)). A rather odd feature of these definitions is that they strictly seem to require that the court is satisfied that the relevant circumstances exist. The purpose of the words in brackets at the end of the warranty is to avoid the argument that neither of these two tests can be met unless a court ruling has actually been obtained. In addition, s.123 provides a number of special cases which result in a company being deemed unable to pay its debts, including non-payment for 21 days after a statutory notice is served by a creditor who is owed more than £750.

The purchaser will be most concerned if a target company is likely to be insolvent. If an insolvency procedure has commenced, and shares in the target company or some or all of its assets are among the assets to be realised in the receivership or liquidation, the purchaser will be keen to ensure that the transaction is valid and that it will receive good title. If a procedure has not begun but may be imminent, any sale may be liable to adjustment or avoidance under the Insolvency Act 1986. The warranty is, therefore, a reasonable one. Inability to pay debts is one of the most common grounds for a court winding-up order and the vendors should have little difficulty in deciding whether the warranty could possibly be infringed. It would be otherwise if the warranty were rephrased so as to refer, instead, to the likelihood of any of the companies becoming insolvent

**7–112     4.9.2 No order has been made, petition presented or resolution passed for the winding-up of the Company; no distress, execution or other process has been levied and remains undischarged in respect of the Company; and there is no outstanding judgment or court order against the Company in connection with the same nor has any application been made for the making of an administration order or notice of intention to appoint an administrator been filed at court, or served on a creditor with the benefit of a floating charge.**

"Distress" is a summary remedy by which a person is entitled, without legal process to take possession of another person's goods, "execution" involves the enforcement of a court judgment or order, "process" includes any document which is served or executed in connection with the purposes of any court. These are all important matters of fact which can readily be checked by the vendors.

**7–113     4.9.3 No steps have been taken for the appointment of an administrator or administrative receiver or receiver over the whole or any part of the Company's assets or undertaking.**

Usually not an issue for the vendors as it is very unlikely that a sale of shares would take place in these circumstances.

**7–114     4.9.4 No event analogous to those described in clauses [4.9.2] or [4.9.3] has occurred outside England.**

A purchaser might seek to include this warranty if the company is established overseas. Given the importance of the solvency of the target company, the vendors should be prepared to give such a warranty.

**4.9.5 No floating charge created by the Company has crystallised and [so far as the Vendors are aware] there are no circumstances likely to cause such a floating charge to crystallise.**    **7–115**

Events of "crystallisation" are usually myriad and it is possible that the target company may have inadvertently triggered one or more. It would be unusual for these to give rise to a loss unless the holder of the charge sought to enforce their rights. The vendors would usually seek to qualify the warranty by the addition of the words in brackets. A letter of non-crystallisation can be obtained on completion if necessary from any floating charge holder.

### 4.10 Compliance with statutes

**4.10.1 Neither the Company nor [so far as the Vendors are aware] any of its officers, agents or employees (during the course of their duties), have done or omitted to do anything, the doing or omitting of which is, or could be, in contravention of a statute, regulation or the like giving rise to a penalty, default proceedings or other liability [which could have a material adverse effect on the business of the Company].**    **7–116**

This clause is extremely widely drawn and would cover even such matters as parking offences relating to a vehicle belonging to the target company or driven by an employee of the target company. The vendors should certainly seek to exclude trivial matters, perhaps by putting a minimum level on any fine or penalty below which a breach of warranty will not occur. The purchaser might well reply to any proposed exclusion, if a floor for warranty claims has been agreed as discussed in para.3–20, that the floor protects the vendors from trivial claims and that it is accordingly not necessary to also amend the warranty. The vendors should, in addition, alter the clause so that it relates only to the position at the date of the agreement and not also to the past. The vendors may also wish to limit the warranty by reference to their knowledge given the extension of its scope to the target company's officers, agents and employees.

If the target company has significant overseas activities, the warranty is unlikely to be satisfactory for either party. The purchaser will wish for more detailed warranties relating to the particular overseas obligations while the vendors may well consider that the warranty, as drafted, is too broad to enable them to carry out proper verification. The vendors may also wish to modify the clause by adding words along the lines of those contained in the square brackets, and they should also consider carefully whether the words **"or could be"** are acceptable.

An alternative form of the warranty, which is likely to be more acceptable, would be:    **7–117**

**The Company has conducted and is conducting its business in all [material] respects in accordance with all applicable laws and regulations.**

It would be reasonable for the vendors to refuse to give warranties such as those above unless the purchaser specifies the legislation in respect of which it requires warranty cover.

*4.11  Documents stamped*

7–118    **4.11.1 All documents which affect the title or interest of the Company to or in any of its assets, or to which the Company is a party, have been duly stamped.**

The only significant penalty for failing properly to stamp a document arises under the Stamp Act 1891, s.14. This provides that a document which is not properly stamped is not available to be given in evidence or for any other purpose until duly stamped. The judge is required to take notice of the omission to stamp or the insufficiency of the stamp duty. Sections 15, 15A and 15B give further force to the legislation by providing for (limited) interest and penalty payments. Although the warranty is, on the face of it, reasonable, it is in practice most unlikely that the purchaser would ever suffer a loss by reason of a document being incorrectly stamped or not stamped at all. There is therefore no generally convincing reason why the vendors should be required to make good any defects in stamping which have occurred to date. The only common exception to this is where the unstamped documents affect title, which could create difficulty on a subsequent dealing with the asset concerned. The vendors, if they are unable to persuade the purchaser to delete the warranty, may therefore wish to confine its application to documents of title or, at least, to restrict the clause to documents executed during, say, the preceding six years. It might also be appropriate to make it clear that the warranty only covers United Kingdom stamp duty. In any case, the warranty may be void under the Stamp Act 1891, s.117 as being an agreement for assuming liability on account of absence or insufficiency of stamp duty or indemnifying against such liability. It might, however, be successfully argued that s.117 does not affect an agreement between the vendor and the purchaser of a company but requires the company itself (as the party directly involved in the liability) to have the benefit of the agreement.

7–119    **4.11.2 There is no document held outside the United Kingdom which, if brought within the United Kingdom, would result in the Company incurring a liability to pay stamp duty.**

A document which is subject to stamp duty must be stamped within 30 days after execution or, if it was executed outside the United Kingdom, within 30 days after it is received in the United Kingdom (Stamp Act 1891, s.15). A stamp duty avoidance device which has been commonly adopted in transactions where the documentation does not permanently affect the title to assets has been to execute the document and to leave it overseas. Unless the document relates to property situate, or to a thing to be done, in the United Kingdom, it is not stampable at the time of execution (s.14). The expectation in these cases is that the document will never need to be physically produced in the United Kingdom unless the transaction gives rise to litigation or the Inland Revenue insists upon having sight of the original document.

In some cases the amount of stamp duty which could be payable is very large. The purchaser is entitled to have the benefit of the warranty—which ideally should last as long as any document could still be relevant for production—but the vendors should not be responsible if the document is brought to the United Kingdom by the purchaser of its own volition.

## 4.12  Business names

**4.12.1 The Company does not make use of any name other than its corporate    7–120 name.**

Under the Business Names Act 1985 a company cannot, without approval, carry on business in Great Britain under a business name which includes certain words and expressions. The list of words and expressions is contained in the Companies and Business Names Regulations 1981 (SI 1981 No 1685) which also specify which Government department must be approached to obtain approval in any particular case. In addition the law of passing off can give a right of action to a party whose proprietary interest in a name is infringed.

The purchaser has reasonable grounds for satisfying itself that all business names can be used without risk and, as the warranty merely invites disclosure of business names used and does not require the vendors to state that no statutory obligations or proprietary rights are infringed, it should be acceptable to the vendors.

It should be noted that the definition of "Intellectual Property Rights" in para.4–01 includes business names and this should be borne in mind when considering cl.8.7.

## 4.13  Transactions involving directors

**4.13.1 The Company has not been a party to a transaction to which CA 1985,    7–121 ss.320 or 330 might apply.**

The broad effect of s.320 is quite clear and is intended to prohibit substantial property transactions between a company and its directors which are not sanctioned by the shareholders. Where such a transaction has been entered into without the approval of shareholders, the agreement may be avoided by the company. Certain exclusions exist for transactions below a minimum size but the difficulty of the section arises not under its direct impact but in relation to transactions which do not obviously fall within its scope. In particular, the section applies to transactions entered into between a company and a person connected with a director of the company. The wide definition of connected persons contained in CA 1985, s.346 has the effect that a director is connected with a company in which he and his family (including trustees of family settlements) are interested in more than 20 per cent of the share capital. The section could be very important, therefore, if a target company had engaged in a transaction with another company and a director of that other company was connected with a significant proportion of the shareholders in the target company.

Notwithstanding the broad scope of s.320, the vendors might consider that the warranty itself is too widely drawn. The warranty should exclude those transactions for which approval has been obtained in accordance with the provisions of the section. In addition, the warranty is relevant only if the other party to a transaction with a target company might, by reason of the infringement, have a right to avoid the contract.

Section 330 prohibits the making of loans by a company to its directors or the directors of its holding company. The section extends to guarantees of loans to directors and to indirect loans where a third party makes the loan which is then taken over by the company. The part of the warranty relating to this section should not give the vendors any difficulty.

### 4.14  Powers of attorney and authorities

7–122   **4.14.1 No powers of attorney or authorities (express or implied) by which a person may enter into a contract or incur an obligation on behalf of the Company are subsisting [other than by reason of the ostensible or implied authority of directors or employees to enter into routine contracts in the normal course of their duties].**

The purpose of this warranty is to ensure that the purchaser is aware of outstanding powers given to third parties enabling them to bind the target company. A breach of the warranty is, however, unlikely to give rise of itself to a claim for damages.

The vendors will normally have no difficulty in giving this warranty in relation to powers of attorney which are in the form of independent documents. A special point arises, however, where a power of attorney is contained as a provision of a longer document such as a debenture or lease. In such cases, the power of attorney is normally limited to matters relating to the execution of documents and implementation of transactions arising from the debenture or lease itself and therefore should give little concern to the purchaser. The vendors may wish to qualify this warranty so that it does not apply to powers of attorney contained in other documents as merely an incidental provision. With regard to other authorities, if the vendors add the words in square brackets or confine the warranty's scope to express authorities, the warranty will apply only to unusual cases which should be readily capable of being identified and disclosed to the purchaser.

### 4.15  Licences and consents

7–123   **4.15.1 The Company has all necessary licences and consents required for the proper carrying on of its business in the manner in which the business is now carried on (short particulars of each licence and consent being set out in the Disclosure Letter).**

Although most businesses carried on in the United Kingdom do not require any specific licences, there is nevertheless a very large number of activities for which licences are required. In particular, excise licences are required for the carrying on of many trades, for example the manufacture or sale of intoxicating liquors, and various gaming activities. Licences are also required by employment agencies and in connection with certain offensive and dangerous trades.

As drafted, this clause could cover licences to exploit patents and other intellectual property rights. It is preferable for these to be dealt with expressly, as for example in cl.8.7. If this approach is adopted, the wording should be amended by adding after **"licences"** the words **"(other than in respect of Intellectual Property Rights)"**.

The warranty is deliberately drafted in general terms as the purchaser would reasonably be entitled to take the view that the vendors are in a far better position than the purchaser to know whether licences are required for any particular aspect of the target company's activities. If, as for most companies, no licences are required, the vendors may prefer this warranty to be in the following form:

**The Company does not require a licence or consent for the proper carrying on of its business.**

In considering this warranty, the vendors should have particular regard to licences or authorities which are required outside the United Kingdom if the target company has material overseas activities.

**4.15.2 The Company is not in breach of any of the terms and conditions** **7–124**
**of any licence or consent; all licences and consents are effective and there is**
**nothing [known to the Vendors and relating to the Company] that might**
**prejudice the continuation or renewal of a licence or consent.**

This warranty will be inappropriate if a warranty is given in the alternative form suggested above in relation to cl.4.15.1. However, if there are licences or consents in existence, the vendors should consider whether the form of this warranty is unduly onerous as immaterial breaches often take place which are of no practical importance. The purchaser's concern is that there should be no penalties from such a breach and that breaches do not bring the licence or consent to an end or prejudice the prospects of its renewal. This latter point is dealt with in the second half of the clause although the wording may be too wide for the vendors. They may prefer to restrict the second half either by inserting the words in square brackets or by amending the provision so that it applies only to breaches of the terms or conditions of the licences or consents which are likely to render the licence or consent terminated or prevent its renewal. The vendors should appreciate that the implications of a breach of this warranty could be very serious, since the refusal to continue a licence could have a major impact on the goodwill of the target company. If licences relating to intellectual property rights are excluded from cl.4.15.1, this clause should be amended by adding after references to **"a licence or consent"** the words **"falling within clause 4.15.1"**.

7–125 **4.15.3 The Company does not carry on investment business within the meaning of the Financial Services and Markets Act 2000.**

If a company carries on regulated activities in the United Kingdom, it is required under the Financial Services and Markets Act 2000 to obtain permission to do so from the Financial Services Authority (FSA), or otherwise be regulated by a designated professional body (DPB) as an exempt professional firm, under the Financial Services and Markets Act 2000, Pt XX. Regulated activities are very widely defined in various Regulated Activities Orders and it is frequently difficult to be sure that particular activities do not fall within the definition even though they would not normally be thought to comprise a regulated activity. If the target company does in fact carry on regulated activities, it would be appropriate for the warranty to be in the following form:

**The Company has either been granted permission by the Financial Services Authority, or is regulated by a designated professional body as an exempt professional firm, and [so far as the Vendors are aware] is complying and has complied with the rules of the appropriate regulator in relation to its conduct of business.**

The rules issued by the FSA and DPBs are extremely complex and it is consequently difficult for any member to be absolutely sure that no infringement has occurred. The vendors might therefore prefer, if there is scope for doubt, to disclose to the purchaser precisely what activities are carried on and to provide a copy of their Scope of Permission Notice (if applicable), so that the purchaser can reach its own view as to whether an infringement might have occurred. Alternatively they may wish to qualify the warranty by awareness.

*4.16 Subsisting contracts*

7–126 **4.16.1 The Company is not party to any agreement or arrangement which:**

4.16.1.1 **is of an unusual nature or was entered into outside the normal course of business;**

4.16.1.2 **is for a fixed term of more than six months or for an indefinite term which is incapable of termination by it in accordance with its terms on not more than 60 days' notice;**

4.16.1.3 **is of a long-term nature (that is, unlikely to have been fully performed, in accordance with its terms, within six months after the date on which it was entered into);**

**4.16.1.4**   is of a loss-making nature (that is, known to be likely to result in a loss to the Company on completion of performance);

**4.16.1.5**   cannot readily be performed by it on time without undue or unusual expenditure or application of money, effort or personnel;

**4.16.1.6**   involves payment by it by reference to fluctuations in the index of retail prices, or other index, or in the rate of exchange for a currency;

**4.16.1.7**   involves an aggregated outstanding expenditure by it of more than £[ ];

**4.16.1.8**   involves, or is likely to involve, the supply of goods or services the aggregate sales value of which will be more than 10 per cent of its turnover for the preceding financial year;

**4.16.1.9**   is a contract for hire or rent, hire purchase or purchase by way of credit sale or periodical payment;

**4.16.1.10** can be terminated as a result of a change in the control of the Company; or

**4.16.1.11** involves, or is likely to involve, other obligations or liabilities which ought reasonably to be made known to an intending purchaser of the Shares.

This list is intended to be by way of guidance only for a purchaser and the **7–127** business activities of the target company should be reviewed carefully by both the purchaser and the vendors to see whether these provisions are all relevant and whether any others ought to be included. In particular, the vendors will observe that the introductory wording to the clause refers not only to agreements but also to arrangements.

Of the sub-headings covering specific matters, the first, which refers to contracts of an unusual nature or which were entered into outside the normal course of business, is perhaps the most difficult in that a complex business will inevitably involve contracts which are unusual but were nevertheless entered into for the benefit of the target company concerned. The last sub-clause is in the nature of a sweeping-up provision and should be rejected by the vendors for lack of specificity.

Clauses 4.16.1.2 and 4.16.1.3 will extend to many licences of intellectual property rights as these are usually of a long-term nature. The vendors may wish to exclude such agreements from this warranty by inserting the words **"(other than an agreement or arrangement relating to the use of Intellectual Property Rights)"** at the beginning of these provisions, as licences of intellectual property are dealt with in cl.8.7.

**4.16.2 The Company has made all payments due under all contracts to   7–128 which it is a party and [so far as the Vendors are aware] observed and performed all conditions thereof.**

The purchaser is entitled to know that all contractual payments are up to date and that contracts have been complied with. While on the face of it this is a factual warranty which the vendors should be able to check and if necessary disclose against, the vendors would usually wish to limit the warranty to material contracts and, in relation to the observance and performance of all conditions, qualify the warranty by awareness. A purchaser would in any event normally only be concerned with material contracts which were likely to affect the ongoing profitability of the target company and if these were considered fundamental would probably require specific warranties on the relevant contracts.

**7–129**   **4.16.3 [So far as the Vendors are aware] the Company is not, nor will it with lapse of time become, in default of any obligation and no threat or claim of default under any agreement, instrument or arrangement to which it is a party has been made and there is nothing whereby any such agreement, instrument or arrangement may be prematurely terminated or rescinded by another party or whereby the terms may be worsened to the Company's detriment.**

This is extremely wide-ranging and to some extent duplicates cl.4.16.2. The vendors would usually wish to limit the warranty by the inclusion of the words in square brackets.

### 4.17  Other parties' default

**7–130**   **4.17.1 [So far as the Vendors are aware] no party to an agreement with the Company is in default, being a default which would be material in the context of the Company's financial or trading position; and there are no circumstances likely to give rise to a default.**

While the first part of this warranty should be broadly acceptable to the vendors, it should be amended by the insertion of the qualification in square brackets and careful consideration should be given as to whether the phrase **"financial or trading position"** is sufficiently specific. The final part of the warranty, referring to circumstances likely to give rise to a default, is extremely wide and is unlikely to be acceptable to the vendors.

### 4.18  Outstanding offers

**7–131**   **4.18.1 No offer or tender is outstanding which is capable of being converted into an obligation of the Company by acceptance or some other act of another person.**

The intention of this clause is clear and it would normally only apply to special cases such as tenders in relation to building contracts. Nevertheless, the wording would apply to any case where an order has been placed by the target company but which has not yet been accepted by the other party. It would therefore be appropriate for the vendors to qualify the clause so that it does not apply to offers and the like in the ordinary course of business (although see cl.4.1.1.1 in relation to the scope of that phrase). The purchaser should treat any such amendment with caution if it is in the ordinary course of the activities of the target company to make sizeable tenders. In such a case, a qualification of the warranty so that it applies to offers in the ordinary course of business could also be subject to a further qualification that any one offer must not involve an expenditure of more than a specified sum.

## 4.19 Defective products

**4.19.1 The Company has not manufactured, sold or supplied products which were, are or will become, in a material respect faulty or defective, or which do not comply in a material respect with warranties or representations expressly or impliedly made by it and all applicable regulations, standards and requirements in respect thereof.**    7–132

This is potentially an extremely onerous warranty for the vendors, particularly because of the absolute liability imposed by the Consumer Protection Act 1987 upon manufacturers, own-branders and importers in respect of defective products. The scope of the provision should accordingly be a matter for specific negotiation between the parties. The problem will be reduced if, as will often be the case, the target company has limited its liability for product defects by way of exclusions in its normal terms of sale although liability under the Act for damage caused by defective products, that is products whose safety is not such as persons generally are entitled to expect, cannot be excluded. Additionally, there may be product liability insurance which would cover most claims. Subject to these qualifications, however, the parties should consider very carefully precisely what liability is covered by the warranty and where the risks should lie. It is particularly difficult to allocate risk in relation to future defects as, although the original owners may have permitted the existence of the circumstances creating the defect, the purchaser would normally accept business risks as from completion.

**4.19.2 The Company has not given any guarantee or warranty [or made any representation] in respect of goods or services supplied or contracted to be supplied by it save for any warranty or guarantee implied by law and (save as aforesaid) has not accepted any obligation which could give rise to any liability after any such goods or services have been supplied by it.**    7–133

This warranty seeks to elicit details of any warranties or guarantees offered over and above those required by law. The vendors would usually wish to qualify the warranty so as to exclude representations.

**4.19.3 The Company has not received notification that any products supplied by it are defective or unfit and [so far as the Vendors are aware] no circumstances exist which could give rise to such a claim.**    7–134

The first part of this warranty should not give the vendors any difficulty. The second part amounts to a "product guarantee" to the purchaser and would not normally be acceptable to the vendors without the addition of the words in brackets.

**7–135    4.19.4 The Company has not received a prohibition notice, a notice to warn or a suspension notice under the Consumer Protection Act 1987.**

A prohibition notice may be served upon a company to prohibit it from supplying, or offering to supply, goods which are considered to be unsafe. A notice to warn requires the recipient to publish at his own expense, in a formal manner and on occasions specified in the notice, a warning that specified goods are considered to be unsafe. A suspension notice prohibits the recipient, for a specified period, from supplying or offering specified goods and can be issued where the enforcement authority for consumer safety has reasonable grounds for suspecting that safety provisions have been contravened in relation to the goods.

The importance of these obligations is obvious and, as they involve a simple question of fact for the vendors, they should have no difficulty in giving the warranty.

### 4.20 Service liabilities

**7–136    4.20.1 The Company is not obliged (save as implied by law) to repair, maintain, take back or otherwise do or not do anything in respect of goods that have been, or will be [pursuant to existing agreements], delivered by it.**

This warranty essentially involves merely questions of fact but, to avoid extensive disclosures, the vendors may wish to amend the warranty so that it does not apply to obligations undertaken in the normal course of business. Furthermore, liability in respect of future deliveries should be restricted, for example by adding the words in square brackets, to those which are the result of agreements subsisting at the date of the sale agreement.

### 4.21 Purchases and sales from or to one party

**7–137    4.21.1 The Company does not obtain or make more than 25 per cent of the aggregate amount of its purchases from, and not more than 25 per cent of the aggregate amount of its sales to, the same supplier or customer (including a person connected with the supplier or customer); and no material source of supply to the Company, or material outlet for the sales of the Company, is in jeopardy.**

The part of this warranty which quantifies purchases and sales from or to a specific supplier or customer will not involve difficulty unless a target company exceeds or is close to the specified percentages. In that case, the vendors should consider carefully how the quantities in question are to be identified. In particular, they may wish to specify more clearly how the amount of the purchases or sales is valued and over what period the relevant figures are calculated. The reference to **"connected"** parties may be unacceptable to the vendors without a clearer definition of the word. The last part of the warranty, referring to the sources of supply or outlets being in jeopardy, is a different question involving matters of judgment and, unless the vendors are quite clear as to whether in fact the warranty may be breached, they should resist giving it.

## 4.22  Data protection

**4.22.1 The Company has, if so required by law, a current entry in the**   7–138
**register maintained by the Information Commissioner under the Data Pro-**
**tection Act 1998 which complies with the requirements of that Act, and**
**particulars of the entry are set out in the Disclosure Letter.**

The Data Protection Act 1998 requires data controllers to notify details of their processing of personal data to the Information Commissioner unless they fall within one of the exemptions from notification. The application for notification must state the purposes for which the data is used as well as other information, including those places outside the European Economic Area to which data is transferred. The notification entry must be accurate and it must be kept up to date. Failure to notify or to notify properly is a criminal offence and it is, therefore, reasonable for the purchaser to seek warranty protection.

**4.22.2 The Company has not carried out nor does it intend to carry out**   7–139
**assessable processing within the terms of the Data Protection Act 1998.**

Some personal data must be notified to the Commissioner before processing of such data can commence. The processing of such data is referred to as "assessable processing". This imposes a more onerous burden than ordinary notification and it may, therefore, be appropriate to address the issue only in circumstances where such data may be being processed by the target company.

**4.22.3 The Company has complied with the data protection principles**   7–140
**applicable to all the processing of personal data carried out by it and**
**collected, processed and disclosed personal data only in accordance with the**
**terms of a privacy policy, details of which are set out in the Disclosure**
**Letter.**

**4.22.4 The Company has not carried out nor does it plan to carry out any**
**processing of [sensitive] personal data in respect of which it does not have**
**grounds under the Data Protection Act 1998, Schedule[s] 2 [or 3].**

**4.22.5 Where the Company uses a data processor to carry out the process-**
**ing of personal data, the processor has provided sufficient guarantees in**
**relation to security measures and compliance with those measures and there**
**is in existence a written contract between the Company and the data**
**processor which complies with the requirements of principle 7 and the Data**
**Protection Act 1998, Part 2, Schedule 1, paragraphs 9–12.**

**4.22.6 The Company does not transfer personal data to jurisdictions outside the European Economic Area.**

7–141     The Data Protection Act contains eight principles which are contained in Schs 1 to 4 of the Act and cover a range of obligations. They include requirements for the data to be accurate and up to date, for the controller to collect information fairly, to use it lawfully and to maintain proper security. Specific warranties relating to the grounds for processing data/sensitive personal data, compliance with the security obligations and restrictions on overseas transfers are given above as well as a general warranty of compliance with the principles. Schedules 2 and 3 detail the requirements for data processing, Schedule 3 relating to sensitive personal data. (If the Company is not involved in the processing or other use of sensitive personal data then the wording in square brackets can be taken out.) One or more of the specific warranties could be employed in addition to the general warranty where significant personal data is involved in the transaction and the data is a particularly valuable asset. If there is non-compliance with the principles the Commissioner can serve an Enforcement Notice which may prohibit particular uses of data or require the data controller to amend his processing. Alternatively, individuals who suffer damage because of the breach of principles may claim compensation. The data protection principles are wide-ranging and are broadly stated. It is therefore difficult for a data controller to be certain that no infringement has occurred. The vendors should therefore be cautious about accepting the general warranty in cl.4.22.3 and could suggest the following as an alternative:

7–142     **The Company has not received a statutory notice served by the Registrar under the Data Protection Act 1984 or by the Information Commissioner under the Data Protection Act 1998.**

These notices may be information notices, requiring further information, or enforcement notices described above. The vendors will know whether such a notice has been received or not.

7–143     **4.22.7 No individual has claimed or taken or has a right to claim compensation or take action for breach of his rights, including actions for rectification or other remedy in respect of inaccurate personal data, against the Company under the Data Protection Act 1998 and the Company has not received any notice, letter or complaint alleging a breach of data protection legislation.**

Individuals have rights to compensation if they suffer damage as a result of a breach of the data protection principles by the data controller. In such a case they may also claim for associated distress. Individuals may also take court action for breach of their right to subject access, their right to object to automated processing of data, their right to object to direct marketing, their right to object to automated decision making or to seek rectification and other remedies where personal data are shown to be inaccurate. In cases where personal data involve the special purposes of journalistic, artistic and literary endeavours, compensation may be claimed for distress without damage having been suffered. The warranty covers both potential claims for compensation and potential claims for breach of the other individual rights.

The warranty is reasonable in so far as it relates to claims which have been made but is onerous to the extent that it covers possible claims.

**4.22.8 [So far as the Vendors are aware] the Company has complied with** **7–144** **all other requirements of the Data Protection Act 1998 and all subordinate legislation, guidance and codes of practice.**

This warranty is in the way of a sweeper warranty for anything not caught by the prior specific ones. The vendors would usually ask to qualify this by awareness, particularly when the prior specific warranties are given in absolute terms.

### 4.23 Guarantees and indemnities

**4.23.1 There is no subsisting guarantee or agreement for indemnity or** **7–145** **suretyship given by, or for the accommodation of, the Company.**

This warranty is to some extent similar to cl.3.4.5. A guarantee is normally to be distinguished from an indemnity by the fact that a guarantee is a collateral contract to be responsible for the default of another party. A guarantee is thus ancillary or subsidiary to another contract. An indemnity is a contract by which the party giving the indemnity undertakes an original and independent obligation.

### 4.24 Insider contracts

**4.24.1 The Company is not, nor has it during the past three years been, a** **7–146** **party to an agreement or arrangement (whether legally binding or not) in which a Vendor, or Associate of a Vendor, or director of the Company, or Associate of a director of the Company, is or has been interested.**

The essential purpose of this warranty is as a check to establish whether any insider contracts have in the recent past been entered into or are currently subsisting. If any such contracts are brought to light, the purchaser will wish to ensure that the terms are satisfactory notwithstanding the interest of the vendors or the directors. The vendors would not normally have any reasonable ground for objecting to this warranty but they should ensure that its scope is clearly understood. In particular, the reference to **"arrangement"** is vague and essentially unnecessary. The vendors may wish, in addition, to provide that interests are deemed to be relevant for this warranty only if they are such that, if they involved a director, they would have to be disclosed for the purpose of CA 1985, s.317. It would also be appropriate for the vendors to exclude obvious agreements such as employment contracts.

**4.24.2 The Company is not a party to, and its profits and financial position** **7–147** **during the past three years have not been affected by, an agreement or**

**arrangement (whether legally binding or not) which is not of an arm's length nature.**

The precise wording of this warranty is unsatisfactory for the vendors in a number of respects. In the first place, the purchaser should be interested only in transactions which have artificially either increased the profits or improved the apparent financial position of the target company or which have given rise to excessive liabilities. In addition, contracts may not be at arm's length but may be on fully commercial terms. The vendors should also consider whether the word **"arrangement"** is acceptable and the reference to **"financial position"** lacks clarity. Unless the warranty is amended to exclude gifts, it will be necessary for the vendors to disclose all charitable and similar donations made by the target company.

7–148    **4.24.3 None of the Company's assets have been acquired for a considera-tion other than market value (at the time of acquisition).**

This is a related warranty to cl.4.24.2 in the sense that it seeks disclosure of any transaction which involved the acquisition of an asset at less than market value. It is difficult to see how the purchaser could suffer loss as a result of any breach except in the limited circumstances where the transaction could be set aside by a liquidator or trustee in bankruptcy of the seller of the relevant asset.

*4.25 Sensitive payments*

7–149    **4.25.1 No officer or [so far as the Vendors are aware] employee of the Company has made or received any Sensitive Payment in connection with any contract or otherwise.**

By the use of the wide-ranging definition of Sensitive Payments this warranty catches the payment of any commission, inducement or bribe of whatever nature. This is usually only a major concern when the target company has significant dealings with local authorities. The vendors will usually be reluctant to give the warranty unless caveated by their knowledge. Even where the warranty were to be given it would be prudent to disclose that no actual enquiry can be made of any relevant employees (given that at the time of provision of the warranty it is most unlikely that such enquiry will have been made given the likely confidential nature of the transaction).

*4.26 Consultants' reports*

7–150    **4.26.1 No financial or management consultants have, within the past three years, given a report in relation to the Company.**

The purchaser will be interested in any management reports which have been obtained by the target company in that they will highlight problems that have arisen and solutions that have been proposed. The vendors might feel that such a report could prejudice their negotiations with the purchaser and should resist producing it.

## 5 Environmental

The most common way of dealing with environmental risks in any transaction is    **7–151**
to try to allocate responsibility for that risk between the parties. This is achieved
through the use of warranties, indemnities and/or other contractual terms in the
transaction. It should always be remembered that a warranty or indemnity is only
as good as the person giving it.

There is no standard approach to the allocation of environmental risk. The
purchaser will try to achieve full protection but the degree of success will vary
and depend on the bargaining position of the parties. Liability for environmental
matters usually arises due to a failure to comply with a statute or a licence issued
under a statute, the presence of a pollutant on or under land requiring clean up,
or under common law (negligence, nuisance etc.). The vendors would usually be
reluctant to accept full environmental responsibility particularly when they have
only recently bought the site or when they have a leasehold interest only. The
usual approach is to require the purchaser to undertake a full environmental
survey and to only provide environmental warranties which relate to pollution
caused by the target company.

### 5.1 Required licences

**5.1 The Company has obtained all Environmental Licences which it requires    7–152
and has complied with all applicable Environmental Laws and with the
terms and conditions of the Environmental Licences and there is no reason
why the Environmental Licences should not continue to be complied with.
True copies of such Environmental Licences are attached to the Disclosure
Letter.**

Protection of the environment has become a key issue within EU and United
Kingdom policy and, as a result, there has been a vast amount of legislation (both
primary and secondary) introduced into the United Kingdom in the last 10–15
years. The United Kingdom approach to regulating the environment is by way of
consents in order that polluting activities are controlled by way of licensing.
There are various regulatory controls including integrated pollution control,
waste management and water that are regulated mainly by the Environment
Agency but in some situations by the local authority. It is important for the
purchaser to ensure that all licences have been complied with in the past and that
the target company has the ability to continue to comply with the licences.
Usually a breach of a condition of a licence is a criminal strict liability
offence.

### 5.2 Breaches

**5.2.1 The Company has not received notification or communication from    7–153
which it appears it is, or may be alleged to be, in violation of any Environmental Laws or Environmental Licences or that any Environmental
Licences may be subject to modification, suspension, revocation or appeal
and there are no circumstances likely to give rise to violation, modification,
suspension, revocation or appeal.**

It is important to ensure that not only has there been no breach or violation of a licence or licence condition in the past but also that no regulatory body, for example the Environment Agency, has notified the target company that it is investigating an incident with a view to a possible prosecution. It is also important to ensure that the relevant regulatory body is not considering modification, suspension, revocation or appeal of any licences as this could affect the operation of the target company going forward.

## 5.3 Audits and surveys

**7–154**    **5.3.1 The Company has disclosed all environmental audits and surveys in relation to the Properties or land previously owned or occupied by it.**

It is now commonplace when acquiring a company, particularly if that company's assets include land, to ensure that environmental audits and surveys have been carried out and have been disclosed. Again, it is important to consider exactly what is contained in the environmental audits and surveys as the warranty is sought in respect of matters that have not been disclosed.

Under the contaminated land regime there is an exclusion for liability if the land has been sold or bought with full information. If the company faces action in respect of land it no longer owns or occupies but can prove that before the sale took place it provided to the buyer full information on the condition of the land, it may be able to take advantage of this exclusion and avoid liability. A purchaser should seek an appropriate warranty from the vendors if during due diligence it becomes apparent that there has been a prior relevant transaction.

## 5.4 Prosecutions

**7–155**    **5.4.1 The Company has not been prosecuted or notified of a possible prosecution for a breach of any Environmental Laws.**

Again it is important to note whether the target company has been prosecuted and in particular if it has been prosecuted by the Environment Agency or another regulatory body on a regular basis as it may appear on what has been termed "the hall of shame". The Environment Agency publish (on its web site) a list of companies which are regularly prosecuted and this can have negative public relations consequences for that company. It is also important to know whether the Environment Agency or another regulatory body are in the process of issuing proceedings or have issued proceedings but the matter has not yet come to court.

## 5.5 No claims

**7–156**    **5.5.1 No Environmental Claims exist against the Company or have been made within the previous [ ] years and there are no circumstances which may lead to a claim.**

It is important that any past claims against the target company for environmental matters are dealt with, as are any pending claims and the possibility of future claims. If this type of claim is to be included in the warranty then the parties will have to decide the length of period in the future within which claims can be made and the procedure for identifying the cause of the claim and making the requisite claim. It may also be necessary to introduce a cap or overall maximum limit on any claim to be made under the warranty.

## 5.6 Hazardous Substances

**5.6.1 Neither the Company nor any other person has deposited, used,**   7–157
**treated, kept, disposed of, released or emitted any Hazardous Substances at,**
**on, from or under any of the Properties now or previously owned, leased,**
**occupied or controlled by the Company.**

This is perhaps the most contentious environmental warranty discussed, as accumulation of the substances contained with the wide definition of Hazardous Substances may not have involved a breach of environmental law. On the other hand, it may result in considerably increased risks of contamination and liability.

While this warranty commences with what appears to be a list of unnecessary verbs, it is usual to use such terminology as it tracks that used in environmental legislation and there is case law as to the nuances between the activities identified.

## 5.7 Notices

**5.7.1 No notices under Environmental Laws have been served against the**   7–158
**Company and no work has been carried out under a notice by a regulatory**
**body whereby the Company must reimburse the regulatory body for the**
**costs of the work carried out.**

This would cover notices served under the contaminated land regime as well as Anti Pollution Works Notices under the Water Resources Act 1991, s.161.

## 5.8 Prior use

**5.8.1 The Company is not aware that there has been any potentially con-**   7–159
**taminative use that has been made of any of the Properties or any land**
**previously owned or occupied by the Company.**

This seeks disclosure from the vendors that, while the target company's property to date has not been used for any contaminative use, there is no possibility that it has been used for something potentially contaminative such that it could fall within any regulatory regime now or at some stage in the future.

This may elicit disclosure of more than would be forthcoming in respect of cl.5.5.1, which deals with past, present or future claims, and the vendors may argue that disclosure of audits and surveys coupled with the warranty given in cl.5.5.1 sufficiently protects the purchaser's interests. Under the contaminated land regime an owner or occupier can be held liable for the clean up of contamination it caused on land it no longer owns or occupies.

## 6 Employment

### 6.1 Employees and terms of employment

**7–160**  **6.1.1 The Disclosure Letter contains accurate and complete particulars of the identities, dates of birth, dates of commencement of employment or appointment to office, and terms of employment or appointment of all the employees and officers of the Company, including details of all remuneration (including pensions, whether to be delivered by occupational or personal schemes) and other benefits, such as profit sharing, commission and bonus arrangements (whether or not contractual), sufficient to allow the financial obligations of the Company to be ascertained.**

Normally the purchaser will want to pay close attention to the terms and conditions of employment of all the employees and will require as much detail as possible. However, if the target company has an unusually large number of employees it may not be realistic for the terms of employment of all of them to be included in the disclosure letter. It may therefore be appropriate either to exclude from the warranty employees whose salary is below a certain level or to make the disclosure on the basis of broad categories of employee. This may be appropriate where there are "standard" terms and conditions of employment for certain classes of employee. In either case, it will be necessary to amend the detailed wording of the warranty. There may also be difficulty in identifying and describing discretionary arrangements if no fixed rule or pattern exists for exercising the discretion although, in such a case, the purchaser is less likely to be legally bound by the arrangements.

**7–161**  **6.1.2 There is no contract of service between the Company and a director or employee for which approval was required but not obtained under CA 1985, s.319.**

Section 319 prohibits the incorporation by a company of a term in a service contract with a director, which has the effect that the contract cannot be terminated within a period of five years, unless the term is first approved by the company in general meeting. A term incorporated in a service agreement which contravenes the section is, to the extent of the contravention, void. The reference to **"employee"** is required because the section extends not only to a service contract between a company and one of its directors but also to a service contract with a subsidiary where the employee is a director of the holding company. It is unlikely that the purchaser would suffer a disadvantage if the section had been contravened and the warranty operates mainly as a reminder to the parties to check whether any infringement may have occurred.

**7–162**  **6.1.3 There are no contracts for services (including without limitation consultancy agreements) between the Company and any individual.**

One of the effects of employment legislation in recent years has been to considerably narrow the gap between employees and the self-employed. Nevertheless the distinction remains vital in terms of taxation matters (principally in so far as PAYE and national insurance contributions are concerned) and also so far as the right to claim unfair dismissal is concerned. This warranty is designed to flush out any arrangements which masquerade as "consultancy agreements" or "contracts for services" but which on closer examination are in fact more like employment arrangements.

**6.1.4 No employee of the Company who has or may have a statutory or contractual right to return to work, is absent on maternity leave, paternity leave, parental leave, adoption leave or other leave of absence. No employee of the Company is absent on sick leave which has or is expected to last longer than 4 weeks.**   7–163

Employees have statutory rights to maternity, paternity, adoption and parental leave. Broadly speaking, employees returning from such leave have the right to return to the same or a similar job on no less favourable terms and conditions as those that they enjoyed immediately before commencing leave. The vendors should consider and make any necessary disclosures in respect of any employee or officer who is absent on sickness grounds or on other leave of absence.

**6.1.5 No employee or former employee of the Company has or may have a right to be reinstated or re-engaged under the Employment Rights Act 1996.**   7–164

An employee who has been unfairly dismissed may be entitled to reinstatement (where the employee is treated in all respects as if he had not been dismissed) or re-engagement (where the employee does not necessarily return to the same post). An order for reinstatement or re-engagement will not be made where it is not practicable for the employer to comply or where to make it do so would be unjust. In practice these remedies are rarely appropriate and orders are made infrequently.

## 6.2 Claims and potential employee claims

**6.2.1 There are no outstanding claims nor [so far as the Vendors are aware] are there any potential claims against the Company by any person who is now or has been an officer or employee of the Company and no liability has been incurred and remains undischarged for breach of any employment contract or for redundancy payments (including protective awards) or for damages or compensation for wrongful dismissal or unfair dismissal or otherwise or for failure to comply with any order for the reinstatement or re-engagement of any person.**   7–165

Although there is likely to be a warranty in respect of litigation generally, cl.6.2.1 will elicit specific information regarding employee claims. The vendors may well consider the expansion of the warranty to **"potential claims"** to be unreasonable and will be most unlikely to accept it without the addition of the wording in square brackets. This should be acceptable to the purchaser as it will at least oblige the vendors to make enquiries as to whether circumstances exist which are likely to give rise to such litigation.

7–166    **6.2.2 There have not within the period of 12 months prior to the date of this Agreement been any claims under the provisions of the Employment Rights Act 1996, the Trade Union Reform and Employment Act 1993, the Health and Safety at Work etc. Act 1974, the Equal Pay Act 1970, the Sex Discrimination Act 1975, the Disability Discrimination Act 1995, the Race Relations Act 1976, the Gender Reassignment Regulations 1999, the Transfer of Undertakings (Protection of Employment) Regulations 1981, the Trade Union and Labour Relations (Consolidation) Act 1992, the Protection from Harassment Act 1997, s.3, the Working Time Regulations 1998, the National Minimum Wage Act 1998, the Employment Relations Act 1999, the Part-Time Workers (Prevention of Less Favourable Treatment) Regulations 2000, the Fixed-Term Employees (Prevention of Less Favourable Treatment) Regulations 2002, the Employment Act 2002, the Employment Equality (Religion or Belief) Regulations 2003 or the Employment Equality (Sexual Orientation) Regulations 2003 relating to any employee or former employee of the Company nor [so far as the Vendors are aware] are there any circumstances which are likely to give rise to such claims.**

The list of Acts and regulations set out in the warranty details the principal legislative instruments under which employment claims are made. The wording of the first part of the warranty should not cause the vendors too much difficulty as it simply requires disclosure of claims made, however they may well consider the extension of the warranty to "potential claims" to be unreasonable and will be unlikely to accept it without the addition of the wording in square brackets.

7–167    **6.2.3 The Company has performed all [material] obligations required to be performed by it in respect of its officers and employees whether arising under contract, statute, at common law or in equity including, without limitation, all obligations arising under the Working Time Regulations 1998 and all obligations under all health and safety legislation.**

Clause 6.2.3 is very broad in its nature, aiming from the purchaser's point of view to prompt disclosure of any breach or non-compliance by the target company of the terms of any contract of employment or employment legislation. It is also designed to elicit details of outstanding liabilities to officers or employees. However, the vendors may view the wide scope of this warranty as unreasonable and seek to resist its inclusion or, as a minimum, qualify it by awareness. It will be noted that the inclusion of the word "material" would be a significant dilution. The Working Time Regulations are referred to specifically because it is these regulations which by and large give rise to the most frequent instances of non-compliance; indeed it appears that many employers remain largely unaware of their scope.

**6.2.4 The Company has paid to the Inland Revenue and any other appro-**    7–168
**priate Taxation Authority all taxes, national insurance contributions and other levies due in respect of the employment of the employees of the Company.**

The nature and benefit of this warranty is obvious. The vendors might seek to resist the warranty on the basis it will be duplicated in the tax warranties and any unpaid tax will be covered by the tax deed.

**6.2.5 There are no enquiries or investigations existing, pending or threat-**    7–169
**ened in relation to the Company by the Equal Opportunities Commission, the Commission for Racial Equality or the Disability Rights Commission.**

The purpose of this warranty is twofold; first to identify any such investigations which may be embarrassing should they proceed and second to identify any potential discrimination claims. This second element will be important particularly where warranty 6.2.2 is not extended to cover "potential" claims. It is intended that the Commission for Equality and Human Rights (which is expected to be established in 2006) will replace the three other commissions.

## 6.3 Changes in remuneration

**6.3.1 During the period to which the Accounts relate and since the Balance**    7–170
**Sheet Date or (where employment or holding of office commenced after the beginning of the period) since the commencement date of the employment or holding of office:**

**6.3.1.1 no change has been made in the rate of remuneration, or the emoluments of employment or pension benefits, of any officer, ex-officer or senior executive of the Company (a senior executive being a person in receipt of remuneration in excess of £[ ] per annum); and**

**6.3.1.2 no [material] change has been made in the other terms of employment of any officer or senior executive.**

The warranty is limited to changes in remuneration of "senior" executives to avoid extensive disclosures where changes have taken place in relation to employees at a comparatively low salary level. There will of course be occasions where it would be inappropriate to limit the warranty in this way. The insertion of the word **"material"**, as indicated in square brackets, may also help to minimise unnecessary disclosures. This warranty is relevant to the purchaser, even if a warranty equivalent to cl.6.1.1 is given, as it will wish to know what changes have occurred in the payroll which are not fully reflected in the last accounts.

**7-171**    **6.3.2 No agreement has been reached with any officers, employees, trade union or other body representing employees that will or may on a future date result in any changes to the terms and conditions of employment of any of the officers or employees of the Company (including without limitation any increase in the rate of remuneration or enhancement of the emoluments of employment or pension benefits of such persons); and no negotiation relating to the terms and conditions of employment of any officer or employee of the Company (including without limitation for any increase in the remuneration or enhancement of the emoluments of employment or pension benefits of such person) are current or likely to take place within the next six months.**

The purpose of this warranty is to identify commitments which have already been or which might be incurred by the target company by reason of negotiations but which will result in changes only after completion. Whether the vendors would be willing to allow the clause to extend to negotiations which are not current but are merely **"likely"** would depend upon the nature of the business. If the target company is unionised, the timing of negotiations for changes in remuneration is likely to be well understood and capable of disclosure to the purchaser.

*6.4 Bonus and share options schemes*

**7-172**    **6.4.1 There are no schemes (whether contractual or discretionary) in operation by or in relation to the Company under which any employee or director of the Company is entitled to any shares in the Company or to any bonus, profit share, commission or remuneration of any other sort (whether calculated by reference to the whole or part of the turnover, profits/losses or sales of the Company or otherwise).**

**6.4.2 The Company is not under any legal or moral obligation to make nor is it accustomed to making any bonus payments to or for the benefit of any officer or employee of the Company.**

Bonus schemes can be problematic particularly in the case of senior executives (whose bonus packages are often a key part of their remuneration package) who tend to negotiate bonuses on an annual basis and where entitlement is often expressed to be discretionary in some way. These warranties catch both contractual and discretionary schemes as well as those arrangements which are informal and ad hoc but to which an employee might nevertheless be able to establish a contractual right. The purchaser should ensure that it fully understands the target company's commitments in relation to this.

*6.5 Termination of contracts of employment*

**7-173**    **6.5.1 All subsisting employment contracts to which the Company is a party are determinable at any time on three months' notice or less without compensation (other than compensation for unfair dismissal in accordance with the Employment Rights Act 1996).**

In the ordinary course of events an employee with more than one year's continuous service has the right to bring a claim for unfair dismissal, even where his employment is terminated on proper notice. In certain limited cases (for example where the employee has been dismissed because he has indicated an intention to join a trade union, has raised concerns about health and safety matters or has asserted a statutory right) the right is extended to those with less than one year's service. Unfair dismissal compensation is based principally on loss of earnings and, in accordance with the provisions of the Employment Rights Act 1996, is to be such amount as the employment tribunal considers just and equitable in all the circumstances of the case.

To some extent, this warranty overlaps cl.6.1.1 but it also covers the position where the notice period specified in the contract is at odds with the statutory minimum period laid down in the Employment Rights Act 1996. The warranty should in practice cause no difficulty for the vendors.

**6.5.2 No employee of the Company, who is in receipt of remuneration in     7–174 excess of £[ ] per annum, and no officer of the Company has given or received notice terminating his employment, except as expressly contemplated in this Agreement and no such employee or officer will be entitled or, so far as the Vendors are aware, is likely to leave his employment or office prematurely, nor to receive any payment from the Company as a result of the sale of the Shares.**

The main purpose of this warranty is to identify senior employees who are still with the target company but under notice of termination. The circumstances of the target company may make it desirable, from the purchaser's point of view, to extend the warranty to all employees, regardless of seniority. The second part of the clause would be more acceptable to vendors if it covered cases where the employee **"will"** leave rather than being **"likely"** to leave and if the wording in brackets were inserted. The warranty refers to being entitled to leave prematurely to cover employment contracts which give the employee a right to leave if there is a change in the control of the employer. In the absence of express provision, there would be no specific right of termination simply by reason of a change of control of the employer as the Transfer of Undertakings (Protection of Employment) Regulations 1981 (SI 1981 No. 1794), which give such rights in the event of a transfer of a business, do not apply to a sale of shares.

### 6.6 Industrial relations

**6.6.1 The Company does not recognise any trade unions, works or staff     7–175 councils or associates of trade unions and there are no collective agreements or other agreements (whether or not legally binding and whether in writing or arising by virtue of custom or practice) between the Company and any trade union or other body representing employees.**

If the target company's employees are represented by one or more trade unions it will be important for the purchaser to have full disclosure of all arrangements which have been entered into with the unions and the extent to which each union has been recognised. A variety of other arrangements may be in place for the purposes of informing, consulting or negotiating with the workforce, including staff and works councils. The purchaser should also bear in mind that in the case of certain trades and industries remuneration, holidays and other terms and conditions of employment may be regulated at industry level by a bargaining mechanism involving a panel of unions' and employers' representatives.

**7–176    6.6.2 The Company has not done anything which might be construed as recognition of a trade union and has not received an application for recognition from a trade union.**

Recognition of a trade union for collective bargaining purposes can occur by agreement or following a request by an independent trade union for recognition by an employer. Recognition requests are considered by the Central Arbitration Committee who in the vast majority of cases will order that a ballot takes place. Recognition will in broad terms follow where both a majority of voters and at least 40 per cent of all workers in the appropriate bargaining unit support recognition. Where a trade union is recognised, an employer will be committed to collective bargaining in respect of matters such as pay, hours and holidays. Although this warranty serves a useful function in bringing out information which could be of considerable commercial relevance to a purchaser, it is not clear how the purchaser would be able to easily establish loss for breach.

**7–177    6.6.3 Neither the Company nor any of its employees is or has been in the last two years involved in an industrial dispute and so far as the Vendors are aware there is nothing which might suggest that there may be an industrial dispute involving the Company, or that this Agreement may lead to an industrial dispute.**

The importance of this clause depends on the nature of the businesses of the target company. If the target company is unionised it will be imperative to know whether there are existing industrial disputes. The purchaser will also want to know something of the industrial relations history of the target given that the future profitability of it could be affected by poor industrial relations. The purchaser will also be anxious to be informed of any circumstances which are likely to result in a dispute but the vendors may feel that the wording of the second half of this clause is too broad. If they are to give a warranty as to the possibility of future industrial disputes, the vendors might wish to limit the warranty so that it applies only to disputes that are **"likely"** to occur and to add the wording in brackets. The closing words of the clause, relating to disputes which could arise from the sale of the target company, are unlikely to be acceptable to the vendors as they may reasonably feel in most cases that the purchaser would have at least as clear an idea as they do as to whether such disputes would arise by reason of the change in ownership of the target company. This part of the warranty might alternatively be included in the items covered by cl.4.3.1.

## 6.7 Redundancies

**6.7.1 No employee of the Company will become redundant and be entitled to a redundancy payment as a result of this Agreement.**                    7–178

If the agreement specifically provides for redundancies, or if redundancies are a clear and inevitable consequence of the sale of the target company, then the warranty is incorrect and inappropriate. The implications of redundancies should be specifically considered in the course of the sale negotiations and the cost allocated between the parties. In any other case there is no particular reason why the vendors should make a representation on this question. The only reasonable value of the warranty is as a reminder so that the possibility of redundancies is not overlooked.

This clause could, as an alternative to being a separate warranty, be included in cl.4.3.1.

**6.7.2 There is no plan, scheme or commitment or established practice relating to the termination of employment affecting an employee or officer of the Company which is more generous than the statutory redundancy entitlement or such sum as may be properly payable by way of damages for breach of contract.**                    7–179

The purchaser will want to know if the target company operates an enhanced redundancy scheme or is morally obliged to make an *ex gratia* payment to an employee or officer on termination of his or her employment. This will be especially relevant if the purchaser envisages job losses following the acquisition of the target company.

## 7 Pensions

Significant changes to pensions legislation are in the pipeline. New requirements are expected to be in force from April 2005 in relation to salary-related scheme funding and from April 2006 in relation to pension scheme tax relief. Reference should be made to such new legislation once implemented to determine whether new warranties are required in relation to these areas. The current format of warranties takes no account of anticipated changes.                    7–180

## 7.1 Full particulars

**7.1.1 Full particulars of the retirement benefits scheme ("the Scheme"), of which the employees of the Company are entitled to become members, have been disclosed in writing to the Purchaser, including the governing trust deeds, rules, announcements, explanatory literature, details of assets held by the Scheme, insurance policies and contracts, funding arrangements, current membership list and the latest actuarial report.**                    7–181

If the target company has a pension scheme, this clause covers straightforward matters of fact of which the purchaser will need to have details so that it can familiarise itself with the scheme and make an assessment of the nature and extent of current and future liabilities in connection with it.

## 7.2 Trustees

7–182     **7.2.1 The persons named in the Disclosure Letter as the trustees of the Scheme are all its present trustees and not less than one third of the trustees are member-nominated trustees appointed in accordance with the provisions of the Pensions Act 1995, s.16 and the regulations made under it.**

Pension schemes consist of assets held upon irrevocable trust by the trustees of the scheme who are not parties (in their capacity as trustees at any rate) to the sale agreement. This warranty is designed to identify the trustees and to ensure that the member-nominated trustee provisions of s.16 have been complied with. If the trustee is a body corporate then reference should instead be made to the member-nominated director provisions of the Pensions Act 1995, s.18.

## 7.3 Pensions Act 1995

7–183     **7.3.1 No order under the Pensions Act 1995, s.3 has been made in respect of any trustee of the Scheme nor has any trustee been requested to pay any penalty under s.10.**

This warranty identifies whether or not OPRA (the Occupational Pensions Regulatory Authority often known as the Pensions Regulator) has made a prohibition order under s.3 or imposed a penalty against the trustees under s.10.

## 7.4 Appointments

7–184     **7.4.1 The trustees of the Scheme have made written appointments of an auditor, an actuary, a fund manager, a legal adviser and any other professional adviser whose appointment is required to be made under the Pensions Act 1995, s.47 and do not rely upon the advice of an adviser not appointed by them in relation to the Scheme.**

This warranty identifies whether or not written appointments of professional advisers, as listed in the clause, are in place as required by s.47.

## 7.5 Books and records

7–185     **7.5.1 The trustees of the Scheme have complied with the requirements of the Pensions Act 1995, s.49 and regulations made under it for the keeping of accounts, books and records in relation to the Scheme.**

This warranty is designed to achieve early identification of any failure to maintain a separate bank account, books and records, including records of meetings and of determinations in connection with the winding-up of a pension scheme, as required by s.49.

## 7.6 Details of the Scheme

**7.6.1 The Scheme is:**                                                    **7–186**

**7.6.1.1  a defined benefit Scheme;**

**7.6.1.2  contracted out for the purposes of the Pension Schemes Act 1993, Part III and the Pensions Act 1995; and**

**7.6.1.3  an exempt approved scheme within the meaning of ICTA 1988, Chapter 1, Part XIV and [so far as the Vendors are aware] there is no reason why approval may be withdrawn.**

This warranty is primarily designed to identify key features of the Scheme. Do    **7–187**
members have to contribute? Is it contracted out? Is it an exempt approved
scheme? In each case further details will be required. For example, with regard
to contracting out, is it contracted out by reference to the provision of guaranteed
minimum pensions or protected rights or by the reference test? The reference test
is described in the Pension Schemes Act 1993, s.12B and is a quality test that
schemes must satisfy in order to contract out of the State Earnings Related
Pension Scheme after April 6, 1997. The guaranteed minimum pensions or
protected rights provisions applied to contracting out prior to that date. The
warranty, particularly if amended by the words in square brackets or if **"may be"**
is replaced by **"is likely to be"**, should not pose a problem to the vendors.

## 7.7 No other obligations

**7.7.1 Save in accordance with the terms of the Scheme the Company does    7–188
not have any obligation (whether or not legally binding) to pay or provide or
secure the provision of a pension or other payment on retirement or disability or after death or otherwise to provide relevant benefits within the
meaning of ICTA 1988, Part XIV in respect of a person who is now or has
been an officer or employee of the Company.**

Pension obligations have a habit of being both extremely expensive (often a
multiple of the consideration in a transaction) and sometimes, quite innocently,
hidden from view. This warranty is designed to flag up any pension obligations
however informal and whether giving rise to moral rather than legal obligations.
The purchaser will need to make good those obligations or face a commercial
cost perhaps by reference to a loss of employee goodwill. Hence the very widely
cast net of this warranty.

## 7.8 Members

**7.8.1 No persons other than employees of the Company are or are entitled to    7–189
be active members of the Scheme.**

It would be unfortunate indeed if the purchaser were to find itself responsible for
the provision of pension benefits for employees with whom it has never had any

connection. While this would be unusual, this warranty is designed to identify whether or not that is the case, and the vendors should be prepared to give it.

## 7.9 Contributions paid

7–190   **7.9.1. All contributions payable by the Company and every other participating employer in accordance with the terms of the Scheme in order to secure or provide for the benefits for and in respect of members (including pensioners, deferred members and other persons prospectively or contingently entitled to benefit under it) have been duly paid to the Scheme.**

If there is a history of non-payment of contributions the purchaser should be made aware of this. Non-payment may have led to industrial relations problems and may have been notified to the Pensions Regulator.

## 7.10 Schedule of contributions

7–191   **7.10.1 The trustees of the Scheme have prepared and maintained and have revised from time to time (as appropriate) a schedule of contributions of the nature required by the Pensions Act 1995, s.58 and all contributions due from members of the Scheme have been duly paid to the Scheme at the rate stipulated by its actuary (and in accordance with the schedule of contributions) as being required to fund the benefits to be provided by the Scheme on the basis of the actuarial method and assumptions used by the actuary in the most recent actuarial valuation of the Scheme.**

Section 58 requires the trustees to ensure that there is prepared, maintained and from time to time revised a schedule showing the rate of contributions payable to the Scheme on behalf of the employer and members and the dates on or before which such contributions are to be paid. This warranty is concerned with compliance with that statutory provision.

## 7.11 Assets sufficient

7–192   **7.11.1 The investments or policies or other assets held by the Trustees of the Scheme are sufficient to meet in full all the liabilities and obligations (current, future and contingent) which the Scheme has to its members, the value or amount of the assets, liabilities and obligations have been calculated in accordance with the actuarial assumptions in, and are held pursuant to, an investment policy formulated in accordance with, a written statement of principles governing decisions about investments for the purposes of the Scheme in compliance with the Pensions Act 1995, s.35 which has been prepared, maintained and from time to time revised as required by that section.**

This warranty is concerned with whether or not a "Statement of Investment Principles" as required by s.35 has been prepared and that the investments are in accordance with those principles. Since these are matters of fact, this should not cause any difficulties for the vendors.

However, the clause also states that the assets are sufficient to meet the scheme's liabilities. The vendors should be cautious about giving such assurance and in preference should produce and warrant factual information regarding the value of the scheme, on the basis that the purchaser and its actuary will be able to reach their own conclusions.

## 7.12 Maintenance of funding

**7.12.1 The combined contribution rates of the Company and all other**   7–193
**participating employers and its and their respective employees are sufficient**
**to maintain the funding of the Scheme at a level which satisfies the minimum**
**funding requirements of the Pensions Act 1995, ss.56 and 57 and will secure**
**the benefits to which the members are entitled under the Scheme.**

The Pensions Act 1995 includes minimum funding requirement provisions, which set out a statutory basis for funding. If the minimum funding requirements are not met resulting in a shortfall, certain consequences, including a requirement that the company makes an immediate cash payment into the scheme, may follow. It is therefore reasonable for the purchaser to seek protection in the form of warranty cover, but the vendors should ensure that this warranty is only given on the basis of appropriate actuarial advice.

## 7.13 Employer-related investments

**7.13.1 The assets of the Scheme do not include employer-related investments**   7–194
**(as defined in the Pensions Act 1995, s.40).**

Section 40 prohibits over-investment in property or shares related to the employer. The mischief which s.40 seeks to address is that if the Scheme holds employer-related assets and the employer suffers an event such that, for example, its shares become worthless, pension scheme members may suffer a double disadvantage. In the case of insolvency, for example, they lose their employment and suffer because the asset holding under the pension scheme has become less valuable. The sanctions for breach of s.40 include the imposition of fines and, in certain circumstances, imprisonment.

## 7.14 Discontinuance of the Scheme

**7.14.1 In the event of the discontinuance of the Scheme before, at or within**   7–195
**six months after Completion, the assets of the Scheme (valued in such a**
**manner as to represent their realisable cash value, taking account where**
**appropriate of surrender penalties) will be of such a value that they will be**
**sufficient to secure in full all benefits accrued due under it up to the date of**
**the discontinuance by purchase of deferred annuity policies on a full buy-out**
**basis.**

This clause requires confirmation that there are sufficient assets to wind up the scheme and discharge all the trustees' obligations to provide benefits in that event. It also requires confirmation that funding is sufficient for discharge to be effected by annuity purchase. This may be the expected method, but the scheme rules may allow alternatives. The vendors should be cautious about this clause, because even if discontinuance is not anticipated it might nonetheless be effected. One approach would be for the vendors to exclude any discontinuance after completion which arises as a consequence of the voluntary actions of the purchaser. Alternatively, they may argue that compliance with minimum funding requirements (see cl.7.12.1) ought to give the purchaser sufficient comfort.

### 7.15 Scheme surpluses or refunds

**7–196**    **7.15.1 No refunds of surplus have been made to and no contribution holidays have been taken for the benefit of the Company or any other person in relation to the Scheme.**

This will identify refunds of surplus or contribution holidays. This information will enable the purchaser to assess whether the target has historically borne the true cost of pension provision and whether its financial performance has been enhanced either by a refund of surplus or a holiday from contribution.

### 7.16 Latest actuarial valuation

**7–197**    **7.16.1 Certified copies of the latest actuarial valuation of and report on the Scheme (being that dated [ ]) and of the latest accounts of the Scheme (being those made up to [ ]) have been delivered to the Purchaser and individually and together give a true and fair view of the state and method of funding of the Scheme and do not contain any material errors or omissions.**

This clause is concerned with the actuarial valuation and accounts of the scheme. The vendors might, with some justification, be concerned about its extension to the **"true and fair view"** of a valuation (which may routinely be three years old) and the inclusion of **"material omissions"**.

### 7.17 Proposed amendments to the Scheme

**7–198**    **7.17.1 No proposal has been announced by the Company either:**

**7.17.1.1**    **to modify, amend, alter or improve the Scheme which proposal remains outstanding and has not been formally implemented (by deed) (in whole or in part); or**

**7.17.1.2**    **regarding its continuation, closure to new members, closure to new benefit accruals, discontinuance or winding-up.**

This is designed to identify any changes which are being planned and ought to be acceptable to the vendors. The purchaser should be wary of any attempt to delete any of the words **"modify, amend, alter"** in cl.7.17.1.1 on the basis of duplication, as they do have different connotations: the power to modify being derived from the Pensions Act 1995, s.67, while powers to amend and alter are usually specifically granted in scheme rules.

## 7.18 No other changes prior to Completion

**7.18.1 The Scheme will not be modified, amended, altered or improved**    **7–199**
**before Completion; no winding-up of the Scheme will be commenced; it will**
**not be wound up or terminated or cease to admit new members on or before**
**Completion; and the Trustees of the Scheme have undertaken in writing to**
**refer and apply to the Purchaser at and from Completion in respect of all**
**aspects of the Scheme.**

This warranty is designed to prevent the vendors from moving the goal posts by changing or by winding the scheme up before completion. It cannot, of course, bind the trustees of the scheme, who will, in any event, owe fiduciary duties to the members, the fulfilment of which may require them to take action of the sort contemplated in the clause, and the vendors may prefer to restrict its scope to a commitment that the target company will not take actions of the type contemplated in this provision. The purchaser should seek an undertaking in like terms applicable at Completion. See also the comments made in relation to cl.7.17.1 above. This clause will only be relevant where there is to be a gap between contracts and completion.

## 7.19 Scheme operated properly

**7.19.1 The Scheme has been operated and administered in accordance**    **7–200**
**with:**

**7.19.1.1    the preservation requirements contained in the Pension Schemes**
**Act 1993, Part IV;**

**7.19.1.2    the equal treatment requirements identified in the Pensions Act**
**1995, ss.62–66;**

**7.19.1.3    the equal pay provisions of the Treaty of Rome; and**

**7.1.91.4    all applicable laws and the documents constituting and governing**
**it (including notices, announcements and explanatory literature**
**and the contracting out requirements of the Pension Schemes Act**
**1993) and all decisions made by the Trustees of the Scheme have**
**been made in accordance with their powers and duties as Trustees**
**of the Scheme.**

Broadly speaking, by virtue of the provisions and requirements listed in    **7–201**
cll.7.19.1.1 to 7.19.1.3, pension schemes are treated as containing rules which have the effect of modifying any aspect of the scheme which treats one sex less favourably than the other, with the effect that if something is done which would be discriminatory, it is invalid. This could give rise to a greater funding liability. The clause also deals with legal requirements generally.

The vendors should not contemplate giving this warranty without the benefit of specialist pensions advice. Furthermore, the vendors may, in any event, feel unable to give comfort in respect of the trustees who may be completely independent of the target company and who are in any case fiduciaries.

## 7.20 Discretions and powers

7–202    **7.20.1 No discretion or power has been exercised under the Scheme in respect of a member (whether active, deferred or a pensioner) (or a beneficiary claiming through or under a member) to:**

**7.20.1.1    augment benefits under it;**

**7.20.1.2    admit to membership of it a director or employee who would not otherwise have been eligible for admission to membership;**

**7.20.1.3    provide under it in respect of a member a benefit which would not otherwise be provided under it in respect of the member; or**

**7.201.4    pay a contribution to it which would not otherwise have been paid;**
**and no undertaking, assurance or intimation has been given pursuant to which a discretion or power will or may be exercised.**

This warranty is designed to identify special treatment for certain categories of member and to flush out any assurances made, even if not properly recorded, as these could give rise to industrial relations problems, if unfulfilled, or greater funding requirements. The vendors should be willing to give such a warranty.

## 7.21 Augmentation of benefits

7–203    **7.21.1 No augmentation of benefits has been made under the Scheme and no additional benefits have been granted without the actuary's confirmation in each case that such augmentation or addition can be borne by the Scheme within the existing funding rate without detriment to the benefits of other members or the payment of any additional contributions which the actuary deems necessary to secure such augmented or additional benefits.**

This warranty is designed to ensure that any benefit increase is funded, as the employer would have to make up any funding shortfall directly or indirectly.

## 7.22 No disputes

7–204    **7.22.1 No claim:**

**7.22.1.1    for benefits under the Scheme has been refused by the Trustees or has been the subject of dispute or delay in settlement or reduction in amount or value paid or payable below that claimed; or**

**7.22.1.2    has been made or threatened against the Company or the Trustees or administrators (if different) of the Scheme or against any other**

**person whom the Company or any of the Trustees of the Scheme is or may be liable to indemnify or compensate in connection with the Scheme (other than routine claims for benefits) and the Vendors are not aware of any circumstances which may give rise to a claim.**

This is designed to identify potential disputes in their earliest stages, along with any disputes which have reached a more advanced stage and more specifically any costs related to them. It is reasonable for the purchaser to be made aware of these matters and the vendors should be willing to give this warranty.

### 7.23 Lump sum benefits insured

**7.23.1 All lump sum death in service benefits which may be payable under the Scheme are fully insured and all premiums due in respect of such insurance have been paid.**  7–205

This is a housekeeping warranty designed to ensure that death benefit cover is in place.

### 7.24 Charges paid

**7.24.1 All actuarial, consultancy, legal and other charges in respect of the Scheme, whether payable by the Company or by the Trustees, have been paid and no services have been rendered in respect of the Scheme in relation to which an account or other invoice has not been rendered.**  7–206

This warranty seeks disclosure of outstanding fees to service providers and, since it deals with matters of fact, the vendors should be willing to give it.

### 7.25 Employee membership

**7.25.1 The Company offers Scheme membership to all its employees (part time, full time, fixed term and permanent) and all employees who have accepted offers to participate in the Scheme have been duly admitted to participation in the Scheme and the Company has fulfilled in all material respects its obligations under it.**  7–207

This clause aims to identify any tidying up with employer participation in the Scheme that may be required, and the vendors ought to be willing to give it.

### 7.26 Members' data

**7.26.1 The membership data in respect of the Scheme for active members, deferred pensioners and pensioners was when given and remains complete and accurate in all material respects.**  7–208

While this warranty principally requires the warranting of matters of fact, much of the data will be provided from a variety of sources, including employers and members themselves and the vendors might with some justification be reluctant to warrant all details. Restriction of the warranty to particular types of information might, however, be acceptable. Alternatively, if such information is included in that disclosed pursuant to cl.7.1.1, the vendors may argue that this provision is not required.

### 7.27 Debts arising

**7-209**    **7.27.1 The Company is not nor has it been an employer (as defined in the Pensions Act 1995, s.124(1)) in relation to an occupational pension scheme (as defined in s.176) (not being a money purchase scheme) in respect of which a relevant insolvency event (as described in s.75(4)) has occurred; or if earlier, which has commenced winding-up.**

This warranty is designed to identify whether or not there is any possibility of a debt on employer liability under s.75 coming back to haunt the target company. Such a debt could result from its previous participation in a scheme which later winds up in deficit. Since the clause deals with the possibility of a debt arising, the vendors might be tempted to seek to qualify it by awareness. However, for there to be a potential liability an insolvency event must have occurred or the scheme commenced winding-up—matters of fact of which the vendors ought to be aware. The better approach, if such an event has occurred but the debt not yet been calculated, would be for the vendors to disclose the relevant facts.

### 7.28 Pensions Act liabilities

**7-210**    **7.28.1 There are no liabilities which, under the Pensions Act 1995, s.75, can be imposed on the Company as a debt due from it to the trustees of an occupational pension scheme in which the Company has participated as an employer (within the definition thereof in s.124(1)).**

While cl.7.27.1 is concerned with whether a debt on employer liability might arise, this is designed to identify whether there are any actual current debts on employer liabilities. It is a matter of fact as to whether such liabilities exist and as such the vendors ought to give this warranty.

### 7.29 No Occupational Pensions Regulatory Authority reports

**7-211**    **7.29.1 No report in relation to the Scheme has been made to the Occupational Pensions Regulatory Authority under the Pensions Act 1995, s.48 and no circumstances exist in which it would be appropriate for a report to be made.**

The Pensions Act 1995 imposes obligations upon the auditor, actuary and other named professional advisers to a pension scheme to report to OPRA any failure to comply with certain requirements, such as the requirement upon the employer to make contributions into a scheme by a specified date.

The purpose of this clause is to identify whether any such reports have been made. It is reasonable for the purchaser to require this information, as a reporting history may disclose potential industrial relations problems and will give an indication as to the extent to which OPRA has been made aware of the scheme.

# 8 Assets

## 8.1 Ownership of assets

**8.1.1 At the Balance Sheet Date the Company owned (free from options,**    7–212
**charges, liens or Encumbrances) and (except for current assets subsequently**
**sold or realised in the normal course of business) still owns all the [tangible]**
**assets included in the Accounts and all [tangible] assets acquired since the**
**Balance Sheet Date and not subsequently sold or realised as above.**

The vendors should consider whether the properties owned by the target company should be excluded from this clause, as normally separate extensive warranties will apply in relation to them (see Ch.6). Furthermore, it is possible that many assets as shown in the last accounts will be subject to reservation of title clauses in view of the guidance statement issued by the Consultative Committee of Accountancy Bodies in September 1976. This recommended that, where the circumstances indicate that the reservation of title is regarded by the parties as having no practical relevance except in the event of insolvency, it would prevent the accounts showing a true and fair view if the stock subject to reservation of title were omitted from the balance sheet of the purchasing customer. Normally a note in the accounts would explain the position. Another relevant point is that equipment leased on finance leases will usually be shown as assets under SSAP21.

The vendors should consider separately each asset appearing in the last accounts to determine whether this warranty can fairly be given in respect of it. They should be alert to the possibility of property being occupied by a company but owned by trustees of a directors' pension arrangement. As debts are normally covered by a separate group of warranties, it would be preferable for the vendors to exclude them from this clause and, indeed, to amend the wording so that intangible assets generally are not included.

**8.1.2 The Company has not created or granted, or agreed to create or**    7–213
**grant, any Encumbrance in respect of any of the fixed assets included in the**
**Accounts, or acquired or agreed to be acquired since the Balance Sheet Date,**
**except in the normal course of business.**

This warranty should give no difficulty to the vendors and clearly is of interest to the purchaser. To some extent, there will be an overlap with cl.1.11.2 in relation to security interests which require registration under CA 1985, Pt XII.

## 8.2 Assets sufficient for the business

**8.2.1 The assets owned by the Company, together with the Intellectual**    7–214
**Property Rights and assets held under the hire purchase, leasing and rental**

**agreements listed in the Disclosure Letter, comprise all assets necessary for the continuation of its business [in substantially the same manner] as now carried on, and no assets are shared with another person.**

The first part of this clause involves matters of judgment, and its accuracy will be tested only by the conduct of the business of the target company after completion. The vendors would therefore normally be reluctant to accept this part of the provision and, if they did so, they might wish to amend the wording as indicated. The second part is concerned with matters of fact and ought not pose a difficulty to the vendors.

### 8.3 Stocks and work in progress

7–215    **8.3.1 The stocks of raw materials, packaging materials and finished goods held by the Company are not excessive and are adequate in relation to its current trading requirements and, save where written down or provided for, none of such stock is obsolete, slow moving, unusable, in poor condition, defective, unmarketable or inappropriate or of limited value in relation to the current business of the Company.**

As with cl.8.2.1, this provision is largely subjective and its accuracy will be tested only once the purchaser has control of the target company. The vendors should accept the warranty only in so far as the matters covered have been taken into account in the negotiations determining the consideration paid for the target company.

7–216    **8.3.2 [So far as the Vendors are aware] the work in progress of the Company is adequate to maintain cash flow and profitability at a level not less than that disclosed in the Disclosure Letter.**

The precise wording of this warranty will depend upon the form of any cash flow and profit projections which have been produced to the purchaser. If the terms of the acquisition have been negotiated on the basis of projections, both the purchaser and the vendors will wish to consider carefully what representations should be warranted in relation to them. This clause deals only with a limited aspect and might serve as a pointer to a suitable warranty. If projections have not been made or, if made, have not formed a basis for negotiating terms, the vendors should resist giving the warranty.

7–217    **8.3.3 The stock in trade of the Company is in good condition and is capable of being sold by it in the normal course of its business in accordance with its current price list, without rebate or allowance to a purchaser.**

Again, this is a subjective question and the vendors would generally prefer the purchaser to satisfy itself by inspection prior to contracts. As drafted, the warranty will in all normal circumstances be far too onerous to be acceptable without substantial qualification.

## 8.4 *Insurance*

**8.4.1 All the assets of the Company of an insurable nature are, and have at**   7–218
**all material times been, insured in amounts representing their full replace-**
**ment or reinstatement value against fire and other risks normally insured**
**against by persons carrying on similar businesses or owning property of a**
**similar nature.**

The interest of the purchaser is to ensure that no loss of assets has occurred since
the balance sheet date which is not fully covered by insurance. It would therefore
be appropriate for this warranty to relate only to circumstances since that date.
The vendors might have difficulty in satisfying themselves as to what is the full
replacement or reinstatement value of assets and what risks are normally covered
by insurance by persons carrying on similar businesses. An alternative approach
to this warranty, therefore, is for the vendors to produce particulars of all
insurance to the purchaser with a warranty that the particulars are correct and that
the policies are in force. Provided that the purchaser has sufficient time to review
the policies, it would be reasonable to accept this alternative. In such circumstances the following wording would be appropriate:

**Full particulars of all insurance policies in which the Company has an**
**interest are given in the Disclosure Letter; all the insurances are in force**
**[and will be maintained in force without alteration pending completion] and**
**all premiums have been paid on time.**

The wording in square brackets would be appropriate if contracts and completion
were not going to be simultaneous.

**8.4.2 The Company is, and has at all material times been, adequately**   7–219
**insured against accident, damage, third party loss (including product liabil-**
**ity), loss of profits and other risks normally insured against by persons**
**carrying on the same type of business as that carried on by it.**

This is an extension of cl.8.4.1 and similar comments apply.

**8.4.3 Nothing has been done or omitted or has occurred which could make**   7–220
**a policy of insurance taken out by the Company void or voidable or which**
**is likely to result in an increase in premium.**

An insurance contract will generally be void if there is a fundamental mistake of
fact relating to the contract (such as the non-existence of the asset purportedly
insured), if the contract is illegal, if the contract of insurance is in the nature of
a gaming contract or if the insured has no insurable interest. A policy is voidable
if it is obtained by misrepresentation or non-disclosure of material facts. While
it would normally be reasonable for the vendors to accept responsibility for the
policies not being void or voidable, it is generally unreasonable for them to be
required to warrant that nothing has occurred which could lead to a rise in

premium. If the purchaser insists on this, the vendors might restrict the warranty to circumstances where the insurance company has intimated that an increase of premium will result from events which have occurred.

**7–221    8.4.4 None of the insurance policies is subject to special or unusual terms or restrictions or to the payment of a premium in excess of the normal rate.**

This clause involves matters of judgment and the vendors cannot readily satisfy themselves as to whether the warranty is acceptable. They should ask the purchaser to inspect the policies and determine for itself whether the terms of the policies are unusual or the premiums excessive.

**7–222    8.4.5 No claim is outstanding, threatened or may be made, under any of the policies and no circumstances exist which could give rise to a claim.**

On the face of it this is a reasonable warranty to request and give, although it may not be easy to be sure what circumstances fall within the scope of the second half. Nevertheless, it is unclear as to what disadvantage the purchaser would suffer if the warranty were breached. So long as the insurance cover is satisfactory, there will be no financial loss. Any inconvenience caused to the business of the target company in the circumstances giving rise to a claim will generally be covered by other warranties.

### 8.5 Leased assets

**7–223    8.5.1 Nothing has occurred or is likely to occur in relation to an asset held by the Company, under a lease or similar agreement, whereby the rental payable has been, or is likely to be, increased.**

It is customary for finance leases of plant and equipment to include a tax adjustment clause providing for an increase in the rental in certain circumstances. The main events normally giving rise to an increase are a change in the corporation tax rate or in the extent of the capital allowances and accordingly the warranty should be acceptable in relation to past events. The vendors should delete the words **"or is likely to occur"** and **"or is likely to be"**.

### 8.6 Plant in working order

**7–224    8.6.1 The plant, machinery, vehicles and other equipment used in connection with the business of the Company:**

**7–225        8.6.1.1 are [subject to normal wear and tear] in a good and safe state of repair and satisfactory working order [taking into account their age, use and value] and have been properly serviced and maintained;**

This clause, even when qualified by the words in the first set of square brackets, is onerous. With the addition of the words in the second set of square brackets the clause is less onerous and the vendors should be more inclined to give it. Whether the vendors will be obliged to give the warranty will depend upon the circumstances of the transaction but in any case it is desirable from the point of view of both parties that the purchaser should inspect the premises of the target company and satisfy itself, so far as possible, as to the state of repair and condition of the equipment.

### 8.6.1.2  are not surplus to requirements;                    7–226

The purchaser cannot reasonably object to surplus plant unless the purchase price is based upon the asset value of the target company. In any case, it is likely to be a difficult matter of judgment to decide whether plant is surplus at any given moment and the vendors will generally find this clause unacceptable. It is difficult to see how the purchaser could suffer loss in most cases.

### 8.6.1.3  are in the possession and control of, and are the absolute    7–227
unencumbered property of, the Company, except for those items the subject of the hire purchase, leasing or rental agreements listed in the Disclosure Letter, and in respect of each of which the outstanding payments do not exceed £[ ]; and

This warranty is largely a question of fact and the vendors should, in principle, have no difficulty with giving it.

### 8.6.1.4  [So far as the Vendors are aware and on the assumption that the    7–228
Company carries on its business in the same manner as carried on prior to Completion] are not expected to require replacements or additions at a cost in excess of £[ ] within the next six months.

It is difficult for the vendors to satisfy themselves in connection with this clause and they should take into account the fact that any need to replace or add to equipment after completion will largely be within the control of the purchaser. The vendors are likely to find this clause acceptable only if the value of the plant has been taken into account in determining the purchase consideration for the shares being sold. With the inclusion of the words in brackets the warranty becomes more reasonable. Even with the awareness qualification the vendors ought to consider a disclosure against this warranty that they have not arranged an inspection or survey of the relevant plant and equipment if in fact that is the case.

### 8.6.2  There are maintenance contracts with independent specialist con-    7–229
tractors in respect of all assets of the Company for which it is normal or prudent to have maintenance agreements and in respect of all assets which

**the Company is obliged to maintain or repair under a lease or similar agreement.**

This warranty can be dealt with more satisfactorily from the vendors' point of view by producing copies of all maintenance contracts to the purchaser and warranting that they are in force. Alternatively the warranty could be amended to make it clear that the company has maintenance agreements in force for those assets which the vendors consider it prudent or necessary to do so taking account of the age, condition and value of the relevant assets and the use to which they are put.

### 8.7 Intellectual Property Rights

7–230    In seeking intellectual property warranties, the purchaser has two primary objectives. First, to ensure that it fully understands the strength of the intellectual property portfolio (such as the technical and geographical scope of the rights, their validity and enforceability, whether or not the rights may be subject to attack and the strength of competing third party registered rights). Second, to fully understand the existing potential liabilities which have been or may be incurred by the target company as a result of the past and continued use of the intellectual property rights.

If the value of the intellectual property rights of the target company are particularly significant to the purchaser (for example, in the case of high technology companies), the purchaser may require more extensive and comprehensive intellectual property warranties including specific warranties pertinent to particular intellectual property rights. The purchaser may also decide to undertake its own assessment as to the technical and commercial value of the intellectual property.

If applications for registered intellectual property rights have significant potential commercial value the purchaser may wish to extend the warranties relating to such applications.

7–231    **8.7.1 Full details of all Intellectual Property Rights (registered and unregistered) owned or used by the Company are set out in the Disclosure Letter [   ] and are complete and accurate. The Intellectual Property Rights are:**

**8.7.1.1 used exclusively in the business of the Company;**

**8.7.1.2 legally and beneficially owned by the Company and not held jointly or in common with any other person;**

**8.7.1.3 valid, subsisting and enforceable and nothing has been done or omitted to be done by which they may cease to be valid and enforceable;**

**8.7.1.4 not subject to infringement, challenge, opposition or attack or the subject of any claim for ownership or compensation by any third party or competent authority and the Vendors know no reason why**

**any of them may be subject to challenge, opposition or attack or claim; and**

**8.7.1.5 where capable of registration are registered in the name of the Company in all jurisdictions relevant to its business.**

This warranty is intended to deal with all intellectual property rights owned by   7–232
the target company, whether or not registered, rather than any third party
intellectual property rights which are licensed to the target company and which
are dealt with in cl.8.7.4. The definition of intellectual property rights is very
wide and as such the vendors may wish to limit their obligations to registered
intellectual property rights and material unregistered intellectual property
rights.

The purchaser will want assurance that all intellectual property rights owned
by the target company are valid. However, this is an onerous warranty which
most vendors will refuse to give. They will argue that they are not in a position
to say whether or not intellectual property rights may be invalid for technical or
other reasons and so will seek the deletion of cl.8.7.1.3. However, vendors will
normally warrant that intellectual property rights have not been subject to any
challenge or attack and they may also warrant that they know of no reason why
they should be.

**8.7.2 The renewal and registration fees for the protection of the registered**   7–233
**Intellectual Property Rights of the Company have been paid and all other**
**steps required for their prosecution, maintenance and protection have been**
**taken.**

If intellectual property rights are particularly valuable to the purchaser then this
clause could be expanded to cover specific types of intellectual property. For
example, in respect of patent applications, the warranty could state that there has
been no prior disclosure of the claimed invention except under obligations of
confidentiality, or, in relation to trade marks, that the trade marks have not lost
their distinctiveness and are therefore liable to attack.

**8.7.3 The Vendors are not aware of any factors which would cause any**   7–234
**applications for registration of any Intellectual Property Rights to be unac-**
**ceptable to any body to whom the application is being made.**

The vendors will wish to restrict this warranty to specific actual applications to
specific bodies, and to disclose any and all known problems. If the purchaser
does not wish to bear the risk that the applications will not succeed for reasons
unknown to the vendors, this warranty may be made absolute rather than subject
to the vendors' knowledge.

**8.7.4 Copies of the licences of Intellectual Property Rights owned by third**   7–235
**parties which have been granted to the Company are attached to the**
**Disclosure Letter. The Company is not in breach of any of the licences and**

**the Vendors are not aware of and have no reason to believe that there is cause for a licence to come to an end or be restricted.**

The vendors will want to limit this warranty solely to licences expressly granted to the target company, rather than to any implied licence of intellectual property rights such as those granted in relation to goods which embody protected rights. The warranty will still extend to a large number of agreements such as computer agreements and software contracts. In large transactions the vendors may wish to limit the obligation to licences which are "material" to the business. In such a case materiality should extend not only to the amount of fees or licence payments but also to licences of low monetary value, the enjoyment of which is critical to the business of the target company. The vendors may also wish to exclude from the warranty off-the-shelf software licences, which may be dealt with as a separate category under the computer systems warranties.

The vendors may find it difficult to be sure that the target company is not in breach of all licence agreements and may, therefore, seek to limit the clause such that the company has not received any notice or claim of any breach of any such agreements.

7–236     **8.7.5 Copies of the licences of Intellectual Property Rights owned by the Company which have been granted to third parties are attached to the Disclosure Letter. The Company is not in breach of any of the licences and the Vendors are not aware and have no reason to believe that there is cause for a licence to come to an end or be restricted.**

Again, the vendors may wish to limit this warranty to material licences and to those which are subsisting.

7–237     **8.7.6 The Intellectual Property Rights referred to in clause [8.7.1] and the third party Intellectual Property Rights referred to in clause [8.7.4] are all the Intellectual Property Rights necessary for the Company to carry on its business and the Company has not charged or encumbered or created an equity, lien or other adverse interest over any of them or agreed to grant an option, right, licence, sub-licence or other adverse right over any of them to any other person and is not obliged to do the same.**

If all licences of intellectual property are not disclosed, then the purchaser may want this clause extended by the words **"and none of the Intellectual Property Rights is subject to a restriction or right of termination"**.

7–238     **8.7.7 None of the activities of the Company, its products, business methods, processes or services infringe third party Intellectual Property Rights. In the past six years the Company has not been a party to or received a threat of litigation or a claim relating to Intellectual Property Rights, passing off or unfair competition. The Vendors are not aware and have no reason to believe that a third party is infringing the Intellectual Property**

**Rights of the Company or that the Company has acquiesced to an infringement.**

This warranty is very far reaching and it is likely that the vendors will, as a minimum, wish to have the first sentence of it deleted. In addition, they may seek to qualify the second limb by their knowledge and awareness. The third element of the clause is effectively similarly qualified but the vendors should ensure that the wording is no broader than any definition agreed in respect of "awareness".

**8.7.8 No licences of Intellectual Property Rights will terminate or become capable of termination or otherwise be adversely affected by [the execution and completion of] this Agreement.**                7–239

Clause 4.3.1.4 will extend to any licence of third party intellectual property rights granted to the target company, but this separate clause dealing specifically with all intellectual property rights may be preferable for the purchaser; not least because it is likely to focus the minds of the vendors. The vendors should see the comments on cl.4.3.1.4.

**8.7.9 There are no pending or outstanding claims against the Company for compensation under the Patents Act 1977, s.40.**                7–240

Section 40 provides for compensation to be payable if an employee makes an invention which is of outstanding commercial benefit to his employer. If the vendors are in any doubt as to whether or not this warranty could apply they should seek to include a suitable disclosure in the disclosure letter.

**8.7.10 The Confidential Business Information which have been developed by or acquired by the Company has been kept secret and has not been disclosed to or used by another person except under obligations of confidentiality. The Vendors are not aware and have no reason to believe that a third party is in breach of confidentiality obligations.**                7–241

The first sentence of this clause is far reaching giving the definition of "Confidential Business Information". The vendors may wish to exclude information which is over five years old, on the basis that such information is unlikely to be of significant commercial value and is likely to have entered the public domain. However where some or all of the matters encompassed by the definition are particularly valuable, this exclusion would be inappropriate and should be resisted by the purchaser. The vendors may also want to exclude any information required to be disclosed to professional advisers or by law or regulatory authority.

The purchaser will wish to extend this warranty to state that the "Confidential Business Information" is **"in the lawful possession of the vendors"** and has not been acquired, for example, in breach of confidence.

7–242    **8.7.11 The Company is not a party to a secrecy agreement or other agreement or arrangement which restricts the use or disclosure of confidential information.**

The vendors may wish to exclude restrictions within the commercial agreements of the target company which have been disclosed to the purchaser.

7–243    **8.7.12 [So far as the Vendors are aware] all moral rights in respect of the Company's Intellectual Property Rights have been waived in favour of the Company.**

Under English law, moral rights consist of the right to be identified as the author of a work (paternity right), the right to not have a work subjected to derogatory treatment (integrity right), the right not to have a work falsely attributed to another person (right of non-attribution) and the right to privacy of photographs and films commissioned for private and domestic purposes. Moral rights may be infringed unless the right-holder has consented to the act, waived his rights by a signed instrument in writing, or the act is permitted under the relevant provisions of the Copyright Designs and Patents Act 1988. Moral rights subsist for the duration of the copyright in the work, except for the right of non-attribution which subsists for 20 years following the right-holder's death. Moral rights may not be assigned but are transmitted on death, except for the right of non-attribution which is actionable for its duration by the right-holder's personal representatives.

This warranty is of particular importance to the purchaser where individuals have been contracted by the target company to create intellectual property rights on its behalf. The vendors will usually wish to qualify this warranty by reference to knowledge.

### 8.8 Computer Systems

7–244    As companies become increasingly reliant on the use of information technology and computer systems, specific warranties may be required in relation to them. The purchaser will want to ensure that during its due diligence it has fully understood what computer systems are used by the target company, how they are used and their robustness and functionality. It will need to understand whether those systems are shared with anyone, whether it will be necessary to separate them and whether it is practical to do so. Furthermore, it will wish to establish whether it will require the use of any computer systems retained by the vendors on a transitional basis following completion. Finally, it will want to ensure that it is aware of all the software licences which apply and the provision, support, maintenance and other services provided by third parties in respect of the computer systems (such as telecommunications services, outsourcing, escrow and facilities management services). The purchaser will aim to ensure that it is aware of the terms of all material agreements so that it may establish whether it can transfer and separate the computer systems or whether new licences and other arrangements need to be put in place. If the purchaser intends to link its own systems to those of the target company post-completion, consideration should be given to covering that with separate warranties.

If the purchaser does intend to do this it will require substantial planning and the parties will need to understand and agree the cost of any transition and separation issues and the apportionment of such costs.

### 8.8.1 The Computer Systems:                                    7–245

**8.8.1.1 are used exclusively by the Company and under its sole control;**

The purpose of this clause is to elicit information as to the extent that the target company may be dependent upon shared use of computer systems or third party services, and it should not pose any difficulties for the vendors.

**8.8.1.2 are, in respect of the hardware, firmware, peripherals, network-    7–246 ing and other equiment comprised in those Computer Systems, legally and beneficially owned by the Company;**

The purpose of the clause is to elicit information as to ownership of hardware, in so far as this is not already covered by the asset warranties earlier.

**8.8.1.3 are in full working order and performing the functions for    7–247 which they were acquired efficiently and without material errors or downtime;**

The vendors will need to disclose any known problems with or limitations of the systems and may wish to qualify or replace the broad subjective phrase **"performing the functions for which they were acquired"** by references to reasonableness, specific intended functions and actual performance.

**8.8.1.4 have not, within the two years immediately preceding Comple-    7–248 tion, unduly interrupted or hindered the operation of the business of the Company;**

The normal warranties as to the condition of plant, machinery, vehicles and other equipment are not appropriate for computer systems which by their nature may include many minor errors or "bugs" which do not materially adversely affect performance. The purchaser may seek to extend the warranty to include a statement that there are no defects in the computer systems, whereas the vendors may wish to avoid such a warranty or limit it to material defects and by reference to their knowledge and awareness.

**8.8.1.5 have adequate capacity for the Company's present and (taking    7–249 into account the extent to which the Computer Systems are expandable) future needs;**

This clause assures the purchaser that the computer systems are suitable and have sufficient capacity for the anticipated growth of the target company. However, the vendors are unlikely to underwrite the future performance or needs of the target company; they will, as a minimum, seek to qualify the target company's future needs as those which are **"foreseeable"** or limit them to those occurring in a short specified period following completion, and may seek to delete the second half of this clause in its entirety.

7–250     **8.8.1.6 have been satisfactorily and appropriately maintained and supported and have the benefit of appropriate maintenance and support agreements (copies of which are attached to the Disclosure Letter), which agreements include emergency support;**

This clause may be inserted in support of cl.8.8.1.3.

The vendors are likely to resist the breadth of this warranty and will look to restrict it to a factual statement only that certain specified maintenance agreements are actually in place, and on the terms disclosed.

7–251     **8.8.1.7 [so far as the Vendors are aware] have not been used in such a way as would invalidate any manufacturer's or supplier's guarantee or warranty or entitle the provider of maintenance or support for the Computer Systems to exclude, suspend or terminate those services;**

This clause is intended to highlight problems with cover for hardware and for proprietary and bespoke software, rather than standard packaged software which is usually only warranted for 90 days from purchase. The vendors will wish to qualify the warranty by inclusion of the wording in brackets. However, the purchaser will resist this, wanting a clear indication of whether it can expect additional costs of repairing or replacing hardware and software which is no longer covered by guarantee or contract. Certain types of hardware maintenance performed by anyone not authorised by the manufacturer to do so, for example by employees of the target company, may commonly invalidate any guarantee or breach the applicable maintenance agreement. So may failure to comply with the manufacturer's instructions. For example, some types of hardware may be required to be kept in a clean environment or within a certain temperature range. Software guarantees and support contracts may also be invalidated or breached by failure to use the software in accordance with its licence terms. If the target company's computer systems contain systems which are key to the successful operation of the business then the purchaser may wish to take specific warranties for those items.

7–252     **8.8.1.8 have, in conjunction with the support and maintenance agreements referred to in clause [8.8.1.6], adequate security measures, back-up systems, disaster recovery arrangements, measures to protect them from viruses and other harmful code and trained personnel to ensure that so far as reasonably practicable:**

The scope of this warranty is wide, and the vendors will wish to restrict its scope to a statement of specified measures that the target company has taken.

### 8.8.1.8.1  the authenticity, integrity and confidentiality of all data held        7–253
by or transmitted by the Computer Systems are preserved;

The vendors will wish to qualify this clause by reference to knowledge, to limit it to confidential, sensitive or material data, and to restrict **"transmitted"** to material sent by the target company. They will need to disclose failure to take appropriate measures, for example to encrypt or digitally sign external email and confidential internal email, if that is the case.

### 8.8.1.8.2  no more than one day's data would be lost in the event of a        7–254
failure of the Computer Systems;

The target company's back-up systems will normally be designed to enable this. The vendors should ensure that back-up data can, in practice, be retrieved and restored. Any problems should be disclosed.

### 8.8.1.8.3  breaches of security, errors and breakdowns are kept to a        7–255
minimum and that in the event of the occurrence of any such
event there will not [so far as the Vendors are aware] be a
material disruption to the Company;

The vendors will seek either to delete the second half of this warranty or to qualify it by reference to knowledge.

### 8.8.1.9  enable all records and data stored by electronic means which        7–256
relate to the Company to be readily accessible by appropriate
personnel; and

This warranty is wide in scope and few vendors will accept it as drafted. They will seek either to delete it or to qualify it by reference to knowledge, or to specified "material" records and data. The vendors will need to disclose problems with the speed of data delivery, whether due to load on the system or to system design. If certain systems do not permit the setting of appropriate access levels to information, that will also need to be disclosed.

### 8.8.1.10  will correctly carry out all calculations relating to or in con-        7–257
nection with the Euro and display all symbols adopted by any
government or European body in connection with the Euro.

A purchaser will wish to know about non-compliant systems if either the target company currently trades in the Euro or makes calculations or conversions by reference to the Euro, or if the purchaser intends that the target company will do so post completion. There will be a cost for the purchaser in making computer systems Euro-compliant, and this clause is intended to highlight any such issue.

**7–258**    **8.8.2 All software used or stored or resident in the Company:**

The vendors may wish to reduce the scope of this warranty by removing the words **"stored or resident"** thereby restricting the following clauses to software actually used in the target company. The vendors may be prepared to include software which is stored or resident in the target company in relation to specific warranties.

**7–259**    **8.8.2.1 [so far as the Vendors are aware] is free from any defect or feature which may adversely affect its performance or the performance of any other software in the future;**

The vendors will be very unlikely to agree to the second half of this warranty as it relates to matters outside of their control. They will normally seek to restrict the first half of the warranty to their knowledge.

**7–260**    **8.8.2.2 performs in accordance with its specification;**

This warranty is inappropriate for standard packaged software, where the licensee will rarely have access to the specification. However, a purchaser should insist on the warranty for any bespoke software which has been written or commissioned by the target company.

**7–261**    **8.8.2.3 has been (if copied) lawfully copied;**

The vendors may seek to restrict this warranty by reference to knowledge. The purchaser should resist this, given the serious consequences if unlawful copying has taken place.

**7–262**    **8.8.2.4 is lawfully held and [so far as the Vendors are aware] does not infringe the Intellectual Property Rights of any person;**

The first half of this warranty should not pose any difficulties for the vendors, but they will want to qualify the second half by reference to knowledge, or remove it altogether.

**7–263**    **8.8.2.5 as to the copyright therein:**

Copyright is the main intellectual property right which protects software.

**7–264**    **8.8.2.5.1 in the case of software written or commissioned by the Company, is owned solely by the Company, no other person has rights therein or rights to use or make copies of the software or source codes;**

This warranty is of fundamental importance to the purchaser and as such it would be unlikely to accept any qualification by the vendors by reference to knowledge.

If the target company licenses software to third parties, or has developed or commissioned software which is important to the business, the purchaser will normally wish to seek further appropriate warranties.

**8.8.2.5.2 in the case of standard packaged software purchased outright,** 7–265 **is validly licensed to the Company in perpetuity (other than in the event of breach or insolvency) on written terms which do not require the Company to make any further payments and no licences will terminate on change of control; and**

This warranty puts the onus on the vendors to check standard licence terms, which can be a laborious task if the target company's use of software is extensive. The mechanisms for software licensing are no longer restricted to a single one-off fee for use in perpetuity. The vendors may seek to shift the risk back to the purchaser by replacing this warranty by a statement that the licence terms are as disclosed.

**8.8.2.5.3 in the case of all other software, is licensed to the Company on** 7–266 **the terms of a written licence which requires payment by the Company of a fixed annual licence fee the terms of which are set out in the Disclosure Letter.**

The vendors will need to remove this warranty if it not relevant, or to make suitable disclosures.

**8.8.3 No software owned by or licensed to the Company is licensed or sub-** 7–267 **licensed by the Company to (or otherwise used by) any other person.**

This clause is wide and its purpose is to elicit information on any and all third party use of the target company's software. Unless these activities constitute the target company's business, the vendors should be able to give this warranty without too many difficulties. The purchaser will resist any attempt by the vendors to qualify the clause by reference to their knowledge, particularly in relation to software licensed to the target company, as sub-licensing will normally be a breach of the licensor's terms.

**8.8.4 No action will be necessary to enable the Company to continue to use** 7–268 **any software currently used by it to the same extent and in the same manner as it has been used prior to Completion.**

Some licence terms require the target company to give notice of change of control, although this is more frequently the case where the software is actually transferred. As with cl.8.8.2.5.2, this clause will require the vendors to check the licence terms. The vendors will argue this is properly part of the purchaser's due diligence and will wish to replace the warranty by a reference to disclosed licence terms.

**7–269**    **8.8.5 The terms of all software licences have been complied with and no notices of breach or termination have been served on the Company in respect of any such licence.**

The vendors may wish to qualify the target company's compliance by reference to knowledge, particularly if the licence terms are not in writing or cannot be located. The purchaser should resist this.

**7–270**    **8.8.6 Details of all Company domain names and websites are set out in the Disclosure Letter. The Company is the registrant and beneficial owner of those domain names and is the legal and beneficial owner of all Intellectual Property Rights in the websites.**

This clause is intended to elicit information which the vendors will normally be able to provide without qualification. However, if the websites are particularly complex or large and have been developed over a number of years, the vendors may not be able to give an absolute assurance on ownership, and will seek to qualify the second part of the warranty by reference to knowledge. The purchaser will wish to know if any domain names have been registered in the name of a third party, commonly an employee or hosting provider, rather than the Company, and to require these to be transferred to the Company pre-completion, so that it can exercise effective control over them. If intellectual property rights in the website are owned by a third party rather than the Company, the purchaser will need to establish the terms on which those rights may be used.

# CHAPTER 8

# Warranties and Indemnities on the Sale of a Business

## INTRODUCTION

The sale of a business is a transaction which involves the sale of a varied **8–01** collection of assets having different characteristics:

(1) some of the assets will be physical goods, such as stock, machinery, equipment, motor vehicles and computer systems some of which may be subject to finance or leasing agreements;

(2) usually there will be freehold or leasehold properties to be transferred;

(3) intangible assets will include the goodwill of the business, and commonly the benefit (subject to the burden) of customer and supply contracts, know how and confidential business information, the customer and employee database and intellectual property rights;

(4) rights may be sold, such as to the current order book or the vendor's rights against third parties, including all rights under warranties, conditions, guarantees or indemnities which are barely assets in the normal sense. Depending on the agreed position between the parties the assets may also include the book debts of the business, although increasingly book debts are being excluded from business sales and retained by the vendor following completion, albeit with some assistance from the purchaser in their collection.

The transaction will not normally involve the purchaser taking over liabilities and these will not generally pass unless there is an express acceptance by the purchaser (for example in respect of contracts). This broad principle needs, however, to be qualified in a number of respects:

(1) liabilities in relation to properties may run with the land and accordingly automatically bind the purchaser;

(2) pursuant to the Transfer of Undertakings (Protection of Employment) Regulations 1981 (SI 1981 No 1794) ("TUPE") on the transfer of a business or other economic entity (other than by way of a sale of shares), responsibility for the contracts of employment of those persons employed in the business immediately before the transfer is automatically assumed by

the purchaser who may neither change the terms and conditions of employment nor dismiss the employees for a reason connected with the transfer;

(3) partly completed goods, the manufacture of which is completed by the purchaser, will give rise to a liability on the purchaser if they prove to be defective even though the defect arises from work done by the vendor; and

(4) from a practical point of view, it is often necessary for the purchaser to perform warranty obligations of the vendor in relation to goods sold slightly before the transfer of the business.

**8–02**     Despite these exceptions, the general rule is that the purchaser does not take over any liabilities of the business for which it does not wish to be responsible. This significantly affects the scope of the warranties and indemnities which the purchaser will seek and, broadly, a number of the warranties on share sales dealing with potential liabilities, and in particular those concerning taxation, will be unnecessary. Nevertheless, not all potential liabilities are irrelevant in determining whether the purchaser has acquired what it thought it was buying. Accordingly, the purchaser will wish to be sure that:

(1) the vendor owns the assets to be transferred to the purchaser absolutely, that there are no encumbrances over any of them and that they are all in working order;

(2) there has been no breach or default by the vendor in respect of any of the contracts to be transferred to the purchaser, or, in so far as there has been, the purchaser does not assume responsibility for such breach or default;

(3) the vendor has complied with the information and consultation provisions set out in TUPE, regulation 10;

(4) no employee other than those which the purchaser is aware of will transfer to it pursuant to TUPE;

(5) there has been full and effective disclosure of all of the transferring employees' terms and conditions of employment and that such employees do not, for example, have any contractual right to enhanced salary, pension or other benefits that the purchaser is not aware of;

(6) there are no present or past disputes with employees or liabilities to employees or former employees of which the purchaser is not aware but for which responsibility will pass to the purchaser under TUPE;

(7) the accounts of the vendor correctly reflect the profitability of the business and that liabilities reducing the profits are fully taken into account; and

(8) there are no disputes with suppliers and customers or in respect of any of the intellectual property rights of the business as these could adversely affect the goodwill of the business.

Given that a business sale would not normally involve the purchaser taking over existing liabilities it is usual for the purchaser to seek indemnities from the vendor in respect of the few areas where liability may pass from the vendor to the purchaser. The most notable example of this is in relation to employment matters, where the operation of TUPE means that the purchaser becomes liable for the acts and omissions of the vendor. Here the appropriate indemnities will provide the purchaser with comfort that it has acquired only what it thought it was acquiring (supported by appropriate warranties). This approach is adopted by purchasers to avoid the need to have to rely on warranties and prove loss in one of the few areas of major concern on a business sale.

## Defined Terms

To facilitate the drafting of the warranties and indemnities it is normal to make use of a number of defined terms. Examples of the definitions used in the warranties and indemnities on the sale of a business are contained in Part 1 of Appendix 5. Paragraph 4–01 provides a commentary on a number of these definitions (which apply to both a share sale and a business sale) highlighting particular points that should be borne in mind on a business sale. However, there are also a number of additional definitions set out in Appendix 5 which are only relevant to the warranties and indemnities on a business sale. Where these definitions require any special consideration they are discussed below.  **8–03**

## Scope of Indemnities

The areas detailed below will generally be the areas in which the purchaser has a legitimate interest in receiving indemnities.  **8–04**

(1) Against all losses, liabilities, obligations and outgoings of the business prior to completion. Legally these liabilities would not ordinarily pass to the purchaser but a "sweeping" indemnity often catches minor liabilities which pass as part of another obligation. Often there will be a "mirror" indemnity in favour of the vendor for any such obligations arising after completion.

(2) Against any pre-completion breach of a contract to be transferred to the purchaser or any default, negligence or misrepresentation concerning any such contract by the vendor. It is also usual for the vendor to require that the purchaser provide a similar indemnity in respect of the purchaser's performance of the obligations it has agreed to perform under contracts following completion.

(3) That the vendor has complied with the information and consultation requirements of TUPE in relation to all affected employees and that there are no other employees entitled to transfer to the purchaser other than those known to the purchaser. (The transferring employees are commonly listed in the sale agreement.) In return, the vendor will usually require that the purchaser warrants and/or provides an indemnity that it too has complied

with its TUPE obligations by providing all relevant information in respect of any measures it anticipates taking in respect of the transferring employees.

(4) Against any pre-completion act or omission by the vendor in relation to the contract of employment of any transferring employee. Again it is usual for the purchaser to grant a reciprocal indemnity to the vendor to cover any post-completion acts or omissions by the purchaser.

Depending on the particular circumstances of a transaction and the nature of the business there may be other specific indemnities that a purchaser may legit-imately require, for example in respect of compliance with the data protection principles on the transfer of a customer database or in respect of any value added tax later determined to be payable on goods or vehicles which are classified and sold by the vendor as value added tax exempt.

## CONSIDERATION OF INDIVIDUAL INDEMNITIES

**8–05**   As discussed above, the specific indemnities are designed to cover the key areas of risk for a purchaser on a business sale without having to rely upon the need to prove loss as a result of a breach of warranty. The indemnities will also be supported by warranties. Examples of suitable indemnities are given in Pt 2 of Appendix 5 and are discussed below.

### Creditors and liabilities

**8–06**   It is a widely accepted principle of a business sale that the liabilities and outgoings of the business up to completion are the responsibility of the vendor and, to the extent that they are transferred to the purchaser, that following completion they are the responsibility of the purchaser. Clauses 1.1 and 1.2 provide indemnities between the vendor and the purchaser to ensure that such a clean break is achieved.

### Contracts

**8–07**   The purchaser has the following concerns in respect of the contracts it is agreeing to take over from the vendor:

(1) that the vendor is not in breach of its obligations under any of the contracts at completion;

(2) that a contract may not be capable of being effectively assigned or novated and as a result remains with the vendor causing a loss of profit for the purchaser;

(3) that the vendor has not been negligent or made any misrepresentation in respect of the contracts; and

(4) that the purchaser is aware of all the obligations it will assume under the contracts.

It is legitimate for the purchaser to expect to be indemnified in respect of matters (1) to (3) above. These matters are covered in cll.2.1 to 2.3. It is, however, normal practice for the purchaser to be expected to rely upon its due diligence supported by limited warranties in respect of (4). Any contracts that the purchaser is assuming will be defined in the definition of "Contracts", which is separately broken down into "Customer Contracts", "Finance Agreements" and "Supply Contracts".

In return for providing the indemnities in cll.2.1 to 2.3 it would be reasonable for the vendor to expect to receive an indemnity back from the purchaser in respect of the purchaser's performance of the contracts following completion, again to reflect the clean break principle of a business sale. This indemnity is covered in cl.2.2.2.

## Employees

TUPE will apply to the sale or other "relevant transfer" of an "economic entity" **8–08** and will therefore apply to virtually all transfers of businesses or parts of businesses. The question of precisely when TUPE does or does not apply is perhaps the most vexed question in employment law. Specialist advice should be obtained early in the course of the transaction to ascertain whether TUPE does or does not apply.

Where TUPE applies, the contracts of employment of those persons who were employed in the business immediately before the transfer are automatically transferred to the purchaser on the same terms and conditions. As such, the purchaser will almost invariably take over responsibility for all employees and this, depending of course on the size of the business and number of employees, can give rise to a sizeable liability.

It is becoming increasingly common for vendors with more than one trading division or those who are selling only part of their business to exclude or "cherry pick" certain employees from the transfer. These employees may serve a multi-functional role across a number of the vendor's businesses or the vendor may simply want to transfer a skilled employee of the transferring business to one of its other businesses. Technically, to be excluded from automatic transfer, such excluded employees should be deployed elsewhere in the vendor's other business prior to completion so that at the point of completion they are not employed in the part to be transferred. Alternatively, TUPE allows employees to formally object to being transferred and appropriate evidence of such objection should be satisfactory. It is normal practice for the agreement to include a list of the transferring employees (defined as the "Employees") and, for the avoidance of doubt, a list of the employees specifically excluded from the transfer (defined as "the Excluded Employees"). The purchaser will normally insist upon an indemnity from the vendor in respect of any liability accruing to it under TUPE in connection with the "Excluded Employees".

Regulation 10 has been mentioned above. It sets out a framework for informing affected employees of the transfer, the reasons for it and the implications of it. Although it is commonly thought that the only affected employees are those whom it is intended to transfer, this is not the case. The purchaser may well have employees who are "affected" by the transfer, for example if the acquisition of the new business will lead to a redundancy situation or changes in terms of employment of the purchaser's existing workforce. Such people are equally entitled to the protection of regulation 10.

So far as transferring employees are concerned, the normal approach is for the vendor to formally ask the purchaser whether it intends taking any "measures" in respect of them. "Measures" are not defined but a sensible starting point is to consider whether any dismissals or significant changes in working practices are contemplated. If the purchaser indicates that some are contemplated then this will trigger a secondary duty to consult with the employees over the proposed measures. If the purchaser indicates that there are not then there is no need for the vendor to consult with the employees who merely need to be told that no measures are contemplated.

Where consultation is necessary, regulation 10 sets out how—and with whom—this should be carried out. The rules are complicated and specialist advice will normally be required.

An employer who fails to comply with its information and (where appropriate) consultation obligations risks Employment Tribunal claims for "protective awards", which can be for up to 13 weeks' gross pay per employee.

It is now settled law that liability in respect of a vendor's failure to inform and consult itself passes to the purchaser under TUPE. It will therefore be crucial that the purchaser obtains an indemnity in respect of any such failure.

**8–09** For the reasons discussed above, the potential employee liability is usually the largest risk for a purchaser on a business sale. The purchaser will therefore wish to be comfortable on a number of areas of key concern in order to ensure that it can quantify the obligations it proposes to assume. Commonly the purchaser will want comfort that:

(1) the vendor has complied with TUPE, regulation 10;

(2) the vendor has not done anything or omitted to do anything before the date of completion in respect of any contract of employment which could give rise to a liability;

(3) the vendor has not failed to pay any sum due to the transferring employees prior to completion;

(4) the vendor has not breached any obligation to any trade unions;

(5) there are no persons entitled to transfer to the purchaser other than the listed employees; and

(6) the purchaser is fully informed as to the terms of employment of the transferring employees.

It is legitimate for the purchaser to expect to be indemnified in respect of matters (1) to (5). The indemnities in cll.3.1.1 to 3.1.6 cover these matters. Again, it is normal practice for the purchaser to be expected to rely upon its due diligence supported by appropriate warranties in respect of matter (6), namely the terms and conditions of employment. Appropriate warranties are discussed separately below.

In return for providing the indemnities in cll.3.1.1 to 3.1.6 it would be reasonable for the vendor to expect to receive indemnities from the purchaser in respect of the following matters:

(1) any claim against the vendor by a transferring employee that the transfer of his employment to the purchaser amounted to a substantial detrimental change to his conditions of employment;

(2) any liability for post-transfer acts or omissions of the purchaser in respect of any transferring employee; and

(3) any liability under TUPE, regulation 10 arising from the failure or delay of the purchaser to notify the vendor of the "measures" the purchaser envisaged taking in relation to the transferring employees following completion (to allow the vendor comply with its own obligations under TUPE, regulation 10).

These indemnities from the purchaser to the vendor are covered in cl.3.2.

## Pensions

In contrast to a share transaction, on a business sale the purchaser does not inherit **8–10** all of the vendor's obligations to provide pensions to the staff. There is at present an exclusion (due to be reduced but to survive in part) where the business provides an occupational pension scheme (i.e. one run by trustees on behalf of the pre-transfer employer). Here, the purchaser is not obliged by law to continue to provide this pension scheme (although from April 2005 it will have to provide a replacement scheme that meets prescribed criteria). A common approach is for that particular trust-based scheme to "stay behind" post-transfer, and to continue to be sponsored by the pre-transfer employer.

Clearly, the purchaser will usually try to provide a replacement which will avoid industrial relations difficulties and also to prevent the remote risk of an aggrieved member of staff successfully challenging the law in the courts. There are exceptions to the current no-transfer rule where the occupational pension scheme provides non-core benefits that do not relate to old age, invalidity or the members' survivors (for example if it provides benefits such as an early pension on redundancy). The purchaser will be obliged to continue to provide those benefits (but they are relatively rare). Any such benefits should have been identified in the purchaser's due diligence.

An alternative approach is for the purchaser to replace the pre-transfer employer as sponsor (or "Principal Employer") of the pension scheme. This the purchaser should only do if the transferring employees account for substantially the whole of the scheme liabilities and if it is very clear as to the extent of such liabilities and how it will fund them. Such clarity is more often gained by taking its own actuarial advice, rather than using material (often out of date and done for a different purpose) from the scheme actuary, whose first duty in law is to scheme members, not a purchaser.

If there are no trust-based schemes and the business makes payments only to contract-based personal pensions, a group personal pension plan or a stakeholder scheme (i.e. run by insurance companies on behalf of the members), the purchaser will be obliged by law to make similar payments to the existing arrangements or to provide replacement arrangements. Similarity often takes the form of the purchaser continuing to provide the same contributions at the same percentage of salary as the vendor did. Not doing so would open the purchaser to claims for constructive dismissal. The due diligence process should establish the extent of the vendor's liability to pay such input contributions. These contributions must be distinguished from employer contributions made to trust-based schemes promising salary-related benefits. While such contributions will also usually be expressed as percentages of salary, the vendor may have an additional "balance of cost" liability.

**8–11**    Assuming that the purchaser has been informed that the business has only standard group personal pension plans or stakeholder schemes (which now seem to be more common than occupational schemes) the purchaser has two key concerns on an assets deal:

(1) that it has been informed of all schemes which affect the transferring employees so that it can properly assess the obligations to provide pensions to the transferring employees; and

(2) that other than in relation to benefits relating to old age, invalidity or survivors, the schemes provide no other benefits (which the purchaser will be obliged to continue to provide).

These concerns are covered in the indemnities in cl.4.1. Any pension scheme which the vendor has disclosed to the purchaser will be defined in the definition of "Schemes". The vendor may try and resist giving such indemnities but the purchaser can always justify its inclusion on the basis that the information is in the control of the vendor and the purchaser does not wish to have to rely on warranties (which will in most instances be subject to limitations) and have to prove loss to protect itself in respect of any pension entitlement of a transferring employee that it was not made aware of. It is a reasonable approach for the purchaser to expect to be informed of all schemes and non-retirement benefits and to be indemnified in respect of any obligation it has not been informed of. These indemnities will be supported by specific warranties in respect of the pension schemes (i.e. payment of contributions), which are discussed below.

## SCOPE OF WARRANTIES

**8–12**    In addition to the specific indemnities in cll.1 to 4 of Pt 2 of Appendix 5 (as discussed above) the matters detailed below will generally be the areas in which the purchaser has a legitimate interest in receiving warranties:

(1) The accounts of the business will be warranted. The form of these warranties will closely follow those that are sought by the purchaser of shares of a company. The primary purpose of the warranties is to enable the purchaser to have a claim if the value which it attributes to goodwill, and which in practice will have been greatly influenced by the accounts, was excessive because the accounts were inaccurate. This is not so straightforward in circumstances where part only of the business is being purchased. In such circumstances the accounts of the enlarged business may not be much help and a more detailed warranty which relates to the part of the business being sold will be more appropriate.

(2) The assets, including stock, information technology systems, debtors (where these are to be assigned to the purchaser) and intellectual property rights, will be covered.

(3) Most of the warranties relating to the trading activities of the business will correspond to those adopted on a share sale.

(4) The purchaser will only assume responsibility for those contracts it elects to do so and any breach or default by the vendor under the contracts will be covered by the specific indemnities at cll.2.1 to 2.3 of Pt 2 of Appendix 5. As such not all of the warranties included in a share purchase agreement in relation to contracts will be relevant. However, some basic warranty cover on the nature, terms and performance of the contracts should be sought, partly to back up any due diligence exercise and partly to elicit disclosure of any issues in respect of the contracts.

(5) As discussed above the rights of employees will be important both commercially and legally. The employment and pensions indemnities at cll.3 and 4 of Pt 2 of Appendix 5 will be supported by fairly long form warranties confirming the accuracy of the details and terms of employment for each employee and any disputes or other potential liabilities.

(6) The purchaser will wish to be sure that the vendor has all necessary and desirable licences and consents in respect of the business and has carried the business on in accordance with applicable law and that there are no statutory restrictions on the business as these factors could effect the value the purchaser has attributed to goodwill.

(7) The taxation warranties—to the extent any taxation warranties are included—will largely be restricted to capital allowances in respect of the transferring assets, value added tax and PAYE and national insurance deductions in respect of the transferring employees.

(8) The contractual aspect of the purchase of any assets which are properties will be dealt with in accordance with normal conveyancing practice. As, however, there may be factors relating to the properties which affect the value of the goodwill of the business but which would not normally be relevant on a property purchase which is unrelated to a business purchase, a few of the warranties that are included in a share purchase agreement may

be relevant. Depending on the nature of the business the purchaser may also seek either full or modified environmental warranties or indemnities when a property is included as part of the deal.

## OMITTED WARRANTIES

**8–13**    The warranties, other than in relation to properties, which are suitable for a business sale are set out in Pt 3 of Appendix 5 and closely follow those for a share sale which are discussed in para.7–03. The warranties omit a number of categories which are adopted on a share sale. These include the following.

### Preliminary

**8–14**    The warranties dealing with the information regarding the share capital of the company and its directors will not be relevant.

### Accounts

**8–15**    The clauses dealing with liabilities will be irrelevant except in so far as they affect the profits shown in the accounts on the basis of which the purchaser has valued the goodwill of the business.

### Finance

**8–16**    The purchaser will not need to be satisfied about the financial facilities available to the vendor for running the business as it would be most unusual for it to take these over. The warranties in this section relating to book debts are dealt with as part of the warranties concerning the assets which are being acquired.

### Trading and contracts

**8–17**    The aspects of the business which merely give rise to liabilities will not concern the purchaser except in so far as they affect the contracts which are to be transferred or are relevant in valuing its goodwill.

### Employees

**8–18**    Liabilities to former employees will rarely be taken over by the purchaser.

## CONSIDERATION OF INDIVIDUAL WARRANTIES

**8–19**    The commentary which follows deals only with those aspects of the warranties in Pt 3 of Appendix 5 which give rise to special considerations in the case of a business sale. In considering whether the warranties are satisfactorily worded or need amendment, regard should be given to the comments in para.7–03 (which are not repeated here).

## Information disclosed to the purchaser

The asset sale agreement will usually contain a number of schedules some or all **8–20** of which are likely to contain information that the purchaser is relying upon being correct. The asset schedule will likely include the net book value of the assets, the employee schedule should include the identities of each employee and a summary of their terms and conditions, the contracts schedule will usually contain a list of contracts and a summary of the key terms, and the intellectual property rights schedule will contain a list of the registered and unregistered intellectual property rights used by the business. The purchaser will have a legitimate interest in requesting that the accuracy of these schedules be warranted so that it can properly assess the assets it is acquiring and the potential liabilities for employees and contracts it is assuming.

## Accounts

### The last accounts

The approach adopted is that the purchaser has an interest in the profit and loss **8–21** accounts for recent periods as these will have influenced its valuation of the goodwill of the business. The warranties relating to the financial position of the vendor and to the provisions for liabilities are omitted.

### The management accounts

If the business being acquired is only part of the business carried on by the **8–22** vendor company, its last accounts will be of limited value to the purchaser. In these circumstances, it is reasonable for the purchaser to seek warranties of the sort set out in cl.2.3 in respect of any management accounts produced for the target.

### Books and records

The purchase agreement will often provide for the books of the business to be **8–23** transferred to the purchaser, in which case the purchaser will require reassurance that they are accurate. This warranty (cl.2.4) will also be appropriate if the purchaser has inspected the books during the pre-contract investigation of the business and if the vendor is to retain the books after completion, perhaps because they relate to more than one business, with the purchaser being granted a right of access to them.

## Assets

### Ownership of assets

The warranties relating to the vendor having good title to the assets and their **8–24** being free from security interests or other encumbrances (cll.3.1.2, 3.1.3 and

3.1.4) will be redundant if the vendor is expressed to sell with full title guarantee (see para.4–07).

## Fixed assets

**8–25**    The purchaser does not have a direct interest in the existence of maintenance contracts (cl.3.3.2) except in the event of its taking over and retaining those contracts—in which case the agreements will be included in the "Contracts" and will be covered by the warranties in cl.4. But if the fixed assets include leased equipment and the purchaser is taking over the leases, it will need to be satisfied that the lease covenants have been satisfied. However, from a commercial perspective, if the purchaser is paying more than net book value for the assets it will be concerned to ensure that the assets it is acquiring have been properly maintained.

## Book debts

**8–26**    It is unusual for the purchaser to acquire the book debts of the business although it often adopts the convenient role of collecting the debts for the benefit of the vendor. In such cases, the purchaser will not be concerned as to the value of the debts and cl.3.5 can be omitted. If, however, the debts are acquired by the purchaser, it is likely that the price paid for them will be determined, at least in part, by the amount they realise on collection. The relevance of these warranties may be minimal.

## Insurance

**8–27**    Risk in relation to assets passes to the purchaser on the signing of the contract unless there is express provision to the contrary. The purchaser will accordingly need to have insurance cover in place at the time contracts are exchanged even if there is to be a gap between contracts and completion. Depending on the circumstances of the transaction the purchaser may take over the vendor's existing policies. The purpose of the warranties in cl.3.6 are to protect the purchaser in such cases. The vendor might reasonably resist giving the warranties on the basis that the purchaser should either make its own insurance arrangements or inspect the policies before contracts to satisfy itself that they are in order.

## Intellectual property rights

**8–28**    These will frequently constitute a significant element of the assets which are being acquired. If, however, no material part of the purchase price is allocated to the rights, there may be difficulty for the purchaser in making an effective claim for damages in the event of a breach of the warranties relating to them. This question is discussed in para.3–06.

## Knowhow

**8–29**    Knowhow is an intangible asset which is increasingly being treated separately to goodwill. Knowhow is the confidential or secret information relating to trade secrets, business methods, development plans and marketing (and in a share sale is often defined as "Confidential Business Information"). Whether these warranties are appropriate will depend both on the nature of the business being acquired and the price (if any) being paid for goodwill.

### Information technology

Businesses are increasingly becoming more reliant on information technology systems to run all aspects of their business and as such computer systems are often a significant asset. If there are any problems with these systems following completion then this could cause expense and loss of profit/goodwill to the purchaser in having to rectify the problems and/or replace any equipment or software not operating correctly. The purpose of these warranties (cl.3.10) is to provide comfort to the purchaser that the computer systems are in operating order and fulfil the purpose for which they were acquired, have adequate capacity, that there are no potential issues in respect of security breaches, failure, breakdown or breaches of software or other intellectual property rights. In a business where the computer systems are non-core or where the purchaser is not paying above net book value for the computer systems or not making a significant payment for goodwill then it is likely that the vendor might reasonably resist giving the warranties or may only be prepared to give more limited warranties, usually qualified in respect of knowledge. In such circumstances the purchaser will need to assess the potential liabilities if the information technology systems do not operate correctly and should consider whether to carry out an information technology audit as part of its due diligence process.

**8–30**

## Contracts

### Nature of contracts

The contracts taken over by a purchaser will generally represent a combination of work in progress and customer contracts, supply contracts and finance agreements (and accordingly the definition of "Contracts" is broken down into these elements). The sale agreement will usually provide that except for the obligations arising from a default on the part of the vendor, the purchaser will duly perform the contracts. If this approach is adopted, the purchaser will usually require the protection of the indemnities contained in cll.2.1 to 2.3 of Pt 2 of Appendix 5 in respect of any post completion breach or omission by the vendor in respect of the contracts and any negligence or misrepresentation concerning them. The purchaser will also require the protection of the warranties in cl.4 concerning the nature of obligations it is taking on under the contracts. However, the vendor may resist these warranties on the basis that the purchaser is likely to review the terms of the contracts it is taking on during due diligence. Whether the vendor is prepared to give these warranties will depend on the circumstances, what other options the vendor has to discharge the obligations under the contract following completion and whether the purchaser needs the benefit of the contracts to allow it to operate the business going forward. If the purchaser is paying more than a nominal sum for the contracts in order to buy the benefit of profitable customer

**8–31**

contracts, then appropriate additional warranties should be included in respect of the continuation of these contracts and/or their profit or revenue stream.

### Defaults and agreements concerning the business

**8–32**    The purchaser would normally expect to receive the indemnity contained in cl.2.1 of Pt 2 of Appendix 5 from the vendor in respect of any default or omission by the vendor under any of the contracts and therefore there is an overlap between this indemnity and the warranties. However, the warranties in cl.4.3 also cover default by a third party under the contracts and will be used by the purchaser to illicit disclosure of any issues in respect of the businesses contracts or agreements.

### Defective products

**8–33**    The purchase agreement will commonly provide that the purchaser assumes responsibility for rectifying defects in products of the business sold by the vendor. This will be because of the practical difficulty which the vendor would otherwise experience in dealing with these once the business has been sold. The agreement will generally provide a mechanism for compensating the purchaser if this obligation proves to be unduly onerous and the warranties in cl.4.4 need to be reviewed in parallel with any other terms of the agreement which deal with this. The purchaser will also be concerned about defects in products sold by the vendor, apart from any obligation it has accepted to remedy them, because customer dissatisfaction with the products could reduce the value of the goodwill of the business.

### Service liabilities

**8–34**    The vendor might reasonably adopt the position that the purchaser is entitled to this warranty (cl.4.6) only if it takes over the responsibility for discharging the vendor's obligations. However, the purchaser's perspective it is important to identify possible causes of customer dissatisfaction and the need to protect goodwill may necessitate the purchaser accepting responsibilities to the vendor's customers which it does not have legally. The vendor is unlikely to find the concept of moral obligations sufficiently convincing to make it willing to give this warranty.

## Trading

### Vendor's other interests

**8–35**    The purchaser will wish to protect the goodwill of the business by identifying— and then, if possible, restricting, competing activities of the vendor. The vendor will argue that this warranty (cl.5.2) is unnecessary and that the purchaser should obtain whatever protection is reasonable by the covenants restricting future activities of the vendor which will feature in almost every sale agreement.

### Joint ventures and partnership

This warranty (cl.5.4) has information value only and it is difficult to see how the **8–36** purchaser can suffer loss if it is breached. On that basis the vendor might reasonably take the position that it is willing to provide the information but not to warrant it.

### Undertakings restricting the business

The purchaser is entitled to this warranty (cl.5.6) only in relation to undertakings **8–37** which are likely to affect it as successor to the business and which are not purely personal to the vendor.

### Unfair trade and restrictive practices

The reason for the purchaser requiring this warranty (cl.5.7) is that it will need **8–38** to know if the ability of the business to achieve the anticipated results is to any extent dependent on practices which are potentially illegal or likely to attract an attack from the authorities.

### Litigation, disputes and winding-up

The interest of the purchaser in litigation relating to the business is limited to **8–39** cases that affect the assets which it is acquiring or the goodwill of the business. The solvency of the vendor is a concern if there is any possibility that the sale is not on arm's length terms or that it might constitute a preference in relation to the purchaser as one of the creditors of the vendor. These circumstances would be unusual and, although the vendor should have no difficulty in checking the facts underlying the warranties contained in cl.5.8, it might reasonably object to giving them as a matter of principle. Furthermore the purchaser will derive some protection from the warranty in cl.1.1.

### Compliance with statutes

A default by the vendor in relation to the statutory obligations applicable to the **8–40** business could affect the purchaser's prospects of getting any licences or other statutory authorities it requires—although this is more specifically covered by the warranties in cl.5.11. The warranty in cl.5.11 is, however, so widely drawn that the vendor will normally be justified in refusing to give it unless it is made much more specific.

### Branches

This warranty (cl.5.12) is unlikely to serve any other function than that of **8–41** providing information. Although the vendor should have no difficulty in deciding whether the warranty is factually correct, it may reasonably consider that there is no reason why it should commit itself to a warranty.

## Employment

### *Employees and terms of employment*

**8–42**    The reasons why it is imperative for the purchaser to have full and accurate details of all the transferring employees and their terms and conditions of employment (cll.6.1.1 and 6.1.2) are, having regard to the operation of TUPE, fairly obvious.

    The purchaser should ask the vendor to warrant (cl.6.1.4) that all employees have been employed exclusively in the business (or part being transferred) for the previous 12 months to ensure that the vendor has not reassigned underperforming or troublesome employees from its other businesses or divisions in order that the obligations in respect of such employees pass to the purchaser.

### *Changes in remuneration*

**8–43**    The purchaser is legally bound only by the actual terms of employment but, from a commercial point of view, it will wish the employees to be supportive of the sale. For this reason it will want to be informed about the employees' expectations but the vendor will need to ensure that the warranty (cl.6.2) relates to factual questions which are easily verified.

    Of course, under TUPE, if the vendor has promised a pay rise to take effect at some point following completion—perhaps with effect from the end of the financial year—then the purchaser will be bound to honour that promise. The same applies where the expectation of a pay rise arises by custom and practice.

### *Termination of contracts of employment and redundancies*

**8–44**    As the purchaser will assume liabilities for the employees (including any claims for unfair, wrongful or constructive dismissal or for redundancy payments) it will be reasonable for the vendor to warrant (cl.6.3) that no employees have given notice or been given notice of termination or have any dispute or grievance with the business and that there are no reasonably foreseeable circumstances likely to give rise to such a matter.

### *Industrial agreements, disputes and negotiations*

**8–45**    In law the purchaser is not affected by disputes involving the vendor but in practice these are likely to have a significant impact on the purchaser's relations with its new employees. It must be remembered that rights and duties under collective agreements will be binding on the purchaser following completion.

### *Compliance with laws*

**8–46**    The purchaser will wish to receive fairly wide warranties from the vendor that it has met all contractual obligations and complied with all relevant legislation and codes of practice in respect of the employees. These are contained in cl.6.5.

## Sub-contractors, agency workers and the self-employed

The purchaser will need to scrutinise the terms on which all consultants, sub-    **8–47**
contractors, agency workers and other self-employed personnel are engaged in
the business in order to be sure that there is no risk of them asserting that they
are in fact employees and therefore availing themselves of the protection
afforded by TUPE. It is usual for the purchaser to expect to receive a fairly wide
warranty (cl.6.6) to cover this.

## Pensions

As discussed in para.8–10 the purchaser will either take over the existing pension    **8–48**
scheme or take a transfer value from it. In either case it will need to know the
rights of the employees and, if it takes over the scheme, it will also have to satisfy
itself as to the legal structure and the actuarial valuations. Specialist actuarial
advice should be taken regarding the pension "exclusion" from TUPE, wherever
employees of the business were members of a defined benefit, final salary
scheme.

## Taxation

Except in the rare case of the purchaser taking over the vendor's VAT registra-    **8–49**
tion, tax liabilities will not transfer to the purchaser. As the purchaser is not
taking over any liabilities, the vendor may resist giving any taxation warranties.
However, the purchaser will usually want taxation warranties to get information
both as to how the business has been run and any potential tax problems.

A number of the suggested taxation warranties in cl.7 relate to PAYE and VAT
compliance. As noted, it can be argued that these warranties are irrelevant as the
purchaser does not take over any liabilities to which they relate. However, the
purchaser will be interested in the compliance record, as a poor record may
indicate that there will need to be investment in systems and training to ensure
future compliance. (A poor record may also indicate that the Inland Revenue and
Customs and Excise will continue to take a strict line on compliance matters
despite the change in ownership.) Where these warranties are given it is difficult
to see how a claim for breach of these warranties would provide any recovery of
expenses incurred as a result of any new investment required. If as a result of
disclosure the purchaser has a concern it should address this directly in negotiations or seek a more direct warranty on the point.

The other warranties in cl.7 give information to the purchaser so that it can
plan its tax affairs and be aware of any inherent tax problems. These include
information regarding assets held under the capital goods scheme (cl.7.1.8),
electing to charge VAT on supplies of property (cl.7.1.9), irrecoverable input tax
(cl.7.1.10) and the capital allowances position (cll.7.1.11 and 7.1.12).

Finally, as noted in para.5–112, in certain circumstances a charge in respect of
unpaid inheritance tax may attach to the assets of the business. Although any
problems are likely in any event to be caught under the general warranties as to
title, it may be worth in appropriate circumstances having a specific warranty so
that the vendor specifically addresses the issue.

# Chapter 9

# Disclosure Letters

## Purpose

**9–01**  It has long been the custom that, in contrast to the practice in relation to purchases of land, the first draft of an agreement for the purchase of the shares or business of a company is prepared by the solicitors for the purchaser. This arises from the fact that a major part of the document consists of the warranties and the purchaser's solicitors will wish to prepare the first draft of these. If the draft is sent out too early, that is to say before receipt of legal due diligence, the document will often have been prepared by somebody who has comparatively little information about the target company or the business that is being acquired. In these circumstances the warranties will often be drafted in an absolute form which will require amendment to comply with the actual circumstances of the target company or business.

The information which is specific to the target company or the business falls into two broad categories. In the first place, there is information which is the subject of express warranties (which for convenience is referred to as "warranted items"). An example is a warranty that the listed names of the employees and their terms of employment are accurate and comprehensive. Secondly there is information which operates in derogation of a warranty (referred to as "excepted items"). An example might arise in the case of a warranty that no employee is entitled to more than one month's notice—the warranty would have to be modified so as to exclude named employees who were in fact entitled to longer notice.

**9–02**  Warranted items will normally be dealt with by listing the relevant details either in a schedule to the sale agreement or, more often, in the disclosure letter. Where the warranty concerned is very rigorous, the details to be provided in relation to the warranted items may be extremely extensive and of comparatively little relevance to the transaction as a whole. It is therefore common to reduce the extent to which warranted items have to be listed by qualifying the warranties so as to remove from their scope items of a trivial nature. Thus, for example, the warranty referred to above with regard to employees might be qualified by specifying that the warranty applies only to employees receiving a salary in excess of a particular amount.

So far as the excepted items are concerned, the warranties can either be expressly qualified by suitable amendments or left in absolute terms with the qualifications collected together in a disclosure letter. Use of a disclosure letter for this purpose is greatly to be preferred if the amendments which have to be made to the warranties are anything but very slight. The agreement will contain a clause that the warranties are to apply **"save as [set out] [or] [as fairly disclosed] in the Disclosure Letter"** (see para.4–05, cl.4C for a more detailed discussion of these points).

It is usual practice to attach to the disclosure letter a disclosure bundle which   **9–03** comprises copies of all documents which are referred to in the warranties—for example, the warranted copies of the memoranda and articles of association—unless, as with the warranted accounts, they are unambiguous documents of record. This procedure avoids the doubt that could arise if a warranty relates to a document "which has not been attached". Two copies of the disclosure letter and bundle should be prepared: one to be delivered to the purchaser and one to be retained by the vendors. Usually the bundles will be compared to ensure they are identical and will be initialled as evidence of that.

It is sometimes suggested that the main purpose and function of the disclosure letter is to bring together all relevant information which might affect the purchaser in making an evaluation of the target company. While this is certainly an important aspect, in the final analysis the effect of the disclosures in relation to excepted items is to transfer to the purchaser the commercial risks which arise from the matters disclosed. If the purchaser is not willing to accept the disclosures in this sense, it will generally be necessary to amend the sale agreement so that, notwithstanding the disclosures, the risk of any loss resulting from these matters is clearly re-imposed on the vendors. This is normally done by way of a specific indemnity.

## Effect of Disclosures

The function of a disclosure letter is therefore to set out the details that are   **9–04** required in relation to the warranted items and to specify how the warranties need to be qualified to deal with excepted items. While ideally the excepted items should relate specifically to the particular warranty which they qualify, it is largely unrealistic to adopt this approach, as warranties have developed in their scope and operation such that with a full set of warranties it will usually be the case that a particular item will be the subject of several of the warranties. For example, if a claim against the target company is disclosed, it can affect separately the warranties relating to the accounts, liabilities and litigation.

The vendors and the purchaser will have the following concerns in relation to the disclosure letter:

(1) The vendors will wish to ensure that a disclosure of an excepted item is effective to remove liability in relation to that item under any of the warranties which could be applicable.

(2) The vendors will wish to pass to the purchaser the burden of understanding the implication of all disclosures made so that if, for example, a complex agreement is disclosed to the purchaser, there cannot subsequently be a complaint by the purchaser that the full effect and repercussions were not understood.

(3) The purchaser will wish to ensure that disclosures are fairly made and that the vendors do not avoid a liability which they have apparently accepted by swamping the purchaser with massive disclosures which cannot readily be absorbed and whose implications cannot easily be appreciated. The purchaser will usually seek to include in the sale agreement a warranty relating to the disclosure letter in the following terms, it being assumed that "Disclosure Letter" and "Warranties" are defined terms (see para.4–01):

## [9A] Disclosures accurate

**The disclosures contained in the Disclosure Letter and the details contained in the accompanying documents are [true], accurate and [fairly] [fully, clearly and accurately] disclose every matter to which they relate [and the Warranties which are affected; and there are no other matters which have not been disclosed and which may render the disclosures incomplete, inaccurate or misleading].**

The vendors will need to consider carefully whether they are prepared to give the warranty which in simple terms warrants the accuracy of the disclosures. The vendors may argue that if, as is usual, the sale agreement provides that the disclosures are only effective to the extent that they "fairly disclose" a matter, if the relevant disclosure fails to satisfy this requirement then the disclosure against the relevant warranty fails, leaving the original warranty intact. The purchaser will usually argue that it has relied on the disclosures contained in the disclosure letter in evaluating the warranties and the risk that it is prepared to assume and as such if the disclosures are inaccurate and as a result it suffers loss it ought to be able to claim for such loss. Ultimately whether the warranty is given will depend upon the bargaining position of the parties. Since the purchaser is not able to "undo" any knowledge gleaned from disclosure, even if inaccurate, there is probably more logic on the purchaser's side. If the vendors are prepared to accept the warranty they will wish to consider carefully whether they are willing to accept the burden, which this clause imposes upon them, of stating clearly which specific warranty is qualified, and in what respects, by each disclosure of the excepted items. They may also reasonably consider that the second half of the clause, which contains a representation that there are no other matters which should be disclosed, is unduly wide and burdensome. The words in brackets detail different standards that can be applied to this warranty.

(4) The purchaser will sometimes wish to ensure that, by accepting a disclosure, it does not reduce its prospective right to damages if the associated warranty is breached. The general proposition is that the purchaser will have difficulty in proving loss if it entered into the contract in the knowledge that deficiencies existed (see para.4–25). While it would seem that this is a perfectly fair result as between the parties if the purchaser has all the details—either through its own investigations or as a result of the disclosure process—which it needs to evaluate the problem, the position will be less clear if the information it receives or which is available is not sufficient to permit this. An example would be if the purchaser was aware that there

might be problems over land contamination but the reality or scope of the risk could not be realistically determined. The vendors will take the view that the purchaser is accepting the risk by deciding to proceed with the transaction once the potential problem has been identified; the purchaser will maintain that the vendors must accept responsibility for a problem existing at the time of the sale if there are no realistic means available to the purchaser to carry out a full investigation. The outcome of the argument will depend upon the relative bargaining strengths of the parties but, if the purchaser's approach is adopted, a suitable clause to protect its rights would be the following:

### [9B] Purchaser's rights not affected by disclosures

**Although the Purchaser is aware that there are or may be matters which cause or will cause a breach of paragraph [ ] in Schedule [ ], it does not know whether there will be a breach or what damage it will suffer from a breach. The Purchaser's remedies in respect of a breach are therefore not to be affected by its awareness and clause [ ] of the agreement will not apply to disclosures made in relation to the above-referenced paragraph.**

An alternative and safer way to deal with the issue given the uncertainty on the effect of knowledge in relation to disclosure is for the purchaser to cover the issue by way of a specific indemnity.

9–05   It will be seen that the disclosure letter therefore requires very careful drafting and consideration by both the vendors and the purchaser. The vendors should be persuaded to provide an early draft of the disclosure letter and associated disclosure bundle so that any disclosures can be properly considered and reviewed. Any attempt by the vendor to adopt last minute bulk or general disclosure of masses of documents without explanation should be resisted by the vendors.

If the disclosure letter is sent by the vendors' solicitors and addressed to the purchaser's solicitors, as is sometimes the case, they should take care to avoid any professional responsibility in relation to the disclosures and to state that they are making the disclosures to the purchaser on the instructions of the vendors.

## Is Disclosure Letter Part of Sale Agreement?

9–06   In the vast majority of cases it will not, save where a US purchaser is involved when they may seek to incorporate the disclosure letter as a specific schedule. Generally the disclosure letter is a separate letter addressed by the vendors to the purchaser.

If, as is normally the case, the disclosure letter is a document which is physically separate from the sale agreement, the question may arise as to whether it is nevertheless part of the agreement. This will be relevant where the agreement has to be filed at the Companies Registry under CA 1985, s.88, or where documents are made available for inspection under the rules of the Stock

Exchange. It is suggested that a disclosure letter does not form part of the sale agreement if the disclosures are of a normal routine nature. If, however, the disclosures are so fundamental that they render the sale agreement misleading on its face, it is considered that it would be wrong to treat the sale agreement as being complete unless the disclosure letter is attached.

## PRECEDENT

**9–07**    A typical form of disclosure letter from the vendors is as follows:

**Dear Sirs,**
   **[ ] Limited ("the Company")**
   **This letter is the Disclosure Letter referred to in clause [ ] of the agreement ("the Agreement") between us dated [ ] relating to the sale and purchase of the [Company] [the business of the Company]. Unless the context otherwise requires, the definitions in the Agreement apply to this letter.**

**9–08**    The adoption of the definitions contained in the sale agreement is useful but requires care. Although the definitions in para.4–01, which are used in the following paragraphs, will not cause difficulty, this will not always be the case. For example, some sale agreements adopt wholesale the definitions appearing in certain statutes—a procedure which is not to be encouraged—and as a result apparently innocuous phrases can be given quite unexpected meanings. The disclosure letter is normally divided into two parts, namely, "general disclosures" and "specific disclosures". The general disclosures are usually much shorter than the specific disclosures and take effect so as to disclose certain matters which appear in public records or are such that the purchaser ought to be aware of them on the basis of searches which have been or are normally carried out. The purchaser should ensure that before accepting general disclosures it has actual knowledge of the matters disclosed.

   The specific disclosures disclose matters which if they were not disclosed would constitute a breach of warranty.

**9–09**    **We wish to make the following general disclosures:**

   **(1) You are deemed to be aware of, and the Warranties [and the indemnities in Schedule [ ] of the Agreement] accordingly do not apply to, anything which was disclosed or [reasonably apparent from] [or referred to in] the accounts of [the [ ] Company] [the Vendor] for all financial periods up to the Balance Sheet Date [to the extent of the disclosure or reference].**

While it is fair and reasonable for the vendors to expect the purchaser to give careful consideration to the contents of the published accounts, nevertheless the purchaser should not be expected to deduce from items appearing in the accounts matters which would not normally flow from the disclosures as made. The words in the last set of square brackets are unlikely to be included by the vendors in the draft of the disclosure letter but the purchaser would wish to have those words added. The purchaser might also prefer to delete the words **"or referred to in"** as being too vague and add the other amendments in brackets so as to moderate the disclosure.

It would not be usual to seek to qualify the tax indemnities on share sales by the disclosure letter but, if they are to be covered by the disclosures, the bracketed words referring to the indemnities should be included.

**(2) Anything apparent from the deeds of the Properties or which would be disclosed by local searches or physical inspection of the Properties is deemed to have been disclosed.**

The effect of this disclosure is largely to nullify many of the warranties in relation to the properties owned by the target company or which are included in the business assets which are being purchased. As discussed in Ch.6, the parties must decide whether property warranties are to be given or whether the purchaser is to rely on its own investigation or a certificate of title. In the former case the first part of the disclosure, relating to title deeds and searches, is inappropriate and in the latter there will be effectively no warranties to which that part of the disclosure relates.

The rest of the disclosure which relates to matters apparent from a physical inspection is likely to be unacceptable to the purchaser unless it has been agreed between the parties that the purchaser will obtain, and rely upon, a survey of the properties in which case it would be usual to refer to the actual surveyor's report so as to obtain certainty in relation to the scope of this disclosure.

**(3) Anything appearing on the file at the Companies Registry [as at [ ]] in respect of the Company is deemed to have been disclosed.**

The purchaser would be expected to make searches of the Companies Registry and it is fair for the vendors to exclude liability for matters which would appear from those searches. The parties should, however, bear in mind that the file may not, in practice, be fully up-to-date in view of the inevitable interval which occurs between lodging and registration of documents.

Furthermore, if the target company or business is old, there will be a vast amount of material at the Companies Registry and it may be almost impossible to evaluate it all in the context of the warranties. In such circumstances it would be reasonable for the purchaser to require that the disclosure is restricted to entries made within a specified prior period, for example, the last two years. It would also be usual to have a date on which the disclosure was deemed to apply to ensure that last minute filings are excluded. Often the search itself will be attached to the disclosure letter.

**(4) You and your accountants and other agents have been given facilities for the inspection of the plant books of account and records of [the Com-**

**pany] [the Business] and accordingly anything which would be apparent from inspection of them is deemed to have been disclosed.**

Where the target company or the business has been the subject of a detailed investigation, the vendors would wish to exclude matters which have been disclosed in the course of the investigation or which would be apparent to the purchaser and its agents. The purchaser, on the other hand, would be concerned to ensure that there is certainty as to what items are covered by this disclosure and, while the principle may not be unacceptable to the purchaser, the wording is much too wide. The purchaser, if faced with this qualification, should insist upon the vendors specifying the particular items which they consider will have been disclosed by the inspection. More often the contents of any due diligence reports that have been produced as a result of such investigations by the purchaser's financial and/or legal advisers will be deemed to be disclosed instead.

**(5) The contents of, and everything referred to in, the documents in the attached bundle (copies of which have been initialled by us and you for the purposes of identification) are deemed to have been disclosed.**

It is, unfortunately, not unusual for vendors to deliver to the purchaser, sometimes only shortly before the signing of the purchase contract, large bundles of documents which cannot be fully assimilated and analysed by the purchaser without inordinate effort. The vendors should be required to specify the precise purpose of the disclosure of the bundles and the modifications to the warranties which the disclosure is intended to achieve. The purchaser if faced with this would usually insist that specific disclosure rather than general disclosure of such documents were made. Alternatively, the purchaser should consider amending the sale agreement to provide for a more limited basis of disclosure to apply to such documents.

**(6) Everything which is in the public domain is deemed to have been disclosed.**

This disclosure is particularly useful where the vendors are required to warrant, for example, that there has been no change in the financial position or prospects of the target company or business (see cl.4.1.1.2 in para.7–81 and cl.5.1.1.2 in Appendix 5). The purpose of the disclosure is to avoid the warranty being breached by reason of circumstances or events of general application (such as changes in interest or tax rates) as opposed to those relating specifically to the target company or business. The disclosure nevertheless should not be accepted by the purchaser, even if confined in its application to those warranties where it is most appropriate, as the purchaser cannot be expected to be aware of everything in the public domain and might not be aware of, or may have overlooked, information regarding the target company or business which has been made public but in a low-key manner. The purchaser might reasonably require the vendors instead to make specific disclosure of any pertinent events.

**(7) Where brief particulars only of a matter are set out or referred to in this letter, or a document is referred to but not attached, or a reference is made to a particular part only of a document, full particulars of the matter and the full contents of the document are deemed to have been disclosed and it is assumed that you do not require any further details.**

The purchaser should resist any attempt to achieve disclosures which are more extensive in their impact than appears on the face of them. If the vendors wish to qualify a warranty, they should be required to state expressly the way in which the qualification is to operate. Normally a disclosure in this form would be resisted on the basis it does not meet the standard of fair disclosure.

**We wish also to make the following specific disclosures and for convenience only reference is made to particular paragraphs in Schedule [ ] of the Agreement. Each item disclosed is nevertheless deemed to be a disclosure in respect of all of the Warranties and is not limited to the paragraph which is referred to below [but subject always to the provisions of clause [ ] of the Agreement].**

The detailed disclosures will normally specify the principal warranty to which each disclosure most particularly relates. In view of the extensive nature of the warranties, it will be difficult in practice, as previously stated, for the vendors to ensure that all the warranties affected by each disclosure are expressly indicated and the vendors will therefore wish to protect themselves by general wording of the kind set out above. Although this may seem to be fair, a problem arises if the relevance of a disclosure to any other warranty is not apparent. If, for example, a licence agreement is disclosed and it contains a provision that a large minimum royalty is to be paid for a considerable number of years, the vendors might disclose it in relation to a warranty which relates only to licence agreements. This disclosure would, by virtue of the general words, also qualify a warranty, for example, that no outstanding liabilities under subsisting contracts involve more than a specified amount (for example cl.4.16.1.7 in para.7–126). It would be unreasonable for the vendors to achieve a disclosure in this oblique manner. The problem can be dealt with in part by the warranty suggested above at cl.9A to the effect that the disclosures are full and clear. The words in square brackets, which are intended to cross-refer to the clause in the sale agreement which sets the standard that disclosures will have to meet to be effective (usually "fair disclosure"), might well be inserted by the purchaser so as to avoid that clause being overridden by the first part of the sentence to which the words are added.

The specific disclosures which are made in practice, including in particular the disclosure of excepted items, vary so greatly that it is not possible to give meaningful examples. What is of the utmost importance, however, is that the vendors and the purchaser should realise that the drafting of the disclosure letter, in relation both to the opening general paragraphs and to the specific disclosures themselves, should be treated with as much care and attention as the sale agreement itself. In so far as the disclosure letter contains excepted items, it operates to reduce the scope and impact of the warranties and both parties should understand the extent to which this occurs.

## PREPARATION OF DISCLOSURES

**9–10**    The preparation of the material to be covered by the disclosures can be an extremely onerous task for the vendors' solicitors who will need to work closely with the appropriate executives of the target company/business to undertake a thorough review of the warranties. When the sale agreement is received by the vendors' solicitors, it is generally unrealistic for them to send the agreement to the vendors with a bare request for comments on the warranties as unless the vendors are exceptionally experienced, it will normally be impossible for them to appreciate the meaning and implications of the warranties without expert guidance.

**9–11**    It is in the interests of the purchaser and the vendors that all disclosures made are fair. The purchaser will want as accurate a picture of the target company as possible prior to completion, at a time when the terms of the transaction are still in the course of negotiation, and the vendors will want to obviate the risk of a later claim for breach of warranty. Last minute "bad news" disclosures are generally not a good idea from the point of view of the vendors as they risk the purchaser walking away from the deal at a stage when significant professional costs will have been expended.

**9–12**    As mentioned above, it is common for the sale agreement to provide that the warranties given are qualified by matters "fairly disclosed" in the disclosure letter. In such circumstances, if the disclosure is not precise enough, a court may find that it is insufficient to prevent a successful claim for breach of warranty (see, for example, *Levison and others v Farin and others* [1978] 2 All E.R. 1149) and, if it is not specific and accurate, it might not constitute a fair disclosure. What amounts to fair disclosure has been considered in the case of *Daniel Reeds Ltd v EM ESS Chemists Ltd* [1995] C.L.C. 1405 and the Scottish case of *New Hearts Ltd v Cosmopolitan Investments Ltd* [1997] 2 B.C.L.C. 249. In the first of these cases, the vendor warranted that the target company had valid product licences for its products. This was not the case and the vendor sought to argue that because it had positively disclosed all existing licences it had in effect disclosed that the licence to which no reference had been made did not exist. The court did not regard this as a fair disclosure of the missing licence. In the latter case, the court cast doubt upon the practice of making deemed disclosure of all matters "set out in or referred to" in the accounts and concluded that simply referring to a complex body of information would not be a fair disclosure, even if a diligent reader might be able to identify relevant information.

## DELIBERATE NON-DISCLOSURE

**9–13**   A practical problem can arise where vendors who are extremely anxious to effect a sale of the target company know that a breach of warranty will arise if an adverse circumstance—such as the existence of outstanding litigation—is not disclosed, but are apprehensive about making a disclosure in case it causes the purchaser to withdraw. The vendors might be quite happy to compensate the purchaser in due course and might therefore consider that there is no question of fraud, arising from deliberate concealment, as there is every intention to make the purchaser's position good. Nevertheless, the purchaser will have been induced to enter into the sale agreement by a deliberate misrepresentation or concealment and this in general terms would constitute fraud. Furthermore, it is a criminal offence under the Financial Services and Markets Act 2000, s.397(1) for a person knowingly or recklessly to make a false statement (or one that is deceptive in a material particular) or to dishonestly conceal any material facts for the purpose of inducing another person to enter into an investment agreement—in this context, the sale agreement. The offence carries an unlimited fine and/or seven years' imprisonment. While there is no civil remedy available for a buyer under the section, an action for civil remedies can be brought by the Financial Services Authority under the Act.

The vendors' solicitors should also note that a court could order them to pay compensation to a purchaser who suffered loss as a result of the vendors' breach of s.397(1) if they were "knowingly concerned" in such breach (see the Court of Appeal's decision in *Securities and Investments Board v Pantell SA and others (No. 2)* [1992] 3 W.L.R. 896 which related to the Financial Services Act 1986, s.47(1), the predecessor to s.397(1)).

If the vendors decide to remain silent regarding a problem, then, since there is **9–14** no general duty to disclose relevant facts, this would not constitute a misrepresentation under general law, as total non-disclosure does not amount to misrepresentation (*Percival v Wright* [1902] 2 Ch. 421). However, if the silence of the vendors distorts a positive representation, the vendors would not be entitled to keep quiet. Therefore, if a warranty requires disclosure for it to be accurate and not misleading, non-disclosure would constitute misrepresentation.

Where a warranty constitutes a misrepresentation of a material fact, it is considered that the only correct way to proceed is either to amend the warranty, so as to eliminate the misrepresentation, or to make a full disclosure of the relevant circumstances.

# CHAPTER 10

# Tax Deeds

## INTRODUCTION

**10–01**  As indicated in para.1–06, the original idea of indemnities, as distinguished from warranties, was to provide the target company with a means of recovering tax for which it had only a secondary liability without a statutory right of recovery from the person primarily liable. The main examples related to surtax apportionments (later replaced by shortfall assessments) and estate duty under FA 1940, s.46, where a liability attributable to a shareholder could be imposed on the company. This narrow concept is still occasionally accepted, with the tax deed being confined to cases where, although the primary liability is not that of the company, a secondary liability is imposed upon it by statute.

The clear principle upon which tax deeds were originally based became eroded with the introduction of the corporation tax regime and the development of the practice of adding additional statutory provisions to which the indemnity would expressly relate. Eventually, tax deeds became of inordinate length with a large number of specific provisions set out in the body of them. (It is still occasionally the case that tax deeds are seen in this form.)

**10–02**  The next stage of development of the form of the tax deed was when an attempt was made to shorten the document by having a blanket indemnity against any taxation liability. The scope of the indemnity was spread even further by an increasingly wide definition of the kinds of taxation covered by the indemnity (considered in more detail below). Then came the case of *Zim Properties Limited v Procter (Inspector of Taxes)* [1985] 58 T.C. 371 after which ESC D33 was issued (as described in paras 3–26 and 3–27). Following this, as a payment to the target company could be taxable whereas a payment to the purchaser was unlikely to be taxable, the tax deed was redrafted as a deed of covenant under which a covenant was given directly to the purchaser. This is the most common approach today, with only the vendors and the purchaser being parties (although the target company is occasionally a party for specific purposes, such as conduct of claims). It is technically inaccurate to refer to this as a tax indemnity as an indemnity is not given to the target company. It is often referred to as a tax covenant or, as in this book, a tax deed.

A more recent development has been to cease drafting the tax deed as a separate document and to have it as a covenant contained in one of the schedules to the sale agreement. It is also sometimes the case that all tax provisions, definitions, warranties, covenants and limitations are all contained in a single tax deed schedule.

The position adopted here is the one which is still most common, namely a separate tax deed to which only the vendors and the purchaser are party.

The modern tax deed will generally raise numerous complex and obscure questions. Normally the purchaser's solicitors will make use of a standard comprehensive form and the covenantors' solicitors will face the task of providing amendments which reflect the liabilities which the covenantors should reasonably expect to accept. This task has been to some extent simplified by the recent trend for first drafts of the tax deed to be more balanced with the purchaser's lawyers including many of the amendments which the covenantors' lawyers would historically have been expected to make. The tax deed given here is a reasonably balanced draft although some of the provisions in favour of the covenantors may not be appropriate in every case.

## SUMMARY OF DEED

Before giving detailed consideration to the contents of a typical tax deed, it might **10–03** be helpful to summarise the main points which will or should be dealt with. Some of the main points that will typically need addressing are listed below:

(1)  The deed will generally be in favour of the purchaser for the reasons set out above. If for any reason the deed is in favour of the target company, this will generally be unacceptable to the covenantors.

(2)  The deed will cover unexpected liabilities to taxation which relate to events or transactions prior to completion.

(3)  The deed may cover the loss of an expected right to a tax repayment, it being a matter for negotiation as to whether the covenantors should accept this liability.

(4)  The purchaser may seek a covenant against the withdrawal of anticipated tax reliefs. It is, however, a complex matter to determine whether this particular covenant is appropriate and, if so, how the covenant should operate.

(5)  Subject to which matters are covered by the covenant, a payment by the covenantors will be required:

(5.1)  when the unexpected liability, or loss of expected relief, results in a payment of tax;
(5.2)  when the expected repayment would have been received;
(5.3)  when a payment of tax occurs which would have been avoided if an expected relief had not been withdrawn; and
(5.4)  when a payment of tax would have occurred but for the availability of other reliefs.

(6)  The deed will not normally extend to liabilities which result in no net loss to the target company, for example because of the availability of otherwise unclaimed reliefs which could be called upon to shelter the liability.

(7) Conduct of negotiations with and litigation against the Inland Revenue will often be given to the covenantors.

(8) As with the warranties, minimum and maximum levels of liability may apply, although usually only the latter.

## Security

**10–04**   The parties should appreciate that, in the absence of express arrangements to the contrary, the covenant involves unsecured liabilities of both the covenantors and (where the covenant provides for repayment by the purchaser in certain circumstances) the purchaser. Where a taxation liability is in dispute, tax may be paid and repaid at various stages, possibly with interest or repayment supplement, as the dispute progresses through the courts. In such a case, payments under the covenant would have to be made and refunded and each party runs the risk of default.

Unless the question is dealt with in the tax deed, neither party will have a right to call for security at a later stage. Both the purchaser and the covenantors should therefore in appropriate circumstances consider the issue of security.

## Checklist

**10–05**   In determining what amendments to require when faced with the usual comprehensive standard form of tax deed, the covenantors' solicitor may find the following checklist helpful:

(1) Does the tax deed adequately protect the interests of the covenantors by providing for payments to be made to the purchaser (see para.3–26 and the discussion below at para.10–08 relating to parties)?

(2) What forms of taxation are to be covered by the tax deed (see para.10–16)?

(3) Who is to bear the risk of retrospective changes in tax legislation (see para.10–31)?

(4) Is the purchaser entitled to recover if carry-forward losses turn out not to be available, even if no immediate taxation liability arises (para.10–74)?

(5) What form of "combined events" wording is used (see para.10–21)?

(6) Are the covenantors to bear additionally any tax liability which the purchaser suffers on the indemnity payments themselves (para.10–61)?

(7) Which of the exclusions in cl.3 (para.10–29) are appropriate?

(8) Is an adequate obligation imposed upon the purchaser to mitigate liability?

(9) Should a representative of the covenantors be appointed to control the conduct of claims (cl.4)?

(10) Should the covenant lapse if the purchaser ceases to own the relevant company?

(11) Should provisions be included as to how liability is to be shared amongst the covenantors (see para.10–22)?

(12) Are minimum and maximum levels of liability covered (see para.10–28)?

(13) Should there be a shorter period than the statutory period of limitation for bringing claims (see paras 10–06 and 10–28)?

## DETAILED CONSIDERATION

A typical form of tax deed is set out in Appendix 6 and considered below clause **10–06** by clause. It is usually produced as a separate deed, though as noted above it may sometimes appear in the form of a schedule to the sale agreement. While the limitation period for claims under a deed is 12 years, as opposed to six years under a contract, it is common for the parties to nevertheless agree a limitation period of between six and seven years to cover the six-year period in which the Inland Revenue may make an assessment. It will be seen that the tax deed is in the modern general form which would obviously be preferred by most purchasers. While from the covenantors' point of view a tax deed is easier to handle if the specific provisions which it is intended to cover are spelled out, the current practice means that a general form must normally be accepted.

The words included within square brackets are unlikely to appear in the purchaser's solicitors' first draft and the covenantors' solicitors may wish to include all or most of them.

### This Agreement to be executed as a deed is made the [ ] day of [ ] 200[ ].

It is universal practice for the deed to be executed and dated at completion. **10–07** When there is a gap between contracts and completion, the issue of who is to bear the risk of unexpected tax issues arising between contracts and completion is much the same issue as who bears the risk of warranty claims between contracts and completion. This is dealt with in relation to the sale agreement at para.4–14. Tax arising on transactions in the ordinary course of business between contracts and completion would normally be excluded.

### Parties:

**1. [ ] of [ ] and [ ] of [ ] (the "Covenantors"); and**
**2. [ ] (registered number [ ]) whose registered office is at [ ] (the "Purchaser").**

As indicated in para.2–20, although the covenantors will usually be all the **10–08** vendors, in special cases—for example, where the vendors include trustees—some of the vendors may be excluded. The purchaser will usually not object as long as it has joint and several covenants from a number of vendors who have the means to meet potential claims.

As noted above, it is now usual for the tax deed to be between the covenantors and the purchaser and for the target company not to be a party. This should ensure that any payment under the tax deed is not taxable in the hands of the purchaser and that the covenantors will receive an adjustment to the amount of the purchase consideration which is brought into account for capital gains tax purposes to the extent of any payments made to the purchaser, whether pursuant to the warranties or under the tax deed.

## Recital:

**10–09** **This Deed is entered into in accordance with the Agreement.**

Although the tax deed largely stands on its own, it is not wholly independent of the sale agreement. Thus, for example, the interplay of the deed with the tax warranties needs to be covered. Additionally, the allocation of liability among several covenantors, who give joint and several covenants to the purchaser, may depend on the sale agreement. It is therefore desirable to relate the deed to the sale agreement so that, if the documents become separated, the context can nevertheless be established.

## Operative provisions:

*1 Definitions*

**In this Deed:**

**10–10**    **1.1 Words and expressions defined in the Agreement shall have the same meaning in this Deed except where otherwise provided or expressly defined below.**

As reference is made to the sale agreement, it is clearly convenient to adopt the definitions contained in the sale agreement and the provisions dealing with construction and interpretation without setting them out again in full. The parties must take care to ensure that these provisions and the definitions are equally appropriate for the tax deed. The comments on the definitions in para.4–01 should be borne in mind.

**10–11**    **1.2 "Agreement" means an agreement of today's date made between the Covenantors and the Purchaser relating to the sale of the Shares.**

If not all the vendors are covenantors or if completion is not simultaneous with exchange of contracts, this definition will need slight amendment.

**10–12**    **1.3 "Claim for Taxation" includes a notice, demand, assessment or other document issued, or action taken, by or on behalf of a Taxation Authority and whether issued before or after Completion, whereby it appears that the**

**Company is, or may be, subject to a Liability to Taxation (whether or not it is primarily payable by the Company and whether or not the Company has a right of reimbursement).**

Although the basic indemnity (contained in cl.2.1.1) is against any liability to taxation, as defined, cl.2.1.2 contains a covenant relating to the costs of dealing with claims for taxation. Further, the conduct of claims provisions in cl.4 are triggered by a "Claim for Taxation". Accordingly, the purchaser will wish the definition to be drawn as widely as possible while the covenantors will seek to restrict its scope. The parties will therefore need to give particular consideration to the phrase **"whereby it appears that the Company is or may be subject to a Liability to Taxation"**, the covenantors at the very least preferring **"may be"** to be replaced by **"will be"** or **"likely to be"**.

**1.4 "Event" includes any disposition, action or omission (whether or not the Company or the Purchaser is a party), the earning, accrual or receipt of any income, profits or gains, the declaration, payment or making of any dividend or other distribution (in each case whether actual or deemed) on or before Completion and includes any events which are deemed to have occurred for any Taxation purpose.**   10–13

The primary covenant contained in cl.2.1.1 operates by reference to events on or before completion. The purchaser will want this definition to be drafted as wide as possible. In practice, this definition is rarely subject to substantial amendment; the main issues tend to occur on the so called "combined events wording" contained at cl.1.10 (see para.10–21 below).

**1.5 "Liability to Taxation" includes:**   10–14

**1.5.1      any liability of the Company to make a payment in respect of or in the nature of Taxation;**

**1.5.2      the set-off or utilisation of a Purchaser's Relief or a Pre-Completion Relief against the liability of the Company to make a payment of or in respect of Taxation where but for the set-off or utilisation a liability would have arisen under clause 1.5.1;**

**1.5.3      the loss, disallowance, counteracting or clawing back of a Pre-Completion Relief which would otherwise have been available to the Company other than as set out in clause 1.5.2;**

**1.5.4      the loss, disallowance or set-off of a right to repayment of Taxation which would otherwise have been available to the Company;**

This is one of the key definitions as the primary covenant contained in cl.2.1.1 turns on the definition of "Liability to Taxation".

One of the principal issues that arises on the definition of "Liability to Taxation" is the extent to which the covenantors will compensate the purchaser for the non-availability of tax reliefs of the target company.

The circumstances of the transaction as negotiated between the parties will generally reveal whether or not the consideration paid by the purchaser has been influenced by the expected availability of relief. If, for example, the purchase price reflects the value of carry-forward losses then the purchaser would expect to have a claim if the losses were not available to the extent anticipated, whether or not this gives rise to an immediate taxation liability. It should be noted that even in such cases a fair level of compensation may be less than a full indemnity. If, on the other hand, the purchaser is not paying for expected losses, the covenantors can reasonably argue that the purchaser should not be compensated if any reliefs are unavailable.

The definition contained here represents a middle approach which is often adopted. It allows the purchaser to recover only where certain reliefs which the purchaser could reasonably expect to be available prove to be unavailable.

The three situations in which the loss of a relief may give rise to a liability are:

(1) the use of a purchaser's relief;

(2) the loss or use of a pre-completion relief; and

(3) the loss of a right to repayment of tax. (Although a right to repayment of tax is strictly speaking not a relief as normally understood, it is often treated as such for the purposes of the tax deed.)

Purchaser's reliefs and pre-completion reliefs are dealt with under their respective definitions in paras 10–17 and 10–18. As regards the right to repayment of taxation (cl.1.5.4) the covenantors would usually seek to restrict this to rights of repayment which are contained in the accounts on the basis that, if a right to repayment did not appear in the accounts, the purchaser could not be expecting the repayment, would not have paid for it and so should not be compensated if it is not available.

**10–15**    **and the amount of the Liability to Taxation is:**

   **1.5.5**    **in the case of a liability falling within clause 1.5.1 or a liability not falling within any of the preceding sub-clauses of this clause, the amount of Taxation payable;**

   **1.5.6**    **in the case of a liability falling within clause 1.5.2, the amount of Taxation which would have been payable but for the set-off or utilisation;**

   **1.5.7**    **in the case of a liability falling within clause 1.5.3, the value attributed in the Accounts to the Pre-Completion Relief so lost, counteracted or clawed back; and**

**1.5.8** **in the case of a liability falling within clause 1.5.4, the amount of repayment which would otherwise have been available.**

Although when the liability to taxation constitutes an actual payment of taxation, the amount which the covenantors are liable to pay is fairly obvious, it is less clear where the liability to taxation is a loss of a relief and accordingly these clauses are necessary.

In the case of a loss of a purchaser's relief or the loss of a pre-completion relief by way of set-off, it is usual for the covenantors' liability to be the amount of tax that would have been saved by the use of the purchaser's relief or pre-completion relief. In the case of loss of pre-completion relief in any other circumstances, it is sometimes proposed by the purchaser that the covenantors liability should be the amount of the relief lost. This is difficult because it raises issues such as what rate of corporation tax is to be assumed when putting a value on the relief lost and whether or not it is fair for the covenantors to have to pay if, in practice, it is most unlikely that the target company would not within a reasonable time be in a position to use the relief. It is also suggested that the clause is conceptually wrong. The approach that has been adopted in the clause is that it is fair for pre-completion losses to be included because they have been given a value in the accounts. If those reliefs are lost, therefore, the appropriate level of compensation is the amount by which the assets of the company would have been less if the loss of the reliefs had been known when the accounts were prepared.

Note that there is no definition of "Taxation" in the tax deed despite its **10–16** obvious fundamental importance. This is because taxation is defined in the definition section of the sale agreement and definitions contained in the sale agreement are incorporated by reference into the tax deed. The definition of "Taxation" in the sale agreement and, indeed, any other tax-related definitions in the sale agreement must be considered carefully when looking at the tax deed.

The definition of "Taxation" in the sale agreement is very wide. Nonetheless, a wide definition is usually accepted by the covenantors. However, issues do sometimes arise, particularly in relation to the following matters:

(1) Rates: It is often argued that rates should not be covered by the tax deed—they will, in any case, normally be dealt with fully under the warranties.

(2) National Insurance Contributions: These are not strictly speaking tax, however, it is usual to treat them in the same way as tax.

(3) Stamp Duty, Stamp Duty Reserve Tax and SDLT: Including stamp duty within the tax deed can cause problems, particularly as stamp duty (unlike stamp duty reserve tax or SDLT) is effectively an optional tax. Further, an indemnity against stamp duty may be ineffective under the Stamp Act 1891, s.117. Such considerations have less force in relation to Stamp Duty Reserve Tax and SDLT because of their compulsory nature.

It is often found in practice that the definition "Taxation" includes taxes which are almost certainly of historical interest only but which, if there has been fraudulent evasion of a tax assessment, may remain a theoretical possibility indefinitely. A note of certain taxes which are no longer in force (and of some taxes which are of limited relevance) is included in para.5–118. The covenantors will find it difficult to insist on the deletion of specific taxes on the grounds of irrelevance since the purchaser may reasonably argue that any risk of a liability, however slight, should fall on the covenantors.

**10–17**    **1.6 "Pre-Completion Relief" means any Relief which arises as result of or by reference to any Event occurring on or before Completion and which has either been treated as an asset in the Accounts or is taken into account in computing (and so reducing or eliminating) a provision for deferred taxation which appears in the Accounts or which would have appeared in the Accounts but for the presumed availability of the Relief.**

The concept behind pre-completion relief is that it is fair for the covenantors to give a covenant in respect of such reliefs since they are reliefs which were taken into account in the balance sheet in the accounts and therefore the purchaser can be assumed to have taken the availability of those reliefs into account in setting the purchase price.

In practice, it is rare for a tax relief to be given a value in the accounts of a company and therefore the first part of the definition will not often be relevant. The position in relation to deferred taxation is more difficult. A provision for deferred taxation may be reduced or eliminated on the basis that when the tax liability becomes actual there will be available to the company some relief, such as carrying forward losses or capital allowances, to off-set against the tax liability. If those assumed reliefs prove to be unavailable, the provision for deferred taxation should have been greater and consequently the net assets of the company would have been less. The purchaser will seek compensation on that basis. The covenantors may argue that it is unreasonable to expect them to compensate the purchaser in respect of a liability that may never arise—deferred taxation is, by its very nature, not an actual liability and may never become an actual liability. If an actual tax liability does subsequently arise, the covenantors may argue that the purchaser should recover either under the tax deed (if the tax liabilities are covered under the tax deed) or under an appropriate warranty (for example, a warranty that adequate provision for tax is made in the accounts).

**10–18**    **1.7 "Purchaser's Relief" means any Relief which arises as a result or by reference to an Event occurring after the Balance Sheet Date.**

It is usual to exclude from the scope of the tax deed any tax liabilities arising in the normal course of trading after the balance sheet date (see cl.3.1.2). On that basis, any tax reliefs occurring after the balance sheet date should also be for the benefit of the purchaser. If those reliefs are lost by being used to reduce another tax liability of the target company then the purchaser should be able to recover from the covenantors.

**1.8 "Relief" includes any relief or allowance, exemption, set-off or deduc-   10–19
tion from or credit available from, against or in relation to Taxation or in the
computation of income, profits or gains for a Taxation purpose.**

This definition is of considerable significance if the covenant is extended to cases
which, while not giving rise to immediate liability to make a tax payment,
involve a loss of relief. The kinds of relief covered are:

(1) Relief as such—for example, group relief or relief from stamp duty.

(2) Allowances—such as capital allowances.

(3) Exemption—for example, the exemption from capital gains tax enjoyed by
    investment trusts.

(4) Set-off—which occurs, for example, in relation to set-off of losses in
    succeeding accounting periods under ICTA 1988, s.393 and by a claimant
    company in respect of group relief under ICTA 1988, ss.403(2A)–403(2E)
    and s.403ff (as amended by FA 1998, Sch.5, Pt II).

(5) Deduction—which arises most commonly in computing taxable profits or
    gains.

(6) Credit—for example under ICTA 1988, s.231, which confers a tax credit for
    certain recipients of qualifying distributions, and credits for foreign tax.

**1.9 "Saving" means a reduction of liability of the Company to Taxation by   10–20
virtue of the set-off against the liability or against any income, profits or
gains of any Relief arising as a result of a Liability to Taxation in respect of
which the Covenantors have made a payment under clause 2.**

Sometimes a liability to taxation can give rise to a corresponding saving in
taxation of the target company. This can arise because of timing issues. For
example, if a deduction has been claimed in one tax period which should have
been claimed for a later tax period, there will be a liability to taxation in respect
of the earlier period. However, the taxation for the later period may be reduced
as the deduction is allowable for the later period. Therefore, the only loss the
target company suffers is in respect of penalties and interest for having claimed
the deduction in the wrong period. In other cases, payment of one form of
taxation may lead to a deduction in payment of another form of taxation. For
example, stamp duty will be deductible when calculating chargeable gains.
Where there is a group of companies, sometimes deductions may be claimed in
the wrong company with the result that the tax liability of one group company
increases, but the tax liability of the group company in which the deduction
should properly have been claimed is reduced. These matters are dealt with in
cl.7.

**1.10 References to any Event occurring on or before Completion include   10–21
a combination of two or more Events the first of which occurred or is
deemed to have occurred on or before Completion.**

This is often a controversial provision. The purchaser will not want its claim defeated on the basis that some part of the Event which gave rise to the claim arose after Completion. For example, if there was a contract which had been largely performed prior to Completion the fact that payment was received after Completion should not prevent a claim. Secondly, there are a number of specific tax situations where a later act combined with an earlier act can give rise to a tax charge, for example, a charge under TCGA 1992, s.179 (see para.5–70) or a claw back of stamp duty or SDLT relief (see para.5–113). However, the covenantors will argue that the clause as drafted is far too wide; for example, this wording may leave the covenantors liable for capital gains tax in respect of a disposal of an asset acquired before completion if that acquisition is combined with the subsequent disposal. This clause also does not address the position where there has been something "unusual" in tax terms about the original acquisition, for example where the asset was not acquired on arm's length terms, or an earlier gain was rolled over into the asset. The covenantors will therefore usually try to either delete this clause or qualify it by wording such as:

**"provided that the Event occurring on or before Completion occurred outside the ordinary course of business of the Company and the Event occurring after Completion occurred in the ordinary course of business of the Company."**

Alternative wording which favours the purchaser more is:

**"provided that the Event occurring after Completion occurred either (a) pursuant to a binding contract entered into on or before Completion or (b) in the ordinary course of business after Completion."**

*2 Covenant*

**10–22**   **2.1 The Covenantors jointly and severally undertake to pay to the Purchaser the amount of:**

The Covenantors will normally be required to accept joint and several liability and, in the absence of express contrary provision, they will ultimately bear the liability amongst themselves in proportion to their rights in the total consideration. For further discussion of this point see para.3–15.

**10–23**    **2.1.1 any Liability to Taxation which has arisen or arises as a result of or in connection with an Event which occurred on or before Completion;**

This is the basic covenant, the scope of which depends to a large extent on the definition of "Liability to Taxation".

**10–24**    **2.1.2 the costs incurred by the Company or the Purchaser in relation to Liability to Taxation or Claims for Taxation;**

The purchaser will normally wish to ensure that the covenant to pay costs covers not only liabilities to taxation in respect of which the covenantors are liable but all claims for taxation, even if the relevant tax authority's claim is subsequently found to be groundless. The justification for this is that any claim for taxation will arise as a result of a problem created by the covenantors and therefore the covenantors should be responsible for the costs of dealing with that problem.

The covenantors should ensure that this clause only relates to liabilities to taxation and claims for taxation to the extent that they arise from events on or before completion. The covenantors will also usually want to build in an element of reasonableness.

**2.1.3 any depletion in or reduction of value of the assets of the Company**   **10–25**
**or an increase in its liabilities as a result of inheritance tax which:**

   **2.1.3.1    is at Completion a charge on the Shares or the assets of the**
   **Company or gives rise to a power to sell, mortgage or charge**
   **the Shares or the assets of the Company; or**

   **2.1.3.2    after Completion becomes a charge on or gives rise to a**
   **power to sell, mortgage or charge any of the Shares or the**
   **assets of the Company being a liability in respect of addi-**
   **tional inheritance tax payable on the death of the person**
   **within seven years after a transfer of value;**

**but a right to pay by instalments shall be disregarded and the provisions of**
**ICTA, s.213 shall not apply to payments to be made under this Deed;**

As set out in paras 5–111 and 5–112, in certain circumstances a charge can arise over the shares in or the assets of the target company in respect of unpaid inheritance tax. It is reasonable for the covenantors to give this covenant.

**2.1.4 any liability of the Company to make a payment in respect of**   **10–26**
**Taxation under any indemnity, covenant, guarantee or charge entered into**
**on or before Completion; and**

This is potentially wide-ranging and the covenantors need to consider the matter carefully before they give the covenant. It covers not only situations where there is a statutory right of reimbursement (see the examples set out at para.5–25) but also where there is a contractual right. For example, if the target company had previously sold a subsidiary, it could cover any continuing liability under the tax deed given at that time. The covenantors may want to argue that it is inappropriate that those types of arrangements are dealt with in the tax deed.

**2.1.5 any Liability to Taxation which arises from the Company being**   **10–27**
**called upon to make a payment for group relief surrendered to it or a**
**clawback of amounts previously paid to it in exchange for a surrender of**
**group relief.**

As noted at para.5–66, a company to whom group relief is surrendered normally pays to the surrendering company an amount equal to the tax saved. The purchaser can argue, therefore, that a payment made in order to reduce the tax liability of the target company should be treated in the same way as a tax liability. Similarly, a clawback of a payment paid to the target company for the surrender of group relief can be viewed as similar to the clawback of a repayment of tax. This clause will clearly only be of relevance where the target company is or has been a member of a group.

10–28    **2.2 The provisions of Schedule [ ] of the Agreement apply to claims under this Deed where they are expressed to do so.**

All of the limitations on liability under the tax deed can be set out in the tax deed itself. Alternatively, as done here, certain limitations can be included by incorporating the appropriate provisions of the sale agreement. The financial limitations on liability are usually set out in a schedule to the sale agreement. In practice, most of the obligations are already contained in the tax deed. The matters dealt with in the sale agreement in relation to the tax deed are usually limited to:

(1)  time limits: it is usual to provide that claims under the tax deed must be brought within a time period of between six and seven years from completion. This equates to the six year period in which, in normal circumstances, the Inland Revenue can raise an enquiry.

(2)  overall cap: it is usual for claims under the tax deed to be included in the overall cap on claims of, usually, the amount of consideration received by the vendors. (Please see comments at para.3–23 for further discussion of this point.) The purchasers may argue that where there are specific known tax problems, these should be excluded from the cap.

(3)  small claims: a purchaser will often argue that there should be no small claims exclusions for claims under the tax deed on the basis that the tax deed should give a straight pound for pound indemnity. The covenantors may argue that there is no logical reason why claims under the tax deed should be treated differently from claims under the warranties. This is usually a matter of commercial negotiation. (Please see comment at para.3–20 for further discussion of this point).

*3 Exclusions*

10–29    **3.1 The undertaking in clause 2.1 does not apply to a Liability to Taxation:**

**3.1.1 to the extent that specific provision or reserve or allowance has been made in the Accounts for the Liability to Taxation;**

If the vendors have provided management accounts for periods subsequent to the last accounts date which contain provisions for taxation on the profits shown, the clause should extend to also include those accounts. If there are to be completion accounts, this clause should refer to the completion accounts rather than the accounts.

The purchaser cannot fairly complain about a liability which arises after completion where a specific provision or reserve was made in the accounts, although a note in the accounts may not of itself provide a quantification of the anticipated liability.

Deferred taxation, which is discussed in relation to cl.2.1.2.7 in para.7–40, needs careful consideration. If no reference is made to deferred taxation, the covenantors will normally not be liable if it becomes a current liability as this will be the result of post-completion events (although there may be liability if the adequacy of the deferred taxation is as a result of the loss of a pre-completion relief). The purchaser should specifically consider the nature of any deferred tax provision to see if it is acceptable for the liability, if it arises, to be outside the scope of the tax deed.

The covenantors will often seek to delete **"specific"** on the grounds that if the provision or reserve for tax is sufficient in aggregate to cover all the tax liabilities, it should not matter whether the provision or reserve has been allocated to a specific liability.

### 3.1.2 for which the Company is, or may become, liable wholly or primarily as a result of transactions in the usual course of its business after the Balance Sheet Date;                                                               10–30

A general exclusion for liabilities arising from transactions in the usual course of the company's business is fair having regard to the broad principle that the indemnities should relate to unexpected liabilities and that the purchaser is effectively getting the benefit of profits earned in that period. Furthermore, the purchaser has the protection of the warranties. This exclusion is not appropriate if there are to be completion accounts and cl.3.1.1 has been amended to include reference to completion accounts as any such liability should be picked up in the completion accounts.

### 3.1.3 if it would not have arisen but for a new form of Taxation, a change in the rates of Taxation or a statutory variation in methods of applying or calculating rates of Taxation, in each case occurring after Completion with retrospective effect;                                                               10–31

Until 1984, the corporation tax rate was fixed annually in arrears and there is always the possibility that this practice will be restored. The exclusion remains correct in principle as it has become established practice for the purchaser to accept the risk of an increased liability and, conversely, for the covenantors to allow the purchaser the benefit of a reduction in the tax rate.

The part of this clause relating to changes in the law will not be necessary if the definition of relevant statutory provisions is limited to those which are in force at the date of the sale agreement or result from a mere consolidation. However, if the definition allows for future changes in the law then it is a matter for negotiation between the parties as to whether retrospective liability imposed upon the target company should be borne by the covenantors or by the purchaser.

The purchaser should bear in mind that provisions in Finance Acts are often retrospective, at least to the date of the budget speech.

The covenantors may wish to try to extend the exclusion to avoid a liability which results, for example, from a recognised interpretation of the law being reversed by the ruling of a higher court.

**10–32     3.1.4 to the extent that it would not have arisen but for the fact that the treatment in future accounts of the Company of assets and liabilities, or of the Taxation attributable to timing differences, is different from the treatment in the Accounts;**

If a change in accounting policy after the purchaser acquires control of the target company gives rise retrospectively to a taxation liability which would not otherwise relate to the pre-completion period, the covenantors might reasonably consider that they should not be required to meet that liability. For example, treatment of an asset as a fixed asset rather than trading stock could affect the deductibility of expenditure incurred on the asset.

There is a considerable subjective element involved in quantifying timing differences and the covenantors should not be penalised if a change of treatment taking place after the sale of the target company results in an unexpected liability.

A purchaser will often qualify this exclusion to exclude changes in accounting policy that are necessary because the target company's accounts have not previously been prepared in accordance with accounting standards.

**10–33     3.1.5 to the extent of any recovery by the Purchaser under the Warranties in respect of, or arising from, the same Liability to Taxation;**

This clause adopts the definition of "Warranties" which appears in the sale agreement (see para.4–01).

In principle it should not be objectionable as its aim is to avoid double recovery. The purchaser will generally want to bring a claim under the tax deed as this gives a better basis for recovery unless warranty claims are to be quantified on an indemnity basis as discussed in para.3–06.

Conflicts of interest may arise under this clause if the vendors and covenantors differ (see also para.2–20). The clause deliberately does not specify from whom the recovery is made in case not all the vendors are also covenantors.

**10–34     3.1.6 to the extent that a Relief other than a Pre-Completion Relief or a Purchaser's Relief is available to reduce such Liability to Taxation;**

As discussed at para.10–14, the position adopted in this tax deed is that the purchaser should only be entitled to the benefit of reliefs if the availability of those reliefs was assumed in deciding the purchase price. If the availability or otherwise of such reliefs is not reflected in the purchase price, then it is fair that the covenantors should have the benefit of them to reduce any potential claim under the tax deed. This exclusion would cover a situation where, for example, there was a liability to taxation but there were carry-forward losses to offset against that liability.

### 3.1.7 if it results from the cessation of the trade of the Company after Completion; 10–35

Cessation of a trade will usually result in the crystallisation of various tax liabilities, some of which might be caught under the tax deed. The covenantors can fairly argue that, unless it is expressly contemplated at the time of entering into the agreement, cessation of trade is outside the reasonable contemplation of the parties and therefore the covenantors should not be liable for the consequences of it.

The exclusions set out above are ones which it is considered reasonable for a purchaser to include in a first draft. The covenantors may want to include other exclusions, as set out below. **10–36**

### 3.1.8 to the extent that it has been made good or otherwise compensated for by the Purchaser or the Company but after deducting costs incurred by them directly as a result of doing so; 10–37

In certain circumstances, particularly where there is a corporate vendor, a liability may be counteracted by making retrospective claims for relief. If this can be achieved without cost to the purchaser or the target company, then it is fair that the covenantors should benefit from any saving that is made. There may be considerable difficulty in quantifying the cost to the purchaser or the company of taking mitigating action and it could be appropriate to provide a certification procedure—for example, by the target company's auditors.

### 3.1.9 which is attributable to the Company ceasing to be entitled to the small companies' rate of corporation tax as a result of the purchase of the Shares by the Purchaser; 10–38

If the taxable profits of a company do not exceed a maximum amount as fixed by Parliament from time to time, a reduced rate of corporation tax applies under ICTA 1988, s.13. This maximum is allocated equally among "associated" companies (that is, companies under common control) and accordingly the acquisition of the target company by a corporate purchaser could reduce the maximum applicable to the target company. If this results in loss of the small companies' relief, it is unreasonable that the covenantors should be penalised.

### 3.1.10 in respect of value added tax relating to supplies made and imports received since the Balance Sheet Date or in respect of stamp duty or stamp duty land tax the liability for which has been incurred in the course of the Company's business since the Balance Sheet Date; 10–39

Value added tax has to be accounted for both in respect of supplies made by a taxable person and also on imports.

It is appropriate for the covenantors to seek to exclude these liabilities, which amount to expenses in the course of business. Similar exclusions would be appropriate if the definition of "Taxation" extends to cover such matters as rates and national insurance. This clause may be unnecessary if the exclusion at cl.3.1.2 is accepted. However, it could still usefully be included if there might be an argument as to whether, for example, the acquisition or disposal of a major capital asset was in the ordinary and usual course of business.

**10–40    3.1.11 specifically disclosed in the Disclosure Letter;**

It is unusual to have a disclosure letter which affects the tax deed. In general it is better practice to detail the exclusions so that the tax deed can largely stand on its own. This is particularly so if there is a likelihood that the purchaser will cease to own the target company, in which event access to the disclosure letter may be impractical.

**10–41    3.1.12 which would not have arisen but for a voluntary act or omission of the Company or the Purchaser [which could reasonably have been avoided] carried out, or occurring, after the date of this Deed, otherwise than in the usual course of business, [(unless under an obligation, whether legally binding or not, incurred prior to the date of this Deed, or taking place with the approval of any of the Covenantors) and which the Purchaser or the Company was, or ought reasonably to have been, aware could give rise to a Liability to Taxation]; or**

**10–42**    On the face of it, it would appear fair that the covenantors should not be responsible for a liability which arises as a result of voluntary acts on the part of the target company after completion. An example of this that could arise where the target company was a member of a group of companies is where there has been a transfer of assets within the target group and, during the period of six years after the transfer, the transferee ceases to be a member of the group. In that event, a tax charge arises retrospectively to the date at which the group transfer took place (TCGA 1992, s.179) (as amended). Unless the transaction was one that was specifically contemplated at the time of the purchase of the target group, it is unreasonable for the purchaser to expect the covenantors to be responsible for this liability. The purchaser would often accept this clause with the inclusion of the words in brackets.

It is to be noted that the exception, even without the bracketed amendments, applies only to transactions effected outside of the usual course of business as the purchaser cannot be expected to absolve the covenantors from liabilities that arise from activities carried out in the ordinary course. The parties may wish to clarify the effect on this clause of post-completion changes in the nature of the target company's business, for example by excluding liability which results from a change in the nature of, or manner of conducting, the business.

**3.1.13 if the Company fails, after due warning, to act in accordance with     10–43
the reasonable instructions of the Covenantors in conducting a dispute (as
referred to in clause 4) in respect of a Claim for Taxation;**

It is of considerable importance to the covenantors that they should control the
conduct of negotiations and litigation with the Inland Revenue in accordance
with cl.4. The clause itself provides no special sanction if the target company
fails to comply with its obligations. The covenantors will therefore sometimes
seek to exclude from the scope of the covenant liability which arises in circumstances where they have not been responsible for the negotiations but, from the
purchaser's point of view, this sanction may be considered to be excessive.
Clause 4.1 contains contrary wording of the type the purchaser will often want.
The purchaser will also need to consider what effect there will be if one of the
covenantors complains that the consultation clause has not been properly
observed in relation to him or her while the others have been consulted. In that
event, there is no reason why those covenantors who have been consulted should
be released from liability simply because of failure to consult another one of the
covenantors. The position of the covenantor who has not been consulted may be
different, but complex questions will then arise as to the impact on the joint and
several liability of the covenantors if one of them is released from liabilities. See
also the discussion of this question in para.3–15.

### 4 Conduct of Claims

**4.1 The Purchaser shall notify the Covenantors in writing of any Claim for     10–44
Taxation which comes to its notice, whereby it appears that the Covenantors
are, or may become, liable to pay the Purchaser under this Deed. Failure to
comply with this clause shall not affect the Purchaser's rights and the
Covenantors' only remedy for the failure shall be a claim for such damages
as they suffer directly as a result of it.**

The basic proposition that the covenantors should have conduct of negotiations
with and litigation against the Inland Revenue or other taxation authorities is
normally unobjectionable.
    Careful consideration needs to be given to the following points:          **10–45**

(1)  The clear identification of items which require notification to the covenan-
     tors. In this context, the target company will wish to avoid a constant
     correspondence with the covenantors but the covenantors are entitled to
     ensure that no significant matter is dealt with without their having an
     opportunity to intervene.

(2)  Where there is more than one covenantor, it is desirable to have a simple
     system for giving notice and for ensuring that a collective decision is
     reached and is communicated to the target company. It may be helpful to
     appoint a representative for this purpose.

(3)  The covenantors may wish to insert a time period in which they must be
     notified to enable the covenantors to consult together, take advice and reach

a view well before any time limit for contesting the claim with the relevant tax authority could lapse.

(4) All parties should bear in mind that a variety of liabilities not normally thought of as "taxation" may fall within that term as defined.

(5) The wording in the final sentence is important for the purchaser to ensure that it does not lose the right to recover from the covenantors because it failed to give notice. The covenantors may seek to delete it (see the discussion at para.10–43).

**10–46**      **4.2 The Purchaser shall ensure that a Claim for Taxation to which this Deed applies is, so far as reasonably practicable, dealt with separately from claims to which it does not apply.**

To minimise some of the potential complexities, the purchaser is expressly required to attempt to deal with matters which can be the subject of a claim under the Tax Deed separately from the target company's general tax affairs. This should also in principle suit the target company as it will not want the covenantors to have access to information regarding its taxation affairs generally by reason of the right of the covenantors to have the conduct of claims.

**10–47**      **4.3 Provided that the Covenantors indemnify and secure the Company and the Purchaser to the reasonable satisfaction of the Purchaser against all losses, costs, damages and expenses (including interest on overdue Taxation) which may be incurred thereby, the Purchaser will procure that the Company at the Covenantors' cost and expense takes such action and gives such information and assistance in connection with its Taxation affairs as the Covenantors reasonably and promptly request to dispute, appeal or settle a Claim. This obligation will not apply where a Taxation Authority alleges dishonest or fraudulent conduct by the Covenantors or by the Company before Completion.**

The covenantors should consider whether it would be helpful when entering into the tax deed to make it clear among themselves as to how liability for costs should be apportioned. It might well be, for example, that in a particular case one covenantor would wish to agree to a certain settlement with the relevant taxation authority while another would prefer to litigate. In that case, several possible choices exist. A basis of majority votes could determine whether or not the settlement should be accepted, the majority being determined either purely on numbers of persons or on amounts of sale consideration received. Another possibility is that a covenantor prepared to accept a compromise could pay his contribution into a suspense account on the basis that such payment would then discharge him from any subsequent liability. If the ultimate liability from a contest of the claim was less than the amount paid into the suspense account, the covenantor who made the payment into that account would receive back only the net amount after deducting an appropriate contribution to the costs incurred.

Alternatively the covenantor willing to accept a settlement could pay his proportion of the amount of the settlement into a common fund the benefit of which would accrue to those covenantors contesting the claim and any surplus would be handed back to the covenantor.

It is nevertheless unusual to spell out these provisions in detail but, where there are covenantors who have distinctly different interests and it is known that a tax liability might arise, it is desirable for these points to be resolved from the start. The purchaser should be aware that litigation can involve heavy demands on executive time and, particularly in any case where there is a likelihood of disputes arising, it would be desirable to have a clear understanding as to whether a charge for time is to be made in this respect and, if so, on what basis.

Purchasers occasionally seek to extend the final sentence to cover allegations of negligent conduct. This is unreasonable. It is easy for the Revenue to allege negligence whenever a mistake in calculating tax has been made, even if only as a negotiating technique.

**4.4 The Purchaser shall procure that the Covenantors (and their advisers)**   **10–48**
**are given full and prompt access to all documents, records and personnel of**
**the Company and the Purchaser and their advisers to enable the Covenan-**
**tors promptly and effectively to evaluate, dispute and deal with a Claim for**
**Taxation to which this Deed applies and enforce their rights under this**
**clause 4.**

The covenantors will, in practice, often require documentary and executive assistance in handling claims. In principle the purchaser should not object as long as the demands are not excessive. If litigation requires the attendance of employees of the target company at court, there could be considerable costs involved and as such it might be fair for the covenantors to pay a suitable attendance fee.

**4.5 In connection with the conduct of a dispute relating to a Claim for**   **10–49**
**Taxation to which this Deed applies:**

**4.5.1 the Covenantors and the Purchaser [or the Company (as the case**
**may be)] shall keep the other parties informed of all relevant matters and**
**shall promptly forward or procure to be forwarded copies of all material**
**correspondence and other written communications;**

Again, where there is more than one covenantor, it would be advisable for them to provide a mechanism for reaching decisions amongst themselves so that one covenantor cannot be penalised for a failure in co-operation on the part of another covenantor.

**4.5.2 the Covenantors shall not settle or compromise the dispute, or agree**   **10–50**
**any thing in its conduct which is likely to affect the amount involved or the**
**future Liability to Taxation of the Company, or the Purchaser, without the**
**prior approval of the Purchaser, such approval not to be unreasonably**
**withheld or delayed;**

Although in principle the target company and the purchaser are unlikely to be concerned about the terms of a settlement or compromise, nevertheless they do have a legitimate interest in case the compromise affects any of their other taxation affairs. For example, the target company may have agreed procedures with the Inland Revenue in relation to such matters as determination of disallowed expenses which it would not wish to be disturbed by the disputed matters. It would also be concerned to ensure that the covenantors are able to discharge the agreed liability.

10–51    **4.5.3 if a dispute arises between the Purchaser and the Covenantors as to whether a Claim for Taxation should be settled in full or contested, the dispute shall be referred to the determination of a senior tax counsel of at least 10 years standing ("Counsel"), appointed by agreement between the Purchaser and the Covenantors, or (if they do not agree) upon the application by either party to the President for the time being of the Law Society, whose determination shall be final. Counsel shall be asked to advise whether, in his opinion, an appeal against the Claim for Taxation would, on the balance of probabilities, be likely to succeed. Only if his opinion is in the affirmative shall that Claim for Taxation be contested. Any further dispute arising between the Covenantors and the Purchaser as to whether a further appeal should be pursued following determination of an earlier appeal (whether or not in favour of the Covenantors) shall be resolved in a similar manner.**

The purchaser may wish to impose some restraint on the freedom of the covenantors in relation to the conduct of claims. This clause substantially limits the rights of the covenantors.

10–52    **4.6 Nothing contained in this clause 4 shall require the Purchaser to prevent the Company from making a payment of Taxation at the time necessary to avoid incurring a fine, penalty or interest in respect of unpaid Taxation.**

Self explanatory.

*5 Dates for payments*

10–53    **5.1 This clause applies solely for determining the date on which payments are to be made by the Covenantors under this Deed.**

It might be thought that there would be no need to provide for the time at which payments under a tax deed are made. However, special provision is required given the complexity of the normal arrangements entered into with the Collector of Taxes in relation to corporation and income tax.

When a company makes a return to the Inland Revenue following the end of its financial year it will pay the tax shown in the return. There will normally be many matters, small and large, which need to be agreed and, as these are resolved, various payments may be made to and by the Collector of Taxes. Claims for allowances and reliefs may be made and withdrawn if it becomes apparent that the claims have to be made, or need not have been made, to minimise the tax burden. It is therefore frequently almost impossible in respect of some payments to determine the moment at which the target company has incurred an actual liability to make them. Further complexity arises when the tax deed covers loss of reliefs, as discussed in more detail at para.10–19.

**5.2 The Covenantors shall make a payment to the Purchaser in cleared   10–54
funds on the date falling five clear Business Days after the date on which the
Purchaser has notified the Covenantors of the amount of the payment
required to be made or, if later, three clear Business Days prior to the date
on which the Company discharges, or is deemed to discharge, a Liability to
Taxation in respect of which the Purchaser is entitled to make a claim under
this Deed.**

This states the general rule and is amplified by cl.5.3.

**5.3 For the purposes of clause 5.2, the Company is deemed to discharge a   10–55
Liability to Taxation:**

**5.3.1 on the date on which the Company makes an actual payment of
Taxation in respect of the Liability to Taxation;**

This deals with the simple case where the target company makes a specific taxation payment.

**5.3.2 in the case of a Liability to Taxation falling within clause 1.5.2, the date
on which the Taxation would have been payable but for the set-off or
utilisation of the Purchaser's Relief or the Pre-Completion Relief; or**

This deals with the situation where a relief which the purchaser was expecting is used to reduce a taxation liability of the target company. The logical date for payment in those circumstances is the date on which the tax which has been saved would have been payable.

**5.3.3 in the case of a Liability to Taxation falling within clause 1.5.4, the date
on which the repayment would otherwise have been made to the Company.**

Note that there is no specific provision dealing with the position where a pre-completion relief is lost otherwise than by being used to reduce another tax liability. The result is that where there is a claim for the loss of a pre-completion relief of this nature this will fall within the general wording in cl.5.2 and will be payable within five days of notification.

**5.4 If a payment by the Covenantors under this Deed is not made on the   10–56
date referred to in clause 5.2 it shall carry interest from the due date of**

**payment at the rate of 4% above the base rate from time to time of Barclays Bank plc until payment is received by the Purchaser.**

This is a standard interest clause and should reflect the equivalent clause, if any, in the sale agreement.

10–57    **5.5 Interest shall be payable on costs incurred under clause 2.1.2 in accordance with clause 5.4 from the date the Company or the Purchaser is invoiced for the costs.**

This ensures that interest in respect of costs runs from the date on which the costs were incurred.

10–58    **5.6 Disputes in relation to the provisions of clauses 5.3 and 5.4 may be referred by the Purchaser or the Covenantors to the auditors of the Company, acting as experts and not as arbitrators, whose certificate shall in the absence of manifest error be final.**

In view of the complexity of circumstances that can arise in practice and the difficulty that exists in many cases of identifying clearly the taxation liabilities which are covered by a specific payment, it is considered to be sensible to provide for a simple method of determination. While the purchaser will be happy to rely on the certificate of the auditors of the target company, the covenantors may wish to ensure that the auditors are a firm of sufficient standing to carry out the determination competently. Although in relation to "taxes", such as stamp duty and rates, the auditors might not be the appropriate experts, it is to be expected that they would obtain suitable professional advice in resolving the matter.

10–59    *6 Deduction from Payments and Right of Set-off*

**6.1 Except as required by law payments under this Deed shall be made gross, free of rights of counterclaim or set-off.**

This excludes the covenantors' right of set-off. Although usually accepted, this could potentially cause problems for the covenantors. If the purchaser's wording in cl.4.1 is accepted, the purchaser's failure to follow the conduct of claims procedure does not reduce the covenantors' liability—it only allows them to bring a claim against the purchaser for breach of contract. Under the wording of this cl.6.1 the purchaser could claim that the covenantors' breach of contract claim cannot be offset against amounts due to the purchaser.

10–60    **6.2 If a deduction or withholding is required by law to be made from a payment by the Covenantors under this Deed, there shall be paid to the Purchaser such additional amount as is necessary to ensure that the net receipt by the Purchaser is equal to the amount which it would have received and retained had the payment in question not been subject to deduction or withholding.**

In practice this is limited to very few situations, mainly tax related, where there is an obligation on the payer to make a deduction at source. An example is payment of interest to persons overseas in certain circumstances. In circumstances where this does apply, the covenantors should consider amending the clause to ensure that any corresponding benefit to the purchaser (for example a tax credit) is taken into account.

**6.3 If the Purchaser or the Company is liable to Taxation in respect of a**    **10–61**
**payment under this Deed (or would have been liable but for the availability**
**of Relief or a right to repayment of Taxation), there shall be paid to the**
**Purchaser an additional amount as if the Taxation had been a deduction or**
**withholding from the payment and the provisions of clause 6.2 shall apply**
**accordingly to the payment.**

This is a fairly standard tax gross-up clause. It is usually accepted by the covenantors where, as is normally the case, payments are made to the purchaser. ESC D33 clarifies that in most cases, such payments will not be taxable in the hands of the purchaser and so the clause is largely academic. If, for whatever reason, payments are to be made to the target company or there is a real risk that ESC D33 will not apply, the covenantors should consider amending or deleting this clause.

## 7 Savings    10–62

**7.1 If (at the request and expense of the Covenantors) the Company's**
**auditors certify that the Company or the Purchaser has obtained a Saving,**
**the Purchaser shall as soon as reasonably practicable repay to the Covenan-**
**tors the lesser of:**

**7.1.1**    **the amount of the Saving less costs incurred in obtaining it (as**
       **certified by the Company's auditors); and**

**7.1.2**    **the amount paid by the Covenantors to the Purchaser under clause**
       **2.**

**7.2 If the amount referred to in clause 7.1.1 exceeds that referred to in clause**
**7.1.2, the excess shall be carried forward to be offset against (and so as to**
**reduce or eliminate) the future liability of the Covenantors under clause**
**2.**

As noted above (see para.10–20) in certain circumstances a tax liability may give rise to a saving of tax in the target company. In those circumstances it is fair for the covenantors to have the benefit of that saving. However, the benefit will only be by way of repayment of claims already paid or a reduction in future liabilities—it does not give rise to a net cash payment to the covenantors.

   The purchaser may object to cl.7.2 on the grounds that the benefit of a saving should only relate to the liability to taxation which gave rise to the saving.

**7.3 If the Company or the Purchaser becomes aware that the Company or**    **10–63**
**the Purchaser has obtained or may obtain a Saving, the Purchaser shall as**

soon as reasonably practicable give notice of that fact to the Covenantors. Provided that the Covenantors have paid the Purchaser in respect of the Liability to Taxation which gave rise to the Saving, the Purchaser shall take and procure the taking by the Company of reasonable steps to obtain the Saving.

10–64       **7.4 In certifying a Saving under clause 7.1, the Company's auditors shall act as experts and not as arbitrators and their certificate shall in the absence of manifest error be final.**

In practical terms, the problem for the covenantors will be in finding out whether the target company has made a saving. Clause 7.2 is therefore important from the covenantors' perspective, although in practice it may be difficult to enforce.

*8 Recovery from Third Party*

10–65   **8.1 If the Company or the Purchaser recovers or becomes aware that it is entitled to recover from a third party (including a Taxation Authority) an amount which is referable to a Liability to Taxation in respect of which the Covenantors are liable under this Deed, the Purchaser shall as soon as reasonably practicable give notice of that fact to the Covenantors. It shall then take or procure that the Company takes such reasonable action as is necessary to effect the recovery as the Covenantors request in writing.**

If the target company or the purchaser has the right to be reimbursed by a third party in relation to a liability which is discharged by the covenantors, it is appropriate to give the covenantors the benefit of this right by accounting for sums received or by assigning the right. This clause covers not only recovery from taxation authorities but also, for example, recovery where the target company has a right of reimbursement. An example of a statutory right of reimbursement is TCGA 1992, s.190 where corporation tax on a chargeable gain accruing to a group company may be recovered from the principal company in the group. The principal company, which has only a secondary liability, has a right of reimbursement against the group company which is primarily liable.

10–66       **8.2 The actions taken by the Purchaser under clause 8.1 shall be at the Covenantors' expense and shall be subject to the Covenantors securing the Purchaser and the Company to the reasonable satisfaction of the Purchaser against all resultant losses, expenses and Taxation relating to that recovery.**

The same considerations apply here as in para.10–47 above.

10–67       **8.3 If the Covenantors have made a payment under clause 2, the Purchaser shall repay to the Covenantors the lesser of:**

**8.3.1       the amount recovered together with any interest (net of Taxation) or repayment supplement received in respect of it (net of any losses,**

costs, damages, expenses and tax relating to the amount recovered not previously recovered from the Covenantors); and

**8.3.2**    **the amount paid by the Covenantors under clause 2 in respect of the Liability to Taxation or Claim for Taxation in question.**

**8.4 If the amount provided for under clause 8.3.1 exceeds that under clause 8.3.2, the excess shall be set against, and so reduce or eliminate, any liability of the Covenantors under clause 2 which arises after the recovery.**

The same considerations apply here as in para.10–62 above. As with cl.7.2 the purchaser may object to cl.8.4.

## 9 General

**9.1 Payments by the Covenantors under this Deed shall be treated as repayments of the consideration paid for the Shares under the Agreement but this clause does not limit the liability of the Covenantors.**                    10–68

In the light of ESC D33 this clause may not strictly be necessary, but is usually included to add weight to the argument that payments under the deed are not themselves taxable but rather they adjust the capital base cost of the shares bought and the sale proceeds of the seller.

**9.2 This Deed shall be binding on the respective successors and personal representatives of the Covenantors.**                    10–69

This clause will have a meaningful effect in relation to the personal representatives of a deceased covenantor or successor trustees where the covenantors include trustees.

**9.3 The benefit of this Deed may be assigned in whole but not in part by the Purchaser.**                    10–70

In general, the assignment of the benefit of the tax deed would be most unusual and could relate only to the right to receive the sums payable by the covenantors. The covenantors will wish to ensure that they are dealing only with the purchaser and amend the clause accordingly, although generally it may be necessary for them to accept the purchaser's right to assign intra-group. Please see the discussion at para.2–12 in relation to subsequent disposals by the purchaser.

**9.4 The provisions of the Agreement relating to notices apply to notices to be given under this Deed.**                    10–71

It might be more convenient, if there is a material possibility that the tax deed will become separated from the sale agreement, for the notice provisions to be set out at length. It may also be desirable, if there are several covenantors, to specify a single representative to whom notices should be sent.

**10–72**    **9.5 The construction, validity and performance of this Deed shall be governed by the laws of England.**

**9.6 The parties submit to the non-exclusive jurisdiction of the English courts.**

These provisions will be appropriate only if one of the parties has a connection with a country other than England and Wales. In this context, it must be borne in mind that the laws of Scotland differ from those of England and Wales.

# CHAPTER 11

# Warranties, Undertakings and Indemnities by Purchaser

## INTRODUCTION

Upon receipt of the first draft of the sale agreement, the vendors' solicitors will find that their task in relation to amending the document will fall into two broad categories, namely altering the form of the provisions as drafted with a view to minimising the obligations imposed upon the vendors and inserting additional provisions for the protection of the vendors. So far as the second category is concerned, it is helpful for the vendors' solicitors to have available a checklist of clauses whose addition may be appropriate. **11–01**

## DEALING IN LAND

This issue may be of some concern where the target company holds land as trading stock which has increased in value, such as property development companies, but is unlikely to be of great concern in most cases. **11–02**

One of the wide-ranging anti-avoidance provisions affecting property companies is ICTA 1988, s.776 which, among other consequences, can treat as income a profit which arises on the sale of shares of a land-owning company. Section 777 enables transactions to be traced through a variety of indirect routes. Nevertheless, liability can be avoided if the land is held as trading stock and is sold in the normal course of trade, with all opportunity of profit arising to the company. The vendors would wish to cover any potential risk under this section by including the following provision in the contract:

### [11A] Land to be sold in course of trade

**The Purchaser shall procure that all land and interests in land held as trading stock by the Company at Completion are disposed of in the normal course of trade so as to procure that all opportunity of profit, in respect of the land and interests (within the meaning of ICTA 1988, s.776(10)), arises to the Company.**

The purchaser is likely to have difficulty with this clause as drafted on a number of grounds: **11–03**

(1) The purchaser has no particular way of knowing what is the normal course of trade of the target company. It would therefore be preferable from the

purchaser's point of view for a specific procedure to be spelled out by which any land held by the target company would be sold. The purchaser could then give an undertaking to procure that the sale took place in accordance with the specified procedure. Alternatively, the purchaser could agree to seek the consent of the vendors before implementing the sale of any land and in that case a provision should be included that, if consent was unreasonably withheld, it should be deemed to have been given.

(2) Although in general it is clear when all opportunity of profit arises to the company selling the land, in complex cases this may not be apparent and the purchaser may prefer to delete that part of the undertaking.

As a matter of caution, the purchaser will wish to maintain control of the litigation arising from a claim under either of the above clauses and as such the provisions of the tax deed relating to control of the conduct of claims by the covenantors should be adopted by the purchaser when giving this clause.

## ADJUSTMENT FOR CORRESPONDING TAX SAVINGS OR RECOVERIES

**11–04** The purchaser of the shares of a company may be entitled to make a claim under the warranties for a tax liability which, in the event, proves to involve only a cash flow disadvantage to the target company.

An example of this is where a close company makes a loan to a participator or his or her associate; in which case the company is liable to account for tax at the rate of 25 per cent under ICTA 1988, s.419. The tax will be repaid as and when the loan is repaid.

Previously this issue was particularly important in relation to advance corporation tax distribution. As advance corporation tax was abolished from April 6, 1999, advance corporation tax is now unlikely to be an issue.

**11–05** In principle, the vendors should be liable only for the ultimate loss to the target company, whether in the nature of cash flow disadvantage or a net tax liability. The difficulty in practice is that it may not be possible to determine, at the time that a warranty claim is made, whether there is a permanent or merely temporary loss by the target company.

A clause which is intended to deal generally with all cases of this kind, including ICTA 1988, s.419, is as follows:

### [11B] Refund when tax repaid or relieved

**If the Vendors are liable to the Purchaser under the Warranties in respect of an obligation of the Company to pay Taxation and in certain circumstances the payment will be repaid or some other liability of the Company to Taxation reduced as a result of the payment, the liability of the Vendors shall be reduced, and amounts paid to the Purchaser in respect of the liability shall be refunded, when and to the extent that the Company obtains the benefit of a repayment or reduction in liability. The Purchaser shall procure**

that the Company does everything necessary to result in the repayment or
reduction being obtained as soon as reasonably possible.

This clause does not deal with the effect of a clause relating to a minimum   **11–06**
level of claims in circumstances where the claim under the relevant warranties
did not result in an actual payment to the purchaser because the floor was not
exceeded. The subsequent tax saving or recovery might then have the effect of
restoring the cushion. For further discussion of this point see para.11–09 and
cl.11E.

## DEBT COLLECTION

If the vendors agree to give a warranty in respect of outstanding debts, they will   **11–07**
have to rely on the purchaser to procure that the debt collecting proceeds with
due vigour. After completion of the purchase, the target company will not only
have no inducement to collect the debts efficiently, as the cost of a failure to do
so will be borne by the vendors except to the extent of any floor to claims, but
may even have a positive incentive to be lax about collecting so as to avoid
upsetting its customers. Another difficulty may arise if a customer incurs debts
both before and after completion and makes a general payment on account of its
total indebtedness. The target company should not be free to apply the payment
to later, rather than earlier, debts.

A clause to cover these points is as follows:

### [11C] Collection of warranted debts

**The Purchaser shall procure that the Company uses all reasonable efforts
[consistent with the maintenance of the goodwill of its business] [in accordance with its ordinary debt collection procedures prior to Completion] to
collect promptly all debts to which clause [ ] relates ("warranted debts")
and, if a person is indebted to the Company in respect of warranted debts
and other debts, a general payment on account of the indebtedness shall be
applied in or towards discharging the warranted debts in priority to the
other debts.**

The clause in the warranties which is referred to above will be the one   **11–08**
corresponding to cl.3.5.2 in para.7–69. The purchaser should find this obligation
acceptable, subject to the addition of the words in the first set of square brackets.
If this wording is proposed, the vendor may seek the addition of the words in the
second set of square brackets as an alternative, since the latter approach offers the
vendor greater certainty as to the obligation upon the purchaser and is less
subjective than the former. Provided that the purchaser is aware of the practices
referred to and is of the opinion that they are acceptable, the wording in the
second set of square brackets ought to satisfy both parties.

This clause will not generally be directly relevant in the case of the purchase
of a business. It is unusual for debtors of the business to be included in the sale

but, instead, the purchaser commonly agrees to act as collecting agent for the vendor. The principle embodied in cl.11C will nevertheless often be useful in defining the scope of the obligations of the purchaser in that case and its wording may be adopted with appropriate modification.

## ASSIGNMENT OF RIGHTS AGAINST THIRD PARTIES

**11–09**   In many cases on a share sale where there is a liability under the warranties or indemnities, the target company will have a right of recovery from a third party. A typical example arises in relation to the usual warranty as to debtors—late payment by the debtor will frequently give rise to a breach of warranty even though the debt may eventually prove good (see cl.3.5.2 in para.7–69). The vendors will wish the target company to pursue its rights of recovery or reimbursement to the full before making a claim. Suitable wording for achieving this is as follows:

### [11D] Rights of recovery or reimbursement to be enforced

**Where the Company is entitled to recover from a third party or claim reimbursement of all or part of a sum in respect of which it has a claim or potential claim under the Warranties, the Purchaser shall procure that it takes all possible steps to enforce the recovery or reimbursement before making a claim under the Warranties.**

**11–10**   This clause imposes a severe restriction on the purchaser, not least because the agreed time limits for making a claim under the warranties may expire before all possible steps against the third party have been completed. Additionally, the purchaser, if it is to accept the clause, would wish to replace "all possible" with "reasonable". A far more acceptable approach is for the purchaser to procure the transfer of the debt or right of reimbursement to the vendors once they have discharged the liability. The following general provision is suitable for this purpose:

### [11E] Assignment of rights of reimbursement

**Where the Vendors are liable in respect of a breach of the Warranties and the Purchaser, or the Company, has a right of reimbursement (in whole or in part) against another person, the Purchaser shall [upon discharge by the Vendors of their liability and at their request and cost] assign, or procure to be assigned, to them for no consideration the benefit of the right.**

**11–11**   A similar clause to 11E is included in the Tax Deed discussed in para.10–06 (see cl.8). The purchaser will wish to add the words in square brackets. In the absence of commercial reasons which might cause the purchaser to prefer that the vendors do not engage in litigation with the third party, there should otherwise be no objection in principle to the clause.

In the case of a warranty relating to debts, this clause does not deal adequately with the question of the consideration to be paid to the target company to which the debt or right of reimbursement is owed. If the vendors satisfy the purchaser's claim under the relevant warranty, they will be entitled to receive an assignment of the debt or right without the payment of any further amount. If, however, the debt or right has some value, the target company will be making an *ex gratia* disposal of an asset and a liquidator of the target company could well upset the transfer. A possible remedy would be for the purchaser to be required to pay to the target company the market value of the asset but, in the case of a debt, this would generally give it a rather pointless taxable receipt. Furthermore, the vendors will have acquired the asset for no cost and any amount received will be liable to capital gains tax (see TCGA 1992, s.251).

A more satisfactory approach is for the asset to be transferred to the vendors **11–12** for a consideration equal to the amount which they would have been liable to pay to the purchaser under the warranties, after making an appropriate deduction for any claims floor. An express provision should be included to the effect that this payment should constitute satisfaction of the corresponding right of the purchaser under the warranties.

An alternative way of dealing with the problem, which although more complex gives full recognition to the fact that in many cases the purchaser is really entitled to receive compensation only for what amounts to a cash flow disadvantage, is to provide that:

(1) if a debt or right of reimbursement is still outstanding after an agreed period of grace, the vendors make a payment to the purchaser for breach of warranty, subject to any claims floor;

(2) if the target company subsequently makes a recovery, an adjustment is made by a refund to the vendors or a restoration of the claims floor or both;

(3) if, after a longer period, the debt or right of reimbursement is still outstanding, it is assigned to the vendors for a nil consideration (which would then be likely to be a fair estimate of its value) and no further adjustments are made under para.(2).

This still leaves the effect of the floor on claims somewhat unresolved. The **11–13** following possibilities exist:

(1) Because of the floor, no payment is made under the relevant warranty but the level of the floor available to cover other warranty claims is reduced.

(2) Because of the reduction, a payment is made under another claim which would otherwise have fallen wholly or partly within the floor.

(3) The liability under the warranty is so great that a payment has to be made despite the floor.

A complex clause which attempts to cover all these points is as follows:

### [11F] Vendors' rights to acquire warranted debts or rights of reimbursement

**[11F.1] In this clause:**

"claims floor" means a provision of the Agreement exempting the Vendors from liability under the Warranties unless the liability exceeds a specified amount;

"doubtful debt" means a debt due to the Company, in respect of which the Vendors have warranted that payment in full, or of a specified amount or proportion, will be received by the Company within a specified period or by a specified date;

"relevant liability" means a liability of the Company in respect of which it has a right of reimbursement against a third party.

**[11F.2]** If the Vendors are (or but for a claims floor would have been) liable to the Purchaser under the Warranties in respect of a doubtful debt or a relevant liability and, after their liability arises, a payment is received by the Company in or towards discharge of the doubtful debt or in or towards satisfaction of the obligation to make reimbursement, payments made by the Vendors shall be repaid and any reduction in the exemption under the claims floor shall be cancelled to the extent that the payments would not have been made or the reduction would not have occurred if the payment in respect of the doubtful debt or reimbursement in respect of the relevant liability had been received at Completion.

**[11F.3]** If a doubtful debt or obligation to make reimbursement in respect of a relevant liability remains outstanding, in whole or in part, on the expiration of 12 months from Completion, the Purchaser, at the request and cost of the Vendors, shall procure that the Company assigns the debt or right, or the outstanding balance, to the Vendors for no consideration.

## CONDUCT OF CLAIMS

**11–14**   It is common practice for the conduct of claims in relation to matters arising under the tax deed to be given to the covenantors (see cl.4 of the deed considered in para.10–06). This is normally acceptable to the purchaser as taxation matters can generally be dealt with separately from the other affairs of the target company.

The position is less simple in relation to the warranties. Many aspects which are the subject of warranties can have considerable importance in relation to the goodwill of the target company and casual litigation to enforce rights could be very harmful. Additionally, it is more difficult to treat individual commercial problems separately from the general business activities of the target company.

Nevertheless the vendors will wish, if possible, to have the conduct of claims so that they can ensure that rights against third parties are pursued properly and not treated as being of secondary importance on the basis that the liability can simply be passed on to them. A clause covering this is as follows:

## [11G] Conduct of claims

**Where a claim will or may be made under the Warranties and the amount of the claim will or could be affected by the outcome of a dispute with a third party, the Purchaser shall procure that the Vendors are fully and promptly informed about the dispute or potential dispute and that its conduct, negotiation, settlement or litigation are, so far as is reasonably practicable, carried out in accordance with the wishes of a majority of the Vendors and at their cost [subject to their giving timely instructions to the Purchaser and providing reasonable security for costs and expenses which might be incurred by the Purchaser or the Company].**

The words in square brackets would be added by the purchaser to make sure   **11–15**
that the target company's position is not adversely affected simply by delay on the part of the vendors in deciding how to proceed. The purchaser is likely to object to the clause in principle, for the reasons discussed above, but there should be no problem in its agreeing to claims in relation to taxation matters being dealt with by the vendors in the same way as they are dealt with by the covenantors under the tax deed. A suitable short clause, which adopts the lengthy provisions in the tax deed is as follows:

## [11H] Conduct of claims in relation to Taxation Warranties

**The provisions of clause [ ] of the Tax Deed apply in relation to a claim which could be made under the Taxation Warranties as they apply to Claims for Taxation (as defined in the Deed) and as if references to the "Covenantors" and to liability under the Tax Deed were replaced by references to the "Vendors" and to liability under the Warranties.**

The need for a corresponding approach in the case of a business sale will rarely arise as the vendor will inherently remain entitled to pursue litigation with third parties.

## LIABILITIES OF GROUPS

If the vendor of shares is a company, it may find that, as former principal   **11–16**
company of the target company, it has statutory liabilities for tax which are primarily the liability of the target company. This secondary liability may also fall upon other subsidiaries of the vendor.

The primary provisions, which are briefly summarised in Appendix 8 are ICTA 1988, ss.767A and 767AA, TCGA 1992, ss.139 and 190 and VATA 1994, s.43. The new rules contained in TCGA 1992 by virtue of FA 2000, which govern the circumstances in which a company can become liable for unpaid tax of other companies with which it is or was associated represent a significant extension of the Inland Revenue's collection powers.

The Inland Revenue is, for example, entitled to claim unpaid corporation tax   **11–17**
on chargeable gains from the company that was the principal company of the

group at the time the gain accrued, or from any other company which, in any part of the 12-month period ending with the time the gain accrued, was a member of that group and owned the relevant asset (in whole or in part) or held an interest or right in or over it. In addition, for accounting periods ending on or after April 1, 2000, if the United Kingdom corporation tax liability of a non-resident company remains unpaid more than six months after the due date, that tax liability can be recovered from another group or consortium company under FA 2000, Sch.28. The definition of group for this purpose changed with effect from April 1, 2000 with the notable result that a company can be liable for the unpaid tax of a company with which it was not treated as a member of a group for the purposes of tax on chargeable gains. This is because the basic 75 per cent subsidiary test has been amended so that a company can be treated as a member of a group if the principal company or another group member holds more than 50 per cent of the ordinary share capital.

11–18     Appendix 8 also refers to a number of other sections which may be considered but which will not generally be relevant. Although each of these provisions includes a right of recovery from the company having the primary liability, this right may in practice be worthless. The vendor will accordingly wish to have the benefit of the purchaser's undertaking as additional protection.

An appropriate clause to cover these provisions is as follows (it is assumed that **"Group Companies"** and **"Subsidiaries"** are appropriately defined):

### [11I] Indemnity against secondary tax liabilities

**The Purchaser shall indemnify the Vendor, and those of its Subsidiaries which are not Group Companies, against claims for tax recoverable from the Vendor or any of the Subsidiaries by reason of:**

**[11I.1] ICTA 1988, s.767AA in respect of corporation tax assessed on a Group Company or TCGA 1992, ss.139 and 178 in respect of chargeable gains accruing, or deemed to accrue, to a Group Company;**

**[11I.2] FA 2000, Schedule 28, in respect of corporation tax payable by a Group Company;**

**[11I.3] VATA 1994, s.43 and ss.43A-C in respect of value added tax attributable to imports or supplies by a Group Company;**

**and the Purchaser shall procure that an application is made, under VATA 1994, s.43(7), immediately after Completion for the Group Companies to cease to be treated for value added tax purposes as members of a group which includes the Vendor or any of its Subsidiaries.**

A clause like this is often contained in the tax deed.

11–19     The purchaser will generally find this clause acceptable provided that the primary liability is known to it and has been taken into account in valuing the target group. It may, however, wish to have the benefit of an assignment by the vendor or its subsidiaries of the statutory right of recovery against the company with primary liability in case there is a later disposal of that company.

It should be noted that once the application for changing the group registration for value added tax purposes has been made, the Commissioners have 90 days from receipt of it to refuse it but, if granted, it will have effect from the date it was made, or such other date as the Commissioners may specify (VATA 1994, s.43B).

## SUBSEQUENT DISPOSALS OF TARGET COMPANY

**11–20** The vendors may be willing to rely on the various provisions set out in this chapter being observed, even though no security is provided by the purchaser, provided that the purchaser retains control of the target company. To deal with possible future disposals, the vendors might request the following undertaking:

### [11J] Undertakings from future purchaser of the Company

**The Purchaser shall not, whilst any of the provisions of this Schedule are applicable or capable of taking effect, cease to control the Company without procuring from the person acquiring control an enforceable undertaking, in favour of the Vendors and the Covenantors (as appropriate), to be bound by those provisions, so far as they affect the Company, to the same extent as the Purchaser is bound.**

**11–21** This draft assumes that all the relevant provisions are contained in a separate schedule. Although this clause may give comfort to the vendors, its value is in fact limited. The purchaser will in any case remain bound by the obligations even if it ceases to control the target company and, as a matter of prudence, it should anyway oblige the new owners to observe the outstanding obligations. If the purchaser fails to comply with its obligations under this clause, it is not clear that the vendors would be entitled to damages simply by reason of this failure. Furthermore, even though the clause has little real effect, the purchaser might object to a clause which imposes, however modestly, a fetter on its free right to dispose of the target company.

## GROUP RELIEF CLAIMS AND CLAIMS FOR CAPITAL ALLOWANCES

**11–22** Under the pay-and-file system, claims for group relief have to be for specified amounts and require an appropriate letter of consent from the surrendering company. It is likely that adjustments will be needed from time to time as the initial estimates of liability to corporation tax become more closely agreed with the Inland Revenue. Where the vendor is itself a company, it will have to consider whether surrenders of group relief which have been made to or by the target company prior to the sale will need subsequent amendment. If this is a possibility, the co-operation of the target company will be required after the sale has taken place.

Similarly, claims for capital allowances must be made for specific amounts and provisional claims or amounts "to be advised" are not acceptable. It is, therefore, necessary in many cases for claims which are made in the first instance to be refined as the precise tax liability becomes more clearly identified.

To cover these points, it is appropriate for a corporate vendor to request the following clause:

### [11K] Surrenders of group relief and claims for capital allowances

**The Purchaser will procure that the Company co-operates with the Vendor [at the Vendor's expense] in making such surrenders of or claims for group relief and such claims for capital allowances as are reasonably required by the Vendor, subject to the Purchaser being reasonably satisfied that either there is no net cost to it or the Company in doing so or that the cost is borne by the Vendor. If there is a dispute between the parties as to this clause, the procedure for resolving disputes set out in clause [ ] of the Tax Deed shall be adopted.**

In reviewing this clause, the purchaser will need to understand precisely what surrenders of group relief have been made and what claims for capital allowances are not finalised and to be satisfied that any adjustments which are made are intended to accrue to the benefit of the vendor.

## Obsolete Provisions

**11–23**    Until the abolition in 1989 of apportionments of the income of close companies (see the commentary in para.5–120), vendors of shares in close companies could be adversely affected by certain post-completion events. It was therefore not unusual for the vendors, in appropriate cases, to seek undertakings from the purchaser (a) not to allow the company to cease to trade or be wound up within 12 months of the last accounts date; and (b) to procure that certain levels of distribution were made for the last two complete accounting periods. These undertakings are no longer required.

**11–24**    For many years it was commonplace for a stamp duty reorganisation (often called "the pref-trick") to be effected where there was a sale of a company by private treaty. The reorganisation typically involved converting the existing share capital into effectively valueless preference shares with a small bonus issue of new ordinary shares being made on renounceable letters of allotment. The benefit arose from the fact that, until the passing of FA 1986, renounceable letters of allotment were exempt from stamp duty. The bulk of the consideration was attributed to the new shares and only the small part allocated to the preference shares resulted in a stamp duty liability.

Although these reorganisations can no longer achieve a saving, standard form documents may still contain provisions—such as the indemnity customarily given by the purchaser to the vendors—relating to them. Such clauses can now be omitted or deleted.

# CHAPTER 12

# Completion Accounts

## PURPOSE IN THE CASE OF SHARE PURCHASES

Completion accounts are a set of non-statutory accounts drawn up shortly **12–01** following completion which are used to "test" the price to be paid for the target company, usually by reference to levels of profit and/or net assets existing at completion. They do so by adjusting the price paid after completion if the target levels have not been met either on a £1 for £1 basis for net assets and/or on a multiplier of profit for any diminution in the level of anticipated profit.

The appropriateness or otherwise of these adjustments can usually be determined by reference to how the target company was valued and whether the vendors and the purchaser are able to reach agreement on the suggested basis of their preparation. Usually vendors will not know how the purchaser has valued the target company and should be very reluctant to agree specific adjustment mechanisms which are based upon unknown valuation criteria.

## WHEN ARE THEY USED?

The most common use for completion accounts is where the last set of audited **12–02** accounts are historic or the business of the target company has changed substantially since them. Sometimes they are also used to make a share transaction reflect an assets based deal, particularly in the case of property based transactions where the target company has been used as a vehicle to "house" the assets.

Where the transaction has been negotiated around agreed levels of profit (or more commonly earnings before interest, tax, depreciation and amortisation "EBITDA") and/or levels of net assets or some element of the latter (by reference to "cash free" and "debt free" deals), completion accounts will be used to provide a contractual price adjustment mechanism that will operate to give the purchaser certainty and comfort on price. Such a mechanism will always be a better option for the purchaser rather than having to rely on a claim for breach of warranty, as to bring a successful warranty claim loss will have to be proved and, more often than not, various layers of warranty protection have to be surpassed before there is any actual price adjustment.

## ADVANTAGES AND DISADVANTAGES

From a purchaser's perspective the provision of completion accounts will almost **12–03** invariably be of advantage to it and in the most extreme cases will allow it to artificially reduce the price based upon its own subjective accounting treatment. While the purchaser will usually have the benefit of meaningful warranties on the last set of audited accounts (and in terms of consistency at least the two prior sets of audited accounts), deterioration warranties and management accounts (covering the period from the last accounts date to completion), such warranties will often provide limited comfort for the purchaser in ensuring that it is getting the target company in at least as good financial shape as was reflected in the last audited accounts. Completion accounts allow the purchaser to ensure that the value is based on up-to-date financial information.

From the vendors' perspective completion accounts will rarely result in an increase in the price to be paid and at the very least will require the vendors to expend accounting and legal fees (sometimes significant) in ensuring that the mechanisms contained in the sale agreement are fair and in having their accountants review and agree the completion accounts after completion.

In the context of the provision of warranties and indemnities by the vendors, completion accounts are often overlooked with the result that a risk that the purchaser had agreed to accept (either by way of fair disclosure against the relevant warranty or on the basis of a provision of an appropriate indemnity in its favour) then causes an actual price adjustment to be made through the completion accounts so that the vendors effectively pay for the issue. To understand how this works it is necessary first to look at some standard completion accounts provisions.

## ANALYSIS OF COMPLETION ACCOUNTS PROVISIONS

**12–04**    Sample wording for a completion accounts mechanism which adjusts the price paid for the target company by reference to both the level of net assets and EBITDA is set out below. The following definitions are used (other defined terms having the meanings set out in para.4–01):

**"Accounting Standards" means SSAPS, FRSs, UTIF Abstracts, SORPs and all other generally accepted accounting principles applicable to a United Kingdom company.**

This definition essentially encapsulates UK GAAP.

**"Completion Accounts Procedure" means the procedure set out in clause [ ] and Schedule [ ] governing the preparation of the Completion Balance Sheet, and Profit and Loss Account and the issue of the Net Asset and EBITDA Statement.**

This is a consolidating definition which brings together the completion accounts mechanisms in the main body of the sale agreement with the particular accounting requirements or adjustments set out in the relevant schedule to the sale agreement.

"Completion Balance Sheet" means the statement of assets and liabilities of the Company as at Completion prepared in accordance with the Completion Accounts Procedure.

"EBITDA" means the Operating Profit before interest, tax, depreciation, amortisation, exchange gains or losses and management fees of the Company for the financial period following the Balance Sheet Date up to and including the date of Completion calculated in accordance with the Completion Accounts Procedure.

Sometimes the purchaser will take the view that depreciation should be deducted from earnings as a true cost of running the business. In such circumstances the definition simply excludes depreciation and becomes "EBITA".

"Net Asset and EBITDA Statement" means the statement to be prepared as part of the Completion Accounts Procedure and being the statement showing the Net Asset Value and EBITDA.

"Net Asset Value" means the net assets of the Company as shown in the Completion Balance Sheet calculated in accordance with the Completion Accounts Procedure.

Given the nature of the specific accounting obligations or practices that can be included in the schedule, the net asset value calculated in accordance with this will often bear little resemblance to the actual net assets of the target company or business.

"Operating Profit" means the operating profit of the Company computed in accordance with the accounting principles adopted in the Accounts.

"Profit and Loss Account" means the profit and loss account of the Company reflecting the Operating Profit of the Company for the period commencing on the day after the Balance Sheet Date and ending on the Completion Date.

"The Purchaser's Accountants" means [ ].

"The Vendors' Accountants" means [ ].

The definitions would usually be inserted at the definitions section of the sale agreement rather than seeking to define these matters in the clause itself.

## COMPLETION ACCOUNTS PROCEDURE

After Completion the Vendors and the Purchaser shall procure that the Net Asset Value and EBITDA are determined in accordance with the Completion Accounts Procedure.      **12–05**

**12–06**    **The Vendors shall [procure that the Vendors' Accountants] prepare and deliver to the [Purchaser [and the] [Purchaser's Accountants] within 60 Business Days of Completion, drafts of the Completion Balance Sheet and Profit and Loss Account together with a draft Net Asset and EBITDA Statement.**

This clause is drafted on the basis that the vendors' accountants will prepare the first draft of the completion accounts (on the basis that they will usually be more familiar with the target company's accounting). A more aggressive approach by the purchaser may substitute the purchaser's accountants as preparing the first draft. Sometimes the completion accounts will be dealt with solely between the respective accountants. Where the purchaser or vendors have significant internal accounting resource they may wish to have a more active involvement. These options are catered for by inclusion in this and the subsequent clauses of the purchaser as well as the purchaser's accountants and the vendors as well as the vendors' accountants.

**12–07**    **If the [Purchaser or the] [Purchaser's Accountants] shall notify the [Vendors or the] [Vendors' Accountants] in writing within 30 Business Days of receipt of the draft Completion Balance Sheet, Profit and Loss Account and the Net Asset and EBITDA Statement that they do not accept the terms thereof and specify in reasonable detail the nature of the objection or disagreement the parties shall then use their reasonable endeavours to reach agreement on any disputed items within a further 10 Business Days of receipt of any such notice. If the [Purchaser or the] [Purchaser's Accountants] do not so notify the [Vendors or the] [Vendors' Accountants] within the said period then the Purchaser shall be deemed to accept the correctness of the draft Completion Balance Sheet, the Profit and Loss Account and the Net Asset and EBITDA Statement which shall become the Completion Balance Sheet, the Profit and Loss Account and the Net Asset and EBITDA Statement for the purposes of this Agreement and shall be final and binding on the parties (in the absence of manifest error).**

Obviously the time periods within these provisions are flexible and should be tailored to suit the particular transaction. This clause provides for the completion accounts to be deemed to have been agreed if no objections are received. If the completion accounts are not agreed to by the purchaser/the purchaser's accountants then the notice that is given of this must specify the grounds for objection.

**12–08**    **If the parties are unable to reach agreement within 20 Business Days following the notification of objections by [the Purchaser or] [the Purchaser's Accountants] to [the Vendors or] [the Vendors' Accountants] the matter in dispute may be referred on the application of either party to an independent chartered accountant to be appointed by agreement or (in default of nomination by agreement) on application by either party by the President for the time being of the Institute of Chartered Accountants in**

**England and Wales. In giving his decision such independent accountant shall state what adjustments (if any) are necessary to the draft Completion Balance Sheet, Profit and Loss Account and the Net Asset and EBITDA Statement in order to comply with the requirements of this Agreement. The draft Completion Balance Sheet, Profit and Loss Account and the Net Asset and EBITDA Statements as so adjusted or not (as the case may be) shall become the Completion Balance Sheet, Profit and Loss Account and the Net Asset and EBITDA Statement for the purposes of this Agreement which shall be final and binding on the parties (in the absence of manifest error) upon the giving of such decision to the Vendors and the Purchaser.**

This clause provides for a short period in which the parties may be able to agree the outstanding points between themselves without the need for a referral to an independent accountant. If a referral is necessary it can be initiated by either party.

**Any determination by an independent accountant appointed pursuant to clause [ ] shall be conclusive and binding on the parties (in the absence of manifest error) and shall be given by him as an expert and not as an arbitrator and the Arbitration Act 1996 shall not apply. The expenses of the independent accountant shall be borne as determined by the independent accountant having regard to the relevant merits of each party's position in relation to the matter or matters in dispute, failing which equally between the Vendors and the Purchaser.**   12–09

This sets out the basis upon which the independent accountant will be appointed. It is important to ensure that the appointment is as an expert and not arbitrator and that there is a fall back provision on costs if the independent accountant does not wish to make a costs award according to the relative merits of the parties. Without these provisions it is unlikely that an independent accountant would be prepared to act and that could frustrate the completion accounts mechanism.

**The Vendors and the Purchaser shall procure to the extent within their respective powers that the Vendors' Accountants, the Purchaser's Accountants and the independent accountant (as the case may be) shall have full access to all relevant papers, documents, records and personnel and shall be provided with such access and information upon request together with all reasonable assistance and information (as necessary) including the right to make copies and take extracts of such books, records and working papers (as necessary) for the purpose of preparing or agreeing or determining the Completion Balance Sheet, Profit and Loss Account and the Net Asset and EBITDA Statement.**   12–10

This provision provides extensive rights of access. It does not however change the basis of the determination of the completion accounts which must be in accordance with the completion accounts procedure.

**12–11**    **Each party shall be entitled to make written representations concerning the matter or matters in dispute to any such independent accountant appointed pursuant to Clause [ ].**

Self explanatory.

**12–12**    **Subject to Clause [ ] the Vendors and the Purchaser shall each bear their own costs and expenses incurred pursuant to this Clause [ ]. For the avoidance of doubt the Purchaser shall be responsible for the cost and expenses of the Purchaser's Accountants and the Vendors shall be responsible for the costs and expenses of the Vendors' Accountants.**

This provision is designed to make it clear that the costs of each party's accountants are borne by them. It is only the independent accountant's costs which are shared equally or as he otherwise directs.

**12–13**    **If following the agreement or determination of the Net Asset Value under this Clause [ ] the Net Asset Value is lower than £[ ] [target amount of net assets to be inserted] the Consideration shall be reduced by the amount of such shortfall on a £1 for £1 basis. Any payment required to be made by the Vendors to the Purchaser as a result of there being such a shortfall shall be paid within 7 days of agreement or determination of the Net Asset Value.**

If the targeted levels of net assets should fairly include the profit since the last accounts date then the target levels should be uplifted to reflect this. When there is a separate EBITDA adjustment as in these provisions then that would result in an unfair adjustment, given any profit diminution would be caught on a £1 for £1 basis on the net asset adjustment and on a multiplier basis on the EBITDA adjustment. Where there are both it would usually be appropriate to strip out the profit from the net asset target and leave profits to be dealt with under the EBITDA adjustment.

**12–14**    **If following the agreement or determination of the EBITDA under this Clause the EBITDA is lower than £[ ] [target amount of EBITDA to be inserted] the Consideration shall (in addition to any adjustment required to the Consideration pursuant to Clause [ ]) be reduced by a sum equating to £[ ] [appropriate multiplier to be inserted calculated by a reference to the number of £s] for each £1 of shortfall of EBITDA below £[ ] [target amount of EBITDA to be inserted]. Any payment required to be made by the Vendors to the Purchaser as a result of their being such a shortfall shall be paid within 7 days of agreement or determination of the EBITDA.**

The mechanism works by reference to the mechanics set out in this clause and by the general and specific accounting requirements which, as mentioned previously, are usually set out in a separate schedule.

The provisions provide for drafts of the various financial statements to be produced within a set timeframe and agreed, or, in the event of disagreement, be determined by an independent accountant. In all cases the financial statements have to be prepared by reference to the accounting requirements of the schedule, an example of which is set out below. Following agreement or determination in accordance with the contractual mechanics the price is then adjusted by reference to the target levels of net assets and/or EBITDA. In the example wording the adjustment is only in favour of the purchaser, as no additional consideration is payable for any excess of either net assets or EBITDA over the targeted minimums. Where the target company has been valued by reference to assumed levels of these it would usually be fair to provide for an upwards adjustment as well in the event that the target levels are exceeded.

Where there is a concern that there could be a significant adjustment to the price as a result of the completion accounts mechanism it is usual to provide for some of the purchase price to be paid into a retention account (controlled by the vendors' solicitors and the purchaser's solicitors), the terms of which will provide for automatic payments to be made once the target levels of net assets and/or EBITDA have been agreed or determined.

**Schedule [ ]**                                                           **12–15**

**The Completion Balance Sheet, Profit and Loss Account and the Net Asset and EBITDA Statement shall be prepared by the Vendors' Accountants consistently with the Accounts but only to the extent that they comply with the Accounting Standards or, to the extent they do not, in accordance with the Accounting Standards subject to the following specific adjustments or practices in respect of the Net Asset and EBITDA Statement which shall override both prior bases:**

(1) **Profits or losses of a capital nature arising on the disposal of, or on the revaluation of, assets or investments by the Company shall be deducted or added back.**

(2) **No value shall be attributed to goodwill or any other intangible asset.**

(3) **No value shall be attributed to any computer equipment not used by the Company as at Completion.**

(4) **Provision shall be made for the cost of remedial works required pursuant to the recommendations of [ ] in connection with the Company's obligations under the Control of Asbestos at Work Regulations 2002 to the extent that such recommendations require the immediate removal of any asbestos found.**

These are a few examples of some of the matters that might be dealt with in the specific accounting mechanisms. There are numerous other matters that could either be protected or altered in favour of the purchaser. To ensure that all relevant matters are addressed a careful analysis of the balance sheet and/or profit and loss account of the target company or business should be undertaken in conjunction with accountancy advisers.

The wording works by firstly providing for consistency with the Accounts (which will have been warranted by the vendors) but then provides for an exception to such consistency where the Accounts do not comply with the Accounting Standards (essentially UK GAAP) and then a further exception to both prior bases by reference to the specific adjustments or practices listed.

It is usually in the specific accounting requirements where the vendors will either protect their position or where the purchaser will provide for specific adjustments or practices that suit its purposes. A few examples are given below which help illustrate some of the issues from both viewpoints.

**12–16**     The vendors seek to disclose a potential litigation liability against the relevant warranty in the sale agreement. The purchaser views the disclosure and concludes that it is happy to accept the risk and does not require an indemnity or, alternatively, that it is not and requests a specific indemnity in its favour in respect of the risk. The relevant transaction has been negotiated by reference to a target level of net assets and the sale agreement contains a similar mechanism to the one outlined above. In the former case where the purchaser has accepted the risk, the vendors would need to ensure that the completion accounts did not provide for the liability disclosed. In the latter case the purchaser could still require a provision for the liability in the completion accounts notwithstanding the provision of the indemnity in its favour. In those circumstances, if the liability crystallised there would be nothing to stop the purchaser seeking redress under the indemnity, even though a provision had already been made in the completion accounts and the price been adjusted through the relevant diminution in the target net asset value.

The only way for the vendors to ensure that no provision is made is to note the matter as a specific adjustment or practice in the schedule. Suitable wording for these purposes would be as follows:

**"No provision shall be made in respect of the litigation detailed at [ ] of the Disclosure Letter".**

Using the same example but where there was less probability in terms of the litigation liability, for example where perhaps a note to the accounts (rather than an actual provision) would suffice for UK GAAP, an unscrupulous purchaser might seek to modify UK GAAP or even consistency with the Accounts by requiring a specific adjustment along the following lines:

**"Full provision shall be made for any liabilities disclosed in the Disclosure Letter."**

This phrase potentially overrides UK GAAP and requires a provision to be made where in the ordinary course it would not need to be.

More obvious examples of specific adjustments overriding normal accounting on either a consistent basis or by reference to UK GAAP might be in relation to bad or doubtful debts. For example, a disclosure is made against the relevant warranty in the sale agreement by reference to a schedule detailing the aged debtors with a view to escaping any liability pursuant to the warranty. Given the subjective interpretation of doubtful or bad debts the purchaser decides that a specific adjustment ought to be made in the completion accounts as follows:

**"Full provision shall be made for all debts over [60] [90] [120] days."**

In those circumstances, far from the vendors escaping liability by reference to the relevant matters in the disclosure letter, the purchaser is able to adjust the price to take account of its preferred policy of provision for aged debtors rather than the target company's prior practice. To protect themselves, the vendors might provide an alternative to ensure that the accounting is in line with the target company's usual practice by effectively reversing the wording to make it clear that no provision will be made for any aged debt unless it exceeds a certain age.

The most common areas (in addition to trade debtors or contingent liabilities) where interpretation issues arise on UK GAAP are in relation to fixed assets and stock and work in progress. Great care needs to be taken to achieve certainty in relation to these areas. The vendors' legal advisors should always ensure that they work hand in hand with the target company's auditors so that between them the disclosure process, due diligence and the negotiation of indemnities do not give rise to any unforeseen adjustments to the price by reference to a completion accounts mechanism where no such adjustment had either been intended or contemplated.

# CHAPTER 13

# Valuation

## RELEVANCE IN THE CONTEXT OF WARRANTIES AND INDEMNITIES

**13–01**   In order to understand the use of warranties and indemnities in the context of the sale and purchase of companies and businesses it is necessary to have an understanding of the way that such businesses are valued, as without this the negotiation of the warranties and indemnities will be undertaken in a vacuum. The purchaser's legal advisors will need to understand the valuation mechanism that has been used or they will not be able to ensure that likely losses to the purchaser (which affect the valuation of the target company or business) have been properly addressed. From the vendors' perspective, it will be important to ensure that an unscrupulous purchaser cannot gain from artifical adjustments to the price through warranties and indemnities or by the use of a completion accounts adjustment mechanism when such adjustments bear no relevance to the purchaser's valuation of the target company or business. Insight into and an understanding of the valuation mechanism that has been used are therefore important to ensure that these issues are addressed.

## BASIC CONCEPTS

**13–02**   This chapter is by no means intended to be a complete guide to how companies or businesses are valued. Reference should be made to any of the established works in the area for a more detailed analysis. Instead this chapter is intended to give the practitioner a useful insight into the more common methodologies that are likely to be encountered in valuing most trading companies.

The three most common bases are by reference to the net assets of the target company or business, a multiple of historical earnings, usually by reference to EBITDA (earnings before interest, taxation, depreciation and amortisation), or by reference to future earnings on a discounted cashflow basis.

## THE NET ASSETS BASIS

**13–03**   This is one of the simplest methods and simply looks at the difference between the total assets and total liabilities as recorded in the accounts or books of the target company or business. Often this methodology is only appropriate for the smallest of businesses and even then will in most cases need adjustment to reflect the value of any intangible assets and to take account of the extraction of cash and other assets for the owner's use. It is very rare for any business or target company to be worth significantly less than its net asset value on anything other than an insolvency valuation. Where a business has been valued by reference to its net assets then any adjustments to the price either by reference to warranty claims, indemnity claims or through a completion accounts mechanism should follow suit.

## Multiple of Historic Earnings

The most common method of valuation is by reference to a multiplier of **13–04** EBITDA or occasionally EBITA (where in the latter case the valuer believes that depreciation should be treated as a cost to be deducted from the earnings). The earnings are arrived at by looking at historical earnings over the last two or three years and then combining them with some element of future earnings either for the current or following year, calculating an average of those and then multiplying that by reference to an appropriate multiplier.

The multiplier will usually be based upon a sector average PE ratio (derived from public company sector indices) discounted by as much as 60 per cent to reflect the fact that the target company or business is a private one. That gives an enterprise value for the target company from which is then deducted any debt and added any excess cash in the target company or business (over and above that required for ordinary working capital purposes). What is included in debt and cash is always the subject of much debate and can significantly affect the net price. For this type of valuation it would normally be appropriate to ensure that any price adjustment mechanism, whether through warranty, indemnity or completion accounts, relates to the earnings of the target company and by reference to the actual mutliplier used to arrive at the enterprise value, as slightly adjusted by the impact of the netting off of any debt or the addition of any cash.

## Discounted Cashflow Basis

The generally accepted definition of the value of any business interest (whether **13–05** in shares in a company or by ownership of a business) is that it must equal the future benefits, usually cash, that attach or will accrue to that business interest discounted back to a present value at an appropriate discount rate.

A discounted cashflow valuation follows this definition and involves three steps. The first is determining the period over which cashflow should be forecast. As in most valuation matters there are no hard and fast rules, although there are sector norms which can be obtained and used as a benchmark. The second stage in the process involves the preparation of a cashflow forecast which will take account of economic assumptions throughout the forecast period and then sales, purchases, payroll and other operating expenditure, capital and financing costs and tax costs for the entity projected forward over the forecast period. The final stage involves discounting that by an appropriate discount rate. The rate should reflect the anticipated level of return on alternative investments with comparable risk. Once again there are established rates for different categories of investment but these will need to be tailored to reflect the perceived risk rather than the industry standard.

If this method of valuation has been used then any price adjustment mechanism should follow the valuation methodology to match the loss with the value actually paid.

## AN EXAMPLE

**13–06**  "Target co ltd", an active trading company in the print and packaging sector, has net assets of £3.8m, EBITDA of £1.2m, debt of £1m and surplus cash (over and above working capital requirements) of £350k.

On a multiple of historic earnings basis (this being an appropriate valuation method used for companies in this sector) an appropriate multiplier is 6 times EBITDA. Using the key financial information provided for target co ltd and assuming that any offer made for the company would be on a "debt and cash free" basis gives a value for target co ltd of £6.55m (being 6 times £1.2m, less £1m debt plus £350k of surplus cash).

A purchaser would usually structure any offer on terms that required EBITDA on completion of no less than £1.2m, net assets of £3.8m and phrase its offer by reference to a "debt and cash free" basis.

It would be difficult for the vendors' advisers to resist completion accounts which adjusted the actual price paid by reference to these elements by simply suggesting that these matters were warranted as this would not give the purchaser the contractual certainty that it would usually seek. Care would need to be taken to ensure that an adjustment to the price based upon any diminution in the EBITDA level was not caught twice, once as part of the net assets and once as part of the multiplier adjustment (which in this case would be £6 for every £1 of diminution).

By comparison, a net assets based valuation for target co ltd would give an indicative valuation of £3.8m which amounts to a substantial discount on the likely open market value of the company.

From the information provided it is not possible to produce a discounted cashflow valuation for target co ltd but it is likely that such a valuation would fall somewhere between a net assets valuation and that derived from the historic earnings basis.

## SUMMARY

**13–07**  While these valuation methodologies can give an insight into how a purchaser may have approached its valuation of the target company or business, the actual price paid may well have been determined by external commercial factors such as the target company or business operating in a niche sector, which could cause higher or lower pricing, significant interest being shown in the target company or business, which would usually result in a higher than desktop price being paid, or simply a strategic purchaser, where the value of the target company or business represents to that particular purchaser far more than any desktop valuation would ever suggest.

Where a transaction involves completion accounts with a specific adjustment mechanism, perhaps by reference to the levels of net assets or a multiple of earnings as in the example provided, then if there is a breach of warranty it is likely that the courts will use the adjustment basis in the completion accounts as a basis for determining the loss for breach of warranty. The completion accounts mechanism in such circumstances will be taken as evidence as to how the parties valued the target company.

# Legal Due Diligence Enquiries

[See para.1–12]

This legal due diligence questionnaire is designed to be of general application to most companies. However, before using it consideration should be given as to whether any of the enquiries should be removed and, in particular, whether any Competition, Accounts and Taxation enquiries are to be included. More usually Accounts and Taxation enquiries will be dealt with as part of the financial due diligence. Short form Accounts and Taxation enquiries which may be useful are included in ss.17 and 18. The Competition enquiries are included in s.16 so that they can easily be deleted if not required (as will often be the case).

## Acquisition of [ ] Limited ("the Company")

Please supply full details/copies of all the items specified below including, where documents are requested, accurate and up to date copies of those documents. (Where a full understanding of the position cannot be obtained from the copy document(s) alone please also provide an explanation.)

In the event that items are not applicable to the Company please state so.

Please identify replies using the same numerical reference system.

All references to "the Company" include references to its subsidiaries (if any). Please therefore reply to each enquiry for the Company and all of its subsidiaries.

### 1 Incorporation and statutory matters

| | |
|---|---|
| 1.1 | The current Memorandum and Articles of Association of the Company (with any amending resolutions). |
| 1.2 | Certificate of incorporation and any certificate on change of name of the Company. |
| 1.3 | Registered office and other trade addresses. |
| 1.4 | The statutory books of the Company. |

### 2 Share capital

| | |
|---|---|
| 2.1 | The authorised and issued share capital of the Company (including details of classes of shares and number of shares in each class), together with names and addresses of all registered shareholders in the Company, showing numbers of shares held and whether held beneficially or otherwise. |
| 2.2 | All shareholder agreements, pre-emption rights, conversion rights or agreements under which any person may acquire the right to subscribe for or purchase shares in the Company. |
| 2.3 | All buy-backs or redemptions of the Company's share capital (and all agreements to buy back or redeem any of the Company's share capital) and of all financial assistance given by the Company. |

## 3 Subsidiaries

3.1 All subsidiaries of the Company and the Company's interests in other companies, partnerships or businesses together with particulars of such shareholdings or interests.

3.2 An organisational chart showing the group structure.

## 4 Officers

4.1 Names and addresses of all directors and the secretary of the Company, stating job title, whether or not they are employed by the Company and any other directorships.

4.2 Service agreements/contracts of employment with officers of the Company. (Where no written documentation exists please supply details of the officer's obligations and duties, date of commencement, remuneration and benefits, unexpired term of office and applicable notice periods.)

4.3 Fringe benefits provided to officers of the Company.

4.4 Arrangements between the Company and its officers or former officers (or any other person connected with such an officer within the meaning of Section 346 of the Companies Act 1985) which relate to or affect the capital, business, property, assets or liabilities of the Company and/or its group undertakings.

4.5 Loans granted by the Company and/or any group undertaking to any of the Company's directors or former directors (or any person connected with such a director within the meaning of Section 346 of the Companies Act 1985), and/or vice versa.

## 5 Employees

5.1 Names of all employees of the Company specifying position, age, date of commencement of employment, hours of work (specifying which employees work part time), contractual notice period (on either side), length of any fixed term contracts, current salary and other contractual and non-contractual benefits such as entitlement to a bonus, company car and medical insurance.

5.2 All employment contracts of employees and all variations to employees' contracts that have been notified to employees by means of notice/circular. If there is more than one contract indicate which contract applies to which employees.

5.3 Staff handbooks, policies, procedures and/or circulars (including disciplinary and grievance procedures).

5.4 Next pay review date and negotiations currently in progress or due for implementation in the next 12 months.

5.5 All share option, share incentive, profit sharing, commission or bonus arrangements, with details of all outstanding entitlements and all bonuses paid in the last 12 months.

5.6 *Ex gratia* payments made in the last 12 months and all current arrangements for the making of *ex gratia* payments to current or former employees. All current or former employees to whom the directors consider the Company to be under a moral obligation to provide *ex gratia* payments or to provide retirement, death, accident or sickness disability benefits.

5.7 Holiday arrangements, including the basis of calculation of holiday pay and date on which holiday year commences.

5.8 Systems in place to record/confirm compliance with the Working Time Regulations 1998 (including opt out agreements, details of any "night workers" and means by which the time worked by employees, rest breaks provided, holiday taken or holiday pay received is recorded together with sample records).

5.9     Systems in place to record/confirm compliance with the National Minimum Wage Regulations 1999 (including agreements entered into in connection with the Regulations).

5.10    Job offers made/about to be made and job vacancies currently been advertised.

5.11    Employees on/about to go on leave and nature of leave (e.g. sick, maternity etc.).

5.12    Resignations/dismissals in the last 4 months (including name of employee and reason for dismissal/resignation) and employees on notice.

5.13    For employees working shift patterns, full details of the shift patterns worked (including start and finish times, details of variable shift patterns and daily and weekly rest breaks).

5.14    Company redundancy policy and details of any significant redundancy programs in the last 3 years.

5.15    All agreements or arrangements with trade unions or employee associations and details of all labour disputes within the last [five] years.

5.16    Names and addresses of all consultants, self-employed persons and sub-contractors retained/engaged by the Company and copies of agreements with them (or if not available a summary of the agreed terms (including termination provisions)).

5.17    Training schemes/qualifications that employees are required to undertake/have.

5.18    All outstanding disciplinary or grievance procedures.

5.19    All outstanding disputes between the Company and all employees including matters already referred to an employment tribunal or anticipated to be so referred or settled by payment of money.

## 6   Pensions

6.1     All pension schemes, share schemes, insurance schemes and all other employee benefit arrangements (including, but not limited to, life assurance, death in service and health, medical expense, income continuation and keyperson insurance) effected by the Company or in which the Company or any of its directors or employees have an interest (confirming which of the employees are covered and contributions made by the Company).[1]

6.2     Confirmation of whether each pension scheme is a defined benefit or money purchase scheme.

## 7   Finance and Grants

7.1     Name and branch address of all banks in which the Company has an account.

7.2     All financial facilities and accounts (including facility letters, account numbers, current balances and all existing bank mandates).

7.3     All legal charges, debentures, mortgages and other financial or security documents affecting the Company.

---

[1] This legal due diligence questionnaire is structured so that preliminary information can be obtained on this aspect and then tailored specific enquiries raised once knowledge of the existing schemes has been obtained. Different considerations will apply depending on whether the identified schemes are defined benefit or money purchase schemes.

7.4 Details or copies of all guarantees or indemnities given by or in respect of the Company and by directors, including intra-group arrangements.

7.5 Loans made to or by the Company including all inter-company loans and all loans to or from the Company's officers.

7.6 All off-balance sheet commitments.

7.7 Copies of debt facilities (including loan notes) issued by or to the Company.

7.8 All dividends and other distributions of the Company made or declared since the date of the last audited accounts or any bonus issues or repayments of capital on, before or after that date (including details of the amount of dividend payable in respect of each class of shares, how such dividends are calculated and when they are payable).

7.9 All grants (including investment, employment, local authority and central government grants) paid or awarded to the Company with all associated agreements and documentation.

## 8 Properties[2] and Environmental

8.1 All properties owned by, leased to, licensed to or otherwise used by the Company (or in which the Company has any interest) specifying tenure and providing title deeds, any relevant leases or licences and plans for the purposes of making searches.

8.2 Property transactions in the course of negotiation/to be completed before completion.

8.3 Leasehold properties previously occupied by the Company where contingent liabilities may exist.

8.4 All insurance policies, planning permissions, planning restrictions, building regulation consents, approvals, licences, permits and certificates (including fire certificates) relating to any of the Company's properties.

8.5 All mortgages, deeds of trust, security agreements and the like over any of the Company's properties.

8.6 Existing use of the Company's properties.

8.7 Details of Company properties or other facilities shared or used in common with other persons (including all relevant agreements and other documentation relating to the same).

8.8 Notices relating to the Company's properties which have been served upon or received by the Company.

8.9 Non-domestic rateable value of the Company's properties.

8.10 Major works of repair in the last 3 years or anticipated (with copies of any building contract, certificate, guarantee, insurance policy etc. relating to the design or construction of the properties or any subsequent works).

8.11 All valuations, reports and appraisals in the last 5 years of any of the Company's properties.

8.12 All environmental audits, surveys and reports carried out by or on behalf of the Company or in respect of the Company's operations.

8.13 Non-compliance with environmental laws (for the purposes of this paragraph including all statutes, regulations, instruments, judgments, by-laws or decrees pertaining to occupational health and safety or the environment); disputes with/outstanding recommendations from agencies regarding compliance with environmental or health and safety law;

---

[2] As with the pensions enquiries the property enquiries are desinged to obtain preliminary information with a view to any required pre-contract property enquiries following.

pending or threatened administrative, judicial or civil investigations, proceedings or actions with respect to environmental or health and safety law; and all notices served on the Company of breach of environmental or health and safety law including details of any potential costs.

8.14    The Company's environmental and health and safety policies.

8.15    All hazardous substances, polluted or contaminated materials that have been or are used, stored, generated, treated, handled, released or disposed of, including off-site, by the Company and all documents, transfer notes, consignment notes and registered carriers certificates relating to such hazardous substances including their use, treatment and disposal.

8.16    All permits, licences, registrations, notices, approvals, consents, certifications, contingency plans, certificates of destruction and other authorisations of the Company relating to environmental law.

8.17    All emission monitoring or sampling test results pertaining to the Company or property owned by it at any time.

8.18    All pollution control equipment used by the Company.

8.19    All PCBs, asbestos, toxic substances or other contaminated materials present in equipment, structures or premises that the Company owns or operates, or has owned or operated, along with all inspection reports or surveys.

8.20    Maintenance and inspection programmes relating to environmental compliance or control, including all spill or release reports, pertaining to the Company.

8.21    All contracts involving the handling, treatment, storage, transportation, recycling, reclamation or disposal of substances subject to regulation.

8.22    Complaints or claims by owners or occupiers of neighbouring land in respect of activities carried on by the Company or in respect of the condition of land currently or previously owned, occupied, used or held by the Company.

8.23    Confirmation that the Company does not need to register under the Producer Responsibility Obligations (Packaging Waste) Regulations 1997.

## 9    Trading Matters and Contracts

9.1    All licences or consents, agreements or arrangements (including hire purchase, leasing, credit sale or deferred payment, maintenance, agency, distribution or factoring agreements or arrangements) to which the Company is party specifically identifying in the replies those which:

9.1.1    involve a capital commitment or annual expenditure or receipts of £[5,000] or more; or

9.1.2    have an unexpired term in excess of 6 months; or

9.1.3    cannot be terminated on 3 months' notice or less without payment of compensation; or

9.1.4    are onerous or unusual.

9.2    A summary of the terms of all verbal agreements, arrangements, commitments or understandings which would fall within paragraph 9.1 above and details of all proposals or negotiations which may if accepted or concluded result in a written or verbal agreement, arrangement, commitment or understanding which if already entered into would fall within that paragraph.

9.3 Company brochures/pamphlets giving details of products/services and principle activities.

9.4 All standard terms of business issued by the Company and details of how and when such terms and conditions are used.

9.5 All standard terms of business issued by third parties and which affect the Company and details of how and when such terms are used.

9.6 If the Company deals with any customer or third party on a non-standard basis, details of all significant agreements/arrangements currently in place.

9.7 All agreements, arrangements or transactions to which the Company has been a party in the last 6 years for either the transfer of assets at an undervalue or which were not at arms length.

9.8 All contracts relating to the acquisition or disposal of shares in the Company, its business or major assets since incorporation.

9.9 All outstanding quotations or tenders made by or to the Company of a value of £[ ] or over.

9.10 All credit arrangements in favour of a customer of the Company granting more than [30] days terms of payment or providing for special discounts.

9.11 Registrations necessary or desirable to conduct the Company's business and confirmation/copies of those which the Company has.

9.12 All Government or trade regulations applicable to the Company together with all significant correspondence and details of all recent regulatory visits.

9.13 All trade associations of which the Company is a member and all rules or codes of conduct with which the Company is expected to comply.

9.14 All agreements or arrangements by which the Company is a member of a joint venture, buying group, consortium, partnership or incorporated or unincorporated association (other than a trade association).

9.15 All non-competition agreements or arrangements/agreements or arrangements with competitors (whether legally enforceable or not) to which the Company is a party and all documentation relating to the same.

9.16 Products in the course of development and expected launch date (whether the new products represent a new product range or modification of an existing range).

9.17 The Company's quality assurance controls in terms of its own services/products and those applied in the procurement of the services/products of others.

9.18 All after sales services and potential liability under warranties, guarantees or recourse arrangements.

9.19 Major suppliers and customers of the Company (i.e. those accounting for more than [5]% of goods or materials purchased or sold) and the value of purchases from or sales to each in the last three years.

9.20 All rebate arrangements with suppliers in the last three years.

9.21 Details of all suppliers or customers where the relationship is likely to change with or because of the sale of the Company or for other reasons (including full details of the last 12 months' purchases or sales and orders in hand).

9.22 All significant capital or reserve commitments.

9.23 All existing powers of attorney granted by the Company.

## 10 Plant, Equipment and Stock

10.1      All machinery, equipment (including fixtures and fittings), plant, tooling and motor vehicles used by the Company in its business differentiating between those which are owned by the Company and those which are subject to lease, hire purchase, conditional sale or similar arrangements.

10.2      Material assets of the Company to be disposed of prior to completion or excluded from the sale.

10.3      All notices or directions issued in respect of the safety or operation of any plant, equipment or Company premises.

10.4      The Company's obsolescence policy or other policy dealing in whole or in part with the valuation of stock.

## 11 Litigation

11.1      All existing, pending or threatened litigation, arbitration claims, or judgments with amounts involved.

11.2      All general or special provisions made by the Company in relation to the recovery of outstanding book debts.

11.3      All litigation, arbitration or claims in the last [five] years and an indication of the amounts involved.

11.4      All outstanding complaints or disputes involving the Company in relation to any materials or goods (or class of materials or goods) supplied by the Company, all services (or class of services) rendered by the Company and/or any other aspect of the business of the Company.

11.5      All accidents at work which have or could give rise to a claim against the Company. The Company's accident book.

11.6      All material breaches that have occurred under any agreements or arrangements to which the Company is a party.

11.7      All formal insolvency proceedings including any bankruptcy, liquidation, receivership, administration, arrangement or scheme with creditors affecting the Company.

## 12 Intellectual Property and Information Technology

12.1      All intellectual property rights vested in, or used by, the Company (whether registered or not and including all trade marks, trade names, brand names, patents, design rights, registered designs, copyright and service marks).

12.2      All certificates (including registration and renewal certificates) for all registered intellectual property rights vested in the Company and all agreements, licences or arrangements to which the Company is a party affecting intellectual property rights vested in, or used by, the Company (or where such agreements, licences or arrangements are not in writing a summary of their terms, including the names of the parties, commencement date, termination date and termination provisions).

12.3      Confirmation that all fees payable by the Company to third parties in relation to intellectual property have been paid.

12.4      All correspondence and other documentation relating to claims of infringement by the Company of the intellectual property rights of others or by others of the intellectual property rights of the Company.

12.5      Disclosures to persons (other than those who owe the Company duties of confidentiality) of intellectual property or other confidential information (including copies of all agreements relating to the same).

12.6   All computer facilities and other information technology hardware or system (including make, model, specification and capacity) in the possession of and/or used by the Company in the operation of its business specifying which is owned by the Company, which is subject to hire purchase, leasing, rental or deferred payment agreement, and which is otherwise provided by a third party.

12.7   All communications facilities (wireless or otherwise) owned or used by the Company including those for landline, mobile and ISP services (together with copy agreements and/or documentation).

12.8   Software owned or used by the Company (including nature, description, version, number of copies licensed, author and details of any source code escrow arrangements for software used under licence) and all licences.

12.9   Company rules or policies concerning intellectual property rights and computers, security, unauthorised use of the Company's computer systems, Company databases and the Internet.

12.10  Domain names registered by the Company (including registration certificates and associated documentation).

12.11  Web site(s) operated by or hosted on behalf of the Company, CD ROMs used by the Company in connection with its business and the promotion of the Company, and all terms and conditions for the use by third parties of such new media.

12.12  All software and new media (including web sites and CD ROMS) development, commissioning, hosting and maintenance agreements used by or developed by or on behalf of the Company.

## 13  Data Protection

In this section the terms "personal data", "data subject", "data processor", "data controller", "fair processing" and "processing" have the meanings ascribed to them in the Data Protection Act 1998 ("the Act").

13.1   The Company's entry in the Information Commissioner's register of data controllers.

13.2   The Company's internal data protection policy for officers and employees.

13.3   Purposes for which data subjects' personal data is used by the Company ("the Purposes").

13.4   All fair processing notices used by the Company in relation to third parties from whom it collects personal data (including without limitation from its customers), including all website privacy policies, cookie statements, notices on application forms, telephone scripts and any other form of notice.

13.5   All direct marketing opt-in or opt-out notices used to collect and update data subjects' direct marketing preferences stating by which method direct marketing is undertaken by the Company (fax, email, telephone, post, SMS, other) and whether the direct marketing is in relation to the Company's own products and services, group products and services and/or third party products and services, providing a separate description for each of these categories of products and services.

13.6   Confirmation of whether the Company has bought mailing lists from or exchanged mailing lists with any third party including a copy of all contracts with those third parties or, if none, details of those third parties and mailing lists.

13.7   Steps taken by the Company to enable data subjects to update their records/profiles and change their preferences, the frequency of this, all standard wording or forms used (including retention policies) and all other steps taken by the Company to ensure its records are adequate, relevant, not excessive in relation to the Purposes, accurate, up to date and not kept longer than is necessary for the Purposes.

13.8    All data processing contracts entered into between the Company and data processors who process personal data on its behalf, including, without limitation, all contracts with the Company's suppliers, sub-contractors, mailing houses and hosting companies.

13.9    Transfers of personal data outside the European Economic Area (the EU member states, Norway, Iceland and Liechtenstein) and steps taken to ensure an adequate level of protection for the rights and freedoms of data subjects in relation to the processing of personal data in the recipient country.

13.10   All complaints made by data subjects or notices received from the Information Commissioner regarding the Company's processing of personal data and confirmation that the Company has processed personal data in accordance with data subjects' rights under Part II of the Act.

## 14  Insurance

14.1    All insurance policies currently in effect and owned by or providing coverage to the Company, its directors, officers and employees, in each case giving details of renewal date, annual premium, risk covered, name of insurance company and policy number.

14.2    All claims filed during the last [three] years under all insurance policies with a description of the claim (including claimant, amount, current status and expected settlement date).

14.3    Insurance coverages cancelled or not renewed during the last [five] years.

14.4    All proposals or requests for insurance in the last six years which were declined or which were accepted subject to the imposition of special terms/payment of a high premium.

14.5    Confirmation of payment of all insurance premiums for current policies and the name and address of the Company's insurance brokers.

## 15  Miscellaneous

15.1    All consents the shareholders must obtain prior to completion.

15.2    All consents the Company must obtain, or permits or licences that will expire consequent upon the change of ownership of the Company.

15.3    All agreements to which the Company is a party which contain change of control provisions.

15.4    All brokers or finders agreements.

## [16  Competition

For the purposes of this section "competition law" shall mean all directly or indirectly effective competition legislation governing the conduct of the Company in the jurisdictions in which it operates.

16.1    The Company's main products and geographic markets.

16.2    Market share per product and turnover of the Company within the United Kingdom and within each country in which the Company operates.

16.3    The Company's main competitors in each geographic market in which it operates and their market shares.

16.4 All infringements or notices or allegations of infringement of competition law.

16.5 All actual or potential investigations by any competition authority, government body, agency or court in relation to the Company's actual or potential breach of competition law.

16.6 All actual or potential complaints by any third party alleging that the Company is breaching/has breached competition law.

16.7 All agreements or arrangements to which the Company is a party and which it is believed may infringe competition law.]

## [17 Accounts

17.1 The last three audited accounts of the Company.

17.2 Most recent management accounts of the Company.

17.3 Current accounting reference date of the Company and all changes which have been made within the last three years.

17.4 Operating projections (including profit and loss and cash flow forecasts) for the next [12] months including all planned or required capital expenditure.

17.5 Current debtors, period of debt and amount and current creditors, period of credit and amount.]

## [18 Taxation

18.1 All agreements with the Inland Revenue as to the latest tax computations of the Company.

18.2 All corporation tax outstanding and due to the Inland Revenue.

18.3 All deferred taxation provisions, including any rollover relief claimed in respect of corporation tax on capital gains relating to the last set of audited accounts.

18.4 Confirmation of whether the Company is or has been a close company and if it is or has been a close company confirmation that it is not and has not been a close investment company.

18.5 All tax clearances obtained and all tax indemnities taken.

18.6 Particulars of VAT group registrations.

18.7 The last [six] tax computations and returns for the Company and any correspondence with the Inland Revenue/Customs and Excise in relation thereto.

18.8 Dates to which tax returns have been settled.

18.9 Dates to which tax has been deducted under PAYE/VAT and been accounted for and paid over.

18.10 PAYE: All recent or ongoing audits or investigations in relation to employee taxes and potential exposures in this respect.

18.11 VAT: All recent or ongoing audits or investigations in relation to VAT, sales taxes and customs duties, and potential exposures in this respect.

18.12 All correspondence with the Inland Revenue concerning shortfall assessments or apportionment of income.

18.13 All stamp duty or stamp duty land tax exemptions in which the Company may have been involved within the last [five] years.

18.14 Stock relief and capital allowances claimed.

18.15 Disputes with the Inland Revenue and unagreed assessments.

18.16 Confirmation of tax losses, if any, available for carrying forward.

18.17 Intra-group dividends and group relief structures or group income and management fee arrangements for the last [six] years (including associated documentation).

18.18   All covenants entered into since 6th April 1965 for annual payment of any nature.

18.19   Analysis of the tax provision in the latest audited accounts with explanation of key components and calculation of deferred tax.

18.20   All special arrangements with, or dispensations by, any tax authority.

18.21   All overseas trading via non-statutory entities or agents, and details of controls and procedures for compliance with overseas filing requirements.]

# APPENDIX 2

# Restrictions on Activities Prior to Completion

[See paras 3–04, 4–14 and 4–16]

The suggested restrictions are fairly comprehensive and of generic application to most companies but consideration should be given as to the suitability of them in relation to the target company and as to whether additional specific restrictions would also be appropriate.

Pending Completion the Vendors undertake to procure that save with the prior written consent of the Purchaser:

1  the business of the Company is carried on in the normal course in all respects in the same manner as prior to today's date without alteration to its location or operations which would or might in the reasonable opinion of the Purchaser materially prejudice its trade;

2  the Purchaser is informed as soon as reasonably practicable of any matter of which the Vendors become aware which [may] [is likely to] [will] materially adversely affect the business of the Company and is consulted with thereon;

3  they will use their best endeavours to procure that the employees and customers of the Company do not cease to be employed by or have dealings with the Company;

4  the Purchaser is consulted in advance on all material decisions taken in relation to the Company;

5  the Company keeps proper accounting records and makes true and complete entries in such records of all of its dealings and transactions;

6  the Company shall not:

   6.1  create or issue, or agree to create or issue, any securities, or agree to grant, any rights in respect of its share or loan capital;

   6.2  repay or redeem or agree to repay or redeem any of its share capital or reduce any of its share capital;

   6.3  enter into any agreement or arrangement whereby another company becomes its subsidiary;

   6.4  enter into any loan [outside of the normal course of business];

   6.5  borrow any monies or give or allow to exist any charge or other security over its assets or undertaking except for charges and other security existing as at today's date (on the same terms as at today's date) [or arising in the normal course of its business and operation of bank overdrafts and facilities within existing limits as required in the normal course of business];

   6.6  give any financial guarantees for any purpose whatsoever;

   6.7  prematurely repay any loans, borrowings or other form of funding;

   6.8  declare, make or pay a dividend or other distribution;

   6.9  enter or agree to enter into any long-term or abnormal contract or other agreement outside of the normal course of business;

6.10 enter or agree to enter into any contract involving capital expenditure or a capital commitment in excess of £[ ] in any one case or £[ ] in aggregate;

6.11 pass a resolution of its members;

6.12 appoint new auditors;

6.13 change (save as required by law) the terms and conditions of employment (whether contractual or not) of any of the officers of the Company or any of the Company's employees;

6.14 appoint or dismiss any officers or employees [on salaries in excess of £[ ]];

6.15 appoint any directors in addition to the current directors of the Company;

6.16 acquire or agree to acquire assets on hire purchase or deferred sale terms, otherwise than in the normal course of business;

6.17 sell, transfer or otherwise dispose of or agree to dispose of its business, undertaking or assets or any material part thereof;

6.18 permit liens to arise on any of its assets, otherwise than in the normal course of business;

6.19 commence, compromise or discontinue any disputes or legal or arbitration proceedings or claims (other than routine debt collection and price negotiations in the normal course of business);

6.20 write off or release any debts [of a value of £[ ] or over] or deal with any of its debtors or creditors in an inconsistent manner to how it has dealt with them in the period from the Balance Sheet Date to today's date; or

6.21 knowingly permit any of its normal insurance policies to lapse or do anything to make any insurance policy void or voidable, cause any increase in the insurance premium payable in respect of any insurance policy or prejudice the ability of the Company to effect insurance (on the same or better terms) in the future (save that this shall not prevent the notification to insurers of claims and/or circumstances which might give rise to claims under any of the current insurance policies in accordance with their relevant terms provided that the Vendors inform the Purchaser of any notification to insurers at or before the time that it is made).

# APPENDIX 3

# Warranties Relating to the Purchaser

[See para.1–05]

Save as otherwise defined in this Appendix, the definitions in para.4.1 are used.

1 The audited balance sheets and profit and loss accounts of the Purchaser and its Subsidiaries, consolidated where applicable, ("the Accounts") for the year ended [ ] ("the Balance sheet Date") have been properly prepared on a consistent basis in accordance with generally accepted accounting principles, standards and practices so as to give at the Balance Sheet Date a true and fair view of the then state of affairs of the Purchaser and its Subsidiaries and of their profit and losses for the period ended on that date.

2 The Accounts contain either provisions adequate to cover, or particulars and notes of, all liabilities (whether quantified or contingent) and all capital commitments of the Purchaser and its Subsidiaries at the Balance Sheet Date.

3 Since the Balance Sheet Date:

   3.1 the Purchaser and its Subsidiaries have carried on their respective businesses in the normal and proper course;

   3.2 there has been no material adverse change in the financial or trading position or prospects of the Purchaser or any of its Subsidiaries;

   3.3 neither the Purchaser nor any of its Subsidiaries has entered into a contract or commitment otherwise than in the normal course of business; and

   3.4 no dividends or other distributions have been declared, made or paid by the Purchaser.

4 The Purchaser and its Subsidiaries have good title to all of their fixed assets as shown in the Accounts, subject only to disposals in the normal course of business.

5 No order has been made, petition presented or resolution passed for the winding up of the Purchaser or any of its Subsidiaries; no distress, execution or other process has been levied in respect of the Purchaser or any of its Subsidiaries during the past three years; there are no outstanding or unsatisfied judgments or Court orders against the Purchaser or any of its Subsidiaries; and there has been no material delay by the Purchaser or any of its Subsidiaries in the discharge of any monetary obligation due to be discharged by it.

6 Neither the Purchaser nor any of its Subsidiaries nor a person for whom any of them is or may be liable, vicariously or otherwise, is engaged in or affected by criminal or civil litigation or arbitration proceedings which, individually or collectively, are or are likely to be of material importance, and no proceedings are threatened or pending.

7 There is no material fact or circumstances known or which, on reasonable enquiry, would be known to the Purchaser which, if disclosed to the Vendors, might have influenced them in determining whether to accept the allotment of shares of the Purchaser in satisfaction of the whole or part of the consideration for the Shares.

# Full Commercial Warranties

## PART 1 TAXATION WARRANTIES

[See para.5–02]

Note: for the purpose of this Appendix, the definitions in Chapter 4.1 are used.

Before using this precedent consideration should be given as to whether or not the warranties should be tailored to meet the specifics of the transaction (the warranties currently reflect a comprehensive "hard" purchaser's first draft) and whether all of the warranties are applicable. For example, the warranties at cll.7, 16 and 17 of Pt 1 would only be relevant when the target company has been or is part of a group of companies, and the warranty at cl.2.6 should only be included if there is a risk that dividends have were paid intra-group prior to April 6, 1999. Reference should be made to the commentaries on the individual warranties in chs 5, 6 and 7 in connection with this.

There is an element of overlap in certain areas between the warranties in Parts 1, 2 and 3, for example the insurance warranties at cll.7 of Pt 2 and 8.4 of Pt 3. A vendor may resist the inclusion of both sets of warranites on the basis that they duplicate each other.

Whilst the warranties are up to date as at the time of writing, there will inevitably be developments in a number of areas that will necessitate changes to them. For example, significant changes to pensions legislation are in the pipeline, with new requirements expected to be in force from April 2005 in relation to salary-related scheme funding and from April 2006 in relation to pension scheme tax relief. The current format of warranties takes no account of these anticipated changes. Care should be taken to ensure that the warranties are up to date.

### 1 Returns and Clearances

1.1    All returns, notifications, computations and payments which should have been made or given by the Company for a Taxation purpose were made or given within the requisite periods and were up-do-date, correct and on a proper basis; and none of them is, or is likely to be, the subject of a dispute with the Inland Revenue or other Taxation Authorities.

1.2    All particulars furnished to the Taxation Authorities, in connection with an application for consent or clearance on behalf of the Company, or affecting the Company, fully and accurately disclosed everything material to their decision; the consent or clearance is valid and effective; and the transactions for which the consent or clearance was obtained have been carried into effect (if at all) only in accordance with the terms of the application and the consent or clearance.

1.3    The Company has not taken any action which has had, or might have, the result of altering or prejudicing for a period commencing after the Balance Sheet Date an arrangement or agreement which it has with a Taxation Authority.

1.4    There has been no determination under TMA 1970, s.41A. (Determination procedure) or FA 1998, Schedule 18, Part V (Revenue determinations and assessments) of the amount of tax payable by the Company.

1.5    The Company is not obliged to pay corporation tax in quarterly instalments under the provisions of Corporation Tax (Instalment Payments) Regulations 1998 (SI 1998 No. 3175) and TMA 1970, s.59E.

1.6    The Company has not entered into any group payment arrangements under FA 1998, s.36.

## 2    PAYE and other deductions at source

2.1    The Company has properly operated the PAYE system, by duly deducting tax from all payments made, or treated as made, to its employees or former employees, and accounting to the Inland Revenue for all tax deducted by it and for all tax chargeable on benefits provided for its employees or former employees.

2.2    The Company has complied fully with all its obligations relating to Class 1 and Class 1A National Insurance Contributions, both primary and secondary.

2.3    The Company has complied with the following sections and regulations made under them:

FA 1995, ss.126 (U.K. Representatives of non-residents), 127 (Persons not treated as U.K. Representatives) and Schedule 23 (Obligations Etc. imposed on U.K. Representatives);

ICTA 1988, s.349 (Payments not out of profits or gains brought into charge to income tax, and annual interest) and s.350 (Charge to tax where payments made under s.349);

ICTA 1988, s.524 (Taxation of receipts from sale of patent rights);

ICTA 1988, s.536 (Taxation of royalties where owner abroad);

ICTA 1988, ss.555–558 (Entertainers and sportsmen);

ICTA 1988, ss.559–567 (Sub-contractors in the construction industry);

ICTA 1988, s.582 (Funding bonds issued in respect of interest on certain debts);

ICTA 1988, s.733 (Persons entitled to exemptions);

ICTA 1988, s.736A and Schedule 23A (Manufactured dividends and interest);

ICTA 1988, s.777 (Provisions supplementary to ss.775 and 776).

2.4    No liability to National Insurance Contributions or obligation to account for income tax under the PAYE system could fall on the Company as a result of a chargeable event (within the meaning of IT(EP)A 2003, Part 7), before, at or after Completion in respect of securities and interests in securities made available or securities options granted to an employee or director prior to Completion.

2.5    No officer or employee of the Company participates in any scheme approved under IT(E)PA 2003, Schedules 2 (Approved share incentive plans), 3 (Approved SAYE option schemes) or 4 (Approved CSOP schemes) or has any unapproved options (whether under IT(EP)A 2003, Schedule 5 (Enterprise Managing Incentives) or otherwise) or is a beneficiary or potential beneficiary of a qualifying employee share ownership trust as defined in FA 1989, Schedule 5 (employee share ownership trust).

2.6    The Disclosure Letter contains full particulars of all elections in force in relation to the Company under ICTA 1988, s.247 (Dividends, etc., paid by one member of a group to another) and no assessment may be made under that section on the Company in respect of advance corporation tax which ought to have been paid or income tax which ought to have been deducted.

## 3   Penalties

3.1     The Company has not paid or, since the Balance Sheet Date, become liable to pay a penalty or interest under any statute relating to Taxation.

3.2     The Company has not been the subject of an investigation, discovery or access order by or involving a Taxation Authority and there are no circumstances which make it likely that an investigation, discovery or order will be made.

## 4   Claims, elections, liabilities and reliefs

4.1     The Disclosure Letter contains full details of all matters relating to Taxation in respect of which the Company (either alone or jointly with another person) is, or at Completion will be, entitled:

4.1.1     to make a claim (including a supplementary claim) for, disclaimer of or election for relief under any statute relating to Taxation;

4.1.2     to appeal against an assessment to or a determination affecting Taxation;

4.1.3     to apply for the postponement of Taxation.

4.2     The Company has not made a claim under TCGA 1992, s.24(2) (Disposals where assets lost or destroyed, or become of negligible value) or exercised an option to pay tax by instalments under s.280 (Consideration payable by instalments).

4.3     The Company is not, nor will it become, liable to pay, or to reimburse or indemnify another person in respect of, Taxation in consequence of the failure by any other person (not being the Company) to discharge the Taxation, where the Taxation relates to a profit, income or gain arising or deemed to have arisen or anything occurring or deemed to have occurred (whether wholly or partly) prior to Completion.

4.4     No relief from Taxation has been claimed by or given to the Company, or taken into account in determining the provision for Taxation in the Accounts, which could be withdrawn, postponed or restricted as a result of anything occurring after Completion.

## 5   Unremittable income and capital gains

5.1     The Company has not received or become entitled to income which is "unremittable income" within the meaning of ICTA 1988, s.584 (Relief for unremittable overseas income) or a gain to which TCGA 1992, s.279 (Foreign assets: delayed remittances) could apply.

## 6   Tax avoidance

6.1     The Company has not, since the Balance Sheet Date, engaged in, or been a party to, a scheme or arrangement of which the main purpose, or one of the main purposes, was the avoidance of, or a reduction in liability to, Taxation.

6.2     The Company has not been a party to, or otherwise involved in, a transaction to which any of the following could apply:

ICTA 1988, s.56 (Transactions in deposits with and without certificates or in debts);

ICTA 1988, s.399 (Dealings in commodity futures, etc.: withdrawal of loss relief);

ICTA 1988, ss.116 (Arrangements for transferring relief), 395 (Leasing contracts and company reconstructions) and 410 (Arrangements for transfer of company to another group or consortium);

ICTA 1988, s.730 (Transfers of income arising from securities);

ICTA 1988, ss.731–735 (Purchase and sale of securities);

ICTA 1988, s.736 (Company dealing in securities: distribution materially reducing value of holding);

ICTA 1988, s.767A (Change in company ownership: corporation tax);

ICTA 1988, s.774 (Transactions between dealing company and associated company);

ICTA 1988, s.779 (Sale and lease-back: limitation on tax reliefs);

ICTA 1988, s.781 (Assets leased to traders and others);

ICTA 1988, s.786 (Transactions associated with loans or credit);

CAA 2001, Part 2, Chapter 17, ss.218, 221–224, 232 (1), 241–243 or 246(1) (Anti Avoidance);

CAA 2001, s.5 (When capital expenditure is incurred);

TCGA 1992, s.29 (Value shifting: General provisions);

TCGA 1992, s.106 (Disposal of shares and securities by company within prescribed period of acquisition).

6.3    The Company has not, since the Balance Sheet Date, been a party to a transaction to which any of the following provisions have been, or could be, applied other than transactions in respect of which all necessary consents or clearances were obtained:

ICTA 1988, ss.703–709 (Cancellation of tax advantages from certain transactions in securities);

ICTA 1988, s.765 (Migration, etc., of companies);

ICTA 1988, s.776 (Transactions in land: taxation of capital gains);

TCGA 1992, ss.135–138 (Company reconstructions); or

TCGA 1992, s.139 (Reconstruction involving transfer of business).

## 7    Depreciatory transactions and value shifting

7.1    No allowable loss, which may accrue on the disposal of an asset by the Company, is likely to be reduced by reason of TCGA 1992, s.176 (Depreciatory transactions within a group) or s.177 (Dividend stripping).

7.2    No chargeable gain or allowable loss arising on a disposal by the Company is likely to be adjusted under TCGA 1992, s.30 (Tax-free benefits).

7.3    No reduction in the value of the shares of the Company has occurred as a result of:

7.3.1    the payment of a dividend after March 13, 1989 out of chargeable profits within the meaning of TCGA 1992, s.31 (Distributions within a group followed by a disposal of shares) as extended by TCGA 1992, s.31A (Asset-holding company leaving the group); or

7.3.2 a transfer of an asset in circumstances within TCGA 1992, s.32(2) (Disposals within a group followed by a disposal of shares).

## 8 Disallowance of deductions

8.1 No rents, interest, annual payments or other sums of an income nature paid, or payable, since the Balance Sheet Date by the Company or which the Company is under an obligation to pay are, or may be, wholly or partially disallowable as deductions in computing profits or as charges on income, for the purposes of corporation tax, by reason of ICTA 1988, s.74 (General rules as to deductions not allowable), s.125 (Annual payments for non-taxable consideration), ss.338–338B (Charges on income deducted from total profits), s.770A (Transaction not at arm's length), s.779 (Sale and lease-back: limitation on tax reliefs), s.781 (Assets leased to traders and others), s.787 (Restriction of relief for payments of interest) or otherwise.

## 9 Transactions not at arm's length

9.1 The Company has not carried out, or been engaged in, a transaction or arrangement to which ICTA 1988, s.770A (Transaction not at arm's length) and Schedule 28AA (Provision not at arm's length) has been or may be applied.

9.2 The Company has not disposed of or acquired an asset in such circumstances that TCGA 1992, s.17 (Disposals and acquisitions treated as made at market value) could apply.

## 10 Disallowance of losses

10.1 There has not been in the past three years a major change in the nature or conduct of the trade or business of the Company such as might prevent the carry forward or back of trading losses or excess management expenses by reason of the application of ICTA 1988, s.768A (Change in ownership: disallowance of carry back of trading losses) or s.768B (Change in ownership of investment company: deductions generally).

## 11 Loan relationships

11.1 If the Company is a party to a loan relationship (within the meaning of FA 1996, s.81 (Meaning of "loan relationship" etc.)) it uses as respects the loan relationship in its statutory accounts a basis of accounting which is or equates to an authorised accounting method under FA 1996, s.85 (Authorised accounting methods).

11.2 The Company has not, in respect of a loan relationship within the meaning of FA 1996, s.81 (Meaning of "loan relationship" etc.), applied:

11.2.1 an authorised accounting method inconsistently or otherwise in a materially different way in successive accounting periods; or

11.2.2 used a different authorised accounting method for the same or successive accounting periods; as provided by FA 1996, s.89 (Inconsistent application of accounting methods).

11.3 The Company is not required to use an authorised accruals basis of accounting as respects a creditor relationship by virtue of FA 1996, s.87 (Accounting method where parties have a connection).

11.4 The Company is not subject to a restriction as to the amount of the loss that it may bring into account in respect of a loan relationship by virtue of FA 1996, Schedule 9, paragraph 10 (Imported losses, etc.).

11.5 The Company has not acquired or disposed of rights or liabilities in respect of a loan relationship where the company from which it made the acquisition or to which it made the disposal was a member of the same group of companies within the meaning of FA 1996, Schedule 9, paragraph 12 (Continuity of treatment: groups, etc.).

11.6 The Company has not been a party to a loan relationship which had an unallowable purpose within the meaning of FA 1996, Schedule 9, paragraph 13 (Loan relationships for unallowable purposes).

## 12 Distributions

12.1 The Company has not repaid, or agreed to repay, or redeemed, or agreed to redeem, any of its shares, or capitalised, or agreed to capitalise, in the form of redeemable shares or debentures, any profits or reserves.

12.2 No outstanding security, within the meaning of ICTA 1988, s.254 (Interpretation of Part VI (Company distributions, tax credits, etc.)) of the Company was issued in such circumstances that the interest payable on it, or any other payment in respect of it, falls to be treated as a distribution under ICTA 1988, s.209 (Meaning of "distribution").

12.3 The Company has not received a capital distribution to which TCGA 1992, s.189 (Capital distribution of chargeable gains: recovery from shareholder) could apply.

## 13 Close companies

13.1 The Company is not, nor was it at any time during the six years ended on the Balance Sheet Date, a close company as defined in ICTA 1988, s.414 (Close companies).

13.2 No distribution within ICTA 1988, s.418 ("Distribution" to include certain expenses of close companies) has been made by the Company.

13.3 No loan or advance within ICTA 1988, Part XI, Chapter II (Charges to tax in connection with loans) has been made, or agreed to, by the Company, and the Company has not, since the Balance Sheet Date, released or written off the whole or part of the debt in respect of such a loan or advance.

## 14 Sale and leaseback of land

14.1 The Company has not, since the Balance Sheet Date, entered into a transaction to which the provisions of ICTA 1988, s.780 (Sale and lease-back: taxation of consideration received) have been, or could be, applied.

## 15 Payments from pension funds

15.1 The company has not received a payment out of funds held for the purposes of an exempt approved scheme in respect of which an amount is recoverable by the Inland Revenue under ICTA 1988, s.601 (Charge to tax: payments to employers).

## 16 Group relief and group surrenders

16.1 The Group Companies comprise a group for the purposes of ICTA 1988, s.402 (Surrender of relief between members of groups and consortia) and there is nothing in ICTA 1988, s.410 (Arrangements for transfer of company to another group or consortium) which precludes a Group Company from being regarded as a member of the group.

16.2 The Company has not, since the Balance Sheet Date, made or agreed to make, otherwise than to or from another Group Company a surrender of, or claim for, group relief under ICTA 1988, Part X, Chapter IV (Group relief).

16.3 No Group Company is liable to make or entitled to receive a payment for group relief otherwise than to or from another Group Company.

16.4 The Company has not made or received a payment for group relief (otherwise than to or from another Group Company), which may be liable to be refunded in whole or in part.

16.5 If any member of the Group Company only became a member after the Balance Sheet Date, the apportionment of profits and losses will be made under ICTA 1988, s.403B (Apportionment under s.403A) on a time basis according to the respective lengths of the component accounting periods.

16.6 The Company is not restricted in relation to the surrendering of group relief by ICTA 1988, s.404 (Limitation of group relief in relation to certain dual resident companies).

16.7 The Company has not agreed to surrender, otherwise than to another Group Company, any right to receive a tax refund under FA 1989, s.102 (Surrender of company tax refund, etc., within group).

## 17 Acquisitions from group members

17.1 The Company does not own an asset which was acquired from another company, which was, at the time, a member of the same group of companies (as defined in TCGA 1992, s.170 (Groups of companies: interpretation of ss.170–181)) as the relevant Group Company, and which owned that asset otherwise than as trading stock within TCGA 1992, s.173 (Transfers within a group: trading stock).

17.2 The execution or completion of this Agreement will not result in profit or gain being deemed to accrue to the Company for Taxation purposes, whether under TCGA 1992, s.179 (Company ceasing to be member of group: post-appointed day cases) or otherwise.

## 18 Demergers and purchase of own shares

18.1 The Company has not been engaged in, or been a party to, any of the transactions set out in ICTA 1988, ss.213–218 (Demergers), nor has it made or received a chargeable payment as defined in s.214 (Chargeable payments connected with exempt distributions).

18.2 The Company has not redeemed, repaid or purchased or agreed to redeem, repay or purchase, any of its own shares.

## 19 Stock dividends

19.1 The Company has not issued share capital to which the provisions of ICTA 1988, s.249 (Stock dividends treated as income) or TCGA, s.142 (Capital gains on stock dividends) could apply and the Company does not own any such share capital.

## 20 Capital allowances

20.1 All expenditure which the Company has incurred or may incur under a subsisting commitment on the provision of machinery or plant has qualified or will qualify (if not deductible as a trading expense of a trade carried on by the Company) for writing-down allowances under CAA 2001, Part 2, Chapter 5 (Allowances and Charges).

20.2 No event has occurred since the Balance Sheet Date which may be treated as a notional sale by the Company of machinery or plant pursuant to CAA 2001, ss.61 (Disposal events and disposal values) or 72 (Disposal values).

20.3 No capital allowances made or to be made to the Company in respect of capital expenditure already incurred or to be incurred under a subsisting commitment arise from special leasing (as defined in CAA 2001, s.19) or qualifying non-trade expenditure (as defined in CAA 2001, s.469) on patents.

20.4 Since the Balance Sheet Date the Company has not done, or omitted to do, or agreed to do, or permitted to be done, an act as a result of which a balancing allowance or a balancing charge may be brought into account for capital allowances purposes, or there may be a recovery of excess relief under CAA 2001, s.111 (Excess allowances: standard recovery mechanism).

20.5 The Company is not in dispute with any person as to any entitlement to capital allowances under CAA 2001, Part 2, Chapter 14 (Fixtures) and at the date of this Agreement as far as the Vendors are aware there are no circumstances which might give rise to such a dispute.

## 21 Base values and acquisition costs

21.1 If each of the capital assets of the Company was disposed of at Completion for a consideration equal to its book value in, or adopted for the purpose of, the Accounts, no liability to corporation tax on chargeable gains and, on the assumption that the expenditure on each asset was incurred for the purpose of a separate trade, no balancing charge under CAA 2001 would arise; and, for the purpose of determining the liability to corporation tax on chargeable gains, there shall be disregarded reliefs and allowances available to the Company other than amounts falling to be deducted under TCGA 1992, s.38 (Acquisition and disposal costs, etc.).

21.2 The Company has not made an election under TCGA 1992, s.35 (Assets held on 31 March, 1982 (including assets held on 6 April, 1965)) for capital gains and losses on all the assets held by it on 31 March, 1982 to be computed by reference only to their market value on that date.

21.3 The Company has not since the Balance Sheet Date engaged in a transaction in respect of which there may be substituted, for Taxation purposes, a different consideration for the actual consideration given or received by it.

21.4 In determining the liability to corporation tax on chargeable gains in respect of any asset which has been acquired by the Company, or which the Company has agreed to acquire (whether conditionally, contingently or otherwise):

21.4.1 the sums allowable as a deduction will be determined solely in accordance with TCGA 1992, ss.38 (Acquisition and disposal costs, etc.) and 53 (The indexation allowance and interpretative provisions);

21.4.2 the amount or value of the consideration, determined in accordance with s.38(1)(a), will not be less than the amount or value of the consideration actually given by the Company for the asset; and

21.4.3 the amount of any expenditure on enhancing the value of that asset, determined in accordance with s.38(1)(b) will not be less than the amount or value of all expenditure actually incurred by the Company on the asset.

21.5 No asset owned, or agreed to be acquired, by the Company (other than plant and machinery in respect of which it is entitled to capital allowances) is a wasting asset within TCGA 1992, s.44 (Meaning of "wasting asset").

21.6 The Company has not joined in the making of a claim under TCGA 1992, s.140A (Transfer of a U.K. trade) in relation to the transfer to it of the whole or part of a trade carried on within the United Kingdom.

## 22 Replacement of business assets

22.1 The Company has not made a claim under TCGA 1992, ss.23 (Receipt of compensation and insurance money not treated as a disposal), 152 (Replacement of business assets: Roll-over relief), 153 (Assets only partly replaced), 154 (New assets which are depreciating assets), 175 (Replacement of business assets by members of a group) or 247 (Roll-over relief on compulsory acquisition) which would affect the amount of the chargeable gain or allowable loss which would, but for the claim, have arisen on a disposal of any of its assets.

## 23 Chargeable gains: special cases

23.1 The Company is not owed a debt (not being a debt on a security), upon the disposal or satisfaction of which a liability to corporation tax on chargeable gains will arise under TCGA 1992, s.251 (Debts: General provisions).

23.2 The Company has not claimed nor is it entitled to claim under TCGA 1992, ss.253 (Relief for loans to traders) or 254 (Relief for debts on qualifying corporate bonds) that an allowable loss has accrued in respect of a loan made by it.

23.3 The Company does not own rights, or an interest in rights, under a policy of assurance or contract for a deferred annuity on the life of any person of which it is not the original beneficial owner.

23.4 No part of the consideration given by the Company for a new holding of shares (within the meaning of TCGA 1992, s.126 (Reorganisation or reduction of share capital: Application of ss.127–131) will be disregarded by virtue of s.128(2) (Consideration given or received by holder).

23.5 No asset owned by the Company has been the subject of a deemed disposal under TCGA 1992, Schedule 2 (Assets held on 6 April, 1965), so as to restrict the extent to which the gain or loss, over the period of ownership, may be apportioned by reference to straightline growth.

## 24 Capital losses and limited partnerships

24.1 The Company has not incurred a capital loss to which TCGA 1992, s.18(3) (Transactions between connected persons) is applicable.

24.2   The Company is not treated as a limited partner under ICTA 1988, s.118 (Restriction on relief: companies).

## 25  Gifts involving group companies

25.1   The Company has not received assets by way of gift as mentioned in TCGA 1992, s.282 (Recovery of tax from donee).

## 26  Foreign businesses

26.1   The Company has not made a claim under TCGA 1992, s.140 (Postponement of charge on transfer of assets to non-resident company) or s.140C (Transfer of a non-U.K. trade) in relation to the transfer of the whole or part of a trade which it carried on outside the United Kingdom through a branch or agency.

26.2   No notice under ICTA 1988, s.747 (Imputation of chargeable profits and creditable tax of controlled foreign companies) has been received by the Company and no circumstances exist which would entitle the Inland Revenue to apportion profits of a controlled foreign company to the Company under ICTA 1988, s.752 (Apportionment of chargeable profits and creditable tax) as extended by ICTA 1988, ss.752A (Relevant interests), 752B (s.752(3): the percentage of shares which a relevant interest represents) and 752C (Interpretation of apportionment provisions).

## 27  Foreign loan interest

27.1   The Company has not received foreign loan interest on which double taxation relief will, or may, be restricted under ICTA 1988, ss.798 (Restriction of relief on certain interest and dividends), 798A (Adjustments of interest and dividends for spared tax etc.) and 798B (Meaning of "financial expenditure").

## 28  Value added tax

28.1   In relation to value added tax the Company:

28.1.1   has duly registered and is a taxable person;

28.1.2   has complied, in all material respects, with all statutory requirements, orders, provisions, directions and conditions;

28.1.3   maintains complete, correct and up-to-date records as required by the applicable legislation;

28.1.4   has not been required by the Commissioners of Customs and Excise to give security;

28.1.5   has not applied for treatment as a member of a group which includes another company; and

28.1.6   is not, nor has it agreed to become, an agent (for the purposes of VATA 1994, s.47 (Agents, etc.)) for the supply of goods for a person who is not a taxable person.

28.2   The Disclosure Letter sets out accurate and complete particulars of claims for bad debt relief which have been made and remain outstanding, or which may be made, by the Company under VATA 1994, s.36 (Bad debts) and of any debts which, if written off, would give a right to claim relief.

28.3   The Company has not, during the past 12 or 24 months respectively, received a surcharge liability notice under VATA 1994, s.59 (The default surcharge) or a penalty liability notice under s.64 (Repeated misdeclarations) nor may it be liable to a penalty under s.63 (Penalty for misdeclaration or neglect resulting in VAT loss for one accounting period equalling or exceeding certain amounts).

28.4   No election to waive exemption from value added tax in relation to any of the Properties has been made by the Company or a predecessor in title under VATA 1994, Schedule 10, paragraph 2 (Election to waive exemption).

## 29  Inheritance tax

29.1   The Company has not made a transfer of value (as defined in IHTA 1984, s.3 (Transfers of value)).

29.2   No Inland Revenue charge for unpaid inheritance tax (as provided by IHTA 1984, ss.237–238 (Inland Revenue charge for unpaid tax)) exists over an asset of the Company or in relation to shares in the capital of the Company.

## 30  Stamp duty and stamp duty land tax

30.1   The Company has not within the past three years made a claim for relief or exemption under FA 1930, s.42 (Relief from transfer stamp duty in case of transfer of property as between associated companies), FA 1995, s.151 (Leases etc. between associated bodies corporate) or FA 1986, ss. 75–77 (Acquisitions: reliefs)).

30.2   All documents in the posession of the Company, or which the Company is entitled to require the production of, and which confer any right upon the Company or are necessary to establish the title of the Company to any asset, have been stamped and any applicable stamp duties or charges in respect of such documents have been accounted for and paid, and no such documents which are outside of the United Kingdom would attract stamp duty if they were brought into the United Kingdom.

30.3   Stamp duty land tax has been paid in full in respect of all estates or interests in land acquired on or after December 1, 2003 by the Company and there are no contingent liabilities or requirements to submit a further land transaction return in relation to:

30.3.1   properties acquired as a going concern for the purposes of VATA s.49 (Taxation of going concerns);

30.3.2   unascertainable future consideration;

30.3.3   transactions capable of being treated as linked for the purposes of FA 2003, s.108 (Linked transactions);

30.3.4   turnover leases;

30.3.5   leases subject to a rent review within five years of grant;

30.3.6   leases the assignment of which would be deemed to be the grant of a new lease; or

30.3.7   any other arrangement capable of giving rise to a further charge to stamp duty land tax.

30.4   The Company has not claimed relief from stamp duty land tax under FA 2003, Schedule 7, Parts 1 or 2 (Stamp Duty Land Tax: group relief and reconstruction and acquisition reliefs) in relation to any estate or interest in land that has been transferred to it.

## 31  Disclosure Requirements

31.1   The Company has not notified the Inland Revenue of any notifiable arrangement (Meaning of "notifiable arrangements" and "notifiable proposal") or notifiable proposal (as defined by FA 2004, s.306) for the purposes of the Tax Avoidance Schemes (Information) Regulations 2004 and there are no circumstances in which any such disclosure should have been made by the Company.

31.2    The Company has not implemented any proposal or entered into any arrangements which are notifiable pursuant to FA 2004, ss.309 (Duty of person dealing with promoter outside United Kingdom) or 310 (Duty of parties to notifiable arrangements not involving promoter) and has not included any scheme reference on any of its tax returns pursuant to FA 2004, s.313 (Duty of parties to notifiable arrangements to notify Board of number, etc.) and there are no circumstances in which such notification or inclusion of a reference should have been made by the Company.

## PART 2 PROPERTY WARRANTIES

[See para.6–18]

### 1   Title

1.1    The Properties comprise all the properties owned, occupied or otherwise used by the Company in connection with its business.

1.2    Those of the Properties which are occupied or otherwise used by the Company in connection with its business are occupied or used by right of ownership or under lease or licence, the terms of which permit the occupation or use.

1.3    The Company is the legal and beneficial owner of the Properties.

1.4    The information contained in Schedule [ ] as to the tenure of each of the Properties, the principal terms of the leases or licences held by the Company and the principal terms of the tenancies and licences subject to and with the benefit of which the Properties are held, is complete and accurate.

1.5    The Company has a good and marketable title to each of the Properties.

1.6    [The Company is the proprietor of the Properties registered at HM Land Registry with absolute title.] [None of the Properties is registered at HM Land Registry.]

1.7    Each lease of the Properties granted for more than 7 years is either registered at HM Land Registry with absolute title or not registered because it was not registrable at the time of grant and no event has occurred in consequence of which first registration of title should have been effected.

### 2   Encumbrances

2.1    The Properties are free from mortgages, debentures, charges, rent charges, liens or other encumbrances.

2.2    The Properties are not subject to outgoings, other than business rates, water rates and insurance premiums and, additionally, in the case of leasehold properties, rent and service charges.

2.3    The Properties are free of restrictive covenants, stipulations, easements, *profits à prendre*, wayleaves, licences, grants, restrictions, overriding interests or other similar rights vested in third parties.

2.4     Where any of the matters referred to in clauses [2.1, 2.2 and 2.3] are disclosed in the Disclosure Letter, the obligations and liabilities imposed and arising under them have been performed and discharged and no payments in respect of them are outstanding.

2.5     The Properties are free of options or rights of pre-emption.

2.6     There are no local land charges, land charges, cautions, inhibitions or notices registered against the Properties and there is nothing which is capable of registration against them.

## 3  Planning matters

3.1     The use of each of the Properties is the permitted use for the purposes of the Planning Acts.

3.2     Planning permission has been obtained, or is deemed to have been granted, for the purpose of the Planning Acts with respect to the development of the Properties; no planning permission has been suspended or called in and no application for planning permission is awaiting a decision.

3.3     Building regulation consents have been obtained with respect to all development of and alterations and improvements to the Properties.

3.4     The Company has complied and is complying with planning permissions and statutory orders and regulations with respect to the Properties.

3.5     The Company has complied and is complying with all agreements and all planning obligations made in respect of the Properties under the Town and County Planning Act 1971, s.52 and under the Town and Country Planning Act 1990, s.106.

3.6     The Company has complied and is complying with all agreements made under the Highways Act 1980, s.38 with respect to the Properties.

3.7     None of the Properties is listed as being of special historic or architectural importance or located in a conservation area.

## 4  Statutory obligations

4.1     The Company has complied and is complying with all applicable statutory and by-law requirements with respect to the Properties of the Public Health Acts, the Shops Acts 1950 to 1965, the Factories Act 1961, the Offices, Shops and Railway Premises Act 1963, the Fire Precautions Act 1971, the Health and Safety at Work etc. Act 1974, the Environmental Protection Act 1990 Part IIA, the Sunday Trading Act 1994, the Disability Discrimination Act 1995 and any other legislation current or previous currently affecting the Properties and any other relevant orders, regulations or directions of a competent authority affecting the Properties.

4.2     There is no outstanding or unperformed obligation with respect to the Properties, compliance with which is necessary to satisfy the requirements (whether formal or informal) of a competent authority exercising statutory or delegated powers.

4.3     No licences are required in relation to any of the Properties.

## 5  Adverse orders

5.1     There are no compulsory purchase notices, orders or resolutions affecting the Properties and there are no circumstances likely to lead to any being made.

5.2     There are no closing, demolition or clearance orders, enforcement notices or stop notices affecting the Properties and there are no circumstances likely to lead to any being made.

## 6   Condition of the Properties

6.1     The buildings and other structures on the Properties are in good and substantial repair and fit for the purposes for which they are used.

6.2     No structure on the Properties has been affected by structural damage or electrical defects or by timber infestation or disease.

6.3     No structure on the Properties contains in its fabric high alumina cement, blue asbestos, calcium chloride accelerator, wood wool slabs used as permanent shuttering or other deleterious material.

6.4     There are no disputes with a neighbouring owner with respect to boundary walls and fences, or with a third party with respect to easements or rights over or benefitting the Properties.

6.5     The principal means of access to the Properties are over roads which have been taken over by the local or other highway authority and which are maintainable at the public expense, and no means of access to the Properties is shared with another party or subject to rights of determination by another party.

6.6     Each of the Properties enjoys the mains services of water, drainage, electricity and gas.

6.7     None of the Properties is located in an area or subject to circumstances particularly susceptible to flooding.

6.8     The Properties are not subject to rights of common.

6.9     The Properties are not affected by mining activity.

## 7   Insurance

7.1     The Properties are covered by insurance of a type usually available in the United Kingdom insurance market against a comprehensive range of risks (including subsidence and terrorism) in their full reinstatement values and against third party and public liabilities and professional fees to an adequate extent and, where any of the Properties are let, for not less than three years' loss of rent or such greater period as may be specified in the tenancies affecting the Properties.

7.2     All premiums due in respect of insurance policies relating to the Properties have been duly paid and, where the Properties are let, the premiums are recoverable in full from the tenants pursuant to the tenancies affecting the Properties and nothing has arisen which would vitiate the policies or permit the insurers to avoid them.

7.3     The information in the Disclosure Letter with respect to insurance policies is complete and accurate.

## 8   Leasehold properties

8.1     The Company has paid the rent and performed the covenants on the part of the tenant and the conditions contained in any leases (which expression in this clause [8] includes underleases) under which the Properties are held, the last demands for rent (or receipts, if issued) were unqualified and all the leases are in full force.

8.2     All licences, consents and approvals required from the landlords and any superior landlords under leases of the Properties have been obtained, and the tenant's covenants therein have been performed.

8.3    There are no rent reviews in progress under leases of the Properties held by the Company.

8.4    No obligation necessary to comply with a notice or other requirement given by the landlord under a lease of any of the Properties is outstanding and unperformed.

8.5    There is no obligation to reinstate any of the Properties by removing an alteration made to it by the Company or a predecessor in title to the Company.

8.6    The Company has not entered into an authorised guarantee agreement under the Landlord and Tenant (Covenants) Act 1995, s.16 in respect of any property.

8.7    The Company has not had the right to call for an overriding lease of any property under the Landlord and Tenant (Covenants) Act 1995, s.19.

8.8    The Company has not entered into an agreement with the lessor of any of the Properties specifying circumstances in which it would be reasonable for the lessor to withhold its consent to an assignment in accordance with the Landlord and Tenant Act 1927, s.19(1A).

## 9   Tenancies

9.1    The Properties are held subject to and with the benefit of the tenancies (which expression in this clause [9] includes subtenancies) as set out in Schedule [ ] and no others.

9.2    With respect to the tenancies, the Disclosure Letter contains particulars of:

9.2.1    the rent and any rent reviews and, with respect to rent reviews, the date for giving notice of exercise of the reviews and the operative review date;

9.2.2    the term and rights to break or renew the term;

9.2.3    the obligations of the landlord and tenant in respect of outgoings, repairs, insurance, services and service charges;

9.2.4    options or pre-emption rights;

9.2.5    the user required or permitted;

9.2.6    the entitlement of a tenant of the Properties to compensation either on quitting the premises, for improvements or otherwise;

9.2.7    any unusual provisions; and

9.2.8    short particulars of subtenancies derived out of the tenancies.

9.3    The Vendors are not aware of a material or persistent breach of covenant by a tenant of the Properties.

9.4    The Company has not at any time:

9.4.1    surrendered any lease, licence or tenancy to the landlord without first satisfying itself that the landlord had good title to accept such surrender and without receiving from the landlord an absolute release from all liability arising under such lease, licence or tenancy;

9.4.2    assigned, or otherwise disposed of, any lease, licence or tenancy without receiving a full and effective indemnity from the assignee or transferee in respect of its liability under such lease, licence or tenancy;

9.4.3    been a guarantor of a tenant's liability under any lease, licence or tenancy; or

9.4.4 assigned or otherwise disposed of any leasehold property in such a way that it retains any other residual liability in respect thereof.

# PART 3 COMMERCIAL WARRANTIES

[See para.7–03]

## 1 Preliminary

### 1.1 Capacity and authority of Vendors

1.1.1 Each Vendor has full power and authority to enter into and perform this Agreement, the Tax Deed and all other documents to be executed by them pursuant to this Agreement which constitute, or when executed will constitute, obligations binding on each Vendor in accordance with their terms.

### 1.2 Ownership of Shares

1.2.1 The Shares are fully paid or credited as fully paid and will, at Completion, constitute the whole of the issued and allotted share capital of the Company.

1.2.2 The Vendors have the right to transfer to the Purchaser (without the consent of any third party) and will on Completion transfer the legal and beneficial title to the Shares.

1.2.3 There is not now existing nor is there any agreement to create any Encumbrance on or affecting shares of the Company.

1.2.4 None of the Shares was, or represents assets which were, the subject of a transfer at an undervalue (within the meaning of the Insolvency Act 1986, ss.238 or 339) within the past five years.

1.2.5 None of the Shares was allotted at a discount.

### 1.3 Share capital

1.3.1 No share or loan capital has been issued or allotted or agreed to be issued or allotted by the Company since the Balance Sheet Date.

1.3.2 The Company has not at any time repaid, redeemed or purchased any of its own shares, reduced its share capital or capitalised any reserves or profits (or agreed to do the same).

1.3.3 The Company has not at any time provided financial assistance pursuant to CA 1985, ss.151 and 158.

### 1.4 Details of the Company

1.4.1 The information relating to the Company in Schedule [ ] is accurate and complete.

1.4.2 The Company has not at any time had only one member.

### 1.5 Directors and shadow directors

1.5.1 The only directors of the Company are the persons listed as such in Schedule [ ].

1.5.2 No person is or has been a shadow director (within the meaning of CA 1985, s.741) of the Company but not treated as one of its directors for all the purposes of CA 1985.

**1.6        Subsidiaries and branches**

1.6.1    The Company:

1.6.1.1    is not the holder or beneficial owner of, nor has it agreed to acquire, share or loan capital of a body corporate; and

1.6.1.2    has not outside the United Kingdom a branch, agency or place of business, or a permanent establishment (as that expression is currently defined in the relevant double taxation relief order).

**1.7        Options over the Company's capital**

1.7.1    Apart from this Agreement, there are no agreements or arrangements which provide for the issue, allotment or transfer of, or grant a right (whether conditional or otherwise) to call for the issue, allotment or transfer of share or loan capital of the Company. No claim has been made by any person to be entitled to any of the foregoing.

**1.8        Commissions**

1.8.1    No one is entitled to receive from the Company a finder's fee, brokerage or other commission in connection with the sale and purchase of the Shares under this Agreement.

**1.9        Elective and written resolutions**

1.9.1    The Company has not passed an elective resolution under CA 1985, s.379A which remains in force.

1.9.2    The Company has complied with CA 1985, s.381B by giving notice to its auditors of all written resolutions passed or to be passed by it from April 1, 1990 to June 18, 1996 and the auditors gave no notice of objection.

**1.10      Memoranda and articles of association, statutory books and resolutions**

1.10.1    The copy of the memorandum and articles of association of the Company attached to the Disclosure Letter is accurate and complete and has embodied in it, or attached to it, a copy of every resolution which is referred to in CA 1985, s.380(2).

1.10.2    The register of members and other statutory books of the Company have been properly kept and contain an accurate and complete record of the matters with which they should deal.

1.10.3    No notice or allegation has been received that the statutory books of the Company are incorrect or should be rectified.

1.10.4    Since the Balance Sheet Date, no alteration has been made to the memorandum or articles of association of the Company and no resolution has been passed by its shareholders (other than resolutions relating to routine business at annual general meetings).

**1.11      Documents filed**

1.11.1    All returns, particulars, resolutions and documents required by CA 1985 or other legislation to be filed with the Registrar of Companies or other authority in respect of the Company have been duly filed and were accurate and complete.

1.11.2    All charges in favour of the Company have (if appropriate) been registered in accordance with the provisions of CA 1985, Part XII.

**1.12 Possession of documents**

1.12.1 All the title deeds relating to the assets of the Company, an executed copy of all agreements to which the Company is a party and the original copies of all other documents which are owned by, or which ought to be in the possession of, the Company are in its possession.

**1.13 Investigations**

1.13.1 No investigation or enquiry by, or on behalf of, a governmental or other body in respect of the affairs of the Company is taking place or pending and the Vendors are not aware of any fact or matter that could lead to any such investigation or enquiry.

**1.14 Information disclosed to Purchaser correct**

1.14.1 All information given by any of the Vendors, the Vendors' solicitors or the Company's auditors to the Purchaser, the Purchaser's solicitors or the Purchaser's accountants relating to the business, affairs, assets and liabilities of the Company was and is accurate and complete and opinions, expectations and beliefs included in the information are honestly held and have been arrived at on a reasonable basis after full enquiry.[1]

1.14.2 There are no material facts or circumstances in relation to the assets, business or financial condition of the Company which have not been fully and fairly disclosed in writing to the Purchaser or the Purchaser's solicitors and which, if disclosed, might reasonably have been expected to affect the decision of the Purchaser to enter into this Agreement.[2]

## 2 Accounts

**2.1 The Accounts**

2.1.1 The Accounts were prepared in accordance with the historical cost convention and with the requirements of all relevant statutes and generally accepted accounting practices; and on the same bases and policies of accounting as adopted for the purpose of preparing the audited accounts of the Company in respect of the preceding three accounting periods.

2.1.2 The Accounts

2.1.2.1 give a true and fair view of the assets and liabilities and state of affairs of the Company at the Balance Sheet Date and its profits and cash flow for the period ended on that date;

2.1.2.2 comply with the requirements of CA 1985;

2.1.2.3 comply with current Accounting Standards;

2.1.2.4 are not affected by extraordinary, exceptional or non-recurring items;

2.1.2.5 fully disclose all the assets of the Company on the Balance Sheet Date;

---

[1] Please see comments at para.7–31 in relation to this warranty and the alternative form of wording that well-advised vendors are likely to insist on.

[2] Please see comments at para.7–32 in relation to this warranty which is the infamous "sweeping-up" warranty which is likely to be strongly resisted by vendors.

2.1.2.6    provide or reserve in full for all liabilities and capital commitments of the Company outstanding at the Balance Sheet Date, including contingent, unquantified or disputed liabilities; and

2.1.2.7    provide or reserve, in accordance with the principles set out in the notes included in the Accounts, for all Taxation liable to be assessed on the Company, or for which it may be accountable, in respect of the period ended on the Balance Sheet Date.

2.1.3    The amount included in the Accounts in respect of each asset, whether fixed or current, did not exceed its purchase price or production cost (within the meaning of CA 1985, Schedule 4) or (in the case of current assets) its net realisable value at the Balance Sheet Date.

## 2.2    Valuation of stock in trade and work in progress

2.2.1    In the Accounts and in the accounts of the Company for the three preceding financial years, the stock in trade and work in progress of the Company was treated in accordance with SSAP 9.

2.2.2    In the Accounts slow-moving stock in trade was written down as appropriate and redundant, obsolete, obsolescent and defective stock was wholly written off and the value attributable to any other stock did not exceed the lower of cost and net realisable value at the Balance Sheet Date.

2.2.3    In valuing work in progress in the Accounts no value was attributed in respect of eventual profit and adequate provision was made for such losses as were at the time of signature of the Accounts by the directors of the Company foreseeable as arising or likely to arise on completion and/or realisation thereof.

## 2.3    Depreciation of fixed assets

2.3.1    In the Accounts and in the accounts of the Company for the three preceding financial years, the fixed assets of the Company were depreciated in accordance with FRS 15.

## 2.4    Deferred Taxation

2.4.1    Where provision for deferred Taxation is not made in the Accounts, full details of the amounts of deferred Taxation have been disclosed in the Disclosure Letter.

## 2.5    Accounting reference date

2.5.1    The accounting reference date of the Company for the purposes of CA 1985, s.224 is, and has always been, [ ].

## 2.6    Management Accounts

2.6.1    The Management Accounts have been prepared in accordance with accounting policies consistent with those used in the preparation of the Accounts, with all due care and on a basis consistent with the management accounts of the Company prepared in the preceding [year]. The cumulative profits, assets and liabilities of the Company stated in the Management Accounts have not been misstated.

**2.7    Books and records**

2.7.1    The accounting and other records of the Company:

    2.7.1.1    are in its exclusive ownership and direct control;

    2.7.1.2    have been fully, properly and accurately kept and completed;

    2.7.1.3    are accurate in all material respects; and

    2.7.1.4    show a true and fair view of its trading transactions and its financial, contractual and trading position.

2.7.2    Full disclosure has been made to the Company's auditors and all previous auditors of the Company of all matters relevant to the preparation of the Accounts and any previous audited financial statements of the Company.

# 3    Finance

**3.1    Capital commitments**

3.1.1    No commitments on capital account were outstanding at the Balance Sheet Date and, since then, the Company has not made, or agreed to make capital expenditure, incurred or agreed to incur capital commitments, or disposed of or agreed to dispose of capital assets (or any interest in them).

**3.2    Bank and other borrowings**

3.2.1    Particulars of all money borrowed by the Company are set out in the Disclosure Letter. The Company does not have any bank borrowings which exceed applicable overdraft limits (and has not had any that have done so during the last 12 months).

3.2.2    The total amount borrowed by the Company (as determined in accordance with the provisions of the relevant documents) does not exceed any limitation on borrowing powers contained in its articles of association or in a debenture or other document.

3.2.3    The Company does not have outstanding nor has it agreed to create or issue any loan capital nor has it factored or discounted its debts or engaged in financing of a type which would not require to be shown or fully reflected in the Accounts or borrowed money which it has not repaid, save for borrowings not exceeding the amounts shown in the Accounts.

3.2.4    The Company has not since the Balance Sheet Date repaid or become liable to repay any loan or other indebtedness in advance of its stated maturity.

3.2.5    The Company has not received notice (whether formal or informal) from any lenders of money, requiring repayment or intimating the enforcement of security which it holds over assets of the Company; and there are no circumstances likely to give rise to such a notice.

**3.3    Bank accounts**

3.3.1    Statements of all the bank accounts of the Company, showing their balances as at a date not more than seven days before today's date, have been supplied to the Purchaser.

3.3.2    Since the date of each statement, there have been no payments out of the account to which the statement relates, except for payments in the normal course of business; and the balances on current accounts are not substantially different from the balances shown in the statements.

**3.4     Continuation of facilities**

3.4.1     The Disclosure Letter sets out full details of (and there are attached to it accurate copies of all documents relating to) all debentures, acceptance credits, loans or other financial facilities outstanding or available to the Company (referred to in this clause as the "Facilities") and of any limits or restrictions to which they are subject.

3.4.2     There has been no contravention of, or non-compliance with, the terms of the Facilities.

3.4.3     No steps for the early repayment of sums outstanding under the Facilities have been taken or threatened and no circumstances have occurred which give rise to an obligation to make, or would permit the calling for, early repayment.

3.4.4     There have not been and are no circumstances known to the Vendors whereby the continuation of any of the Facilities might be prejudiced or their terms altered.

3.4.5     None of the Facilities is dependent on the guarantee or indemnity of, or security provided by, a third party.

**3.5     Debts**

3.5.1     No part of the amounts included in debtors in the Accounts, or subsequently recorded in the books of the Company as owing by a debtor, is overdue by more than 90 days, has been released on terms that the debtor pays less than the full book value of his debt, has been written off, has had a credit issued against it or has proved to be, or is regarded as, wholly or partly irrecoverable.

3.5.2     The amounts due from debtors as at Completion will be recoverable in full, in the normal course of business, and in any event not later than 60 days after Completion; and none of the debts is subject to a right of counterclaim or set-off, or withholding on other deduction except to the extent of the provision or reserve.

3.5.3     Complete and accurate details, including repayment terms, of loans made by the Company which remain outstanding are set out in the Disclosure Letter and all the loans will be repaid in full by their maturity dates.

3.5.4     The Company has not made a loan or quasi-loan contrary to CA 1985.

3.5.5     The Company has not made a loan, which remains outstanding, on terms entitling it to receive either a rate of interest varying with, or a share of, the profits of a business.

**3.6     Liabilities**

3.6.1     The Company has no outstanding liabilities (including disputed or contingent liabilities) other than the liabilities disclosed in the Accounts or incurred, in the normal course of business, since the Balance Sheet Date.

3.6.2     The Company has not been the tenant of, or a guarantor in respect of, a leasehold property which is not one of the Properties.

3.6.3    There has been no exercise, purported exercise or claim for any Encumbrance over any of the assets of the Company and there is no dispute directly or indirectly relating to any assets.

### 3.7    Working capital

3.7.1    Having regard to the Facilities (as defined in clause [3.4.1]), the Company has sufficient working capital to carry on its business, in its present form and at its present level of turnover, for 12 months after Completion and to carry out, in accordance with their terms, all outstanding commitments.

### 3.8    Dividends and distributions

3.8.1    Since the Balance Sheet Date, no dividend or other distribution (as defined in ICTA 1988, Part VI and s.418) has been, or is treated as having been, declared, paid or made by the Company.

3.8.2    All dividends and distributions declared, made or paid by the Company were declared, made or paid in accordance with its articles of association and the applicable provisions of CA 1985 and in accordance with any agreements or arrangements between the Company, its shareholders or any third party regulating the payment or declaration of dividends.

### 3.9    Government grants

3.9.1    No Group Company has in the last 6 years applied for, or received, a grant, subsidy or financial assistance from any government department or agency, or a local or other authority.

## 4    Trading and contracts

### 4.1    Changes in business activities and financial position since the Balance Sheet Date

4.1.1    Since the Balance Sheet Date:

4.1.1.1    the business of the Company has been continued in its normal course with a view to maintaining the businesses as a going concern and without entering into any transaction assuming any liability or making any payment which is not provided for in the Accounts or which is not in the normal course of its business;

4.1.1.2    there has been no deterioration in the turnover, or financial or trading position or prospects, of the Company;

4.1.1.3    the Company has not by doing, or omitting to do, anything prejudiced its goodwill;

4.1.1.4    the Company has not entered into any capital transaction as seller, purchaser, lessor or lessee or otherwise undertaken any material commitment on its capital account;

4.1.1.5    of the plant, machinery, fixtures, fittings, equipment, vehicles, furniture, property, materials and other assets (not being included in the current assets) included in the Accounts or acquired by the Company since the Balance Sheet Date:

4.1.1.5.1 none has been sold or disposed of at a figure lower than book value or an open market arm's length value whichever is the higher;

4.1.1.5.2 none has been or has been agreed to be let on hire or hire purchase or sold on deferred terms; and

4.1.1.6 the Company has paid its creditors in accordance with their respective credit terms; and there are no amounts owing by it which have been due for more than 60 days.

4.1.2 The value of the net realisable assets of the Company is not less than at the Balance Sheet Date.

## 4.2 Vendors' other interests and liabilities

4.2.1 The Vendors and their Associates are not, directly or indirectly, interested in any business, other than that now carried on by the Company, which is or is likely to be competitive with the business of the Company, apart from interests in securities listed on the London Stock Exchange, or dealt in on its alternative investment market, and in respect of which the Vendors, with their Associates, are interested in less than three per cent of any class of the securities in that company.

4.2.2 None of the Vendors, or their Associates, is indebted to the Company.

## 4.3 Effect of sale of Shares

4.3.1 The Vendors are not aware, and have no grounds for believing, that after Completion (whether by reason of an existing agreement or arrangement or as a result of the acquisition of the Company by the Purchaser):

4.3.1.1 a supplier of the Company will cease, or be entitled to cease, supplying it or may substantially reduce its level of supplies;

4.3.1.2 a customer of the Company will cease, or be entitled to cease, to deal with it or may substantially reduce its level of business;

4.3.1.3 a supplier or customer of the Company will seek to impose or negotiate materially different terms of trading from those currently enjoyed by the Company;

4.3.1.4 the Company will lose a right or benefit which it enjoys; or

4.3.1.5 any officer or senior employee of the Company will leave its employment.

4.3.2 Compliance with this Agreement will not:

4.3.2.1 breach or constitute a default under an agreement or arrangement to which the Company is a party, or any provision of the memorandum or articles of association of the Company, or any security interest, lease, contract or order, judgment, award, injunction, regulation or other restriction or obligation of any kind affecting the Company;

4.3.2.2　relieve any person from any obligation to the Company (whether contractual or otherwise), or enable any person to determine any such obligation or any right or benefit enjoyed by the Company, or to exercise a right in respect of the Company;

4.3.2.3　result in any present or future indebtedness of the Company becoming, or becoming capable of being declared, due and payable prior to its stated maturity or loan facilities being withdrawn; or

4.3.2.4　result in the creation, imposition, crystallisation or enforcement of any Encumbrance on any of the assets of the Company.

## 4.4　Business conducted properly

4.4.1　The Company has carried on business and conducted its affairs in compliance with CA 1985 and all other statutory obligations and in accordance with its memorandum and articles of association and all other documents to which it is, or has been, a party.

4.4.2　The Company has the power and is duly qualified to carry on business in all jurisdictions in which it carries on business.

## 4.5　Joint ventures and partnerships

4.5.1　The Company is not, nor has it agreed to become, a party in or member of a joint venture, consortium, partnership or other unincorporated association or other profit or income sharing arrangement.

## 4.6　Agency agreements and agreements restricting business

4.6.1　The Company is not a party to an agency, distributorship, marketing, purchasing, manufacturing or licensing agreement or arrangement, or a restrictive agreement or arrangement, under which part of its business is carried on or which restricts its freedom to carry on its business as it thinks fit.

4.6.2　The Company is not subject to any undertaking or assurance which it has given to a court or government agency which is still in force.

## 4.7　Unfair trade and restrictive practices

4.7.1　The Company is not nor has it been a party to or concerned in any agreement, practice or arrangement (whether legally binding or not) which is or was:

4.7.1.1　in contravention of the Trade Descriptions Act 1968;

4.7.1.2　in contravention of the Fair Trading Act 1973, Part XI as amended by the Trading Schemes Act 1996;

4.7.1.3　in contravention of the Consumer Credit Act 1974;

4.7.1.4　in contravention of or invalidated (in whole or in part) by, the Competition Act 1998;

4.7.1.5　in contravention of the Enterprise Act 2002;

4.7.1.6　in contravention of the Treaty of Rome; or

4.7.1.7 in contravention of any regulations, orders, notices or directions made thereunder, or otherwise registerable, unenforceable or void or renders the Company or any of its officers liable to administrative, civil or criminal proceedings under any anti-trust, anti-monopoly or anti-cartel, trade regulation or similar legislation or regulation in any jurisdiction where the Company carries on business.

## 4.8 Litigation

4.8.1 Neither the Company nor any person for whose acts or defaults the Company is or may be vicariously liable are engaged in litigation, arbitration, administrative or criminal proceedings; there are no proceedings pending or threatened, either by or against the Company or such persons; and there is nothing which is likely to give rise to such proceedings.

4.8.2 The Company is not subject to any order or judgment given by any court or governmental agency (local or national).

4.8.3 There are no claims pending or threatened or capable of arising against the Company by an employee or workman or third party in respect of any accident or injury which are not fully covered by valid insurance.

4.8.4 There is no dispute with any government (local or national) or agency or body acting on behalf of such government or other authority in the United Kingdom or elsewhere in relation to the affairs of the Company and there are no facts or circumstances which may give rise to such a dispute.

4.8.5 Neither the Company nor any current or former employee, officer or agent of the Company has been convicted of an offence in relation to the Company and no employee or officer has been convicted of an offence that reflects upon the reputation of the Company or their suitability for holding the position that they hold in the Company.

## 4.9 Winding-up

4.9.1 The Company is not insolvent or unable to pay its debts within the meaning of the Insolvency Act 1986, s.123 (the references in that section to proving to the satisfaction of the court being disregarded).

4.9.2 No order has been made, petition presented or resolution passed for the winding-up of the Company; no distress, execution or other process has been levied and remains undischarged in respect of the Company; and there is no outstanding judgment or court order against the Company in connection with the same nor has any application been made for the making of an administration order or notice of intention to appoint an administrator been filed at court, or served on a creditor with the benefit of a floating charge.

4.9.3 No steps have been taken for the appointment of an administrator or administrative receiver or receiver over the whole or any part of the Company's assets or undertaking.

4.9.4 No event analogous to those described in clauses [4.9.2] or [4.9.3] has occurred outside England.

4.9.5 No floating charge created by the Company has crystallised and there are no circumstances likely to cause such a floating charge to crystallise.

### 4.10    Compliance with statutes

4.10.1    Neither the Company nor any of its officers, agents or employees (during the course of their duties), have done or omitted to do anything, the doing or omitting of which is, or could be, in contravention of a statute, regulation or the like giving rise to a penalty, default proceedings or other liability.

### 4.11    Documents stamped

4.11.1    All documents which affect the title or interest of the Company to or in any of its assets, or to which the Company is a party, have been duly stamped.

4.11.2    There is no document held outside the United Kingdom which, if brought within the United Kingdom, would result in the Company incurring a liability to pay stamp duty.

### 4.12    Business names

4.12.1    The Company does not make use of any name other than its corporate name.

### 4.13    Transactions involving directors

4.13.1    The Company has not been a party to a transaction to which CA 1985, ss.320 or 330 might apply.

### 4.14    Powers of attorney and authorites

4.14.1    No powers of attorney or authorities (express or implied) by which a person may enter into a contract or incur an obligation on behalf of the Company are subsisting.

### 4.15    Licences and consents

4.15.1    The Company has all necessary licences and consents required for the proper carrying on of its business in the manner in which the business is now carried on (short particulars of each licence and consent being set out in the Disclosure Letter).

4.15.2    The Company is not in breach of any of the terms and conditions of any licence or consent; all licences and consents are effective and there is nothing that might prejudice the continuation or renewal of a licence or consent.

4.15.3    The Company does not carry on investment business within the meaning of the Financial Services and Markets Act 2000.

### 4.16    Subsisting contracts

4.16.1    The Company is not party to any agreement or arrangement which:

4.16.1.1    is of an unusual nature or was entered into outside the normal course of business;

4.16.1.2    is for a fixed term of more than six months or for an indefinite term which is incapable of termination by it in accordance with its terms on not more than 60 days' notice;

4.16.1.3    is of a long-term nature (that is, unlikely to have been fully performed, in accordance with its terms, within six months after the date on which it was entered into);

4.16.1.4   is of a loss-making nature (that is, known to be likely to result in a loss to the Company on completion of performance);

4.16.1.5   cannot readily be performed by it on time without undue or unusual expenditure or application of money, effort or personnel;

4.16.1.6   involves payment by it by reference to fluctuations in the index of retail prices, or other index, or in the rate of exchange for a currency;

4.16.1.7   involves an aggregated outstanding expenditure by it of more than £[ ];

4.16.1.8   involves, or is likely to involve, the supply of goods or services the aggregate sales value of which will be more than 10 per cent of its turnover for the preceding financial year;

4.16.1.9   is a contract for hire or rent, hire purchase or purchase by way of credit sale or periodical payment;

4.16.1.10   can be terminated as a result of a change in the control of the Company; or

4.16.1.11   involves, or is likely to involve, other obligations or liabilities which ought reasonably to be made known to an intending purchaser of the Shares.

4.16.2   The Company has made all payments due under all contracts to which it is a party and observed and performed all conditions thereof.

4.16.3   The Company is not, nor will it with lapse of time become, in default of any obligation and no threat or claim of default under any agreement, instrument or arrangement to which it is a party has been made and there is nothing whereby any such agreement, instrument or arrangement may be prematurely terminated or rescinded by another party or whereby the terms may be worsened to the Company's detriment.

## 4.17   Other parties' default

4.17.1   No party to an agreement with the Company is in default, being a default which would be material in the context of the Company's financial or trading position; and there are no circumstances likely to give rise to a default.

## 4.18   Outstanding offers

4.18.1   No offer or tender is outstanding which is capable of being converted into an obligation of the Company by acceptance or some other act of another person.

## 4.19   Defective products

4.19.1   The Company has not manufactured, sold or supplied products which were, are or will become, in a material respect faulty or defective, or which do not comply in a material respect with warranties or representations expressly or impliedly made by it and all applicable regulations, standards and requirements in respect thereof.

4.19.2   The Company has not given any guarantee or warranty or made any representation in respect of goods or services supplied or contracted to be supplied by it save for any warranty or guarantee implied by law and (save as aforesaid) has not accepted any obligation which could give rise to any liability after any such goods or services have been supplied by it.

4.19.3 The Company has not received notification that any products supplied by it are defective or unfit and no circumstances exist which could give rise to such a claim.

4.19.4 The Company has not received a prohibition notice, a notice to warn or a suspension notice under the Consumer Protection Act 1987.

**4.20 Service liabilities**

4.20.1 The Company is not obliged (save as implied by law) to repair, maintain, take back or otherwise do or not do anything in respect of goods that have been, or will be, delivered by it.

**4.21 Purchases and sales from or to one party**

4.21.1 The Company does not obtain or make more than 25 per cent of the aggregate amount of its purchases from, and not more than 25 per cent of the aggregate amount of its sales to, the same supplier or customer (including a person connected with the supplier or customer); and no material source of supply to the Company, or material outlet for the sales of a the Company, is in jeopardy.

**4.22 Data protection**

4.22.1 The Company has, if so required by law, a current entry in the register maintained by the Information Commissioner under the Data Protection Act 1998 which complies with the requirements of that Act, and particulars of the entry are set out in the Disclosure Letter.

4.22.2 The Company has not carried out nor does it intend to carry out assessable processing within the terms of the Data Protection Act 1998.

4.22.3 The Company has complied with the data protection principles applicable to all the processing of personal data carried out by it and collected, processed and disclosed personal data only in accordance with the terms of a privacy policy, details of which are set out in the Disclosure Letter.

4.22.4 The Company has not carried out nor does it plan to carry out any processing of sensitive personal data in respect of which it does not have grounds under the Data Protection Act 1998, Schedules 2 or 3.

4.22.5 Where the Company uses a data processor to carry out the processing of personal data, the processor has provided sufficient guarantees in relation to security measures and compliance with those measures and there is in existence a written contract between the Company and the data processor which complies with the requirements of principle 7 and the Data Protection Act 1998, Part 2, Schedule 1, paragraphs 9–12.

4.22.6 The Company does not transfer personal data to jurisdictions outside the European Economic Area.

4.22.7 No individual has claimed or taken or has right to claim compensation or take action for breach of his rights, including actions for rectification or other remedy in respect of inaccurate personal data, against the Company under the Data Protection Act 1998 and the Company has not received any notice, letter or complaint alleging a breach of data protection legislation.

4.22.8   The Company has complied with all other requirements of the Data Protection Act 1998 and all subordinate legislation, guidance and codes of practice.

### 4.23   Guarantees and indemnities

4.23.1   There is no subsisting guarantee or agreement for indemnity or suretyship given by, or for the accommodation of, the Company.

### 4.24   Insider contracts

4.24.1   The Company is not, nor has it during the past three years been, a party to an agreement or arrangement (whether legally binding or not) in which a Vendor, or Associate of a Vendor, or director of the Company, or Associate of a director of the Company, is or has been interested.

4.24.2   The Company is not a party to, and its profits and financial position during the past three years have not been affected by, an agreement or arrangement (whether legally binding or not) which is not of an arms' length nature.

4.24.3   None of the Company's assets have been acquired for a consideration other than market value (at the time of acquisition).

### 4.25   Sensitive payments

4.25.1   No officer or employee of the Company has made or received any Sensitive Payment in connection with any contract or otherwise.

### 4.26   Consultants' reports

4.26.1   No financial or management consultants have, within the past three years, given a report in relation to the Company.

## 5   Environmental

### 5.1   Required licences

5.1.1   The Company has obtained all Environmental Licences which it requires and has complied with all applicable Environmental Laws and with the terms and conditions of the Environmental Licences and there is no reason why the Environmental Licences should not continue to be complied with. True copies of such Environmental Licences are attached to the Disclosure Letter.

### 5.2   Breaches

5.2.1   The Company has not received notification or communication from which it appears it is, or may be alleged to be, in violation of any Environmental Laws or Environmental Licences or that any Environmental Licences may be subject to modification, suspension, revocation or appeal and there are no circumstances likely to give rise to violation, modification, suspension, revocation or appeal.

**5.3 Audits and surveys**

5.3.1 The Company has disclosed all environmental audits and surveys in relation to the Properties or land previously owned or occupied by it.

**5.4 Prosecutions**

5.4.1 The Company has not been prosecuted or notified of a possible prosecution for a breach of any Environmental Laws.

**5.5 No claims**

5.5.1 No Environmental Claims exist against the Company or have been made within the previous [ ] years and there are no circumstances which may lead to a claim.

**5.6 Hazardous Substances**

5.6.1 Neither the Company nor any other person has deposited, used, treated, kept, disposed of, released or emitted any Hazardous Substances at, on, from or under any of the Properties now or previously owned, leased, occupied or controlled by the Company.

**5.7 Notices**

5.7.1 No notices under Environmental Laws have been served against the Company and no work has been carried out under a notice by a regulatory body whereby the Company must reimburse the regulatory body for the costs of the work carried out.

**5.8 Prior use**

5.8.1 The Group Company is not aware that there has been any potentially contaminative use that has been made of any of the Properties or any land previously owned or occupied by the Company.

## 6 Employment

**6.1 Employees and terms of employment**

6.1.1 The Disclosure Letter contains accurate and complete particulars of the identities, dates of birth, dates of commencement of employment or appointment to office, and terms of employment or appointment of all the employees and officers of the Company, including details of all remuneration (including pensions, whether to be delivered by occupational or personal schemes) and other benefits, such as profit sharing, commission and bonus arrangements (whether or not contractual), sufficient to allow the financial obligations of the Company to be ascertained.

6.1.2 There is no contract of service between the Company and a director or employee for which approval was required but not obtained under CA 1985, s.319.

6.1.3 There are no contracts for services (including without limitation consultancy agreements) between the Company and any individual.

6.1.4 No employee of the Company who has or may have a statutory or contractual right to return to work, is absent on maternity leave, paternity leave, parental leave, adoption leave or other leave of absence. No employee of the Company is absent on sick leave which has or is expected to last longer than 4 weeks.

6.1.5   No employee or former employee of the Company has or may have a right to be reinstated or re-engaged under the Employment Rights Act 1996.

## 6.2   Claims and potential employee claims

6.2.1   There are no outstanding claims nor are there any potential claims against the Company by any person who is now or has been an officer or employee of the Company and no liability has been incurred and remains undischarged for breach of any employment contract or for redundancy payments (including protective awards) or for damages or compensation for wrongful dismissal or unfair dismissal or otherwise or for failure to comply with any order for the reinstatement or re-engagement of any person.

6.2.2   There have not within the period of 12 months prior to the date of this Agreement been any claims under the provisions of the Employment Rights Act 1996, the Trade Union Reform and Employment Act 1993, the Health and Safet at Work etc. Act 1974, the Equal Pay Act 1970, the Sex Discrimination Act 1975, the Disability Discrimination Act 1995, the Race Relations Act 1976, the Gender Reassignment Regulations 1999, the Transfer of Undertakings (Protection of Employment) Regulations 1981, the Trade Union and Labour Relations (Consolidation) Act 1992, the Protection from Harassment Act 1997, s.3, the Working Time Regulations 1998, the National Minimum Wage Act 1998, the Employment Relations Act 1999, the Part-Time Workers (Prevention of Less Favourable Treatment) Regulations 2000, the Fixed-Term Employees (Prevention of Less Favourable Treatment) Regulations 2002, the Employment Act 2002, the Employment Equality (Religion or Belief) Regulations 2003 or the Employment Equality (Sexual Orientation) Regulations 2003 relating to any employee or former employee of the Company nor are there any circumstances which are likely to give rise to such claims.

6.2.3   The Company has performed all obligations required to be performed by it in respect of its officers and employees whether arising under contract, statute, at common law or in equity including, without limitation, all obligations arising under the Working Time Regulations 1998 and all obligations under all health and safety legislation.

6.2.4   The Company has paid to the Inland Revenue and to any other appropriate Taxation Authority all taxes, national insurance contributions and other levies due in respect of the employment of the employees of the Company.

6.2.5   There are no enquiries or investigations existing, pending or threatened in relation to the Company by the Equal Opportunities Commission, the Commission for Racial Equality or the Disability Rights Commission.

## 6.3   Changes in remuneration

6.3.1   During the period to which the Accounts relate and since the Balance Sheet Date or (where employment or holding of office commenced after the beginning of the period) since the commencement date of the employment or holding of office:

6.3.1.1    no change has been made in the rate of remuneration, or the emoluments of employment or pension benefits, of any officer, ex-officer or senior executive of the Company (a senior executive being a person in receipt of remuneration in excess of £[ ] per annum); and

6.3.1.2    no change has been made in the other terms of employment of any officer or senior executive.

6.3.2    No agreement has been reached with any officers, employees, trade union or other body representing employees that will or may on a future date result in any changes to the terms and conditions of employment of any of the officers or employees of the Company (including without limitation for any increase in the remuneration or enhancement of the emoluments of employment or pension benefits of such person); and no negotiation relating to the terms and conditions of employment of any officer or employee of the Company (including without limitation for any increase in the rate of remuneration or enhancement of the emoluments of employment or pension benefits of such person) are current or likely to take place within the next six months.

**6.4    Bonus and share option schemes**

6.4.1    There are no schemes (whether contractual or discretionary) in operation by or in relation to the Company under which any employee or director of the Company is entitled to any shares in the Company or to any bonus, profit share, commission or remuneration of any other sort (whether calculated by reference to the whole or part of the turnover, profits/losses or sales of the Company or otherwise).

6.4.2    The Company is not under any legal or moral obligation to make nor is it accustomed to making any bonus payments to or for the benefit of any officer or employee of the Company.

**6.5    Termination of contracts of employment**

6.5.1    All subsisting employment contracts to which the Company is a party are determinable at any time on three months' notice or less without compensation (other than compensation for unfair dismissal in accordance with the Employment Rights Act 1996).

6.5.2    No employee of the Company, who is in receipt of remuneration in excess of £[ ] per annum, and no officer of the Company has given or received notice terminating his employment, except as expressly contemplated in this Agreement and no such employee or officer will be entitled or, so far as the Vendors are aware, is likely to leave his employment or office prematurely, nor to receive any payment from the Company as a result of the sale of the Shares.

**6.6    Industrial relations**

6.6.1    The Company does not recognise any trade unions, works or staff councils or associates of trade unions and there are no collective agreements or other agreements (whether or not legally binding and whether in writing or arising by virtue of custom or practice) between the Company and any trade union or other body representing employees.

6.6.2     The Company has not done anything which might be construed as recognition of a trade union and has not received an application for recognition from a trade union.

6.6.3     Neither the Company nor any of its employees is or has been in the last two years involved in an industrial dispute and so far as the Vendors are aware there is nothing which might suggest that there may be an industrial dispute involving the Company, or that this Agreement may lead to an industrial dispute.

### 6.7     Redundancies

6.7.1     No employee of the Company will become redundant and be entitled to a redundancy payment as a result of this Agreement.

6.7.2     There is no plan, scheme or commitment or established practice relating to the termination of employment affecting an employee or officer of the Company which is more generous than the statutory redundancy entitlement or such sum as may be properly payable by way of damages for breach of contract.

## 7     Pensions

### 7.1     Full particulars

7.1.1     Full particulars of the retirement benefits scheme ("the Scheme"), of which the employees of the Company are entitled to become members, have been disclosed in writing to the Purchaser including the governing trust deeds, rules, announcements, explanatory literature, details of assets held by the Scheme, insurance policies and contracts, funding arrangements, current membership list and the latest actuarial report.

### 7.2     Trustees

7.2.1     The persons named in the Disclosure Letter as the trustees of the Scheme are all its present trustees and not less than one third of the trustees are member-nominated trustees appointed in accordance with the provisions of the Pensions Act 1995, s.16 and the regulations made under it.

### 7.3     Pensions Act 1995

7.3.1     No order under the Pensions Act 1995, s.3 has been made in respect of any trustee of the Scheme nor has any trustee been requested to pay any penalty under s.10.

### 7.4     Appointments

7.4.1     The trustees of the Scheme have made written appointments of an auditor, an actuary, a fund manager, a legal adviser and any other professional adviser whose appointment is required to be made under the Pensions Act 1995, s.47 and do not rely upon the advice of an adviser not appointed by them in relation to the Scheme.

**7.5    Books and records**

7.5.1    The trustees of the Scheme have complied with the requirements of the Pensions Act 1995, s.49 and regulations made
under it for the keeping of accounts, books and records in
relation to the Scheme.

**7.6    Details of the Scheme**

7.6.1    The Scheme is

7.6.1.1    a defined contribution Scheme;

7.6.1.2    contracted out for the purposes of the Pension
Schemes Act 1993, Part III and the Pensions Act
1995; and

7.6.1.3    an exempt approved scheme within the meaning of
ICTA 1988, Chapter 1, Part XIV and there is no
reason why approval may be withdrawn.

**7.7    No other obligations**

7.7.1    Save in accordance with the terms of the Scheme the Company does not have any obligation (whether or not legally
binding) to pay or provide or secure the provision of a pension
or other payment on retirement or disability or after death or
otherwise to provide relevant benefits within the meaning of
ICTA 1988, Part XIV in respect of a person who is now or has
been an officer or employee of the Company.

**7.8    Members**

7.8.1    No persons other than employees of the Company are or are
entitled to be active members of the Scheme.

**7.9    Contributions paid**

7.9.1    All contributions payable by the Company and every other
participating employer in accordance with the terms of the
Scheme in order to secure or provide for the benefits for and
in respect of members (including pensioners, deferred members and other persons prospectively or contingently entitled
to benefit under it) have been duly paid to the Scheme.

**7.10    Schedule of contributions**

7.10.1    The trustees of the Scheme have prepared and maintained and
have revised from time to time (as appropriate) a schedule of
contributions of the nature required by the Pensions Act 1995,
s.58 and all contributions due from members of the Scheme
have been duly paid to the Scheme at the rate stipulated by its
actuary (and in accordance with the schedule of contributions)
as being required to fund the benefits to be provided by the
Scheme on the basis of the actuarial method and assumptions
used by the actuary in the most recent actuarial valuation of
the Scheme.

**7.11    Assets sufficient**

7.11.1    The investments or policies or other assets held by the Trustees of the Scheme are sufficient to meet in full all the
liabilities and obligations (current, future and contingent)
which the Scheme has to its members, the value or amount of
the assets, liabilities and obligations have been calculated in
accordance with the actuarial assumptions in, and are held

pursuant to, an investment policy formulated in accordance with, a written statement of principles governing decisions about investments for the purposes of the Scheme in compliance with the Pensions Act 1995, s.35 which has been prepared, maintained and from time to time revised as required by that section.

### 7.12 Maintenance of funding

7.12.1   The combined contribution rates of the Company and all other participating employers and its and their respective employees are sufficient to maintain the funding of the Scheme at a level which satisfies the minimum funding requirements of the Pensions Act 1995, ss.56–57 and will secure the benefits to which the members are entitled under the Scheme.

### 7.13 Employer-related investments

7.13.1   The assets of the Scheme do not include employer-related investments (as defined in the Pensions Act 1995, s.40).

### 7.14 Discontinuance of the Scheme

7.14.1   In the event of the discontinuance of the Scheme before, at or within six months after Completion, the assets of the Scheme (valued in such a manner as to represent their realisable cash value, taking account where appropriate of surrender penalties) will be of such a value that they will be sufficient to secure in full all benefits accrued due under it up to the date of the discontinuance by purchase of deferred annuity policies on a full buy-out basis.

### 7.15 Scheme surpluses or refunds

7.15.1   No refunds of surplus have been made to and no contribution holidays have been taken for the benefit of the Company or any other person in relation to the Scheme.

### 7.16 Latest actuarial valuation

7.16.1   Certified copies of the latest actuarial valuation of and report on the Scheme (being that dated [ ]) and of the latest accounts of the Scheme (being those made up to [ ]) have been delivered to the Purchaser and individually and together give a true and fair view of the state and method of funding of the Scheme and do not contain any material errors or omissions.

### 7.17 Proposed amendments to the Scheme

7.17.1   No proposal has been announced by the Company either:

7.17.1.1   to modify, amend, alter or improve the Scheme which proposal remains outstanding and has not been formally implemented (by deed) (in whole or in part); or

7.17.1.2   regarding its continuation, closure to new members, closure to new benefit accruals, discontinuance or winding-up.

### 7.18 No other changes prior to Completion

7.18.1   The Scheme will not be modified, amended, altered or improved before Completion; no winding-up of the Scheme will be commenced; it will not be wound up or terminated or cease to admit new members on or before Completion; and the Trustees of the Scheme have undertaken in writing to refer and apply to the Purchaser at and from Completion in respect of all aspects of the Scheme.

### 7.19    Scheme operated properly

7.19.1    The Scheme has been operated and administered in accordance with:

7.19.1.1    the preservation requirements contained in the Pension Schemes Act 1993, Part IV;

7.19.1.2    the equal treatment requirements identified in the Pensions Act 1995, ss.62–66;

7.19.1.3    the equal pay provisions of the Treaty of Rome; and

7.19.1.4    all applicable laws and the documents constituting and governing it (including notices, announcements and explanatory literature and the contracting out requirements of the Pension Schemes Act 1993) and all decisions made by the Trustees of the Scheme have been made in accordance with their powers and duties as Trustees of the Scheme.

### 7.20    Discretions and powers

7.20.1    No discretion or power has been exercised under the Scheme in respect of a member (where active, deferred or a pensioner) (or a beneficiary claiming through or under a member) to:

7.20.1.1    augment benefits under it;

7.20.1.2    admit to membership of it as a director or employee who would not otherwise have been eligible for admission to membership;

7.20.1.3    provide under it in respect of a member a benefit which would not otherwise be provided under it in respect of the member; or

7.20.1.4    pay a contribution to it which would not otherwise have been paid;

and no undertaking assurance or intimation has been given pursuant to which discretion or power will or may be exercised.

### 7.21    Augmentation of benefits

7.21.1    No augmentation of benefits has been made under the Scheme and no additional benefits have been granted without the actuary's confirmation in each case that such augmentation or addition can be borne by the Scheme within the existing funding rate without detriment to the benefits of other members or the payment of any additional contributions which the actuary deems necessary to secure such augmented or additional benefits.

### 7.22    No disputes

7.22.1    No claim:

7.22.1.1    for benefits under the Scheme has been refused by the Trustees or has been the subject of dispute or delay in settlement or reduction in amount or value paid or payable below that claimed; or

7.22.1.2     has been made or threatened against the Company or the Trustees or administrators (if different) of the Scheme or against any other person whom the Company or any of the Trustees of the Scheme is or may be liable to indemnify or compensate in connection with the Scheme (other than routine claims for benefits) and the Vendors are not aware of any circumstances which may give rise to claim.

## 7.23    Lump sum benefits insured

7.23.1    All lump sum death in service benefits which may be payable under the Scheme are fully insured and all premiums due to respect of such insurance have been paid.

## 7.24    Charges paid

7.24.1    All actuarial, constancy, legal and other charges in respect of the Scheme, whether payable by the Company or by the Trustees, have been paid and no services have been rendered in respect of the Scheme in relation to which an account or other invoice has not been rendered.

## 7.25    Employee membership

7.25.1    The Company offers Scheme membership to all its employees (part time, full time, fixed term and permanent) and all employees who have accepted offers to participate in the Scheme have been duly admitted to participation in the Scheme and the Company has fulfilled in all material respects its obligations under it.

## 7.26    Members' data

7.26.1    The membership data in respect of the Scheme for active members, deferred pensioners and pensioners was when given and remains complete and accurate in all material respects.

## 7.27    Debts arising

7.27.1    The Company is not nor has it been an employer (as defined in the Pensions Act 1995, s.124(1)) in relation to an occupational pension scheme (as defined in s.176) (not being a money purchase scheme) in respect of which a relevant insolvency event (as described in s.75(4)) has occurred; or if earlier, which has commenced winding-up.

## 7.28    Pensions Act liabilities

7.28.1    There are no liabilities which, under the Pensions Act 1995, s.75, can be imposed on the Company as a debt due from it to the trustees of an occupational pension scheme in which the Company has participated as an employer (within the definition thereof in s.124(1)).

## 7.29    No Occupational Pensions Regulatory Authority reports

7.29.1    No report in relation to the Scheme has been made to the Occupational Pensions Regulatory Authority under of the

Pensions Act 1995, s.48 and no circumstances exist in which it would be appropriate for a report to be made.

## 8 Assets

### 8.1 Ownership of assets

8.1.1 At the Balance Sheet Date the Company owned (free from options, charges, liens or Encumbrances) and (except for current assets subsequently sold or realised in the normal course of business) still owns all the assets included in the Accounts and all assets acquired since the Balance Sheet Date and not subsequently sold or realised as above.

8.1.2 The Company has not created or granted, or agreed to create or grant, any Encumbrance in respect of any of the fixed assets included in the Accounts, or acquired or agreed to be acquired since the Balance Sheet Date, except in the normal course of business.

### 8.2 Assets sufficient for the business

8.2.1 The assets owned by the Company, together with the Intellectual Property Rights and assets held under the hire purchase, leasing and rental agreements listed in the Disclosure Letter, comprise all assets necessary for the continuation of its business as now carried on, and no assets are shared with another person.

### 8.3 Stocks and work in progress

8.3.1 The stocks of raw materials, packaging materials and finished goods held by the Company are not excessive and are adequate in relation to its current trading requirements and, save where written down or provided for, none of such stock is obsolete, slow moving, unusable, in poor condition, defective, unmarketable or inappropriate or of limited value in relation to the current business of the Company.

8.3.2 The work in progress of the Company is adequate to maintain cash flow and profitability at a level not less than as disclosed in the Disclosure Letter.

8.3.3 The stock in trade of the Company is in good condition and is capable of being sold by it in the normal course of its business in accordance with its current price list, without rebate or allowance to a purchaser.

### 8.4 Insurance

8.4.1 All the assets of the Company of an insurable nature are, and have at all material times been, insured in amounts representing their full replacement or reinstatement value against fire and other risks normally insured against by persons carrying on similar businesses or owning property of a similar nature.

8.4.2 The Company is, and has at all material times been, adequately insured against accident, damage, third party loss (including product liability), loss of profits and other risks normally insured against by persons carrying on the same type of business as that carried on by it.

8.4.3 Nothing has been done or omitted or has occurred which could make a policy of insurance taken out by the Company void or voidable or which is likely to result in an increase in premium.

8.4.4    None of the insurance policies is subject to special or unusual terms or restrictions or to the payment of a premium in excess of the normal rate.

8.4.5    No claim is outstanding, threatened or may be made, under any of the policies and no circumstances exist which could give rise to a claim.

## 8.5    Leased assets

8.5.1    Nothing has occurred or is likely to occur in relation to an asset held by the Company, under a lease or similar agreement, whereby the rental payable has been, or is likely to be, increased.

## 8.6    Plant in working order

8.6.1    The plant, machinery, vehicles and other equipment used in connection with the business of the Company:

8.6.1.1    are in a good and safe state of repair and satisfactory working order and have been properly serviced and maintained;

8.6.1.2    are not surplus to requirements;

8.6.1.3    are in the possession and control of, and are the absolute unencumbered property of, the Company, except for those items the subject of the hire purchase, leasing or rental agreements listed in the Disclosure Letter, and in respect of each of which the outstanding payments do not exceed £[ ]; and

8.6.1.4    are not expected to require replacements or additions at a cost in excess of £[ ] within the next six months.

8.6.2    There are maintenance contracts with independent specialist contractors in respect of all assets of the Company for which it is normal or prudent to have maintenance agreements and in respect of all assets which the Company is obliged to maintain or repair under a lease or similar agreement.

## 8.7    Intellectual Property Rights

8.7.1    Full details of all Intellectual Property Rights (registered and unregistered) owned or used by the Company are set out in the Disclosure Letter and are complete and accurate. The Intellectual Property Rights are:

8.7.1.1    used exclusively in the business of the Company;

8.7.1.2    legally and beneficially owned by the Company and not held jointly or in common with any other person;

8.7.1.3    valid, subsisting and enforceable, and nothing has been done or omitted to be done by which they may cease to be valid and enforceable;

8.7.1.4    not subject to infringement, challenge, opposition or attack or the subject of any claim for ownership or compensation by any third party or competent authority and the Vendors know no reason why any of them may be subject to challenge, opposition or attack or claim; and

8.7.1.5     where capable of registration are registered in the name of the Company in all jurisdictions relevant to its business.

8.7.2     The renewal and registration fees for the protection of the registered Intellectual Property Rights of the Company have been paid and all other steps required for their prosecution, maintenance and protection have been taken.

8.7.3     The Vendors are not aware of any factors which would cause any applications for registration of any Intellectual Property Rights to be unacceptable to any body to whom the application is being made.

8.7.4     Copies of the licences of Intellectual Property Rights owned by third parties which have been granted to the Company are attached to the Disclosure Letter. The Company is not in breach of any of the licences and the Vendors are not aware of and have no reason to believe that there is cause for a licence to come to an end or be restricted.

8.7.5     Copies of the licences of Intellectual Property Rights owned by the Company which have been granted to third parties are attached to the Disclosure Letter. The Company is not in breach of any of the licences and the Vendors are not aware and have no reason to believe that there is cause for a licence to come to an end or be restricted.

8.7.6     The Intellectual Property Rights referred to in clause [8.7.1] and the third party Intellectual Property Rights referred to in clause [8.7.3] are all the Intellectual Property Rights necessary for the Company to carry on its business and the Company has not charged or encumbered or created an equity, lien or other adverse interest over any of them or agreed to grant an option, right, licence, sub-licence or other adverse right over any of them to any other person and is not obliged to do the same.

8.7.7     None of the activities of the Company, its products, business methods, processes or services infringe third party Intellectual Property Rights. In the past six years the Company has not been a party or received a threat of litigation or a claim relating to Intellectual Property Rights, passing off or unfair competition. The Vendors are not aware and have no reason to believe that a third party is infringing the Intellectual Property Rights of the Company or that the Company has acquiesced to an infringement.

8.7.8     No licences of Intellectual Property Rights will terminate or become capable of termination or otherwise be adversely affected by this Agreement.

8.7.9     There are no pending or outstanding claims against the Company for compensation under the Patents Act 1977, s.40.

8.7.10     The Confidential Business Information which has been developed by or acquired by the Company has been kept secret and has not been disclosed to or used by another person except under obligations of confidentiality. The Vendors are not aware and have no reason to believe that a third party is in breach of confidentiality obligations.

8.7.11     The Company is not a party to a secrecy agreement or other agreement or arrangement which restricts the use or disclosure of confidential information.

8.7.12 All moral rights in respect of the Company's Intellectual Property Rights have been waived in favour of the Company.

**8.8 Computer Systems**

8.8.1 The Computer Systems:

8.8.1.1 are used exclusively by the Company and under its sole control;

8.8.1.2 are, in respect of the hardware, firmware, peripherals, networking and other equiment comprised in those Computer Systems, legally and beneficially owned by the Company;

8.8.1.3 are in full working order and performing the functions for which they were acquired efficiently and without material errors or downtime;

8.8.1.4 have not, within the two years immediately preceding Completion, unduly interrupted or hindered the operation of the business of the Company;

8.8.1.5 have adequate capacity for the Company's present and (taking into account the extent to which the Computer Systems are expandable) future needs;

8.8.1.6 have been satisfactorily and appropriately maintained and supported and have the benefit of appropriate maintenance and support agreements (copies of which are attached to the Disclosure Letter), which agreements include emergency support;

8.8.1.7 have not been used in such a way as would invalidate any manufacturer's or supplier's guarantee or warranty or entitle the provider of maintenance or support for the Computer Systems to exclude, suspend or terminate those services;

8.8.1.8 have, in conjunction with the support and maintenance agreements referred to in clause [8.8.1.6], adequate security measures, back-up systems, disaster recovery arrangements, measures to protect them from viruses and other harmful code and trained personnel to ensure that so far as reasonably practicable:

8.8.1.8.1 the authenticity, integrity and confidentiality of all data held by or transmitted by the Computer Systems are preserved;

8.8.1.8.2 no more than one day's data would be lost in the event of a failure of the Computer Systems;

8.8.1.8.3 breaches of security, errors and breakdowns are kept to a minimum and that in the event of the occurrence of any such event there will not be a material disruption to the Company;

8.8.1.9 enable all records and data stored by electronic means which relate to the Company to be readily accessible by appropriate personnel;

8.8.1.10 will correctly carry out all calculations relating to or in connection with the Euro and display all symbols adopted by any government or European body in connection with the Euro.

8.8.2 All software used or stored or resident in the Company:

8.8.2.1. is free from any defect or feature which may adversely affect its performance or the performance of any other software in the future;

8.8.2.2. performs in accordance with its specification;

8.8.2.3 has been (if copied) lawfully copied;

8.8.2.4. is lawfully held and does not infringe the Intellectual Property Rights of any person;

8.8.2.5 as to the copyright therein:

8.8.2.5.1 in the case of software written or commissioned by the Company, is owned solely by the Company, no other person has rights therein or rights to use or make copies of the software or source codes;

8.8.2.5.2 in the case of standard packaged software purchased outright, is validly licensed to the Company in perpetuity (other than in the event of breach or insolvency) on written terms which do not require the Company to make any further payments and no licences will terminate on change of control; and

8.8.2.5.3 in the case of all other software, is licensed to the Company on the terms of a written licence which requires payment by the Company of a fixed annual licence fee the terms of which are set out in the Disclosure Letter.

8.8.3 No software owned by or licensed to the Company is licensed or sub-licensed by the Company to (or otherwise used by) any other person.

8.8.4 No action will be necessary to enable the Company to continue to use any software currently used by it to the same extent and in the same manner as it has been used prior to the Completion.

8.8.5 The terms of all software licences have been complied with and no notices of breach or termination have been served on the Company in respect of any such licence.

8.8.6. Details of all Company domain names and websites are set out in the Disclosure Letter. The Company is the registrant and beneficial owner of those domain names and is the legal and beneficial owner of all Intellectual Property Rights in the websites.

# APPENDIX 5

# Warranties and Indemnities on the Sale of a Business

[See paras 8–03, 8–05, 8–12, 8–13, 8–19, 8–31 and 8–32]

## PART 1–DEFINITIONS

In this Agreement, the following expressions have the meanings stated namely:

"Accounts" means the accounts relating to the Business incorporated into the audited financial statements of the Vendor for the accounting reference period ended on the Balance Sheet Date comprising a balance sheet, profit and loss account, notes, the directors' and auditors' reports and cashflow statements a copy of which is attached to the Disclosure Letter.

"Accounting Standards" means SSAPs, FRSs, UITF Abstracts, SORPs and all other generally accepted accounting practices applicable to a United Kingdom company.

"Agreement" means this agreement for the sale and purchase of the Business and Assets.

"Assets" means all the assets and rights of the Business to be purchased by the Purchaser as described in clause [ ].

"Associates" means a Subsidiary or holding company of the Vendor, and any other Subsidiary of a holding company of the Vendor "holding company" bearing the meaning in CA 1985, s.736.

"Balance Sheet Date" means [ ] (being the date as at and to which the Accounts were prepared).

"Benefit" means any pension, lump sum, gratuity or other like benefit given or to be given on retirement or on death, or in anticipation of retirement, or after retirement or death, or to be given on or in anticipation of or in connection with any change in the nature of the service of the employee in question, including (without limitation) the termination of the employment of the employee, or given or to be given on or in connection with the illness, injury or disability of, or suffering of any accident by, an employee.

"Book Debts" means the trade and other debts owed (whether or not due in accordance with any credit terms) to the Vendor at Completion including all securities, guarantees and all other rights in respect of such debts.

"Business" means the business of [ ] carried on by the Vendor at Completion from the Property under the Name and, where the context so admits, includes the Assets and the Goodwill.

"Business Intellectual Property Rights" means all Intellectual Property Rights owned, used, enjoyed, exploited or held for use by the Vendor in, or in connection with, the Business (including those specified in Schedule [ ]).

"CA 1985" means the Companies Act 1985.

"CAA 2001" means the Capital Allowances Act 2001.

"Completion" means completion of the sale and purchase of the Business and Assets.

"Computer Systems" means all hardware, firmware, peripherals, communication links, storage media, networking equipment and other equipment used in conjunction with it together with all Software.

"Contracts" means the Customer Contracts, the Supply Contracts and the Finance Agreements but not the contracts with employees.

"Creditors" means the aggregate amount owed (whether or not due in accordance with any credit terms) by the Vendor in connection with the Business to or in respect of trade or other creditors and accrued costs, expenses and charges as recorded in the books of account of the Business at Completion.

"Customer Contracts" means those orders, engagements or contracts entered into prior to Completion by or on behalf of the Vendor with customers for the sale of goods or provision of services by the Vendor in connection with the Business which remain (in whole or in part) to be performed by the Vendor (other than in relation to warranty or guarantee obligations or commitments of the Vendor) details of which are set out in Schedule [ ].

"Disclosure Letter" means the disclosure letter of today's date from the Vendor to the Purchaser in the agreed form.

"Employees" means the persons listed in part 1 of Schedule [ ].

"Encumbrance" means any encumbrance or security interest of any kind whatsoever including without limitation a mortgage, charge, pledge, lien, hypothecation, restriction, right to acquire, right of pre-emption, option, conversion right, third party right or interest, right of set-off or counterclaim, equity, trust arrangement or any other type of preferential agreement (such as a retention of title arrangement) having similar effect or any other rights exercisable by or claims by third parties.

"Excluded Assets" means any assets of the Business not comprised in the Assets which are to be purchased by the Purchaser under this Agreement including for the avoidance of doubt those assets listed in Schedule [ ].

"Excluded Employees" means the employees listed in part 2 of Schedule [ ].

"Finance Agreements" means hire purchase, conditional sale, hire, rental, leasing or other agreements of a similar type the details of which are set out in Schedule [    ].

"Fixed Assets" means all plant, machinery, tools, equipment, motor vehicles, fixtures and fittings, fixed IT equipment and other chattels on the Property or otherwise owned by the Vendor at Completion for the purposes of the Business listed in Schedule [ ].

"FRS" means a financial reporting standard issue by the Accounting Standards Board Limited.

"IHTA 1984" means the Inheritance Tax Act 1984.

"Intellectual Property Rights" means all copyright, moral rights, design rights, registered designs, database rights, semiconductor topography rights, patents, utility models, business names, trade marks, service marks, trade names, rights arising in domain names, knowhow, trade secrets and rights in confidential information and any other intellectual property rights or rights of a similar nature (in each case whether or not registered) and all applications for any of them which may subsist anywhere in the world.

"IP Licences" means any licences, authorisations and permissions in any form whatsoever whether express or implied, pertaining to the use, enjoyment and exploitation of the Business Intellectual Property Rights.

"Knowhow" means confidential or secret information relating to trade secrets, knowhow, ideas, business methods, finances and financial information, prices, business plans, marketing plans, development plans, manpower plans, sale targets, sales statistics, customer lists, customer relationships, technical information and other information relating to the Computer Systems of the Business.

"Liabilities" means the liabilities whether actual or contingent of the Business (other than the Creditors) incurred or outstanding at Completion and without limitation all other liabilities of the Vendor.

"Management Accounts" means the unaudited balance sheet of the Vendor relating to the Business and the unaudited profit and loss account for the period ended on [ ] copies of which are attached to the Disclosure Letter.

"Name" means [ ].

"Pension Schemes" means [ ].

"Property" means the [freehold/leasehold] property owned by the Vendor described in Schedule [ ].

"Purchaser's Accountants" means [ ].

"Purchaser's Solicitors" means [ ].

"Regulations" means the Transfer of Undertakings (Protection of Employment) Regulations 1981.

"Software" means all software products together with all related object and source codes and databases used or owned by the Vendor in connection with the Business.

"SSAPs" means a Statement of Standard Accounting Practice published by the Accounting Standards Committee of CCAB Limited and adopted by the Accounting Standards Board Limited.

"Stocks" means the stocks owned or used by the Vendor at Completion for the purpose of or in connection with the Business including without limitation, spare parts, accessories, goods or other assets purchased for resale, raw materials, consumables and components, Work in Progress, partly finished and finished goods, finished but uninvoiced work and including items which although subject to reservation of title by the seller are under the control of the Vendor.

"Subsidiary" means a subsidiary as defined in CA 1985, s.736.

"Supply Contracts" means the orders, engagements or contracts entered into prior to Completion by or on behalf of the Vendor with suppliers for the supply of goods or services in connection with the Business which remain (in whole or in part) to be performed by the supplier details of which are set out in schedule [ ].

"Taxation" means all forms of taxation, duties, imposts, government charges (whether international, national or local) and levies whatsoever and whenever created, enacted or imposed and whether of the United Kingdom or elsewhere and without prejudice to the generality of that expression includes:

(1) income tax, corporation tax, capital gains tax, capital transfer tax, inheritance tax, stamp duty, stamp duty reserve tax, rates, VAT, customs and other import duties, insurance premium tax, national insurance contributions and any payment whatsoever which the Company may be or become bound to make to any Taxation Authority or any other person as a result of any enactment relating to taxation and any other taxes, duties or levies supplementing or replacing any of the above; and

(2) all costs, charges, interests, fines, penalties and expenses incidental or relating to any taxation, duties, imposts, charges and levies whatsoever (including without limitation any such described above).

"Taxation Authority" means the Inland Revenue, HM Customs and Excise or any statutory or governmental authority or body (whether in the United Kingdom or elsewhere) involved in the collection or administration of Taxation.

"UITF Abstract" means an abstract issued by the Urgent Issues Task Force of the Accounting Standards Board Limited or such other body or bodies as are prescribed for the purposes of CA, s.256.

"VAT" means value added tax chargeable under VATA and any similar replacement or additional tax.

"VATA 1994" means the Value Added Tax Act 1994.

"VAT Regulations" means the Value Added Tax Regulations 1995 (SI 1995/2518).

"Vendor's Accountants" means [ ].

"Vendor's Solicitors" means [ ].

"Warranties" means the warranties contained in Schedule [ ].

"Work in Progress" means services partially performed by the Vendor on behalf of the Business but not completed as at the close of business on the date of Completion (whether performed by the Vendor or by a subcontractor of the Vendor) including the parts, accessories and consumables used in the performance of said services.

# Part 2–Indemnities

## 1  Creditors and Liabilities

1.1    Subject to the other provisions of this Agreement:

    1.1.1    all profits and receipts of the Business and all losses, liabilities, obligations and outgoings of the Business up to Completion belong to and are for the account of the Vendor;

    1.1.2    the Vendor shall promptly discharge the Creditors and the Liabilities (at the latest by the expiry of any agreed or statutory credit or payment periods);

    1.1.3    notwithstanding Completion the Vendor shall be responsible for all debts payable by and claims (whether contingent or otherwise) outstanding against it at Completion or that primarily relate to any fact or matter occurring prior to Completion or anything done or omitted to be done on or prior to Completion by the Vendor including, without limitation, all wages, sums payable in respect of Taxation, rent and other expenses or any failure by the Vendor in the performance of any of its obligations falling due on or before Completion in relation to the Business or which relate to any of the Excluded Assets; and

    1.1.4    the Vendor shall indemnify the Purchaser in respect of any breach in whole or part of this sub-clause by the Vendor.

1.2    Subject to the other provisions of this Agreement all profits and receipts of the Business and all losses, liabilities, obligations and outgoings of the Business (to the extent that they are transferred to the Purchaser under this Agreement or relate to, or otherwise arise during the period after the date of Completion) belong to and must be paid and discharged by the Purchaser. Accordingly, and without prejudice to its rights under the Warranties and subject to the other provisions of this Agreement, the Purchaser shall indemnify the Vendor against:

    1.2.1    all liabilities, obligations and outgoings relating to the Assets to the extent that they are referable to the period after the date of Completion; and

    1.2.2    all costs, claims, proceedings, damages and expenses in connection with them.

## 2  Contracts

2.1    Insofar as the benefit of any of the Contracts may be effectively assigned by the Vendor to the Purchaser without the consent of a third party:

    2.1.1    the Vendor hereby agrees to assign and transfer with effect from Completion all the benefit of them to the Purchaser;

    2.1.2    the Purchaser shall perform all of the Vendor's obligations thereunder save any such obligations that were under the terms of the relevant Contract to be performed prior to Completion or any obligations that the Vendor is in breach of as at Completion; and

    2.1.3    the Purchaser shall indemnify the Vendor in respect of any breach of this sub-clause by it.

2.2     Insofar as the benefit of any of the Contracts may not be effectively assigned by the Vendor to the Purchaser without the consent of a third party then:

2.2.1   the Vendor and the Purchaser shall each use their reasonable endeavours to procure a novation of those Contracts or consent to assignment (as the Purchaser may require) and that those Contracts are novated or assigned, provided that:

2.2.1.1   the Purchaser shall not be obliged to make any payment, give any security or provide any guarantee as the basis for, or in connection with, any such assignment or novation; and

2.2.1.2   nothing contained in this Agreement shall or shall be deemed to operate so far as concerns any third party as such an assignment or novation as would or might give rise to any termination or forfeiture of any benefit, right or interest of any person in any of the Contracts in question;

2.2.2   unless and until any such Contracts (but excluding the Supply Contracts) shall be so novated or assigned:

2.2.2.1   the Vendor shall, insofar as may be permissible and lawful, give to the Purchaser the benefit of them as if the same had already been novated to or assigned to the Purchaser:

2.2.2.2   the Purchaser shall after Completion as the Vendor's sub-contractor (or in any way or capacity reasonably open to the Purchaser) perform on behalf of the Vendor all of the Vendor's obligations thereunder arising after Completion save any obligations of the Vendor that under the terms of any of the Contracts were to be performed prior to Completion or any obligations that the Vendor is in breach of as at Completion; and

2.2.2.3   the Purchaser shall indemnify the Vendor in respect of any breach of this sub-clause;

2.2.3   the Vendor shall hold all Supply Contracts in trust for the Purchaser and:

2.2.3.1   as required by the Purchaser all goods to be delivered or services to be provided thereunder shall be delivered or provided as the Purchaser may direct;

2.2.3.2   the Vendor shall permit the Purchaser to have the use of any assets or rights whose use by the Vendor is authorised by any such Supply Contract; and

2.2.3.3   the Purchaser shall, in respect of the period during which the provisions of this sub-clause are followed and to the extent that such Supply Contracts permit (and save insofar as they are not inconsistent with the provisions hereof), perform the obligations of the Vendor and make payments due thereunder (but only insofar as such obligations and payments do not relate to a breach of any of the Vendor's obligations thereunder on or prior to Completion);

2.2.4 in respect of the Contracts to which sub-clauses 2.2.1 and 2.2.2, apply the Vendor shall not do any act in respect of such Contracts without the consent of the Purchaser and shall keep the Purchaser fully and properly informed of all communications and any other relevant information concerning such Contracts; and

2.2.5 in the event of the actions referred to in sub-clauses 2.2.1 and 2.2.2 being unlawful or in breach of the terms of any of the Contracts, all liabilities and obligations relating to such Contracts shall remain with the Vendor which shall indemnify the Purchaser in respect of the loss of profit to the Purchaser in not being able to complete such Contracts and obtain the benefit thereof.

2.3 The Vendor shall indemnify the Purchaser in respect of any default by the Vendor under the Contracts or negligence or misrepresentation concerning all or any of the Contracts.

2.4 The Vendor shall perform all obligations in the Contracts that the Purchaser has not hereunder agreed to perform.

## 3 Employees

3.1 The Vendor shall indemnify the Purchaser in relation to any act or omission by the Vendor or any other event or occurrence prior to the date of Completion in relation to any contract of employment or collective agreement concerning the Employees or under statute pursuant to the Regulations including, without limitation, any such matter relating to or arising out of:

3.1.1 the Vendor's failure to comply with the provision of regulation 10 of the Regulations in relation to all Employees;

3.1.2 the Vendor's rights, powers, duties and/or liabilities under or in connection with any such contract of employment or any such collective agreement or under statute (which rights, powers, duties and/or liabilities are or will be transferred to the Purchaser in accordance with the Regulations);

3.1.3 anything done or omitted before the date of Completion by or in relation to the Vendor in respect of any contract of employment or any such collective agreements or any person employed in the Business which is deemed to have been done or omitted by or in relation to the Purchaser in accordance with the Regulations;

3.1.4 the Vendor's failure to pay to any Employee any sums due in respect of the period prior to the date of Completion;

3.1.5 any claim by any trade union, staff association or staff body recognised by the Vendor in respect of all or any of the Employees arising out of the Vendor's failure to comply with its legal obligations to such trade unions, staff associations or bodies; and

3.1.6 any claim by an Excluded Employee or other former or existing employee of the Vendor (other than the Employees) relating to any matter whatsoever.

3.2 The Purchaser shall indemnify the Vendor in relation to:

3.2.1 any claim by any Employee that in consequence of the sale of the Business to the Purchaser there has been a substantial change in such Employee's working conditions to his detriment;

3.2.2 any act or omission of the Purchaser in relation to any Employee occurring after the date of Completion;

3.2.3 any claim for redundancy payments or protective awards and any liability for wrongful dismissal or unfair dismissal or otherwise in connection with the transfer of the employment of the Employees to the Purchaser; and

3.2.4 any claim arising from the failure or delay of the Purchaser to notify the Vendor pursuant to regulation 10(3) of the Regulations of the measures the Purchaser envisages taking in relation to the Employees.

## 4 Pensions

4.1 The Vendor shall indemnify the Purchaser against:

4.1.1 any claim for any Benefit in respect of any scheme other than the Pension Schemes referable to any period up to and including Completion, including without limitation any order made by any court, tribunal or regulator in respect of such claim and any payment made by the Purchaser to any such person to settle any such claim; and

4.1.2 any claim in respect of the Pension Schemes relating to any benefits other than those relating to old age, invalidity or survivors or relating to any output target on benefits referable to pensionable service in the period up to and including Completion.

# PART 3–WARRANTIES

## 1 Preliminary

### 1.1 Capacity and authority of Vendor

1.1.1 The Vendor has the power and authority to enter into and perform this Agreement, which constitutes a binding obligation on the Vendor in accordance with its terms.

### 1.2 Investigations

1.2.1 No investigations or enquiries by, or on behalf of, a governmental or other body in respect of, or which might affect, the Business are taking place or pending.

### 1.3 Information disclosed to Purchaser correct

1.3.1 All information given by the Vendor, the Vendor's Solicitors or the Vendor's Accountants to the Purchaser, the Purchaser's Solicitors or the Purchaser's Accountants relating to the Business and the Assets was when given and is on Completion true, accurate and complete in all respects and opinions, expectations and beliefs included in the information are honestly held and have been arrived at on a reasonable basis after full enquiry.[1]

---

[1] Please see comments at paragraph 7–31 in relation to this warranty and the alternative form of wording that a well-advised vendor is likely to insist on.

1.3.2 There are no material circumstances in relation to the Business or the Assets which have not been fully and fairly disclosed in writing to the Purchaser or the Purchaser's Solicitors and which, if disclosed, might reasonably have been expected to affect the decision of the Purchaser to enter into this Agreement.

1.3.3 The information contained in Schedule[s] [ ] of this Agreement is true, complete and accurate.

## 2 Accounts

### 2.1 The Accounts

2.1.1 The Accounts were prepared in accordance with the historical cost convention; and the bases and policies of accounting, adopted for the purpose of preparing the Accounts, were the same as those adopted in preparing the audited accounts of the Vendor in respect of the three last preceding accounting periods.

2.1.2 The Accounts:

2.1.2.1 give a true and fair view of the assets and liabilities of the Business at the Balance Sheet Date and its profits for the financial period ended on that date;

2.1.2.2 comply with the requirements of CA 1985;

2.1.2.3 comply with all current Accounting Standards;

2.1.2.5 are not affected by extraordinary, exceptional or non-recurring items.

2.1.3 The amount included in the Accounts in respect of each asset, whether fixed or current, did not exceed its purchase price or production cost (within the meaning of CA 1985, Schedule 4) or (in the case of current assets) its net realisable value at the Balance Sheet Date.

### 2.2 Valuation of stock in trade and work in progress

2.2.1 In the Accounts and in the accounts of the Vendor for the three preceding financial years, stock in trade and work in progress were treated in accordance with SSAP 9.

2.2.2 In the Accounts all redundant, obsolete and slow-moving stock in trade was written off or written down, as appropriate.

### 2.3 Management Accounts

The Management Accounts have been prepared in accordance with accounting policies consistent with those used in the preparation of the Accounts with all due care and on a basis consistent with the management accounts of the Vendor prepared in the preceding year. The cumulative profits, assets and liabilities of the Business stated in the Management Accounts have not been misstated.

### 2.4 Books and records

2.4.1 The accounting and other records of the Business:

2.4.1.1 have been fully and properly kept;

2.4.1.2 are accurate in all material respects;

2.4.1.3     show a true and fair view of its trading transactions and its financial, contractual and trading position; and

2.4.1.4     are in the possession or under the control of the Vendor.

## 3   Assets

### 3.1   Ownership of assets

3.1.1     Apart from current assets acquired or realised by the Vendor in the ordinary course of the Business, the Assets are the same as the assets shown in the Accounts.

3.1.2     The Vendor owns the Assets free from Encumbrances except for those items the subject of Finance Agreements listed in the Disclosure Letter.

3.1.3     None of the Assets is subject to, and there is no agreement to create, an Encumbrance.

3.1.4     None of the Assets was purchased by the Vendor on terms that provided for a reservation of title by the seller.

3.1.5     There has been no exercise or purported exercise of or claim under any Encumbrance over any of the Assets and there is no dispute directly or indirectly relating to any of the Assets.

### 3.2   Assets sufficient for the Business and location

3.2.1     The Assets comprise all assets necessary for the satisfaction of the Vendor's obligations under the Contracts and for the continuation of the Business as now carried on (which without limitation shall include the continuation of the Business in the same scale and manner).

3.2.2     All of the Assets are currently being used exclusively in the Business.

3.2.3     Any of the Assets which are not situated at the Property at Completion are specified together with their actual location in the Disclosure Letter and are clearly identified as assets of the Vendor at such specified locations.

### 3.3   Fixed Assets

3.3.1     The Fixed Assets:

    3.3.1.1     are in a good and safe state of repair and satisfactory working order and have been properly serviced and maintained;

    3.3.1.2     are not surplus to requirements;

    3.3.1.3     would not be expected (if the sale of the Business had not taken place) to require replacement or additions at a cost in excess of £[ ] within the next six months.

3.3.2     There are maintenance contracts with independent specialist contractors in respect of all the Fixed Assets for which it is normal or prudent to have maintenance agreements and in respect of all the Fixed Assets which the Vendor is obliged to maintain or repair under a leasing or similar agreement.

3.3.3     Nothing has occurred or is likely to occur in relation to any of the Fixed Assets under a lease or similar agreement whereby the rental payable has been, or is likely to be, increased.

**3.4      Stock and Work in Progress**

3.4.1      The Stock is not excessive and is adequate in relation to the current trading requirements of the Business and to perform the Contracts.

3.4.2      The Work in Progress included in the Stock is adequate to maintain current cash flow and profitability of the Business at a level not less than as disclosed in the Disclosure Letter.

3.4.3      The Stock is in good condition and is capable of being sold in the normal course of the Business in accordance with the Vendor's current price list, without rebate or allowance to a purchaser.

**3.5      Book Debts**

3.5.1      None of the Book Debts is overdue by more than 12 weeks, or has been released on terms that the debtor pays less than the full book value of his debt, or has been written off or is regarded by the Vendor as wholly or partly irrecoverable.

3.5.2      The Book Debts will be recoverable in full, in the normal course of the Business, and in any event not later than 12 weeks after Completion; and none of them is subject to a right of counter-claim or set-off or withholding or other deduction.

3.5.3      All charges securing any of the Book Debts have (if appropriate) been registered in accordance with the provisions of CA 1985, Part XII.

**3.6      Insurance**

3.6.1      All the Assets which are of an insurable nature are insured in amounts representing their full replacement or reinstatement value against fire and other risks normally insured against by persons carrying on the same type of business as the Business.

3.6.2      The Business and the Assets are and have at all material times been adequately covered against employee's liability, public liability, professional liability and accident, damage, injury, third party loss, loss of profits and other risks normally covered by insurance.

3.6.3      Nothing has been done or omitted or has occurred which could make any of the insurance policies void or voidable or which is likely to result in an increase in premium.

3.6.4      None of the insurance policies is subject to special or unusual terms or restrictions or to the payment of a premium in excess of the normal rate.

3.6.5      The details set out in the Disclosure Letter give all relevant information relating to all claims by the Vendor under any of its insurance policies in the period of two years prior to Completion.

**3.7      Documents**

3.7.1      All the title deeds relating to the Assets will be delivered to the purchaser at Completion.

3.7.2      All documents which affect the title or interest of the Vendor to or in the Assets or which relate to contracts included in the Assets have been duly stamped within the requisite period for stamping.

**3.8**     **Intellectual property rights**

3.8.1     Full details of all the Business Intellectual Property Rights and IP Licences are set out in Schedule [ ]. All such Business Intellectual Property Rights are used, enjoyed and exploited exclusively in connection with the Business.

3.8.2     Except in respect of any Business Intellectual Property Rights which are the subject of a valid and enforceable IP Licence which has been granted to the Vendor, the Vendor is the sole legal and beneficial owner of all Business Intellectual Property Rights (including the subject matter of them) free from all claims, liens, equities, Encumbrances, licences and adverse rights of any description. No Business Intellectual Property Rights are held jointly or in common with any other person.

3.8.3     None of the Business Intellectual Property Rights are subject to any challenge or attack by a third party or competent authority. All renewal and registration fees for the protection of the registered Business Intellectual Property Rights have been paid.

3.8.4     All IP Licences are valid and enforceable. There are no other outstanding agreements or arrangements whereby a licence, sub-licence or other permission to use has been granted to or by, or is obliged to be granted to or by, the Vendor in respect of any of the Business Intellectual Property Rights owned or used by the Vendor.

3.8.5     Neither the Vendor nor any other party is in breach of any IP Licence and all such licences are in full force and effect and will not terminate or be capable of termination by reason of the execution and performance of this Agreement.

3.8.6     None of the activities involved in the conduct of the Business infringe or have infringed any Intellectual Property Rights of any third party, or constitute or have constituted any breach of confidence, passing off or actionable unfair competition in any jurisdiction. No such activities give or have given rise to any obligation to pay any royalty, fee, compensation or any other sum whatsoever.

3.8.7     The Vendor is not, and has not within the six years preceding the date of this Agreement been, party to or threatened with any legal proceedings relating to any Intellectual Property Rights of any third party and the Vendor is not aware of (and has not acquiesced in) any infringement of any Intellectual Property Rights or any breach of confidence, passing off or actionable unfair competition in any jurisdiction.

3.8.8     There are no outstanding or potential claims against the Vendor under any contract or under the Patents Act 1977, s.40 for employee compensation in respect of any Intellectual Property Rights of any third party.

**3.9**     **Knowhow**

3.9.1     The Knowhow is in the Vendor's lawful possession and under its control. No licences or other agreements have been granted or entered into in respect thereof and no circumstances exist under which the Vendor or any of its predecessors in title have granted any rights or interest to any third party or any third party has acquired any rights or interest in connection with the Knowhow.

3.9.2    No disclosure has been made or agreed to be made to any person (other than the Purchaser) of any of the Knowhow of the Business or any customer or client of the Business and the Vendor has not entered into any agreement for the use by any third party of any Knowhow or other Business Intellectual Property Rights held by the Vendor, other than pursuant to written obligations of confidence which have been set out in the Disclosure Letter.

**3.10      Information Technology**

3.10.1    All Computer Systems:

3.10.1.1    are in operating order and are fulfilling the purposes for which they were acquired or established in an efficient manner without material failures, downtime or errors;

3.10.1.2    have adequate capacity for the Business' present needs and (taking into account the extent to which the Computer Systems are expandable) foreseeable future needs;

3.10.1.3    have adequate security, back-up systems, duplication, hardware and software support and maintenance (including emergency cover) and trained personnel to ensure so far as reasonably practicable that:

3.10.1.3.1  breaches of security, errors and breakdowns are kept to a minimum;

3.10.1.3.2  no material disruption will be caused to the Business or any material part thereof in the event of a breach of security, error or breakdown;

3.10.1.3.3  in the event of any fault no more than one day's data would be lost;

3.10.1.3.4  the availability, confidentiality and integrity of data held or transmitted by the Computer Systems are preserved.

3.10.2    All necessary licences within the Computer Sytems have been validly obtained and no act has been committed which would lead to any such licences being terminated. Such licences will not terminate on the transfer of the Business to the Purchaser.

3.10.3    All Computer Systems are in the lawful possession and under the sole control of the Vendor, are located in the Property, are not shared with or used by or on behalf of or accessible by any other person and (save for software licensed to the Vendor) are owned and used solely by the Vendor.

3.10.4    In the year preceding the date of this Agreement the Vendor has not suffered any major failures or bugs in or breakdowns or repeated disruption or loss or interruption in or to its use of the Computer Systems and the Vendor is not aware of any fact or matter which may so disrupt or interrupt or affect the use of such systems on the same basis as presently used.

3.10.5    All Software used on or sorted or resident in the Business:

3.10.5.1    performs in accordance with its specification and does not contain any defect or feature which may adversely affect its performance or the performance of any other software in the future;

3.10.5.2 is lawfully held and used and does not infringe the copyright or other Intellectual Property Rights of any person and all copies held have been lawfully made;

3.10.5.3 as to the copyright therein:

3.10.5.3.1 in the case of software written or commissioned by the Vendor, is owned solely by the Vendor, no other person has rights therein or rights to use or make copies of the software or source codes;

3.10.5.3.2 in the case of standard packaged software purchased outright, is validly licensed to the Vendor in perpetuity (other than in the event of breach or insolvency) on written terms which do not require the Vendor to make any further payments; and

3.10.5.3.3 in the case of all other software, is licensed to the Vendor on the terms of a written licence which requires payment by the Vendor of a fixed annual licence fee the terms of which are set out in the Disclosure Letter.

3.10.6 No software owned by or licensed to the Vendor is licensed or sub-licensed by the Vendor to (or otherwise used by) any other person.

3.10.7 All records and data stored by electronic means which relate to the Vendor are capable of ready access through the Computer Systems.

3.10.8 The Vendor either owns or is validly licensed in perpetuity (other than in the event of breach or insolvency) to use the Software, all sums due under any such licences have been paid, and so far as the Vendor is aware no action will be necessary to enable the Purchaser to continue to use such Software to the same extent and in the same manner as it has been used prior to the date of this Agreement. The terms of all licences of the Software have not been breached and no notices of breach or termination have been served on the Vendor in respect of any such licence.

## 4 The Contracts

### 4.1 The Contracts

4.1.1 The Contracts, true copies of which are annexed to the Disclosure Letter or the full terms of which are set out in the Disclosure Letter, constitute all the contracts and other engagements, whether written or oral, referable to the Business and Assets to which the Vendor is now a party, apart from the contracts of employment of the employees.

4.1.2 All of the Contracts are assignable by the Vendor to the Purchaser without the consent of any other party.

4.1.3   The performance of this Agreement will not relieve any other party to any Contract from its obligations or enable it to determine any of them.

4.1.4   No steps have been taken by any party to the Finance Agreements to terminate the Finance Agreements.

**4.2      Nature of contracts**

4.2.1   None of the Contracts:

4.2.1.1   was entered into in any way otherwise than in the ordinary and normal course of the Business bona fide on an arms-length basis;

4.2.1.2   is of a loss-making nature (that is to say known to be likely to result in a loss to the Business on completion of performance);

4.2.1.3   cannot readily be fulfilled or performed by the Business on time without undue expenditure or application of money, effort or personnel;

4.2.1.4   involves, or is likely to involve, other obligations or liabilities which ought reasonably to be made known to an intending purchaser of the Business;

4.2.1.5   is of an unusual, abnormal or onerous nature; or

4.2.1.6   is of a long term nature (that is to say incapable of performance in accordance with its terms within 6 months after the date on which it was entered into or undertaken).

**4.3      Defaults**

4.3.1   None of the parties to the Contracts is in default, being a default which would be material in the context of the financial or trading position of the Business; and there are no circumstances likely to give rise to a default.

**4.4      Defective products**

4.4.1   The Vendor has not, in the course of carrying on the Business, manufactured, sold or supplied products which were, are or will become, in a material respect, faulty or defective, or which do not comply in a material respect with warranties or representations expressly or impliedly made by it.

4.4.2   The Vendor has not received a prohibition notice, a notice to warn or a suspension notice under the Consumer Protection Act 1987.

4.4.3   All of the products currently sold by the Vendor in respect of the Business comply with all applicable laws, legislation, regulations, orders and standards (including without limitation those relating to or concerned with product safety).

**4.5      Agreements concerning the business**

4.5.1   There have been no arrangements or understandings (whether legally enforceable or not) between the Vendor and any person who is, directly or indirectly, a shareholder or the beneficial owner of any interest in the Vendor, or any company in which the Vendor is interested relating to the management of the Business or the ownership or transfer of ownership or the letting of any of the Assets or the provision of finance, goods, services or other facilities to or by the Vendor or otherwise in any way relating to the Business or the Assets.

4.5.2    The Vendor has not been and is not a party to any agency, distributorship, marketing, purchasing, manufacturing, licensing or restrictive trading agreement or arrangement or any agreement or arrangement pursuant to which any part of the Business has been carried on or any agreement or arrangement which in any way has restricted its freedom to carry on the whole or any part of the Business or to use or exploit any of the Assets in any part of the world in such manner as it thinks fit.

4.5.3    Compliance with the terms of this Agreement does not and will not conflict with, result in the breach of or consitute a default under any of the terms, conditions or provisions of any rules or provisions relating to the membership of any association or body or any arrangement, licence agreement or instrument to which the Vendor is now a party or which affects or relates to the Business or the Assets (including without limitation the Contracts), or give rise to a right exercisable by any person other than the Vendor to terminate or in any way vary the terms of any such membership, arrangement, licence agreement or instrument or excuse performance by such party from the whole or part of its obligations under such agreement or instrument.

**4.6    Service liabilities**

4.6.1    The Vendor is not obliged to repair, maintain, take back or otherwise do or not do anything in respect of goods sold in the course of carrying on the Business.

## 5    Trading

**5.1    Changes in business activities and financial position since the Balance Sheet Date**

5.1.1    Since the Balance Sheet Date:

5.1.1.1    the Business has been continued in its proper, usual and normal course as regards the nature, extent and manner of carrying it on;

5.1.1.2    there has been no deterioration in its turnover, or its trading position or prospects;

5.1.1.3    the Vendor has not done or omitted to do anything which has prejudicially affected (or which is likely to or may prejudicially affect) the Goodwill.

**5.2    Vendor's other interests**

5.2.1    The Vendor and its Associates are not, directly or indirectly, interested in businesses which are or are likely to be competitive with the Business, apart from interests in securities listed on the London Stock Exchange, or dealt in on its alternative investment market, and in respect of which the Vendor, with its Associates, is interested in less than three per cent of any class of the securities in that company.

**5.3    Effect of sale of the Business**

5.3.1    The Vendor is not aware, and has no grounds for believing, that after Completion (whether by reason of an existing agreement or arrangement or as a result of the acquisition of the Business by the Purchaser):

5.3.1.1      a supplier of the Business will cease, or be entitled to cease, supplying it or may substantially reduce its level of supplies;

5.3.1.2      a customer of the Business will cease, or be entitled to cease, to deal with it or may substantially reduce its level of business; or

5.3.1.3      the Business will lose a right or benefit which the Vendor enjoys in relation to it.

5.3.2      Compliance with this agreement will not breach or constitute a default under any agreement or arrangement to which the Vendor is a party, any provision of its memorandum or articles of association or any other restriction affecting it.

**5.4      Joint venture and partnerships**

5.4.1      The Vendor is not, and has not agreed to become, a party to or member of a joint venture, consortium, partnership or other unincorporated association.

**5.5      Outstanding offers**

5.5.1      No offer, tender or the like relating to the Business which is capable of being converted into an obligation of the owner of the Business by an acceptance or other act of some other person, firm or corporation is outstanding.

**5.6      Undertakings restricting the Business**

5.6.1      The Vendor is not subject to an undertaking or assurance which it has given to a court or government agency in relation to the Business.

**5.7      Unfair trade and restrictive practices**

5.7.1      The Vendor is not, nor has it been in relation to the Business, a party to or concerned in any agreement, practice or arrangement (whether legally binding or not) which is or was:

5.7.1.1      in contravention of the Trade Descriptions Act 1968;

5.7.1.2      in contravention the Fair Trading Act 1973, Part XI as amended by the Trading Schemes Act 1996;

5.7.1.3      in contravention of the Consumer Credit Act 1974;

5.7.1.4      in contravention of or invalidated (in whole or in part) by the Competition Act 1998;

5.7.1.5      in contravention of the Enterprise Act 2002;

5.7.1.6      in contravention of the Treaty of Rome; or

5.7.1.7      in contravention of any other anti-trust, anti-monopoly or anti-cartel legislation or regulation.

**5.8      Litigation and winding-up**

5.8.1      The Vendor is not engaged (nor at any time has been engaged) in connection with the Business in any litgation, arbitration, prosecution or any other legal proceedings or claims with any person (including any customers of the Business). No injunction or order for specific performance has been granted against the Vendor in respect of any activity or potential activity of the Business and the Vendor has not given any undertaking to any prospective claimant or defendant or any other governmental or administrative body or court in connection with the Business or any of the Assets. There is no cirumstance which might give rise to the same and there are no circumstances which may give rise to any claims against the Vendor or litigation or arbitration in relation to the Business.

5.8.2    There are no outstanding claims against the Vendor on the part of customers or other parties in respect of defects in quality or delays in delivery or completion of contracts or deficiencies of design or performance or otherwise relating to liability for goods or services sold or supplied by the Vendor in the course of the Business. No such claims are threatened and there is no matter or fact in existence in relation to goods or services sold or supplied by the Vendor in the course of the Business which might give rise to the same.

5.8.3    There are no outstanding claims against the Vendor by suppliers of goods or services to the Vendor in respect of the Business, or disputes between the Vendor and suppliers. There are no such claims by the Vendor against such suppliers and there is no matter or fact in existence which may give rise to any such claims or disputes.

5.8.4    The Vendor is not insolvent or unable to pay its debts within the meaning of the Insolvency Act 1986, s.123 (the references in that section to proving to the satisfaction of the court being disregarded).

5.8.5    No order has been made, petition presented or resolution passed for the winding-up of the Vendor; no distress, execution or other process has been levied and remains undischarged in respect of the Assets; and there is no outstanding judgment or court order against the Vendor in relation to the Business or the Assets.

5.8.6    No event analogous to those described in clauses 5.8.4 or 5.8.5 has occurred outside England.

## 5.9    Compliance with statutes

5.9.1    The Vendor has not done or omitted to do anything in relation to the Business, the doing or omitting of which is, or could be, in contravention of a statute, regulation or the like giving rise to a penalty, default proceedings or other liability.

## 5.10    Business names

5.10.1    The Vendor does not, in relation to the Business, make use of a name other than the Name.

## 5.11    Licences and consents

5.11.1    The Vendor has, in relation to the Business, all necessary or desirable licences and consents required for carrying it on properly (short particulars of each licence and consent being set out in the Disclosure Letter).

5.11.2    The Vendor is not in breach of any licence or consent; all licences and consents are in full force and effect and there is nothing that might prejudice the continuation or renewal of a licence or consent by the Purchaser without the necessity for any expense or special arrangement.

**5.12 Branches**

5.12.1 The Vendor does not carry on any part of the Business outside the United Kingdom through a branch, agency or other place of business. The Disclosure Letter contains full particulars of all telephone and fax numbers and all other electronic addresses and codes used by the Business at or in the 12-month period prior to Completion.

**5.13 Purchases and sales from or to one party**

5.13.1 Not more than 25 per cent of the aggregate amount of all the purchases, and not more than 25 per cent of the aggregate amount of all the sales, of the Business are obtained, or made, from or to the same supplier or customer (including a person connected with the supplier or customer); and no material source of supply to the Business, or material outlet for its sales, is or is likely to be in jeopardy.

5.13.2 The profits of the Business and financial position of the Vendor in relation to it have not been affected during the past three years by an agreement or arrangement which was not at arm's length.

**5.14 Management reports**

5.14.1 No financial or management consultants have, within the past three years, produced a report in relation to the Business.

**5.15 Grants**

5.15.1 The Vendor has not received any grants from any national or supranational body or any governmental or public body which would or might become repayable by virtue of the entering into or completing of this Agreement or for any reason after Completion.

# 6 Employment

**6.1 Employees and terms and conditions**

6.1.1 Full and accurate details are given in Schedule [ ] of the Employees' full names, addresses, national insurance numbers, tax codes, rates of remuneration (or methods of calculating remuneration) (including overtime pay), benefits, bonuses, commissions, periods of notice, pensions, voluntary pensions, annuities and rights under any retirement benefit, life assurance or hospital or medical insurance scheme of the Vendor in respect of the Business and all other benefits (including share option schemes and pre-requisites of any nature) of each of the Employees. Copies of any communication to staff concerning any such matters have been supplied to the Purchaser and are attached to the Disclosure Letter.

6.1.2 The details shown in Schedule [ ] together with the information contained in the Disclosure Letter (including, without limitation, any staff handbook) give full, complete and accurate details of all the terms and conditions of employment of each of the Employees.

6.1.3 There are no loans outstanding from the Vendor to any of the Employees.

6.1.4 All of the Employees are employed by the Vendor, are wholly and exclusively engaged in carrying on the Business and have been so engaged for at least 12 months prior to Completion.

6.1.5 All contracts of employment between the Vendor and the Employees are terminable on not more than 3 months' notice without compensation, other than compensation payable in accordance with the Employment Rights Act 1996.

6.1.6 The Vendor has not recognised any trade union for the purpose of collective bargaining in relation to any of the Employees or done any act that may be construed as recognition.

6.1.7 No past employee of the Vendor has a right to return to work or may have a right to be reinstated or re-engaged under the Employment Rights Act 1996.

6.1.8 The Vendor is not bound (whether legally or morally) to vary any of the terms and conditions of any of the Employees and has not offered any new contract of employment to any of the Employees.

6.1.9 The Vendor is not in breach of any of the terms of the contracts of employment of any of the Employees nor any other duties or obligations owed to the Employees (or any of them) nor (so far as the Vendor is aware) is any Employee in breach of his contract of employment.

6.1.10 There are no employees of the Vendor or any other person engaged or employed in the Business or in carrying on the Business except the Employees. None [of the employees of the Vendor who have within the previous 12 months worked in the Business and none] of the Employees are on sick leave, disability leave, maternity leave, paternity leave, adoption leave, parental leave or any other authorised or unauthorised leave.

6.1.11 No offers of employment have been made to any persons other than the Employees nor any agreements made for any person to become an employee of the Vendor.

6.1.12 There are not in existence and the Vendor has neither proposed nor is proposing to introduce any bonus, profit sharing, share option or share incentive scheme or any other scheme or arrangement under which the Employees or any of them are or is or would be entitled to participate in the profits of the Business.

**6.2 Changes in remuneration**

6.2.1 Since the Balance Sheet Date no change has been made in the rate of remuneration, emoluments, pension benefits or, without limitation, any other terms or conditions of employment of any of the Employees.

6.2.2 No negotiations for any increase in remuneration or benefits or any other changes in the terms and conditions of employment of any of the Employees are current or due within a period of six months from Completion.

**6.3 Termination of contracts of employment and redundancies**

6.3.1 No liability has been incurred by the Vendor and not yet been discharged for:-

6.3.1.1 breach of any contract of service or employment or for redundancy payments (including protective awards);

6.3.1.2 damages or compensation for wrongful dismissal or unfair dismissal or otherwise;

6.3.1.3    failure to comply with any order for reinstatement or re-engagement of any Employee engaged in connection with the Business; or

6.3.1.4    for the actual or proposed termination or suspension of employment or variation of any contract of employment of any present or former director or employee of the Vendor employed in connection with the Business.

6.3.2    None of the Employees have given or been given notice of termination of his employment nor is any of the Employees engaged in any grievance or disciplinary procedure, nor is the Vendor engaged in relation to the Business or any of the Employees in any dispute, litigation or claim arising out of or relating to the provisions of the Employment Rights Act 1996, the Trade Union Reform and Employment Act 1993, the Health and Safety at Work etc. Act 1974, the Equal Pay Act 1970, the Sex Discrimination Act 1975, the Disability Discrimination Act 1995, the Race Relations Act 1976, the Gender Reassignment Regulations 1999, the Regulations, the Trade Union and Labour Relations (Consolidation) Act 1992, the Protection from Harassment Act 1997, s.3, the Working Time Regulations 1998, the National Minimum Wage Act 1998, the Employment Relations Act 1999, the Part-Time Workers (Prevention of Less Favourable Treatment) Regulations 2000, the Fixed-Term Employees (Prevention of Less Favourable Treatment) Regulations 2002, the Employment Act 2002, the Employment Equality (Religion or Belief) Regulations 2003, the Employment Equality (Sexual Orientation) Regulations 2003 or any other law statute or regulation relating to the Employees (or any of them), and there is no matter or fact in existence which can be reasonably foreseen as likely to give rise to the same.

6.3.3    No employees currently or previously employed in the Business have received or been given notice of dismissal during the period of twelve months prior to Completion.

6.3.4    None of the Employees as a result of this Agreement will be entitled to terminate their contracts of employment or will become redundant and be entitled to a redundancy payment.

## 6.4    Industrial agreements disputes and negotiations

6.4.1    There is no dispute between the Vendor and any trade union or any of the Employees existing or pending at the date of this Agreement and there are no circumstances (including without limitation the entry into and carrying out of this Agreement) which may give rise to a dispute with any of the Employees.

6.4.2    There are no enquiries or investigations existing, pending or threatened into the Vendor in relation to the Business by the Equal Opportunities Commission, the Commission for Racial Equality or the Disability Rights Commission or other similar authority.[2]

---

[2] It is intended that the Commission for Equality and Human Rights (which is expected to be established in 2006) will replace the other three Commissions.

**6.5    Compliance with laws**

6.5.1    The Vendor has complied in all material respects with all:

6.5.1.1    obligations imposed on it by all statutes, regulations and codes of conduct and practice relevant to the relations between it, the Employees and any relevant trade union (including without limitation the Working Time Regulations 1998 and any obligations under any health and safety legislation or any legislation relating to the environment);

6.5.1.2    collective agreements and customs and practices for the time being dealing with relations between the Vendor and the Employees or any relevant trade union and the terms and conditions of service of the Employees; and

6.5.1.3    relevant orders, declarations and awards made under any relevant statute, regulation or code of conduct and practice affecting the conditions of service of any of the Employees.

**6.6    Sub-contractors, agency workers and the self-employed**

6.6.1    Full, complete and accurate details are set out in the Disclosure Letter of the terms on which all consultants, sub-contractors, self-employed persons and other independent contractors are engaged in the Business. The Inland Revenue has confirmed in writing that it does not consider any such person to be an employee of the Vendor.

6.6.2    The Vendor has paid to the Inland Revenue and any other appropriate taxation authority all taxes, national insurance contributions and other levies payable prior to Completion in respect of the Employees.

**6.7    Pensions**

6.7.1    The particulars of the Vendor's pension scheme for the benefit of the Employees ("the Scheme"), including details of its assets, funding arrangements and current membership and copies of the trust deeds and latest actuarial report contained in or attached to the Disclosure Letter are accurate and complete.

6.7.2    The assets held by the trustees of the Scheme are sufficient to satisfy its liabilities (both current and contingent).

6.7.3    The Scheme is an exempt approved scheme within the meaning of ICTA 1988, s.592 and there is no reason why approval may be withdrawn.

6.7.4    The particulars of contributions required from the Vendor to the individual or group personal pension schemes which are contained in or annexed to the Disclosure Letter are accurate and state the basis of contribution obligation as a percentage of total earnings.

**7    Taxation**

**7.1    VAT and PAYE**

7.1.1    The Vendor has duly deducted all amounts from any payments from which tax falls to be deducted at source under the PAYE system and national insurance contributions and any other sums required by law to be deducted from wages, salaries or other benefits and the Vendor has duly paid or accounted for such amounts and all other sums due in respect of any benefits that are subject to taxation or similar contributions to the Inland Revenue or any other relevant Taxation Authorities.

7.1.2    There have been no investigations made by the Inland Revenue within 3 years prior to the date hereof into or affecting the payment of tax on benefits in cash or otherwise paid by the Vendor to its employees.

7.1.3    In respect of the Business the Vendor has complied with the provisions of VATA 1994 and with all statutory requirements, regulations, orders, provisions, directions or conditions relating to VAT, including the terms of any agreement reached with the Commissioners of Customs and Excise in respect of the Business and has maintained full, complete, correct and up to date records, invoices and other documents (as the case may be) appropriate or requisite for the purposes thereof and has preserved such records, invoices and other documents in such form and for such periods as are required by the relevant legislation.

7.1.4    The Disclosure Letter contains full details of all current agreements or arrangements between the Vendor and the Commissioners of Custom and Excise.

7.1.5    The Vendor is not liable to any abnormal or non-routine payment, or any forfeiture, penalty, interest or surcharge, or to the operation of any penal provision, in relation to VAT.

7.1.6    The Vendor has not been required by the Commissioners of Customs and Excise to give security for payment of VAT.

7.1.7    There has been no investigation by the Commissioners of Customs and Excise within three years prior to the date hereof into or affecting the payment of VAT in respect of the Business.

7.1.8    The Disclosure Letter contains details (including the cost and percentage of input tax claimed on the item in the first interval as defined in the VAT Regulations, regulation 114) of all land and other capital items which are used in the course of furtherance of the Business to which VAT Regulations, regulation 115 could apply. No such adjustment as is referred to in VAT Regulations, regulations 112–116 has been made or should have been made in respect of the current interval in relation to any such capital items.

7.1.9    No election under VATA 1994, Schedule 10, paragraph 2 to waive exemption from VAT in respect of the grant of any interest in or right over land owned or occupied by the Vendor which is to be transferred to the Purchaser under the terms of this Agreement has been made by the Vendor or by any person making such a grant to the Vendor.

7.1.10   The Vendor has not made exempt supplies such, or of such amount, that it is unable to obtain full credit for input tax paid or suffered by it.

7.1.11   The Disclosure Letter identifies such of the Property on which works have been carried out in respect of which industrial buildings allowances have been claimed and in respect of each such part of the Property contains details of:

7.1.11.1    the amount of capital expenditure concerned;

    7.1.11.2    the aggregate of initial and writing down allowances claimed;

    7.1.11.3    the residue of expenditure available; and

    7.1.11.4    the period of years over which writing down allowances may be available to the Purchaser.

7.1.12    The Disclosure Letter contains details in respect of:

    7.1.12.1    such of the Property as is leasehold; all fixtures, within the meaning of CAA 2001 s.173, which are treated pursuant to that section as belonging to the Vendor;

    7.1.12.2    such of the Property as is freehold; all fixtures, as aforesaid, that are treated pursuant to the said s.173 as belonging to a person other than the Vendor.

## 7.2    Inheritance tax

7.2.1    The Assets hereby agreed to be sold are not subject to an Inland Revenue charge as it mentioned in IHTA 1984, s.237 nor is any unsatisfied liability to inheritance tax attached to or attributable to any of the Assets.

7.7.2    No person is liable to inheritance tax attributable to the value of the Assets hereby agreed to be sold in such circumstances that such person has the power under IHTA 1984, s.212 to raise the amount of such tax by the sale or mortgage or by a terminable charge on the said assets.

# APPENDIX 6

# Tax Deed

[See para.10–06]

This Agreement to be executed as a deed is made the [ ] day of [ ] 200[ ]

## Parties:

(1) [ ] of [ ] and [ ] of [ ] (the "Covenantors"); and
(2) [ ] (registered number [ ]) whose registered office is at [ ] ("the Purchaser").

## Recital:

This Deed is entered into in accordance with the Agreement.

## Operative Provisions:

### 1  Definitions

In this Deed:

1.1     Words and expressions defined in the Agreement shall have the same meaning in this Deed except where otherwise provided or expressly defined below.

1.2     "Agreement" means an agreement of today's date made between the Covenantors and the Purchaser relating to the sale of the Shares.

1.3     "Claim for Taxation" includes a notice, demand, assessment or other document issued, or action taken, by or on behalf of a Taxation Authority and whether issued before or after Completion, whereby it appears that the Company is, or may be, subject to a Liability to Taxation (whether or not it is primarily payable by the Company and whether or not the Company has a right of reimbursement).

1.4     "Event" includes any disposition, action or omission (whether or not the Company or the Purchaser is party), the earning, accrual or receipt of any income, profits or gains, the declaration, payment or making of any dividend or other distribution (in each case whether actual or deemed) on or before Completion and includes any events which are deemed to have occurred for any Taxation purpose.

1.5     "Liability to Taxation" includes:

1.5.1     any liability of the Company to make a payment in respect of or in the nature of Taxation;

1.5.2     the set-off or utilisation of any Purchaser's Relief or a Pre-Completion Relief against the liability of the Company to make a payment of or in respect of Taxation where but for the set-off or utilisation a liability would have under clause 1.5.1;

1.5.3     the loss, disallowance, counteracting or clawing back of a Pre-Completion Relief which would otherwise have been available to the Company other than as set out in clause 1.5.2;

1.5.4     the loss, disallowance or set-off of a right to repayment of Taxation which would otherwise have been available to the Company;

and the amount of the Liability to Taxation is:

1.5.5     in the case of a liability falling within clause 1.5.1 or a liability not falling within any of the preceding sub-clauses of this clause, the amount of Taxation payable;

1.5.6     in the case of a liability falling within clause 1.5.2, the amount of Taxation which would have been payable but for the set-off or utilisation;

1.5.7     in the case of a liability falling within clause 1.5.3, the value attributed in the Accounts to the Pre-Completion Relief so lost, counteracted or clawed back; and

1.5.8     in the case of a liability falling within clause 1.5.4, the amount of repayment which would otherwise have been available.

1.6     "Pre-Completion Relief" means any Relief which arises as a result of or by reference to any Event occurring on or before Completion and which has either been treated as an asset in the Accounts or is taken into account in computing (and so reducing or eliminating) a provision for deferred taxation which appears in the Accounts or which would have appeared in the Accounts but for the presumed availability of the Relief.

1.7     "Purchaser's Relief" means any Relief which arises as a result of or by reference to an Event occurring after the Balance Sheet Date.

1.8     "Relief" includes any relief or allowance, exemption, set-off or deduction from or credit available from, against or in relation to Taxation or in the computation of income, profits or gains for a Taxation purpose.

1.9     "Saving" means a reduction of liability of the Company to Taxation by virtue of the set-off against the liability or against any income, profits or gains of any Relief arising as a result of a Liability to Taxation in respect of which the Covenantors have made payment under clause 2.

1.10     References to any Event occurring on or before Completion include any combination of two or more Events the first of which occurred or is deemed to have occurred on or before Completion.

## 2    Covenant

2.1     The Covenantors jointly and severally undertake to pay to the Purchaser the amount of:

2.1.1     any liability to Taxation which has arisen or arises as a result of or in connection with an Event which occurred on or before Completion;

2.1.2     the costs incurred by the Company or the Purchaser in relation to Liability to Taxation or Claims for Taxation;

2.1.3     any depletion in or reduction of value of the assets of the Company or any increase in its liabilities as a result of inheritance tax which:

2.1.3.1     is at Completion a charge on the Shares or the assets of the Company or gives rise to a power to sell, mortgage or charge the Shares or the assets of the Company; or

2.1.3.2     after Completion becomes a charge on or gives rise to a power to sell, mortgage or charge any of the

Shares or the assets of the Company being a liability in respect of additional inheritance tax payable on the death of the person within seven years after a transfer of value;

but a right to pay by instalments shall be disregarded and the provisions of ICTA 1988, s.213 shall not apply to payments to be made under this Deed.

2.1.4 any liability of the Company to make a payment in respect of Taxation under any indemnity, covenant, guarantee or charge entered into on or before Completion; and

2.1.5 any liability to Taxation which arises from the Company being called upon to make payment for group relief surrendered to it or a clawback of amounts previously paid to it in exchange for a surrender of group relief.

2.2 The provisions of Schedule [ ] of the Agreement shall apply to claims under this Deed where they are expressed to do so.

# 3 Exclusions

3.1 The undertaking in clause 2.1 does not apply to a Liability to Taxation:

3.1.1 to the extent that specific provision or reserve or allowance has been made in the Accounts for the Liability to Taxation;

3.1.2 for which the Company is, or may become, liable wholly or primarily as a result of transactions in the usual course of its business after the Balance Sheet Date.

3.1.3 it would not have arisen but for a new form of Taxation, a change in the rates of Taxation or a statutory variation in methods of applying or calculating rates of Taxation, in each case occurring after Completion with retrospective effect;

3.1.4 to the extent that it would not have arisen but for the fact that the treatment in future accounts of the Company of assets and liabilities, or of the Taxation attributable to timing differences, is different from the treatment in the Accounts;

3.1.5 to the extent of any recovery by the Purchaser under the Warranties in respect of, or arising from, the same Liability to Taxation;

3.1.6 to the extent that a Relief other than a Pre-Completion Relief or a Purchaser's Relief is available to reduce such Liability to Taxation;

3.1.7 if it results from the cessation of the trade of the Company after Completion;

3.1.8 to the extent that it has been made good or otherwise compensated for by the Purchaser or the Company but after deducting costs incurred by them directly as a result of doing so;

3.1.9 which is attributable to the Company ceasing to be entitled to the small companies' rate of corporation tax as a result of the purchase of the Shares by the Puchaser;

3.1.10 in respect of value added tax relating to supplies made and imports received since the Balance Sheet Date or in respect of stamp duty or stamp duty land tax the liability for which has been incurred in the course of the Company's business since the Balance Sheet Date;

3.1.11   which would not have arisen but for a voluntary act or omission of the Company or the Purchaser carried out, or occurring, after the date of this Deed, otherwise that in the usual course of business; or

3.1.12   if the Company fails, after due warning, to act in accordance with the reasonable instructions of the Covenantors in conducting a dispute (as referred to in clause 4) in respect of a claim for Taxation.

## 4   Conduct of Claims

4.1   The Purchaser shall notify the Covenantors in writing of any Claim for Taxation which comes to its notice, whereby it appears that the Covenantors are, or may become, liable to pay the Purchaser under this Deed. Failure to comply with this clause shall not affect the Purchaser's rights and the Covenantors' only remedy for the failure shall be a claim for such damages as they suffer directly as a result of it.

4.2   The Purchaser shall ensure that a Claim for Taxation to which this Deed applies is, so far as reasonably practicable, dealt with separately from claims to which it does not apply.

4.3   Provided that the Covenantors indemnify and secure the Company and the Purchaser to the reasonable satisfaction of the Purchaser against all losses, costs, damages and expenses (including interest on overdue Taxation) which may be incurred thereby, the Purchaser will procure that the Company at the Covenantors' cost and expense takes such action and gives such information and assistance in connection with its Taxation affairs as the Covenantors reasonably and promptly request to dispute, appeal or settle a claim. This obligation will not apply where a Taxation Authority alleges dishonest or fraudulent conduct by the Covenantors or by the Company before Completion.

4.4   The Purchaser shall procure that the Covenantors (and their advisers) are given full and prompt access to all documents, records and personnel of the Company and the Purchaser and their advisers to enable the Covenantors promptly and effectively to evaluate, dispute and deal with a Claim for Taxation to which this Deed applies and enforce their rights under this clause 4.

4.5   In connection with the conduct of a dispute relating to a Claim for Taxation to which this Deed applies:

4.5.1   the Covenantors and the Purchaser shall keep the other parties informed of all relevant matters and shall promptly forward or procure to be forwarded copies of all material correspondence and other written communications;

4.5.2   the Covenantors shall not settle or compromise the dispute, or agree any thing in its conduct which is likely to affect the amount involved or the future Liability to Taxation of the Company, or the Purchaser, without the prior approval of the Purchaser, such approval not to be unreasonably withheld or delayed;

4.5.3   if a dispute arises between the Purchaser and the Covenantors as to whether a Claim for Taxation should be settled in full or contested, the dispute shall be referred to the determination of a senior tax counsel of at least 10 years standing ("Counsel"), appointed by agreement between the Purchaser and the Covenantors, or (if they do not agree) upon the application by either party to the President for the time being of the Law Society, whose determination shall be final. Counsel shall be asked to advise whether, in his opinion, an appeal against the Claim for Taxation would, on the balance of probabilities, be likely to succeed. Only if his opinion is in the affirmative shall that Claim for Taxation be contested. Any further dispute arising between the Covenantors and the Purchaser as to whether a further appeal should be pursued following determination of an earlier appeal (whether or not in favour of the Covenantors) shall be resolved in a similar manner.

4.6 Nothing contained in this clause 4 shall require the Purchaser to prevent the Company from making a payment of Taxation at the time necessary to avoid incurring a fine, penalty or interest in respect of unpaid Taxation.

## 5 Dates for Payments

5.1 This Clause applies solely for determining the date on which payments are to be made by the Covenantors under this Deed.

5.2 The Covenantors shall make a payment to the Purchaser in cleared funds on the date falling five clear Business Days after the date on which the Purchaser has notified the Covenantors of the amount of the payment required to be made or, if later, three clear Business Days prior to the date on which the Company discharges, or is deemed to discharge, a Liability to Taxation in respect of which the Purchaser is entitled to make a claim under this Deed.

5.3 For the purposes of clause 5.2, the Company is deemed to discharge a Liability to Taxation:

5.3.1 on the date on which the Company makes an actual payment of Taxation in respect of the Liability to Taxation;

5.3.2 in the case of a Liability to Taxation falling within clause 1.5.2, the date on which the Taxation would have been payable but for the set-off or utilisation of the Purchaser's Relief or the Pre-Completion Relief; or

5.3.3 in the case of a Liability to Taxation falling within clause 1.5.4, the date on which the repayment would otherwise have been made to the Company.

5.4 If a payment by the Covenantors under this Deed is not made on the date referred to in clause 5.2 it shall carry interest from the due date of payment at the rate of 4% above the base rate from time to time of Barclays Bank plc until payment is received by the Purchaser.

5.5 Interest shall be payable on costs incurred under clause 2.1.2 in accordance with clause 5.4 from the date the Company or the Purchaser is invoiced for the costs.

5.6 Disputes in relation to the provisions of clauses 5.3 and 5.4 may be referred by the Purchaser or the Covenantors to the auditors of the Company, acting as experts and not arbitrators, whose certificate shall in the absence of manifest error be final.

## 6 Deduction from Payments and Right of Set-Off

6.1 Except as required by law payments under this Deed shall be made gross, free of rights of counterclaim or set-off.

6.2 If a deduction or withholding is required by law to be made from a payment by the Covenantors under this Deed, there shall be paid to the Purchaser such additional amount as is necessary to ensure that the net receipt by the Purchaser is equal to the amount which it would have received and retained had the payment in question not been subject to deduction or withholding.

6.3     If the Purchaser or the Company is liable to Taxation in respect of a payment under this Deed (or would have been liable but for the availability of Relief or a right to repayment of Taxation), there shall be paid to the Purchaser an additional amount as if the Taxation had been a deduction or withholding from the payment and the provisions of clause 6.2 shall apply accordingly to the payment.

## 7   Savings

7.1     If (at the request and expense of the Covenantors) the Company's auditors certify that the Company or the Purchaser has obtained a Saving, the Purchaser shall as soon as reasonably practicable repay to the Covenantors the lesser of:

7.1.1     the amount of the Saving less costs incurred in obtaining it (as certified by the Company's auditors); and

7.1.2     the amount paid by the Covenantors to the Purchaser under clause 2.

7.2     If the amount referred to in clause 7.1.1 exceeds that referred to in clause 7.1.2, the excess shall be carried forward to be offset against (and so as to reduce or eliminate) the future liability of the Covenantors under clause 2.

7.3     If the Company or the Purchaser become aware that the Company or the Purchaser has obtained or may obtain a Saving, the Purchaser shall as soon as reasonably practicable give notice of that fact to the Covenantors. Provided that the Covenantors have paid the Purchaser in respect of the Liability to Taxation which gave rise to the Saving, the Purchaser shall take and procure the taking by the Company of all reasonable steps to obtain the Saving.

7.4     In certifying a Saving under clause 7.1, the Company's auditors shall act as experts and not as arbitrators and their certificate shall in the absence of manifest error be final.

## 8   Recovery from third parties

8.1     If the Company or the Purchaser recovers or becomes aware that it is entitled to recover from a third party (including a Taxation Authority) any amount which is referable to a Liability to Taxation in respect of which the Covenantors are liable under this Deed, the Purchaser shall as soon as reasonably practicable give notice of that fact to the Covenantors. It shall then take or procure that the Company takes such reasonable action as is necessary to effect the recovery as the Covenantors request in writing.

8.2     The actions taken by the Purchaser under clause 8.1 shall be at the Covenantors' expense and shall be subject to the Covenantors securing the Purchaser and the Company to the reasonable satisfaction of the Purchaser against all resultant losses, expenses and Taxation relating to that recovery.

8.3     If the Covenantors have made a payment under clause 2, the Purchaser shall repay to the Covenantors the lessor of:

8.3.1     the amount recovered together with any interest (net of Taxation) or repayment supplement received in respect of it (net of any losses, costs, damages, expenses and tax relating to the amount recovered not previously recovered from the Covenantors); and

8.3.2    the amount paid by the Covenantors under clause 2 in respect of the Liability to Taxation or Claim for Taxation in question.

8.4    If the amount provided for under clause 8.3.1 exceeds that under clause 8.3.2, the excess shall be set against, and so reduce or eliminate, any liability of the Covenantors under clause 2 which arises after the recovery.

## 9    General

9.1    Payments by the Covenantors under this Deed shall be treated as repayments of the consideration paid for the Shares under the Agreement but this clause does not limit the liability of the Covenantors.

9.2    This Deed shall be binding on the respective successors and personal representatives of the Covenantors.

9.3    The benefit of this Deed may be assigned in whole but not in part by the Purchaser.

9.4    The provisions of the Agreement relating to notices apply to notices to be given under this Deed.

9.4    The construction, validity and performance of this Deed shall be governed by the laws of England.

9.6    The parties submit to the non-exclusive jurisdiction of the English Courts.

# Appendix 7

# Short Form Warranties

[See paras 5–01, 6–18 and 7–02]

Note: for the purpose of this Appendix, the definitions in para.4–01 are used.

## 1  Corporate matters and capacity

1.1   Each Vendor has full power and authority to enter into and perform this Agreement, the Tax Deed and all other documents to be executed by them pursuant to this Agreement which constitute, or when executed will constitute, obligations binding on each Vendor in accordance with their terms.

1.2   The information contained in Schedules [ ] is true accurate and complete.

1.3   The Shares will at Completion constitute the whole of the issued and allotted share capital of the Company.

1.4   The Vendors are the sole beneficial owners of the Shares.

1.5   There are no agreements or arrangements in force, other than this Agreement, which grant to any person the right to call for the allotment or transfer of any share or loan capital of the Company or any interest therein and no claim has been made by any person to be entitled to the same.

1.6   The register of members and other statutory books of the Company have been properly kept and contain an accurate and complete record of the matters with which they should deal; and no notice or allegation, that any of them is incorrect or should be rectified, has been received.

1.7   All returns, particulars, resolutions and documents required to be filed with the Registrar of Companies in respect of the Company have been duly filed and were correct.

1.8   The Company is not the holder or beneficial owner of, nor has it agreed to acquire, any share or loan capital of any company.

## 2  Possession of documents

2.1   All title deeds relating to the assets of the Company, an executed copy of all agreements to which the Company is a party and the original copies of all other documents which are held by, under the control of or which ought to be in the possession of the Company are in its possession and duly stamped.

## 3  Accounting matters

3.1   The Accounts have been prepared in accordance with the historical cost convention and with the requirements of all relevant statutes and generally accepted accounting principles and on the same bases and policies of accounting as adopted for the purpose of preparing the audited accounts of the Company in respect of the preceding three accounting periods.

3.2 The Accounts:

    3.2.1 give a true and fair view of the assets, liabilities (including contingent, unquantified or disputed liabilities), commitments and state of affairs of the Company at the Balance Sheet Date and its profits and cash flow for the period ended on that date;

    3.2.2 comply with the requirements of CA 1985 and other relevant statutes;

    3.2.3 comply with current Accounting Standards; and

    3.2.4 are not affected by extraordinary, exceptional or non-recurring items.

3.3 All accounting and other records of the Company are in its possession, have been fully, properly and accurately kept and completed and give a true and fair view of its financial contractual and trading position.

3.4 Full disclosure has been made to the Company's auditors or any previous auditors of the Company of all matters relevant to the preparation of the Accounts and any previous audited financial statements of the Company.

3.5 The Management Accounts have been prepared consistently with the Accounts and previous management accounts of the Company and do not contain any material inaccuracies.

## 4 Financial Matters

4.1 Full details of the Company's existing facilities (none of which are dependent on security provided by any third party) ("the Facilities") are set out in the Disclosure Letter. The Facilities provide sufficient working capital for the purposes of the Company continuing to carry on its business in its present form and at its present level of turnover for the period of 12 months after Completion.

4.2 The Company has no outstanding, nor has it agreed to create or issue any, loan capital, nor has it factored or discounted any of its debts or engaged in financing of a type which would not be required to be shown or reflected fully in the Accounts, nor borrowed any money which it has not repaid, save for borrowings not exceeding the amounts shown in the Accounts.

4.3 The Company has not lent any money which has not been repaid to it nor owns the benefit of any debt (whether or not due for payment) other than debts which have arisen in the normal course of its business.

4.4 Full details of all grants, subsidies or financial assistance applied for or received by the Company from any governmental department or agency or any local or other authority are set out in the Disclosure Letter and the Company had complied in full with the terms of such grants, subsidies and financial assistance.

## 5 Business since the Balance Sheet Date

5.1 Since the Balance Sheet Date the Company has:

    5.1.1 not paid, made or declared a dividend or other distribution (as defined in ICTA 1988);

    5.1.2 not repaid, or become liable to repay any indebtedness in advance of its stated maturity;

5.1.3    paid its creditors in accordance with their respective credit terms;

5.1.4    carried on its business in the ordinary and normal course of business and there has been no adverse change in the Company's financial position or trading position and in particular there has been no reduction in the level of turnover;

5.1.5    not entered into any long-term, substantial or abnormal obligations or transactions (including joint venture, consortium or similar arrangements);

5.1.6    not acquired or set up (or agreed to do so) any new branch or subsidiary; and

5.1.7    not made or agreed to make any capital expenditure or incurred or agreed to incur any capital commitments nor has it disposed of or realised any capital assets or any interest in such assets (and there were no commitments on capital account in respect of the Company outstanding at the Balance Sheet Date).

## 6    Effect of Sale of Shares

6.1    The Vendors have no knowledge, information or belief that after Completion (whether by reason of an existing agreement or arrangement or otherwise) or as a result of the proposed acquisition of the Company by the Purchaser any person or third party with whom the Company deals will or will seek to change the manner and/or terms upon which it deals with the Company.

6.2    Compliance with the terms of this Agreement will not so far as the Vendors are aware have a detrimental effect to the Company under the terms of any subsisting contract, agreement, transaction, arrangement, liability, understanding or commitment (howsoever the same may be described) to which it is a party.

## 7    Liabilities

7.1    The Company has no outstanding liabilities (including disputed or contingent liabilities) other than the liabilities disclosed in the Disclosure Letter and the Accounts or incurred in the normal course of trading since the Balance Sheet Date.

7.2    There has been no exercise, purported exercise or claim for any Security Interest over any of the assets of the Company and there is no dispute directly or indirectly relating to any assets.

7.3    The Company has at all times conducted and is conducting its business in all material respects in accordance with all applicable Official Requirements and contractual obligations and has obtained all requisite licences, permits and consents and there are no investigations or enquiries in existence or pending in respect of the affairs of the Company and the Vendors have no knowledge of any fact or matter which could lead to such investigations or enquiries.

7.4    The Company is not under any liability in relation to goods sold or services provided by it and the Vendors know of no reason why it may become so liable in the future in respect of goods already sold and services already provided.

## 8    Guarantees and Indemnities

8.1    There are no subsisting loans, guarantees or agreements for indemnity given by or for the accommodation of the Company.

## 9 Taxation matters

9.1 The Accounts make proper provision (taking account of the relevant Accounting Standards) or reserve for all Taxation (including deferred Taxation) which is liable to be assessed on the Company, or for which it may be accountable, in respect of the period ended on the Balance Sheet Date including distributions made down to such date or provided for in the Accounts.

9.2 All returns, notifications, computations and payments which should have been made or given by the Company for a Taxation purpose in the last 6 years were made or given within the requisite periods and were up to date, correct and on a proper basis.

9.3 There is no material dispute or disagreement outstanding or contemplated at the date of this Agreement with any Taxation Authority regarding liability or any potential liability to any tax or duty (including in each case penalties or interest) recoverable from the Company or regarding the availability of any relief from tax or duty to the Company and so far as the Vendors are aware there are no circumstances which make it likely that any such dispute or disagreement will commence.

## 10 Litigation and insolvency

10.1 Neither the Company nor any person for whose acts or defaults the Company is or may be vicariously liable are engaged in any litigation, arbitration, administrative or criminal proceedings and there are no proceedings pending or threatened or expected by or against such persons or the Company; and there is nothing which is likely to give rise to such proceedings. The Company is not subject to any order or judgment given by any Court or governmental agency (whether local or national) nor has it been a party to any undertaking or assurance given to any court, governmental agency or person which is still in force.

10.2 No insolvent event has occurred in relation to the Company and the Vendors are not aware of any circumstances which may lead to such an event.

## 11 Trading matters

11.1 No authorities (express or implied) by which any person may enter into a contract or commitment to do anything on behalf of the Company are subsisting.

11.2 The Disclosure Letter contains accurate particulars of all subsisting contracts to which the Company is a party at the date of this Agreement and the Vendors know of no breach of or any invalidity, or grounds for determination, rescission, avoidance or repudiation of any such contract or of any allegations of such thing.

11.3 The Company is not a party to, and its profits and financial position during the past three years have not been affected by, a contract or arrangement which is not of an arm's length nature.

11.4 The Company has complied with all Environmental Laws, obtained all relevant Environmental Licences (and complied with the terms of them) and is not subject to any Environmental Liabilities.

## 12 Property matters

12.1 The Company has good and marketable title to all of the Properties which comprise all the estate or interest of the Company in land or premises, and [the Company is the proprietor of each of the Properties registered at HM Land Registry with absolute title][particulars of the titles to the Properties are set out in Schedule [ ].

12.2    The Company has in its possession, or under its control, all duly stamped deeds and documents which are necessary to prove title to each of the Properties.

12.3    There is no option, or agreement for sale, mortgage (whether specific or floating), charge, lien, lease agreement or lease, overriding interest, condition, restrictive covenant, easement or other encumbrance in respect of any of the Properties.

12.4    The Properties are not subject to the payment of any outgoings (except business and water rates).

12.5    The Company has duly and punctually performed and observed all covenants, conditions, agreements, statutory requirements, planning consents, bye-laws, orders and regulations affecting any of the Properties, and no notice of a breach has been received.

12.6    The use of each of the Properties is the permitted use for the purposes of the Town and Country Planning Act 1990.

12.7    There are no compulsory purchase notices, orders or resolutions affecting any of the Properties.

12.8    The Properties have at all times been held by the Company as investments and not as trading stock.

## 13  Employment matters

13.1    Accurate and complete particulars of the identities, dates of commencement of employment or appointment to office and terms and conditions of employment of all the employees and officers of the Company, including without limitation details of all remuneration and other benefits, such as profit sharing, commission and bonus arrangements (whether or not contractual), and details of any outstanding claims or potential claims by any person who is now or has been an officer or employee of the Company (all of which are fully covered by insurance) are fully and accurately set out in the Disclosure Letter.

## 14  Pensions

14.1    Apart from the pension scheme referred to in the Disclosure Letter ("the Scheme") (accurate and complete particulars of which are contained in or attached to the Disclosure Letter), the Company is not under a liability or obligation, or a party to any *ex-gratia* arrangement or promise, to pay, or accustomed to paying, pensions, gratuities, superannuation allowances or the like, or otherwise under any obligation to provide "relevant benefits" within the meaning of ICTA, s.612, to or for any of its past or present officers or employees or their dependants; and there are no retirement benefit, pension or death benefit or similar schemes or arrangements in relation to, or binding on, the Company or to which the Company contributes.

## 15  Asset matters

15.1    Except for assets disposed of by the Company in the ordinary and normal course of business the Company is the owner of and has title to all assets included in the Accounts and all assets which have been acquired by the Company since the Balance Sheet Date (save for those items the subject of hire purchase, leasing or rental agreements listed in the Disclosure Letter) and there is not outstanding any Security Interest (or agreement to grant any such interest) over the whole or any part of the undertaking property or assets of the Company.

15.2    The plant, machinery, vehicles and other equipment used in connection with the business of the Company are in a good and safe state of repair and satisfactory working order and have been properly maintained.

15.3    The Company's stock levels are not excessive and are adequate in relation to current trading requirements, with stock in trade being in good condition and capable of sale in accordance with the Company's current price list, without rebate or allowance to a purchaser.

15.4    All the assets of the Company of an insurable nature are and have at all material times been insured in amounts representing their full replacement or reinstatement value against fire and other risks normally insured against by persons carrying on the same type of business as that carried on by it.

15.5    The Company is, and has at all material times been, adequately covered against accident, damage, third party loss (including product liability), loss of profits and other risks normally insured against by persons carrying on the same type of business as that carried on by it.

15.6    All insurances are currently fully effective (all premiums having been duly paid to date) and nothing has been done or omitted to be done which could make a policy of insurance void or voidable or which is likely to result in an increase in premium.

15.7    No claim is outstanding, or may be made, under any of the insurance policies and no circumstances exist which are likely to give rise to a claim.

## 16  Intellectual Property Rights

16.1    The Company is the sole legal and beneficial owner and exclusive user of the Intellectual Property Rights which have been or are being used by the Company or which are necessary for the carrying on of its business as it has been carried on up to Completion (as accurately detailed in the Disclosure Letter).

16.2    All Intellectual Property Rights are valid, subsisting and enforceable (nothing having been done that could affect this), are not subject to any infringement or challenge (and the Vendors know of no reason why they should be) and, where capable of registration, have been registered by the Company in all jurisdictions relevant to its business with all renewal and registration fees having been paid and all other steps required for the prosecution, maintenance and protection of the Intellectual Property Rights having been taken.

## 17  Information Technology

17.1    All Computer Systems are owned and used exclusively by the Company, do not infringe the Intellectual Property Rights of any third party, are covered by appropriate maintenance and support agreements (details of which are set out in the Disclosure Letter), and are in full working order and performing the functions for which they were acquired without material errors or downtime. The Vendors are not aware of any matters which may interrupt or affect the use of the Computer Systems used by the Company on the same basis as currently used.

17.2    The Computer Systems have adequate capacity for the Company's present needs and adequate security and backup systems to ensure that breaches of security, errors and breakdowns are kept to a minimum and that in the event of such an event that no more than one day's data will be lost and there will not be a material disruption to the Company.

## 18  General matters

18.1    All information given by any of the Vendors, the Vendors' Solicitors or the Company's auditors to the Purchaser, the Purchaser's Solicitors or the Purchaser's accountants relating to the business, activities, affairs, or assets or liabilities of the Company was and is accurate and complete and opinions, expectations and beliefs included in the information are honestly held and have been arrived at on a reasonable basis after full enquiry.[1]

18.2    There are no material facts or circumstances in relation to the assets, business or financial condition of the Company which have not been fully and fairly disclosed in writing to the Purchaser or the Purchaser's Solicitors and which, if disclosed, might reasonably have been expected to affect the decision of the Purchaser to enter into this Agreement.[2]

18.3    No one is entitled to receive from the Company any finder's fee or brokerage or other commission in connection with the sale and purchase of the Shares.

---

[1] Please see comments at paragraph 7–31 in relation to this warranty and the alternative form of wording that a well-advised vendor is likely to insist on.

[2] Please see comments at paragraph 7–32 in relation to this warranty which is the infamous "sweeping-up" warranty which is likely to be strongly resisted by vendors.

# APPENDIX 8

# Statutory Provisions to be Covered by Limited Indemnity

[See paras 5–25, 11–16 and 11–18]

Note: for the purposes of this Appendix, those provisions that are marked with an asterisk provide a statutory right of recovery. Many of the provisions relate to a group situation.

## 1 Corporation tax on chargeable gains

*TCGA 1992, s.189: a company which receives a capital distribution from a connected company, otherwise than on a reduction of capital, representing the proceeds of a disposal which gave rise to a chargeable gain, is liable for the tax on the chargeable gain if it is not paid by the distributing company. The section does not apply if the distribution is taxable as income of the recipient (as would normally be the case) and is therefore of limited significance.

## 2 Group companies

*ICTA 1988, ss.767A and 767AA: if the ownership of a company changes on or after July 2, 1997 and corporation tax for a period which began before the change remains unpaid six months after the date of the corporation tax assessment, the tax may be collected from a person who, during the three years preceding the change of ownership had control of the Company or from a company controlled by that person. For the section to apply there must have been either a major change in the activities of the company which owes the tax associated with a transfer of assets to a connected party or a cessation of the company's trade. The person required to pay the tax has a right of recovery from the company which owed it (s.767B). Any person may be required to supply documents or particulars which may help determine the fact and extent of the vendor's potential liability, or whether the company whose ownership has changed (or an associated company) is or may be liable to any tax in respect of which the vendor is or may be liable (s.767C).
*TCGA 1992, s.190: corporation tax on a chargeable gain accruing to a member of a group can be recovered from the company which was the principal member of the group when the gain accrued or from another group company owning the asset in question.
*TCGA 1992, s.139: if a company's business is transferred to another company for no consideration other than the taking over of liabilities, no gain or loss will arise to the transferor provided that the transfer results from a bona fide reconstruction. If the bona fide requirement is not met, the resulting tax can be recovered from a person holding the relevant assets. This does not apply where all or part of the company's business is being transferred to a venture capital trust.

## 3 Corporation tax on loans

ICTA 1988, s.419: if a close company makes a loan to a participator, a tax charge is imposed upon it equivalent to 25 per cent of the amount of the loan. The tax is repaid when the loan is repaid.

## 4 Non-resident companies

*FA 1988, s.132: a company which intends to cease to be resident in the United Kingdom must notify the Treasury and make arrangements to secure the payment of tax up to the date of emigration (FA 1988, s.130). If the tax is not paid within six months, it can be recovered within three years from a company which is or was a member of the same group.

TCGA 1992, s.187: A company which ceases to be resident in the United Kingdom and a company of which it is a 75 per cent subsidiary may elect to postpone the tax charge on emigration which arises under TCGA 1992, s.185 in so far as it relates to foreign assets. The parent company will become liable for the outstanding tax if the group relationship ends.

## 5 Inheritance tax

IHTA 1984, s.199: if a company was the recipient of a transfer of value, it will be liable for the inheritance tax unless the tax is paid by the transferor.

IHTA 1984, ss.94 and 202: inheritance tax arising on a transfer of value by a close company is apportioned amongst the shareholders as if they had made the transfer. The liability falls in the first instance on the company.

## 6 Capital gains tax

TCGA 1992, s.69(4): capital gains tax which is due from trustees of a settlement of which the company is a beneficiary may be recovered from the company to the extent of tax on the value transferred to it.

TCGA 1992, s.125: if a close company transfers assets at an undervalue, the amount of the difference is apportioned amongst its shareholders (which may include the target company) and their allowable expenditure in relation to their acquisition of the shares of the close company is reduced accordingly.

*TCGA 1992, s.137(4): roll-over relief from capital gains tax is not available unless there is a bona fide commercial transaction. Where, as a result, a tax liability exists, a member of the same group as the company making the disposal may be assessed.

*TCGA 1992, s.282: a donee may be liable for unpaid capital gains tax on a gift to it.

## 7 Value added tax

*VATA 1994, s.43 and ss.43A–43C: where a group registration exists, the members of the group are jointly and severally liable for the tax due from the representative member.

# Miscellaneous Clauses

Note: before using any of these clauses reference should be made to the commentary in the body of the book at the paragraph indicated which will provide a summary of the purpose of the clause, suitable amendments and, where applicable, the arguments for and against these.

## [1A] Claims under Warranties to precede claims under the Tax Deed

If a claim may be made by the Purchaser in respect of an act, event or default, both under the Warranties and under the Tax Deed, the claim shall first be made under the Warranties. Any amount payable under the Tax Deed to the Purchaser in respect of the claim shall be reduced to the extent of the amount payable under the Warranties. The provisions of clause [ ] of the Tax Deed shall apply as if the claim were wholly made under the Tax Deed.
[See para.1–09]

## [2A] Restrictions on distributions by trustee Vendors

The liability of the Trustees under the Warranties is limited to the net value from time to time of the capital of the Trust, after deduction of sums due to the Inland Revenue and costs and fees properly chargeable against the capital of the Trust. The Trustees may not distribute capital of the Trust, other than for the payment of those sums, costs and fees, whilst a claim under the Warranties is outstanding or prior to the expiration of the time limit for making a claim, unless an undertaking in favour of the Purchaser is obtained from a beneficiary, in a form satisfactory to the Purchaser, by which the beneficiary accepts joint and several liability with the Trustees to the extent of the value of the distribution.
[See para.2–06]

## [2B] No assignment of Warranties

The Purchaser shall not be entitled to assign the Warranties and shall not be taken to hold the benefit of the Warranties for its successors in title to [the Shares] [the Assets].
[See para.2–13]

## [2C] Liability of Vendors to assignee

If the benefit of the Warranties is assigned, the liability of the Vendors shall be no greater than it would have been had the Purchaser remained the owner of [the Shares] [the Business] and retained the benefit of the Warranties.
[See para.2–15]

## [2D] Exclusion of the Contracts (Rights of Third Parties) Act 1999

A person which is not a party to this [Agreement] [Tax Deed] has no right under the Contracts (Rights of Third Parties) Act 1999 to enforce any of its terms but this does not affect the rights or remedies of a third party which exist or are available apart from that Act.
[See para.2–17]

## [2E] Sharing of liability between Vendors

Without affecting their joint and several liability under this Agreement, the Vendors agree that, as between themselves, any one person shall bear only his appropriate part of a liability which arises in relation to the Warranties. For this purpose "appropriate part" means:

[2E.1]    in the case of a liability which is fairly attributable to, or which arises by reason of, income or benefits received by, or the act or default of, that person or persons connected with him (not themselves being any of the Vendors): the whole liability; and

[2E.2]    in any other case that proportion of the liability that the number of the Shares sold by him bears to the total number of the Shares.

[See para.2–20]

## [3A] Right to rescind prior to Completion

The Purchaser may rescind this Agreement by notice in writing to the Vendors or the Vendors' solicitors if prior to Completion:

[3A.1]    it appears that the Warranties were not or have ceased to be accurate; or

[3A.2]    an act or event occurs which, had it occurred on or before today's date, would have had the effect that there would have been a breach of the Warranties; or

[3A.3]    there is a breach or non-fulfilment of the Warranties which (being capable of remedy) is not remedied prior to Completion.

[See para.3–04]

## [3B] Purchaser's loss on breach of Warranty

If a Warranty does not relate to the value, or to anything affecting the value, of the Assets other than the Goodwill, the loss suffered by the Purchaser as a result of a breach of the Warranty shall be determined as if the value of each of the Assets (other than the Goodwill) was not that stated in clause [ ] but the lesser value that they would have had if the sale of the Business had been a forced sale and the reduction in the value of those Assets was additional consideration given for the Goodwill. If the parties are unable to agree to the adjustments to be made under this clause, the matter shall be referred to an independent firm of accountants nominated by the President of the Institute of Chartered Accountants in England and Wales for their determination as independent experts and, in the absence of manifest error, their determination shall be final.
[See para.3–06]

## [3C] Measure of damages for breaches of Warranty

Without limiting the rights of the Purchaser or its ability to claim damages on any basis if there is a breach of Warranty or any of the Warranties is untrue or misleading, if [the Company incurs and becomes subject to a liability or an increase in any liability which it would not have incurred or been subject to had the breach not occurred or][1] the value of any asset of the Company is less or becomes less than the value would have been had the breach not occurred then the Vendors undertake to the Purchaser to pay to the Purchaser (as the Purchaser elects) in cash on demand a sum equal to the liability or increased

---

[1] The words in sqaure brackets will not be relevant in the case of the purchase of a business.

liability, or the reduction in the value of the asset (as appropriate), or the reduction in the value of the Shares caused by the breach.
[See para.3–07]

## [3D] Credit for improvements

The liability of the Vendors under the Warranties shall be reduced by:

[3D.1]    an amount equal to the value or additional value of any fixed assets (apart from the Properties and goodwill) owned at Completion which were not included in the Accounts or were included at less than market value after deducting (in the case of assets acquired after the Balance Sheet Date) their costs of acquisition;

[3D.2]    the amount of or by which Taxation for which the Company is accountable is extinguished or reduced as a result of the claim giving rise to the liability;

[3D.3]    the amount by which a provision for Taxation, bad or doubtful debts or contingent or other liabilities contained in the Accounts proves after Completion to have been excessive, except by reason of a reduction in tax rates after Completion;

[3D.4]    the amount of debts paid which had been previously written off;

[3D.5]    the amount of credits, recoveries or other benefits which have been or will be received or obtained by the Company by reason of the matters giving rise to the liability.

[See para.3–10]

## [3E] Time limit for Warranty claims

A claim shall not be brought by the Purchaser in respect of a breach of the Warranties unless notice of the claim (specifying in reasonable detail the circumstances which give rise to the claim, the breach that results and the amount claimed) has been given to the Vendors before the expiration of the appropriate period. The claim shall be deemed to have been withdrawn (if it has not been previously satisfied, settled or withdrawn) one year after the expiration of the appropriate period, unless proceedings in respect of it have commenced by being issued and served on any of the Vendors. For the purpose of this clause, the "appropriate period":

[3E.1]    in respect of claims which could have been brought by the Purchaser under the Tax Deed is seven years from the Balance Sheet Date;

[3E.2]    in respect of claims which arise under clauses [ ] or [ ] of Schedule [ ] is [ ] years from Completion;

[3E.3]    in respect of other claims is two years from Completion.

[See para.3–18]

## [3F] Exclusion of small claims

The Vendors shall not be liable in respect of a claim brought by the Purchaser for a breach of the Warranties unless their liability for all claims would exceed in aggregate £[ ] and in that event they shall be liable only for the excess.
[See para.3–20]

## [3G]  Ceiling on claims

The total liability of [the Vendors and the Covenantors], arising by reason of claims under the Warranties or the Tax Deed, shall not exceed £[ ].
[See para.3–24]

## [4A]  Definitions

In this Agreement, the following expressions have the meanings stated namely:
"Accounts" means the audited balance sheet, as at the Balance Sheet Date, and audited profit and loss account for the year ended on the Balance Sheet Date of the Company together with the directors and auditors reports and notes in relation to them.
"Accounting Standards" means SSAPs, FRSs, UITF Abstracts, SORPs and all other generally accepted accounting principles applicable to a United Kingdom company.
"this Agreement" means this agreement for the sale and purchase of the Shares.
"Associate" means:

>  (1)  (in relation to an individual);

>> (1.1)  the individual's spouse, brother, sister or parent;
>> (1.2)  a company which is directly or indirectly controlled (within the meaning of ICTA 1988, s.840) by the individual or a person who is the individual's spouse, brother, sister or parent, or by any two or more of them;

>  (2)  (in relation to a company) a Subsidiary or holding company of the Company, and any other Subsidiary of a holding company of the Company, "holding company" bearing the meaning in CA 1985, s.736.

"Balance Sheet Date" means [ ] 200[ ] (being the date as at and to which the Accounts were prepared).
"Business Day" means any day other than Saturdays and Sundays and bank holidays during which clearing banks are open for business in the City of London.
"CA 1985" means the Companies Act 1985.
"CAA 2001" means the Capital Allowances Act 2001.
"Companies Acts" means CA 1985, the former Companies Acts (within the meaning of CA 1985, s.735(i)) and the Companies Act 1989.
"Completion" means completion of the purchase of [the Shares] [the Business].
"Computer Systems" means all hardware, firmware, peripherals, communication links, storage media, networking equipment and other equipment used in conjunction with it together with all computer software and all related object and source codes and data-bases.
"Confidential Business Information" means all or any information relating to:

>  (1)  the business methods, corporate plans, management systems, finances, new business opportunities or development projects of the Company;
>  (2)  the marketing or sales of any present of future product of the Company;
>  (3)  any trade secrets of other information relating to the provision of any product or services of the Company to which the Company attaches confidentiality or in respect of which it holds an obligation of confidentiality to any third party.

"Connected Person" has the same meaning as in ICTA 1988, s.839.
"Disclosure Letter" means the disclosure letter of today's date from the Vendors to the Purchaser in the agreed form.
"Encumbrance" means any encumbrance or security interest of any kind whatsoever including without limitation a mortgage, charge, pledge, lien, hypothecation, restriction, right to acquire, right of pre-emption, option, conversion right, third party right or interest, right of set-off or counterclaim, equity, trust arrangement or any other type of preferential agreement (such as a retention of title arrangement) having similar effect or any other rights exercisable by or claims by third parties.

"Environment" means the environment as defined in the Environmental Protection Act 1990, s.1(2) and includes any or all of the following media: air, water and land and the medium of air includes the air within buildings and the air within other natural or man-made structures above or below ground and the medium of water includes ground water and acquifers.

"Environmental Claim" means any claim, notice of violation, prosecution, demand, action, official warning, abatement or other order or notice (conditional or otherwise) relating to any Environmental Matters or Environmental Liabilities and any other notification or order requiring compliance with the terms of any Environmental Licence or Environmental Laws.

"Environmental Damage" means any pollution, contamination, degradation, damage or injury caused by, related to or arising from or in connection with the presence, generation, use, handling, processing, treatment, storage, transportation, disposal or release of any Hazardous Substance.

"Environmental Laws" means any Official Requirements relating to the protection of the Environment or the control or prevention or remedying of Environmental Damage or the control of Hazardous Substances.

"Environmental Liabilities" means any liabilities, responsibilities, claims, losses, costs (including remedial, removal, response, abatement, clean-up, investigative and/or monitoring costs), damages, expenses, charges, assessments, liens, penalties and fines which are incurred by, asserted against or imposed upon a person as a result of or in connection with any violation of or non-compliance with Environmental Laws (including the failure to procure or violation of any Environmental Licence required by Environmental Laws); or any Environmental Damage.

"Environmental Licence" means any permit, licence, authorisation, consent or other approval obtained or which ought to have been obtained pursuant to any Environmental Laws at any time by the Company and/or in relation to the business carried on by the Company.

"Environmental Matters" means any of the following (1) any generation, deposit, keeping, treatment, transportation, transmission, handling or manufacture of any Hazardous Substances; (2) damage to property, nuisances, noise, defective premises or health and safety at work or elsewhere; (3) the carrying out of a development (as defined in the Town and Country Planning Act 1990, s.55(1)); and (4) the pollution, conservation or protection of the Environment whether relating to man or any living organisms supported by the Environment or any other matter whatsoever affecting the Environment or any part of it.

"FA" means the Finance Act.

"FRS" means a financial reporting standard adopted or issued by The Accounting Standards Board Limited or such other body or bodies as are prescribed for the purposes of CA, s.256.

"Hazardous Substances" means any solid, liquid, gas, noise and any other substance or thing which causes or may cause harm (alone or in combination with any other substance) to the Environment or any structure, thing or living organism within the Environment including any substance regulated under any Environmental Law.

"ICTA 1988" means the Income and Corporation Taxes Act 1988.

"Intellectual Property Rights" means all copyright, moral rights, design rights, registered designs, database rights, semi-conductor topography rights, patents, utility models, business names, trade marks, service marks, trade names, rights arising in domain names, knowhow, trade secrets and rights in confidential information and any other intellectual property rights or rights of a similar nature (in each case whether or not registered) and all applications for any of them which may subsist anywhere in the world.

"ITA 1984" means the Inheritance Tax Act 1984.

"IT(EP)A 2003" means the Income Tax (Earnings and Pensions) Act 2003.

"the LPMPA 1994" means the Law of Property (Miscellaneous Provisions) Act 1994.

"Management Accounts" means the unaudited balance sheet of the Company as at [ ] and the unaudited profit and loss account for the period ended on [ ] copies of which are attached to the Disclosure Letter.

"Non Taxation Warranties" means those warranties set out in Schedule 4 other than the Taxation Warranties.

"Official Requirement" means any law, statute, ordinance, pact, decree, treaty, code, rule, regulation, directive, order, notice or official published plan or policy with legal or actual force in any geographical area and/or for any class of persons.

"Planning Acts" means the Town and Country Planning Act 1990, the Planning (Listed Buildings and Conservation Areas) Act 1990, the Planning (Hazardous Substances) Act 1990 (as amended) and the Planning and Compensation Act 1991.

"Properties" means the properties briefly described in Schedule [ ].

"Sensitive Payments" means (whether or not illegal) (1) commercial bribes, bribes or kickbacks paid to any person including central or local government officials, trade union officials or employees; (2) amounts received with an understanding that rebates or refunds will be made in contravention of the laws of any jurisdiction either directly or through a third party; (3) political contributions; (4) payments or commitments (whether made in the form of commissions, payments or fees for goods received or otherwise) made with the understanding or under circumstances that would indicate that all or part thereof is to be paid by the recipient to central or local government officials or as a commercial bribe, influence, payment or kickback; and (5) any payment deemed illegal under the Prevention of Corruption Acts 1889 to 1916.

"Shares" means the whole of the issued and allotted share capital of the Company as at Completion.

"Subsidiary" means a subsidiary as defined in CA 1985, s.736.

"Subsidiary Undertaking" means a subsidiary undertaking as defined in CA 1985, s.258.

"SORP" means a statement of recommended practice issued by The Accounting Standards Board Limited or such other body or bodies as are prescribed for the purposes of CA 1985, s.256.

"SSAP" means a statement of standard accounting practice published by the accounting standards committee of CCAB Limited and adopted by The Accounting Standards Board Limited.

"Taxation" means all forms of taxation, duties, imposts, governmental charges (whether international, national or local) and levies whatsoever and whenever created, enacted or imposed and whether of the United Kingdom or elsewhere and without prejudice to the generality of that expression includes:

(1) income tax, corporation tax, capital gains tax, capital transfer tax, inheritance tax, stamp duty, stamp duty reserve tax, rates, value added tax, customs and other import duties, insurance premium tax, national insurance contributions and any payment whatsoever which the Company may be or become bound to make to any Taxation Authority or any other person as a result of any enactment relating to taxation and any other taxes, duties or levies supplementing or replacing any of the above;

(2) all costs, charges, interests, fines, penalties and expenses incidental or relating to any taxation, duties, imposts, charges and levies whatsoever (including without limitation any such described above).

"Taxation Authority" means the Inland Revenue, HM Customs and Excise or any statutory or governmental authority or body (whether in the United Kingdom or elsewhere) involved in the collection or administration of Taxation.

"Tax Deed" means a tax deed in the form set out in Schedule [ ].

"Tax Warranties" means the warranties in paragraphs [ ] to [ ] of Schedule [ ].

"TCGA 1992" means the Taxation of Chargeable Gains Act 1992.

"TMA 1970" means the Taxes Management Act 1970.

"UITF Abstract" means an abstract issued by the Urgent Issues Task Force of The

Accounting Standard Board Limited or such other body or bodies as are prescribed for the purposes of CA, s.256.

"VATA 1994" means the Value Added Tax Act 1994.

"Warranties" means the [obligations,] warranties[, representations and undertakings] of the Vendors contained in [this Agreement][[clause [ ] and] Schedule [ ]].

"Warranty Claim" means any claim made by the Purchaser for breach of any of the Warranties.

[See para.4–01]

## [4B] Statutory references

References to any statute, or to any statutory provision, statutory instrument, order or regulation made thereunder, includes that statute, provision, instrument, order or regulation as amended, modified, consolidated, re-enacted or replaced from time to time, whether before or after the date of this Agreement and also includes any previous statute, statutory provision, instrument, order or regulation, amended, modified, consolidated, re-enacted or replaced by such statute, provision, instrument, order or regulation.

[See para.4–03]

## [4C] The Warranties

The Vendors jointly and severally warrant and represent to the Purchaser that, save as fairly disclosed in the Disclosure Letter, the Warranties are true in all respects.

[See para.4–05]

## [4D] Restriction on implied covenants

The express assurance in clause [ ] as to freedom from encumbrances and the covenants implied in that clause by sections 2 and 3 of the LPMPA 1994 shall apply to anything falling within the scope of such assurances and covenants notwithstanding that the Vendors do not know or could not reasonably be expected to know about it, or, at the time of transfer, it is within the actual knowledge, or is a necessary consequence of facts then within the actual knowledge of the Purchaser, and the operation of the covenants implied by sections 2 and 3 of the LPMPA 1994 shall be deemed to be extended so as not to exclude the liability of the Vendors thereunder in any such circumstances.

[See para.4–09]

## [4E] Application of Warranties to past events

The Vendors shall not be liable, in relation to a breach of the Warranties, if and to the extent that the breach is primarily attributable to anything which occurred prior to [ ].

[See para.4–11]

## [4F] Effect of post-Completion events

The Vendors shall not be liable for a claim under the Warranties which would not have arisen but for anything occurring after Completion.

[See para.4–12]

## [4G] Events occurring prior to Completion

[Each of the Vendors] [The Vendor] will promptly disclose in writing to the Purchaser any circumstance which arises, or becomes known to [him] [her] [it], prior to Completion and is inconsistent with any of the Warranties or the disclosures in the Disclosure Letter, or which might be material to be known by a purchaser for value of [the Shares] [the Business].

[See para.4–14]

## [4H] Conduct of the Company pending Completion

The Vendors shall procure that, save as may be necessary to give effect to this Agreement, the Company shall not, before Completion, without the prior written consent of the Purchaser do, procure or allow anything which might constitute or result in a breach of the Warranties, or make any of them inaccurate or misleading, if they were given at Completion.
[See para.4–16]

## [4I] Warranties to apply at Completion

Each of the Warranties shall be deemed to be repeated, with any necessary modification, immediately before the time of Completion, with reference to the facts then existing.
[See para.4–17]

## [4J] Full enquiry by the Vendors

Where a Warranty refers to the knowledge, information, awareness or belief of the Vendors, each of the Vendors undertakes that they have made full enquiry into the subject matter of the Warranty and it shall not be a defence that the Vendors did not appreciate the relevance of any particular matter.
[See para.4–19]

## [4K] Knowledge of the Vendor

In determining whether the Vendor has the knowledge referred to in a Warranty it shall be treated as knowing:

[4K.1]   anything which is known to any of its directors; and

[4K.2]   anything which is known to the persons listed in Schedule [ ] but, in respect of each of the individuals named, only in relation to those of the Warranties which are specified against his name in that Schedule.

[See para.4–21]

## [4L] Awareness of one of the Vendors

If one of the Vendors is or could reasonably have been aware that there was a breach of a Warranty which refers to the knowledge, information, awareness or belief of the Vendors, he shall be liable for a fraction of the Purchaser's loss arising from that breach equal to the fraction of the Shares which are sold by him.
[See para.4–22]

## [4M] Effect of investigation or waiver of liability

The remedies of the Purchaser in respect of a breach of the Warranties shall not be affected by any investigation made. or to be made, by or on behalf of the Purchaser into [the affairs of the Company] [the Business]. or by the Purchaser rescinding. or failing to rescind. this Agreement or anything else other than a specific and duly authorised written waiver or release.
[See para.4–24]

## [4N] *Ejusdem generis* rule

In construing this Agreement the so-called "*ejusdem generis* rule" does not apply and accordingly the interpretation of general words is not restricted by:

[4N.1]   being preceded by words indicating a particular class of acts, matters or things; or

[4N.2]   being followed by particular examples.

[See para.4–27]

## [4O] Overseas companies or businesses

The Warranties apply, with any necessary modification, to [that part of the Company's business as is carried on] [any part of the Business carried on] outside England and Wales, and for the purpose of construction:

[4O.1]   a reference to a statutory provision enacted, or accounting principle applying, in England and Wales includes a reference to the corresponding provision in the local legislation and (where relevant) to a generally accepted accounting principle; and

[4O.2]   a reference to a governmental, or administrative, authority or agency includes a reference to the equivalent local governmental, or administrative, authority or agency.

[See para.4–29]

## [4P] Failure to follow Vendors' instructions

The Purchaser shall not be entitled to make a claim in respect of a Warranty if it fails after due warning to act in accordance with the reasonable instructions of the Vendors in conducting a dispute in relation to the subject matter of the claim in accordance with clause [ ].
[See para.4–31]

## [4Q] Information supplied to Vendors

Information supplied by the Company or its professional advisers to the Vendors, or their agents, representatives or advisers, in connection with the Warranties and the Disclosure Letter, or otherwise in relation to the business and affairs of the Company, is not deemed to be a representation by the Company to the Vendors as to its accuracy, and the Vendors may not make a claim against the Company, its officers or employees or its professional advisers in respect of that information.
[See para.4–33]

## [4R] Warranties independent

Each of the Warranties is independent of other Warranties and undertakings and, unless the contrary is expressly stated, no clause in this Agreement limits the extent or application of another clause.
[See para.4–35]

## [4S] Warranties to survive Completion

Each of the Warranties, other than a Warranty fully performed at Completion, shall remain in full force and effect notwithstanding Completion.
[See para.4–36]

## [4T] Delay in enforcing Warranties

A failure by the Purchaser to exercise, or a delay by it in exercising, a right in respect of a Warranty shall not operate as a waiver of the right or Warranty, and a single or partial

exercise of a right shall not preclude another or further exercise of the right or the exercise of another right.
[See para.4–38]

## [4U] Purchaser's warranty

The Purchaser has not already formulated, and does not presently have any actual knowledge (save as fairly disclosed in the Disclosure Letter) of any circumstances which it knows would presently entitle it to make, a Warranty Claim.
[See para.4–39]

# Warranties and Undertakings by the Purchaser

Note: before using any of these clauses reference should be made to the commentary in the body of the book at the paragraph indicated which will provide a summary of the purpose of the clause, suggested amendments and, where appropriate, the arguments for and against these.

## [11A] Land to be sold in course of trade

The Purchaser shall procure that all land and interests in land held as trading stock by the Company at Completion are disposed of in the normal course of trade so as to procure that all opportunity of profit, in respect of the land and interests (within the meaning of ICTA 1988, s.776(10)), arises to the Company.
[See para.11–02]

## [11B] Refund when tax repaid or relieved

If the Vendors are liable to the Purchaser under the Warranties in respect of an obligation of the Company to pay Taxation and in certain circumstances the payment will be repaid or some other liability of the Company to Taxation reduced as a result of the payment, the liability of the Vendors shall be reduced, and amounts paid to the Purchaser in respect of the liability shall be refunded, when and to the extent that the Company obtains the benefit of a repayment or reduction in liability. The Purchaser shall procure that the Company does everything necessary to result in the repayment or reduction being obtained as soon as reasonably possible.
[See para.11–05]

## [11C] Collection of warranted debts

The Purchaser shall procure that the Company uses all reasonable efforts to collect promptly all debts to which clause [ ] relates ("warranted debts") and, if a person is indebted to the Company in respect of warranted debts and other debts, a general payment on account of the indebtedness shall be applied in or towards discharging the warranted debts in priority to the other debts.
[See para.11–07]

## [11D] Rights of recovery or reimbursement to be enforced

Where the Company is entitled to recover from a third party or claim reimbursement of all or part of a sum in respect of which it has a claim or potential claim under the Warranties, the Purchaser shall procure that it takes all possible steps to enforce the recovery or reimbursement before making a claim under the Warranties.
[See para.11–09]

## [11E]  Assignment of rights of reimbursement

Where the Vendors are liable in respect of a breach of the Warranties and the Purchaser, or the Company, has a right of reimbursement (in whole or in part) against another person, the Purchaser shall assign, or procure to be assigned, to them for no consideration the benefit of the right.
[See para.11–10]

## [11F]  Vendors' rights to acquire warranted debts or rights of reimbursement

[11F.1]  In this clause:

> "claims floor" means a provision of the Agreement exempting the Vendors from liability under the Warranties unless the liability exceeds a specified amount;
> "doubtful debt" means a debt due to the Company, in respect of which the Vendors have warranted that payment in full, or of a specified amount or proportion, will be received by the Company within a specified period or by a specified date;
> "relevant liability" means a liability of the Company in respect of which it has a right of reimbursement against a third party.

[11F.2]  If the Vendors are (or but for a claims floor would have been) liable to the Purchaser under the Warranties in respect of a doubtful debt or a relevant liability and, after their liability arises, a payment is received by the Company in or towards discharge of the doubtful debt or in or towards satisfaction of the obligation to make reimbursement, payments made by the Vendors shall be repaid and any reduction in the exemption under the claims floor shall be cancelled to the extent that the payments would not have been made or the reduction would not have occurred if the payment in respect of the doubtful debt or reimbursement in respect of the relevant liability had been received at Completion.

[11F.3]  If a doubtful debt or obligation to make reimbursement in respect of a relevant liability remains outstanding, in whole or in part, on the expiration of 12 months from Completion, the Purchaser, at the request and cost of the Vendors, shall procure that the relevant Group Company assigns the debt or right, or the outstanding balance, to the Vendors for no consideration.

[See para.11–13]

## [11G]  Conduct of claims

Where a claim will or may be made under the Warranties and the amount of the claim will or could be affected by the outcome of a dispute with a third party, the Purchaser shall procure that the Vendors are fully and promptly informed about the dispute or potential dispute and that its conduct, negotiation, settlement or litigation are, so far as is reasonably practicable, carried out in accordance with the wishes of a majority of the Vendors and at their cost.
[See para.11–14]

## [11H]  Conduct of claims in relation to Taxation Warranties

The provisions of clause [ ] of the Tax Deed apply in relation to a claim which could be made under the Taxation Warranties as they apply to Claims for Taxation (as defined in

the Deed) and as if references to the "Covenantors" and to liability under the Tax Deed were replaced by references to the "Vendors" and to liability under the Warranties.
[See para.11–15]

## [11I]  Indemnity against secondary tax liabilities

The Purchaser shall indemnify the Vendor, and those of its Subsidiaries which are not Group Companies, against claims for tax recoverable from the Vendor or any of the Subsidiaries by reason of:

[11I.1]   ICTA 1988, s.767AA in respect of corporation tax assessed on a Group Company or TCGA 1992, ss.139 and 178 in respect of chargeable gains accruing, or deemed to accrue, to a Group Company;

[11I.2]   FA 2000, Schedule 28, in respect of corporation tax payable by a Group Company;

[11I.3]   VATA 1994, s.43 and ss.43A–C in respect of value added tax attributable to imports or supplies by a Group Company;

and the Purchaser shall procure that an application is made, under VATA 1994, s.43(7), immediately after Completion for the Group Companies to cease to be treated for value added tax purposes as members of a group which includes the Vendor or any of its Subsidiaries.
[See para.11–18]

## [11J]  Undertakings from future purchaser of the Company

The Purchaser shall not, whilst any of the provisions of this Schedule are applicable or capable of taking effect, cease to control the Company without procuring from the person acquiring control an enforceable undertaking, in favour of the Vendors and the Covenantors (as appropriate), to be bound by those provisions, so far as they affect the Company, to the same extent as the Purchaser is bound.
[See para.11–20]

## [11K]  Surrenders of group relief and claims for capital allowances

The Purchaser will procure that the Company co-operates with the Vendor in making such surrenders of or claims for group relief and such claims for capital allowances as are reasonably required by the Vendor, subject to the Purchaser being reasonably satisfied that either there is no net cost to it or the Company in doing so or that the cost is borne by the Vendor. If there is a dispute between the parties as to this clause, the procedure for resolving disputes set out in clause [ ] of the Tax Deed shall be adopted.
[See para.11–22]

# APPENDIX 11

# Index to Tax Warranties

# INDEX

# THE COMPANION CD-ROM
## Instructions for Use

### Introduction

These notes are provided for guidance only. They should be read and interpreted in the context of your own computer system and operational procedures. It is assumed that you have a basic knowledge of WINDOWS. However, if there is any problem please contact our help line on 020 7393 7266 who will be happy to help you.

### CD Format and Contents

To run this CD you need at least:
- IBM compatible PC with Pentium processor
- 8mb RAM
- CD-ROM drive
- Microsoft Windows 95

The CD contains data files of Precedent material. It does not contain software or commentary.

### Installation

The following instructions make the assumption that you will copy the data files to a single directory on your hard disk (e.g. C:\Sinclair on Warranties).

Open your **CD ROM drive,** select and double click on **setup.exe** and follow the instructions. The files will be unzipped to your **C drive** and you will be able to open them up from the new **C:\Sinclair on Warranties** folder there.

# LICENCE AGREEMENT

## Definitions

1. The following terms will have the following meanings: "The PUBLISHERS" means Sweet & Maxwell of 100 Avenue Road, London NW3 3PF (which expression shall, where the context admits, include the PUBLISHERS' assigns or successors in business as the case may be) of the other part on behalf of Thomson Books Limited of Cheriton House, North Way, Andover SP10 5BE.

"The LICENSEE" means the purchaser of the title containing the Licensed Material.

"Licensed Material" means the data included on the disk;

"Licence" means a single user licence;

"Computer" means an IBM-PC compatible computer.

## Grant of Licence; Back up copies

2. (1) The PUBLISHERS hereby grant to the LICENSEE, a non-exclusive, non-transferable licence to use the Licensed Material in accordance with these terms and conditions.

(2) The LICENSEE may install the Licensed Material for use on one computer only at any time.

(3) The LICENSEE may make one back-up copy of the Licensed Material only, to be kept in the LICENSEE's control and possession.

## Proprietary Rights

3. (1) All rights not expressly granted herein are reserved.

(2) The Licensed Material is not sold to the LICENSEE who shall not acquire any right, title or interest in the Licensed Material or in the media upon which the Licensed Material is supplied.

(3) The LICENSEE shall not erase, remove, deface or cover any trademark, copyright notice, guarantee or other statement on any media containing the Licensed Material.

(4) The LICENSEE shall only use the Licensed Material in the normal course of its business and shall not use the Licensed Material for the purpose of operating a bureau or similar service or any online service whatsoever.

(5) Permission is hereby granted to LICENSEES who are members of the legal profession (which expression does not include individuals or organisations engaged in the supply of services to the legal profession) to reproduce, transmit and store small quantities of text for the purpose of enabling them to provide legal advice to or to draft documents or conduct proceedings on behalf of their clients.

(6) The LICENSEE shall not sublicense the Licensed Material to others and this Licence Agreement may not be transferred, sublicensed, assigned or otherwise disposed of in whole or in part.

(7) The LICENSEE shall inform the PUBLISHERS on becoming aware of any unauthorised use of the Licensed Material.

## Warranties

4. (1) The PUBLISHERS warrant that they have obtained all necessary rights to grant this licence.

(2) Whilst reasonable care is taken to ensure the accuracy and completeness of the Licensed Material supplied, the PUBLISHERS make no representations or warranties, express or implied, that the Licensed Material is free from errors or omissions.

(3) The Licensed Material is supplied to the LICENSEE on an "as is" basis and has not been supplied to meet the LICENSEE'S individual requirements. It is the sole responsibility of the LICENSEE to satisfy itself prior to entering this Licence Agreement that the Licensed Material will meet the LICENSEE's requirements and be compatible with the LICENSEE's hardware/software configuration. No failure of any part of the Licensed Material to be suitable for the LICENSEE's requirements will give rise to any claim against the PUBLISHERS.

(4) In the event of any material inherent defects in the physical media on which the licensed material may be supplied, other than caused by accident abuse or misuse by the LICENSEE, the PUBLISHERS will replace the defective original media free of charge provided it is returned to the place of purchase within 90 days of the purchase date.

The PUBLISHERS' enure liability and the LICENSEE's exclusive remedy shall be the replacement of such defective media.

(5) Whilst all reasonable care has been taken to exclude computer viruses, no warranty is made that the Licensed Material is virus free. The LICENSEE shall be responsible to ensure that no virus is introduced to any computer or network and shall not hold the PUBLISHERS responsible.

(6) The warranties set out herein are exclusive of an in lieu of all other conditions and warranties, either express or implied, statutory or otherwise.

(7) All other conditions and warranties, either express or implied, statutory or otherwise, which relate in the condition and fitness for any purpose of the Licensed Material are hereby excluded and the PUBLISHERS' shall not be liable in contract or in tort for any loss of any kind suffered by reason of any defect in the Licensed Material (whether or not caused by the negligence of the PUBLISHERS).

## Limitation of Liability and Indemnity

5. (1) The LICENSEE shall accept sole responsibility for and the PUBLISHERS shall not be liable for the use of the Licensed Material by the LICENSEE, its agents and employees and the LICENSEE shall hold the PUBLISHERS harmless and fully indemnified against any claims, costs, damages, loss and liabilities arising out of any such use.

(2) The PUBLISHERS shall be not be liable for any indirect or consequential loss suffered by the LICENSEE (including without limitation loss of profits, goodwill or data) in connection with the Licensed Material howsoever arising.

(3) The PUBLISHERS will have no liability whatsoever for any liability of the LICENSEE or any third party which might arise.

(4) The LICENSEE hereby agrees that

(a) the LICENSEE is best placed to foresee and evaluate any loss that might be suffered in connection with this Licence Agreement;

(b) that the cost of supply of the Licensed Material has been calculated on the basis of the limitations and exclusions contained herein; and

(b) the LICENSEE will effect such insurance as is suitable having regard to the LICENSEE's circumstances.

(5) The aggregate maximum liability of the PUBLISHERS in respect of any direct loss or any other loss (to the extent that such loss is not excluded by this Licence Agreement or otherwise) whether such a claim arises in contract or tort shall not exceed a sum equal to that paid as the price for the title containing the Licensed Material.

## Termination

6. (1) In the event of any breach of this Agreement including any violation of any copyright in the Licensed Material, whether held by the PUBLISHERS or others in the Licensed Material, the Licence Agreement shall automatically terminate immediately, without notice and without prejudice to any claim which the PUBLISHERS may have either for moneys due and/or damages and/or otherwise.

(2) Clauses 3 to S shall survive the termination for whatsoever reason of this Licence Agreement.

(3) In the event of termination of this Licence Agreement the LICENSEE will remove the Licensed Material.

## Miscellaneous

7. (1) Any delay or forbearance by the PUBLISHERS in enforcing any provisions of this Licence Agreement shall not be construed as a waiver of such provision or an agreement thereafter not to enforce the said provision.

(2) This Licence Agreement shall be governed by the laws of England and Wales. If any difference shall arise between the Parties touching the meaning of this Licence Agreement or the rights and liabilities of the parties thereto, the same shall be referred to arbitration in accordance with the provisions of the Arbitration Act 1996, or any amending or substituting statute for the time being in force.

**Disclaimer**

Precedents in this publication may be used as a guide for the drafting of legal documents specifically for particular clients but not for republication. Such legal documents may be provided to clients in print or electronic form, but the distribution to third parties otherwise is prohibited. Precedents are provided "as is" without warranty of any kind, express or implied, including but not limited to fitness for a particular purpose. The publishers and the author cannot accept any responsibility for any loss of whatsoever kind including loss of revenue business, anticipated savings or profits, loss of goodwill or data or for any direct or consequential loss whatsoever to any person using the precedents, or acting or refraining from actions as a result of the material in this publication.